From Day to Day

A Calendar of Notable Birthdays and Events

Second Edition

David E. Johnson

The Scarecrow Press, Inc.
Lanham, Maryland, and London
2001

SCARECROW PRESS, INC.

Published in the United States of America
by Scarecrow Press, Inc.
4720 Boston Way, Lanham, Maryland 20706
www.scarecrowpress.com

4 Pleydell Gardens, Folkestone
Kent CT20 2DN, England

Interior book design by Jeff Spears with Spears Computer Consulting, Inc., Birmingham, AL

British Library Cataloguing in Publication Information Available

Library of Congress Cataloging-in-Publication Data

Johnson, David E.
   From day to day : a calendar of notable birthdays and events / David E. Johnson.—2nd ed.
     p. cm.
  Includes index.
  ISBN 0-8108-3944-X (alk. paper)
   1. Birthdays—Calendars. 2. Anniversaries—Calendars. I. Title.
  CT105 .J64 2001
  394.2—dc21   00-061947

Tomorrow, and tomorrow, and tomorrow,
Creeps in this petty pace from day to day
To the last syllable of recorded time . . .

Macbeth

Contents

Preface

God created the earth. And the nights and the days. But people created dates. They did it by counting and naming the days and the months and counting the years. December 7, 1941, was a date—"a date which will live in infamy," according to President Franklin D. Roosevelt. It was the seventh day of the 12th month of the 1,941st year of the Christian Era. It was also a Sunday, the first day of the week, and the event which FDR referred to, the bombing of Pearl Harbor, began at 7:50 A.M. Hawaii time, or 1:50 P.M. Eastern Standard Time. Thus God gave us the light and the dark and the days, but we developed our own system of keeping and counting time, and, it must be said, of carrying out bombing raids.

A book of dates, such as this, logically could begin with a discussion of how our system of dates came into being and how time came to be measured. Why, for example, do we have seven days in a week and 12 months in a year? Why does a year consist of 365 or 366 days? Who divided a day into 24 hours instead of ten or a hundred, and who decided that 60 minutes constitute an hour? Where did the names of the days come from? Who named the months? Better still, who *misnamed* the months? December, the 12th month, is named for *decem,* the Latin word for ten. The same inconsistencies apply to September, October and November, the ninth, tenth and eleventh months, which are named the seventh, eighth, and ninth months, respectively. How long have we had our system of counting time, and how did it get to us in its present form?

We consider these questions first, by tracing the development of the calendar from the ancient Egyptians and Babylonians, through the Greeks and Romans, to the present. We then present chronologically the highlights in history of each day of the year, and consider which noteworthy events occurred and which famous persons were born on that day, beginning with January 1 and continuing through all 366 days to December 31. These accounts are divided into 12 chapters, one devoted to each month. Each chapter begins with a discussion of that month's history—how it got its name, its length, etc.—and what facts are pertinent to it, such as its flower and its birthstone. The list of notable birthdays and events of the month follows.

The daily lists of birthdays and events, of course, are alive, as much so as any living organism. Every month, and certainly every year, sees the emergence of new figures on the world's stage. New heads of state take office, new sports and entertainment figures burst upon the scene and noteworthy events occur daily. But in compiling the list, we have to stop at some point. We also have to make choices about what to include and what to omit.

We have included all the notable birthdays we could put together, an ongoing task of most of the past two decades, and we have gone to great lengths to assure their accuracy. Those omitted were either deemed less important—an obvious matter of opinion—or their dates of birth were unknown. Some like Socrates, Plato, Columbus, for example, are unknown to *everybody,* and some were unknown to us—Fred Lasswell (the cartoonist of *Snuffy Smith*) and Garry Trudeau (the creator of *Doonesbury*) come to mind—though we tried valiantly to get them.

Accuracy was, and is, a major problem. To compile thousands of entries without making errors is, of course, impossible. Many of the errors are our own fault, and we willingly take the blame. These were compounded by compilation errors of overzealous researchers of the past. For example, the birthdays of Daniel Defoe, Peter Stuyvesant, and Henry Hudson don't seem to be known by the major encyclopedia compilers, but dates are alleged in other sources. Still other sources—trustworthy ones—give these same dates, except for the year, for other events associated with these men, such as the date of Defoe's death, Stuyvesant's surrender of New Amsterdam to the British, and Hudson's discovery of Hudson Bay. Other errors seem deliberate, like the many varied accounts of birthdays of well-known movie stars, put out by studios or agents.

Another source of confusion is the change from the Julian Calendar to the Gregorian Calendar. This change was made by most of the Latin countries in 1582, but England and her colonies did not make the change until 1752. Russia did not make the change until 1917, and Greece waited until 1923. Thus Isaac Newton, born in England, thought his birthday was on Christmas Day, but he was born on the same day and year as others in the Latin countries who thought their birthday was January 4. For years dates were listed as New Style or Old Style to at least identify the discrepancy, but most reputable references have adjusted to the new system. The problem lingers on, however, in many circles.

We have relied on most of the well-known encyclopedias for historical persons and events, and for the more contemporary ones, we have consulted current biographies, autobiographies, Hall of Fame lists, sports encyclopedias, movie biographical books, magazines, newspapers, radio, and television. We have done everything short of writing notable persons and asking for their birthdays. We were afraid of getting a response like one person got when he wired, "How old Cary Grant?" The great actor replied, "Old Cary Grant fine. How you?"

In this second edition we have increased the number of entries from some 15,000 to almost 17,000, adding birthdays that have become important or events that have occurred in the years since the first edition. We have also corrected all the first-edition errors we have found or that have been pointed out to us by our readers, to whom we are deeply grateful.

The Calendar

Everybody at some time or other must have pondered the questions of how our present calendar came into being, how the months and days were named, who decided how many days make a week and how many make a month, how many hours in a day, how many minutes in an hour, and so forth. No one knows all the answers for certain, but we do know that our calendar, with slight modifications, had its origin with the great Roman leader Julius Caesar in the year 45 B.C. The *Julian* Calendar, which he put into effect at that time, over 2,000 years ago, is, with minor modifications, the same one we have today, an amazing fact and a monumental tribute to that remarkable general, historian and politician. The numbers of hours per day and days per week were determined by civilizations even more ancient than Rome, but the names of the days and months, as we know them today, were given to us by the Romans.

From the earliest times, people must have noticed that the seasons came regularly, the rivers flooded periodically, and the moon waxed and waned according to some schedule. It obviously must have occurred to them to count the number of sunrises to place an event, or to count the number of full moons to determine a time to sow and a time to reap, even in their earliest attempts at agriculture. They must have had words for *today, tomorrow,* and *yesterday,* arising in their daily experiences with the sun. The rise of the priesthood must have dictated a need for placing religious festivals at periodic times, which must have been based on the seasons and hence on the sun. In short, it was imperative that the ancients try to reckon time by the positions of the moon and/or the sun.

The moon goes through a complete cycle in about 29½ days, a fact which undoubtedly led to the idea of a month. The sun, on the other hand, takes about 365¼ days to complete its cycle, which inevitably became the basis for a year. The lunations, or periods, of the moon are conveniently short and thus would be excellent time periods on which to base a calendar. But the seasons and therefore the times for planting and the times for harvesting depend on the sun's cycle, and unfortunately 29½ will not divide a whole number of times into 365¼. A *lunar* year of 12 months, or roughly 360 days, is too short to keep in step with the sun, and a year of 13 months is too long. In Caesar's time, for example, the plant-

ing season according to the calendar then in existence was 80 days earlier than it should have been, according to the sun. As we will see, Caesar solved the problem by basing the calendar on a *solar* year of 365 or 366 days with different lengths for the 12 months.

The earliest Roman calendar year, in the time of Romulus, the legendary first king of Rome, may have been one of only four months—Martius, Aprilis, Maius and Junius or, as we know them, March, April, May and June. At any rate, these were the only months with names, and since they originally had 30 days each, it took three such "years" to approximate a solar year. The Romans had eight-day weeks, with the days unnamed, but simply lettered A, B, C, D, E, F, G and H. March, the first month of the year, thus began with day A, and it was the only month to do so. This may have been the way the early Romans kept track of New Year's Day.

About 738 B.C., Romulus, tradition has it, added six additional months to the original four. These new months had no names, but were simply numbered from five to ten as Quintilis (fifth), Sextilis (sixth), Septembris (seventh), Octobris (eighth), Novembris (ninth) and Decembris (tenth). The latter four are, of course, our September, October, November and December. At first Romulus gave 30 days to each of his ten months, but this resulted in a year of 300 days, which was not divisible by eight, and thus not a whole number of weeks. Four days were then added, one each to March, May, Quintilis and October, so that the new year had 304 days, and therefore precisely 38 weeks. The end of December marked the end of the year, which was followed by an uncounted winter gap, determined so that the new year beginning in March would correspond more or less with the seasons. Romulus and/or his religious leaders probably decided when March 1 had arrived.

Numa Pompilius, the second of the seven legendary kings of Rome (around 715 to 673 B.C.), is credited with creating the 12-month calendar that survived more or less intact until Caesar's day. Numa added two months, Januarius and Februarius, our January and February, to the calendar of Romulus, creating a year of 354 days, just some eight hours short of a true lunar year (12 lunations of the moon). His 50 additional days plus six days, one taken from each of the 30-

day months, were divided equally between the two new months. Thus March, May, Quintilis and October had 31 days, January and February had 28, and the remaining months had 29. Since 354 days contained 44 eight-day weeks with two days left over, three consecutive days of December were labeled F days, so that the year would end with an H day and the new year would begin with an A day. Both March 1 and January 1 were A days, however, and an open question existed as to which was New Year's Day. Each day had its supporters, which seems incredible, until we realize that the clash of custom with religious and secular needs has led to wars over smaller things.

The *intercalary* days (days inserted between two days) were resented and immediately neglected, especially by the proponents of March 1 as New Year's Day. This prompted a later reformer, or perhaps Numa himself, to add a day to January, making a year of 355 days. A different kind of intercalation was then used. Five extra days were added between February 23 and 24, which were lettered but not numbered. This was the origin of the festivals of February 23, the *Terminalia,* and February 24, the *Regifugium.*

The Roman calendar now had 360 days, though five were uncounted; the year contained exactly 45 eight-day weeks and began with an A day, as desired, and March 1 regained its place as New Year's Day. Unfortunately, however, a lunar year is not a solar year, and the new calendar soon became incompatible with the seasons. During the period of the Roman Republic, still another intercalation was attempted to keep the lunar year in step with the sun. Instead of the five intercalary days, an intercalary month of 22 or 23 days was added in alternate years, after February 23, to the 355-day year of Numa. The new month was called *Mercedonius,* from a Latin word for *wages,* since its presence meant an extra month's pay. A cycle of four years was thus devised, with 355 days in the first year, 377 in the second, 355 again in the third, and 378 in the fourth. This produced an average length of 366¼ days per year, which was close to a solar year, but almost a day too long.

There were other changes made in the calendar during the days of the Republic which should be mentioned. Originally Numa seems to have placed his new months of January and February at the end of the year and retained March as the first month. The order appeared to be March, April, and so on, down to December, February and January. Thus during the periods when January was considered to be the first month, February was the last. In 452 B.C., however, the Decemvirs, a body of magistrates in ancient Rome, reversed the order of January and February, giving us our present ordering of the months. January seems to have become the first month, in the official political calendar at least, in 153 B.C. when the Roman consuls began to take office on January 1. March 1 continued to be New Year's Day, however, in the eyes of the religious leaders and the populace for a considerable time, probably up to the time of Caesar.

Even if the Roman priests had adhered strictly to the calendar of the Republic it still would have fallen out of step with the sun because the year contained too many days. But because of ignorance and neglect (probably deliberate) by the priests, the calendar, as the great historian Theodor

Mommsen noted, "went on its own way tolerably unconcerned about moon and sun." As a consequence, by the middle of the first century B.C. the calendar was 80 days behind the sun. Drastic measures were called for, but history teaches us that politicians are treading on dangerous ground when they try to tamper with something as sacred as a nation's calendar. The ancient Egyptians, for example, had a 365-day calendar, and their astronomers knew that it needed an additional one-quarter day per year, but when the Egyptian king, Ptolemy III, tried in 239 B.C. to adjust the calendar he was met with such a storm of protest that he wisely gave up.

In 46 B.C. Julius Caesar entered the picture. He was in total control of both the Roman government and the Roman religion. He therefore had the power to adjust the calendar, and the world is fortunate that he also had the will to do so. Caesar's first step was to engage the services of Sosigenes, a learned Greek astronomer from Alexandria, Egypt. Together they introduced the reforms that are still the basis of our calendar.

Caesar first extended the year 46 B.C. to 445 days, bringing the old calendar into agreement with the sun. At the end of this "year of confusion," as the Romans called it, the new calendar went into effect, with January 1, 45 B.C., as the first day of the new year. Each year had 365 days, with every fourth year, a leap year, increased to 366 days by adding a day in February. Caesar also distributed the days among the months better than the old calendar did, giving 31 days each to January, March, May, Quintilis, September and November, and 30 to the remaining months, except for February, which had 29 (30 in leap years). It is not quite clear why Caesar short-changed February rather than one of the 31-day months, but some historians speculate that the Romans thought February was an unlucky month given over to the "infernal gods," and the shorter it was the better. Other authorities theorize that even numbers were considered unlucky, and thus the Romans felt there should be as many odd-numbered months as possible.

The Roman Senate honored Caesar in 44 B.C. by changing the name of Quintilis to Julius (July), and in 8 B.C. the emperor Augustus had Sextilis renamed Augustus (August). Probably because he wanted his month to have as many days as Caesar's, Augustus took still another day from February and added it to August. But this created three consecutive 31-day months (July, August and September), so he reduced September and November to 30 days each, and increased October and December to 31 days each. Despite the efforts of other emperors to rename months after themselves, this arrangement of Augustus has endured to the present day. We remember it by the adage, "Thirty days hath September, April, June and November. All the rest have 31 except February alone, which has 28, rain or shine, and in leap years 29."

The only other change made in the Roman calendar before the 16th century A.D. was made in 527 A.D. when Dionysius Exiguus, the abbot of Rome, moved New Year's from January 1 to March 25. Dionysius is also credited with fixing Christmas at December 25 and for originating the custom of dating events (B.C. and A.D.) from the birth of Christ. Before this time there were many *eras* used in counting the years. For example, the Roman Era, dated from the founding of the city of Rome, supposedly in 753 B.C., was widely used by Roman writers, who abbreviated it A.U.C., for *Anno Urbis Conditae* (the year of the founding of the city). Thus Caesar was assassinated in 709 A.U.C. (44 B.C.) and the Western Roman Empire fell in 1229 A.U.C. (476 A.D.).

The Christian Era is now the dominant dating system in the world, though many people may refer to it in different terms than A.D. and B.C., such as "The Common Era" (C.E.) and "Before the Common Era" (B.C.E.). It took some 200 years, however, for the new system to meet with universal approval. It was popularized by the great British writer, the Venerable Bede, in the early eighth century, but the issue was not settled until the end of that century when Charlemagne, another strong leader like Caesar, adopted the system.

An interesting footnote to the Christian Era is that Dionysius picked the wrong year for the birth of Christ. According to the Gospel of St. Matthew, Herod the Great was alive when Christ was born, and it is an established fact that Herod died in 4 B.C., the year most historians accept as Christ's birth year. Other estimates are as early as 7 B.C. Another interesting fact of the Christian Era is that there is no year labeled zero. The year 1 B.C. is followed by the year 1 A.D.

It would seem that Caesar had solved the world's calendar problems once and for all with his Julian Calendar. It was, after all, too long by only 11 minutes and 14 seconds per year. This seemingly trivial error, however, resulted in a gain of one day every 128 years, which by the 16th century had added up to a total of ten days. Easter, the first Sunday after the first full moon on or after the vernal equinox, taken as March 21, was therefore being celebrated further into the spring, and, of course, Christmas was pushed further into the winter. The Catholic Church dignitaries realized that something had to be done or these sacred holidays would eventually lose their traditional relation to the seasons.

In 1582, Pope Gregory XIII, after consultation with his advisors, decreed that October 5 of that year would be changed to October 15, thus shortening the year by the ten days gained by the Julian calendar. Then, to avoid the problem of Caesar's calendar, Gregory declared every fourth year to be a leap year, as before, except for centurial years (those ending in a double 0) not divisible by 400. That is, 1600 and 2000 would be leap years (divisible by 400), but 1700, 1800, 1900, 2100 and so on would not be. Finally, Gregory's calendar restored January 1 as New Year's Day. The new *Gregorian* Calendar reduced the annual error to approximately 26 seconds, or one day every 3,323 years.

The Catholic countries adopted the Gregorian Calendar almost immediately, but because of the Protestant Reformation many other countries did not. England and her colonies, for example, waited until 1752 to adopt the new calendar and by then 11 days had to be dropped. George Washington, who was born on February 11, 1732, very sensibly switched his birthday to February 22. Russia adopted Gregory's "New Style" calendar in 1918 and Greece followed in 1923, the last European country to do so.

As we have noted, the Romans further divided the year into eight-day weeks, but they seemed to have reckoned the time of the month in an even more peculiar way. The first day of the month was the *calends* (or kalends), from which we get our word *calendar,* and the day at or near the middle of the month was the *ides.* The ides was the 15th day of the months of March, May, July and October, and the 13th day of the remaining months. Caesar, it may be recalled, was assassinated on the ides of March in 44 B.C. The ninth day before the ides, counting the ides as one day, was the *nones* (nine), which fell on the seventh day of March, May, July and October, and on the fifth of the other months. The Romans would count backward from these key days to place an event occurring on other days. For example, such and such happened on the second day before the ides, or on the fourth day before nones, or on the seventh day before calends.

The seven-day week was first used by the Babylonians, perhaps because they regarded the number seven as magical, but more likely because of the phases of the moon, seven being approximately one-fourth of a lunar cycle. The days of the week were named for the planets, which in ancient times were conceived to be Saturn, Jupiter, Mars, Sol (the sun), Venus, Mercury and Luna (the moon). The earth was not counted, since it was believed to be stationary and the center of the universe, and the planets Pluto, Neptune and Uranus were, of course, unknown. The Roman Emperor Constantine introduced the seven-day week into the Roman calendar in the third century A.D., using for the days the Latin names *Saturni dies* (Saturn's day), *Solis dies* (Sun's day), *Lunae dies* (Moon's day), *Martis dies* (Mars' day), *Mercurii dies* (Mercury's day), *Jovis dies* (Jove's, or Jupiter's, day) and *Veneris dies* (Venus's day). Our English equivalents of Saturday, Sunday and Monday are easily recognized as the first three of these, and the other four English weekday names were taken from Norse gods: Tuesday is *Tiw's day* (for Tiw, the god of war), Wednesday is *Woden's day* (for Woden, or Odin, the chief Norse god), Thursday is *Thor's day* (the god of lightning and thunder) and Friday is *Frigga's day* (Odin's wife and the chief Norse goddess). Today our week begins with Sunday and ends with Saturday, a custom inherited from the Hebrews, who considered Saturday (the *Sabbath,* or day of rest) to be the seventh day.

A *solar* day is the length of time it takes the earth to turn around once on its axis, but it is now thought of as a *day* of daylight and a *night* of darkness. The Sumerians, between 3,000 and 2,000 B.C., were the first to divide the days into parts, their day consisting of 12 *danna* (perhaps about two of our hours), each of 30 *ges.* It is to the Egyptians, however, that we owe our present system of 24-hour days, though the word *hour* was coined much later from a Greek word meaning "time of day." The Egyptians had 12 hours of day marked by the progress of the sun and 12 hours of night distinguished by the appearance of certain stars or constellations on the eastern horizon. The lengths of the hours varied with the lengths of the daylight periods, which varied with the seasons. Thus on the spring and autumn equinoxes (equal nights), around March 21 and September 23, the day and night hours were equal, but they differed on every other day. The differences were the greatest on the summer and winter solstices (the times when the sun is farthest from the equator, either north or south, and seems to "stand still"). These are usually the longest and the shortest days, respectively, occurring around June 21 and December 22.

Uniform hours came into general use soon after 1300 A.D. when the mechanical clock was invented. The first of these were large devices set in the towers of cathedrals, and the hours were announced by the ringing of bells. In fact, the word *clock* comes from the French *clocke,* an original word for "bell." As clocks became more accurate and their sizes scaled down considerably, due to the invention of the hair spring by the Dutch astronomer Christiaan Huygens in 1675, soldiers and sailors were able to carry them on their night watches. For this reason these portable clocks became known as *watches,* the name they have today.

Most scientific work today is done using the metric system, a beautiful measuring system handed down to us by the Greeks, which allows us to change from one unit to another by simply moving a decimal place (or multiplying by a power of ten). For example, one kilometer is 1000 meters. Our time measuring system, however, differs spectacularly from the orderly metric system, containing as it does, multiples of 60 rather than of 10. We have, of course, 60 minutes (from a Latin word for "small") in an hour and 60 seconds (the *second* subdivision) in a minute (3600 in an hour). These numbers were handed down to us by the Babylonians, through the Greeks, who did not tamper with them, despite their zeal for the metric system. The Babylonians were good mathematicians and were fascinated with numbers. They particularly liked numbers like 6, which is divisible by 1, 2 and 3. They were enamored even more by 60; which is divisible by 1, 2, 3, 4, 5, 6, 10, 12, 15, 20 and 30; and 360 must have driven them out of their minds with ecstasy, since it has all the divisors of 60 plus 18, 24, 36, 40, 45, 60, 72, 90, 120 and 180. From the Babylonians we also get 360 degrees in a circle (each of which could have represented to them a day in the full circle of a solar year).

The planets move relative to the sun, but thousands of stars are fixed in the night sky and are visible from earth. They seem to move only because the motion of the earth gives us a different view of the sky from hour to hour and season to season. This panorama of stars that we see during the course of a year is called a *zodiac,* from a Greek word meaning "circle of animals." The name arose because the ancients, particularly the Babylonians and later the Greeks, imagined patterns of stars to form animals in the sky. They divided the zodiac into 12 equal parts, or constellations, of 30 degrees each, called *signs of the zodiac.* Each sign is prominent in its turn in the night sky and then fades and disappears, becoming part of the day sky as the earth makes its yearly journey around the sun. The Latin names of the signs of the zodiac, which are still used today, are Aries (the Ram), Taurus (the Bull), Gemini (the Twins), Cancer (the Crab), Leo (the Lion), Virgo (the Virgin or Maiden), Libra (the Scales), Scorpio (the Scorpion), Sagittarius (the Archer), Capricorn or Capricornus (the Goat), Aquarius (the Water Bearer) and Pisces (the Fish).

Astrology is the study of the sun, moon, planets and stars in the belief that these heavenly bodies control the affairs of human beings and can be used to predict the future. Astrology probably had its origins with the Chaldeans, who occupied Babylonia in the 700s and 600s B.C. From the Chaldeans the knowledge of astrology was carried into Egypt and Greece from whence it eventually reached Rome and the Arab world. It flourished in Europe in the Middle Ages and reached its peak in the 15th century, prior to the discoveries of Copernicus, Galileo and Kepler that the sun and not the earth was the center of the solar system.

Astrologers today, as in ancient times, cast *horoscopes,* which are diagrams showing the relative position of the planets and the signs of the zodiac. The sign in which the sun is located at the time of a person's birth is his or her *sign of the zodiac* (or more precisely, his or her sun sign). Thus you are a Leo if the sun was in Leo when you were born, and this is supposed to determine your character to a large extent. Astrologers are interested in the other planet signs, as well, such as moon signs, etc., to give them the complete picture, but for a less detailed, general interest the sun sign is the one usually considered. It is also the one given in the daily newspaper astrology columns.

1

January

January, the first month of the year, was added to the calendar around 700 B.C. by Numa Pompilius, the second of the legendary kings of Rome. At the same time he also added February to bring the number of months in the Roman calendar to our present total of 12. January was originally the 12th month, with February preceding it as the 11th month and March following it as the first month of the new year. January first had 28 days and then 29 in the calendar of Numa, but Julius Caesar gave it 31 days in his Julian Calendar of 45 B.C., and this length has come down to us. In 452 B.C. the Decemvirs reversed the order of January and February, giving us the present ordering of the months.

March 1 was originally the Roman New Year's Day, but after the addition of January to the calendar there was a continuous battle between the adherents of March 1 and January 1 as to which day would begin the year. January 1 got a big boost in 153 B.C. when the new Roman consuls started the tradition of taking office on that day, and also Caesar made January the first month in his calendar. The issue, however, was not finally settled until 1582 when the Gregorian Calendar made January 1 the official New Year's Day.

January was taken from the Latin *Januarius* in honor of the Roman god Janus, who was always depicted as having two faces, one facing the past and one the future, an appropriate symbol for the beginning of the new year. Janus was also the god of gates and doors and held dominion over the beginnings of all human enterprises.

In addition to New Year's Day, January includes such holidays as *Epiphany*, the coming of the wise men (January 6); the birthday of Martin Luther King Jr. (the nearest Monday to January 15); and in some southern states the birthday of Robert E. Lee (January 19). Also January 20 following each Presidential election is Inauguration Day, when the President of the United States takes the oath of office. January, in addition, is the birth month of U.S. Presidents Millard Fillmore, William McKinley, Franklin D. Roosevelt, and Richard M. Nixon.

The birthstone for January is the garnet, and the snowdrop and the carnation are the special flowers for the month.

January 1 – Birthdays

1449   **Lorenzo the Magnificent.** The most famous member of the Medici family, who made Florence the most powerful and most beautiful city of his time

1467   **Sigismund I (the Old).** King of Poland, 1506-1548

1484   **Huldreich Zwingli.** The most important reformer in the Swiss Protestant Reformation

1618   **Bartolome Esteban Murillo.** Spanish painter noted as the best interpreter of the gentle, optimistic side of Christianity, and known for works such as *The Immaculate Conception*

1735   **Paul Revere.** American silversmith and Revolutionary War hero who made the famous midnight ride warning the patriots that the British were coming

1745   **Anthony Wayne.** American Revolutionary War general, known as "Mad Anthony" because of his reckless courage

1750   **Frederick Augustus Conrad Muhlenberg.** American statesman, clergyman, member of the Continental Congress, and speaker of the House of Representatives in the first and third Congresses

1752   **Betsy Ross.** American seamstress who some believe made the first U.S. flag that had stars and stripes

1767   **Maria Edgeworth.** Anglo-Irish writer known for her children's stories and novels such as *Castle Rackrent* (1800)

1819   **Arthur Hugh Clough.** English poet, noted for works such as *The Latest Decalogue*, an irreverent version of the Ten Commandments

1819   **Philip Schaff.** Swiss-born ecumenical leader and theologian

1834   **Ludovic Halevy.** French librettist and novelist who with Henri Meilhac wrote the librettos for most of the operettas of Jacques Offenbach

1854   **Sir James George Frazer.** Scottish anthropologist, noted for the famous book *The Golden Bough* (1922), one of the great works of world literature

1856 **Tim Keefe.** Hall of Fame baseball pitcher with a record 19 consecutive victories in 1883

1859 **Michael J. Owens.** American inventor of an automatic bottle-making machine, patented in 1904

1863 **Baron Pierre de Coubertin.** Frenchman who single-handedly revived the Olympic Games in 1896

1864 **Alfred Stieglitz.** American pioneer photographer and "father of modern photography," whose photographs are among the greatest ever produced

1879 **E.M. Forster.** English novelist noted for works such as *Howards End* (1910) and *A Passage to India* (1924)

1879 **William Fox.** Hungarian-born founder of Fox Film Corporation which later became 20th Century Fox

1883 **Roy Wilson Howard.** American co-founder of the Scripps-Howard newspaper chain

1884 **George W. Meyer.** American composer noted for songs such as "For Me and My Gal," "In the Land of Beginning Again," and "There Are Such Things"

1888 **John Cantius Garand.** American rifle designer and inventor of the Garand, or M1, semiautomatic rifle, which served as the official rifle of the U.S. Army from 1936 to 1960

1889 **Charles Bickford.** American stage, screen, and television actor and commanding character player in over 80 films

1895 **J. Edgar Hoover.** First director of the FBI, who served from 1924 to 1972

1900 **Xavier Cugat.** Spanish-born bandleader and "Rhumba King" of the Big Band Era of the 1930s and 1940s

1909 **Dana Andrews.** American motion-picture and television actor with a 40-year career

1909 **Barry Goldwater.** U.S. senator and presidential candidate in 1964

1911 **Hank Greenberg.** Hall of Fame baseball player who hit 58 home runs in 1938

1913 **Eliot Janeway.** American economist, author, lecturer, and columnist

1919 **J.D. Salinger.** American novelist noted for *The Catcher in the Rye* (1951)

1919 **Carole Landis.** American motion-picture actress

1922 **Ernest Hollings.** U.S. senator

1923 **Milt Jackson.** American jazz musician

1924 **Earl Torgeson.** Professional baseball player

1925 **Idi Amin.** Dictator of Uganda in the 1970s

1925 **Valentina Cortese.** Italian actress

1925 **George Connor.** Hall of Fame professional football player

1927 **Doak Walker.** Professional football player and Hall of Famer

1939 **Willye White.** Noted long jumper and the only American woman to compete in five Olympic Games

1940 **Frank Langella.** American motion-picture actor

1943 **Don Novello.** U.S. comedian known as Father Guido Sarducci

1943 **Jerilyn Britz.** Professional golfer who won the U.S. Women's Open in 1979

1950 **Steve Ripley.** Country music singer with The Tractors

1955 **Lamarr Hoyt.** Professional baseball player

January 1 – Events

43 BC Cicero delivered his "Fifth Philippic" (fifth of a series of speeches condemning Mark Antony) in the Roman Senate.

27 BC Octavian became the first emperor of Rome, and took the name Caesar Augustus.

69 Roman legions in Germany refused to renew the oath of allegiance to Emperor Galba.

1399 Tamerlane, the Mongol conqueror, left Delhi, India, after sacking it, massacring most of its inhabitants, and occupying it for a year.

1492 The Moors offered to surrender Granada to the Spanish. The actual surrender took place the next day, ending the Moorish hold in Europe.

1502 Portuguese explorer Goncalo Coelho entered Guanabara Bay, on the Atlantic coast of South America. Believing it was a river mouth, he named it Rio de Janeiro ("River of January").

1503 Columbus spent the day anchored off the site of present-day Coco Solo, Canal Zone, in Panama, on his fourth voyage to America. He never learned how close he was to the Pacific.

1651 Charles II was crowned King of the Scots at Scone. He was to become King of England in 1660 after the death of Oliver Cromwell.

1660 Samuel Pepys began his *Diary* with the words "Blessed be God, at the end of the last year I was in very good health, without any sense of my old pain, but upon taking of cold."

1772 Thomas Jefferson married Martha Wayles Skelton.

1824 James K. Polk married Sarah Childress.

1824 Haiti was proclaimed an independent country by General Jean Jacques Dessalines, the leader in the struggle against the French.

1863 President Abraham Lincoln issued the Emancipation Proclamation, freeing the slaves.

1892 The Ellis Island Immigrant Station in New York Harbor was officially opened.

1901 The Commonwealth of Australia was established by the British Parliament.

1902 The first Rose Bowl football game was played, with Michigan beating Stanford, 49-0.

1913 The U.S. parcel post service began.

1916 The Rose Bowl game became an annual event with the game between Washington State and Brown in the new 101,385-seat stadium in Pasadena, California.

1925 The Norwegian capital of Christiania was renamed Oslo.

1931 The comic strip *Joe Palooka,* by Ham Fisher, first appeared, in the New York *Mirror.*

1935 The Sugar Bowl game was played for the first time, with Tulane beating Temple, 20-14.

1935	The Orange Bowl game was played for the first time, with Bucknell defeating Miami, 26-0.
1937	The Cotton Bowl game was played for the first time, with Texas Christian University beating Marquette, 16-8.
1954	The Tournament of Roses parade in Pasadena, California, became the first program to be televised in color on a nationwide network.
1959	Cuban dictator Fulgencio Batista resigned and fled to Dominica, as rebel leader Fidel Castro captured Santiago.
1975	Richard Nixon's aides, H.R. Haldeman, John Ehrlichman, and John Mitchell, were convicted in the Watergate cover-up trial.
1979	President Jimmy Carter opened United States diplomatic relations with the People's Republic of China.
1984	The breakup of AT&T took place as the telecommunications giant was divested of its 22 Bell System companies under terms of an antitrust agreement.
1993	Czechoslovakia split into two new political states: the Czech Republic and Slovakia.

January 2 – Birthdays

1647	**Nathaniel Bacon.** American planter who led Bacon's Rebellion in Virginia in 1676 against the English colonial government
1727	**James Wolfe.** British general and hero of the Battle of Quebec in 1759, which won Canada for the British Empire
1752	**Philip Freneau.** Early American poet and journalist, known by many as the "Poet of the American Revolution"
1822	**Rudolf Clausius.** German physicist who in 1850 formulated the second law of thermodynamics: "Heat cannot of itself pass from a colder to a hotter body"
1828	**Jeremiah E. Rankin.** Composer of the hymn "God Be with You till We Meet Again"
1831	**Justin Winsor.** American historian, librarian and co-founder of the American Library Association
1857	**Frederick Burr Opper.** American cartoonist and creator of *Happy Hooligan, Maud,* and *Alphonse and Gaston*
1857	**Martha Carey Thomas.** American educator, suffragist and author of *Sir Gawain and the Green Knight*
1861	**Helen Herron Taft.** Wife of President William Howard Taft
1863	**Lucia Zarate.** The world's lightest recorded adult, at 5.7 pounds when she was 17 years old
1865	**William Lyon Phelps.** American author, educator, and literary critic who was influential in shaping American literary tastes of his time, and who taught the first American course in modern fiction
1866	**Gilbert Murray.** British classical scholar best known for translation of the Greek plays

1870	**Ernst Heinrich Barlach.** German sculptor noted for works such as *The Reunion* (1930)
1885	**Marcel Andre.** Distinguished character actor of the French stage and screen
1893	**Lillian Leitzel.** German-born trapeze artist and "Queen of the Circus," who performed for both Barnum and Bailey and the Ringling Brothers
1894	**Arthur C. Nielsen.** American tennis philanthropist
1895	**Count Folke Bernadotte.** Swedish humanitarian and U.N. diplomat who was murdered in Jerusalem in 1948 while trying to bring about peace between the Arabs and the Jews
1896	**Lank Leonard.** American comic strip artist and creator of *Mickey Finn*
1899	**Charles Howard.** American painter
1904	**Sally Rand.** American strip-tease artist and inventor of the fan dance
1920	**Isaac Asimov.** American biochemist and novelist, noted for his worldwide bestsellers in science fiction
1922	**Renata Tebaldi.** Italian operatic soprano and one of the great stars of her day
1925	**William J. Crowe.** U.S. admiral and Chairman of the Joint Chiefs of Staff under Presidents Reagan and Bush
1927	**Gino Marchetti.** Professional football player
1928	**Dan Rostenkowski.** U.S. congressman
1930	**Julius LaRosa.** American singer and television entertainer
1933	**Richard Riley.** Secretary of Education under President Clinton
1936	**Roger Miller.** American singer
1939	**Jim Bakker.** American television evangelist defrocked in 1987 because of a sex scandal involving a church secretary
1942	**Marvin Fleming.** Professional football player
1947	**Calvin Hill.** Professional football player
1949	**Mike Newlin.** Professional basketball player
1963	**David Cone.** Professional baseball pitcher who pitched a perfect game (no baserunners) in 1999
1963	**Edgar Martinez.** Professional baseball player
1965	**Diane Lane.** American stage, screen and television actress
1968	**Cuba Gooding.** American motion-picture actor

January 2 – Events

1492	The last Moorist stronghold in Europe was wiped out as the forces of Ferdinand and Isabella of Spain occupied Granada.
1788	Georgia ratified the Constitution becoming the fourth state of the Union.
1842	The first U.S. wire suspension bridge was opened, spanning the Schuylkill River at Fairmont, near Philadelphia.
1900	U.S. Secretary of State John Hay announced the "Open-Door Policy" to facilitate trade with China.

1905 The Russians surrendered at Port Arthur in Manchuria in the last major military engagement of the Russo-Japanese War.

1921 Religious services were first broadcast over the radio, by Station KDKA of Pittsburgh.

1942 The Japanese occupied Manila in World War II.

1948 The American Federation of Musicians under James C. Petrillo started a recording strike.

1949 American comedian Jack Benny began his Sunday night radio program over CBS, after moving from NBC.

1959 The Russians launched the moon probe *Luna I*, which missed the moon and became the first spacecraft to orbit the sun.

1968 South African surgeon Dr. Christiaan Barnard performed his, and the world's, second heart transplant. The patient in this case left the hospital and lived for more than a year.

1974 President Nixon signed the bill requiring a 55 mph speed limit on all U.S. highways by March 2, 1974. The Congress repealed the law in 1995.

1984 W. Wilson Goode was sworn in as Philadelphia's first black mayor.

January 3 – Birthdays

106 BC **Marcus Tullius Cicero.** Noted Roman statesman and orator, and the greatest of the ancient writers

1591 **Le Valentin.** French painter

1698 **Pietro Metastasio.** Italian poet and librettist

1793 **Lucretia Mott.** American reformer, co-founder of the American Anti-Slavery Society (1833), and pioneer in the women's rights movement

1803 **Douglas Jerrold.** English dramatist and journalist

1823 **Robert Whitehead.** British engineer who invented the Whitehead submarine torpedo

1835 **Larkin Goldsmith Mead.** American sculptor noted for the Lincoln monument in Springfield, Illinois

1840 **Henry Holt.** American publisher who founded Henry Holt Company publishers in 1866

1840 **Joseph Damien de Veuster.** Belgian priest who gave his life to the care of lepers in Molokai, Hawaii

1879 **Grace Goodhue Coolidge.** Wife of President Calvin Coolidge

1883 **Clement Attlee.** British prime minister, 1945-1951, who succeeded Winston Churchill

1886 **Raymond Ames Spruance.** American admiral, commander of the Fifth Fleet in World War II, and leader of the great victory in the Battle of Midway, which many think was the turning point in the Pacific war with Japan

1887 **August Macke.** German painter

1892 **J.R.R. Tolkien.** English fantasy writer and author of the monumental work *The Lord of the Rings* (1954-1956)

1897 **Marion Davies.** American stage and motion-picture actress, noted for her leading roles of the 1920s and for her 30-year affair with the famous journalist William Randolph Hearst

1898 **John Loder.** English stage and screen actor

1898 **ZaSu Pitts.** American motion-picture and television actress, who appeared in over 100 silent and talking pictures in a 45-year career

1901 **Ngo Dinh Diem.** First president of South Vietnam, 1955-1963

1905 **Ray Milland.** Welsh-born motion-picture and television leading man and character actor in over 150 films in a 50-year career

1909 **Victor Borge.** Danish comedian and pianist

1911 **Joseph Rauh.** American lawyer and liberal political activist

1915 **Jack Levine.** American painter noted for works such as *Gangster Funeral* (1953)

1916 **Betty Furness.** American television performer and consumer advocate

1918 **Buddy Kaye.** American author, saxophonist, and producer, noted for such lyrics as "Till the End of Time," "A-You're Adorable," and "Full Moon and Empty Arms"

1918 **Maxine Andrews.** One of the singing Andrews Sisters, a highly popular harmony trio of the 1940s

1919 **Jesse White.** American stage, screen, and television character actor with a career of over 40 years

1924 **Hank Stram.** Professional football player, coach, and sportscaster

1926 **George Martin.** Producer for The Beatles, 1962-1969

1930 **Carla Anderson Hills.** Secretary of Housing and Urban Development under President Ford

1930 **Robert Loggia.** American stage, screen and television actor

1932 **D.X. Fenton.** American author of children's stories

1932 **Dabney Coleman.** American motion-picture and television actor

1935 **Millard Fuller.** American lawyer and President of Habitat for Humanity

1936 **Betty Rollin.** American journalist and author

1939 **Bobby Hull.** One of the greatest goal scorers in National Hockey League history and its first player to score 50 or more goals in more than one season

1945 **Stephen Stills.** American singer and guitarist with Crosby, Stills, Nash, and Young

1946 **John Paul Jones.** British bassist with the Led Zeppelin musical group

1948 **David Lloyd.** English tennis player

1950 **Victoria Principal.** American actress noted for her role in the long-running television series *Dallas*

1956 **Mel Gibson.** American motion-picture actor with ten Academy Award nominations

1963 **Jim Everett.** Professional football player

1964 **Cheryl Miller.** Hall of Fame basketball player

January 3 – Events

1521 Pope Leo X excommunicated Martin Luther from the Roman Catholic Church.

1777 George Washington, in one of his most brilliant triumphs, defeated the British in the Battle of Princeton, N.J., in the Revolutionary War.

1841 Herman Melville boarded the whaler *Acushnet,* beginning his career of naval adventures that gave him the background for his novels, particularly his masterpiece *Moby Dick.*

1847 The village of Yerba Buena in California officially changed its name to San Francisco.

1870 Construction of the Brooklyn Bridge began. It was the largest suspension bridge in the world when it was completed 13 years later.

1871 Henry W. Bradley of Binghampton, New York, received a patent for oleomargarine.

1882 Oscar Wilde, the famous Irish poet and wit, on docking at New York and being asked by customs if he had anything to declare, replied, "Nothing but my genius."

1920 Babe Ruth signed with the New York Yankees, having just been acquired from the Boston Red Sox.

1935 In a special plebiscite conducted by the League of Nations, the residents of the Saar Basin voted overwhelmingly for reunion with Germany.

1938 "The March of Dimes" campaign to fight infantile paralysis was organized.

1942 The American defenders of the Philippines retreated to the Bataan Peninsula in World War II.

1959 Alaska was admitted to the Union as the 49th state.

1961 The United States severed diplomatic relations with Fidel Castro's Cuba.

January 4 – Birthdays

1581 **James Ussher.** Anglo-Irish archbishop who claimed by his research that the world was created in 4,004 B.C.

1643 **Sir Isaac Newton.** English giant of science, who discovered the law of gravity, invented the calculus, and discovered the secrets of light and color

1710 **Giovanni Battista Pergolesi.** Italian composer noted for the comic opera *La Serva Padrona* (1733) and the religious work *Stabat Mater* (1729)

1784 **François Rude.** French sculptor

1785 **Jakob Grimm.** German scholar who with his brother Wilhelm wrote the *German Dictionary* and compiled *Grimm's Fairy Tales* (1812, 1815)

1809 **Louis Braille.** Inventor of the braille system of printing and writing for the blind (1829)

1813 **Sir Isaac Pitman.** British schoolmaster who invented phonetic shorthand

1831 **E.P. Dutton.** American publisher and founder of E.P. Dutton publisher (1858)

1838 **Tom Thumb (Charles S. Stratton).** Famous 40-inch, 70-pound "little person" with the P.T. Barnum show in the mid-19th century

1858 **Carter Glass.** American statesman and sponsor of the Federal Reserve Act of 1913

1859 **George Washington Carver.** Noted black American scientist who revolutionized the agriculture of the South and made more than 300 products from the peanut

1877 **Marsden Hartley.** American painter known as "the painter from Maine," and noted for works such as *Earth Warming, Mexico* (1932)

1878 **Augustus John.** British painter known principally for his portraits of prominent people, such as David Lloyd George and George Bernard Shaw

1881 **Wilhelm Lehmbruck.** German sculptor noted for works such as *Seated Youth* (1918)

1887 **Edwin Emil Witte.** American economist who wrote the Social Security Act of 1935

1895 **Leroy Randle Grumman.** American aircraft manufacturer who founded Grumman Aerospace Corporation in 1929

1896 **Everett McKinley Dirksen.** U.S. senator and Minority Leader, 1959-1969

1905 **Sterling Holloway.** American motion-picture actor who appeared in some 100 films and provided voice-overs for many Walt Disney cartoon characters

1906 **William Bendix.** American motion-picture and television actor

1907 **Joe Marsala.** American composer, author, and conductor, noted for songs such as "Little Sir Echo"

1908 **George Selkirk.** Professional baseball player who succeeded Babe Ruth in right field in 1934 for the New York Yankees

1914 **Jane Wyman.** American motion-picture and television superstar, who won the Academy Award in 1948 for *Johnny Belinda*

1920 **William Colby.** Director of the CIA under Presidents Nixon and Ford

1925 **Johnny Lujack.** Professional football superstar

1927 **Barbara Rush.** American motion-picture and television actress, and leading lady of the 1950s and 1960s

1930 **Sorrell Booke.** American stage, screen, and television actor

1930 **Don Shula.** One of the most successful football coaches in the history of the National Football League

1932 **Carlos Saura.** Spanish motion-picture director and one of the leading figures of the new Spanish cinema

1935 **Floyd Patterson.** First boxer in history to hold the world heavyweight championship twice (1956-1959 and 1960-1962)

1937 **Grace Bumbry.** American mezzo-soprano

1937 **Dyan Cannon.** American stage, screen, and television actress

1941 **Maureen Reagan.** Daughter of President Ronald Reagan and actress Jane Wyman

1943 **Doris Kearns Goodwin.** American historian and writer, noted for works such as *Lyndon Johnson and the American Dream* (1976) and *Wait Till Next Year* (1997)

1951 **Barbara Ann Cochran.** Professional skier

1961 **Clifford Eugene Levingston.** Professional basketball player

1965 **Guy Forget.** French tennis player

January 4 – Events

48 BC Julius Caesar arrived in Greece in pursuit of his rival, Pompey, whom he later defeated at Pharsalus.

1076 Henry IV, King of Germany, convened the Synod of Worms, which declared Pope Gregory VII deposed.

1877 Cornelius Vanderbilt, the famous American financier, died at age 82, leaving an estate of $100 million, a prodigious sum for that time.

1885 The first successful U.S. appendectomy was performed, by Dr. William West Grant in Davenport, Iowa. The patient was 22-year-old Mary Gartside.

1893 President Benjamin Harrison issued a proclamation granting amnesty for polygamists "who had abstained from unlawful cohabitation of a polygamist marriage since November 1, 1890."

1896 Utah was admitted to the Union as the 45th state.

1937 Italian troops landed in Spain to help Generalissimo Francisco Franco's rebels in the Spanish Civil War.

1948 Britain granted independence to Burma.

1960 Albert Camus, the noted French writer, was killed in a car accident near Sens, France, at age 46.

1965 T.S. Eliot, the famous American-born English poet, died in London at age 76.

1979 The Shah of Iran appointed Shahpour Bakhtiar prime minister, to appease his critics.

January 5 – Birthdays

1548 **Francisco Suarez.** Noted Spanish theologian and a founder of the philosophy of international law

1779 **Zebulon Montgomery Pike.** American general and explorer, famous for his discovery in 1806 of Pikes Peak

1779 **Stephen Decatur.** One of the most daring officers of the U.S. Navy during its early years, who is remembered for the famous toast, "Our country, right or wrong"

1782 **Robert Morrison.** First Protestant minister in China

1786 **Thomas Nuttall.** Pioneer English botanist

1794 **Edmund Ruffin.** American agriculturist and Southern secessionist who fired the first shot on Fort Sumter

1855 **King Camp Gillette.** Inventor and manufacturer of the safety razor and blade

1864 **Ban Johnson.** Organizer and first president of baseball's American League

1871 **Frederick Shepherd Converse.** American romantic music composer

1875 **J. Stuart Blackton.** English-born pioneer motion-picture director, screenwriter, and actor, who co-founded the Vitagraph Company in 1897

1876 **Konrad Adenauer.** First chancellor of the West German Republic, 1949-1963

1877 **Henry Sloane Coffin.** Noted American clergyman, author, and educator

1879 **Jack Norworth.** American composer, author, and actor, noted for songs such as "Shine On, Harvest Moon" and "Take Me Out to the Ball Game"

1887 **Courtney Hodges.** American World War II general

1887 **Bernard Leach.** English ceramist

1893 **Spencer Gordon Bennet.** American motion-picture director who started in 1912 as a stuntman and actor in Edison action pictures and had a career of over 50 years

1900 **Yves Tanguy.** French-born surrealist artist noted for works such as *Fear*

1902 **Hubert Beuve-Mery.** French publisher, editor and founder of the famous newspaper *Le Monde* (1944)

1905 **Francis Henry.** English-American composer, author, and guitarist, noted for songs such as "Little Girl," "Ain't It a Shame," and "Sugar Bun"

1906 **Dame Kathleen Kenyon.** English archaeologist who excavated the ancient city of Jericho

1909 **Jean-Pierre Aumont.** French actor and durable leading man of French, American, and international films with a 50-year career

1913 **Kemmons Wilson.** American financier who founded the Holiday Inn chain

1914 **Nicolas de Stael.** French painter

1918 **Jeanne Dixon.** American astrologer and newspaper columnist

1926 **Maria Schell.** Austrian stage and motion-picture actress and sister of actor-director Maximilian Schell

1928 **Walter F. Mondale.** U.S. vice president under President Carter, and presidential candidate in 1984

1928 **Ali Bhutto.** President of Pakistan, 1971-1977

1931 **Alvin Ailey.** American choreographer and dancer

1931 **Alfred Brendel.** Austrian pianist

1931 **Robert Duvall.** American stage and motion-picture actor

1932 **Umberto Eco.** Italian author noted for works such as *In the Name of the Rose*

1932 **Chuck Noll.** Professional football player and coach

1932 **Raisa Gorbachev.** Wife of former Soviet leader Mikhail Gorbachev

1935 **Earl Battey.** Professional baseball player

1938 **Juan Carlos I.** King of Spain who was installed in 1975 following the death of dictator Francisco Franco

1938 **Jim Otto.** Hall of Fame professional football player

1941 **Charles McKinley.** American tennis player

1942 **Charlie Rose.** American television interviewer and talk-show host

1946 **Diane Keaton.** American stage and motion-picture actress

1947 **Eugene "Mercury" Morris.** Professional football player

1948 **Charlie Hough.** Professional baseball player and pitching coach

1951 **Don Gullet.** Professional baseball player

1953 **Pamela Sue Martin.** American motion-picture and television actress

1954 **Alex English.** Professional basketball player with over 20,000 career points

1954 **Jim Gantner.** Professional baseball player

1957 **Steve Fuller.** Professional football player

1958 **Joe Cribbs.** Professional football player

1966 **Kate Schellenbach.** Rock musician with the group Luscious Jackson

January 5 – Events

1066 Edward the Confessor, the last English king descended from Alfred the Great, died at age 64. The dispute over his successor led to the Norman conquest of England.

1477 The Swiss defeated the Burgundians and Charles the Bold at Nancy, France.

1776 New Hampshire became the first colony to form a government independent of Great Britain, adopting a temporary constitution.

1895 Captain Alfred Dreyfus, unjustly convicted of espionage, was stripped of his badges and buttons in Paris.

1914 Because of his great success with the Model T, Henry Ford raised his workers' pay from $2.40 to $5.00 per day and reduced the working day from nine to eight hours.

1919 The National Socialist Party, the forerunner of the Nazis, was founded in Germany.

1925 Mrs. Nellie Tayloe Ross, the first U.S. woman governor, was sworn in as governor of Wyoming.

1933 Calvin Coolidge died in Northampton, Massachusetts, at age 60.

1943 George Washington Carver, the great black American scientist, died at an approximate age of 84.

1948 Dr. Alfred C. Kinsey published his *Sexual Behavior in the Human Male.*

1949 President Harry S. Truman labeled his administration the "Fair Deal" in his State of the Union Address.

January 6 – Birthdays

1367 **Richard II.** King of England, 1377-1399, and son of the great English warrior, Edward the Black Prince

1412 **Joan of Arc.** French national heroine and beloved saint of the Roman Catholic Church, who led the French army to victory at the siege of Orleans in 1429

1425 **Henry IV (the Impotent).** King of Castile before the time of Ferdinand and Isabella

1580 **Captain John Smith.** Leader of the English colonists who settled Jamestown, Va., in 1607 (His birthday is speculation, but he was baptized on January 9 when he was probably three days old.)

1799 **Jedediah Smith.** American explorer, fur trader, and one of the first white men to enter California from the east

1811 **Charles Sumner.** American statesman and noted abolitionist, and one of the founders of the Republican Party

1822 **Heinrich Schliemann.** German archaeologist who became famous for discovering and excavating the ruins of ancient Troy

1828 **Ward Hill Lamon.** American statesman and law partner of Abraham Lincoln

1832 **Gustave Dore.** French painter and sculptor, who illustrated a large number of literary masterpieces, such as Dante's *Divine Comedy,* Cervantes' *Don Quixote,* and Poe's "The Raven"

1838 **Max Bruch.** German composer noted for works such as *Kol Nidrei* for cello and orchestra

1872 **Alexander Nikolaievitch Scriabin.** Russian composer and pianist, whose last six sonatas for piano (1908 to 1913) are considered masterworks

1878 **Dame Adeline Genee.** Noted German-English ballet dancer

1878 **Carl Sandburg.** American poet, biographer, and folk song collector, whose six-volume *Abraham Lincoln* (1926, 1939) is considered by many to be the great biography of the 20th century

1879 **Joseph Medill Patterson.** Publisher of the Chicago *Tribune,* 1914-1925

1880 **Tom Mix.** Legendary cowboy star of Hollywood silents and early talkies

1882 **Sam Rayburn.** U.S. congressman who served 49 consecutive years (1912-1961) and was Speaker of the House longer than any other person (nearly 17 years)

1883 **Khalil Gibran.** Lebanese writer and painter, noted for his great philosophical work *The Prophet* (1923)

1910 **Wright Morris.** American novelist

1911 **Joey Adams.** American comedian

1913 **Loretta Young.** American motion-picture and television actress, Hollywood leading lady of the 1930s and 1940s, and star of television in the 1950s

1914 **Danny Thomas.** American motion-picture and television actor, singer, and comedian

1920 **Early Wynn.** Hall of Fame baseball pitcher who won 300 career games

1920 **Sun Myung Moon.** Korean evangelist and leader of the "Moonies"

1920 **Jean Ipousteguy.** French sculptor

1921 **Cary Middlecoff.** Professional golfer

1921 **Lou Harris.** American public opinion pollster

1924 **Earl Scruggs.** American banjo player and songwriter with Flatt and Scruggs

1926	**Kid Gavilan.** World welterweight boxing champion, 1951-1954
1926	**Ralph Branca.** Professional baseball pitcher who threw the famous home-run pitch to Bobby Thomson that gave the New York Giants the 1951 pennant over the Brooklyn Dodgers
1929	**Vic Tayback.** American actor noted for his role as Mel in the long-running TV series *Alice*
1931	**E.L. Doctorow.** American novelist and editor, noted for works such as *The Book of Daniel* and *Ragtime*
1931	**Dickie Moore.** Professional hockey player
1933	**Capucine (Germaine Lefebvre).** French motion-picture actress and model
1936	**Darlene Hard.** Top-ranked U.S. tennis player in 1962
1937	**Lou Holtz.** Noted football coach
1944	**Bonnie Franklin.** American television actress and star of the long-running show *One Day At a Time*
1944	**Henry R. Kravis.** American businessman and partner in Kolberg, Kravis, Roberts and Co., which specializes in leveraged buyouts
1946	**Harold Jackson.** Professional football player
1946	**Syd Barrett.** Original guitarist with the Pink Floyd musical group
1950	**Louis J. Freeh.** Director of the FBI under President Clinton
1953	**Jett Williams.** American singer and daughter of singer Hank Williams
1957	**Nancy Lopez.** Professional golfer and superstar
1959	**Kathy Sledge.** American musician and member of Sister Sledge, noted for their 1979 hit, "We Are Family"
1960	**Howie Long.** Professional football player
1962	**Michael Houser.** American rock musician with the group Widespread Panic
1964	**Charles Lewis Haley.** Professional football player

January 6 – Events

1266	Charles d'Anjou was crowned King of Naples and Sicily.
1540	King Henry VIII of England married his fourth wife, Anne of Cleves, despite his opinion that she had no looks and was "no better than a Flanders mare."
1759	George Washington married Martha Dandridge Custis in New Kent County, Virginia.
1872	Jim Fisk, famous American Robber Baron, was shot to death on the stairs of the Grand Central Hotel in New York by Edward S. Stokes, a rival for the favors of Fisk's mistress.
1898	Simon Lake, the developer of the method of submerging by negative buoyancy, used in today's submarines, became the first person to talk by telephone from under water.
1912	New Mexico was admitted to the Union as the 47th state.

1919	Theodore Roosevelt died at Oyster Bay, New York, at age 60.
1941	President Franklin D. Roosevelt called for a world with the Four Freedoms—of speech, of religion, from want, and from fear.
1975	The long-running television show *Wheel of Fortune* made its debut. Pat Sajak became the host in 1981.

January 7 – Birthdays

1718	**Israel Putnam.** American pioneer and Revolutionary War general
1745	**Jacques Etienne Montgolfier.** French balloonist who with his brother Joseph invented the first balloons to carry men into the air
1768	**Joseph Bonaparte.** King of Naples, 1806, King of Spain, 1808, and brother of Napoleon Bonaparte
1800	**Millard Fillmore.** 13th U.S. president
1830	**Albert Bierstadt.** One of the greatest American romantic landscape painters
1844	**Saint Bernadette of Lourdes.** Roman Catholic visionary to whom the Virgin Mary is said to have appeared 18 times in 1858 and told her to make known the healing powers of the springs of water in Lourdes
1845	**Louis III.** King of Bavaria
1873	**Charles Peguy.** French writer noted for works such as the poem "Jeanne d'Arc" (1897)
1873	**Adolph Zukor.** Hungarian-born film pioneer and co-founder and early president of Paramount Pictures
1890	**Maurice Evans McLoughlin.** American Hall of Fame tennis player and national champion in 1912 and 1913
1899	**Francis Poulenc.** Member of "Les Six," a group of French composers in the 1920s that rejected romanticism and impressionism
1906	**Herbert Adolph Magidson.** American composer and author, noted for songs such as "Enjoy Yourself," "Black-Eyed Susan Brown," "I'll Buy That Dream," "The Continental," and "Music, Maestro, Please"
1910	**Orval Faubus.** American politician and governor of Arkansas who refused to allow court-ordered integration of a Little Rock high school in 1957, causing President Eisenhower to order in the National Guard
1912	**Charles Addams.** American cartoonist famous for his macabre humor and his amusing monsters in the *New Yorker* magazine
1913	**Johnny Mize.** Hall of Fame baseball player who hit 51 home runs in 1947
1922	**Vincent Gardenia.** Italian-American stage, screen, and television actor
1922	**Alvin Dark.** Professional baseball player and manager

1928 **William Peter Blatty.** American screenwriter, director and author, noted for works such as *The Exorcist* (1970)

1929 **Terry Moore.** American motion-picture actress

1930 **Eddie Le Baron.** Professional football superstar

1930 **Douglas Kiker.** American television news correspondent and host

1934 **Reg Murphy.** American journalist and editor

1938 **Lou Graham.** Professional golfer

1939 **Maury Povich.** American television host and son of sportswriter Shirley Povich

1943 **Leona Williams.** American singer and songwriter

1945 **Alena Palmeova-West.** Czechoslovakian tennis player

1948 **Kenny Loggins.** American singer, songwriter, and recording artist

1950 **Ross Grimsley.** Professional baseball player

1957 **Katie Couric.** *Today Show* hostess

1959 **Kathy Valentine.** Rock musician with The Go-Go's

1964 **Nicolas Cage.** American television and motion-picture actor

January 7 – Events

1327 King Edward II of England was forced by Parliament to abdicate. He was murdered soon after.

1536 Catherine of Aragon, the first wife of King Henry VIII of England, died at age 50.

1610 Galileo, the great Italian scientist, discovered the four moons of Jupiter through his telescope. He named them the Medicean stars, after the Medici family.

1714 The first patent for a typewriter was given to English engineer Henry Mills.

1782 The Bank of North America, the first commercial bank in the United States, opened in Philadelphia.

1789 The first American presidential election was held, with George Washington an easy winner.

1830 Commercial railroad service was started in the United States by the Baltimore and Ohio Railroad Company.

1896 Fannie Farmer published her famous cookbook, *Boston Cooking School Cook Book,* one of the best sellers of all time.

1924 George Gershwin, the great American composer, completed the piano score of *Rhapsody in Blue.*

1927 Transatlantic telephone service from New York to London began.

1927 The Harlem Globetrotters, the famous black basketball team, was founded by Abe Saperstein in Hinckley, Illinois.

1929 The comic strip *Buck Rogers*, by Phil Nowland and Dick Callins, first appeared.

1929 *Tarzan of the Apes*, created by Edgar Rice Burroughs and illustrated by Harold Foster, first appeared in newspapers.

1934 The comic strips *Flash Gordon* and *Jungle Jim*, both by Alex Raymond, first appeared.

1942 The Japanese began their three-month siege of Bataan in World War II.

1952 General Dwight D. Eisenhower announced that he would accept the Republican nomination for president if it were offered to him.

1953 President Harry S. Truman announced in his State of the Union Address that the United States had developed a hydrogen bomb.

1999 The impeachment trial of President Clinton began in the U.S. Senate with Chief Justice William Rehnquist presiding.

January 8 – Birthdays

1587 **Jan Pieterszoon Coen.** Chief founder of the Dutch East Indies

1638 **Elisabetta Sirani.** Italian painter

1705 **Jacques François Blondel.** French architect

1735 **John Carroll.** First Roman Catholic bishop in the U.S. (1790) and founder in 1789 of Georgetown University

1786 **Nicholas Biddle.** American financier, early president of the U.S. Bank, and author, noted for *History of the Expedition of Captains Lewis and Clark*

1792 **Lowell Mason.** American hymnwriter, who wrote more than 1,650 religious compositions, one of the best known of which is "Nearer My God to Thee," reportedly played by the band on the *Titanic* as it was going down

1821 **James Longstreet.** Confederate general in the Civil War

1823 **Alfred Russel Wallace.** British naturalist and explorer, noted for reaching independently the same explanation for evolution as Charles Darwin did.

1824 **Wilkie Collins.** English detective story writer noted for works such as *The Woman in White* (1860) and *The Moonstone* (1868), one of the world's greatest detective stories

1825 **Henri Giffard.** French inventor of the first successful airship, a steam-powered craft which he flew in 1852

1862 **Frank N. Doubleday.** American publisher and founder of Doubleday and Company

1881 **William Thomas Piper.** American airplane manufacturer

1883 **Patrick J. Hurley.** American statesman and soldier and secretary of war, 1929-1933

1885 **John Curtin.** Prime minister of Australia during World War II

1891 **William Kiplinger.** Founder of the *Kiplinger Letter*

1902 **Georgi Malenkov.** Premier of Russia, 1953-1955, who succeeded Joseph Stalin

1904 **Peter Arno.** American cartoonist who drew primarily for the *New Yorker* magazine

1911 **Butterfly McQueen.** American theater and motion-picture actress, noted for her role of Prissy in *Gone With the Wind*

1912	**Jose Ferrer.** Puerto Rican-born stage and motion-picture actor and director
1915	**Walker Cooper.** Professional baseball catcher, who with his brother, pitcher Mort Cooper, formed one of baseball's best-known brother batteries
1923	**Larry Storch.** American actor and comedian
1924	**Ron Moody.** English singer and stage, screen, and television actor
1928	**Sander Vanocur.** American broadcast journalist
1928	**Slade Gorton.** U.S. senator
1930	**Doreen Wilbur.** Professional archer
1930	**Soupy Sales.** American comedian and television personality
1933	**Charles Osgood.** American television news correspondent and host of CBS's *Sunday Morning*
1934	**Alexandra Ripley.** American novelist and author of *Scarlett: The Sequel to Margaret Mitchell's Gone with the Wind* (1991)
1935	**Elvis Presley.** "The King" of American rock and roll singers, and rock music's first multi-millionaire superstar
1937	**Dame Shirley Bassey.** Welsh singer
1939	**Yvette Mimieux.** American stage, screen, and television actress
1941	**Graham Chapman.** British actor and screenwriter, who with John Cleese conceived the idea of the hit TV show *Monty Python's Flying Circus*
1942	**Stephen W. Hawking.** British theoretical physicist, considered by many to be the greatest since Albert Einstein, and author of *A Brief History of Time*
1946	**Robbie Krieger.** American guitarist with The Doors rock group
1947	**David Bowie.** British rock singer and musician
1953	**Bruce Sutter.** Professional baseball player and one of the game's great relief pitchers
1957	**Dwight Clark.** Professional football player

January 8 – Events

1198	Innocent III, the greatest of the medieval Roman Catholic popes, was elected.
1337	Giotto di Bondone, the Italian painter, died in Florence at age 70.
1642	Galileo, the great Italian astronomer and physicist, died in Florence at age 77.
1798	Amendment 11 to the Constitution was proclaimed, prohibiting any citizen of one state from suing another state.
1815	General Andrew Jackson defeated the British in the Battle of New Orleans in the War of 1812, two weeks after the peace treaty had been signed.
1835	President Andrew Jackson paid off the final installment of the national debt, the only president ever to do so.
1845	Felix Mendelssohn's "Hear My Prayer" was sung publicly for the first time, in London.
1918	Mississippi became the first state to ratify the Prohibition Amendment to the Constitution.

1918	President Woodrow Wilson announced his Fourteen Points as a basis for a post-World War I settlement.
1926	Ibn Saud was crowned King of Hejaz and Nejd, which he was to rename Saudi Arabia in 1932.
1959	Charles de Gaulle was inaugurated president of France's Fifth Republic.
1964	President Lyndon B. Johnson committed the U.S. to a "War on Poverty."
1976	Chou En-Lai, Chinese premier since 1949, died at age 78.

January 9 – Birthdays

1554	**Gregory XV.** Roman Catholic pope, 1621-1623
1590	**Simon Vouet.** French painter
1658	**Nicolas Cousteau.** French sculptor
1819	**William Powell Frith.** English artist noted for paintings such as *Derby Day* (1858)
1854	**Jennie Jerome Churchill.** American socialite and mother of Winston Churchill
1856	**Lizette Woodward Reese.** American poet
1859	**Carrie Chapman Catt.** American pioneer leader in the campaign for woman suffrage, and founder in 1920 of the National League of Women Voters, now the League of Women Voters
1864	**Alvah Curtis Roebuck.** American merchant and partner with Richard W. Sears in founding Sears, Roebuck and Co. (1887)
1870	**Joseph Baerman Strauss.** Designer of the Golden Gate Bridge
1881	**Lascelles Abercrombie.** British poet and critic
1890	**Karel Capek.** Czech writer, best known for his play *R.U.R. (Rossum's Universal Robots)* (1921), in which he introduced the word *robot* to the language
1897	**Felisa Rincon de Gautier.** Puerto Rican statesman
1898	**Dame Gracie Fields.** English actress, singer, and comedienne, and the top box office draw in Britain in the 1930s
1900	**Richard Halliburton.** American adventurer, author, and lecturer, noted for works such as *New Worlds to Conquer* (1929) and *The Orient* and *The Occident* (both in 1937)
1901	**Chic Young.** American cartoonist and creator in 1930 of *Blondie,* one of the most popular comic strips of all time
1902	**Rudolf Bing.** Manager of the Metropolitan Opera Association of New York City, 1950-1972
1904	**George Balanchine.** Russian-born American choreographer and founder of the New York City Ballet
1908	**Simone de Beauvoir.** French philosopher and novelist, noted for works such as *The Second Sex* (1949)
1910	**Dick Henry Jurgens.** American composer, author, and orchestra leader, noted for songs such as "Elmer's Tune" and "One Dozen Roses"

1913 Richard M. Nixon. 37th U.S. president and the only president to resign the office

1914 Gypsy Rose Lee. American actress and writer, and burlesque queen of the 1930s, the best-known stripper of her day

1915 Fernando Lamas. Argentine motion-picture actor and sporty Latin lover of Hollywood films of the 1950s

1915 Henning Dahl Mikkelsen. American cartoonist

1917 Herbert Lom. Czech motion-picture and stage actor with a 50-year career

1922 Vic Mizzy. American composer and author, noted for songs such as "The Whole World Is Singing My Song," "Three Little Sisters," "My Dreams Are Getting Better All the Time," and "The Jones Boy"

1922 Sekou Toure. First president of the Republic of Guinea

1925 Lee Van Cleef. American television and motion-picture actor who starred often as an ideal villain

1928 Judith Krantz. American author noted for works like *Mistral's Daughter* (1982)

1934 Bart Starr. Professional football superstar and Hall of Famer

1935 Bob Denver. American actor noted for his role as Gilligan in the long-running television series *Gilligan's Island*

1935 Dick Enberg. American television sportscaster

1936 Ralph Terry. Professional baseball player

1941 Joan Baez. Noted American folk singer and guitarist

1941 Susannah York. English stage, screen, and television actress

1944 Jimmy Page. British guitarist with the Led Zeppelin musical group

1950 Bob Newhouse. Professional football player

1951 Crystal Gayle. American country singer

1953 Ivan De Jesus. Professional baseball player

1965 Muggsy Bogues. Professional basketball player

January 9 – Events

1324 Marco Polo, the famous Venetian traveler, died in Venice at approximately 70 years of age.

1580 John Smith, the future captain of the English colony in Jamestown, Virginia, was baptized.

1788 Connecticut ratified the Constitution, becoming the fifth state of the Union.

1793 The first successful balloon flight in the U.S. originated in Philadelphia with George Washington, Thomas Jefferson, John Adams, Henry Clay, and Paul Revere in the audience. John Pierre Blanchard, a Frenchman, piloted the balloon to Woodbury, New Jersey.

1799 The world's first successful income tax was introduced, by British Prime Minister William Pitt to help finance the war between Britain and France.

1839 Louis Jacques Daguerre, the French inventor and painter, announced his perfection of the technique of making daguerreotypes, the first popular form of photography.

1861 Mississippi seceded from the Union, the second state, after South Carolina, to do so.

1873 Victoria Woodhull, the famous free love advocate, labeled the Reverend Henry Ward Beecher an adulterer in a speech in New York, repeating charges she had made earlier in print.

1942 The U.S. Joint Chiefs of Staff was created.

1945 Allied troops invaded the Philippine Island of Luzon in World War II, fulfilling General MacArthur's promise, "I shall return."

1960 Construction began on the Aswan High Dam in the Nile River in Egypt.

1970 The *Cosmos 318* space vehicle was launched by Russia.

1977 The Oakland Raiders beat the Minnesota Vikings, 32-14, in Super Bowl XI in Pasadena, California.

January 10 – Birthdays

1480 Margaret of Austria. Duchess of Savoy

1538 Louis of Nassau. Leader of The Netherlands revolt in 1581 against Spain

1737 Ethan Allen. American patriot and soldier who led the Green Mountain Boys in the capture of Fort Ticonderoga from the British in the Revolutionary War

1747 Abraham Louis Breguet. French inventor and one of the greatest watchmakers of all time

1760 Johann Zumsteeg. German composer and conductor

1769 Michel Ney. The most famous of Napoleon's generals

1834 Lord John Acton. British historian best remembered for his statement "All power tends to corrupt, and absolute power corrupts absolutely"

1843 Frank James. Noted American Western outlaw of the late 1800s, and brother of the famous outlaw Jesse James

1850 John W. Root. American architect noted for works such as Chicago's Rookery building (1886)

1862 Walter Travis. Hall of Fame golfer

1869 Grigori Rasputin. Russian "Mad Monk," who exerted great influence on Czar Nicholas II and Czarina Alexandra in the years before Nicholas abdicated

1883 Francis X. Bushman. America's first screen idol, in the pre-1920s, whose acting career spanned 60 years

1887 Robinson Jeffers. American poet noted for works such as "Tamar" (1924) and "Medea" (1946)

1889 John Held Jr. American illustrator and cartoonist noted for his *New Yorker* magazine cartoons and for the strip *Merely Margy*

1898 **Arthur James Johnston.** American composer, conductor, and pianist, noted for songs such as "Cocktails for Two," "Troubled Waters," "One, Two, Button Your Shoe," and "Pennies From Heaven"

1908 **Ray Bolger.** American dancer and actor, who played the scarecrow in *The Wizard of Oz*

1908 **Paul Henreid.** Austrian-American stage and motion-picture actor and director

1910 **Galina Ulanova.** Russian prima ballerina

1927 **Gisele MacKenzie.** Canadian singer

1927 **Johnnie Ray.** American singer, composer, and author, noted for songs such as "The Little White Cloud That Cried"

1931 **Marlene Sanders.** American broadcast journalist

1931 **Ron Galella.** American photographer famous for his pursuit to photograph Jackie Onassis

1938 **Sherrill Milnes.** American opera singer

1938 **Willie McCovey.** Hall of Fame baseball player who hit over 500 career home runs

1938 **Frank Mahovlich.** Professional hockey player and superstar

1939 **William Toomey.** American decathlon champion

1939 **Sal Mineo.** American stage, screen, and television actor

1943 **Jim Croce.** American rock singer and songwriter, noted for works such as "Bad, Bad Leroy Brown"

1944 **Frank Sinatra Jr.** American singer and son of the noted crooner

1945 **Rod Stewart.** British rock singer and musician

1948 **Donald Fagen.** American singer and songwriter

1949 **George Foreman.** World Heavyweight Boxing Champion, 1973-1974

1953 **Pat Benatar.** American singer

1959 **Dick Dotson.** Professional baseball player

1962 **Julie Moran.** American sports reporter and first female host of ABC's Wide World of Sports

1964 **Brad Roberts.** Rock singer with the group Crash Test Dummies

January 10 – Events

1356 Holy Roman Emperor Charles IV had the Reichstag of Nuremberg pass an act regulating imperial elections. This act became a part of the famous Golden Bull issued in December, 1356.

1645 Archbishop William Laud of the Church of England was beheaded for treason on orders of the Long Parliament.

1776 Thomas Paine published his famous pamphlet *Common Sense,* which played a principal role in leading the American colonies to revolt. A half million copies were sold within a few months.

1861 Florida seceded from the Union, and later joined the Confederacy.

1863 The world's first subway system, called the Metropolitan Railway, opened in London, using steam locomotives.

1870 The Standard Oil Company was incorporated by John D. Rockefeller.

1901 Oil was first discovered in Texas, near Beaumont.

1917 Buffalo Bill Cody, the great frontiersman of the American West, died at age 70.

1920 The League of Nations was established, with headquarters in Geneva, Switzerland.

1925 "Ma" Ferguson was sworn in as governor of Texas, the second woman governor in U.S. history, after Nellie Tayloe Ross of Wyoming (1925).

1929 The comic strip *Little Annie Rooney,* by Brandon Walsh, first appeared.

1946 Man first made contact with the moon, as radar signals were bounced off the lunar surface.

1946 The first United Nations General Assembly met, in London.

1984 The United States and the Vatican established diplomatic relations after a break of 117 years.

January 11 – Birthdays

1503 **Francesco Mazzuolli Parmigianino.** Italian painter

1757 **Alexander Hamilton.** Brilliant American statesman and first secretary of the treasury

1807 **Ezra Cornell.** American businessman, philanthropist, founder of Western Union Telegraph Company, and a guiding force in the establishment of Cornell University

1815 **Sir John MacDonald.** First prime minister of the Dominion of Canada, 1867-1873, and later in 1878-1891

1842 **William James.** American philosopher and psychologist, author of the classic work *The Principles of Psychology* (1890), and brother of the famous novelist Henry James

1859 **Lord George Curzon.** British foreign secretary noted for the Curzon Line between Poland and Russia

1870 **Alice Rice.** Author of *Mrs. Wiggs of the Cabbage Patch*

1872 **Wilfred Baddeley.** British tennis player and Wimbledon singles champion in 1891, 1892, and 1895

1873 **Dwight Whitney Morrow.** American lawyer, diplomat, U.S. ambassador to Mexico, and father of poet Anne Morrow (Mrs. Charles A. Lindbergh)

1876 **Elmer Flick.** Hall of Fame baseball player

1888 **Chester Conklin.** American comedian and silent film actor who started his 50-year career as a Keystone Cop in 1913

1890 **Monte Blue.** American motion-picture actor in over 200 films, beginning with *The Birth of a Nation* in 1915

1890 **Max Carey.** Hall of Fame baseball player

1895 **Laurens Hammond.** American inventor noted for the development of the electric organ

1896 **Paddy Driskoll.** Hall of Fame professional football player

1897 **Bernard DeVoto.** American writer, editor, and critic, who won the Pulitzer Prize in 1948 for *Across the Wide Missouri*

1899 **Eva Le Gallienne.** English actress, theatrical director, and producer

1903 **Alan Paton.** South African writer and author of *Cry, the Beloved Country* (1948)

1905 **Manfred B. Lee.** American mystery writer, who with co-author Frederic Dannay, wrote under the pen name Ellery Queen

1905 **Oveta Culp Hobby.** First secretary of Health, Education, and Welfare (1953-1955)

1907 **Pierre Mendez-France.** French premier of the Fourth Republic in the 1950s

1910 **Schoolboy Rowe.** Professional baseball player

1911 **Zenko Suzuki.** Post-World War II prime minister of Japan

1911 **Jumping Jack McCracken.** Hall of Fame basketball player

1912 **Don "Red" Barry.** American motion-picture actor who was for many years one of the "Top Ten Money-Making Western Stars"

1915 **Veda Ann Borg.** American motion-picture actress whose name has become a favorite quiz item among nostalgia buffs

1921 **Juanita Kreps.** Secretary of commerce under President Carter

1926 **Grant Tinker.** American television producer

1928 **David Wolper.** American film executive and founder of Wolper Productions

1929 **Rod Taylor.** Australian-born motion-picture and television actor

1934 **Gerald Rafshoon.** American political media expert

1934 **Jean Chrétien.** Prime minister of Canada, elected in 1993

1942 **George Mira.** Professional football player

1946 **Naomi Judd.** American country singer and partner with her daughter Wynonna in the mother and daughter Judd duo

1948 **Madeline Manning.** Professional runner

1949 **Chris Ford.** Professional basketball player

1951 **Brenda Kirk.** South African tennis player

1952 **Ben Crenshaw.** Professional golfer and superstar

1953 **Freddie Solomon.** Professional football player

1954 **Gary Brokaw.** Professional basketball player

1957 **Darryl Dawkins.** Professional basketball player

1963 **Tracey Caulkins.** American gold medalist swimmer and member of the International Women's Sports Hall of Fame

1971 **Tom Rowlands.** American musician with The Chemical Brothers

January 11 – Events

1861 Alabama seceded from the Union and declared itself the Republic of Alabama, before later joining the Confederacy.

1878 Milk was delivered for the first time in glass bottles, by New York milkman Alexander Campbell.

1913 The sedan, a four-door automobile, was first introduced, at the National Automobile Show in New York, by the Hudson Car Company.

1915 Brewer Jacob Ruppert and engineer Tillinghast Houston purchased the New York Yankees franchise for $460,000, and began building it into baseball's greatest dynasty.

1923 France and Belgium occupied the Ruhr valley to force Germany to pay World War I reparations.

1928 Thomas Hardy, the great English novelist, died at Max Gate, near Dorchester, at age 87.

1935 American aviator Amelia Earhart left Honolulu for Oakland, California, to become the first woman to fly solo across the Pacific Ocean.

1942 The Japanese invaded the Netherlands East Indies in World War II.

1964 Surgeon General Luther L. Terry linked cigarette smoking to cancer.

1966 Alberto Giacometti, the noted Swiss sculptor, died at Chur, Switzerland, at age 64.

1970 The Kansas City Chiefs beat the Minnesota Vikings, 23-7, in Super Bowl IV in New Orleans.

1973 The Watergate break-in trial began in Washington, D.C.

1973 American League owners voted to adopt the designated hitter rule, allowing a tenth player in the lineup to bat for the pitcher.

1975 The Russians launched *Soyuz 17* with two cosmonauts aboard.

January 12 – Birthdays

1580 **Jan Baptista van Helmont.** Belgian scientist believed to be the one who coined the word "gas"

1588 **John Winthrop.** Puritan governor of the Massachusetts Bay Colony, 1629-1630

1591 **Jusepe de Ribera.** Spanish artist nicknamed "Lo Spagnoletto" (Little Spaniard) in Italy where he spent most of his life, and noted for his paintings of Christian martyrs and saints

1628 **Charles Perrault.** French poet and fairy-tale writer, best known for collecting the famous *Tales of Mother Goose* (1697), including "Little Red Riding Hood," "Sleeping Beauty," and "Puss in Boots"

1729 **Lazzaro Spallanzani.** Italian experimental biologist, who was the first to show that the air carries microscopic life

1729 **Edmund Burke.** Noted British statesman, orator, and writer, whose ideas became the philosophy of the British Conservative Party

1737 **John Hancock.** American patriot who was the first to sign the Declaration of Independence, writing his name boldly so "King George could read it without his spectacles"

1746 **Johann Heinrich Pestalozzi.** Pioneer Swiss educator and great contributor to the development of educational practices and theory

1751 **Ferdinand IV.** King of Naples

1810	**Ferdinand II.** King of Sicily
1852	**Joseph Jacques Cesaire Joffre.** French World War I general and the first French soldier to be named Marshal of France
1853	**Curbastro Gregorio Ricci.** Italian mathematician noted as the developer of tensor analysis
1854	**Albert Nelson Marquis.** American publisher
1856	**John Singer Sargent.** American painter best known for his portraits of fashionable people
1876	**Feozi Cakmak.** Turkish marshal and statesman
1876	**Jack London.** American author noted for works such as *The Call of the Wild* (1903) and *The Sea Wolf* (1904)
1878	**Ferenc Molnar.** Hungarian playwright and novelist, known for *Liliom* (1903) and *The Paul Street Boys* (1907)
1879	**Ray Harroun.** Winner of the first Indianapolis 500 automobile race (in 1911)
1884	**William Barr Friedlander.** American composer noted for songs such as "Nikki" and "Araby"
1891	**Raeburn Van Buren.** American comic strip writer and creator with Al Capp of *Abbie an' Slats* (1937)
1893	**Alfred Rosenberg.** Idealogist of the German Nazi movement
1893	**Hermann Goering.** German World War II air force commander and second to Adolf Hitler as a leader of Nazi Germany
1895	**Bo McMillin.** Hall of Fame football player
1899	**Fritz Crisler.** Noted college football coach
1899	**Paul Muller.** Swiss-born American chemist who won the Nobel Prize (1945) for his discovery of the insect-killing powers of DDT
1902	**Joe E. Lewis.** American comedian
1904	**Edgar Delange.** American composer noted for songs such as "Along the Navajo Trail," "A String of Pearls," and "All This and Heaven, Too"
1905	**Tex Ritter.** American singer, cowboy actor, and "America's Most Beloved Cowboy" of the 1930s and 1940s
1906	**Henny Youngman.** American comedian and master of the one-liners, such as "Take my wife. Please"
1910	**Luise Rainer.** Austrian stage and motion-picture actress, who won two consecutive Academy Awards, for *The Great Ziegfield* (1936) and *The Good Earth* (1937)
1915	**Martin Agronsky.** American broadcast journalist
1916	**Pieter Willem Botha.** Prime minister of South Africa who succeeded Balthazar Johannes Vorster in 1978
1926	**Ray Price.** American country music singer
1930	**James Farmer.** American civil rights leader of the 1960s
1940	**Bob Hewitt.** South African tennis player noted for his doubles play with Frew McMillan
1944	**Joe Frazier.** World heavyweight boxing champion, 1970-1973

1947	**Tom Dempsey.** Professional football player who once kicked a 63-yard field goal (for the New Orleans Saints versus the Detroit Lions)
1949	**James W. Dietz.** Professional rower
1950	**Randy Jones.** Professional baseball player
1950	**Patrice Dominguez.** French tennis player
1951	**Rush Limbaugh.** Right-wing radio talk show host
1951	**Bill Madlock.** Professional baseball player
1951	**Drew Pearson.** Professional football superstar
1952	**Campy Russell.** Professional basketball player
1953	**Terry Whitfield.** Professional baseball player
1954	**Howard Stern.** Irreverent television talk show host
1955	**Kirstie Alley.** American motion-picture and television actress (*Cheers*)
1960	**Dominique Wilkins.** Professional basketball player
1960	**Mike Marshall.** Professional baseball player

January 12 – Events

532	The second Cathedral of Santa Sophia in Constantinople was destroyed by fire in the Nika insurrection.
1519	Holy Roman Emperor Maximilian I died at Augsburg, Germany, at age 60.
1687	Robert Cavalier, Sieur de La Salle, the distinguished French explorer, began his last exploration, on the coast of Texas.
1755	Moscow University was established by Czarina Elizabeth Petrovna.
1773	The first public museum in America was established, in Charleston, South Carolina.
1848	The Italian Revolution began in Sicily, the first of a number of 1848 European revolutions that ended the old political order.
1918	The Distinguished Service Medal was instituted by Congress.
1932	Mrs. Hattie Caraway of Arkansas became the first woman to be elected to the U.S. Senate.
1969	The New York Jets beat the Baltimore Colts, 16-7, in Super Bowl III in Miami. Jets quarterback Joe Namath "guaranteed" the victory before the game started.
1971	The long-running comedy *All in the Family* premiered on CBS television.
1975	The Pittsburgh Steelers beat the Minnesota Vikings, 16-6, in Super Bowl IX in New Orleans.
1976	The great English mystery writer Agatha Christie died at age 85.
1986	The space shuttle *Columbia* was launched with a crew of seven including Bill Nelson, the first U.S. Representative to fly in space.

January 13 – Birthdays

1381	**Saint Colette.** Founder of the Coletine Poor Clares
1596	**Jan Josephszoon Van Goyen.** Dutch painter who specialized in landscapes

1749 **Charles James Fox.** Brilliant English statesman who supported the American colonies in their fight for independence

1804 **Gavarni.** French caricaturist, lithographer, and illustrator (born Sulpice Guillaume Chevalier)

1808 **Salmon P. Chase.** U.S. statesman who was secretary of the treasury under President Lincoln and later Chief Justice of the Supreme Court

1832 **Horatio Alger.** American author of more than 100 "rags-to-riches" books, such as *Ragged Dick* (1867) and *Tattered Tom* (1871)

1867 **Francis Everett Townsend.** American physician who proposed the Townsend Plan, an old age pension, for all citizens over 60 in the 1930s

1882 **Domenico Savino.** Italian-born composer and conductor, noted for songs such as "Anchors Aweigh"

1884 **Sophie Tucker.** American stage actress and "the last of the red hot mamas"

1885 **Alfred Carl Fuller.** American businessman who founded the Fuller Brush company (1906)

1885 **James V. Monaco.** Italian-born composer and pianist, noted for songs such as "You Made Me Love You," "Six Lessons From Madam La Zonga," "I'm Making Believe" and "I Can't Begin to Tell You"

1886 **A.H. Ross.** Inventor of the net and puck used in the National Hockey League

1890 **Elmer Davis.** American news broadcaster and writer of the 1940s and 1950s

1903 **Kay Francis.** American stage and motion-picture actress in over 60 films

1904 **Richard Addinsell.** English composer best known for his *Warsaw Concerto*

1919 **Robert Stack.** American motion-picture and television actor, who was "the first boy to kiss Deanna Durbin" (in *First Love,* 1939)

1922 **Army Archerd.** Hollywood columnist

1925 **Gwen Verdon.** American singer and actress, and top star of Broadway musicals in the 1950s

1931 **Charles Nelson Reilly.** American actor and director

1933 **Tom Gola.** Professional basketball player and Hall of Famer

1933 **Frank Gallo.** American artist

1943 **Richard Moll.** American television actor (*Night Court*)

1949 **Brandon Tartikoff.** American television executive

1950 **Bob Forsch.** Professional baseball player

1961 **Julia Louis-Dreyfus.** American actress noted for her role in *Seinfeld*

1962 **Kevin Mitchell.** Professional baseball player

1964 **Penelope Ann Miller.** American motion-picture and television actress

January 13 – Events

1733 James Oglethorpe arrived at Charleston, South Carolina, with a charter to establish a colony in Georgia.

1864 Stephen Foster, the great American songwriter, died in New York at age 37 a few days after writing "Beautiful Dreamer."

1898 French novelist Emile Zola's famous headline "J'accuse" appeared in the French newspaper *L'Aurore,* charging that Alfred Dreyfus was unjustly convicted in the Dreyfus Trial.

1930 The comic strip *Mickey Mouse,* by Walt Disney, first appeared.

1941 James Joyce, the great Irish novelist, died in Zurich at age 58.

1947 The comic strip *Steve Canyon,* by Milton Caniff, first appeared.

1953 The Russian government announced the arrest of nine Soviet physicians accused of plotting to kill leading Communist officials in the "Doctors' Plot."

1964 "I Want to Hold Your Hand," the first Beatles' record in America, was released by Capitol Records.

1974 The Miami Dolphins won their second straight Super Bowl, beating the Minnesota Vikings, 24-7, in Super Bowl VIII in New Orleans.

1978 U.S. Senator and former Vice President Hubert H. Humphrey died of cancer at age 66.

1990 L. Douglas Wilder became the nation's first black governor since reconstruction as he took the oath of office in Richmond, Virginia.

January 14 – Birthdays

1131 **Vlademar I.** King of Denmark, 1157-1182

1730 **William Whipple.** American Revolutionary War general and New Hampshire signer of the Declaration of Independence

1741 **Benedict Arnold.** American Revolutionary War general and the most infamous traitor in American history

1791 **Calvin Phillips.** The shortest recorded adult male, at 26½ inches tall

1806 **Matthew Fontaine Maury.** U.S. naval officer and scientist, whose wind and current charts of the oceans resulted in his being called the "Pathfinder of the Seas"

1836 **Henri Fantin-Latour.** French painter and printmaker noted for his still lifes with flowers and for his portraits

1841 **Berthe Morisot.** French painter

1847 **Wilson Carlile.** English clergyman and founder of the Church Army, a group of laymen in the Anglican Church concerned with social work as much as with the work of preaching

1850 **Pierre Loti.** French novelist noted for works such as *An Iceland Fisherman* (1886)

1863 **R.F. Outcault.** American cartoonist and creator of *Buster Brown* and the first true comic strip, *At the Circus in Hogan's Alley,* featuring the Yellow Kid

1866 **Robert L. MacCameron.** American painter

1874   **Thornton Waldo Burgess.** American author of children's books, best known for his stories about Peter Rabbit

1875   **Albert Schweitzer.** Brilliant German philosopher, physician, musician, clergyman, missionary, and writer

1882   **Henrik Willem Van Loon.** Dutch-American illustrator noted for books such as *R.v.R.*, a fictionalized biography of Rembrandt and *The Story of Mankind*

1886   **Hugh Lofting.** English-born writer and creator of Dr. Doolittle

1892   **Hal Roach.** Pioneer American motion-picture producer and director whose career spanned over 50 years

1896   **John Dos Passos.** American novelist noted for works such as *Three Soldiers* (1921) and the trilogy *U.S.A.* (1930, 1932, and 1936)

1901   **Bebe Daniels.** American motion-picture actress who was one of the most popular stars of the silent era and also a leading lady of the talkies

1901   **Carlos Romulo.** Filipino diplomat and author, who served as president of the U.N. General Assembly in 1949

1904   **Cecil Beaton.** British photographer, noted for *Winged Squadrons*, a photographic book about the Battle of Britain

1909   **Joseph Losey.** American motion-picture director with a career of over 40 years

1919   **Giulio Andreotti.** Prime minister of Italy, 1972-1973

1919   **Andy Rooney.** American writer, producer, and television entertainer

1920   **George Herman.** American broadcast journalist

1926   **Tom Tryon.** American motion-picture and television actor, screenwriter, and novelist

1938   **Jack Jones.** American singer

1940   **Julian Bond.** American state legislator (Georgia) and civil rights leader

1941   **Faye Dunaway.** American stage and motion-picture actress, and Academy Award winner in 1976 for *Network*

1944   **Nina Totenberg.** American broadcast journalist with National Public Radio

1947   **Gene Washington.** Professional football player

1949   **Lawrence Kasdan.** American director and screenwriter noted for films such as *The Big Chill* (1983) and *The Accidental Tourist* (1988)

1951   **Derrel Thomas.** Professional baseball player

1952   **Terry Forster.** Professional baseball player

1952   **Maureen Dowd.** Controversial American newspaper columnist and Pulitzer Prize winner who has been called brilliant and at the same time vicious and poison-penned

1963   **Steven Soderberg.** American motion-picture director noted for works such as *Kafka* (1991)

1967   **Emily Watson.** British stage, screen and television actress

1969   **Jason Bateman.** American actor and brother of actress Justine Bateman

1969   **David Grohl.** Rock singer-musician with the group Foo Fighters

January 14 – Events

1639   The Connecticut Colony adopted its first constitution, the "Fundamental Orders," which was the first written constitution in history.

1742   English astronomer Edmond Halley, for whom Halley's Comet was named, died at age 85.

1784   Congress ratified the peace treaty with Great Britain granting independence to the American Colonies.

1898   The great English author Lewis Carroll (Charles L. Dodgson) died 13 days before his 66th birthday.

1900   Giacomo Puccini's great opera *Tosca* had its world premiere at Rome's Teatro Costanzi.

1914   Henry Ford inaugurated his assembly line technique of manufacturing cars. With this new procedure, Ford workers were able to build a Model T in an hour and a half.

1943   President Franklin D. Roosevelt and Prime Minister Winston Churchill opened the Casablanca Conference in World War II.

1952   The *Today* show made its debut on NBC television stations, with Dave Garroway serving as host.

1954   Joe DiMaggio, the great baseball player, and Marilyn Monroe, the star movie actress, were married in San Francisco's City Hall.

1954   The Nash and Hudson automobile companies merged to become American Motors.

1957   Humphrey Bogart, the great motion-picture actor and screen legend, died in his sleep in Hollywood just short of his 58th birthday.

1964   In her first television appearance since the assassination of President Kennedy, former First Lady Jacqueline Kennedy thanked the public for some 800,000 messages of sympathy.

1968   The Green Bay Packers beat the Oakland Raiders, 33-14, in Super Bowl II in Miami.

1973   The Miami Dolphins beat the Washington Redskins, 14-7, in Super Bowl VII in Los Angeles.

1999   The U.S. Senate heard the opening presentations from both sides in President Clinton's impeachment trial.

January 15 – Birthdays

1622   **Molière.** French dramatist, born Jean Baptiste Poquelin, who was the greatest French writer of comedy

1654   **Paul Potter.** Dutch painter and etcher

1675   **Duc de Saint-Simon.** French memoirist and courtier (born Louis de Rouvroy)

1716   **Philip Livingston.** A New York signer of the Declaration of Independence and member of the Continental Congress

1803 **Nathan Marcus Adler.** Chief rabbi of the British Empire and founder of Jew's College and the United Synagogue

1809 **Pierre Joseph Proudhon.** French socialist, reformer, and writer, who believed in anarchism, a social order without government

1823 **Mathew B. Brady.** Noted pioneer American photographer who became famous for his photographic record of the Civil War

1844 **Cole Younger.** American outlaw of the 1870s and a member of the Younger Brothers gang

1850 **Jim Younger.** American outlaw of the 1870s and member of the Younger Brothers gang

1877 **Lewis Madison Terman.** American psychologist, who developed the Stanford-Binet Intelligence Tests

1891 **Ray Chapman.** The only professional baseball player ever killed by being hit with a pitched ball, by Carl Mays in 1920

1891 **Osip Emilyevich Mandelstam.** Russian poet

1892 **William Beaudine.** American motion-picture director who began with D.W. Griffith and had a career of 50 years

1892 **Hobey Baker.** Hall of Fame hockey player

1899 **Ace Goodman.** American radio and television writer, actor, humorist, and according to the great comedian Fred Allen, "America's greatest wit"

1902 **Saud.** Saudi Arabia's second king, 1953-1964, after his father Ibn Saud

1905 **Allie Wrubel.** American composer and author, noted for songs such as "Zip-A-Dee-Doo-Dah," "The Lady from Twenty-Nine Palms," "I'll Buy that Dream," and "Music, Maestro, Please"

1908 **Edward Teller.** Hungarian-born American physicist and father of the hydrogen bomb

1909 **Gene Krupa.** American drummer of the Big Band Era of the 1930s and 1940s

1913 **Lloyd Bridges.** American stage, screen, and television actor, with a career of over 40 years

1918 **Gamal Abdul Nasser.** Egyptian nationalist who led the revolt that overthrew King Farouk and established Egypt as a republic, and who served as prime minister and president, 1954-1970

1920 **Bob Davies.** Professional basketball player

1920 **John Joseph O'Connor.** American Roman Catholic cardinal and controversial anti-abortionist

1926 **Rod MacLeish.** American journalist and news commentator

1929 **Martin Luther King Jr.** The greatest of the American civil rights leaders of the 1950s and 1960s, who received the 1964 Nobel Peace Prize for his "nonviolent resistance" struggle for equal rights

1930 **Joe Grabowski.** Professional basketball player

1933 **Ernest Gaines.** American novelist noted for *The Autobiography of Miss Jane Pittman*

1934 **Walter Marks.** American composer and author, noted for songs such as "I've Gotta Be Me," "Getting On," and "Must It Be Love?"

1937 **Margaret O'Brien.** Noted child star of Hollywood films of the 1940s, who won an Academy Award in 1944 as the "Outstanding Child Actress" of her day

1941 **Captain Beefheart (Don Van Vleit).** American rock singer

1943 **Mike Marshall.** Professional baseball player

1945 **Ronnie Van Zant.** American rock singer and musician with Lynyrd Skynard

1949 **Howard Twitty.** Professional golfer

1949 **Bobby Grich.** Professional baseball player

1951 **Ernie Digregorio.** Professional basketball player

1951 **Charo.** Mexican actress and singer

1953 **Randy White.** Professional football player

1975 **Mary Pierce.** French-American tennis player

January 15 – Events

69 Otha was proclaimed Emperor of Rome.

1559 Queen Elizabeth I of England was crowned in Westminster Abbey.

1701 Prussia was proclaimed a kingdom.

1759 The British Museum, the oldest of the great national museums, was opened to the public in Montague House in London, a site it still occupies.

1777 Vermont settlers declared their territory the independent republic of New Connecticut. The name was changed to Vermont the following July.

1842 The University of Notre Dame was founded by a group of French missionaries headed by the Reverend Edward F. Sorin.

1870 The donkey symbol of the Democratic Party first appeared, in a cartoon by Thomas Nast, depicting "A live Jackass kicking a dead lion."

1879 Gilbert and Sullivan's *H.M.S. Pinafore* had its U.S. debut.

1890 The *Sleeping Beauty* ballet, by Peter Ilich Tchaikovsky, had its premiere at the Maryinski Theater in St. Petersburg.

1896 Mathew Brady, the great pioneer photographer of 21 United States presidents, died in poverty in New York at age 73.

1919 Ignace Paderewski, the great pianist and statesman, became the first premier of the newly created state of Poland.

1929 The U.S. ratified the Kellogg-Briand Peace Pact, which condemned the use of war to solve international problems.

1943 The Pentagon, the world's largest office building, was completed, on the Virginia side of the Potomac River in Washington, D.C.

1953 President Harry S. Truman made his farewell address to the nation.

1967 Professional football's Super Bowl I was played in Los Angeles with the Green Bay Packers defeating the Kansas City Chiefs, 35-10.

1972	Margrethe II was proclaimed Queen of Denmark, as she became the first reigning queen in Denmark's history.
1978	The Dallas Cowboys beat the Denver Broncos, 27-10, in Super Bowl XII in New Orleans.

January 16 – Birthdays

1409	**Rene I.** King of Naples, Sicily, and Jerusalem
1697	**Richard Savage.** British poet and satirist
1749	**Vittorio Alfieri.** Italian dramatist and poet, noted for works such as *Filippo* (1775), *Saul* (1782), and *Oreste* (1786)
1752	**George Cabot.** American Federalist Party leader
1757	**Samuel McIntire.** American architect
1767	**Anders Gustav Ekeberg.** Swedish chemist and discoverer in 1802 of the element tantalum
1815	**Henry W. Halleck.** U.S. military scholar and Union general in the Civil War
1845	**Charles Dwight Sigsbee.** U.S. admiral during the Spanish-American War, who commanded the battleship *Maine* when it blew up in Havana harbor
1853	**Andre Michelin.** French industrialist and cofounder with his brother Edouard of the Michelin Tire Company, noted for the world's first pneumatic automobile tires (1895)
1870	**Jimmy Collins.** Hall of Fame baseball player
1874	**Robert William Service.** Canadian poet and author of "The Shooting of Dan McGrew"
1878	**Harry Carey.** American motion-picture actor in almost 400 films, called by the noted director John Ford the "bright star of the early Western sky"
1894	**Irving Mills.** American composer, author, and singer, noted for songs such as "When My Sugar Walks Down the Street," "Sophisticated Lady," "Mood Indigo," and "Moon Glow"
1897	**Joseph Bodis.** Hall of Fame bowler
1901	**Fulgencio Batista.** Cuban dictator who was deposed by Fidel Castro in 1959
1907	**Alexander Knox.** Canadian actor and writer with a 40-year career
1909	**Ethel Merman.** American singer and actress with a career of over 50 years
1911	**Eduardo Frei.** First Christian Democratic president of Chile
1911	**Dizzy Dean.** Hall of Fame baseball pitcher who won 30 games in 1934
1927	**Katy Jurado.** Mexican motion-picture actress
1928	**William Kennedy.** American author noted for his Pulitzer Prize-winning novel *Ironweed* (1983)
1930	**Norman Podhoretz.** American author and editor
1932	**Dian Fossey.** American naturalist, gorilla expert, and author of *Gorillas In the Mist* (1983)
1932	**Jim Berry.** American cartoonist noted for the strip *Berry's World*, begun in 1963
1934	**Marilyn Horne.** American operatic soprano
1935	**A.J. Foyt.** American automobile racing driver and four times winner of the Indianapolis 500
1941	**Christine Janes.** English tennis player
1942	**Barbara Lynn.** American soul singer and guitarist
1946	**Ronnie Milsap.** American country singer
1948	**John Carpenter.** American motion-picture director noted for films such as *Halloween* (1978) and its sequels
1948	**Peter Kanderal.** Australian tennis player
1950	**Debbie Allen.** American motion-picture and television actress, dancer, choreographer and sister of actress Phylicia Rashad
1954	**Dave Stapleton.** Professional baseball player
1957	**Steve Balboni.** Professional baseball player
1960	**Sade (Adu).** Nigerian-English vocalist

January 16 – Events

1066	Harold II became the last Anglo-Saxon king of England.
1493	Columbus sailed from Samana Bay in present-day Haiti, starting his return trip on his first voyage to America.
1547	Ivan IV became the first Russian ruler to be crowned Czar (Caesar).
1556	Charles V, Holy Roman Emperor and King of Spain, abdicated rule of Spain.
1599	Edmund Spenser, the great English poet and author of *The Faerie Queene,* died in London at an approximate age of 47.
1778	France recognized the independence of the United States.
1794	Edward Gibbon, the great British historian, died in London at age 56.
1883	The U.S. Civil Service System was established.
1896	The University of Chicago defeated the University of Iowa, 15-12, in Iowa City, Iowa, in a basketball game that established the five-man basketball team.
1920	The 18th Amendment to the Constitution went into effect, prohibiting the sale of alcoholic beverages in the U.S.
1939	*Superman,* by Jerry Siegel and Joe Shuster, first appeared in newspapers.
1942	Carole Lombard, noted screen actress and wife of actor Clark Gable, was killed in a plane crash on Table Mountain, Nevada, near Las Vegas.
1944	General Dwight D. Eisenhower took command of the Allied Invasion Force in London.
1964	The long-running musical *Hello, Dolly!* starring Carol Channing opened on Broadway.
1972	The Dallas Cowboys beat the Miami Dolphins, 24-3, in Super Bowl VI in New Orleans.
1979	Shah Mohammed Reza Pahlavi left Iran on "vacation," never to return.
1991	The U.S. and its allies began the Persian Gulf War against Iraq with massive air strikes in Operation Desert Storm.

January 17 – Birthdays

1342 Philip the Bold. Duke of Burgundy and youngest son of French king John II the Good, who ruled France as regent for his nephew Charles VI (1380-1422)

1501 Leonhard Fuchs. French botanist for whom the fuchsia is named

1504 Pius V. Roman Catholic pope, 1566-1572, who was made a saint in 1712

1600 Pedro Calderon de la Barca. Spanish dramatist and poet who wrote over 120 plays including his best known, *Life Is a Dream* (1635)

1612 Thomas Fairfax. British general who as commander of Oliver Cromwell's forces defeated King Charles I's English Cavaliers in the Battle of Naseby (1645)

1657 Peeter van Bloemen. Flemish painter

1706 Benjamin Franklin. American statesman, inventor, one of the most admired men of the Western world during his time, and one of the half-dozen greatest Americans of all time

1732 Stanislaw Poniatowski. The last king of an independent Poland (1764)

1771 Charles Brockden Brown. America's first important novelist, and the first American to make literature his major profession

1806 James Madison Randolph. Grandson of President Thomas Jefferson, and the first baby born in the White House

1820 Anne Brontë. English novelist noted for *Agnes Grey* (1847) and *The Tenant of Wildfell Hall* (1848), and sister of novelists Emily and Charlotte Brontë

1834 August Weismann. German biologist known chiefly for his theories of heredity and evolution

1860 Douglas Hyde. Irish scholar, statesman, and first president of Eire (1938-1945)

1863 David Lloyd George. British prime minister during World War I

1867 Carl Laemmle. German-American film pioneer and tycoon who in 1912 founded the forerunner of Universal Pictures

1871 Earl Beatty David. First Sea Lord of England

1876 Frank Hague. Jersey City mayor and political boss, noted for the remark, "I am the law in Jersey City"

1880 Mack Sennett. American pioneer director, producer, and actor, who was the father of American slapstick motion-pictures and the creator of the famous Keystone Kops

1884 Noah Beery. American stage and motion-picture actor, brother of actor Wallace Beery, and father of actor Noah Beery, Jr.

1886 Glenn L. Martin. American pioneer airplane designer and manufacturer, whose Martin B-10 bomber was standard in the Army Air Force for many years

1886 Ronald Firbank. English novelist

1899 Al Capone. American gangster who controlled the Chicago underworld in the 1920s

1899 Robert Maynard Hutchins. American educator and administrator who was noted for his unconventional theories about higher education

1899 Nevil Shute. English novelist noted for works such as *Pied Piper* (1942) and *On the Beach* (1957)

1900 George Sperti. American inventor and holder of the patent on Preparation H

1901 Olin Dutra. Hall of Fame professional golfer

1911 Jackson Busher. Hall of Fame hockey player

1917 Ulysses Simpson Kay. American composer

1922 Nicholas Katzenbach. U.S. attorney-general under President Lyndon Johnson

1924 Betty White. American comedienne and actress

1928 Vidal Sassoon. English hairdresser and designer

1929 Jacques Plante. Hall of Fame hockey player

1931 James Earl Jones. American stage, screen, and television actor

1931 Don Zimmer. Professional baseball player and manager

1931 L. Douglas Wilder. First black governor of Virginia, 1990-1994

1933 Sheree North. American stage, screen, and television actress

1934 Shari Lewis. Noted American puppeteer

1942 Muhammad Ali (Cassius Clay). One of the greatest world heavyweight boxing champions, who held the title an unprecedented three times, in the 1960s and 1970s

1945 Preston Pearson. Professional football player

1948 Mick Taylor. British guitarist with The Rolling Stones, 1969-1974

1949 Andy Kaufman. American comedian and actor

1952 Darrell Porter. Professional baseball player

1953 Mark Littell. Professional baseball player

1956 David Caruso. American motion-picture and television actor (*NYPD Blue*)

1956 Paul Young. British vocalist

1960 Chili Davis. Professional baseball player

1962 Jim Carrey. Canadian-born motion-picture and television actor and comedian

January 17 – Events

395 The Roman Empire was split into eastern and western parts upon the death of Emperor Theodosius I, whose will provided that his two sons would inherit the two parts.

1793 French King Louis XVI was condemned to death by the National Convention. He was guillotined four days later.

1794 Andrew Jackson and Rachel Donelson Robards were remarried in Nashville, Tennessee, after learning that their first marriage was invalid.

1893 Rutherford B. Hayes died in Fremont, Ohio, at age 70.

1910   Thomas Crapper, the man who revolutionized the world's flush toilets and was "Plumber By Appointment to King Edward VII," died near London at age 73.

1917   The U.S. bought the Virgin Islands from Denmark for $25 million.

1925   "The business of America is business," proclaimed President Calvin Coolidge to a group of businessmen.

1929   Popeye the Sailor made his debut as a character in E.C. Segar's comic strip, *Thimble Theater*.

1945   Warsaw was liberated from the Nazis by Soviet and Polish soldiers in World War II.

1950   Eleven bandits robbed the Brink's headquarters in Boston of $2.5 million. They were apprehended nearly six years later, just a week before the statute of limitations expired.

1961   Patrice Lumumba, the first president of the Congo, was murdered by unknown assailants.

1961   In his farewell address, President Dwight D. Eisenhower warned the nation against the rise of the "military-industrial complex."

1971   The Baltimore Colts beat the Dallas Cowboys, 16-13, in Super Bowl V in Miami.

January 18 – Birthdays

1689   **Montesquieu.** Outstanding French political philosopher, whose major work, *The Spirit of the Laws* (1748), greatly influenced the writing of the U.S. Constitution

1754   **Vicente Martin y Soler.** Spanish composer

1779   **Peter Mark Roget.** British physician and scholar who invented the slide rule, but is best known as the compiler of Roget's *Thesaurus of English Words and Phrases* (1852)

1782   **Daniel Webster.** The best-known American orator, and one of the ablest lawyers and statesmen of his time

1813   **Joseph Farwell Glidden.** American farmer noted for the invention in 1873 of barbed wire

1825   **Edward Frankland.** British chemist who co-discovered helium in the sun and formulated the doctrine of chemical valence

1841   **Emmanuel Chabrier.** French composer noted for works such as *Espana* (1883) and the music for *The Reluctant King* (1887)

1854   **Thomas Augustine Watson.** Alexander Graham Bell's assistant who first heard Bell's words, "Mr. Watson, come here. I want you," on his newly-invented telephone in 1875

1863   **Konstantin Stanislavski.** Well-known Russian stage director and actor, whose attempt to have the actor live the life of the character became known as the "Stanislavski method"

1867   **Ruben Dario.** Nicaraguan poet and short-story writer, who was one of the most important poets in the Spanish language

1879   **Henri Honoré Giraud.** French World War II general selected by the Allies as French leader in North Africa

1882   **A.A. Milne.** English writer noted for *Winnie the Pooh*

1886   **Antoine Pevsner.** Russian-born painter and sculptor noted for works such as *Construction in the Egg* (1948) and *Peace Column* (1954)

1887   **W. Franke Harling.** English-born composer and conductor, noted for songs such as "Beyond the Blue Horizon"

1888   **Sir Thomas Octave Murdoch Sopwith.** British aircraft designer and founder of the Sopwith Aviation Company, Ltd. (1912)

1892   **Oliver Hardy.** Member with Stan Laurel of the Laurel and Hardy team, the most fabulously successful comedy duo the screen has ever known

1894   **Richard E. Berlin.** American newspaper publisher and president of the Hearst Corporation

1896   **Art Kassel.** American composer, author, and conductor, noted for songs such as "Don't Let Julia Foolya" and "You Never Say Yes, You Never Say No"

1904   **Cary Grant.** American motion-picture actor and perennial favorite of movie audiences for more than three decades

1908   **Jacob Bronowski.** Polish-American mathematician, author, and television host

1909   **Leo Hurwitz.** American documentary filmmaker noted for works such as *Native Land* (1942)

1913   **Danny Kaye.** American comedian, actor, and superstar in a career of more than 40 years

1922   **Constance Moore.** American band vocalist, radio singer, and motion-picture actress

1925   **Sol Yurick.** American novelist

1932   **Joe Schmidt.** Professional football player and coach

1933   **Ray Dolby.** American inventor, noted for the noise reduction system known as Dolby sound

1933   **John Boorman.** British motion-picture director noted for films such as *Deliverance* (1972)

1938   **Curt Flood.** Professional baseball player whose lawsuit led to the modification of baseball's reserve clause and allowed players to negotiate new contracts periodically

1941   **Bobby Goldsboro.** American singer and songwriter

1950   **Pat Sullivan.** Professional football player

1953   **Brett Hudson.** American comedian, singer and musician

1954   **Steven DeBerg.** Professional football player

1954   **Scott McGregor.** Professional baseball player

1955   **Kevin Costner.** American motion-picture actor and director

1957   **Tom Bailey.** British musician and singer with the Thompson Twins musical group

1961   **Mark Messier.** Professional hockey player

1964   **Brady Anderson.** Professional baseball player

January 18 – Events

1486 King Henry VII of England married Elizabeth of York, uniting the Houses of Lancaster and York.

1535 Francisco Pizarro, the Spanish conquestador who conquered the Inca Indians, founded Lima, Peru.

1778 Captain James Cook, the great British naval explorer, discovered the Hawaiian Islands, which he named the Sandwich Islands, in honor of the Earl of Sandwich.

1862 John Tyler died at age 71.

1871 Wilhelm I of Prussia was crowned the first "kaiser" of the new united Germany.

1873 Edward Bulwer-Lytton, the noted English novelist, died at Torquay at age 69.

1911 Pilot Eugene Ely landed his plane on the USS *Pennsylvania,* in San Francisco harbor, for the first landing in history of an aircraft on a ship.

1912 English explorer Robert Scott reached the South Pole only to find that Norway's Roald Amundsen had arrived first.

1919 The Versailles Conference opened to draft a World War I peace treaty.

1936 Rudyard Kipling, the great English writer, died in London at age 70.

1943 Moscow announced that the 900-day siege of Leningrad in World War II had been lifted.

1943 The U.S. banned the sale of presliced bread for the duration of World War II to save on labor costs and equipment.

1976 The Pittsburgh Steelers beat the Dallas Cowboys, 21-17, in Super Bowl X. It was their second consecutive Super Bowl victory.

1980 The price of gold hit a record $845 per ounce.

January 19 – Birthdays

1544 **Francis II.** King of France, 1559-1560, during whose reign began the long and bitter rivalry between the noble houses of Guise and Bourbon

1736 **James Watt.** Scottish inventor who developed the steam engine and for whom the power unit, the watt, is named

1749 **Isaiah Thomas.** American printer and publisher of *The Massachusetts Spy,* an influential newspaper during the American Revolution

1798 **Auguste Comte.** Noted French social thinker and philosopher, who founded the philosophy known as positivism

1807 **Robert E. Lee.** Commander of the Confederate Army in the Civil War and one of the great generals in U.S. history

1809 **Edgar Allan Poe.** One of America's greatest poets and short-story writers, noted for works such as the poems "The Raven" and "To Helen" and the short story "The Fall of the House of Usher"

1813 **Sir Henry Bessemer.** British inventor and manufacturer, who developed the Bessemer process of converting pig iron to steel

1839 **Paul Cezanne.** Noted French painter and leader of the post-impressionism school, whose style of composition changed the course of art

1863 **Edgar J. Helms.** American clergyman who developed Goodwill Industries

1866 **Harry Davenport.** American stage and screen actor who appeared in over 100 films

1887 **Alexander Woollcott.** American journalist and taleteller, known for his unusual personality and sharp tongue

1887 **Clementine Hunter.** American artist noted for rural, primitive paintings

1917 **John Raitt.** American singer

1919 **Ray Eberle.** American vocalist with the Glen Miller Band, and brother of singer Bob Eberle

1922 **Guy Madison.** American motion-picture and television actor

1923 **Jean Stapleton.** American actress who played Edith Bunker in the long-running television show, *All in the Family*

1926 **Fritz Weaver.** American stage, screen, and television actor

1931 **Robert MacNeil.** American broadcast journalist

1932 **Richard Lester.** American motion-picture director noted for films such as *A Funny Thing Happened on the Way to the Forum* (1966)

1935 **Tippi Hedren.** American motion-picture actress

1939 **Phil Everly.** American singer and guitarist and one of the Everly Brothers

1942 **Shelley Fabares.** American motion-picture and television actress

1942 **Michael Crawford.** British stage, screen and television actor

1943 **Janis Joplin.** American blues singer, composer, and author, noted for songs such as "Mercedes Benz" and "Down On Me"

1943 **Princess Margriet Francisca.** Daughter of Queen Juliana of The Netherlands

1946 **Dolly Parton.** American singer, songwriter, and actress

1946 **Tom Gorman.** American tennis player

1947 **Ann Woodruff Compton.** American broadcast journalist

1948 **Terrence Hanratty.** Professional football player

1950 **Jon Matlack.** Professional baseball player

1953 **Desi Arnaz Jr.** American actor and singer, and son of entertainers Lucille Ball and Desi Arnaz

1957 **Ottis Anderson.** Professional football player

1966 **Stefan Edberg.** Swedish tennis player and superstar

January 19 – Events

1825 Ezra Daggett and his nephew Thomas Kensett received a patent for their process of storing food in cans.

1830 The famous Hayne-Webster debates began in the U.S. Senate on whether a state could nullify a federal law.

| 1853 | Giuseppe Verdi's great opera *Il Trovatore* premiered in Rome. |

1853   Giuseppe Verdi's great opera *Il Trovatore* premiered in Rome.

1861   Georgia became the fifth southern state to secede from the Union.

1881   The Western Union Telegraph Company was created by a consolidation by financiers Jay Gould and William Vanderbilt of the Western Union Company with two smaller companies.

1929   Leon Trotsky, the ex-Bolshevist leader, left Moscow for exile to Alma Alta in Kazakstan after his expulsion from the Politburo by Joseph Stalin.

1955   President Dwight D. Eisenhower held the first presidential press conference ever televised.

1966   Indira Gandhi was chosen prime minister of India, succeeding Lal Bahadur Shastri, who had died of a stroke.

1978   The last Volkswagen "Bug" was manufactured, as the Volkswagen Company changed over to the Volkswagen Rabbit. The move ended a production run since 1938 of over 19 million "Bugs."

January 20 – Birthdays

1554   **Sebastian I.** King of Portugal, 1557-1578, who was killed and his army annihilated in the watershed Battle of Al-Kasr al-Kebir in Northwest Africa (August 4, 1578)

1723   **John Goddard.** Early American cabinetmaker noted for developing the block front on desks

1732   **Richard Henry Lee.** American patriot and signer of the Declaration of Independence, who introduced the resolution declaring the American colonies independent on June 7, 1776

1804   **Eugene Sue.** French physician and author noted for works such as the ten volume novel *The Wandering Jew* (1846)

1814   **David Wilmot.** U.S. congressman who sponsored the Wilmot Proviso to prohibit slavery in new territories, and who helped found the Republican Party in 1854

1876   **Josef Hofmann.** Polish-born American pianist and composer

1877   **Ruth Saint Denis.** Noted American dancer, dance teacher, and choreographer, with a 70-year career

1891   **Mischa Elman.** Noted Russian-American concert violinist

1892   **Roscoe Ates.** American stage and motion-picture actor

1893   **Bessie Coleman.** American flyer and first black woman to obtain a pilot's license (1921)

1894   **Harold Gray.** American cartoonist and creator in 1924 of *Little Orphan Annie*

1894   **Walter Piston.** American composer, noted for works such as the ballet *The Incredible Flutist*

1896   **George Burns.** Highly popular American comedian and actor in vaudeville, on radio, and in television and motion pictures

1897   **Mae Busch.** Australian-born American actress, who was a leading lady in silent films in the 1920s and a comic foil for Laurel and Hardy in the 1930s

1903   **Leon Ames.** American stage, screen, and television actor, who appeared in some 100 films

1904   **Alexandra Danilova.** One of the great Russian ballerinas of the 1920s through the 1950s

1906   **Aristotle Onassis.** Greek shipowner and businessman, one of the wealthiest men of his time, and second husband of Jacqueline Kennedy

1910   **Joy Adamson.** Austrian-born naturalist, author, and artist, noted for her work with wild animals in Kenya, such as her pet lion Elsa

1912   **Walter Briggs.** American baseball executive and long-time owner of the Detroit Tigers

1920   **DeForrest Kelley.** American actor noted for his role as the doctor in the long-running television series *Star Trek*

1920   **Frederico Fellini.** Italian motion-picture director, noted for films such as *La Strada* (1954) and *La Dolce Vita* (1960)

1922   **Ray Anthony.** American bandleader of the Big Band Era

1926   **Patricia Neal.** American stage, screen, and television actress

1928   **Harold Prince.** Noted Broadway producer

1930   **Edwin "Buzz" Aldrin Jr.** U.S. astronaut and the second man, after Neil Armstrong, to set foot on the moon

1934   **Arte Johnson.** American television actor and comedian

1934   **Camilo Pascual.** Professional baseball player

1937   **Bailey Howell.** Professional basketball superstar with over 14,000 career points

1937   **Dorothy Provine.** American motion-picture and television actress, dancer, and singer

1940   **Carol Heiss.** Hall of Fame figure skater

1946   **David Lynch.** American motion-picture director noted for works such as *Elephant Man* (1980)

1949   **Paul Stanley.** American musician with the rock group KISS

1956   **Bill Maher.** American television talk-show host (*Politically Incorrect*)

1958   **Lorenzo Lamas.** American actor and son of actors Fernando Lamas and Arlene Dahl

1969   **Melissa Rivers.** American actress, stage director, TV gossip show hostess, and daughter of comedienne Joan Rivers

January 20 – Events

1265   The English Parliament met for the first time.

1479   Ferdinand, husband of Isabella and benefactor of Columbus, assumed the throne of Aragon at age 26.

1649   The treason trial of English King Charles I opened in Westminster Hall in London.

1788   The first Australian settlers, mostly convicts from England, arrived in New South Wales.

1801 President John Adams appointed John Marshall, "the great chief justice," to the Supreme Court.

1892 The first official basketball game was played, in Springfield, Massachusetts, by YMCA students of Dr. James Naismith, the game's inventor.

1936 King George V of England died at age 70 and was succeeded by his son Edward VIII. In 1987 it was revealed that his physician, Lord Dawson, poisoned the mortally-ill king to hasten his death, and that his last words to his physician were not "How is the empire?" but "God damn you."

1937 As a result of the 20th Amendment, President Franklin D. Roosevelt was inaugurated, and all future presidents will be inaugurated on this date, which was changed from March 4.

1941 President Franklin D. Roosevelt was inaugurated for an unprecedented third term.

1942 The Nazis held their notorious Wannsee conference in Berlin, at which they decided on their "final solution" of exterminating Europe's Jews.

1945 President Franklin D. Roosevelt was inaugurated for an unprecedented fourth term.

1954 The lowest temperature ever recorded in the lower 48 states, 70 below zero, occurred at Rogers Pass, Montana.

1961 John F. Kennedy, at his inaugural, said, "Ask not what your country can do for you, but ask what you can do for your country."

1971 The first nation-wide postal strike in British history began.

1977 Jimmy Carter was inaugurated as the 39th president, and set a precedent by walking down Pennsylvania Avenue from the Capitol to the White House.

1980 The Pittsburgh Steelers beat the Los Angeles Rams, 31-19, in Super Bowl XIV in Pasadena, California.

1981 The Iranians released the American hostages they had held for a year only minutes after Ronald Reagan was sworn in as the 40th president.

January 21 – Birthdays

1337 **Charles V.** King of France (1364-1380) known as The Wise, who was perhaps the best of the Valois kings

1659 **Adriaen van der Werff.** Dutch painter

1721 **James Murray.** Soldier, statesman and first British governor of Canada

1743 **John Fitch.** American inventor and metal craftsman, who built and operated a mechanically successful steamboat 20 years before Robert Fulton built his *Clermont*

1813 **John C. Fremont.** U.S. explorer and first Republican presidential candidate, in 1856

1815 **Horace Wells.** American dentist and the first to use an anesthetic (on himself in 1844) in dentistry

1821 **John C. Breckenridge.** U.S. vice president under President Buchanan, and candidate for president in 1860

1824 **Thomas J. "Stonewall" Jackson.** The South's greatest Civil War general, after Robert E. Lee

1829 **Oscar II.** King of Sweden and Norway, 1872-1907, during whose reign the Norwegians gained their independence from Sweden (1905)

1854 **John Moses Browning.** American inventor of pistols, rifles, and shotguns, noted especially for the Browning automatic rifle, or BAR

1855 **Ernest Chausson.** French composer of the late 18th century

1871 **Bartley C. Costello.** American lyricist noted for songs such as "El Rancho Grande"

1879 **Gilmour Dobie.** Hall of Fame football player

1884 **Roger Baldwin.** Founder of the American Civil Liberties Union

1886 **John M. Stahl.** American motion-picture director noted for works such as *The Keys of the Kingdom* (1944)

1887 **Wolfgang Kohler.** German-American psychologist and chief exponent of the Gestalt theory

1888 **Leadbelly (Huddie Ledbetter).** Black American singer and guitarist who had an enormous influence on the folk music revival of the 1950s and 1960s

1892 **Robert Forsythe Irwin.** Sponsor of Talking Books for the blind

1899 **Lew Fonseca.** Professional baseball player

1900 **John T. Scopes.** American teacher who was the defendant in the famous Scopes Trial, or "Monkey Trial," for teaching evolution

1900 **J. Carroll Naish.** American motion-picture and television actor

1905 **Christian Dior.** Noted French fashion designer

1905 **Karl Wallenda.** American circus performer and patriarch of the family of high wire performers, the Flying Wallendas

1910 **Patsy Kelly.** American dancer, actress, and highly talented comedienne, with a career of over 50 years

1912 **Konrad Emil Bloch.** American biochemist and Nobel Prize winner (1964) for his discovery of how animal cells produce cholesterol

1919 **Jinx Falkenburg.** American motion-picture actress

1922 **Paul Scofield.** English stage and motion-picture actor who won the Academy Award in 1966 for *A Man for All Seasons*

1925 **Telly Savalas.** American television and motion-picture actor, and star of the long-running television series *Kojak*

1925 **Benny Hill.** British comedian and actor

1939 **Wolfman Jack.** American radio and television personality

1940 **Jack Nicklaus.** One of the greatest professional golfers of all time, and the first to win all four major golf titles at least twice

1941 **Richie Havens.** American singer and guitarist

1941 **Placido Domingo.** Noted Spanish operatic tenor

1942 **Mac Davis.** American singer and songwriter

1947 **Jill Eikenberry.** American stage, screen, and television actress

1950 **Billy Ocean.** Trinidadian-born singer and song-writer
1952 **Mike Krukow.** Professional baseball player
1955 **Peter Fleming.** American tennis player
1956 **Robby Benson.** American motion-picture and television actor
1957 **Geena Davis.** American motion-picture and television actress
1963 **Hakeem Olajuwan.** Professional basketball player
1978 **Emma "Baby Spice" Bunton.** British singer with The Spice Girls

January 21 – Events

1793 French King Louis XVI was guillotined by the French revolutionaries.
1846 The London *Daily News* began publication.
1861 Jefferson Davis resigned from the U.S. Senate to join Mississippi in secession.
1908 The Sullivan Ordnance was enacted in New York City making it illegal for women to smoke in public. The punishment was a fine of $5 to $25 and up to 10 days' imprisonment.
1915 The first Kiwanis Club was founded, in Detroit.
1924 V.I. Lenin, Russian Communist leader and founder of the Soviet state, died of a brain hemorrhage at age 53.
1950 Alger Hiss was convicted of perjury, and subsequently sentenced to five years in prison.
1950 George Orwell, the noted British writer, died in London at age 46.
1954 The *Nautilus,* the world's first atomic-powered submarine, was launched at Groton, Connecticut.
1961 The American nuclear submarine *George Washington* completed a journey under the Arctic ice.
1979 The Pittsburgh Steelers defeated the Dallas Cowboys, 35-21, in Super Bowl XIII in Miami.
1994 Lorena Bobbitt was charged with cutting off her husband's penis in retaliation for his abuse. She was later acquitted by reason of insanity.
1997 Speaker of the House Newt Gingrich was reprimanded and fined as the House voted for the first time in history to discipline the Speaker for ethical misconduct.
1998 President Clinton denied allegations that he had a sexual relationship with Monica Lewinsky, a young White House intern, and that he had asked her to lie about the affair.

January 22 – Birthdays

1440 **Ivan III (The Great).** Grand Duke of Muscovy, who freed Russia in 1480 from its 240-year rule by the Tartars, laid the basis for a unified Russia, and was considered by many to be the first Russian czar though Ivan IV was the first to adopt that title

1561 **Francis Bacon.** Great English philosopher, statesman, and writer, noted for works such as *The Advancement of Learning* (1605) and *Novum Organum* (1620)
1690 **Nicolas Lancret.** French painter noted for works such as *The Dancer LaCamargo* (1730) and *The Pleasure Party* (1735)
1729 **Gottfried Ephraim Lessing.** German dramatist and philosopher, often considered to be the father of modern German literature, and whose play *Minna von Barnhelm* (1767) is one of the greatest German comedies
1775 **Andre Marie Ampere.** French physicist who discovered the laws of electromagnetism in the 1820s, and for whom the ampere, the unit of electric current, was named
1788 **Lord Byron.** The most colorful of the English romantic poets (born George Gordon Byron), noted for works such as "Childe Harold's Pilgrimage" (1812-1816) and *Don Juan,* left unfinished in 1824
1797 **John Harper.** One of the four Harper brothers who founded the famous publishing house of Harper and Brothers
1802 **Richard Upjohn.** American architect
1849 **August Strindberg.** Swedish dramatist and novelist, one of the key figures in the history of modern drama, and according to many, Sweden's greatest playwright
1850 **Robert Somers Brookings.** American manufacturer, philanthropist and founder in 1927 of the Brookings Institution
1858 **Beatrice Webb.** Noted British reformer and Fabian Socialist, who with her husband Sidney helped lead the British socialist movement in the late 1800s and early 1900s
1874 **Edward Stephen Harkness.** American businessman and philanthropist who devoted his life to giving away the fortune his father made as a partner of John D. Rockefeller
1875 **D.W. Griffith.** The single most important figure in the history of American films, and director of the 1915 classic, *The Birth of a Nation*
1877 **Hjalmar Schacht.** German financier, economic advisor to Hitler, and later a plotter to assassinate him
1879 **Francis Picabia.** French artist
1890 **Fred M. Vinson.** Chief Justice of the U.S. Supreme Court, 1946-1953
1893 **Fulton Oursler.** American journalist and author noted for *The Greatest Story Ever Told* (1949)
1897 **Rosa Melba Ponselle.** American dramatic soprano, who was a leading star with the Metropolitan Opera in New York City in the 1920s and 1930s
1907 **Douglas "Wrong Way" Corrigan.** American aviator who in 1938 left New York for California and wound up in Dublin, Ireland (Some said on purpose)
1909 **U Thant.** Burmese statesman and third United Nations secretary general

1909 Ann Sothern. American stage, screen, and television actress with a career of over 40 years

1916 Howard Miles Teichmann. American biographer and dramatist noted for *The Solid Gold Cadillac* (1953)

1920 Irving Kristol. American editor and founder of *Public Interest* magazine

1928 Birch Bayh. U.S. senator in the 1960s and 1970s

1931 Sam Cooke. American soul singer

1932 Piper Laurie. American leading lady of Hollywood films of the 1950s and character actress of the 1970s and 1980s

1935 Pierre S. DuPont. Governor of Delaware

1937 Joseph Wambaugh. American writer noted for novels such as *The New Centurions*, *The Onion Field*, and *The Glitter Dome*

1940 John Hurt. British-born motion-picture actor noted for the title role in *Elephant Man*

1952 Teddy Gentry. Country singer-musician with the group Alabama

1955 Lester Hayes. Professional football player

1957 Mike Bossy. Professional hockey player

1959 Linda Blair. American motion-picture actress

January 22 – Events

1789 The first American novel, *The Power of Sympathy,* by Sarah Wentworth Morton (*Philenia*), was published in Boston.

1840 The first British colonists landed in New Zealand.

1881 Cleopatra's Needle, an ancient Egyptian obelisk, was erected in New York's Central Park.

1901 Queen Victoria of England died at age 81, ending a reign of nearly 64 years, the longest of any British monarch.

1905 "Bloody Sunday" occurred in St. Petersburg, on which Czar Nicholas II of Russia bloodily suppressed an assault on the Winter Palace.

1907 Richard Strauss's opera *Salome* made its debut at the Metropolitan Opera in New York, shocking the audience with its "Dance of the Seven Veils."

1917 President Wilson asked for an end to World War I, saying that there must be "peace without victory."

1944 Allied troops landed near Anzio, Italy, 33 miles south of Rome, in World War II.

1972 Denmark, Great Britain, Ireland, and Norway signed the Treaty of Brussels, agreeing to join the European Common Market.

1973 Lyndon B. Johnson died of a heart attack in Johnson City, Texas, at age 64.

1973 The U.S. Supreme Court legalized abortions for women during the first three months of pregnancy in the landmark *Roe v. Wade* decision.

January 23 – Birthdays

1598 François Mansart. French architect

1730 Joseph Hewes. Member of the Continental Congress, North Carolina signer of the Declaration of Independence, and executive head of the U.S. Navy who appointed John Paul Jones a navy officer

1762 Christian August Vulpius. German historical novelist and brother-in-law of the great German writer Johann Wolfgang von Goethe

1783 Stendhal (Marie Henri Beyle). One of the leading 19th-century French novelists, noted for works such as *The Red and the Black* (1831), one of the great books of world literature

1832 Edouard Manet. French artist who revolutionized painting in the mid-1800s by using subject matter for visual effect rather than for telling a story

1840 Ernst Abbe. German physicist who with Carl Zeiss developed the Zeiss works into the world's leading manufacturer of optical goods

1862 David Hilbert. German mathematician noted for his classic work *Foundations of Geometry* (1902)

1863 Samuel Henry Kress. American merchant and founder in 1907 of the Kress dime store chain

1869 Herbert David Croly. American political philosopher and founder in 1914 of the *New Republic* magazine

1878 Edwin Plimpton Adams. American physicist and author of *The Quantum Theory*

1884 George McManus. American cartoonist and creator of *Bringing Up Father* and the characters Maggie and Jiggs

1887 Percy Wenrich. American composer and pianist, noted for songs such as "Put on Your Old Gray Bonnet," "Silver Bell," "Moonlight Bay," and "When You Wore a Tulip and I Wore a Big Red Rose"

1898 Randolph Scott. American motion-picture actor, who was a strong and silent Western star, and the ideal of two generations of filmgoers

1898 Sergei Mikhailovitch Eisenstein. Latvian-born motion-picture director and one of the giant creative talents and theorists of the screen

1899 Joseph Nathan Kane. American historian and author noted for works such as *Facts about the Presidents* (1976)

1906 Bob Steele. American motion-picture and television actor and cowboy star of the 1930s

1907 Hideki Yukawa. Physicist and first Japanese to win the Nobel Prize (1949), for predicting the existence of the meson, a particle with a mass between the electron and the proton

1907 Dan Duryea. American motion-picture and television actor in over 60 films

1915 Potter Stewart. U.S. Supreme Court justice, 1958-1981, who on his appointment was the second youngest justice in 105 years

1919 Ernie Kovacs. American actor and zany, creative comic of television and motion pictures

1924 Frank R. Lautenberg. U.S. senator

1928 Jeanne Moreau. French stage and motion-picture actress and director

1932   **George Aliceson Tipton.** American composer noted for scores for films and TV, such as *Phantom of the Paradise, Soap,* and *Benson*

1933   **Chita Rivera.** American singer

1943   **Gary Burton.** Hall of Fame American musician noted for *Alone at Last* (1971) and *Dust* (1979)

1944   **Rutger Hauer.** Dutch motion-picture actor sometimes called the "Dutch Paul Newman"

1947   **Kurt Bevacqua.** Professional baseball player

1950   **Pat Simmons.** American singer and songwriter with The Doobie Brothers

1953   **Pat Haden.** Professional football player

1957   **Princess Caroline.** Daughter of Prince Rainier and Princess Grace of Monaco

January 23 – Events

27 BC   Augustus Caesar (Octavian) founded the Roman Empire that would last until A.D. 476.

1294   Boniface VIII was elected Roman Catholic pope.

1516   Ferdinand of Aragon, husband of Queen Isabella and sponsor of Columbus, died at age 63 and was succeeded by his grandson Charles I.

1789   Georgetown University was founded in the colonial village of Georgetown, which later became a part of Washington, D.C.

1845   Congress established election day in the United States as the first Tuesday after the first Monday in November.

1849   Elizabeth Blackwell graduated from the Geneva (New York) College of Medicine to become America's first woman physician.

1893   Phillips Brooks, American clergyman who composed "O Little Town of Bethlehem," died at age 57.

1943   The British Eighth Army under General Bernard L. Montgomery took Tripoli from Field Marshal Irwin Rommel's Afrika Corps in World War II.

1948   General Dwight D. Eisenhower refused to run in 1948 for president.

1950   The Israeli parliament proclaimed Jerusalem the capital of Israel.

1960   Dr. Jacques Picard and Lieutenant Donald Walsh touched the ocean bottom at 35,820 feet in the Pacific's Mariana Trench in the U.S. Navy bathysphere *Trieste.*

1968   The U.S. reconnaissance ship *Pueblo* was seized by the North Koreans.

1973   President Nixon announced that an accord had been reached to end the Vietnam War.

January 24 – Birthdays

76   **Hadrian.** Roman Emperor, A.D. 117-138, who was one of the "five good emperors"

1544   **Gillis van Coninxloo.** Flemish painter

1664   **Sir John Vanbrugh.** English playwright and architect who satirized the manners of his day in works such as *The Relapse* (1696) and *The Provoked Wife* (1697), and who designed Blenheim Palace

1670   **William Congreve.** English dramatist who wrote in his play, *The Mourning Bride* (1697), the famous line, "Music has charms to soothe a savage breast," and the well-known quote, paraphrased as "Hell hath no fury like a woman scorned"

1679   **Christian Freiherr von Wolff.** German philosopher and mathematician

1705   **Farinelli (Carlo Broschi).** Noted Italian Castrato soprano

1712   **Frederick II (The Great).** King of Prussia, 1740-1786, and one of the great Prussian heroes of the 18th century

1732   **Pierre Augustin C. de Beaumarchais.** French dramatist noted for his comedies, *The Barber of Seville* (1775) and *The Marriage of Figaro* (1781)

1746   **Gustavus III.** King of Sweden, 1771-1792

1776   **E(rnst) T(heodor) A(madeus) Hoffman.** German writer, composer, painter and pioneer of German romantic literature, whose *Mademoiselle de Scudery* (1818) was a forerunner of the detective story

1818   **John Mason Neale.** English hymn writer and prolific translator of such hymns as "O Come, O Come, Immanuel"

1828   **Ferdinand Julius Cohn.** German botanist who founded bacteriology

1855   **Charles Henry Niehaus.** American sculptor noted for his statues of Presidents Garfield, McKinley and Lincoln

1860   **Bernard Henry Kroger.** American businessman who in 1883 founded the Kroger chain of grocery stores

1862   **Edith Wharton.** Noted American novelist and author of such works as *Ethan Frome* (1911) and *The Age of Innocence* (1920)

1870   **William G. Morgan.** American YMCA physical director who in 1895 invented volleyball

1885   **Umberto Nobile.** Italian airship designer, aviator and arctic explorer who piloted Amundsen and Ellsworth across the North Pole in his dirigible (1926)

1888   **Henry King.** American motion-picture director with a 50-year career, who directed such films as *Twelve O'Clock High* (1949) and *Tender Is the Night* (1962)

1899   **Hoyt Vandenberg.** U.S. World War II general and Air Force chief of staff, 1948-1953

1915   **Mark Goodson.** American television producer

1917   **Ernest Borgnine.** American motion-picture and television actor, who won the Academy Award in 1955 for his role in *Marty*

1918   **Oral Roberts.** Noted American evangelist

1922   **Ava Gardner.** American motion-picture actress and Hollywood's "love goddess" in the 1940s and 1950s

1925   **Maria Tallchief.** American ballerina of North American Indian descent, and one of the first American ballerinas to gain international fame

1926   **Alfredo Poveda Burbano.** Head of Ecuador's ruling junta

1927   **Paula Hawkins.** U.S. senator

1928   **Desmond Morris.** British zoologist and author, noted for *The Naked Ape* (1967)

1930   **Ernest Sheldon Lieberman.** American composer, author, and singer, noted for songs such as "The Windows of Your Mind," "The Best Is Yet to Come," and "Baby the Rain Must Fall"

1936   **Doug Kershaw.** American country violinist

1937   **Monte Clark.** Professional football player

1941   **Neil Diamond.** American singer and composer, noted for works such as "Song Sung Blue," "Jonathan Livingston Seagull," and "September Morn"

1943   **Sharon Tate.** American motion-picture actress

1949   **John Belushi.** American motion-picture and television actor and comedian

1958   **Atlee Hammaker.** Professional baseball player

1961   **Nastassja Kinski.** German-born motion-picture actress

1968   **Mary Lou Retton.** American gymnast and darling of the 1984 Olympics

January 24 – Events

41   Rome's insane emperor Caligula was murdered by a tribune of the guard after he had insulted the army and threatened to kill the members of the Roman Senate.

1556   The greatest loss of life in history from an earthquake occurred in Shensi, China, when 830,000 people were killed.

1848   A gold nugget was discovered by James Wilson Marshall at Sutter's Mill in California, leading to the Gold Rush of 1849.

1894   Lobster thermidor was first served, in Paris.

1908   The first Boy Scout troop was organized, by Sir Robert Baden-Powell in England.

1916   The U.S. Supreme Court ruled that the federal income tax was constitutional.

1922   Eskimo Pie was patented by Christian K. Nelson, of Onawa, Iowa.

1924   The Russian city of Petrograd was renamed Leningrad in honor of the revolutionary leader, Vladimir I. Lenin, who had died three days earlier. The name was changed back to the original St. Petersburg in 1991.

1935   Canned beer went on sale for the first time, in Richmond, Virginia.

1943   The Casablanca Conference in World War II concluded, with President Roosevelt's call for "unconditional surrender" of the Axis powers.

1945   Russian soldiers crossed the Oder River into German soil for the first time in World War II.

1965   Sir Winston Churchill, Britain's great World War II leader, died at age 90 of a stroke suffered on January 15.

January 25 – Birthdays

1540   **Edmund Campion.** English Jesuit who was hanged in 1581 on orders of Queen Elizabeth for his attacks on the Anglican Church and for allegedly conspiring to dethrone her

1585   **Hendrick van Avercamp.** Dutch painter

1627   **Robert Boyle.** Irish chemist and physicist who formulated Boyle's law of gases

1708   **Pompeo Batoni.** Italian painter

1736   **Joseph Louis Lagrange.** Noted French mathematician and author of the famous work *Analytical Mechanics* (1788)

1743   **Friedrich Heinrich Jacobi.** German philosopher

1759   **Robert Burns.** The national poet of Scotland, noted for works such as "To a Louse," "Auld Lang Syne," and "Comin' Thro' the Rye"

1783   **William Colgate.** American industrialist who founded the Colgate Soap Co. (the forerunner to Colgate-Palmolive) and Colgate University

1814   **Francis Harrison Pierpont.** Governor during the Civil War of the "Restored Government of Virginia," the western part that remained loyal to the U.S., which under his guidance became West Virginia in 1863

1825   **George Edward Pickett.** Confederate general whose charge (Pickett's Charge) in the Battle of Gettysburg ranks as one of the great events in American history

1860   **Charles Curtis.** U.S. vice president under President Hoover

1874   **W. Somerset Maugham.** One of the most popular British authors of the 1900s, noted for works such as *Of Human Bondage* (1915) and *Cakes and Ale* (1930)

1874   **Hewlett Johnson.** English religious leader known by his enemies as the "Red Dean of Canterbury"

1881   **Emil Ludwig.** German-born author who wrote famous biographies of Bismarck, Napoleon, Lincoln, Beethoven, and Goethe

1882   **Virginia Woolf.** British novelist and critic, noted for works such as *Mrs. Dalloway* (1925) and *Between the Acts* (1941)

1886   **Wilhelm Furtwangler.** Noted German conductor with the Berlin Philharmonic Orchestra and the New York Philharmonic Symphony

1896   **Harry Link.** American composer and publisher, noted for songs such as "These Foolish Things"

1899   **Paul-Henri Spaak.** European statesman, leader of the Socialist Party in Belgium, and secretary-general of NATO, 1957-1961

1906   **Mildred Dunnock.** American stage, screen, and television actress

1919   **Edwin Newman.** American television journalist and author

1924 **Lou Groza.** Professional football superstar who scored 1,608 points in a 21-year career

1928 **Eduard Shevardnadze.** Soviet foreign minister under Gorbachev and second president of Georgia (of the old USSR)

1933 **Corazon Aquino.** President of the Philippines, who succeeded Ferdinand Marcos in 1986

1935 **Dean Jones.** American stage, screen, and television actor and singer

1937 **Don Maynard.** Professional football player

1938 **Etta James.** American blues singer

1943 **Jack Snow.** Professional football player

1944 **Leigh Taylor-Young.** American motion-picture actress

1952 **Alfred Jenkins.** Professional football player

1959 **Mark Duper.** Professional football player

1969 **Kina Cosper.** Rhythm-and-blues singer with the group Brownstone

January 25 – Events

1533 King Henry VIII of England secretly married Anne Boleyn, his mistress of the past six years.

1554 Sao Paulo, Brazil, was founded by the Jesuits on the site of an Indian village. It was named for St. Paul because the date was the anniversary of his conversion to Christianity.

1579 The Union of Utrecht was formed, which later became the Dutch Republic or The Netherlands.

1787 Shays' Rebellion occurred in which Daniel Shays, a Massachusetts farmer, led 1200 men in an attack on the Federal arsenal in Springfield, Massachusetts.

1858 Felix Mendelssohn's famous "Wedding March" was played in a wedding for the first time—the wedding of Queen Victoria's daughter.

1871 William McKinley married Ida Saxton.

1890 Nellie Bly (reporter Elizabeth Cochrane) returned to New Jersey, completing a 72-day trip around the world, beating the record of the hero of *Around the World in Eighty Days.*

1915 Transcontinental telephone service began as Alexander Graham Bell in New York again spoke the famous words, "Watson, come here, I want you," to Thomas Watson in San Francisco.

1934 John Dillinger, Public Enemy Number One on the FBI's list, was captured in Tucson, Arizona. He later escaped in March but was killed in July.

1956 The atomic submarine U.S.S. *Swordfish* was launched.

1959 American Airlines made the first scheduled transcontinental flight of a Boeing 707, opening the jet age in U.S. commercial aviation.

1961 President Kennedy held the first live presidential press conference on television.

1964 *Echo II,* the U.S. communications satellite, was launched in the first joint Russian-U.S. experiment.

1971 Idi Amin seized power in Uganda, ousting President Apollo Milton Obote.

1981 The Oakland Raiders beat the Philadelphia Eagles, 27-10, in Super Bowl XV in the Superdome in New Orleans.

January 26 – Birthdays

1582 **Giovanni Lanfranco.** Italian painter

1714 **Jean Baptiste Pigalle.** Court sculptor to King Louis XV of France

1715 **Claude Adrien Helvetius.** French philosopher and author of *De l'Esprit* (*Of the Spirit*), which raised a storm of protest and was publicly burned

1810 **Joseph Rogers Brown.** American inventor and founder of the Brown and Sharpe Co.

1826 **Julia Dent Grant.** Wife of President U.S. Grant

1831 **Mary Mapes Dodge.** American author noted for the famous children's book *Hans Brinker, or, The Silver Skates* (1865)

1832 **Rufus H. Gilbert.** Noted elevated railroad builder

1852 **Pierre Paul F.C.S. de Brazza.** Founder of the French Congo

1877 **Kees van Dongen.** French painter

1880 **Douglas MacArthur.** One of the leading American generals of World War II, and commander of all American Army forces in the Pacific

1884 **Roy Chapman Andrews.** Famous American explorer and leader of expeditions for the American Museum of Natural History, and a leading authority on whales

1905 **Al Goodhart.** American composer and pianist, noted for songs such as "Auf Wiedersehen, My Dear" and "I Apologize"

1905 **Maria von Trapp.** Austrian musician and matriarch of the singing von Trapp family who inspired the famous motion-picture *The Sound of Music*

1912 **Howard W. Cannon.** U.S. Senator, 1968-1981

1912 **Alfred Sheinwold.** American bridge expert, columnist, and author

1913 **Jimmy Van Heusen.** American popular composer noted for songs such as "Moonlight Becomes You," "Swinging on a Star," "High Hopes," and "Personality"

1918 **Nicolae Ceausescu.** Romanian head of state

1923 **Sid Wayne.** American composer and author, noted for songs such as "I'm Gonna Knock on Your Door," "Two Different Worlds," and "It's Impossible"

1923 **Anne Jeffreys.** American motion-picture and television actress

1925 **Paul Newman.** American stage and motion-picture actor, director, producer, and superstar

1925 **Joan Leslie.** American stage and screen actress and dress designer

1926 **Moira Shearer.** Scottish ballerina and motion-picture actress

1928 **Roger Vadim.** French motion-picture director noted for such works as the sensational *And God Created Woman* (1956), starring his then wife Brigitte Bardot

1928 **Eartha Kitt.** American stage and screen actress and singer

1929 **Jules Feiffer.** American cartoonist and author

1935 **Bob Uecker.** Professional baseball player who used his unheralded career to become a television personality

1944 **Angela Davis.** American black militant philosophy professor

1946 **Gene Siskel.** American motion-picture critic and coauthor with Roger Ebert of a movie review column

1946 **Christopher Hampton.** English playwright noted for the Academy Award-winning picture, *Dangerous Liaisons* (1988), which he adapted from his own stage play

1950 **Jack Youngblood.** Professional football player

1952 **Tom Henderson.** Professional basketball player

1957 **Eddie Van Halen.** American rock singer

1958 **Ellen DeGeneres.** American actress and comedienne

1961 **Wayne Gretzky.** Professional hockey superstar known as "The Great Gretzky"

1963 **Andrew Ridgeley.** British guitarist with the Wham! musical group

January 26 – Events

1699 The Peace of Karlowitz (Hungary) marked the eclipse of the Ottoman Empire, as the Turks were forced to give up nearly all of Hungary and the Turkish part of Ukraine.

1784 In a letter to his daughter, Benjamin Franklin expressed unhappiness over the choice of the eagle as the symbol of America and expressed his own preference for the turkey.

1788 Sydney, Australia, was founded by Captain Arthur Phillip and a cargo of convicts from England.

1802 Congress authorized a national library, the forerunner of the Library of Congress.

1808 William Bligh, the captain of the *Bounty* during the famous mutiny in 1789, was arrested for tyranny in his capacity as governor of New South Wales, Australia.

1837 Michigan was admitted to the Union as the 26th state.

1861 Louisiana seceded from the Union.

1905 The 3,106-carat Cullinan diamond, the largest ever discovered, was found in the Premier mine of South Africa by Captain M.F. Wells.

1917 The U.S. Army Tank Corps was created.

1942 The first American Expeditionary Force of World War II arrived in Northern Ireland.

1945 Larry MacPhail and Dan Topping bought the New York Yankees baseball team for $3 million.

1950 India became a republic, as the new constitution went into effect.

1962 The U.S. lunar probe, *Ranger III,* was launched.

1971 Charles Manson and three of his followers were convicted for the first-degree murder of actress Sharon Tate.

1980 Frank Sinatra sang before 175,000 people at the Maracana Stadium in Rio de Janeiro, the largest crowd ever assembled for one performer.

January 27 – Birthdays

1571 **Abbas I (The Great).** Shah of Persia, 1588-1629, and the greatest of the Safavid kings

1756 **Wolfgang Amadeus Mozart.** One of the world's three or four greatest composers, who wrote over 600 works, including 41 symphonies and *Don Giovanni,* perhaps the world's greatest opera

1775 **Friedrich Wilhelm J. von Schelling.** German philosopher whose works are considered to be a major link between Immanuel Kant and G.W.F. Hegel

1805 **Samuel Palmer.** British painter and engraver, who was one of the founders of the group known as "The Ancients"

1814 **Eugène Emmanuel Viollet-le-Duc.** French architect, restorer, and writer, who in the 1840s directed the restoration of Notre Dame Cathedral in Paris

1823 **Edouard Lalo.** French composer noted for works such as the violin concerto *Symphonie Espagnole* (1873)

1832 **Lewis Carroll (Charles L. Dodgson).** English author of the famous story *Alice's Adventures in Wonderland* (1865) and its continuation, *Through the Looking Glass and What Alice Found There* (1871)

1850 **Samuel Gompers.** U.S. labor leader and principal organizer of the American Federation of Labor

1859 **Wilhelm II.** World War I leader and last emperor, or kaiser, of Germany, 1888-1918, whose reign marked the end of the great Hohenzollern dynasty that had ruled Prussia since 1701

1872 **Learned Hand.** Judge of the U.S. Court of Appeals, 1924-1951, and one of the most able judges in American history

1885 **Jerome Kern.** Famous American composer noted for songs such as "Smoke Gets in Your Eyes," "Ol' Man River," "All the Things You Are," and "Why Do I Love You?"

1895 **George Gard Desylvia.** American composer noted for songs such as "April Showers," "Somebody Loves Me," "If You Knew Susie," "Button Up Your Overcoat," and "Sonny Boy"

1895 **Harry Ruby.** American composer, author, and pianist, noted for songs such as "Who's Sorry Now?" "I Wanna Be Loved By You," "A Kiss to Build a Dream On," and "Three Little Words"

1899 **Philip Strong.** American author noted for works such as *State Fair* (1932)

1900 **Hyman G. Rickover.** American admiral and father of the nuclear-powered submarine

1908 **William Randolph Hearst Jr.** American newspaper publisher and son of the founder of the Hearst chain

1918 **Skitch Henderson.** English-American bandleader

1921 **Donna Reed.** American motion-picture and television actress

1936 **Troy Donahue.** American motion-picture and television actor

1940 **Bob Wynn.** Professional golfer

1945 **Nick Mason.** British drummer of the Pink Floyd rock group

1947 **John Lowenstein.** Professional baseball player

1948 **Mikhail Baryshnikov.** Noted Russian-born ballet dancer

1952 **Brian Gottfried.** American tennis player

1959 **Cris Collinsworth.** Professional football player

1961 **Margo Timmons.** Rock singer with the Cowboy Junkies

1964 **Bridget Fonda.** American motion-picture actress, daughter of actor Peter Fonda and granddaughter of actor Henry Fonda

January 27 – Events

1302 The great Italian writer Dante Alighieri was expelled from Florence forever by the Guelphs, one of the two contending political factions in the city.

1521 The Diet of Worms was opened to hear the charges against Martin Luther.

1689 Peter, the future great czar of Russia, was forced into a marriage at age 17 with the beautiful but stupid Eudoxia Lopukhina.

1851 John James Audubon, the great American naturalist, died in New York City at age 65.

1854 The Canadian Great Western Railway began operations.

1870 Kappa Alpha Theta, the first Greek-letter sorority, was founded at Indiana University, now De Paul University.

1880 Thomas A. Edison patented his incandescent lamp.

1888 The National Geographic Society was founded in Washington, D.C.

1910 Thomas Crapper, English plumber and prime developer of the flush toilet mechanism, died. In his honor January 27 was named Thomas Crapper Day.

1943 The U.S. Eighth Air Force staged the first all-American air raid on Germany in World War II, bombing Wilhelmshaven in broad daylight.

1944 The Russians broke the German siege of Leningrad in World War II.

1967 In the first U.S. space disaster, three American astronauts, Virgil Grissom, Edward White, and Roger Chaffee, were killed in an Apollo launching-pad fire.

1973 A cease-fire accord was signed in Paris by the United States and North Vietnam, ending the Vietnam War.

January 28 – Birthdays

1457 **Henry VII.** First English king of the House of Tudor, 1485-1509, who came to the throne as a result of his killing Richard III at Bosworth Field, which ended the Wars of the Roses

1582 **John Barclay.** Scottish satirist and Latin poet

1611 **Johann Hevelius.** German astronomer

1706 **John Baskerville.** English printer and inventor of the Baskerville printing type, whose first book from his press, an edition of Virgil in 1757, amazed readers by its elegance

1784 **George Hamilton-Gordon.** British prime minister of the Victorian Age

1825 **Benedetto Cairoli.** Italian statesman who served three times as premier of Italy

1841 **Sir Henry Morton Stanley.** Noted British explorer of the African continent, who, upon finding the British explorer David Livingstone, greeted him with the famous line: "Dr. Livingstone, I presume?"

1847 **George Wright.** Hall of Fame baseball player who was the first batter in National League history, leading off the opening game on April 22, 1876

1855 **William Burroughs.** American inventor noted for the first commercially successful adding machine (patented in 1883)

1858 **Eugene Dubois.** Dutch anatomist and anthropologist, who in 1891-1892 discovered the fossilized bones of Java Man, believed to have walked erect on the earth a million years ago

1864 **Charles William Nash.** U.S. automobile manufacturer who formed Nash Motors in 1916

1873 **Colette.** One of the outstanding French woman writers of the 20th century (born Sidonie-Gabrielle Colette), noted for works such as *The Vagabond* (1910) and *Gigi* (1945)

1882 **Alice Tisdale Nourse Hobart.** American author noted for *Oil for the Lamps of China* (1933)

1884 **Jean Piccard.** Swiss chemist, pioneer in stratospheric balloon exploration, and twin brother of physicist Auguste Piccard

1884 **Auguste Piccard.** Swiss physicist, pioneer in the use of the bathyscaph for underwater research, and twin brother of chemist Jean Piccard

1887 **Arthur Rubinstein.** Polish-born American concert pianist and one of the greatest keyboard virtuosos of the 20th century

1892 **Ernst Lubitsch.** Noted German-American motion-picture director of such classics as *Ninotchka* (1939) and *To Be or Not to Be* (1942)

1903 **Samuel Manuel Lerner.** Romanian-born composer, author, and publisher, noted for songs such as "Popeye the Sailor Man" and "Is It True What They Say About Dixie?"

1911 **Lee Metcalf.** U.S. senator, 1958-1978

1912 **Jackson Pollock.** American painter and exponent of Abstract Expressionism, noted for works such as *One* (1950)

1913	**Judith Allen.** American stage and motion-picture actress and leading lady of the 1930s

1913 **Judith Allen.** American stage and motion-picture actress and leading lady of the 1930s

1915 **Kermit Goell.** American lyricist noted for songs such as "Near You," "Ever True Evermore," and "Huggin' and Chalkin'"

1918 **Bob Hilliard.** American lyricist noted for songs such as "Mention My Name in Sheboygan," "Civilization," "Be My Life's Companion," and "Dear Hearts and Gentle People"

1929 **Claes Oldenburg.** American sculptor

1932 **Parry O'Brien.** The greatest shot-putter in history

1933 **Susan Sontag.** American author, noted for the collection of essays, *Against Interpretation* (1966)

1934 **Bill White.** Professional baseball player and president of the National League, 1989-1994

1936 **Alan Alda.** American stage, screen, and television actor, son of actor Robert Alda, and star of the long-running television comedy *M*A*S*H*

1943 **Susan Howard.** American television actress

1944 **Marthe Keller.** Swiss stage, screen, and television actress

1950 **Barbi Benton.** American motion-picture and television actress

1957 **Nick Price.** Zimbabwe-born professional golfer who won 11 PGA events in 1992-94

1959 **Dave Sharp.** Welsh guitarist with The Alarm musical group

January 28 – Events

814 The great Holy Roman Emperor Charlemagne died of pleurisy in Aachen at age 72.

1547 King Henry VIII of England died at age 55 of syphilis and cirrhosis of the liver.

1596 Sir Francis Drake, the great English seaman, died of the plague near Nombre de Dios in the West Indies, and was buried at sea by his crew.

1807 The first gas-lit street was illuminated in Pall Mall, London.

1871 Paris surrendered to the Germans, ending the fighting in the Franco-Prussian War.

1878 The *Yale News,* the first daily college newspaper, began publication in New Haven, Connecticut.

1902 The Carnegie Institution was established in Washington, D.C.

1915 Congress created the U.S. Coast Guard, by combining the Revenue Cutter Service and the Lifesaving Service.

1916 Louis D. Brandeis was appointed as the first Jewish justice to the Supreme Court.

1938 President Franklin D. Roosevelt asked Congress to permit the building of a two-ocean U.S. Navy.

1939 William Butler Yeats, the noted Irish poet, died at Roquebrunne, France, at age 73.

1958 Roy Campanella, the great Los Angeles Dodger catcher, was seriously injured in an automobile accident in New York, ending his baseball career.

1973 Hostilities officially ended in the Vietnam War.

1986 The U.S. space shuttle *Challenger* exploded at Cape Canaveral, 73 seconds after liftoff, killing all seven crew members.

January 29 – Birthdays

1688 **Emanuel Swedenborg.** Swedish scientist, philosopher, and theologian, whose followers founded the Church of the New Jerusalem based on his biblical interpretations

1737 **Thomas Paine.** American Revolutionary War patriot, whose writings, such as the famous pamphlet *Common Sense* (1776), encouraged the Continental Army during the darkest days of the war

1749 **William Sharp.** English printmaker

1756 **Henry "Light-Horse Harry" Lee.** American Revolutionary War officer, father of Civil War general Robert E. Lee, and author of the famous epitaph of George Washington, "First in war, first in peace, and first in the hearts of his countrymen"

1761 **Albert Gallatin.** American financier, Secretary of the Treasury under Presidents Jefferson and Madison and a founder of New York Universssity

1782 **Daniel Auber.** French composer

1835 **Sarah Chauncy Woolsey.** American author known for the Kady Did series for children

1838 **Edward Williams Morley.** American scientist noted for research on the atomic weights of hydrogen and oxygen

1843 **William McKinley.** 25th U.S. president

1860 **Anton Chekhov.** Russian playwright noted for works such as *The Seagull* (1896) and *The Cherry Orchard* (1904)

1862 **Frederick Delius.** English composer noted for works such as "Over the Hills and Far Away" (1895) and "Appalachia" (1902)

1866 **Romain Rolland.** Nobel Prize-winning French novelist best known for his ten-volume novel *Jean-Christophe* (1904-1912)

1874 **John D. Rockefeller Jr..** American financier, only son of the founder of the Standard Oil Company, builder of Rockefeller Center in New York City, and restorer of Williamsburg, Virginia

1878 **Barney Oldfield.** Famous American automobile racer who was the first to drive an automobile a mile a minute (1903) and whose name became synonymous with speeders

1880 **W.C. Fields.** American actor and comedian who played swindling characters whose beliefs were "Never give a sucker an even break" and "Anyone who hates children can't be all bad"

1884 **John Schommer.** Hall of Fame basketball player

1891 **Richard Norris "Dick" Williams.** Swiss-American Hall of Fame tennis player and National Champion in 1914 and 1916

1900 **Dynamite Sonnenberg.** "King of Wrestlers," who introduced the flying tackle

1901 **Allen B. Du Mont.** American engineer who perfected the cathode-ray tube and who founded the Du Mont Television company

1912 **"Professor" Irwin Corey.** American comedian

1913 **Victor Mature.** American motion-picture actor and leading man of the 1940s and 1950s

1918 **John Forsythe.** American stage, screen, and television actor

1918 **Bill Rigney.** Professional baseball player and manager

1923 **Paddy Chayefsky.** American playwright and screenwriter who won Academy Awards for the scripts of *Marty* (1955), *The Hospital* (1971), and *Network* (1976)

1923 **Jack Burke Jr.** Professional golfer who won the Masters and the PGA in 1956

1933 **Ron Towson.** Member of the 5th Dimension singing group

1939 **Germaine Greer.** Australian-born feminist and author, noted for works such as *The Female Eunuch*

1942 **Claudine Longet.** Motion-picture actress

1942 **Katharine Ross.** American motion-picture and television actress

1942 **Scott Glenn.** American stage and screen actor

1945 **Donna Maria Caponi.** Professional golfer

1945 **Tom Selleck.** American television actor, noted for the long-running series *Magnum, P.I.*

1952 **Tommy Ramone.** American musician with The Ramones musical group

1953 **Oprah Winfrey.** American actress and television hostess

1954 **Tony Galbreath.** Professional football player

1955 **Jonathan Smith.** English tennis player

1960 **Steve Sax.** Professional baseball player

1960 **Greg Louganis.** U.S. Olympic diving champion, 1984 and 1988

1964 **Roddy Frame.** British musician and singer with the Aztec Camera musical group

1967 **Stacy King.** Professional basketball player

January 29 – Events

1327 Edward III was crowned King of England.

1819 Singapore was founded by English colonial officer Thomas S. Raffles of the East India Company.

1820 George III, King of England during the American Revolution, died insane at Windsor Castle.

1845 Edgar Allan Poe's famous poem, "The Raven," was first published, in the New York *Evening Mirror*.

1850 Henry Clay introduced his omnibus bill in the U.S. Senate, which was later passed as the famous series of acts known as the Compromise of 1850.

1861 Kansas was admitted to the Union as the 34th state.

1886 The first successful gasoline-driven car, the Motorwagen, was patented by Karl Benz, a German engineer.

1900 Baseball's American League was organized in Philadelphia by Ban Johnson.

1936 The first five players were elected to the Baseball Hall of Fame. They were Ty Cobb, Walter Johnson, Christy Mathewson, Babe Ruth, and Honus Wagner, who were formally inducted, along with 21 more players chosen in subsequent elections, when the Hall opened in 1939.

1956 H.L. Mencken, the noted American writer and critic, died in Baltimore at age 75.

1963 Robert Frost, the noted American poet, died in Boston at age 88.

1968 Adolphe Rupp became the winningest basketball coach in history as the University of Kentucky beat the University of Mississippi for his 772nd victory.

January 30 – Birthdays

1628 **George Villiers.** English politician, writer, and second Duke of Buckingham

1687 **Balthasar Neumann.** German architect

1720 **Bernardo Bellotto.** Italian painter

1775 **Walter Savage Landor.** English poet, essayist, and novelist, whose best-known work is *Imaginary Conversations* (1824-1848)

1866 **Gelett Burgess.** American writer and illustrator, noted for "I Never Saw a Purple Cow"

1882 **Franklin D. Roosevelt.** 32nd U.S. president, and the only president to be elected to a third and a fourth term

1894 **Boris III.** King of Bulgaria, 1918-1943

1900 **Martita Hunt.** English stage and screen actress with a movie career of almost 50 years

1911 **Hugh Marlowe.** American stage, screen and television actor

1911 **Roy Eldridge.** American trumpeter and musician

1912 **Barbara Tuchman.** American novelist and biographer, noted for works such as *The Guns of August*

1914 **David Wayne.** American stage, screen, and television actor

1914 **John Ireland.** American stage and motion-picture actor

1923 **Walt Dropo.** Professional baseball player

1923 **Dick Martin.** American comedian and co-star of television's long-running Rowan and Martin's *Laugh In*

1925 **Dorothy Malone.** American motion-picture and television actress

1927 **Olof Palme.** Prime minister of Sweden, 1969-1976 and 1982-1986, who was murdered in a Stockholm street in 1986, the first major Swedish official to be assassinated since King Gustav III in 1792

1928 **Harold Prince.** Noted Broadway producer-director

1931 **Gene Hackman.** American stage, screen, and television actor, who won the Academy Award for *The French Connection* (1971)

1933 **Louis Rukeyser.** American television commentator and stock market analyst

1933 **Richard Brautigan.** American author and poet (*Trout Fishing in America*, 1967)

1934	**Tammy Grimes.** American stage and motion-picture actress
1937	**Vanessa Redgrave.** British stage, screen, and television actress, and daughter of actor Michael Redgrave
1937	**Boris Spassky.** Russian world champion chess player
1941	**Dick Cheney.** Secretary of Defense under President Bush
1943	**Dave Johnson.** Professional baseball player and manager
1943	**Martin Balin.** American singer with The Jefferson Airplane musical group
1945	**Michael Dorris.** American writer noted for works such as *The Broken Cord* (1989)
1949	**William King.** Rhythm-and-blues musician with The Commodores
1955	**Curtis Strange.** Professional golfer who won the U.S. Open in 1988 and 1989
1955	**Nolan Cromwell.** Professional football player
1955	**Mychal Thompson.** Professional basketball player
1958	**Brett Butler.** American TV actress and star of the sitcom *Grace Under Fire*

January 30 – Events

1649	King Charles I of England was beheaded at Whitehall for treason.
1730	Czar Peter II of Russia died of smallpox on his wedding day.
1815	The U.S. Congress authorized the purchase of Thomas Jefferson's library as the nucleus of the new Library of Congress, the original having been burned by the British in 1814.
1835	The first assassination attempt on a U.S. president occurred as an insane gunman, Richard Lawrence, tried unsuccessfully to fire two pistols at Andrew Jackson. Neither went off.
1917	The first jazz record, "The Darktown Strutters' Ball," was cut, by "The Original Dixieland Jazz Band" in New York.
1933	The long-running radio program *The Lone Ranger* was aired for the first time.
1933	German President Paul von Hindenburg named Adolf Hitler Chancellor.
1937	German chancellor Adolf Hitler publicly repudiated the Versailles Peace Treaty.
1940	The first U.S. Social Security checks went out, totalling $75,844.
1948	Orville Wright, the great American aviation pioneer, died in Dayton, Ohio, at age 76.
1948	Mahatma Gandhi, India's great spiritual and political leader, was assassinated by a Hindu fanatic in New Delhi.
1965	The state funeral of Sir Winston Churchill was held in London.

1968	North Vietnamese forces launched surprise attacks against South Vietnamese provincial capitals in what became known as the "Tet Offensive" in the Vietnam War.

January 31 – Birthdays

1624	**Arnold Geulincx.** Dutch metaphysician and logician
1734	**Robert Morris.** Pennsylvania signer of the Declaration of Independence and "financier of the American Revolution"
1735	**J. Hector Crevecoeur.** French-American essayist
1752	**Gouverneur Morris.** American statesman and diplomat, member of the Continental Congress, and one of the key figures in the Constitutional Convention in 1787
1769	**Andre Jacques Garnerin.** The first man to drop from a balloon in a parachute, over the Parc Monceau in Paris on October 22, 1797
1797	**Franz Schubert.** Great Austrian composer whose *Symphony in C major* and *Unfinished Symphony* (*Symphony No. 8 in B minor*) are two of the immortal works of music
1806	**Fletcher Harper.** One of the four Harper brothers who founded the famous publishing house of Harper and Brothers
1812	**William Hepburn Russell.** American pioneer freighter and founder of the Pony Express (1860)
1830	**James G. Blaine.** Influential 19th-century American political leader and U.S. presidential candidate in 1884
1831	**Rudolph Wurlitzer.** American bank clerk who founded the Wurlitzer organ company in 1856
1848	**Nathan Straus.** American merchant and philanthropist, who did more for New York City's welfare in the first quarter of the 20th century than any other person
1860	**James Gibbons Huneker.** American critic and author
1868	**Theodore William Richards.** American Nobel Prize winner (1914) for determining the atomic weights of 30 chemical elements
1875	**Zane Grey.** American novelist who wrote over 60 popular books about the American West, such as *Riders of the Purple Sage* (1912)
1881	**Alfred Harcourt.** American publisher and founder in 1919 of Harcourt, Brace, Inc.
1885	**Anna Pavlova.** Russian ballerina and most famous dancer of her generation, best known for the three minute solo, "The Dying Swan," that often moved audiences to tears
1892	**Eddie Cantor.** American stage and screen comic actor and singer
1894	**Isham Jones.** American composer, conductor, and pianist, noted for songs such as "On the Alamo," "It Had to Be You," and "I'll See You in My Dreams"

1902 **Edward Beverly Mann.** American writer of Western novels

1902 **Leo Corday.** American composer noted for songs such as "There's No Tomorrow" and "See the USA in Your Chevrolet"

1903 **Tallulah Bankhead.** One of the American theater's most brilliant and legendary actresses, daughter of U.S. Representative William B. Bankhead, and granddaughter of U.S. Senator John Bankhead

1905 **John O'Hara.** American novelist and short-story writer, noted for works such as *Appointment in Samarra, Butterfield 8,* and *Ten North Frederick*

1913 **Don Hutson.** Professional football superstar, Hall of Famer and member of the great Isbell to Hutson passing combination.

1914 **Jersey Joe Walcott.** World heavyweight champion, 1951-1952

1915 **Thomas Merton.** American poet and religious writer, noted for "The Seven Storey Mountain" (1948)

1915 **Garry Moore.** Noted American television personality of the 1950s and 1960s

1915 **Alan Lomax.** American musician and preeminent folklorist

1915 **Bobby Hackett.** American trumpeter

1916 **Frank Parker.** American Hall of Fame tennis player who ranked in the top ten for 17 consecutive years (1933-1949)

1919 **Jackie Robinson.** The first black major league baseball player (1947) and Hall of Famer

1920 **Stewart Udall.** Secretary of the Interior under President Kennedy

1921 **John Agar.** American motion-picture actor, better known as the first husband of the famous child actress Shirley Temple

1921 **Mario Lanza.** American singer and motion-picture actor

1923 **Norman Mailer.** American novelist, noted for works such as *The Naked and the Dead* (1948) and *The Armies of the Night* (1968)

1923 **Carol Channing.** American comic actress, entertainer, and singer of stage, screen, and television

1923 **Joanne Dru.** American model and motion-picture actress, and sister of TV host Peter Marshall

1925 **Charles E. Silberman.** American author

1925 **Benjamin Hooks.** American civil rights leader and executive director of the NAACP

1929 **Jean Simmons.** English-born motion-picture and television actress

1929 **Rudolf Ludwig Mossbauer.** German physicist and Nobelist whose discoveries helped lead to Einstein's general theory of relativity

1931 **Ernie Banks.** Hall of Fame baseball player with 512 career home runs

1934 **James Franciscus.** American television and motion-picture actor

1937 **Suzanne Pleshette.** American stage, screen, and television actress

1937 **Philip Glass.** American musician and composer noted for works such as *Songs from Liquid Days*

1938 **Beatrix.** Queen of The Netherlands

1940 **Jessica Walter.** American stage, screen, and television actress

1941 **Richard Gephardt.** U.S. Congressman

1943 **James Watt.** Secretary of the Interior under President Reagan

1944 **Szabolcs Baranyi.** Hungarian tennis player

1947 **Nolan Ryan.** Professional baseball pitcher who struck out 383 men in one season and 5,668 in his career, both records

1951 **Phil Collins.** Record producer and lead singer and drummer with the rock group Genesis

1953 **Roosevelt Leaks.** Professional football player

1953 **Louie Wright.** Professional football player

1955 **Virginia Ruzici.** Romanian tennis player

1956 **Johnny Rotten.** Singer (born John Lydon) with the Sex Pistols musical group

1957 **Shirley Babashoff.** American Olympic swimmer with eight Olympic medals, and member of the U.S. Olympic Hall of Fame

1959 **Kelly Lynch.** American actress and leading lady of Hollywood films of the 1980s and 1990s

1971 **Minnie Driver.** English motion-picture and television actress

January 31 – Events

1606 Guy Fawkes, the ringleader in the Gunpowder Plot against the English Parliament, was hanged in London.

1865 Jefferson Davis, President of the Confederacy, appointed General Robert E. Lee commander-in-chief of all Confederate armies.

1917 Germany served notice that it would begin a policy of unrestricted submarine warfare in World War I.

1934 President Franklin D. Roosevelt fixed the price of the U.S. dollar in terms of gold at $35 per ounce.

1945 U.S. Army Private Eddie Slovick was shot for desertion by a firing squad. He was posthumously pardoned nearly 40 years later.

1949 NBC broadcast *These Are My Children,* the first daytime soap opera on television.

1950 President Harry S. Truman announced the order to develop the hydrogen bomb.

1958 The first U.S. satellite, *Explorer I,* was launched, leading to the discovery of the Van Allen radiation belt.

1971 U.S. spacecraft *Apollo 14* was launched with the third crew of astronauts (Alan Shepard, Edgar Mitchell, and Stuart Roosa) to land on the moon.

1999 The Denver Broncos and quarterback John Elway beat the Atlanta Falcons 34-19 in Super Bowl XXXIII for their second consecutive Super Bowl victory.

2
February

February, the second month of the year, got its name from *Februarius,* which is derived from the Latin verb *februare,* meaning "to purify." The Romans celebrated a "Feast of Purification" during the month at which the people repented of their wrongdoing and offered sacrifices to the gods.

February, along with January, was added to the Roman calendar by Numa Pompilius, the second king of Rome, around 700 B.C., at which time it had 28 days. Its length was increased to 29 days in Caesar's Julian Calendar of 45 B.C., and reduced back to 28 days when Emperor Augustus made his adjustments in 8 B.C. This is, of course, its present length, except in leap years when it has 29 days. February originally preceded January in the early calendar, but in 452 B.C. the Decemvirs interchanged the two months. Thus when January became the first month, February became the second.

Special days of February include Ground Hog's Day (February 2), when legend has it that six weeks of winter weather will follow if the ground hog sees its shadow; Abraham Lincoln's Birthday (February 12); Saint Valentine's Day (February 14); Susan B. Anthony's Birthday (February 15); George Washington's Birthday (February 22), which is a legal holiday celebrated on the third Monday of February; and, of course, every four years, February 29 is Leap Year Day. Presidents William Henry Harrison and Ronald Reagan were also born in February.

The birthstone for February is the amethyst, and its special flowers are the violet and the primrose.

February 1 – Birthdays

1552   **Sir Edward Coke.** Brilliant English courtroom lawyer who in 1594 was selected over Sir Francis Bacon as Queen Elizabeth's attorney general

1787   **Richard Whately.** English archbishop and social reformer

1797   **John Bell.** One of the three major candidates defeated by Lincoln in 1860

1801   **Thomas Cole.** Early American painter who was a leader of the Hudson River school, the first American group of landscape painters, and who was noted for works such as *The Voyage of Life*

1828   **Meyer Guggenheim.** American industrialist and philanthropist who founded the Guggenheim fortune in mining and smelting

1859   **Victor Herbert.** American conductor, composer, and "prince of operetta," noted for works such as *Babes in Toyland* (1903) and *Naughty Marietta* (1910)

1869   **Frederick Allen "Kerry" Mills.** American composer, author, and violinist, noted for songs such as "Meet Me in St. Louis" and "Red Wing"

1871   **Harry K. Thaw.** American murderer who killed noted architect Stanford White in a sensational case in 1906 apparently over Thaw's wife, Evelyn Nesbit Thaw, who before her marriage was White's mistress

1874   **Hugo von Hofmannsthal.** Austrian poet and dramatist best known for writing the words for the operas of the German composer Richard Strauss

1878   **Hattie Wyatt Caraway.** The first woman elected to the U.S. Senate (1932)

1882   **Louis S. Saint Laurent.** Prime Minister of Canada, 1948-1957

1887   **Charles Bernard Nordhoff.** American novelist and traveler, noted with James Norman Hall for *Mutiny on the Bounty, Pitcairn's Island,* and *Men Against the Sea*

1887   **Harry Scherman.** Co-founder with Maxwell Byron Sackheim in 1926 of the Book-of-the-Month Club

1891   **James P. Johnson.** American composer and pianist, noted for songs such as "If I Could Be With You One Hour Tonight" and "Runnin' Wild"

1894   **Herman Hupfeld.** American composer, author, and singer, noted for songs such as "As Time Goes By," which was revived and used in the great movie *Casablanca*

1895   **John Ford.** The first motion-picture director to win Academy Awards for four movies (*The Informer, The Grapes of Wrath, How Green Was My Valley,* and *The Quiet Man*)

1896   **Anastasio Somoza Garcia.** Dictator of Nicaragua, 1936-1956

1900   **Stephen Potter.** English author noted for works such as *Gamesmanship* and *One-upmanship*

1901   **Clark Gable.** "The King" of Hollywood in the 1930s and 1940s, who won the 1934 Academy Award for *It Happened One Night,* and whose most famous role was Rhett Butler in *Gone With the Wind*

1902   **Langston Hughes.** American poet and short-story writer, noted for works such as *The Weary Blues* (1926) and *The Best of Simple* (1961)

1904   **S.J. Perelman.** American writer known for his humorous satires, many of which are collected in *The Most of S.J. Perelman* (1958)

1905   **Emilio Gino Segre.** Italian physicist who shared the 1959 Nobel Prize with Owen Chamberlain for co-discovering the antiproton

1906   **Hildegarde (Loretta Sell).** American singer and actress

1907   **John Canaday.** Noted American art critic

1908   **Albie Booth.** Noted football player and coach at Yale, known as "Little Boy Blue"

1918   **Muriel Spark.** English novelist and short-story writer, noted for works such as *Momento Mori* (1959) and *The Prime of Miss Jean Brodie* (1961)

1922   **Renata Tebaldi.** Italian operatic soprano and one of the great stars of her day

1924   **Pierre Rinfret.** American economist

1926   **Stuart Whitman.** American stage, screen, and television actor

1931   **Boris N. Yeltsin.** President of the Russian Federation, elected in 1991, and the first freely elected leader of Russia in its 1,000-year history

1937   **Garrett Morris.** American actor and comedian

1937   **Don Everly.** American singer and guitarist, and one of the Everly Brothers singers

1938   **Sherman Hemsley.** American television actor noted for his starring role in the long-running show, *The Jeffersons*

1940   **Herve Filion.** The most successful harness racing driver in North America

1944   **Paul Blair.** Professional baseball player

1944   **Dick Snyder.** Professional basketball player

1947   **Karen Krantzche.** Australian tennis player

1948   **Debbie Austin.** Professional golfer

1948   **Rick James.** American soul singer

1965   **Princess Stephanie.** Princess of Monaco and daughter of Prince Rainier and Princess Grace

1968   **Lisa Marie Presley.** Daughter of Elvis and Priscilla Presley

February 1 – Events

1328   King Charles IV, the Fair, of France died at age 33, ending the line of Capetian kings descended from Hugh Capet, that began in A.D. 987.

1691   Roman Catholic pope Alexander VIII died after a two-year reign.

1790   The United States Supreme Court held its first session.

1814   English poet Lord Byron's poem "The Corsair" was first published.

1861   Texas seceded from the Union.

1862   Julia Ward Howe's great poem "The Battle Hymn of the Republic" was published for the first time, in the *Atlantic Monthly.*

1884   The first Oxford English Dictionary was published by James A.H. Murray, who had largely compiled it single-handedly.

1896   *La Boheme,* Giacomo Puccini's great opera, premiered in Turin, Italy.

1898   The Travelers Insurance Company of Hartford, Connecticut, issued the first automobile insurance policy, to Dr. Truman Martin of Buffalo, New York, for $11.25.

1917   Germany began unrestricted submarine warfare in World War I.

1920   The Royal Canadian Mounted Police was formed as a merger of the Northwest Mounted Police and the Dominion Police.

1933   Adolf Hitler ordered the Reichstag dissolved as one of his first acts upon assuming control of Germany.

1949   RCA Records issued the world's first 45 rpm single.

1951   The United Nations General Assembly condemned China as an aggressor in Korea.

1956   Autherine Lucy became the first black student admitted to the University of Alabama.

1958   The United Arab Republic (a union of Egypt and Syria) was proclaimed by Egyptian President Gamal Abdel Nasser and Syrian President Shukri Al-Kuwatli.

1960   Four black students staged the first "sit-in" protest, at a lunch counter in Greenville, North Carolina, which had previously refused to serve them.

1972   Hewlett-Packard's HP-35, the first hand-held scientific calculator, was first marketed at $395.

1979   Ayatollah Ruhollah Khomeini returned to Iran after 15 years in exile.

February 2 – Birthdays

1208   **James I (the Conqueror).** King of Aragon

1522   **Lodovico Ferrari.** Italian mathematician who first solved the general quartic equation

1602   **Michelangelo Cerquozzi.** Italian painter

1650   **Nell Gwyn.** One of England's first actresses, and mistress of King Charles II

1745   **Hannah More.** English writer

1803 **Albert Sidney Johnston.** Confederate general in the Civil War who was killed in the Battle of Shiloh

1852 **Abdulhak Hamid (Tarhan).** One of the greatest Turkish romantic writers

1854 **Stephen H. Horgan.** Inventor of the half-toning method of printing pictures

1859 **Havelock Ellis.** British author and psychologist, noted for his seven-volume work *Studies in the Psychology of Sex* (1897-1928)

1875 **Fritz Kreisler.** Austrian-born virtuoso violinist and composer, who ranks as one of the best-loved violinists of all time

1882 **James Joyce.** Irish novelist noted for the two great works *Ulysses* (1922) and *Finnegans Wake* (1939)

1882 **Geoffrey O'Hara.** Canadian-born composer and author, noted for songs such as "K-K-K-Katy"

1884 **S.Z. "Cuddles" Sakall.** Hungarian-born stage and motion-picture actor with a 40-year career

1888 **Frank Lloyd.** Scottish-American motion-picture director with a 40-year career

1891 **Frank Foyston.** Hall of Fame hockey player

1895 **George Halas.** Pioneer of professional football, who organized, owned, and coached the Chicago Bears

1900 **Carroll Righter.** American astrologer and newspaper columnist

1901 **Jascha Heifetz.** Russian-American violin virtuoso

1901 **Louis Kahn.** American architect

1905 **Ayn Rand.** American writer, novelist, and exponent of objectivism, known for works such as *The Fountainhead* and *Atlas Shrugged*

1906 **Gale Gordon.** American motion-picture, radio, and television actor

1909 **Frank Albertson.** American motion-picture actor

1911 **Jussi Bjoerling.** Swedish operatic and concert tenor of the 1930s and 1940s

1912 **Burton Lane.** American composer and author, noted for songs such as "On a Clear Day You Can See Forever," "Feudin' and Fightin'," "How Are Things In Glocca Morra?" and "Everything I Have Is Yours"

1915 **Abba Eban.** Israeli foreign minister and ambassador to the U.N.

1919 **Ann Fogarty.** American fashion designer

1923 **James Dickey.** American poet and novelist, noted for works such as *Madness, Buckhead and Mercy,* and *Deliverance*

1923 **Bonita Granville.** American stage and motion-picture actress and leading lady of the 1940s

1923 **Red Schoendienst.** Professional baseball player and manager

1926 **Valerie Giscard d'Estaing.** President of France in the 1970s

1926 **Elaine Stritch.** American stage, screen and television actress and comedienne

1927 **Stan Getz.** American saxophonist

1927 **Herbert E. Kaplow.** American broadcast journalist

1937 **Tommy Smothers.** One of the two Smothers Brothers, American comedians

1937 **Don Buford.** Professional baseball player

1940 **Helga Hoesl.** West German tennis player

1942 **Graham Nash.** American actor and guitarist with the Crosby, Sills, and Nash group

1942 **Bo Hopkins.** American motion-picture actor

1942 **Barry Diller.** American businessman and television executive

1947 **Christie Brinkley.** American model

1947 **Farah Fawcett.** American model and motion-picture and television actress

1954 **John Tudor.** Professional baseball player

1955 **Ed Simonini.** Professional football player

1966 **Robert DeLeo.** Rock musician with the group Stone Temple Pilots

February 2 – Events

506 The *Brevarium,* a code of laws for the subjects of Alaric II, King of the Goths, was drafted at Toulouse.

1440 Frederick III was crowned Holy Roman Emperor.

1585 Hamnet and Judith, twins of William Shakespeare and Anne Hathaway, were baptized.

1653 New Amsterdam (now New York City) was incorporated.

1709 Alexander Selkirk, a Scotsman whose experiences on a lonely island inspired Daniel Defoe's story of Robinson Crusoe, was rescued from his island by English Captain Woodes Rogers.

1831 Gregory XVI was elected Roman Catholic pope.

1848 The Treaty of Guadalupe Hidalgo ended the Mexican War and gave all the Mexican land north of the Rio Grande River to the United States.

1876 Baseball's National League was founded under the name National League of Professional Base Ball Clubs.

1893 The first motion-picture close-up was filmed at the Edison studio in West Orange, N.J., when cameraman William Dickson photographed comedian Fred Ott sneezing.

1922 James Joyce's great novel *Ulysses* was published in Paris.

1943 The last German troops surrendered in the Stalingrad pocket, completing the Russian victory in World War II. Only 90,000 Germans were left of the original 350,000-man army.

1953 President Dwight D. Eisenhower announced that the Seventh Fleet would no longer block Chinese Nationalist raids from Formosa against the Chinese mainland.

1957 Actress Elizabeth Taylor married movie producer Mike Todd three days after she divorced actor Michael Wilding.

1998 President Clinton proposed the first balanced budget (for fiscal year 1999) in three decades.

February 3 – Birthdays

1795 **Antonio Jose de Sucre.** South American general who liberated Ecuador and Bolivia from Spain and served as the first president of Bolivia

1807 **Joseph E. Johnston.** Confederate general in the Civil War

1809 **Felix Mendelssohn.** German composer, pianist, and conductor, noted for five symphonies and for such other works as the oratorio *Elijah* (1846)

1811 **Horace Greeley.** Prominent American journalist, founder of the New York *Tribune,* and 1872 presidential candidate, who popularized the phrase, "Go west, young man"

1821 **Elizabeth Blackwell.** First woman physician in the United States

1826 **Walter Bagehot.** English economist, political analyst, sociologist, and author

1842 **Sidney Lanier.** One of the greatest American poets, in the view of some critics, noted for works such as "Sunrise," "The Marshes of Glynn," and "Song of the Chattahoochee"

1843 **William Cornelius Van Horne.** U.S.-born Canadian railroad executive who was instrumental in building the Canadian Pacific Railway and whose motto was "I eat all I want, I drink all I want, and don't give a damn about anybody"

1853 **Hudson Maxim.** American inventor of smokeless gunpowder, a self-propelled torpedo, and *maximite,* an explosive more powerful than dynamite

1859 **Hugo Junkers.** German aircraft designer

1865 **David Lawrence Pierson.** Originator of Constitution Day (September 17th)

1874 **Gertrude Stein.** Influential American author, noted for works such as *Three Lives* (1908) and *The Autobiography of Alice B. Toklas* (1933)

1883 **Clarence E. Mulford.** American author noted for *Hopalong Cassidy* (1907)

1883 **Marie Wagner.** American Hall of Fame tennis player

1887 **Georg Trakl.** Austrian poet

1889 **Carl Theodor Dreyer.** Danish motion-picture director noted for works such as *Day of Wrath* (1943)

1890 **Larry MacPhail.** Noted baseball executive who introduced night games in 1935

1894 **Norman Rockwell.** Noted American artist especially known for over 300 *Saturday Evening Post* cover paintings between 1916 and 1963

1895 **Nick A. Kenny.** American lyricist, noted for songs such as "There's a Gold Mine in the Sky," "Love Letters in the Sand," and "Leanin' on the Old Top Rail"

1898 **Alvar Aalto.** Finnish architect, city planner, and furniture designer

1899 **Red De Bernardi.** Hall of Fame basketball player

1901 **Pretty Boy Floyd.** American criminal who was gunned down by the FBI in 1934

1907 **James A. Michener.** American novelist, noted for works such as *Tales of the South Pacific* (1949), *Sayonara* (1954), *Hawaii* (1960), and *The Source* (1965)

1907 **Walt Morey.** American author noted for *Gentle Ben* (1965)

1912 **Jacques Soustelle.** French anthropologist and politician

1918 **Helen Stephens.** American Olympic gold medalist and member of the U.S. Track and Field Hall of Fame

1918 **Joey Bishop.** American comedian, motion-picture actor, and television personality

1918 **Stanley Earl Cowan.** American composer noted for songs such as "Do I Worry"

1920 **Henry Jay Heimlich.** American physician who developed the anti-choking "Heimlich Maneuver"

1926 **Shelley Berman.** American comedian

1931 **Peggy Ann Garner.** American stage, screen, and television actress, and noted child star of the 1940s

1933 **Paul Sarbanes.** U.S. senator

1938 **Emile Griffith.** World welterweight (1961) and middleweight (1966-1967) boxing champion

1940 **Fran Tarkenton.** Professional Hall of Fame football superstar and television personality

1941 **Carol Mann.** Professional golfer and Hall of Famer

1943 **Dennis Edwards.** American singer with The Temptations

1943 **Blythe Danner.** American stage, screen and television actress and mother of actress Gwyneth Paltrow

1945 **Bob Griese.** Professional football superstar and Hall of Famer

1947 **Dave Davies.** British guitarist with The Kinks musical group

1949 **Bake McBride.** Professional baseball player

1950 **Morgan Fairchild.** American motion-picture and television actress

1951 **Eddie Dibbs.** American tennis player

1952 **Ben Malone.** Professional football player

1952 **Fred Lynn.** Professional baseball player

1953 **Keith Hancock.** Australian tennis player

1956 **John Jefferson.** Professional football player

1957 **Tony Butler.** Irish bassist with the Big Country musical group

February 3 – Events

590 Gregory I, the Great, was elected Roman Catholic pope.

1468 Johannes Gutenberg, the famous pioneer printer of the *Gutenberg Bible,* died at age 72.

1793 Spain recognized U.S. independence from Britain.

1889 The notorious American Western outlaw, Belle Starr, was shot and killed by an unknown assailant.

1898 The National Biscuit Company was incorporated by a consolidation of four baking companies.

1917 The United States broke diplomatic relations with Germany because of the German announcement of unrestricted submarine warfare.

1924 Woodrow Wilson died in Washington, D.C., at age 67.

1930 President Herbert Hoover appointed Charles Evans Hughes chief justice of the Supreme Court.

1945 U.S. troops entered Manila in World War II.

1959 Buddy Holly, influential American rock star, was killed in a plane crash near Mason City, Iowa, at age 22.

February 4 – Birthdays

1688 **Pierre Carlet de Marivaux.** French playwright, novelist, and essayist, best known for his comedies, such as *The Game of Love and Chance* (1730)

1693 **George Lillo.** English playwright noted for *The London Merchant* (1731), which became a model for dramatists in 18th-century Europe

1802 **Mark Hopkins.** Famous American college teacher and president of Williams College, 1836-1872

1864 **Louis Michel Eilshemius.** American landscape painter

1865 **Abe Isoo.** One of the founders of the Japanese socialist movement

1869 **William "Big Bill" Haywood.** American labor organizer and early leader of the Industrial Workers of the World (IWW)

1871 **Friedrich Ebert.** First president of the German Weimar Republic, established after the defeat of Germany in World War I

1873 **George Bennard.** American composer noted for "The Old Rugged Cross"

1877 **Herman "Germany" Schaefer.** Professional baseball player and the only runner to steal first base (in 1908 when it was legal to do so, but nobody ever did, he went from second to first hoping to steal second again on the next pitch to allow a runner on third to score)

1881 **Kliment Yefremovich Voroshilov.** Russian World War II general

1881 **Fernand Leger.** French painter noted for such works as *Three Women* (1921)

1889 **Walter Catlett.** American stage and motion-picture actor

1897 **Ludwig Erhard.** West German statesman and chancellor, 1963-1966

1902 **Charles A. Lindbergh.** American aviator who in 1927 made the first nonstop solo flight across the Atlantic Ocean

1904 **MacKinlay Kantor.** American novelist, noted for *Long Remember* (1934) and *Andersonville* (1955)

1905 **Eddie Foy Jr.** American stage and motion-picture actor, and son of the celebrated vaudeville star Eddie Foy

1906 **Clyde William Tombaugh.** American astronomer who discovered the planet Pluto in 1930

1906 **Dietrich Bonhoeffer.** Noted Protestant theologian executed by the Nazis

1911 **Byron Nelson.** Professional golfer and one of the game's immortals

1913 **Rosa Lee Parks.** Alabama black woman whose refusal to move to the back of the bus precipitated the civil rights movement in Alabama in the 1960s led by Martin Luther King

1915 **Ray Evans.** American songwriter, who with Jay Livingston wrote popular songs such as "Buttons and Bows," "Mona Lisa," "Golden Earrings," and the TV theme for *Bonanza*

1917 **Yahya Khan.** President of Pakistan, 1969-1971

1918 **Ida Lupino.** American motion-picture and television actress, director, and screenwriter

1921 **Betty Friedan.** Prominent American feminist, author, and journalist

1923 **Conrad Bain.** American television and motion-picture actor

1929 **Neil Johnston.** Professional basketball superstar with over 10,000 career points

1938 **Donald Riegle.** U.S. senator

1943 **La Rue Florence.** Member of the 5th Dimension singing group

1943 **Cheryl Miller.** American motion-picture and television actress

1945 **David Brenner.** American actor and comedian

1947 **J. Danforth Quayle.** U.S. vice president under President Bush

1948 **Alice Cooper.** American rock and roll singer

1948 **Ron Jessie.** Professional football player

1952 **Lisa Eichorn.** American motion-picture and television actress

1959 **Lawrence Taylor.** Professional football player

February 4 – Events

1789 The first U.S. Electoral College unanimously elected George Washington as the first president, and it also elected John Adams as the first vice president.

1801 John Marshall, "the great chief justice," began his term on the U.S. Supreme Court.

1861 The Confederate States of America was formed in Montgomery, Alabama.

1881 Thomas Carlyle, the great Scottish essayist and historian, died at age 85.

1894 Adolphe Sax, the inventor of the saxophone, died in poverty. There were no saxophones at his funeral.

1899 The Philippine Rebellion against the United States began, led by Philippine patriot Aguinaldo. The revolt was put down in March, when Aguinaldo was captured.

1915 Germany declared the waters around Britain to be a war zone, with the intention of attacking any ships it found there in World War I.

1926 John Giola of New York City danced the Charleston for 22 hours and 30 minutes, a record.

1941 The United Service Organizations (USO) was founded.
1945 The World War II Yalta Conference began, with Franklin D. Roosevelt, Winston Churchill, and Joseph Stalin attending.
1957 The comic strip *Miss Peach,* by Mell Lazarus, first appeared.
1964 The 24th Amendment was proclaimed, banning poll taxes in the United States.
1971 Rolls-Royce, Ltd., the famous English automobile company, declared bankruptcy.
1974 Patricia Hearst, granddaughter of William Randolph Hearst, was kidnapped by a group called the Symbionese Liberation Army.

February 5 – Birthdays

1534 **Giovanni Bardi.** Florentine musician, writer, and scientist
1626 **Marquise Marie de Sevigne.** French noblewoman, noted for the famous letters she wrote in the mid-1600s, in which she belittled such things as coffee, Racine's poetry, and the use of condoms as a contraceptive
1723 **John Witherspoon.** Member of the Continental Congress and a signer of the Declaration of Independence
1725 **James Otis.** One of the most forceful leaders and orators in the American colonies' struggle for independence from Great Britain
1788 **Sir Robert Peel.** Famous British statesman and prime minister, who founded the London police force and the British Conservative Party
1808 **Carl Spitzweg.** German painter
1837 **Dwight L. Moody.** American evangelist, who founded the Moody Bible Institute and the Moody Press in Chicago
1838 **Abram Joseph Ryan.** Southern American poet known as the "Poet of the Confederacy"
1840 **John Boyd Dunlop.** Scottish veterinarian who developed and manufactured the first pneumatic (air-filled) tire
1840 **Sir Hiram Stevens Maxim.** American-born inventor of the Maxim machine gun, and brother of inventors Hudson and Hiram Percy Maxim
1848 **Joris Karl Huysmans.** French-born Dutch novelist, noted for works such as *Marthe* (1876) and *Against Nature* (1884)
1848 **Belle Starr.** Notorious American horse thief and outlaw of the 1870s and 1880s
1871 **Maxine Elliott.** American stage actress
1878 **Andre Gustave Citroen.** French manufacturer of the famous Citroen automobile
1892 **Elizabeth Ryan.** Hall of Fame tennis player whose 19 Wimbledon titles stood as a record for more than 40 years
1894 **Ange Lorenzo.** American composer, conductor, and pianist, noted for such songs as "Sleepy Time Gal"

1898 **Ralph Emerson McGill.** American journalist and long-time editor of the *Atlanta Constitution*
1900 **Adlai E. Stevenson.** U.S. Democratic presidential candidate in 1952 and 1956 against General Dwight D. Eisenhower in both years
1903 **Joan Payson.** First owner of the New York Mets baseball team
1906 **John Carradine.** American stage, screen, and television actor, who appeared in more than 170 motion pictures in a career of over 50 years
1907 **Norton Simon.** American industrialist
1914 **William Seward Burroughs.** American writer and chief spokesman for the "beat generation" and author of works such as *Naked Lunch* (1959) and *Queer* (1985)
1915 **Robert Hofstadter.** American physicist who shared the 1951 Nobel Prize in physics
1918 **Tim Holt.** American Western motion-picture actor and son of actor Jack Holt
1919 **Andreas Papandreou.** Greek statesman
1919 **Red Buttons.** American stage, screen, and television comedian and actor
1922 **Bernard Kalb.** American television newsman and U.S. State Department spokesman under President Reagan
1926 **Arthur Sulzberger.** Publisher of the *New York Times*
1934 **Hank Aaron.** Most prolific home run hitter in professional baseball, with a career total of 755
1937 **Stuart Damon.** American television actor
1937 **Lionel Tiger.** American anthropologist and author
1938 **John Guare.** American playwright
1939 **Jane Bryant Quinn.** American writer and financial columnist
1942 **Roger Staubach.** Professional football superstar
1942 **Cory Wells.** Singer with Three Dog Night
1943 **Eddie Belmonte.** American jockey
1943 **Craig Morton.** Professional football player
1945 **Charlotte Rampling.** British motion-picture actress
1948 **David Wallechinsky.** American author noted for *The Book of Lists,* which he co-authored with his father and sister, Irving and Amy Wallace (1977)
1948 **Barbara Hershey.** American motion-picture and television actress
1950 **Jan Hordijk.** Dutch tennis player
1951 **Elizabeth Swados.** American composer, writer, and director
1962 **Jennifer Jason Leigh.** American motion-picture actress and daughter of actor Vic Morrow and TV writer Barbara Turner
1964 **Duff McKagan.** American rock musician with the group Guns N' Roses
1968 **Roberto Alomar.** Professional baseball player and son of baseball player Sandy Alomar Sr.

February 5 – Events

46 BC Marcus Cato, the Roman philosopher, committed suicide by stabbing himself, on learning of the victory of his enemy, Julius Caesar, over Pompey at Thapsus.

1631 Roger Williams, future founder of Rhode Island, arrived in Boston from England.

1826 Millard Fillmore married his former teacher, Abigail Powers.

1861 Coleman Sellers, a Philadelphia inventor, patented his *kinematoscope,* a motion picture device.

1881 Phoenix, Arizona, was incorporated.

1887 Italian composer Giuseppe Verdi's greatest tragic opera, *Otello,* was first performed, at Milan's La Scala.

1929 The comic strip, *They'll Do It Everytime,* by Jimmy Hatlo, first appeared.

1937 President Franklin D. Roosevelt proposed that up to six additional Supreme Court justices be appointed, prompting his critics to charge him with trying to "pack" the Court.

1945 The U.S. Third Army under General George S. Patton broke through the Germans' Siegfried Line in World War II.

1951 Sylvia Green Wilks, the daughter of Hettie Green, the miserly "Witch of Wall Street," died, leaving an estate of over $90 million.

1971 U.S. astronauts Alan Shepard and Edgar Mitchell landed on the moon while astronaut Stuart Roosa remained in the command module of the *Apollo 14* mission.

February 6 – Birthdays

1665 **Queen Anne.** Queen of England, 1702-1714, first queen of the joint kingdom of Great Britain and Ireland, 1707-1714, and the last monarch of the House of Stuart

1756 **Aaron Burr.** U.S. vice president, 1801-1805, whose promising career ended disastrously when he killed Alexander Hamilton in a duel in 1804

1802 **Sir Charles Wheatstone.** English physicist and inventor best known for his work on electrical measuring devices, the best example of which is the Wheatstone bridge

1807 **Hiram Sibley.** American financier who with Ezra Cornell in 1856 organized the Western Union Company

1833 **J.E.B. "Jeb" Stuart.** Confederate Civil War general who distinguished himself in the first Battle of Bull Run and in the Wilderness Campaign

1838 **Sir Henry Irving.** One of the greatest stage actors and most successful theater managers of the 19th century

1845 **Isador Straus.** German-American merchant killed on the *Titanic,* who with his wife chose to drown together in their bed

1857 **Ernest Flagg.** American architect who designed the U.S. Naval Academy

1887 **Ernest Gruening.** American politician, U.S. senator, governor of Alaska, and author of "The State of Alaska"

1888 **Haven Gillespie.** American composer noted for songs such as "That Lucky Old Sun" and "Santa Claus Is Coming to Town"

1895 **Babe Ruth.** The greatest slugger in baseball history, whose records of 714 career home runs and 60 single-season home runs stood for nearly 40 years

1899 **Ramon Novarro.** Romantic idol of Hollywood silent films of the 1920s

1902 **Louis Nizer.** Prominent English-born lawyer and author, noted for his autobiography, *My Life in Court*

1902 **Leon T. Rene.** American composer and author, noted for songs such as "When the Swallows Come Back to Capistrano"

1903 **Claudio Arrau.** Chilean pianist and teacher noted for his many concerts and recordings

1908 **Amintore Fanfani.** Three-time premier of Italy, 1954, 1958-1959, and 1960-1963

1911 **Ronald Reagan.** American actor and 40th U.S. president

1912 **Eva Braun.** Mistress of Adolf Hitler who reportedly married him in 1945, the day before they both committed suicide

1913 **John Lund.** American stage and screen actor

1918 **Zsa Zsa Gabor.** Hungarian-born stage, screen, and television actress, and sister of actress Eva Gabor

1920 **William Jovanovich.** American publisher and one of the founders of Harcourt, Brace, Jovanovich

1922 **Patrick Macnee.** English television and motion-picture actor

1927 **Smokey Burgess.** Professional baseball player noted in his later years as a highly effective pinch-hitter

1927 **Hugh Haynie.** American editorial cartoonist

1931 **Mamie Van Doren.** American stage and motion-picture actress

1931 **Rip Torn.** American stage, screen, and television actor

1932 **François Truffaut.** French motion-picture director

1939 **Mike Farrell.** American motion-picture and television actor noted for his role in the long-running TV series *M*A*S*H*

1940 **Tom Brokaw.** American television host and newscaster

1941 **Gigi Perreau.** American child star of Hollywood films of the 1940s and early 1950s

1941 **Fabian (Forte).** American teeny-bopper idol, singer, and actor

1942 **Sarah Brady.** American gun control activist and wife of James S. Brady, White House press secretary who was gravely wounded in the March 1981 attempted assassination of President Reagan

1945 **Bob Marley.** Jamaican reggae singer and musician with The Wailers

1945	**Donald Cockroft.** Professional football player
1947	**Charles Hickcox.** Professional swimmer
1947	**Rik Massengale.** Professional golfer
1949	**Manuel Orantes.** Spanish tennis player
1949	**Richie Zisk.** Professional baseball player
1950	**Natalie Cole.** American singer and daughter of the noted singer Nat King Cole
1962	**Axl Rose.** American rock singer with the group Guns 'N Roses

February 6 – Events

1685	King Charles II of England, the first of the restored Stuart line, died at age 54.
1778	France signed an alliance with the United States to help fight the British in the Revolutionary War.
1788	Massachusetts ratified the U.S. Constitution, becoming the sixth state.
1843	"The Virginia Minstrels," the first minstrel show produced in America, was staged in New York City.
1862	General U.S. Grant's Union troops captured Fort Henry in Tennessee in the Civil War.
1899	The U.S. Senate ratified the Treaty of Paris, formally ending the Spanish-American War.
1911	The Rolls-Royce mascot, "The Spirit of Ecstasy," was cast for the first time.
1933	The 20th Amendment to the U.S. Constitution was proclaimed, moving the date of the president's inauguration from March 4 to January 20.
1943	General Dwight D. Eisenhower was appointed commander-in-chief of all the Allied forces in North Africa.
1952	King George VI of England died of lung cancer at age 56, and was succeeded by his daughter, Elizabeth II.
1959	The U.S. first successfully test-fired the Titan intercontinental ballistic missile from Cape Canaveral.
1964	Britain and France agree to build a "Euro-Tunnel," or English Channel Tunnel, or "Chunnel," which would connect Folkestone, England, to Calais.

February 7 – Birthdays

1477	**Sir Thomas More.** Great English author, statesman, and scholar, known for the famous book *Utopia* (1516)
1741	**Henry Fuseli.** Anglo-Swiss painter noted for works such as *The Nightmare* (1781)
1804	**John Deere.** American manufacturer and inventor who invented the first steel plow and became the most famous plowmaker in the world
1812	**Charles Dickens.** England's greatest novelist and one of the most popular writers of all time
1814	**George Palmer Putnam.** American publisher who founded G.P. Putnam's Sons

1817	**Frederick Douglass.** American slave who escaped and became a noted author and speaker and the leading spokesman of American Negroes in the 1800s
1834	**Dmitri Ivanovich Mendeleev.** Noted Russian chemist who devised the Periodic Table of the elements
1837	**James A.H. Murray.** English scholar who edited the *Oxford English Dictionary*, published in 1884
1863	**Sir Anthony Hope-Hawkins.** English author known for *The Prisoner of Zenda* (1894)
1867	**Laura Ingalls Wilder.** American author of pioneer stories for children, such as *Little House on the Prairie* (1935)
1870	**Alfred Adler.** Austrian psychiatrist who introduced the term *inferiority feeling*
1883	**Eubie Blake.** American pianist and "grand old man of ragtime," who wrote "I'm Just Wild about Harry," and was active to age 100
1885	**Sinclair Lewis.** One of America's greatest novelists, noted for works such as *Main Street* (1920), *Babbitt* (1922), and *Arrowsmith* (1925)
1898	**Jean Charlot.** French-American illustrator, author and painter noted for his many illustrations of children's books
1911	**Josef Mengele.** Nazi physician and Auschwitz "Angel of Death," who performed ghastly experiments on Jewish prisoners and was accused of killing 400,000 people in World War II
1918	**Ruth Sager.** Noted American geneticist
1920	**Oscar Brand.** Canadian-born folksinger and authority on the songs written for all the American presidential campaigns
1920	**Eddie Bracken.** American stage, screen, and television actor
1923	**Keefe Brasselle.** American motion-picture actor, television producer, and author
1926	**Bill Hoest.** American cartoonist noted for *The Lockhorns* and *Agatha Crumm*
1932	**Alfred M. Worden.** U.S. astronaut and pilot of the Command Module of *Apollo*
1932	**Gay Talese.** American author and journalist
1935	**Herbert Kohl.** U.S. senator
1950	**Marilyn Cochran.** Professional skier
1950	**Burt Hooton.** Professional baseball player
1953	**Robert Brazile.** Professional football player
1954	**Dan Quisenberry.** Professional baseball player and one of the greatest relief pitchers of all time
1957	**Carney Lansford.** Professional baseball player
1960	**James Spader.** American stage, screen and television actor
1960	**Steve Bronski.** British singer and songwriter with the Bronski Beat musical group
1962	**Garth Brooks.** American country music singer
1962	**David Bryan.** American rock musician with Bon Jovi

February 7 – Events

1613	Michael Romanov was elected czar of Russia, becoming the first of the Romanov czars.
1827	The first ballet group formed in the United States performed the ballet *The Deserter* at the Bowery Theatre in New York City.
1878	Pope Pius IX died at age 85, ending a term of 32 years as pope, the longest reign in papal history.
1901	Queen Wilhelmina of The Netherlands married Henry, Duke of Mecklenburg-Schwerin.
1904	A fire began in Baltimore that lasted for 30 hours and destroyed some 1,500 buildings.
1936	A special flag for the office of vice president was created on executive order of President Franklin D. Roosevelt.
1940	Walt Disney's motion picture *Pinocchio* had its world premiere.
1948	General Dwight D. Eisenhower resigned as army chief of staff and was succeeded by General Omar Bradley.
1950	The United States recognized South Vietnam.
1964	The Beatles arrived in America for the first time, and were greeted by 10,000 fans at New York's Kennedy Airport.
1971	Women in Switzerland were given the right to vote.
1974	The island of Grenada was given its independence from Great Britain.

February 8 – Birthdays

1577	**Robert Burton.** English scholar and poet
1580	**William Herbert.** Earl of Pembroke
1591	**Guercino (Giovanni F. Barbieri).** Italian painter
1612	**Samuel Butler.** English satirist, who in his famous poem, "Hudibras," popularized such proverbs as "Spare the rod and spoil the child"
1819	**John Ruskin.** English writer on art, literature, and social issues, who was probably the most influential critic of Victorian England
1820	**William Tecumseh Sherman.** U.S. Civil War general, famous for his "March to the Sea" in Georgia in 1865, for his declaration that "War is hell," and for his absolute refusal to run for president: "If nominated, I will not run, and if elected, I will not serve"
1828	**Jules Verne.** French novelist and pioneer science fiction writer, noted for works such as *Twenty Thousand Leagues Under the Sea* (1870) and *Around the World in Eighty Days* (1873)
1866	**John Henry Whitley.** Noted Speaker of the English House of Commons
1868	**Lionel Walter Rothschild.** English zoologist, member of the House of Commons, and founder of the Rothschild Natural History Museum
1878	**Martin Buber.** Israeli philosopher and Zionist leader, noted for his studies of Hasidism and for more than 20 books on Jewish life
1886	**Charlie Ruggles.** American stage and motion-picture actor who appeared in some 100 films
1888	**Dame Edith Evans.** English stage, screen, and television actress
1894	**King Vidor.** Famous American motion-picture director, noted for films such as *Duel in the Sun* (1947) and *Solomon and Sheba* (1959)
1903	**Tunku Abdel Rahman.** First prime minister of the Federation of Malaya
1906	**Chester Floyd Carlson.** American inventor noted for the photocopying process xerography used by the Xerox company in its copying machines
1911	**Elizabeth Bishop.** American poet who won the Pulitzer Prize for *North and South: A Gold Spring* (1955)
1914	**Bill Finger.** American comic book writer, who with Bob Kane created *Batman*
1919	**Buddy Morrow.** American trombonist
1920	**Lana Turner.** American stage, screen, and television actress, and glittering star of the 1940s
1921	**Willard Marshall.** Professional baseball player
1921	**Hoot Evers.** Professional baseball player
1924	**Audrey Meadows.** American television actor (Alice Kramden in *The Honeymooners*) and sister of actress Jane Meadows
1925	**Jack Lemmon.** American stage, screen, and television actor who won Academy Awards for his work in *Mister Roberts* (1955) and *Save The Tiger* (1973)
1931	**James Dean.** American motion-picture actor and object of posthumous adulation unequaled since Valentino
1932	**John Williams.** American composer and successor to Arthur Fiedler as conductor of the Boston Pops Orchestra
1937	**Clete Boyer.** Professional baseball player
1940	**Ted Koppel.** American television broadcast journalist
1941	**Nick Nolte.** American motion-picture and television actor
1942	**Robert Klein.** American comedian
1949	**Brooke Adams.** American stage, screen, and television actress
1956	**Marques Johnson.** Professional basketball player
1968	**Gary Coleman.** American television actor

February 8 – Events

1587	Mary Queen of Scots was beheaded at Fotheringay Castle on orders of England's Queen Elizabeth I.
1693	The College of William and Mary, the second oldest in the United States to Harvard, was chartered by King William III and Queen Mary II of England.
1800	A ceremony was held at the Church of the Invalides in Paris to mourn the death of George Washington, which had occurred some two months earlier.
1837	For the only time in its history, the U.S. Senate chose the vice president, selecting Richard Mentor Johnson after none of the candidates received a majority of electoral votes.

1861 The Confederate States of America was founded when seven states that had seceded agreed to a constitution in Montgomery, Alabama.

1904 The Japanese attacked and decimated the Russian fleet at Port Arthur in a surprise assault that started the Russo-Japanese War.

1910 The Boy Scouts of America was incorporated in the District of Columbia by U.S. businessman William D. Boyce and others.

1915 The great D.W. Griffith movie, *The Birth of a Nation*, premiered at Clune's Auditorium in Los Angeles, marking the beginning of modern movie-making. At the time it was entitled *The Clansman*.

1918 *The Stars and Stripes*, the American Expeditionary Force's official newspaper, was published for the first time.

1924 The first execution by gas chamber took place at the Nevada State Prison in Carson City, Nevada, when Chinese-American Gee Jon was executed for murder.

1932 Jack Dempsey, the great heavyweight boxer, defeated two opponents, Buck Everett and Jack Roper, in exhibition bouts in Milwaukee.

1940 The Nazis shot every tenth person in two villages near Warsaw in reprisal for the deaths of two German soldiers in World War II.

1943 Allied troops took Guadalcanal in the Solomon Islands from the Japanese in World War II.

1952 Elizabeth II was proclaimed Queen of England.

1955 Georgi Malenkov, Joseph Stalin's successor, in a surprise move, resigned, to be succeeded as Soviet premier by Nikolai Bulganin.

1974 The U.S. *Skylab* mission ended after a record-breaking 84 days in space.

February 9 – Birthdays

1700 **Daniel Bernoulli.** Noted Swiss mathematician and member of the famous family of mathematicians that included his father John and his uncle Jacob Bernoulli

1773 **William Henry Harrison.** Ninth U.S. president and grandfather of the 23rd president, Benjamin Harrison

1789 **Franz Gabelsberger.** Inventor of the calculating machine

1814 **Samuel J. Tilden.** U.S. presidential candidate in 1876 who probably had the election stolen from him by the followers of Rutherford B. Hayes

1826 **John Alexander Logan.** Union Civil War general who helped organize the Grand Army of the Republic, and who was credited with naming May 30, 1868, as the first Memorial Day

1863 **Anthony Hope.** English author noted for *The Prisoner of Zenda*

1866 **George Ade.** American humorist and playwright, noted for works such as *Fables in Slang* and *County Chairman*

1874 **Amy Lowell.** American poet and critic, best known for "Sword Blades and Poppy Seeds" (1914) and the biography *John Keats* (1925)

1885 **Alban Berg.** Austrian composer noted for works such as the opera *Wozzeck* (1925) and *Three Orchestral Pieces* (1914)

1891 **Ronald Colman.** English stage and motion-picture actor and leading man in both silents and talkies

1899 **Brian Donlevy.** Irish-born stage and motion-picture actor in nearly 100 films

1902 **Fred Harman.** American cartoonist and creator of *Red Ryder* (1938)

1902 **Chester Lauck.** American actor who portrayed Lum Edwards in the radio show *Lum and Abner* of the 1930s and 1940s

1907 **Dit Clapper.** Hall of Fame hockey player

1908 **Seymour "Sy" Miller.** American composer, author, and pianist, noted for songs such as "Let There Be Peace on Earth (And Let It Begin With Me)"

1909 **Heather Angel.** English stage, screen, and television actress

1909 **Carmen Miranda.** Portuguese-born singer, dancer, and actress of the 1930s and 1940s, billed as the "Brazilian Bombshell"

1909 **Dean Rusk.** U.S. secretary of state under Presidents Kennedy and Johnson

1914 **Ernest Tubb.** One of America's leading country music singers and songwriters of the 1940-1980 era, noted for songs such as "Walking the Floor over You" (1941)

1914 **Bill Veeck.** Noted American baseball executive

1922 **Kathryn Grayson.** American singer and actress of the 1940s and early 1950s

1925 **Vic Wertz.** Professional baseball player

1928 **Frank Frazetta.** American cartoonist and artist known for his drawings of cartoon characters Tarzan, Buck Rogers and Flash Gordon

1928 **Roger Mudd.** American television newscaster and commentator

1939 **Barry Mann.** American songwriter

1942 **François Jauffret.** French tennis player

1942 **Carole King.** American songwriter and singer

1943 **Joe Pesci.** American motion-picture actor and Academy Award winner for *Goodfellas* (1990)

1944 **Alice Walker.** American novelist, noted for works such as *The Color Purple* (1982)

1945 **Mia Farrow.** American stage, screen, and television actress, and daughter of director John Farrow and actress Maureen O'Sullivan

1951 **Dennis "D.T." Thomas.** Rhythm-and-blues musician with the group Kool and the Gang

1952 **Danny White.** Professional football player

1963 **Travis Tritt.** American country music singer and songwriter

February 9 – Events

1119 Calixtus II was crowned Roman Catholic pope.

1825 The House of Representatives elected John Quincy Adams president, after the 1824 election in which Andrew Jackson led the popular voting but did not get an electoral majority.

1861 Jefferson Davis was elected president of the Confederacy.

1870 The United States Weather Service was established.

1881 Fyodor Dostoevsky, the great Russian novelist, died in St. Petersburg at age 59.

1893 *Falstaff,* the last opera of the great Italian composer, Giuseppe Verdi, had its world premiere at Milan's La Scala.

1895 The Minnesota State School of Agriculture defeated Hamline College, 9-3, in the world's first college basketball game.

1942 The French luxury liner *Normandy,* while being refitted as a transport ship, burned and capsized in New York Harbor.

1943 U.S. troops under Major General Alexander Patch finally won the World War II Battle of Guadalcanal, begun the previous August.

1950 U.S. Senator Joseph McCarthy started a four-year "witch-hunt" by charging in a Wheeling, West Virginia, speech that the State Department was riddled with Communists.

1964 The Beatles made their American television debut on the *Ed Sullivan Show.*

1969 The first Boeing 747, the world's largest airplane, began its first flight, from Paine Field in Seattle, Washington.

1971 California's San Fernando Valley was rocked by an earthquake that measured 6.5 on the Richter scale.

1984 Soviet premier Yuri Andropov died, only 15 months after he had succeeded Leonid Brezhnev.

February 10 – Birthdays

1499 **Thomas Platter.** Swiss writer and humanist

1775 **Charles Lamb.** Noted British essayist and critic of the romantic movement of the early 1800s, who used the pen name *Elia* for many of his essays

1846 **Ira Remsen.** American chemist and founder in 1879 of the *American Chemical Journal,* the first American journal in the field of science

1858 **Walt McDougall.** American comic strip and political cartoonist, whose front-page work *The Royal Feast of Belshazzar Blaine and the Money Kings* may have cost James Blaine the 1884 election

1868 **William Allen White.** American journalist and editor, known in the early 1900s as the "Sage of Emporia"

1888 **Harry Beaumont.** American motion-picture director whose film *The Broadway Melody* won the Academy Award as best picture for 1928-29

1890 **Boris Pasternak.** Russian writer noted for the novel *Doctor Zhivago* (1957)

1892 **Alan Hale.** American actor and director who appeared in over 100 films

1893 **William "Big Bill" Tilden.** American tennis player who dominated the game in the decade of the 1920s, winning 138 of 192 tournaments, and who is considered by many to be the greatest player of all time

1893 **Jimmy Durante.** American comedian, songwriter, and entertainer, nicknamed "Schnozzola" for his long, bulbous nose

1894 **Harold Macmillan.** British prime minister, 1957-1963

1894 **Herb Pennock.** Hall of Fame baseball pitcher who worked in 617 games in a 22-year career

1898 **Bertolt Brecht.** German playwright noted for works such as *The Three Penny Opera* (1928) and *The Caucasian Chalk Circle* (1944-1945)

1898 **Dame Judith Anderson.** One of the finest actresses on the 20th-century English-speaking stage

1902 **Walter Houser Brattain.** American physicist who with John Bardeen and William Shockley developed the transistor in 1947

1904 **John Farrow.** American motion-picture director who shared in the Academy Award for the screenplay of *Around the World in 80 Days* (1956)

1905 **Walter Brown.** American basketball executive who organized the Boston Celtics basketball team

1907 **Lon Chaney Jr.** American motion-picture actor in some 150 films, who like his famous father specialized in monster and villain roles

1913 **Merriam Smith.** American author and journalist

1914 **Larry Adler.** American musician

1915 **Allie Reynolds.** Professional baseball pitcher who pitched two no-hit games in 1951

1920 **Alex Comfort.** American gerontologist and author of *The Joy of Sex* (1972)

1927 **Leontyne Price.** American opera singer and one of the most celebrated sopranos of her time

1930 **Robert Wagner.** American motion-picture and television actor

1939 **Roberta Flack.** American soul singer

1941 **Michael Apted.** English motion-picture director noted for films such as *Gorillas in the Mist* (1988)

1946 **Dick Anderson.** Professional football player

1950 **Mark Spitz.** American swimming superstar who won seven gold medals in the 1972 Olympics

1955 **Greg Norman.** Professional golfer

1961 **George Stephanopoulos.** Advisor to President Clinton in his first term

1963 **Lenny Dykstra.** Professional baseball player

1967 **Laura Dern.** American motion-picture actress and daughter of actors Bruce Dern and Diane Ladd

February 10 – Events

1755 Montesquieu (Charles de Secondat), the great French philosopher, died in Paris at age 66.

1763 The Treaty of Paris ended the French and Indian War and gave the French empire in India and North America to the British.

1837   Alexander Pushkin, Russia's most celebrated poet, was killed at age 37 in a duel defending his wife's honor.

1840   Queen Victoria of England married Prince Albert of Saxe-Coburg-Gotha.

1863   Tom Thumb, the star "little person" of P.T. Barnum's circus, married Lavinia Warren, "the smallest woman alive."

1899   Herbert Hoover married Lou Henry.

1904   Japan formally declared war on Russia two days after hostilities had begun in the Russo-Japanese War.

1933   Singing telegrams were introduced in New York by the Postal Telegraph Company.

1942   The first "golden record" was presented by RCA Victor to bandleader Glenn Miller for his recording of "Chattanooga Choo Choo."

1942   The last civilian automobiles rolled off the assembly lines in Detroit as the U.S. geared up for war production.

1949   Arthur Miller's famous play *Death of a Salesman* made its debut, at New York's Morosco Theater.

1957   The comic strip *On Stage,* by Leonard Starr, first appeared.

1971   *Apollo 14* splashed down from its moon voyage.

February 11 – Birthdays

1466   **Elizabeth of York.** Daughter of King Edward IV of England and wife of Henry VII, whose marriage to her united the houses of Lancaster and York

1535   **Gregory XIV.** Roman Catholic pope, 1590-1591

1657   **Bernard de Bouyer Fontenelle.** French man of letters, scientist, and philosopher, noted for works such as *Entretiens sur la Pluralite des Mondes* (1687)

1760   **Richard Allen.** American slave who bought his freedom and founded the African Methodist Church (1816), the first black denomination in the United States

1812   **Alexander Hamilton Stephens.** Vice President of the Confederate States of America during the Civil War

1821   **Auguste Mariette.** French Egyptologist

1839   **J. Willard Gibbs.** One of the greatest American theoretical physicists, thought by some to be the father of modern physical chemistry

1847   **Thomas A. Edison.** Probably the greatest inventor in history, whose 1,100 inventions include the electric light, the phonograph, and the motion-picture projector

1863   **John "Honey Fitz" Fitzgerald.** American businessman and politician, and grandfather of President John F. Kennedy

1881   **Carlo Carra.** Noted 20th-century Italian painter

1889   **John Mills.** American singer and member of the Mills Brothers group

1900   **Tommy Hitchcock Jr.** The greatest polo player of all time

1904   **Sir Keith Jacka Holyoake.** Governor General of New Zealand

1907   **William Levitt.** American industrialist who brought mass production methods to the housing industry, and became the biggest builder of houses in the U.S. in the 1940s and 1950s

1908   **Sir Vivian Ernest Fuchs.** British geologist and Antarctic expert, who commanded the British Commonwealth Trans-Antarctic Expedition in 1957 and 1958, the first to cross Antarctica

1909   **Max Baer.** World heavyweight boxing champion, 1934-1935

1909   **Joseph Mankiewicz.** American director, producer, and screenwriter, who won Academy Awards for *A Letter to Three Wives* (1949) and *All About Eve* (1950)

1912   **Rudolf Firkusny.** Czechoslovakian pianist

1917   **Sidney Sheldon.** American author and screenwriter noted for works such as *The Other Side of Midnight* (1973)

1920   **Farouk I.** King of Egypt, 1936-1952

1921   **Lloyd Bentsen.** U.S. senator and Democratic candidate for vice president in 1988

1923   **Eva Gabor.** Hungarian-born stage, screen, and television actress, and sister of actress Zsa Zsa Gabor

1924   **Budge Patty.** American tennis superstar

1925   **Virginia E. Johnson.** American psychologist noted for human sexuality studies with Dr. William H. Masters

1925   **Kim Stanley.** American stage and motion-picture actress

1926   **Leslie Nielsen.** American stage, screen, and television actor

1934   **Mary Quant.** English fashion designer

1934   **Tina Louise.** American stage, screen, and television actress

1936   **Burt Reynolds.** American motion-picture and television actor, and virile leading man of the 1960s, 1970s, and 1980s

1949   **Ben Ogilvie.** Professional baseball player

1969   **Jennifer Aniston.** American motion-picture and television actress

February 11 – Events

1650   Rene Descartes, the great French mathematician and philosopher, died in Sweden at age 53.

1752   The Pennsylvania Hospital, the first incorporated hospital in the U.S., opened in Philadelphia.

1812   The word *gerrymander* came into the language to describe the political redistricting done by Massachusetts governor Elbridge Gerry.

1858   French schoolgirl Bernadette Soubirous had her first vision of Our Lady of Lourdes in the French town of Lourdes near the foothills of the Pyrenees.

1861   President-elect Abraham Lincoln and his wife left Springfield, Illinois, for Washington, D.C.

1929	Vatican City became a sovereign state with the signing of the Treaty of the Lateran.
1943	General Dwight D. Eisenhower was made a full general in the U.S. Army.
1945	The World War II Yalta Conference concluded with a statement by Roosevelt, Churchill, and Stalin of their intentions to occupy Germany and form the United Nations.
1965	President Lyndon B. Johnson announced U.S. policy to help South Vietnam.
1979	Moslem revolutionaries took over the government of Iran, with Mehdi Bazargan selected as prime minister by Ayatollah Khomeini.
1983	The space shuttle *Challenger* returned to earth after an eight-day mission, featuring the first untethered spacewalk by astronauts.
1990	South African black activist Nelson Mandela was freed after 27 years in prison.

February 12 – Birthdays

1567	**Thomas Campion.** Elizabethan English composer, poet, and physician, noted for his four *Books of Airs*
1606	**John Winthrop Jr.** Colonial governor and later governor of Connecticut, and son of the Puritan governor of the Massachusetts Bay Colony
1663	**Cotton Mather.** Noted American Puritan scholar and minister, son of the Puritan minister Increase Mather, and fanner of the flames of the Salem witchcraft mania
1746	**Thaddeus Kosciusko.** Polish patriot who fought for freedom in America and in Poland, known for this reason as the "Hero of Two Worlds"
1768	**Francis II.** Austrian ruler who became the last monarch to hold the title of Holy Roman Emperor
1775	**Louisa Catherine Johnson.** Wife of President John Quincy Adams
1791	**Peter Cooper.** American inventor and philanthropist who in 1830 built the "Tom Thumb," the first commercial American steam locomotive, and in 1859 founded the Cooper Union
1809	**Abraham Lincoln.** 16th U.S. president, considered by most historians to be the greatest of all the presidents
1809	**Charles Darwin.** English naturalist noted for the theory of evolution
1813	**James Dwight Dana.** American geologist, mineralogist, zoologist, and author
1828	**George Meredith.** English poet and novelist, noted for works such as *The Ordeal of Richard Feverel* (1859) and *Diana of the Crossways* (1885)
1878	**Joseph Edgar Howard.** American composer and actor noted for songs such as "I Wonder Who's Kissing Her Now" (with Will Hough)
1880	**John L. Lewis.** American labor leader who formed the Committee for Industrial Organization (CIO), and who was president of the United Mine Workers from 1919 to 1960
1884	**Alice Roosevelt Longworth.** Daughter of President Theodore Roosevelt
1884	**Max Beckmann.** German painter
1893	**Omar N. Bradley.** U.S. World War II general whose Twelfth Army Group of about 1,000,000 men was the largest fighting force ever amassed in battle under the American flag
1898	**Roy Harris.** American composer whose best-known works are his *Symphony No. 3* and *An American Overture*
1903	**Chick Hafey.** Hall of Fame baseball player
1904	**Ted Mack.** Host of the *Original Amateur Hour* on radio and television
1911	**Silvestre Antonio Guzman Fernandez.** President of the Dominican Republic
1912	**Tex Beneke.** American singer and bandleader who took over the Glenn Miller band after Miller was killed in World War II
1915	**Lorne Greene.** Canadian stage, screen, and television actor, who played Ben Cartwright in the long-running television series *Bonanza*
1916	**Joseph L. Alioto.** Mayor of San Francisco in the 1970s
1917	**Dom DiMaggio.** Professional baseball player and brother of baseball great Joe DiMaggio
1919	**Eddie Robinson.** College football coach at Grambling State University with over 340 career victories, a record in both college and professional football
1919	**Forrest Tucker.** American motion-picture and television actor
1923	**Franco Zeffirelli.** Italian motion-picture director noted for films such as *Romeo and Juliet* (1968)
1926	**Joe Garagiola.** Professional baseball player and television sportscaster
1930	**Arlen Specter.** U.S. senator
1932	**Princess Astrid.** Princess of Norway
1934	**Bill Russell.** Professional Hall of Fame basketball superstar, and one of the greatest defensive centers in basketball history
1935	**Ray Manzarek.** Keyboard player with The Doors rock group
1938	**Johnny Rutherford.** Noted American racing car driver
1938	**Judy Blume.** American writer and author of juvenile fiction
1945	**Maud Adams.** American actress and model
1951	**Kjell Johansson.** Swedish tennis player
1952	**Simon MacCorkindale.** English motion-picture and television actor
1955	**Chet Lemon.** Professional baseball player
1955	**Arsenio Hall.** American actor and television host (*The Arsenio Hall Show*)
1959	**Larry Nance.** Professional basketball player
1970	**Jim Creggan.** Rock musician with the group Barenaked Ladies

February 12 – Events

1541 Santiago, Chile, was founded by Spanish explorer Pedro de Valdivia.

1554 Lady Jane Grey, pretender to the throne of England after the death of Edward VI, was beheaded along with her husband on a charge of high treason.

1733 James Oglethorpe founded Savannah, as Georgia's first colonial settlement.

1736 Maria Theresa, the great queen of Austria, married Francis Stephen, Duke of Lorraine.

1793 The Fugitive Slave Act was passed by the U.S. Congress, allowing owners to recover their runaway slaves merely by presenting proof of ownership before a magistrate.

1804 Immanuel Kant, the great German philosopher, died in Königsberg, East Prussia, at age 79.

1818 Chile gained its independence from Spain.

1878 Frederick Thayer patented the baseball catcher's mask.

1909 The National Association for the Advancement of Colored People (NAACP), America's oldest civil rights organization, was founded in New York City.

1912 The Chinese Republic was formed by Sun Yat-sen.

1915 The cornerstone for the Lincoln Memorial was laid in Washington, D.C.

1917 The comic strip *The Gumps,* by Sidney Smith, first appeared.

1924 George Gershwin's *Rhapsody in Blue* was first performed, with Gershwin himself at the piano, at Aeolian Hall in New York.

1938 Adolf Hitler demanded concessions of Austrian Premier Kurt von Schuschnigg, who had no alternative but to give in. A month later Hitler took over Austria anyway.

1971 J.C. Penney, the noted American merchant, died at age 95.

1999 President Clinton's impeachment trial by the Senate ended in his acquittal on both charges (perjury and obstruction of justice). Neither charge received a majority vote let alone the two-thirds majority required.

2000 Charles Schulz, creator of the famous *Peanuts* comic strip, died at age 77.

February 13 – Birthdays

1457 **Mary of Burgundy.** Wife of Maximilian I of Austria and daughter of Charles the Bold of Burgundy

1674 **Prosper Jolyot Crebillon.** French playwright noted for works such as *Idomeneus* (1705) and *Electra* (1717)

1682 **Giovanni Battista Piazzetta.** Venetian painter and illustrator

1728 **John Hunter.** English surgeon and anatomist, noted as the founder of experimental surgery

1754 **Charles Maurice de Talleyrand.** French statesman noted for his diplomatic achievements under Napoleon and at the Congress of Vienna

1755 **Philibert Louis Debucourt.** French painter

1805 **Peter Gustav Lejeune Dirichlet.** Noted German mathematician

1849 **Randolph Henry Spencer Churchill.** English statesman, son of the Duke of Marlborough and father of Winston Churchill

1873 **Feodor Ivanovich Chaliapin.** Russian opera singer and the leading interpreter of his time of bass roles in Russian and Italian opera

1877 **Sidney Smith.** American comic strip writer and creator in 1917 of *The Gumps*

1883 **Hal Chase.** Professional baseball player and manager

1885 **Bess Wallace.** Wife of President Harry S. Truman

1888 **Georgios Papandreou.** Three-time prime minister of Greece

1892 **Grant Wood.** American artist noted for the famous painting *American Gothic* (1930)

1903 **George Simenon.** French reporter, writer, and creator of "Inspector Maigret"

1908 **Lennie Hayton.** American jazz composer and conductor

1910 **William Bradford Shockley.** American physicist and co-developer of the transistor

1911 **Jean Muir.** American stage, screen and television actress

1915 **Lyle Bettger.** American stage, screen, and television actor

1918 **Patty Berg.** One of the greatest women golfers in history

1919 **"Tennessee Ernie" Ford.** American humorist and singer

1920 **Boudleaux Bryant.** American songwriter noted with his wife Felice for works such as "Bye Bye Love" and "Wake Up Little Susie"

1920 **Eileen Farrell.** American opera singer and "super-soprano"

1923 **Charles E. "Chuck" Yeager.** American test pilot who was the first to break the sound barrier (1947)

1924 **Jean-Jacques Servan-Schreiber.** French journalist, politician, and author

1933 **Emanuel Ungaro.** French fashion designer

1933 **Kim Novak.** American motion-picture actress and number one box-office attraction in the 1950s

1934 **George Segal.** American stage, screen, and television actor

1938 **Oliver Reed.** English motion-picture actor and leading man of British and international films

1941 **Bo Svenson.** American actor

1942 **Carol Lynley.** American motion-picture and television actress

1944 **Sal Bando.** Professional baseball player

1944 **Peter Tork.** American singer and member of the Monkees musical group

1944 **Stockard Channing.** American motion-picture actress

1944 **Jerry Springer.** Irreverent American television talk show host

1947	**Mike Krzyzewski.** Noted college basketball coach (Duke University)
1951	**Jane Seymour.** English stage, screen and television actress, noted for the long-running series *Dr. Quinn, Medicine Woman*
1951	**David Naughton.** American motion-picture and television actor
1960	**Matt Salinger.** American television actor

February 13 – Events

1542	England's King Henry VIII had his fifth wife, Catherine Howard, beheaded on charges of adultery.
1571	Benvenuto Cellini, the great Italian sculptor and writer, died in Florence at age 70.
1635	The Boston Public Latin School, the oldest public school in America, was opened.
1689	William and Mary were formally proclaimed King and Queen-regnant of England.
1728	Cotton Mather, the famous American theologian and preacher, died in Boston at age 65.
1741	*The American Magazine*, the first magazine in America, was published in Philadelphia by Andrew Bradford, three days before Benjamin Franklin published *The General Magazine*.
1883	Richard Wagner, the great German composer, died in Bayreuth at age 69.
1914	The American Society of Composers, Authors, and Publishers (ASCAP) was organized in New York City by composer Victor Herbert and others.
1937	The comic strip *Prince Valiant,* by Harold Foster, first appeared.
1945	The Russians took Budapest from the Germans in World War II after 49 days of fighting.
1945	In the most intense incendiary "terror bombing" of World War II, British and American planes began a two-day air attack which devastated the German city of Dresden.
1960	France exploded its first atom bomb in the Sahara Desert.

February 14 – Birthdays

1404	**Leon Battista Alberti.** Italian Renaissance architect, painter, and author, who designed the Rucellai Palace and the church of Santa Maria Novella in Florence
1602	**Francesco Cavalli.** Italian opera composer noted for works such as *Giasone* (1649) and *Calisto* (1651)
1766	**Thomas Robert Malthus.** English economist noted for his famous "Malthusian theory" that the population will eventually outrun the food supply
1768	**Ivan Krylov.** Russian fable writer
1819	**Christopher Latham Sholes.** American printer and co-inventor of the first practical typewriter
1824	**Winfield Scott Hancock.** Union Civil War general and candidate for U.S. president in 1880

1838	**Edwin Ginn.** Founder in 1866 of Ginn & Company publishers
1856	**Frank Harris.** Journalist and author, noted for the erotic book *My Life and Loves* (1923)
1859	**George Washington Gale Ferris.** U.S. engineer who designed the world's first Ferris wheel, a structure 250 feet tall with 36 passenger cars at the Columbian Exposition in Chicago in 1893
1865	**Carl Thomas Anderson.** American cartoonist and creator in 1932 of the comic strip *Henry*
1882	**George Jean Nathan.** American author, editor, and drama critic
1894	**Jack Benny.** American actor, comedian, and superstar, with a durable and influential career in American comedy that spanned over 60 years
1905	**Thelma Ritter.** American motion-picture performer who was an excellent character actress of the 1950s and 1960s
1907	**Johnny Longden.** Noted American jockey with over 6,000 winners
1913	**Woody Hayes.** Winningest football coach in Big Ten history, with 14 conference titles and three national championships at Ohio State
1913	**Mel Allen.** American sportscaster and author, noted especially for his broadcasts of the New York Yankees' baseball games in their great pennant-winning years
1913	**James R. Hoffa.** American labor leader and president of the Teamsters Union in the late 1950s and 1960s
1913	**James A. Pike.** American clergyman, Episcopal bishop, and outspoken advocate of social justice
1915	**Irving Gordon.** American composer noted for songs such as "Unforgettable" and "Mister and Mississippi"
1921	**Hugh Downs.** American television personality
1923	**Cesare Siepi.** Italian basso
1931	**Bernie "Boom Boom" Geoffrion.** Professional hockey player
1932	**Vic Morrow.** American television and motion-picture actor
1934	**Florence Henderson.** American television actress
1935	**Mickey Wright.** One of the top professional women golfers
1937	**Magic Sam Maghett.** American musician and the "last great original Chicago bluesman"
1941	**Paul Tsongas.** U.S. senator
1944	**Carl Bernstein.** American columnist and author, and one of the principal figures in exposing the Watergate scandals
1946	**Gregory Hines.** American motion-picture actor and dancer
1947	**Gregg Judd.** U.S. senator
1950	**Philip Dent.** Australian tennis player
1951	**Michael Doucet.** Cagun singer and musician
1960	**Meg Tilly.** American stage, screen and motion-picture actress and sister of actress Jennifer Tilly
1966	**Billy Zane.** American motion-picture actor known for his ability to play leading men or villains

1967	**Manuela Maleeva.** Bulgarian tennis player and sister of tennis players Katerina and Magdalena
1968	**Molly Ringwald.** American motion-picture actress
1972	**Drew Bledsoe.** Professional football player

February 14 – Events

44 BC	Julius Caesar was made dictator of Rome for life (which turned out to be for one month).
269	The Roman priest Saint Valentine was beheaded in Rome on Palatine Hill.
1130	Innocent II was elected Roman Catholic pope.
1400	Ex-King Richard II of England died in prison. It is very likely that he was murdered.
1779	Captain James Cook, the famous British navigator, was killed by the natives at Owhyhee, Hawaii.
1849	James K. Polk became the first U.S. president to be photographed while in office when he posed for the noted photographer Mathew Brady in New York City.
1859	Oregon was admitted to the Union as the 33rd state.
1864	Union general William Tecumseh Sherman captured Meridian, Mississippi, in the Civil War.
1876	Elisha Gray filed for a patent on his telephone a few hours after Alexander Graham Bell had filed for his. The Supreme Court eventually ruled Bell was the rightful inventor.
1884	A double tragedy struck Theodore Roosevelt as his wife, Alice, died of childbirth and his mother died of typhoid fever.
1895	Oscar Wilde's masterpiece *The Importance of Being Earnest* premiered in London's St. James Theatre.
1903	The Department of Commerce and Labor was established by Congress at the request of President Theodore Roosevelt.
1912	Arizona was admitted to the Union as the 48th state.
1918	The motion picture *Tarzan of the Apes* was released for the first time.
1929	The "St. Valentine's Day Massacre" occurred in Chicago as seven members of the "Bugs" Moran Gang were murdered in a garage. Police suspected the Al Capone gang did the killing.
1949	Chaim Weizmann was elected first president of Israel.
1966	Wilt Chamberlain set a National Basketball Association scoring record of 20,884 points after only seven years of play.

February 15 – Birthdays

1368	**Sigismund.** King of Hungary and Bohemia and Holy Roman Emperor, 1433-1437
1519	**Pedro Menendez de Aviles.** Spanish sea captain who in 1565 founded St. Augustine, Florida, the oldest city in the U.S.
1564	**Galileo (Galilei).** Italian astronomer, mathematician, and one of the greatest scientists of all time, who discovered the law of falling bodies and first observed the four bright satellites of Jupiter
1571	**Michael Praetorius.** German composer of church music, noted for *Syntagma Musicum* (1615-1620) and two books of hymns
1705	**Charles Andre Van Loo.** French Rococo painter
1710	**Louis XV.** King of France, 1715-1774, noted for his mistresses, Madame de Pompadour and Madame Du Barry, and for his cynical remark, "After me the deluge!"
1726	**Abraham Clark.** New Jersey signer of the Declaration of Independence and member of the Continental Congress, the Congress of the Confederation and the U.S. Congress
1748	**Jeremy Bentham.** English economist and philosopher who founded the philosophy that became known as Utilitarianism
1797	**Henry Englehard Steinway.** Famous German-American piano builder and founder in 1853 of Steinway and Sons
1803	**John Augustus Sutter.** Pioneer settler on whose land gold was discovered, precipitating the 1849 California Gold Rush
1809	**Cyrus Hall McCormick.** American inventor noted for the invention in 1831 of the mechanical reaping machine that revolutionized agriculture
1811	**Domingo Faustino Sarmiento.** Argentine statesman, educator, and writer, noted for works such as *Civilization and Barbarism: Life of Juan Facundo Quiroga* (1845)
1812	**Charles Lewis Tiffany.** American jeweler and founder of Tiffany's jewelry company, whose reputation became so great that his name now stands for the highest quality in jewelry
1817	**Charles François Daubigny.** French painter and etcher noted for works such as *Lever de Lune* (1877)
1820	**Susan B. Anthony.** American reformer and pioneer crusader for woman suffrage
1826	**Johnstone Stoney.** English physicist who coined the word "electron"
1843	**Russell Herman Conwell.** American lawyer, clergyman, and author of the famous lecture, "Acres of Diamonds"
1845	**Elihu Root.** American lawyer, statesman, and Cabinet officer, who won the 1912 Nobel peace prize
1861	**Alfred North Whitehead.** English mathematician and philosopher who with Bertrand Russell wrote the monumental work *Principia Mathematica* (1910-1913)
1875	**Sir Ernest Shackleton.** Irish Antarctic explorer, who led a British expedition to within 97 miles of the South Pole in 1908
1880	**Joseph Hergesheimer.** American novelist noted for works such as *Java Head* (1919)

1882 **John Barrymore.** The youngest of the "Fabulous Barrymores" and the greatest actor of his day

1886 **Sir Cyril Newall.** British Air Marshal

1892 **James V. Forrestal.** First U.S. secretary of defense, 1947-1949, and secretary of the Navy, 1944-1947, who helped to build the United States Fleet into the largest in the world

1893 **Walter Donaldson.** American composer and pianist noted for songs such as "How Ya Gonna Keep 'em Down on the Farm?" "Yes, Sir, That's My Baby," and "My Blue Heaven"

1897 **Earl Blaik.** American college football coach who coached the great Army football teams of the World War II era

1900 **George Earnshaw.** Professional baseball player

1905 **Harold Arlen.** American composer of some 500 songs such as "That Old Black Magic," "Stormy Weather," and his greatest hit, "Over the Rainbow"

1907 **Cesar Romero.** American motion-picture and television actor and "Latin lover" of the 1930s and 1940s, with a career of over 50 years

1911 **Leonard Woodcock.** American labor leader and president of the United Automobile Workers, 1970-1977

1914 **Kevin McCarthy.** American stage, screen, and television actor, and brother of writer Mary McCarthy

1922 **Herman Kahn.** American futurologist and author of *On Thermonuclear War*

1922 **John B. Anderson.** U.S. congressman and third presidential candidate in 1980

1927 **Harvey Korman.** American stage, screen, and television actor

1929 **Graham Hill.** British automobile racing driver and twice winner of the Grand Prix

1929 **James Schlesinger.** First secretary of the Department of Energy

1931 **Claire Bloom.** English stage, screen, and television actress

1933 **Adolfo (Sardina).** Cuban-born fashion expert

1935 **Roger B. Chaffee.** U.S. astronaut who was killed in 1967 when fire and smoke swept through his Apollo spacecraft during a ground test

1935 **Susan Brownmiller.** American writer and feminist leader

1940 **John Hadl.** Professional football player

1941 **Brian Holland.** American musician and songwriter whose Holland-Dozier-Holland partnership had over 30 hits

1942 **Kim Jong Il.** President of North Korea, succeeding his father Kim Il Sung in 1994

1944 **Mick Avory.** American rock musician with The Kinks

1948 **Ron Cey.** Professional baseball player

1948 **Marisa Berenson.** American model and motion-picture actress

1949 **Ken Anderson.** Professional football player

1951 **Melissa Manchester.** American rock and roll singer

1953 **Pat Tilley.** Professional football player

1954 **Matt Groening.** American cartoonist and creator of *The Simpsons*, TV's first animated prime-time series

1964 **Chris Farley.** American motion-picture and television actor and comedian

1973 **Amy Van Dyken.** Noted Olympic swimmer and the first American woman to win four medals in a single Olympics (1996)

February 15 – Events

360 The first Cathedral of Santa Sophia in Constantinople was dedicated.

1145 Eugenius III was elected Roman Catholic pope.

1288 Nicholas IV was elected Roman Catholic pope.

1493 Christopher Columbus arrived aboard the *Nina* at Santa Maria Island in the Azores, on his return trip from discovering America.

1643 Johann Bjornsson Printz and his predominately Finnish colonists landed in Port Christina in what is now Wilmington, Delaware, joining the Swedes who had founded the colony.

1764 St. Louis was established by a French fur trader Pierre Laclede Liguest and his stepson Rene Auguste Chouteau.

1862 The construction of the *Monitor,* the first ironclad vessel of the United States Navy, was completed.

1867 The first performance of "On the Beautiful Blue Danube," the famous waltz of Johann Strauss, Jr., created a sensation in Vienna.

1898 The U.S. battleship *Maine* blew up in Havana harbor, leading to the Spanish-American War.

1933 President Franklin D. Roosevelt narrowly escaped assassination in Miami when a fanatic fired at him and killed Mayor Anton J. Cermak of Chicago, who was riding with Roosevelt.

1942 Singapore surrendered in World War II to the Japanese, who had come in from the Malayan interior, a feat considered impossible, rather than from the sea.

1965 Canada replaced the Union Jack with the Maple Leaf as its national flag.

1971 Great Britain adopted a decimal currency system, ending the 1,000-year history of the pence-and-pound currency.

1978 Leon Spinks defeated Muhammad Ali to become the heavyweight champion of the world.

February 16 – Birthdays

1497 **Philip Melanchthon.** German humanist and scholar who was Martin Luther's chief associate in starting and leading the Protestant Reformation

1519 **Gaspard de Coligny.** French statesman and "Admiral of France," who as a leading Huguenot was the first to be killed in the massacre on St. Bartholomew's Day in 1572

1620	**Frederick William.** Ruler of Brandenburg, 1640-1688, known as the "Great Elector," who laid the foundations for the military greatness of Prussia
1740	**Giambattista Bodoni.** Italian printer and type designer who introduced the "classical" type face into bookmaking
1812	**Henry Wilson.** U.S. vice president under President U.S. Grant and one of the founders of the Republican Party
1822	**Francis Galton.** British anthropologist and founder of eugenics
1834	**Ernst Heinrich Haeckel.** Noted German zoologist and evolutionist and author of the widely-read book, *The Riddle of the Universe* (1899)
1838	**Henry Adams.** American historian and philosopher, noted for the Pulitzer Prize-winning book *The Education of Henry Adams*
1840	**Henry Watterson.** American newspaper editor associated with the Louisville *Courier-Journal* for over 50 years
1843	**Henry Leland.** American automobile manufacturer who founded Cadillac Motor Co. (1902) and Lincoln Motor Co. (1917)
1848	**Hugo De Vries.** Dutch botanist and geneticist, known primarily for his "mutation theory"
1858	**Lon Myers.** American track star who at one time held all U.S. records for distances from 50 yards to a mile
1866	**Sliding Billy Hamilton.** Hall of Fame baseball player who was the pre-modern era stolen base king
1876	**George Macauley Trevelyan.** Famous British historian, noted for *History of England* (1926) and *England Under Queen Anne* (1930-1934)
1884	**Robert J. Flaherty.** American motion-picture director and "father of the documentary"
1886	**Van Wyck Brooks.** American critic, biographer, and historian, noted for the monumental work *Makers and Finders: A History of the Writer in America, 1800-1915*
1888	**Harold R. Medina.** Noted U.S. federal judge who won fame for his fair conduct of the trial of 11 American Communist party leaders in 1949
1895	**Louis Calhern.** American motion-picture actor noted for his romantic leading man roles in the 1920s and for his powerful character roles in the 1950s
1898	**Katharine Cornell.** One of the greatest American stage actresses of the 1920s and 1930s
1901	**Wayne King.** American composer, clarinetist, and bandleader of the Big Band Era, known as the "Waltz King," and known also for the song "The Waltz You Saved For Me"
1903	**Edgar Bergen.** Noted American ventriloquist and creator of Charlie McCarthy and Mortimer Snerd
1904	**George F. Kennan.** American diplomat and architect of the U.S. containment policy of the 1950s
1907	**Alec Wilder.** American composer
1909	**Hugh Beaumont.** American motion-picture and television actor
1914	**Jimmy Wakely.** American actor, singer, and songwriter
1920	**Patti Andrews.** One of the singing Andrews Sisters, a highly popular trio in the 1940s
1926	**John Schlesinger.** English motion-picture director and Academy Award winner for *Midnight Cowboy* (1969)
1934	**Marlene Bauer.** Noted professional golfer
1935	**Sonny Bono.** American singer, comedian, and member of the Sonny and Cher television team
1940	**Tracy Carter.** American motion-picture and television actress
1943	**Anthony Dowell.** American ballet dancer
1944	**Roger Dowdeswell.** Professional tennis player from Zimbabwe
1952	**John Feaver.** English tennis player
1957	**LeVar Burton.** American motion-picture and television actor
1958	**Ice-T.** American rapper known for his controversial song, "Cop Killer"
1959	**John McEnroe.** American tennis player and superstar
1959	**Kelly Tripucka.** Professional basketball player
1961	**Andy Taylor.** Guitarist with the Duran Duran musical group

February 16 – Events

1786	James Monroe married Elizabeth Kortright.
1804	U.S. naval officer Stephen Decatur, in a daring raid, led a picked band into Tripoli Harbor and set fire to the U.S.N. frigate *Philadelphia,* captured by the Tripoli pirates.
1862	Ft. Donelson surrendered unconditionally to Union General U.S. Grant in the Civil War, after Grant had refused to accept any other terms.
1868	The Benevolent and Protective Order of Elks was organized in New York City.
1937	Dr. Wallace H. Carothers, a chemist of the du Pont company, patented nylon.
1938	Austrian Chancellor Kurt von Schuschnigg bowed to pressure and admitted Austrian Nazis into his cabinet, as the prelude to the overthrow of his government by the Germans.
1945	American paratroopers landed on Corregidor in the Philippines in World War II. Within two weeks the Americans retook the fortress from the Japanese.
1947	American Admiral Richard E. Byrd flew over the South Pole for the second time.
1959	Fidel Castro took power as premier of Cuba, following the overthrow of Fulgencio Batista.
1972	Wilt Chamberlain, the basketball superstar, became the first NBA player in history to score 30,000 points.
1978	Japan and China signed an eight-year $20-billion trade pact.

February 17 – Birthdays

1653   **Arcangelo Corelli.** Italian composer and one of the earliest musicians to use the violin, which was replacing the viol in his time

1740   **John Sullivan.** American Revolutionary War hero who seized military supplies from a British fort in New Castle, N.H., in one of the first armed actions by colonists against the British

1740   **Horace Benedict de Saussure.** French physicist and Alpinist

1774   **Raphaelle Peale.** American artist and son of artist Charles Willson Peale

1781   **Rene Theophile Myacinthe Laennec.** French physician who in 1816 invented the stethoscope

1796   **Giovanni Pacini.** Italian composer

1836   **Gustavo Adolfo Becquer.** Spanish poet and writer

1837   **Pierre Auguste Cot.** French painter noted for works such as *The Storm*

1843   **Aaron Montgomery Ward.** American pioneer in the mail-order business and founder in 1872 of the Montgomery Ward Company, the first mail-order house

1854   **Friedrich Alfred Krupp.** Grandson of the founder of the great German Krupp works, and father of Bertha Krupp, for whom the "Big Bertha" lone-range guns of World War I were named

1856   **Frederick E. Ives.** American inventor who developed the Ives halftone process of photoengraving

1857   **Samuel Sidney McClure.** American editor and publisher, who founded the McClure Syndicate in New York City in 1884, one of the first newspaper syndicates

1874   **Thomas J. Watson.** American industrialist whose leadership of IBM from 1914 to 1956 made it into an international powerhouse

1877   **Andre Maginot.** French statesman for whom the heavily-fortified French Maginot Line was named

1879   **Dorothy Canfield Fisher.** American novelist known for works such as *The Deepening Stream* and *Vermont Tradition*

1880   **Alvaro Obregon.** Mexican statesman, soldier, and twice president of Mexico

1889   **H.L. Hunt.** American oil producer who became one of the world's richest men

1892   **Bob Neyland.** One of the greatest college football coaches (at the University of Tennessee)

1893   **Wally Pipp.** Professional baseball player whom Lou Gehrig replaced in the lineup and began a streak of playing in 2,130 consecutive games

1899   **Harvey Oliver Brooks.** American composer noted for such songs as "A Little Bird Told Me"

1902   **Marian Anderson.** American contralto of whom the famous conductor Arturo Toscanini said, "A voice like hers comes once in a century."

1904   **Hans J. Morgenthau.** German-born political scientist and historian

1906   **Billy Hayes.** American composer, author, and guitarist, noted for songs such as "Blue Christmas"

1907   **Charlie Spivak.** American orchestra leader and trumpet player of the Big Band Era

1907   **Buster Crabbe.** American motion-picture and television actor and gold medal swimmer in the 1932 Olympics

1908   **Red Barber.** Noted American sportscaster

1914   **Arthur Kennedy.** American stage and motion-picture actor

1919   **Joseph Hunt.** American Hall of Fame tennis player

1924   **Margaret Truman Daniel.** Daughter of U.S. President Harry S. Truman

1925   **Hal Holbrook.** American stage, screen, and television actor

1929   **Chaim Potok.** American author noted for *The Chosen* (1967)

1934   **Alan Bates.** English stage, screen, and television actor

1936   **Jim Brown.** Professional Hall of Fame football superstar whose career record 12,312 yards gained lasted from 1966 to 1984

1939   **John Leyton.** British musician

1939   **Mary Ann Mobley.** American actress and beauty queen

1942   **Huey P. Newton.** American political activist

1947   **Tim Buckley.** American singer and songwriter noted for the album *Goodbye and Hello* (1967)

1955   **Stanley Morgan.** Professional football player

1959   **Neil Lomax.** Professional football player

1963   **Michael Jordan.** Professional basketball player, superstar, and perhaps the greatest of all time

1972   **Billie Joe Armstrong.** American rock singer and musician

February 17 – Events

1598   Boris Godunov was elected czar of Russia. His regime coincided with "The Time of Troubles."

1621   Miles Standish was appointed military commander of the Plymouth Colony.

1673   Molière, the noted French playwright, died in Paris at age 51.

1801   The U.S. House of Representatives, after 35 ballots, broke the tie in the electoral vote between Thomas Jefferson and Aaron Burr, electing Jefferson the third president.

1817   Baltimore city streets were illuminated by gas lights, the first time gas had been used for this purpose in America.

1856   Heinrich Heine, the great German writer, died in Paris at age 58.

1876   The first sardines were canned, by the Wolff and Reesing cannery in Eastport, Maine.

1897   The National Congress of Mothers, the forerunner of the Parent-Teacher Association, first met, in Washington, D.C.

1904   Giacomo Puccini's great opera *Madama Butterfly* premiered at Milan's La Scala.

1906 Alice Roosevelt, the daughter of President Theodore Roosevelt, married Congressman Nicholas Longworth in the East Room of the White House.

1909 Geronimo, the famous Apache Indian chief, died at approximately 80 years of age.

1933 *Newsweek* magazine had its beginnings with a weekly news magazine published under the name *News-Week* by journalist Thomas John Cardel Martyn.

1936 The comic strip *The Phantom,* by Lee Falk and Ray Moore, first appeared.

1944 American troops landed on Eniwetok Island and naval forces raided Truk Island in World War II.

1958 The comic strip *B.C.,* by Johnny Hart, appeared for the first time.

1959 The U.S. launched *Vanguard II,* the first satellite to send weather information back to earth.

1964 The U.S. Supreme Court issued its "one man, one vote" decision, ruling that congressional districts must be roughly equal in population.

1979 China invaded Vietnam.

February 18 – Birthdays

1516 **Mary I (Bloody Mary).** Daughter of Henry VIII and Catherine of Aragon, and first reigning queen of England, 1553-1558 (her famous nickname was earned from her persecutions of the non-Catholics)

1589 **Sir Henry Vane (the Elder).** English statesman

1609 **Edward Hyde Clarendon.** English earl who played a leading role in restoring the monarchy in England in 1660

1745 **Count Alessandro Volta.** Italian nobleman, who invented the electric battery and for whom the volt, the unit of electromotive force, was named

1775 **Thomas Girtin.** English painter

1790 **Marshall Hall.** British physicist who discovered reflex action

1792 **Jabez Gorham.** American merchant, silversmith and founder of the Gorham Manufacturing Co.

1795 **George Peabody.** American philanthropist for whom George Peabody College was named.

1838 **Ernst Mach.** Austrian physicist for whom "Mach 1," the speed of sound, was named.

1848 **Lewis Comfort Tiffany.** American artist, son of the founder of Tiffany's jewelry store, and developer of Tiffany Favrile glass

1857 **Max Klinger.** German artist

1859 **Sholem Aleichem.** Russian-born writer whose real name was Solomon Rabinowitz, and who is the most widely read of all Yiddish writers

1860 **Anders Leonhard Zorn.** Swedish painter and etcher, noted for works such as *Summer in Sweden* and *Portrait of Ernest Renan*

1885 **Nikos Kazantzakis.** Greek author, dramatist, poet, and philosopher, noted for the epic poem "The Odyssey: A Modern Sequel" and the novel *Zorba the Greek*

1890 **Edward Arnold.** American stage and motion-picture actor, in some 150 films

1890 **Adolphe Menjou.** American stage and motion-picture actor, noted for debonair man-of-the-world roles

1892 **Wendell L. Willkie.** U.S. presidential candidate in 1940

1894 **Andres Segovia.** One of the greatest guitarists of the 20th century

1895 **George Gipp.** First Notre Dame All-American football player

1897 **Edward McNall Burns.** American historian, teacher, and writer, noted for *Western Civilizations: Their History & Their Culture*

1898 **Luis Munoz-Marin.** Four-time governor of Puerto Rico

1907 **Billy De Wolfe.** American motion-picture actor

1909 **Wallace Stegner.** American novelist and critic, noted for works such as *On a Darkling Plain* (1940) and *A Shooting Star* (1961)

1910 **John Jacob Loeb.** American composer and author, noted for songs such as "Boo Hoo," "Rosie the Riveter," and "Seems Like Old Times"

1913 **Dane Clark.** American stage, screen, and television actor

1915 **Joe Gordon.** Professional baseball player and manager

1920 **Jack Palance.** American stage, screen, and television actor

1920 **Bill Cullen.** American television personality and show host

1922 **Helen Gurley Brown.** American author noted for *Sex and the Single Girl*

1925 **George Kennedy.** American motion-picture and television actor who won an Academy Award for *Cool Hand Luke* (1967)

1926 **Len Ford.** Hall of Fame professional football player

1927 **John W. Warner.** U.S. senator

1929 **Len Deighton.** American novelist noted for works such as *The Ipcress File* (1962)

1931 **Toni Morrison.** American Nobel Prize-winning novelist noted for works such as *Song of Solomon* (1977) and *Beloved,* which won the Pulitzer Prize in 1987

1931 **Johnny Hart.** American cartoonist who created *B.C.* and, with Brant Parker, *The Wizard of Id*

1932 **Milos Forman.** Czech-American motion-picture director who won the Academy Award for *One Flew Over the Cuckoo's Nest* (1975), which swept all the top five awards, a feat accomplished only once before (*It Happened One Night* in 1934)

1933 **Yoko Ono.** Japanese film maker, singer, and wife of Beatle John Lennon

1938 **Manny Mota.** Professional baseball player

1945 **Judy Rankin.** Professional golfer and first woman to earn over $100,000 in the sport in a single year (1976)

1950 **Bruce Kison.** Professional baseball player

1950 **John Mayberry.** Professional baseball player

1950	**Cybill Shepherd.** American model and motion-picture actress
1951	**Dick Stockton.** American tennis player
1952	**Maurice Lucas.** Professional basketball player
1954	**John Travolta.** American motion-picture and television actor
1957	**Vanna White.** American television personality noted for her role on the TV game show *Wheel of Fortune*
1959	**Rafael Ramirez.** Professional baseball player
1961	**Alycia Moulton.** American tennis player
1964	**Matt Dillon.** American motion-picture and television actor

February 18 – Events

1546	Martin Luther, the great Protestant Reformation leader, died in Eisleben in Saxony at age 62.
1564	Michelangelo (Buonarroti), the great Italian artist, died in Rome at age 88.
1678	John Bunyan's great work, *The Pilgrim's Progress,* was licensed for publication only a few months after Bunyan was released from prison.
1685	French explorer Robert Cavalier Sieur de La Salle founded Fort Saint Louis, a few miles inland from Matagorda Bay, the first white settlement in Texas.
1735	*Flora, or Hob in the Well,* the first opera presented in the U.S., was performed in Charleston, South Carolina.
1861	Jefferson Davis was sworn in as provisional president of the Confederate States of America.
1885	Mark Twain's famous novel *The Adventures of Huckleberry Finn* was first published in the U.S. (It had already appeared in Britain and Canada in 1884.)
1915	Frank James, brother of notorious outlaw Jesse James, died in Excelsior Springs, Missouri, where he had been living as a respectable farmer.
1924	The comic strip *Boots and Her Buddies,* by Edgar Martin, first appeared.
1930	The planet Pluto was discovered by astronomer Clyde W. Tombaugh, working at the Lowell Observatory in Flagstaff, Arizona.
1939	San Francisco's Golden Gate International Exposition opened.
1953	Lucille Ball and Desi Arnaz were awarded an $8 million contract, an enormous figure for the time, to continue their television program, *I Love Lucy.*
1972	The California Supreme Court ended capital punishment, calling it cruel and unusual punishment.

February 19 – Birthdays

1473	**Nicolaus Copernicus.** Polish astronomer famous for the discovery that the earth rotates around a stationary sun
1526	**Carolus Clusius.** Dutch botanist who helped establish modern botany
1717	**David Garrick.** One of the greatest English actors of all time
1743	**Luigi Boccherini.** Italian composer and cellist noted for *Minuet* and some 500 other works
1818	**Lydia Pinkham.** American housewife who patented "Mrs. Lydia E. Pinkham's Vegetable Compound" in 1876
1819	**William III.** King of The Netherlands, 1849-1890
1843	**Adelina Patti.** Spanish-born coloratura soprano, noted as one of the world's greatest operatic singers
1846	**Charles Simon Clermont-Ganneau.** French orientalist
1859	**Svante August Arrhenius.** Swedish Nobel Prize-winning chemist and physicist
1865	**Sven Anders Hedin.** Swedish explorer of Asia who provided the first maps and information about central Asia
1887	**Paul H. Terry.** American cartoonist noted for the animation of Mighty Mouse
1888	**John G. Adolfi.** American motion-picture director of the silent as well as the talking era
1893	**Sir Cedric Hardwicke.** Noted English stage and motion-picture actor with a career of some 50 years
1895	**Semen Timoshenko.** One of the greatest Russian generals in World War II
1896	**André Breton.** French poet, novelist, and leader of the surrealist movement in Paris in the 1920s and 1930s
1911	**Merle Oberon.** Tasmanian-born leading lady of Hollywood and British films of the 1920s and 1930s
1912	**Saul Chaplin.** American composer, musical director, and producer, noted for *An American in Paris* (1951) and *West Side Story* (1961)
1912	**Stan Kenton.** American bandleader of the Big Band Era
1912	**Ceil Chapman.** American fashion designer
1916	**Eddie Arcaro.** Famous American jockey with five Kentucky Derby winners and two Triple Crown winners: Whirlaway in 1941 and Citation in 1948
1917	**Carson McCullers.** American novelist noted for works such as *The Heart Is a Lonely Hunter* (1940) and *The Member of the Wedding* (1946)
1924	**Lee Marvin.** American stage, screen, and television actor
1930	**John Frankenheimer.** American motion-picture director noted for *The Manchurian Candidate* (1962)
1940	**Smokey Robinson.** American singer, composer, and producer
1940	**Jill Krementz.** American photographer and wife of writer Kurt Vonnegut
1952	**Amy Tan.** American author noted for works such as *The Joy Luck Club* (1989)
1953	**Corrado Barazzutti.** Italian tennis player
1954	**Billy Waddy.** Professional football player
1956	**Marita Redondo.** American tennis player
1957	**Dave Stewart.** Professional baseball player and coach

1959   Sarah Ferguson. Former wife of Prince Andrew of England
1960   Prince Andrew. Second son of Queen Elizabeth II of England
1962   Hana Mandlikova. Czechoslovakian tennis player
1966   Justine Bateman. American motion-picture and television actress

February 19 – Events

1405   Tamerlane, the fierce Mongol leader, died of fever on his way to conquer China. He was 68 years old.
1594   Sigismund III was crowned King of Sweden.
1674   The Treaty of Westminster ceded New York (formerly New Amsterdam) to the British from the Dutch.
1864   The Knights of Pythias was founded in Washington, D.C. by Justus Henry Rathbone.
1878   Thomas A. Edison patented the phonograph.
1881   Kansas became the first state to prohibit alcoholic beverages.
1922   Ed Wynn, "The Perfect Fool" of vaudeville, became the first big show business name to sign up for a starring role in a regular radio program.
1942   President Franklin D. Roosevelt signed the executive order that made possible the detention of Japanese-American citizens in World War II.
1945   The U.S. marines landed on Iwo Jima in World War II.
1977   The U.S. space shuttle *Enterprise* made its first test flight above a Boeing 747 airplane.

February 20 – Birthdays

1500   **Charles V.** King of Spain, 1516-1558, Holy Roman Emperor, 1519-1558, and ruler of The Netherlands and the Burgundian lands in 1506
1726   **William Prescott.** American colonel who served in three wars, led the militia in the Battle of Bunker Hill, and was said to have given the order, "Don't fire until you see the whites of their eyes"
1751   **Johann Heinrich Voss.** German poet and translator of Homer
1829   **Joseph Jefferson.** American comedian and one of the most beloved figures in the American theater
1834   **George Du Maurier.** English novelist and artist, author of *Trilby* (1894), and grandfather of writer Daphne Du Maurier
1844   **Ludwig Eduard Boltzmann.** Austrian theoretical physicist, noted for the Stefan-Boltzmann law of radiated energy and for his contributions to the kinetic theory of gases
1874   **Mary Garden.** Scottish-American soprano famous for her vivid opera portrayals
1887   **Vincent Massey.** The first native-born governor-general of Canada, 1952-1959
1888   **Georges Bernanos.** French author noted for works such as *The Diary of a Country Priest* (1937)

1888   **Marie Rambert.** Polish-born founder of the Ballet Rambert
1896   **Muddy Ruel.** Professional baseball player
1898   **Jimmy Yancy.** American jazz musician and one of the developers of boogie woogie in the 1930s
1898   **Enzo Farrari.** Italian sports car manufacturer
1899   **Cornelius Vanderbilt Whitney.** One of the founders of Pan American Airways
1902   **Ansel Adams.** Noted American landscape photographer
1904   **Aleksei Kosygin.** Russian premier, 1964-1980
1907   **Malcolm Atterbury.** American motion-picture and television actor
1912   **Muriel Buck Humphrey.** U.S. senator and wife of Vice President Hubert Humphrey
1912   **Pierre François Marie-Louis Boulle.** French author noted for works such as *Bridge On the River Kwai* (1952) and *Planet of the Apes* (1963)
1913   **Tommy Henrich.** Professional baseball player
1914   **John Daly.** American television personality and moderator of the long-running panel show, *What's My Line?*
1915   **Chick Harbert.** Hall of Fame professional golfer
1918   **Don Hesse.** American editorial cartoonist
1924   **Sidney Poitier.** American stage and motion-picture actor and director, who was Hollywood's number one black actor in the 1950s and 1960s
1924   **Gloria Vanderbilt.** American heiress and noted clothes designer
1925   **Robert Altman.** American motion-picture and television director, noted for *M*A*S*H* (1970)
1928   **Elroy Face.** Professional baseball pitcher with an 18-1 won-loss record in 1959
1929   **Amanda Blake.** American motion-picture and television actress who played Miss Kitty in the long-running television series *Gunsmoke*
1934   **Bobby Unser.** American racing car driver who won the 1968 Indianapolis 500
1937   **Nancy Wilson.** American popular music singer
1941   **Buffy Sainte-Marie.** English singer
1942   **Philip Esposito.** Professional hockey superstar who scored a record 152 points in 1970-1971
1942   **Mitch McConnell.** U.S. senator
1946   **Sandy Duncan.** American stage, screen, and television actress
1946   **J. Geils.** American rock guitarist and bandleader
1947   **Peter Strauss.** American television and motion-picture actor
1948   **Jennifer O'Neill.** American model and television and motion-picture actress
1951   **Edward Albert.** American motion-picture actor and son of actors Eddie Albert and Margo
1951   **Kathie Baillie.** American country singer
1954   **Glynis Coles.** English tennis player
1954   **Patty Hearst.** American heiress and noted fugitive of the 1970s
1963   **Charles Barkley.** Professional basketball player
1963   **Ian Brown.** American rock musician with Stone Roses

1966   **Cindy Crawford.** American model

1967   **Kurt Cobain.** American musician who founded the group Nirvana (1987)

February 20 – Events

1839   Congress prohibited dueling in the District of Columbia.

1872   The Metropolitan Museum of Art in New York was opened to the public.

1878   Leo XIII was elected Roman Catholic pope.

1921   The motion picture *The Four Horsemen of the Apocalypse,* starring Rudolph Valentino, was released for the first time.

1933   The U.S. House of Representatives voted to repeal Prohibition.

1938   Anthony Eden resigned as British foreign secretary in protest against the "appeasement" policy toward Hitler of Prime Minister Neville Chamberlain.

1962   U.S. astronaut John Glenn became the first American to orbit the earth, circling it three times in less than five hours.

1965   U.S. satellite *Ranger 8* photographed and then landed on the moon.

1976   The Southeast Asia Treaty Organization was formally disbanded in ceremonies in Manila.

February 21 – Birthdays

1728   **Peter III.** Czar of Russia for a short time in 1762 before being succeeded by Catherine the Great

1794   **Antonio Lopez de Santa Anna.** Three-time president-dictator of Mexico who presided over the loss of Texas and the American Southwest to the United States

1801   **John Henry Cardinal Newman.** British Catholic churchman and man of letters, noted for the famous hymn "Lead, Kindly Light"

1821   **Charles Scribner.** American publisher who with Isaac D. Baker founded the New York publishing house of Baker and Scribner in 1846, the forerunner of Charles Scribner's Sons

1836   **Leo Delibes.** French composer known for his opera *Lakme* and his two ballets *Coppelia* and *Sylvia*

1866   **August von Wassermann.** German physician and bacteriologist known for the Wassermann test to detect veneral disease

1876   **Constantin Brancusi.** Romanian sculptor who ranks as one of the greatest sculptors of the 20th century

1895   **Carl Peter Henrik Dam.** Danish chemist and Nobelist who discovered vitamin K

1903   **Anais Nin.** French-born writer of poetic novels such as *Ladders to Fire* (1936) and *The House of Incest* (1949)

1903   **Tom Yawkey.** Owner of the Boston Red Sox baseball team for over 40 years

1907   **W.H. Auden.** English-born poet, known for his ballads, blues, limericks, sonnets, nonsense verse, and dramas, and who won the 1948 Pulitzer Prize for his poem "The Age of Anxiety"

1910   **Douglas Bader.** Britain's most famous air ace who fought in World War II with two artificial legs

1915   **Ann Sheridan.** American motion-picture and television actress and "Oomph Girl" of the 1940s

1921   **Albert Axelrod.** Professional fencer

1924   **Robert Mugabe.** First president of Zimbabwe

1925   **Sam Peckinpah.** American motion-picture and television director and screen-writer, noted for such scripts as television's long-running *Gunsmoke* and such movies as *Ride the High Country* and *The Wild Bunch*

1927   **Erma Bombeck.** American columnist, writer, and humorist

1927   **Guy Mitchell.** American singer noted for "Singing the Blues"

1927   **Hubert de Givenchy.** Influential French fashion designer who designed clothes for First Lady Jackie Kennedy and other celebrities, and who by the 1980s was one of the greatest in his field

1935   **Rue McClanahan.** American television and stage actress noted for her role in the longrunning television series, *The Golden Girls*

1936   **Barbara Jordan.** American congresswoman and political leader

1937   **Prince Harald.** Crown prince of Norway

1937   **Gary Lockwood.** American motion-picture and television actor

1937   **Ron Clarke.** Noted Australian runner and holder of 19 world records

1940   **John Lewis.** American civil rights leader and Congressman

1943   **David Geffen.** American music producer who with Steven Spielberg and Jeffrey Katzenberg created the movie studio DreamWorks SKG

1946   **Tricia Nixon Cox.** Daughter of President Richard M. Nixon

1946   **Tyne Daly.** American television actress (*Cagney and Lacey*) and daughter of actor James Daly

1947   **Olympia J. Snowe.** U.S. senator

1951   **Erik Van Dillen.** American tennis player

1955   **Kelsey Grammer.** American television actor (*Cheers* and *Frasier*)

1958   **Mary Chapin Carpenter.** American singer and songwriter

1958   **Alan Trammell.** Professional baseball player

1961   **Christopher Atkins.** American motion-picture actor

1979   **Jennifer Love Hewitt.** American motion-picture actress

February 21 – Events

1779   Captain James Cook, the great British explorer, was buried at sea, after being killed by the Hawaiian Islanders.

1807   Martin Van Buren married Hannah Hoes.

1848   John Quincy Adams collapsed on the floor of the House of Representatives, went into a coma, and died two days later.

1852   Nikolai Gogol, the great Russian writer, died in Moscow at age 42.

1853   Three dollar gold pieces were authorized by the U.S. government.

1866   Lucy B. Hobbs became the first black woman graduate of a dental school, the Ohio College of Dental Surgery in Cincinnati.

1878   The world's first telephone directory was issued, by the New Haven, Connecticut, Telephone Company. It listed 50 names.

1885   The Washington Monument was dedicated in Washington, D.C.

1904   The National Ski Association of America was founded.

1916   Germany began the World War I Battle of Verdun, which was defended by French General Henri Petain, who made the famous vow, "They shall not pass!"

1925   The *New Yorker* magazine was first published.

1947   American inventor Edwin Land first publicly demonstrated his Polaroid Land camera, which produced an instant photograph in 60 seconds.

1965   Malcolm X, U.S. Black Muslim leader, was assassinated in New York City at age 39.

1972   President Richard M. Nixon arrived in Peking for his historic talks with the Chinese Communist leaders.

1975   President Nixon's aides John D. Ehrlichman, H.R. Haldeman, and John Mitchell were sentenced to from 2½ to 8 years in prison for their parts in the Watergate cover-up.

1978   China spared the "Gang of Four," including Mao Tse-tung's widow, from execution.

February 22 – Birthdays

1403   **Charles VII.** King of France, 1422-1461, and "one of the most contemptible creatures" ever to disgrace the title of king

1440   **Ladislaus V.** King of Bohemia and Hungary

1715   **Charles N. Cochin (the Younger).** The outstanding French engraver of the 18th century

1732   **George Washington.** First U.S. president, "Father of His Country," and the greatest American in history

1778   **Rembrandt Peale.** American painter who painted hundreds of famous portraits and who was the son of the noted painter Charles Willson Peale

1785   **Jean Charles Athanese Peltier.** French physicist who discovered the Peltier effect that current at a juncture of two dissimilar metals will produce heat or cold

1788   **Arthur Schopenhauer.** Noted German philosopher noted for his main work, *The World as Will and Idea* (1819, 1844)

1805   **Sarah Flower Adams.** Writer of the poem "Nearer My God to Thee" (1841), which became famous when Lowell Mason later set it to music

1810   **Frederic Chopin.** Polish composer and pianist, and one of the great masters of piano composition

1819   **James Russell Lowell.** American poet and diplomat noted for his *Biglow Papers* and the famous poem "The Vision of Sir Launfal" (1848)

1857   **Heinrich Rudolph Hertz.** German physicist who discovered electromagnetic waves (between 1886 and 1888), and for whom the frequency unit *Hertz* (cycles per second) was named

1857   **Lord Robert Baden-Powell.** British soldier who in 1907 founded the Boy Scout movement

1868   **Ren Shields.** American composer, author, and actor, noted for songs such as "In the Good Old Summertime" and "Frankie and Johnnie"

1874   **Bill Klem.** Noted professional baseball umpire

1877   **Maurice Costello.** American stage and motion-picture actor who was one of the first stage idols to turn to the screen

1879   **Uncle Charlie Moran.** Major league baseball pitcher, catcher, and umpire, and professional football coach

1892   **David Dubinsky.** American labor leader and president of the International Ladies' Garment Workers' Union, 1932-1966

1892   **Edna St. Vincent Millay.** American poet noted for works such as "A Few Figs from Thistles" and "The Ballad of the Harp-Weaver"

1896   **Nacio Herb Brown.** American composer noted for such songs as "You Were Meant for Me," "Singin' in the Rain," and "Temptation"

1900   **Luis Buñuel.** Spanish motion-picture director with a career of some 50 years and a ranking among cinema's all-time greats

1901   **Charles Newman.** American lyricist noted for songs such as "Six Lessons from Madam La Zonga" and "Why Don't We Do This More Often?"

1904   **Peter Hurd.** American painter and illustrator whose portrait of Lyndon Johnson was said by Johnson to be the "ugliest thing I ever saw"

1906   **Leon Henderson.** American economist and educator who headed the Office of Price Administration during World War II

1907   **Robert Young.** American motion-picture and television actor who appeared in some 100 films and starred in two long-running television series, *Father Knows Best* and *Marcus Welby, M.D.*

1907   **Sheldon Leonard.** American stage, screen, and television actor

1908   **Sir John Mills.** British stage and motion-picture actor with a career of over 60 years

1908   **Romulo Betancourt.** President of Venezuela, 1958-1964

1915   **Gus Lesnivich.** Light heavyweight boxing champion, 1941-1948

1918   **Robert Pershing Wadlow.** Tallest man who ever lived, at 8 feet 11 inches

1918   **Sid Abel.** Professional hockey player

1918   **Charles O. Finley.** American financier and colorful owner in the 1970s of the Oakland A's baseball team

1921   **Jean Bedel Bokassa.** Army colonel who overthrew the government of the Central African Republic in 1966 and proclaimed himself Bokassa I, Emperor of the Central African Empire

1924   **Allen H. Neuharth.** Founder of the newspaper *USA Today*

1926   **Bunker Hunt.** American entrepreneur and son of billionaire H.L. Hunt

1929   **Ryne Duren.** Professional baseball player and drug and alcohol consultant

1929   **Marni Nixon.** American singer whose voice was dubbed in as the singing voice of Deborah Kerr in *The King and I,* Natalie Wood in *West Side Story* and Audrey Hepburn in *My Fair Lady*

1932   **Edward M. Kennedy.** U.S. senator and brother of President John F. Kennedy

1934   **Sparky Anderson.** Professional baseball manager who in 1984 became the first to manage World Series champions from each of the two major leagues

1937   **Tommy Aaron.** Professional golfer

1943   **Dick Van Arsdale.** Professional basketball player and brother of basketball player Tom Van Arsdale

1944   **Tom Van Arsdale.** Professional basketball player and brother of basketball player Dick Van Arsdale

1944   **Tom Okker.** Dutch tennis player

1944   **Jonathan Demme.** American motion-picture director noted for *Silence of the Lambs* (1991)

1949   **Niki Lauda.** Austrian racing driver known as the "Austrian Ace"

1950   **Julius "Dr. J." Erving.** Professional basketball superstar and Hall of Famer

1952   **Bill Frist.** U.S. senator and physician

1956   **John Turner.** Professional football player

1956   **Joe Lefebvre.** Professional baseball player

1964   **Gigi Fernandez.** Puerto Rican tennis player

1972   **Michael Chang.** American tennis player and first American to win the French Open (1989) since 1955

1975   **Drew Barrymore.** American actress and granddaughter of the great actor John Barrymore

February 22 – Events

1276   Innocent V was crowned Roman Catholic pope.

1630   The Massachusetts Bay colonists tasted their first popcorn on their first Thanksgiving dinner.

1819   Spain agreed to turn over Florida to the United States in exchange for a U.S. agreement to pay some $5 million to American citizens in Florida for property damages.

1847   "General Taylor never surrenders" was the American response to the Mexican demand that they surrender in the Battle of Buena Vista in the Mexican War.

1848   The February Revolution of 1848 began in Paris, forcing the abdication of French King Louis Philippe two days later.

1862   Jefferson Davis was inaugurated as regular president of the Confederacy. He had been provisional president before this.

1879   The first "five cent" store was opened, by F.W. Woolworth in Utica, New York.

1892   Oscar Wilde's play *Lady Windermere's Fan* premiered at St. James Theatre in London.

1924   Calvin Coolidge delivered the first presidential radio broadcast from the White House.

1931   One hundred women in Miami, Florida, organized a "Carrie Nation Brigade" to fight against bootleggers and gamblers.

1943   An American commercial plane carrying a company of American entertainers crashed in the Tagus River in Portugal, killing 24 people. One of the survivors was singer Jane Froman.

1973   The United States and the People's Republic of China agreed to establish liaison offices in Washington and Peking.

1980   The unranked U.S. Olympic hockey team, in a stunning upset, defeated the heavily-favored Russians, 4-3, at Lake Placid, New York.

1997   British embryologist Ian Wilmut announced the cloning of the sheep Dolly (born the previous July).

February 23 – Birthdays

1395   **Johannes Gutenberg.** German printer who invented the type mold, which made movable metallic type practical for the first time, and who used his method to print the magnificent Gutenberg Bible

1440   **Matthias Corvinus.** Powerful king of Hungary, known as Matthias I, who ruled between 1458 and 1490

1564   **Christopher Marlowe.** The first great Elizabethan writer of tragedy, noted for works such as *The Tragical History of Doctor Faustus* (The date is a guess since he was baptized three days later.)

1633   **Samuel Pepys.** English author of the most famous diary in the history of the world

1649   **John Blow.** English composer who wrote the anthem "I Was Glad When They Said" for the opening of Christopher Wren's Choir of St. Paul's Cathedral in London in 1697

1685   **George Frederick Handel.** German-English composer who wrote the famous oratorio *Messiah,* one of the most popular works in music

1726   **Sir William Chambers.** English architect noted for his design of Somerset House in London and for his part in founding the Royal Academy in 1768

1744   **Mayer Amschel Rothschild.** German banker and financier, who founded the famous House of Rothschild in the late 18th century

1787   **Emma Hart Willard.** The first American woman publicly to support higher education for women, and who wrote the famous poem "Rocked in the Cradle of the Deep" (1830)

1817   **George Frederic Watts.** English painter noted for his portraits of famous men of his time and for works such as *Sir Galahad*

1865   **Barney Dreyfuss.** American baseball owner and originator of the modern world series

1868   **W.E.B. Du Bois.** One of the most important leaders of black protest in the United States and a co-founder in 1909 of the NAACP

1880   **Roy Dikeman Chapin.** American manufacturer and co-founder with J.L. Hudson and H.E. Coffin of the Hudson Motor Car Co. (1909)

1883   **Karl Jaspers.** German philosopher and author, and leading proponent of existentialism

1904   **William L. Shirer.** American journalist and author of the epic work *The Rise and Fall of the Third Reich* (1959)

1905   **Sally Victor.** American hat designer

1913   **Jon Hall.** American motion-picture and television actor and producer

1927   **Regine Crespin.** French dramatic soprano

1929   **Elston Howard.** Professional baseball player

1938   **Sylvia Chase.** American broadcast journalist

1939   **Peter Fonda.** American motion-picture actor and director, and son of actor Henry Fonda

1940   **Jackie Smith.** Professional football player

1943   **Fred Biletnikoff.** Professional football player and Hall of Famer

1944   **Johnny Winter.** American rock and blues guitarist

1951   **Ed "Too Tall" Jones.** Professional football player

1954   **Sophie Hayden.** American stage actress

1955   **Howard Jones.** British musician, synthesizer, and singer

1958   **John Shelby.** Professional baseball player

1958   **David Sylvian.** British singer with the musical group Japan

1960   **Naruhito Hironomiya.** Crown prince of Japan

1963   **Bobby Bonilla.** Professional baseball player

1965   **Helena Sukova.** Czech tennis player

February 23 – Events

303   Roman Emperor Diocletian ordered a general persecution of the Christians.

532   Work began on the third Cathedral of Santa Sophia in Constantinople.

1505   Christopher Columbus was granted a license to ride a mule in Spain.

1723   Sir Christopher Wren, the great English architect, died in London at age 90.

1792   Sir Joshua Reynolds, the noted English painter, died in London at age 68.

1821   John Keats, the great English poet, died of tuberculosis in Rome at age 25.

1822   Boston was granted a charter to incorporate as a city.

1836   The Mexican Army under General Santa Anna began its siege of the Alamo.

1847   U.S. General Zachary Taylor defeated Mexico's General Santa Anna in the Battle of Buena Vista in the Mexican War.

1848   John Quincy Adams died of a stroke in Washington, D.C., at age 80.

1870   Mississippi was readmitted to the Union.

1905   The first Rotary Club was founded, by Paul P. Harris in Chicago.

1917   The Smith-Hughes Act was passed by Congress, setting up the Federal Board of Vocational Education.

1930   Nazi thug Horst Wessel died of blood poisoning after having been shot in a street brawl, inspiring the Nazis to make a martyr of him in their "Horst-Wessel-Lied."

1932   Franklin D. Roosevelt announced his candidacy for the Democratic presidential nomination.

1942   A Japanese submarine fired on an oil refinery near Santa Barbara, California, the only time in World War II that any state received hostile fire.

1945   The U.S. Marines planted the American flag atop Mount Suribachi in Iwo Jima. Joe Rosenthal's picture showing the action is considered the best picture of World War II.

1954   The first mass inoculations of children with the anti-polio Salk vaccine began in Pittsburgh.

1967   The 25th Amendment to the Constitution was proclaimed, providing for presidential succession and for filling a vacancy in the office of Vice President.

February 24 – Birthdays

1463   **Giovanni C. Pico della Mirandola.** Florentine Platonist philosopher whose writings influenced Sir Thomas More

1597   **Vincent Voiture.** French poet

1613   **Mattia Preti.** Italian painter

1619   **Charles Le Brun.** One of the two outstanding French craftsmen (Andre Charles Boulle was the other) employed to create the Louis XIV furniture of the post-Renaissance period.

1663   **Thomas Newcomen.** English inventor of one of the first practical steam engines in 1712

1709   **Jacques de Vaucanson.** Noted French toymaker who specialized in extraordinary lifelike creations

1766   **Samuel Wesley.** English composer and organist

1772   **William Harris Crawford.** U.S. senator, statesman, and candidate for president in 1824

1786   **Wilhelm Karl Grimm.** German writer who with his brother Jakob was noted for the famous Grimm's *Fairy Tales* (1812, 1815)

1836 **Winslow Homer.** American painter noted for paintings of the sea, such as *The Gulf Stream* (1899), and of rural American life scenes

1840 **John Philip Holland.** Irish-American inventor, who was largely responsible for the submarine

1842 **Arrigo Boito.** Italian composer, librettist, and poet, noted for works such as the opera *Mefistofele* (1868)

1852 **George Augustus Moore.** Irish author noted for works such as *Confessions of a Young Man* (1888) and *Heloise and Abelard* (1921)

1872 **John Jarvis.** British swimming champion who held 108 titles

1874 **Honus Wagner.** Hall of Fame baseball player considered by many experts to be baseball's greatest shortstop

1876 **Victor Moore.** American actor and comedian of vaudeville, the stage, and motion pictures with a 40-year career

1877 **Rudolph Ganz.** Swiss-American pianist, composer, and conductor

1880 **Sir Samuel Hoare.** English statesman

1885 **Chester W. Nimitz.** U.S. admiral and commander in chief of the American Pacific Fleet in World War II

1890 **Marjorie Main.** American stage and motion-picture actress and co-star of the *Ma and Pa Kettle* series of movies

1896 **Richard Thorpe.** American motion-picture director noted for hundreds of films in a 45-year career

1914 **Zachary Scott.** American stage, screen, and television actor

1919 **Richard "Dick" Charles Krieg.** American composer and author, noted for songs such as "Along the Navajo Trail" and "Mad About Him, Sad About Him Blues"

1921 **Abe Vigoda.** American actor noted for his role as Fish in the long-running television series *Barney Miller*

1927 **Mark Lane.** American lawyer and author

1928 **Michael Harrington.** American political activist and writer

1931 **James Abourezk.** U.S. senator

1932 **Michel Legrand.** French singer and movie composer who won an Oscar for the score of *The Summer of '42* (1971)

1932 **Zell Miller.** Governor of Georgia and U.S. senator

1935 **Renata Scotto.** American opera singer

1938 **James Farentino.** American stage, screen, and television actor

1940 **Jimmy Ellis.** World heavyweight boxing champion, 1968-1970

1942 **Joseph Lieberman.** U.S. senator

1946 **Barry Bostwick.** American stage, screen, and television actor

1947 **Edward James Olmos.** Mexican-American motion-picture and television actor

1947 **Rupert Holmes.** English-born composer, author, and recording artist, noted for writing and arranging for the Drifters, the Platters, Gene Pitney, and the Carol Burnett TV show

1952 **Sharon Walsh.** American tennis player

1955 **Eddie Johnson.** Professional basketball player

1956 **Eddie Murray.** Professional baseball player with over 500 career homeruns

1956 **Paula Zahn.** American television anchor (CBS morning show) and reporter

February 24 – Events

303 The first Roman edict for persecution of the Christians was published on the order of Emperor Diocletian.

1525 Holy Roman Emperor Charles V defeated French King Francis I in the famous Battle of Pavia (Italy), which established the superiority of firearms over infantry lance and pike.

1582 Pope Gregory XIII issued the papal bull outlining the reforms of the Gregorian Calendar, which went into effect the following October and is still in use today.

1761 American patriot James Otis, in a speech protesting English search and seizure tactics, coined the famous saying paraphrased as "A man's home is his castle."

1785 John Adams was appointed first United States minister to Great Britain.

1803 The U.S. Supreme Court issued its landmark *Marbury v. Madison* decision, ruling that the court was the final interpreter of constitutional issues.

1821 Mexico declared its independence from Spain.

1848 Louis Philippe abdicated as King of France as a result of the Paris Revolution of 1848.

1868 The U.S. House of Representatives voted 128 to 47 to impeach President Andrew Johnson.

1903 The U.S. leased Guantanamo Bay from Cuba for the site of the Guantanamo Naval Station.

1922 Henri Desire Landru, known as "Bluebeard," was executed in Versailles, France, for murdering ten of his mistresses.

1942 The Voice of America made its first broadcast.

1991 U.S.-led allied forces launched the ground war against Iraq in the Persian Gulf War.

February 25 – Birthdays

1510 **Francisco Vasquez de Coronado.** Spanish explorer of the American Southwest in 1540, whose expedition discovered the Continental Divide and the Grand Canyon

1682 **Giovanni Battista Morgagni.** Italian anatomist and pathologist, and "the father of pathologic anatomy," noted for his great book, *On the Seats and Causes of Diseases* (1761)

1707   **Carlo Goldoni.** Italian playwright noted for works such as *The Servant of Two Masters* (1745) and *The Liar* (1750)

1746   **Charles Cotesworth Pinckney.** American statesman, Revolutionary War soldier, and twice Federalist candidate for president

1778   **Jose de San Martin.** South American liberator of Argentina, Chile, and Peru

1841   **Pierre Auguste Renoir.** One of the most brilliant painters of the French Impressionist movement

1842   **Karl May.** German adventure story writer, who wrote vividly of the American West though he never laid eyes on it

1848   **Edward Henry Harriman.** American financier, one of the leading railroad magnates of the late 19th century, and father of statesman W. Averell Harriman

1866   **Benedetto Croce.** Perhaps the most distinguished Italian philosopher of the 20th century, and author of such works as *Aesthetic* (1902) and *Logic* (1905)

1871   **Oliver Samuel Campbell.** American Hall of Fame tennis player

1873   **Enrico Caruso.** Italian operatic tenor with one of the most brilliant voices in the history of music

1883   **Princess Alice.** Granddaughter of England's Queen Victoria, Countess of Athlone, and the last of the Royal Victorians

1888   **John Foster Dulles.** U.S. secretary of state under President Eisenhower

1890   **Dame Myra Hess.** English pianist noted for her playing of the works of Bach, Mozart, and Scarlatti

1895   **Bert Bell.** Professional football player, coach, and Commissioner of the National Football League

1896   **John McClellan.** U.S. senator, 1943-1977

1901   **Zeppo Marx.** American comedian and member of the Marx Brothers comedy group

1904   **Adelle Davis.** American writer and expert on nutrition

1907   **Mary Coyle Chase.** American dramatist noted for the popular play *Harvey* (1944)

1908   **Frank G. Slaughter.** American physician and author

1910   **Millicent Fenwick.** U.S. congresswoman in the 1980s

1913   **Jim Backus.** American stage, screen, and television actor, and voice of cartoon character Mr. Magoo

1916   **Ralph Baldwin.** Harness racing driver who set 11 major world records

1917   **Anthony Burgess.** English novelist noted for works such as *Clockwork Orange* (1962) and *Nothing Like the Sun* (1964)

1918   **Bobby Riggs.** American Hall of Fame tennis player and 1939 Wimbledon singles champion

1919   **Monte Irvin.** Hall of Fame baseball player

1920   **Philip Habib.** American career diplomat

1921   **Andy Pafko.** Professional baseball player

1927   **Ralph Stanley.** American bluegrass singer, songwriter, and co-founder of Stanley Brothers and Clinch Mountain Boys

1929   **Tommy Newsom.** American musician noted for his role on *The Tonight Show*

1932   **Faron Young.** American country singer

1934   **Tony Lema.** Professional golfer

1937   **Bob Schieffer.** American broadcast journalist

1937   **Tom Courtenay.** English stage and motion-picture actor

1938   **Diane Baker.** American motion-picture and television actress and director

1940   **Ron Santo.** Professional baseball player

1943   **George Harrison.** Member of The Beatles musical group

1943   **Sally Jessy Raphael.** American television talk show hostess

1944   **Karen Grassle.** American actress noted for her role in TV's *Little House on the Prairie*

1947   **Lee Evans.** Professional runner

1951   **Cesar Cedeno.** Professional baseball player

1958   **Kurt Rambis.** Professional basketball player

1959   **Mike Peters.** Welsh singer, guitarist, and harmonica player with The Alarm musical group

1963   **Paul O'Neill.** Professional baseball player

February 25 – Events

1570   Queen Elizabeth I of England was excommunicated by Pope Pius V.

1791   President George Washington met with government department heads at his home in the first U.S. cabinet meeting.

1804   Thomas Jefferson was nominated for a second term as president by his party, the Democratic-Republicans.

1820   Congressman Felix Walker from Buncombe County, N.C., in a long-winded speech about his county, caused the coining of the words *bunk* and *buncombe,* meaning nonsense.

1836   Samuel Colt obtained a U.S. patent on his famous revolver.

1870   Hiram R. Revels became the first black U.S. senator, as he was sworn in to serve out the unexpired term of Mississippi Senator Jefferson Davis.

1901   The United States Steel company was incorporated by Elbert Gary and J.P. Morgan.

1908   The north tunnels, the first tunnels built under the Hudson River in New York City, were opened to the public.

1913   The 16th Amendment to the Constitution was proclaimed, establishing the income tax.

1919   Oregon became the first state to tax gasoline.

1932   Adolf Hitler acted hastily to become a citizen of Germany in time to run for president in an election to be held some two weeks later.

1933   The *Ranger,* the first U.S. aircraft carrier built expressly for that purpose, was launched.

1948   The Communists, in a bloodless coup, seized complete control of the government of Czechoslovakia.

1956 Soviet premier Nikita Khrushchev denounced the late dictator Josef Stalin in a speech before a Communist Party congress in Moscow.

1964 Cassius Clay (Muhammad Ali) knocked out Sonny Liston in the seventh round in Miami Beach to win the heavyweight boxing championship.

1986 President Ferdinand Marcos fled the Philippines in the wake of a tainted election and pressure from the United States. Corazon Aquino succeeded him.

February 26 – Birthdays

1361 **Wenceslaus.** One of the last kings of Germany before the Hapsburgs gained control in 1438

1531 **David Chytraeus.** The last of the "Fathers of the Lutheran Church"

1802 **Victor Hugo.** Noted French writer, whose novels *The Hunchback of Notre Dame* (1831) and *Les Miserables* (1862) rank among the world's most popular fiction

1808 **Honore Daumier.** French artist and caricaturist who was imprisoned for six months for drawing a caricature of King Louis Philippe entitled Gargantua

1829 **Levi Strauss.** Bavarian-born creator of jeans, who with his brothers Jonas and Louis formed Levi Strauss and Co. (1853)

1846 **William F. "Buffalo Bill" Cody.** U.S. army scout, Indian fighter, and "Wild West Circus" owner

1852 **John Harvey Kellogg.** American physician who, with his brother W.K. Kellogg, developed grain cereal flakes (J.K. used the results to help treat patients while W.K. used them to establish the Kellogg Co.)

1861 **Ferdinand.** Bulgarian prince who in 1908 declared Bulgaria independent and made himself king

1866 **Herbert Henry Dow.** American chemist who founded the Dow Chemical Co. in 1897

1869 **Nadezhda Krupskaya.** Wife of Vladimir I. Lenin, the founder of the Russian Communist dictatorship

1877 **Rudolph Dirks.** American cartoonist and creator in 1897 of *The Katzenjammer Kids* comic strip

1878 **Emmy Destinn.** Czechoslovakian soprano

1882 **Husband E. Kimmel.** American admiral in command of the U.S. Naval fleet at Pearl Harbor when the Japanese attacked in 1941

1887 **William Frawley.** American motion-picture, stage, and television actor, noted for his role as a regular in the long-running TV series *I Love Lucy*

1887 **Grover Cleveland Alexander.** One of the greatest pitchers in baseball history, with 373 victories and 90 shutouts in a 20-year career

1890 **Chance Milton Vought.** American aeronautical engineer

1906 **Madeleine Carroll.** English stage, screen, and television actress

1914 **Robert Alda.** American stage, screen, and television actor, and father of actor Alan Alda

1915 **Preacher Roe.** Professional baseball player

1916 **Jackie Gleason.** American stage, screen, and television actor and comedian, and star of the long-running television series *The Honeymooners*

1920 **Tony Randall.** American stage, screen, and television actor and comedian

1921 **Betty Hutton.** American stage and motion-picture singer and actress, and "The Blonde Bombshell" of the 1940s

1922 **Margaret Leighton.** English stage and motion-picture actress

1928 **Fats Domino.** American rock and roll pianist and singer

1931 **Robert Novak.** Member of the Evans and Novak team of political columnists

1932 **Johnny Cash.** American country-music singer and composer

1933 **Godfrey Cambridge.** American stage, screen, and television comedian and actor

1950 **James Bertelsen.** Professional football player

1954 **Bili Sparrow.** American composer, author, and performer, noted for "Star Wars (That's the Politics)"

1954 **Ted McKnight.** Professional football player

1957 **Connie Carpenter.** American skater and cyclist and member of the International Women's Sports Hall of Fame and the U.S. Olympic Hall of Fame

1966 **Jennifer Grant.** American stage and screen actress and daughter of actors Cary Grant and Dyan Cannon

1973 **Jenny Thompson.** American Olympic swimmer who won five gold medals

February 26 – Events

1564 Christopher Marlowe, the great Elizabethan writer and contemporary of William Shakespeare, was baptized, presumably at age three days, as was the custom.

1815 Napoleon Bonaparte escaped from Elba, where he had been in exile, to return to power in France.

1848 The French Second Republic was proclaimed, after the overthrow of King Louis Philippe in the Revolution of 1848.

1855 The first public school system was established in the South, in Nashville, Tennessee.

1919 The Grand Canyon National Park in Arizona was established by Congress.

1951 James Jones' great novel *From Here to Eternity* was published in New York.

1951 The 22nd Amendment to the U.S. Constitution was ratified, limiting a president to two terms in office.

1991 The U.S. and allied ground forces liberated Kuwait in the Persian Gulf War.

February 27 – Birthdays

280   **Constantine I (The Great).** Roman emperor, A.D. 306-337, who made Christianity the religion of the empire, and in A.D. 315 built the Arch of Constantine, which is still a landmark of Rome

1691   **Edward Cave.** English printer who published *Gentleman's Magazine,* the first modern English magazine, in 1731

1744   **John Lawrence Geib.** American piano maker

1807   **Henry Wadsworth Longfellow.** The most popular American poet of the 19th century, noted for works such as "Evangeline, A Tale of Acadie," "The Song of Hiawatha," and "The Cross of Snow"

1823   **Ernest Renan.** French historian and religious scholar, noted for his *Life of Jesus* (1863)

1848   **Dame Ellen Terry.** The greatest actress on the English stage for fifty years in the late 19th and early 20th centuries

1850   **Henry Edwards Huntington.** American railway and transportation system builder, and founder of the Henry E. Huntington Library and Art Gallery in San Marino, California

1850   **Laura Elizabeth Richards.** American writer, biographer (*Florence Nightingale*), and daughter of the noted songwriter Julia Ward Howe

1878   **Manuel Ugarte.** Argentine writer who coined the term, "Colossus of the North," in reference to the United States

1886   **Hugo Black.** U.S. Supreme Court justice who served for 34 years

1888   **Lotte Lehmann.** German operatic soprano, noted for her interpretations of the music of Richard Wagner and Richard Strauss

1888   **Arthur M. Schlesinger.** American historian, teacher, and author, who became known as the dean of American historians

1891   **David Sarnoff.** American pioneer in the development of radio and television broadcasting, and president or chairman of the board of RCA from 1930 to 1970

1892   **William Demarest.** American stage, screen, and television actor who played over 100 character roles in a 50-year career

1898   **Allison Danzig.** Dean of U.S. tennis writers, who wrote for the *New York Times* for 45 years, and was the first writer to be inducted into the tennis Hall of Fame

1899   **Charles Herbert Best.** Canadian physiologist and co-discoverer in 1921 (with Sir Frederick G. Banting) of insulin for the treatment of diabetes

1902   **Gene Sarazen.** American golf immortal who in the 1920s and early 1930s won the Masters, the British Open, the U.S. Open (twice), and the PGA (three times)

1902   **John Steinbeck.** American novelist, noted for works such as *The Winter of Our Discontent, Of Mice and Men,* and one of the most famous books of the 20th century *The Grapes of Wrath*

1904   **James T. Farrell.** American writer noted for the *Studs Lonigan* trilogy (1932-1935)

1905   **Franchot Tone.** American stage, screen, and television actor

1910   **Joan Bennett.** American stage, screen, and television actress, and daughter of actor Richard Bennett and sister of actresses Constance and Barbara Bennett

1910   **Peter De Vries.** American novelist, noted for works such as *The Tunnel of Love, The Mackerel Plaza,* and *The Blood of the Lamb*

1912   **Lawrence Durrell.** English novelist noted for *The Alexandria Quartet, Justine,* (1957), *Balthazar* (1958), *Mountolive* (1959), and *Clea* (1960)

1913   **Irwin Shaw.** American playwright and novelist, noted for works such as *Bury the Dead* (1936) and *The Young Lions* (1948)

1917   **John B. Connally.** Governor of Texas, 1963-1969, and secretary of the treasury under President Nixon

1925   **Kenneth Koch.** American poet and playwright

1927   **James Leo Herlihy.** American actor, playwright, and novelist

1930   **Joanne Woodward.** American stage, screen, and television actress, who won the Academy Award in 1957 for *The Three Faces of Eve*

1932   **Elizabeth Taylor.** English-American motion-picture actress, who won the Academy Award in 1960 for *Butterfield 8* and in 1966 for *Who's Afraid of Virginia Woolf?*

1933   **Malcom Wallop.** U.S. senator

1933   **Raymond Berry.** Professional football player

1934   **Ralph Nader.** American lawyer, writer, and social crusader for public health and safety, noted for the book *Unsafe at Any Speed* (1965), which led to new safety standards for cars

1935   **Mirella Freni.** Italian operatic soprano

1937   **Jay Silvester.** Champion discus thrower

1948   **Munawar Iqbal.** Pakistani tennis player

1951   **Steve Harley.** English musician and songwriter

1961   **James Worthy.** Professional basketball player and superstar

1980   **Chelsea Clinton.** Daughter of President and Mrs. Bill Clinton

February 27 – Events

1801   The District of Columbia was placed under the jurisdiction of the U.S. Congress.

1860   Abraham Lincoln made his famous address at Cooper Union in New York, ending with "Let us have faith that right makes might, . . . and dare to do our duty as we understand it."

1883   Oscar Hammerstein, the grandfather of noted lyricist Oscar Hammerstein II, patented the first practical cigar-rolling machine.

1900   England's Labour Party was founded.

1932   The neutron was discovered by English physicist Sir James Chadwick.

1933	The Nazis burned the Reichstag building in Berlin, and, to consolidate their power, accused the Communists of the act.
1939	Great Britain and France recognized the regime of Generalissimo Francisco Franco in Spain.
1939	The U.S. Supreme Court outlawed sit-down strikes.
1942	The Battle of the Java Sea began in World War II. It ended three days later with the rout by the Japanese of the Allied fleet.
1959	The Boston Celtics scored a record 173 points in an NBA basketball game against Minneapolis.
1972	President Nixon and Chinese Premier Chou En-lai issued the Shanghai Communique at the conclusion of Nixon's visit to the People's Republic of China.
1973	Members of the American Indian Movement occupied Wounded Knee, S.D., the site of the 1890 Sioux Indian massacre, and remained there until early May.
1991	President Bush announced the cessation of offensive military action against Iraq in the Persian Gulf War. He was to declare the war over the next day.

February 28 – Birthdays

1533	**Michel Eyquem de Montaigne.** French author who wrote 107 essays and is considered by many to be the creator of the personal essay
1683	**Rene Antoine Ferchault de Reaumur.** French scientist noted for his work in metallurgy, turquoise mines and opaque glass
1797	**Mary Lyon.** American pioneer in providing higher education for women and the founder of Mount Holyoke College, which opened in 1837 as Mount Holyoke Seminary in South Hadley, Massachusetts
1820	**Sir John Tenniel.** English illustrator and cartoonist, who illustrated Lewis Carroll's *Alice's Adventures in Wonderland* (1865) and *Through the Looking-Glass* (1872)
1824	**Charles Blondin.** French tightrope walker who crossed Niagara Falls three times on a tightrope
1859	**Florian Cajori.** Swiss-American mathematician
1865	**Sir Wilfred Grenfell.** British medical missionary, known as "Grenfell of Labrador," who devoted his life to serving people in Newfoundland, Labrador, and near the Arctic Circle
1865	**Arthur Symons.** English poet and critic noted for his translations and studies of French poet Charles Baudelaire
1869	**Rida Johnson Young.** American lyricist noted for songs such as "Ah, Sweet Mystery of Life" (music by Victor Herbert)
1876	**John Alden Carpenter.** American composer
1890	**Vaslav Nijinsky.** Russian ballet dancer and the most famous male dancer of his time
1894	**Ben Hecht.** American novelist, playwright, screenwriter, and director, noted for works such as *The Front Page* (with Charles MacArthur) and some 70 screenplays

1896	**Philip Showalter Hench.** American physicist who received the Nobel Prize for his discovery of cortisone
1901	**Linus Pauling.** American chemist who was the only person besides Marie Curie to win two Nobel Prizes (the 1954 prize in chemistry and the 1962 peace prize)
1905	**Audrey Wood.** Noted American literary agent who represented such notables as Tennessee Williams, William Inge and Carson McCullers
1906	**Bugsy Siegel.** Well-known American racketeer of the 1940s
1907	**Milton Caniff.** American comic strip artist who created *Terry and the Pirates* and *Steve Canyon*
1908	**Dee Brown.** American author and historian noted for *Bury My Heart At Wounded Knee* (1971)
1909	**Stephen Spender.** English poet and writer noted for "The Express" and the autobiography *World Within World* (1951)
1910	**Josef Myrow.** Russian-born composer and pianist, noted for songs such as "On the Boardwalk in Atlantic City," "You Make Me Feel So Young," and "Marianne"
1910	**Vincente Minnelli.** American motion-picture director and father of actress Liza Minnelli, noted for directing films such as *An American in Paris,* which won the 1951 best picture Academy Award
1915	**Zero Mostel.** American stage and motion-picture actor who won three Tony Awards in four years (1961, 1963, and 1964)
1923	**Charles Durning.** American stage and motion-picture actor
1926	**Svetlana Alliluyeva.** Daughter of Russian dictator Joseph Stalin
1930	**Frank Malzone.** Professional baseball player
1931	**Dean Edwards Smith.** Hall of Fame basketball coach
1931	**Gavin MacLeod.** American television actor noted for his role as the captain in the long-running series *The Love Boat*
1939	**Tommy Tune.** American director and choreographer
1939	**John Fahey.** American blues guitarist
1940	**Mario Andretti.** Italian-American automobile racing driver who won the 1969 Indianapolis 500
1941	**Alice May Brock.** American author and restaurateur about whom Arlo Guthrie's song "Alice's Restaurant" was written
1942	**Frank Bonner.** American television actor (*WKRP in Cincinnati*)
1942	**Brian Jones.** British guitarist with The Rolling Stones musical group
1945	**Bubba Smith.** Professional football player
1948	**Bernadette Peters.** American motion-picture and television actress
1949	**Evan Williams.** Professional golfer
1951	**Gustave Theoni.** Professional skier
1952	**Fred Dean.** Professional football player
1953	**Roland Harper.** Professional football player

1955   **John Grisham.** American lawyer and novelist noted for works such as *A Time to Kill, The Pelican Brief* and *The Firm*
1956   **Adrian Dantley.** Professional basketball player
1957   **John Turturro.** American motion-picture actor

February 28 – Events

590   Gregory I (the Great) became Roman Catholic pope.
1632   Portland, Maine, was first settled.
1827   The Baltimore and Ohio Railroad had its beginnings in a charter granted to build a 380-mile railroad to the West to compete with the Erie Canal.
1844   The U.S. secretary of state and secretary of the Navy were killed when a new "Peacemaker" cannon exploded on the U.S.S. *Princeton.* President John Tyler escaped unharmed.
1845   The U.S. House and Senate passed a joint resolution inviting Texas to join the Union. Her acceptance started the Mexican War later in the year.
1849   The first forty-niners (the gold-rushers of 1849) reached San Francisco aboard the steamer *California.*
1854   Antislavery Whigs passed a resolution at Ripon, Wisconsin, calling for a new party—the Republican Party—if Congress passed the Kansas-Nebraska Bill.
1916   Henry James, the great American novelist, died in London at age 72.
1942   Japanese troops landed on Java in World War II.
1952   Vincent Massey was sworn in as the first Canadian-born governor-general of Canada.
1971   Jack Nicklaus won the PGA Tournament, making him the first golfer to win the world's four major titles—the U.S. Open, the British Open, the Masters, and the PGA—twice.
1972   President Richard Nixon returned to the United States and described his visit to China as the trip that "changed the world."
1974   The United States and Egypt re-established diplomatic relations after a seven-year break.
1991   The Gulf War ended as President Bush ordered a cease fire.
1993   A gun battle erupted at a compound near Waco, TX, when government agents tried to serve warrants on the so-called Branch Davidians. Four agents and six Davidians were killed as a 51-day standoff began.

February 29 – Birthdays

1468   **Paul III.** Roman Catholic pope, 1534-1549, who summoned the Council of Trent, restored the Inquisition, excommunicated Henry VIII, and made Michelangelo chief architect of the Vatican
1712   **Marquis de Montcalm.** French general who was killed in the Battle of Quebec in the French and Indian War

1736   **Ann Lee.** English religious leader who founded the Society of Shakers in America
1756   **Christian F. Hansen.** Noted Danish architect
1792   **Gioacchino Rossini.** Italian operatic composer, noted for *The Barber of Seville* (1816), perhaps the greatest farce opera ever written, and *William Tell* (1829), with its famous overture
1808   **Charles Pritchard.** Noted British astronomer
1860   **Herman Hollerith.** American inventor who pioneered the processing of data in the U.S. census office by the use of punched cards, which were the forerunners of computer cards
1864   **Jan Svatopluk Macher.** Czechoslovakian poet
1900   **Jean Negulesco.** Rumanian-born motion-picture director noted for films such as *Johnny Belinda* (1948) and *Three Coins in the Fountain* (1954)
1904   **Pepper Martin.** Professional baseball player and star of the 1934 St. Louis Cardinals' "Gas House Gang"
1904   **Jimmy Dorsey.** American bandleader of the Big Band Era of the 1930s and 1940s, and brother of bandleader Tommy Dorsey
1908   **Balthus.** French painter noted for works such as *The Children* (owned by his friend Picasso), *Getting Up* (1975-1978), *The Painter and His Model* (1980-1981), and *The Cat with Mirror III* (1989-1994)
1920   **Michele Morgan.** The most popular movie actress in France before World War II
1920   **Arthur Franz.** American stage, screen, and television actor
1920   **Howard Nemerov.** American poet and writer who won the Pulitzer Prize for poetry in 1978 for *The Collected Poems of Howard Nemerov*
1924   **Al Rosen.** Professional baseball player and executive
1924   **William Dodd Hathaway.** U.S. senator
1928   **Joss Ackland.** English motion-picture actor
1936   **Jack Lousma.** American astronaut
1944   **Dennis Farina.** American motion-picture and television actor
1948   **Willi Smith.** American fashion designer
1952   **Reyno Seegers.** South African tennis player
1956   **Mike Compton.** American teacher and mandolin player of bluegrass music

February 29 – Events

1288   A law was passed in Scotland making it legal for women to propose to men.
1504   Columbus used the total eclipse of the moon, which he knew from his almanac would occur, to scare the Jamaica natives into supplying him with food on his fourth voyage to America.
1872   England's Queen Victoria narrowly missed death at the hands of a would-be assassin, Albert O'Connor, an 18-year-old revolutionary.
1940   *Gone With the Wind* won eight Oscars at the Academy Awards ceremony, including Best Picture.

1944 Allied soldiers landed in the Admiralty Islands in World War II.

1956 President Dwight D. Eisenhower announced his candidacy for reelection.

1956 The great blizzard of 1956 in Western Europe finally ended. It had lasted the entire month of February and resulted in 1,000 deaths.

1960 Agadir, Morocco, was hit by a major earthquake, a tidal wave, and fire, resulting in 12,000 deaths.

3

March

March, the third month of the year, was originally the first month of the ancient Roman calendar. Its Latin name was *Martius,* chosen to honor Mars, the Roman god of war. March was the first month of the year until 45 B.C., when Caesar made it the third month of his Julian Calendar. The running battle continued, however, as to which month, January or March, would be first, until the issue was finally settled by the Gregorian Calendar in 1582. Except for a brief period when Romulus issued the first Roman calendar, March has always had 31 days.

St. Patrick's Day is celebrated on March 17, and four American presidents—James Madison, Andrew Jackson, John Tyler, and Grover Cleveland—were born in March. One of the most noteworthy events in world history, the assassination of Caesar, also occurred in the month (on the Ides of March—March 15—in 44 B.C.).

The March birthstones are the bloodstone and the aquamarine, and the special flower is the jonquil.

March 1 – Birthdays

1812 **Augustus Welby Northmore Pugin.** English architect, designer, author, and noted participant in the English Roman Catholic and Gothic revivals

1837 **William Dean Howells.** American novelist, editor, and critic, noted for works such as *The Rise of Silas Lapham* (1885) and *Criticism and Fiction* (1891)

1848 **Augustus Saint-Gaudens.** Foremost American sculptor of the late 19th century, noted for his statue of Admiral David Farragut (1880) and for the lifelike qualities of his work in general

1880 **Lytton Strachey.** English biographer, essayist, and critic, noted for works such as *Eminent Victorians* (1918) and *Queen Victoria* (1921)

1880 **Julian Myrick.** American Hall of Fame tennis player and leader in the development of the game

1883 **Thomas Shelvin.** Yale end who ranked second to Jim Thorpe in 1926 as the greatest college football player of all time

1886 **Oskar Kokoschka.** Austrian painter noted for works such as *The Tempest* and *View of the Thames*

1904 **Glenn Miller.** One of the most notable of the American bandleaders of the Big Band Era of the 1930s and 1940s

1909 **David Niven.** English-American motion-picture and television actor and author, who won an Academy Award in 1958 for *Separate Tables*

1914 **Sidney Lippman.** American composer, author, and publisher, noted for songs such as "A-You're Adorable" and "My Sugar Is So Refined"

1917 **Robert Lowell.** A leading American poet of the 20th century, who won the 1947 Pulitzer Prize for "Lord Weary's Castle"

1917 **Dinah Shore.** American radio, motion-picture, and television singer and actress

1919 **Harry Caray.** American baseball telecaster noted for his coverage of the St. Louis Cardinals and the Chicago Cubs

1920 **Max Bentley.** Professional hockey player and Hall of Famer

1921 **Richard Wilbur.** American poet whose volume *Things of This World* won the 1957 Pulitzer Prize for poetry

1921 **Terence Cardinal Cooke.** Archbishop of New York who was appointed a cardinal of the Roman Catholic Church in 1969

1922 **Yitzhak Rabin.** Prime Minister of Israel who was assassinated Nov. 4, 1995 by a right-wing Israeli extremist

1924 **Donald K. Slayton.** U.S. astronaut

1926 **Pete Rozelle.** Commissioner of the National Football League

1926 **Robert Clary.** American television actor noted for the longrunning series *Hogan's Heroes*

1927 **Harry Belafonte.** American stage, screen, and television singer and actor

1934 **Jean-Michel Folon.** Belgian painter and illustrator

1935 **Robert Conrad.** American motion-picture and television actor

1935 **Judith Rossner.** American novelist, noted for works such as *Looking for Mr. Goodbar*

1942 **Louis Gerstner.** American businessman and CEO of IBM

1942	**Joan Hackett.** American motion-picture and television actress
1944	**John Breaux.** U.S. senator
1945	**Roger Daltrey.** British singer with The Who musical group
1945	**Dirk Benedict.** American television actor (*The A-Team*)
1950	**Riley Odoms.** Professional football player
1952	**Brian Winters.** Professional basketball player
1953	**Jose Higueras.** Spanish tennis player
1953	**Thomas "Hollywood" Henderson.** Professional football player
1954	**Ron Howard.** American television and motion-picture actor and director
1954	**Catherine Bach.** American television actress noted for her role in the long-running TV series *The Dukes of Hazzard*
1956	**Timothy Daly.** American stage, screen, and television actor, son of actor James Daly and brother of actress Tyne Daly
1957	**Johnny Ray.** Professional baseball player
1958	**Nik Kershaw.** British singer and guitarist
1961	**Mike Rozier.** Professional football player
1973	**Chris Webber.** Professional basketball player

March 1 – Events

1638	The first Swedish settlers, and the first to build log cabins in America, arrived at the present site of Wilmington, Delaware.
1781	The Articles of Confederation became effective as the governing documents of the United States as Maryland became the 13th state to sign them.
1790	The first U.S. Census was authorized by Congress.
1803	Ohio was admitted to the Union as the 17th state.
1845	President John Tyler signed a joint House and Senate resolution admitting Texas to the Union. Texas formally joined in December, 1845.
1864	Rebecca Lee became the first black woman to receive a medical degree, from the New England Female Medical College in Boston.
1867	Nebraska was admitted to the Union as the 37th state.
1872	Yellowstone became America's first national park by an act of Congress setting aside a two million acre tract of wilderness in the Wyoming Territory.
1913	The United States income tax law took effect.
1932	Colonel Charles A. Lindberghs' baby was kidnapped from his bed in the Lindbergh's New Jersey home. He was later found dead.
1949	The great heavyweight boxer Joe Louis announced his retirement from the ring after an all-time record of over 11 years as champion.
1951	The 22nd Amendment to the U.S. Constitution was proclaimed, limiting a president to two terms in office.
1954	The United States detonated its first deliverable megaton-class hydrogen bomb, the Bravo.

1961	The Peace Corps was established by President John Kennedy.
1962	The first K-Mart store opened, in Garden City, Michigan.
1974	The Watergate Grand Jury indicted seven of President Nixon's presidential aides, and named Nixon himself as an unindicted co-conspirator.

March 2 – Birthdays

1316	**Robert II.** King of Scotland who succeeded Robert Bruce's son David II
1545	**Sir Thomas Bodley.** English diplomat who rebuilt the Oxford University library (now known as the Bodleian Library) after it was destroyed by King Edward VI in 1550
1578	**George Sandys.** English traveler, poet, and colonizer
1769	**De Witt Clinton.** Governor of New York who promoted the building of the Erie Canal
1793	**Sam Houston.** American statesman who played a leading role in winning the independence of Texas from Mexico
1810	**Leo XIII.** Roman Catholic pope, 1878-1903, best known for his famous encyclical *Rerum Novarum,* which upheld the rights of the working class
1824	**Bedrich Smetana.** Bohemian composer noted for works such as *The Bartered Bride* (1866) and *My Country,* which contains his famous work "The Moldau"
1829	**Carl Shurz.** American statesman of the post-Civil War era
1862	**John Jay Chapman.** American writer
1867	**Homer C. Davenport.** American political cartoonist of the Theodore Roosevelt era
1876	**Pius XII.** Roman Catholic pope, 1939-1958
1897	**Max Lincoln Schuster.** American publisher who with Richard Leo Simon founded the publishing house of Simon and Schuster in 1924
1900	**Kurt Weill.** German composer of music for the stage and motion-picture scores, such as *Lady in the Dark* and *One Touch of Venus*
1902	**Edward U. Condon.** American physicist noted for his application of new quantum theories to radioactive processes
1904	**Dr. Seuss (Theodor Seuss Geisel).** Noted American author of children's books, such as *The Cat in the Hat, Green Eggs and Ham,* and *How the Grinch Stole Christmas*
1909	**Mel Ott.** Hall of Fame baseball player and first National Leaguer to hit over 500 career home runs
1913	**Mort Cooper.** Professional baseball player and member of the brother battery, Mort and Walker Cooper
1917	**Desi Arnaz.** American motion-picture and television actor and musician, who with his wife Lucille Ball formed Desilu Productions
1917	**Jim Konstanty.** Professional baseball player

1919 **Jennifer Jones.** American motion-picture actress who won the 1943 Academy Award for best actress in *The Song of Bernadette*

1923 **Doc Watson.** American country music entertainer and guitarist

1927 **John Brademas.** U.S. congressman, 1959-1981

1931 **Mikhail S. Gorbachev.** General secretary of the Russian Communist Party and leader of the Soviet government, who succeeded Konstantin Chernenko in 1985

1931 **Tom Wolfe.** American author noted for works such as *The Bonfire of the Vanities* (1987)

1934 **Howard "Hopalong" Cassady.** Heisman Trophy winner and noted professional football player

1942 **John Irving.** American novelist noted for works such as *The World According to Garp* (1978) and *A Prayer for Owen Meany* (1989)

1943 **Peter Straub.** American author of horror novels such as *Ghost Story* (1979)

1944 **Lou Reed.** American singer, songwriter, guitarist and member of Velvet Underground

1950 **Karen Carpenter.** American singer of The Carpenters brother and sister duo

1950 **John Reaves.** Professional football player

1952 **Laraine Newman.** American TV actress noted for her work on *Saturday Night Live*

1953 **Russell Feingold.** U.S. senator

1954 **Pete Johnson.** Professional football player

1957 **Earnest Gray.** Professional football player

1958 **Kevin Curren.** American tennis player

1962 **Jon Bon Jovi.** American rock singer

March 2 – Events

1415 Pope John XXIII (the antipope) abdicated under pressure from the Council of Constance.

1791 John Wesley, the founder of the Methodist Church, died in London at age 87.

1836 Texas declared its independence from Mexico.

1867 Russian composer Peter Tchaikovsky made his first appearance as a conductor, in St. Petersburg.

1877 The disputed presidential election of 1876 was decided by a commission, two days before inauguration day. The vote was 8-7 along party lines for Republican Rutherford B. Hayes.

1917 Puerto Ricans became citizens of the U.S. by the second Organic Act, or Jones Act.

1923 *Time* magazine was first published, in New York by Henry Luce and Briton Hadden.

1930 D.H. Lawrence, the noted English novelist, died in Vence, France, at age 44.

1939 Pius XII was elected Roman Catholic pope.

1949 The U.S. superfortress *Lucky Lady II* completed the first nonstop round-the-world flight in 94 hours, 1 minute.

1951 East beat West 111-94 in the first NBA All-Star Game.

1962 Superstar Wilt Chamberlain made a record 100 points in an NBA basketball game between Philadelphia and New York at Hershey, Pennsylvania.

1969 The Concorde, the supersonic transport developed by France and England, made its first test flight.

1972 The U.S. launched *Pioneer 10* on an unmanned flight that will take it past the planet Jupiter and then out of the solar system, where it will travel for 2 million years.

1972 American jockey Willie Shoemaker rode his 555th lifetime winner, breaking Eddie Arcaro's record.

March 3 – Birthdays

1549 **Henric Laurenszoon Spieghel.** Dutch poet

1606 **Edmund Waller.** English poet best known for "Go, Lovely Rose" (1655)

1652 **Thomas Otway.** English playwright best known for *Venice Preserved, or A Plot Discovered* (1682)

1756 **William Godwin.** English philosopher and writer, who wrote the influential book *Political Justice* (1793), and who was the father of Mary Godwin Shelley, the wife of the poet Percy B. Shelley

1793 **Charles William Macready.** English actor, stage manager, and diarist

1831 **George Mortimer Pullman.** American inventor and business who popularized the Pullman sleeping car

1845 **Georg Cantor.** German mathematician and father of set theory

1847 **Alexander Graham Bell.** American scientist and inventor noted for the invention of the telephone (in 1875)

1860 **John M. "Monte" Ward.** Hall of Fame baseball pitcher and manager, who pitched the second perfect game (no one reached base) in baseball history (in 1880)

1869 **Sir Henry Wood.** British composer and conductor

1872 **Willie Keeler.** Hall of Fame baseball player whose philosophy was "Hit 'em where they ain't," and who hit .432 in 1897

1873 **William Green.** American labor leader who succeeded William Gompers as president of the American Federation of Labor in 1924 and held that position until his death in 1952

1878 **Edward Thomas.** Welsh poet and novelist, noted for works such as *The Happy-Go-Lucky Morgans* (1913)

1884 **Fontaine Fox.** American cartoonist who created *Toonerville Folks,* with its famous Toonerville trolley, and drew the strip for 40 years until he retired himself and it in 1955

1884 **Sir Hugh Walpole.** One of the most popular British novelists of the early 20th century, best known for the four novels *The Herries Chronicles* (1930-1933)

1895 **Matthew B. Ridgway.** American general who succeeded General Douglas MacArthur as commanding general of the U.N. forces in the Korean War

1898	**Emil Artin.** Noted Austrian-American mathematician
1900	**Edna Best.** English-born American stage actress
1902	**Isabel Bishop.** American artist
1903	**Adrian.** American costume designer
1911	**Jean Harlow.** American motion-picture superstar and sex symbol of the 1930s
1920	**Julius Boros.** Professional golfer who won the U.S. Open in 1952 and 1963
1920	**Ronald Searle.** English cartoonist and writer, who created the appalling girls' school, St. Trinian's
1921	**Diana Barrymore.** American stage and motion-picture actress, and daughter of the noted actor John Barrymore
1927	**John McLaughlin.** American priest, TV host (*The McLaughlin Group*), and special assistant to Presidents Nixon and Ford
1928	**Dave Dudley.** American musician and songwriter, noted for "Six Days on the Road"
1933	**Lee Radziwell.** American interior decorator and sister of Jackie Kennedy Onassis
1945	**George Miller.** Australian motion-picture director noted for works such as *Lorenzo's Oil* (1992)
1947	**Dennis Shaw.** Professional football player
1950	**Ed Marinaro.** Professional football player and television actor noted for his role in *Hill Street Blues*
1962	**Jackie Joyner-Kersee.** American champion jumper at the 1988 Olympics
1962	**Herschel Walker.** Professional football player and superstar

March 3 – Events

1493	Christopher Columbus, on board the *Nina,* reached Lisbon on his return from the first voyage to America.
1820	The U.S. Congress passed the Missouri Compromise, admitting Maine to the Union as a free state and allowing Missouri to form a state constitution.
1845	Florida was admitted to the Union as the 27th state.
1849	The Department of the Interior was established.
1861	Czar Alexander II emancipated the serfs in Russia. (This was February 19, by the Old Style date then in effect.)
1863	The first draft law in U.S. history was passed by Congress.
1875	George Bizet's famous opera *Carmen* premiered at the Opera-Comique in Paris.
1887	Anne Sullivan began her job of teacher of the blind and deaf six-year-old Helen Keller.
1915	D.W. Griffith's *The Birth of a Nation,* one of the world's greatest silent movies, had its world premiere under that name in New York. It had previously premiered under the name *The Clansman* in Los Angeles.
1918	The Bolsheviks of Russia signed the Treaty of Brest-Litovsk with Germany, in which Russia agreed to withdraw from World War I.

1931	"The Star-Spangled Banner" was officially designated by Congress as the national anthem of the United States.
1934	John Dillinger, the notorious American criminal, escaped from the Crown Point Prison in Indiana, using a fake pistol he had carved out of wood and colored with shoe polish.
1974	Commercial aviation's worst air crash in history occurred as 346 people were killed in the crash of a Turkish DC-10 jumbo jet in a forest near Paris.
1978	Prime Minister Ian D. Smith of Rhodesia and three black leaders signed an agreement to transfer power to Rhodesia's black majority by December 31, 1978.

March 4 – Birthdays

1394	**Prince Henry the Navigator.** Portuguese nobleman who was the leading promoter of exploration and the study of geography in the 15th century
1678	**Antonio Vivaldi.** Italian violin virtuoso and composer who wrote nearly 50 operas
1748	**Count Casimir Pulaski.** Polish soldier who fought and was killed in the service of the American colonies in the Revolutionary War
1756	**Sir Henry Raeburn.** Perhaps the most famous Scottish painter of all time, who was known for works such as the famous *Boy with Rabbit*
1826	**John Buford.** Northern Civil War general
1877	**Garrett Augustus Morgan.** American inventor known for the first effective gas mask and the automatic traffic light
1888	**Knute Rockne.** One of the greatest football coaches of all time, who with Notre Dame, 1918-1931, won 105 games and lost 12, and made the forward pass an integral part of the game
1891	**Dazzy Vance.** Hall of Fame baseball pitcher who led the National League in strikeouts for seven straight years
1897	**Lefty O'Doul.** Professional baseball player and manager who had a lifetime batting average of .349
1901	**Charles H. Goren.** One of the foremost American bridge experts and columnists of the 20th century
1904	**George Gamow.** Russian-American physicist and author, noted for works such as *The Birth of the Sun* (1940), *One, Two, Three...Infinity* (1947), and *A Planet Called Earth* (1963)
1906	**Phil Davis.** American cartoonist who with Lee Falk created the comic strip *Mandrake the Magician*
1913	**John Garfield.** American stage and motion-picture actor
1918	**Margaret Osborne DuPont.** American tennis and superstar of the 1940s
1921	**Joan Greenwood.** British stage and motion-picture actress
1924	**Kenneth O'Donnell.** American government official and aide to President Kennedy
1927	**Dick Savitt.** American tennis player and 1951 Wimbledon singles champion

1936 **Jim Clark.** Scottish racing car driver and superstar, who won the Indianapolis 500 in 1965 and the Grand Prix in 1963 and 1965

1939 **Barbara McNair.** American singer and actress

1939 **Joanne Gunderson Carner.** Professional golfer

1939 **Paula Prentiss.** American motion-picture and television actress

1944 **Mary Wilson.** American musician with The Supremes musical group

1948 **Chris Squire.** American rock musician

1953 **Kay Lenz.** American motion-picture and television actress

1954 **Catherine O'Hara.** Canadian stage, screen and television actress

1954 **Barbara Downs.** American tennis player

1954 **Annette Coe.** English tennis player

1968 **Patsy Kensit.** English television and motion-picture actress who made the transition from child star to adult roles

March 4 – Events

1461 King Henry VI of England was deposed by the Yorkists. He ruled again briefly ten years later before he was murdered.

1681 William Penn was granted a charter by King Charles II to found the colony of Pennsylvania.

1789 The United States Constitution went into effect as the first Congress met in New York City.

1791 Vermont was admitted to the Union as the 14th state.

1793 Washington became the first president to be inaugurated on March 4, the original inauguration date. The date was moved to January 20 by the 20th Amendment beginning in 1937.

1801 Thomas Jefferson became the first president to be inaugurated in Washington, D.C.

1829 The mob at Andrew Jackson's inauguration broke White House furniture and China before being induced to leave by punch served on the White House lawn.

1837 Chicago, with a population of 4,000, was incorporated as a city.

1865 Abraham Lincoln, at his second inaugural, pleaded for national unity "With malice toward none, with charity for all."

1902 The American Automobile Association was founded.

1917 Jeannette Rankin of Montana, the first woman to be elected to the House of Representatives, took her seat as a member of Congress.

1933 Franklin D. Roosevelt, at his first inaugural, said, "The only thing we have to fear is fear itself."

1946 The comic strip *Rip Kirby,* by Alex Raymond, first appeared.

1952 Ronald Reagan married movie actress Nancy Davis.

1968 Joe Frazier knocked out Buster Mathis in the 11th round in New York to become in several states the heavyweight champion. (Other states recognized Jimmy Ellis.)

1974 British Prime Minister Edward Heath resigned and was succeeded by Labour Party leader Harold Wilson.

1976 John Pezzin made a record 33 consecutive strikes in a bowling match at Toledo, Ohio.

March 5 – Birthdays

1324 **David II.** King of Scotland in 1329, and son of Scotland's great king, Robert Bruce

1326 **Louis I (The Great).** King of Hungary, 1343-1370

1512 **Gerhardus Mercator.** The greatest map maker of the 16th century and inventor of the Mercator projection

1574 **William Oughtred.** English mathematician who invented the slide rule and introduced the symbol "X" for multiplication

1656 **Antoine de la Mothe Cadillac.** French soldier and explorer of North America, who in 1701 founded Detroit and in 1711 was governor of Louisiana

1696 **Giovanni Battista Tiepolo.** Italian painter of the Venetian group, noted for works such as *The Meeting of Antony and Cleopatra*

1817 **Sir Austen Henry Layard.** English archaeologist noted for excavations at Nimrod and Kiyunik in Iraq which revealed the remains of the palaces of the Assyrian kings of Nineveh

1824 **James Merritt Ives.** Noted American lithographer who with Nathaniel Currier published the famous Currier and Ives color pictures

1853 **Howard Pyle.** American painter and illustrator, noted for works such as *The Merry Adventures of Robin Hood* (1883) and *The Story of King Arthur and His Knights* (1903)

1860 **Sam Thompson.** Hall of Fame baseball player with a .331 lifetime batting average

1870 **Frank Norris.** American novelist noted for works such as *McTeague* (1899) and *The Octopus* (1901)

1876 **Elisabeth Moore.** Hall of Fame tennis player who played in the last five-set final for women in the U.S. championships (1901)

1882 **Egbert Anson Van Alstyne.** American composer and pianist, noted for songs such as "In the Shade of the Old Apple Tree," "Pretty Baby," and "Drifting and Dreaming"

1887 **Heitor Villa-Lobos.** Brazilian composer, conductor, and educator, noted for the forms *Bachiana Brasiliera* and *Choros* in which he wrote his works

1891 **Daniel R. Fitzpatrick.** American political cartoonist who won the Pulitzer Prize for cartooning in 1926

1891 **Chic Johnson.** American comic actor who with Ole Olsen formed the Olsen and Johnson comedy act in vaudeville and the movies

1903 **Irving Kahal.** American lyricist, noted for songs such as "Let a Smile Be Your Umbrella," "Wedding Bells Are Breaking Up That Old Gang of Mine," and "The Night Is Young and You're So Beautiful"

1908 **Rex Harrison.** English stage and motion-picture actor who won the 1964 Academy Award for *My Fair Lady*

1918 **Paul Christman.** Hall of Fame football player

1921 **Elmer Valo.** Professional baseball player

1927 **Jack Cassidy.** American stage, screen, and television actor, singer, and dancer

1929 **J.B. Lenoir.** American blues singer

1930 **Loren Maazel.** Musical prodigy and conductor

1930 **Del Crandall.** Professional baseball player

1931 **Barry Tuckwell.** The world's premier horn player

1935 **Mal Anderson.** Australian tennis superstar

1936 **Dean Stockwell.** American stage, screen, and television actor who made the transition from child star to adult leading man

1937 **Olusegun Obasanjo.** Head of Nigeria's military government in the 1970s

1938 **Fred Williamson.** Professional football player and actor

1939 **Samantha Eggar.** English motion-picture actress

1945 **Randy Matson.** American shot putter who set the world's record of 71 feet 5½ inches for a 16-pound shot put in 1967

1946 **Rocky Bleir.** Professional football player

1947 **Kent Tekulve.** Professional baseball player

1950 **Eugene Fordor.** American concert violinist

1958 **Andy Gibb.** Australian singer and teenage idol

March 5 – Events

493 German barbarian leader Odovacar (Odoacer), who had ended the Western Roman Empire in A.D. 476, was executed at age 59 by the Ostrogoths.

1625 Charles I succeeded to the English throne upon the death of his father, James I.

1770 The Boston Massacre occurred, in which British troops fired into a crowd on King's Street, leaving five people dead.

1821 President James Monroe was inaugurated for his second term. (The date was moved because March 4 fell on a Sunday.)

1868 The U.S. Senate was organized into a Court of Impeachment to hear the charges against President Andrew Johnson.

1900 The Hall of Fame of Great Americans was established at New York University by Henry Mitchell MacCracken, a former chancellor of the university.

1933 The Nazis won 44% of the popular vote and 52% of the Reichstag seats in the last "free" election in Germany until after World War II.

1945 Marshal Tito became absolute ruler of Yugoslavia.

1946 Winston Churchill, in a speech at Fulton, Missouri, originated the term "Iron Curtain."

1953 Soviet dictator Joseph Stalin died in Moscow at age 73.

1960 Elvis Presley, the rock and roll idol, was released from the U.S. Army.

1963 Country singer Patsy Cline was killed in a plane crash along with fellow performers "Cowboy" Copas and "Hawkshaw" Hawkins.

1979 U.S. space vehicle *Voyager I* came within 172,000 miles of Jupiter and sent back spectacular photographs to the earth.

March 6 – Birthdays

1405 **John II.** King of Castile, 1406-1454

1475 **Michelangelo (Buonarroti).** Great leader of the Italian Renaissance and one of the most famous artists in history

1619 **Savinien de Cyrano de Bergerac.** French author and soldier, noted for his skill in sword fighting and for his long nose

1806 **Elizabeth Barrett Browning.** Wife of English poet Robert Browning and poet in her own right, best known for "Sonnets from the Portuguese" (1850)

1831 **Philip H. Sheridan.** Union cavalry general in the Civil War who fought at Chickamauga, the Battle of Chattanooga, and the Shenandoah Valley

1870 **Oscar Strauss.** Austrian composer best known for *The Chocolate Soldier* and *The Waltz Dream*

1882 **Guy Kibbee.** American stage and motion-picture actor

1884 **Molla Bjurstedt Mallory.** Norwegian-American Hall of Fame tennis player and eight-time U.S. Open champion

1885 **Ring Lardner.** American sports reporter and author of humorous short stories, such as *Alibi Ike* and *You Know Me Al*

1892 **Clark Daniel Shaughnessy.** American football coach who revived the T formation

1896 **Jack Stern.** American composer and author, noted for songs such as "Too Beautiful for Words," "When You're In Love," and "Remember Pearl Harbor"

1897 **John D. MacArthur.** Noted American billionaire

1898 **Jay C. Flippen.** American motion-picture and stage actor

1899 **Richard Leo Simon.** American publisher who with Max Lincoln Schuster founded the publishing house of Simon and Schuster in 1924

1900 **Lefty Grove.** Hall of Fame baseball pitcher who won 300 career games

1905 **Bob Wills.** American bandleader, fiddler, and composer, noted for songs such as "San Antonio Rose," "Take Me Back to Tulsa," and "Time Changes Everything"

1906 **Lou Costello.** American actor and member of the famed Abbott and Costello comedy team

1914 **Rochelle Hudson.** American motion-picture actress in over 70 films

1923	**Ed McMahon.** American television performer and sidekick of Johnny Carson on the *Tonight Show*
1924	**Sarah Caldwell.** American conductor and first woman to conduct a major symphony orchestra
1924	**William H. Webster.** Director of the F.B.I. under Presidents Carter and Reagan, and Director of the C.I.A. under President Reagan
1926	**Alan Greenspan.** American economist, advisor to Presidents Nixon and Ford, and Chairman of the Board of Governors of the Federal Reserve System
1927	**L. Gordon Cooper Jr.** One of the original team of seven U.S. astronauts and participant in the Gemini 5 mission in 1965
1937	**Valentina Vladimirovna Tereshkova.** Russian cosmonaut and first woman to travel in space (1963)
1941	**Willie Stargell.** Professional baseball superstar and Hall of Famer
1944	**Dame Kiri Te Kanawa.** English-New Zealand opera singer
1945	**Rob Reiner.** American actor, son of actor Carl Reiner, and one of the stars of the long-running television comedy *All in the Family*
1945	**Robert Trumpy Jr.** Professional football player
1948	**Stephen Schwartz.** American composer-lyricist, noted for *Godspell*
1952	**Jimmy Allen.** Professional football player
1957	**Vagas Ferguson.** Professional football player
1959	**Tom Arnold.** American comedian and actor
1972	**Shaquille O'Neal.** Professional basketball player and superstar

March 6 – Events

1521	Ferdinand Magellan landed on Guam in his round-the-world voyage.
1629	Holy Roman Emperor Ferdinand II issued the Edict of Restitution, providing that all church possessions acquired by the Protestants were to be returned to the Catholics.
1834	The city of York in the Canadian province of Upper Canada changed its name and was incorporated as Toronto.
1836	The Alamo at San Antonio fell to Mexican General Santa Anna after an 11-day siege. Its entire garrison was killed, including Davy Crockett and Jim Bowie.
1857	Chief Justice Roger B. Taney announced the Dred Scott Decision, refusing the slave Dred Scott the right to sue for his freedom.
1858	The Missionary Society of Saint Paul the Apostle, or the "Paulists," was founded in New York City by Father Isaac Thomas Hecker.
1896	Charles Brady King drove his "Horseless Carriage" on the streets of Detroit, the first automobile to appear in the motor city.
1924	The Egyptian government officially opened Tutankhamen's mummy.

1930	The first frozen foods—developed by Clarence Birdseye—were sold in grocery stores, in Springfield, Massachusetts.
1933	President Franklin D. Roosevelt proclaimed the national bank holiday to save the country's tottering banks.
1935	Oliver Wendell Holmes, Jr., the great Supreme Court justice, died in Washington, D.C., two days before his 94th birthday.
1953	Georgi Malenkov succeeded Joseph Stalin as Soviet premier.
1957	The former British African colonies of Togoland and the Gold Coast became the independent nation of Ghana.
1967	Svetlana Alliluyeva, Josef Stalin's daughter, appeared at the U.S. embassy in India to defect to the West. She returned to Russia in 1984.

March 7 – Birthdays

1556	**Guillaume du Vair.** French philosopher and writer
1671	**Ellis Wynne.** English clergyman and author
1693	**Clement XIII.** Roman Catholic pope, 1758-1769
1707	**Stephen Hopkins.** Governor of Rhode Island and signer of the Declaration of Independence
1785	**Alessandro Manzoni.** One of Italy's greatest novelists because of his only novel, *The Betrothed* (1827), which set the standard for modern Italian prose style
1792	**Sir John Herschel.** British astronomer, son of noted British astronomer Sir William Herschel, and pioneer in the use of hypo in photography
1802	**Sir Edwin Landseer.** The most popular English artist of his time, noted for works such as *Dignity and Impudence* (1839) and *The Stag at Bay* (1846)
1844	**Anthony Comstock.** American crusader against obscenity and imagined obscenity in literature
1845	**Daniel David Palmer.** Founder of chiropractic
1849	**Luther Burbank.** American plant breeder who developed numerous new trees, flowers, vegetables, and grasses, such as the Shasta daisy and the spineless cactus
1850	**Champ Clark.** Speaker of the U.S. House of Representatives, 1911-1919, and chief opponent of Woodrow Wilson for the Democratic nomination for president in 1912
1850	**Tomas Masaryk.** First president and chief founder of Czechoslovakia
1869	**Bertha Townsend Toulmin.** American Hall of Fame tennis player
1872	**Piet Mondrian.** Dutch painter known for his rigidly geometric style
1875	**Maurice Ravel.** The greatest French composer since Claude Debussy, noted for works such as *Bolero* and *Daphnis et Chloe*
1889	**Ben Ames Williams.** American novelist
1893	**Milton Avery.** American painter noted for works such as *Swimmers and Sunbathers* (1945)

1908 **Anna Magnani.** Egyptian-Italian stage, screen, and television actress, referred to by director Vittorio De Sica as "Italy's greatest actress"

1930 **Anthony Armstrong-Jones.** English photographer and former husband of Princess Margaret

1934 **King Curtis.** American rock and roll saxophone player

1934 **Willard Scott.** American television weatherman on NBC's *Today* show

1938 **Janet Guthrie.** American automobile racing driver and first female to compete in the Indianapolis 500

1938 **Homero Blancos.** Professional golfer

1940 **Daniel J. Travanti.** American television actor noted for his role in the popular series *Hill Street Blues*

1941 **John C. Malone.** American telecommunications executive and engineer

1942 **Michael Eisner.** Chairman, Walt Disney Company

1945 **John Heard.** English motion-picture actor

1946 **Peter Wolf.** American rock singer

1950 **Franco Harris.** Professional Hall of Fame football superstar and the second player in history after Jim Brown to rush for over 12,000 yards in a career

1950 **Billy Joe DuPree.** Professional football player

1952 **Lynn Swann.** Professional football superstar

1955 **Tommy Kramer.** Professional football player

1957 **Kenny King.** Professional football player

1960 **Ivan Lendl.** Czechoslovakian tennis player and superstar

1960 **Joe Carter.** Professional baseball player

1963 **Kim Ung-Yong.** South Korean native with an I.Q. of 210, a world's record

1980 **Laura Prepon.** American actress (*That 70s Show*)

March 7 – Events

161 Roman Emperor Antoninus Pius died of fever at age 75, and was succeeded by Marcus Aurelius.

1274 St. Thomas Aquinas, one of the greatest Christian theologians, died at an approximate age of 49.

1277 Christian Averroism (studying questions from philosophical rather than from religious premises) was condemned by Bishop Etienne Tempier, on instructions of Pope John XXI.

1815 Napoleon Bonaparte was acclaimed by soldiers sent to arrest him on his return to France from the island of Elba, where he had been in exile.

1850 U.S. Senator Daniel Webster made a three-hour "Union-saving" speech, endorsing the Compromise of 1850.

1876 Alexander Graham Bell was granted a patent for his telephone.

1936 On orders of Adolf Hitler, German troops occupied the Rhineland, defying the Treaty of Versailles and the Pact of Locarno. Even Hitler was amazed that the French offered no opposition, thus setting the stage for World War II.

1945 The Allies crossed the Rhine into Germany in World War II, using a bridge at Remagen that was still intact in spite of German efforts to blow it up.

1965 Civil rights demonstrators, in an attempted march on Montgomery, Alabama, were confronted in Selma by state troopers who used clubs and tear gas to break up the demonstration.

March 8 – Birthdays

1495 **Giovanni Battista di Jacopo Rosso.** Florentine Mannerist painter who became known as Il Rosso Fiorentino

1714 **Carl Philipp Emanuel Bach.** German composer and second surviving son of the great composer, Johann Sebastian Bach

1748 **William V.** Prince of Orange

1783 **Hannah Hoes Van Buren.** Wife of President Martin Van Buren

1787 **Karl von Grafe.** Father of plastic surgery

1788 **Sir William Hamilton.** Scottish metaphysical philosopher

1799 **Simon Cameron.** Powerful Pennsylvania political boss of the 1800s whose definition of an honest politician was "one who when bought, stays bought"

1841 **Oliver Wendell Holmes Jr.** Noted U.S. Supreme Court justice, 1802-1832, and son of the famous novelist and writer

1858 **Ruggiero Leoncavallo.** Italian opera composer, best known for *Pagliacci* (1892)

1859 **Kenneth Grahame.** Scottish writer noted for the great children's classic *The Wind in the Willows* (1908)

1865 **Frederic William Goudy.** American type designer and printer noted for types such as Goudy Old Style, Forum, and Kennerley

1879 **Otto Hahn.** German radiochemist who with Fritz Strassmann reported the splitting of the uranium atom in 1938

1890 **George Keogan.** Hall of Fame basketball coach with Notre Dame (1924-1943)

1891 **Sam Jaffe.** American stage, screen, and television actor

1902 **Jennings Randolph.** U.S. senator

1902 **Louise Beavers.** American motion-picture and television actress

1909 **Claire Trevor.** American stage, screen, and television actress

1920 **Douglass Wallop.** American author noted for *The Year the Yankees Lost the Pennant* (1954), on which the hit musical *Damn Yankees* was based

1921 **Cyd Charisse.** American motion-picture and television dancer and actress

1922 **Carl Furillo.** Professional baseball player

1936 **Sue Ane Langdon.** American actress

1938 **Charley Pride.** American country music singer

1939 **Jim Bouton.** Professional baseball player and author of *Ball Four*

1939	**Lynn Seymour.** Canadian dancer
1942	**Dick Allen.** Professional baseball player
1943	**Lynn Redgrave.** English stage, screen, and television actress, and daughter of English actor Sir Michael Redgrave
1944	**Susan Clark.** Canadian-born motion-picture actress
1945	**Mickey Dolenz.** American musician with The Monkees musical group
1947	**Carole Bayer Sager.** American singer and lyricist noted for works such as "That's What Friends Are For"
1953	**Jim Rice.** Professional baseball player and superstar
1959	**Aidan Quinn.** American stage, screen and television actor

March 8 – Events

1702	Queen Anne, the last English monarch of the House of Stuart, ascended the throne upon the death of William III.
1869	Hector Louis Berlioz, the noted French composer, died in Paris at age 65.
1874	Millard Fillmore died in Buffalo, New York, at age 74.
1894	New York became the first state to pass a dog licensing law.
1917	The U.S. Senate voted to limit filibusters by adopting the cloture rule.
1917	Count Ferdinand von Zeppelin, German pioneer in lighter-than-air vehicles, died at age 78.
1917	Rioting in St. Petersburg marked the beginning of the Russian February (by the old calendar) Revolution. It would end a week later with the abdication of the czar.
1930	William Howard Taft died in Washington, D.C., at age 72.
1942	The Japanese captured Rangoon, Burma, during World War II.
1950	Russia announced that it possessed the atomic bomb. They had tested their first bomb the previous August.
1965	The first American ground combat unit landed in South Vietnam. The unit consisted of some 3,500 marines.
1971	Joe Frazier defeated Muhammad Ali at Madison Square Garden in 15 rounds to retain his heavyweight championship.
1999	Joe DiMaggio, the great baseball player, died in Florida at age 84.

March 9 – Birthdays

1291	**Can Grande della Scala.** Military leader of Verona
1451	**Amerigo Vespucci.** Italian merchant-explorer for whom the Americas were named
1629	**Alexis (Mikhailovich).** Czar of Russia, 1645-1676, "the gentlest czar," and son of Michael Romanov, the first of the Romanov czars
1749	**Count Honoré de Mirabeau.** French statesman, orator, and one of the principal leaders of the French Revolution
1758	**Franz Joseph Gall.** German anatomist who founded the pseudoscience of phrenology and co-authored the four-volume work *Anatomy and Physiology of the Nervous System* (1810-1820)
1763	**William Cobbett.** English writer, reformer, and publisher, who attacked the Industrial Revolution as an enemy of the working people
1773	**Isaac Hull.** American naval commodore who commanded the U.S.S. *Constitution* when it defeated the British *Guerriere* in the War of 1812 and got the famous nickname "Old Ironsides"
1824	**Leland Stanford.** American statesman, railroad builder, and founder in 1885 of Stanford University
1852	**Mary Outerbridge.** American Hall of Fame tennis player who introduced tennis to the U.S. in 1874 and is often called the founder of American tennis
1856	**Edward Goodrich Acheson.** American inventor who developed the method of making graphite from coke in 1896
1856	**Eddie Foy.** Famous American vaudeville comedian and father of the *Seven Little Foys* of the movie by that name
1883	**James Kendis.** American composer, author, and publisher, noted for lyrics such as "I'm Forever Blowing Bubbles"
1890	**V.M. Molotov.** Foreign minister of Russia until he was demoted in 1957 by Nikita Khrushchev
1892	**Victoria Mary Sackville-West.** English poet and writer known for *The Edwardians* (1930)
1898	**Luther H. Hodges.** U.S. governor and secretary of commerce under President Kennedy
1900	**Howard Hathaway Aiken.** Harvard University professor who in 1944 built the Mark I, the first digital computer
1902	**Edward Durrell Stone.** American architect who designed the John F. Kennedy Center for the Performing Arts in Washington, D.C. and the Museum of Modern Art in New York City
1902	**Will Geer.** American stage, screen, and television actor, noted for his role as Grandpa in the long-running television series *The Waltons*
1904	**Reinhard Heydrich.** Feared Nazi "Hangman of Europe," whose assassination in 1942 led the Germans to kill 300 Czechs and destroy the town of Lidice for revenge
1905	**Rex Warner.** English poet, novelist, and notable translator of the plays of ancient Greece
1906	**David Smith.** American sculptor noted for works with metals, such as *Cubi XIX* (1964)
1910	**Samuel Barber.** American composer noted for works such as the opera *Vanessa, Piano Concerto No. 1,* and the popular *Adagio for Strings*
1912	**Arky Vaughan.** Professional baseball player

| 1914 | **Fred Clark.** American stage and motion-picture actor |

1914   **Fred Clark.** American stage and motion-picture actor

1918   **Mickey Spillane.** American novelist noted for works such as *I, the Jury* (1946) and as the creator of detective Mike Hammer

1918   **George Lincoln Rockwell.** American Nazi leader

1920   **Carl Betz.** American stage, screen, and television actor

1923   **James Buckley.** U.S. senator in the 1970s and brother of columnist William F. Buckley

1925   **G. William Miller.** Chairman of the Board of Governors of the Federal Reserve System in the 1970s

1926   **Jerry Ross.** American songwriter who teamed with Richard Adler to write such songs as "Hey There," "Hernando's Hideaway," and "Whatever Lola Wants"

1927   **Jackie Jenson.** Professional baseball player

1934   **Yuri Gagarin.** Russian cosmonaut and the first man to travel in space (on April 12, 1961)

1934   **Joyce Van Patten.** American stage, screen, and television actress, who made the transition from child star to leading lady

1936   **Marty Ingels.** American stage, screen, and television actor and comedian

1940   **Raul Julia.** Puerto Rican stage, screen, and television actor

1942   **Bert Campaneris.** Professional baseball player

1943   **Bobby Fischer.** First American to win the world chess title (1972-1975)

1943   **Charles Gibson.** American television personality and morning show co-host

1945   **Trish Van Devere.** American stage, screen, and television actress, and wife of actor George C. Scott

1950   **Andy North.** Professional golfer

1950   **Danny Sullivan.** American race car driver who won the Indianapolis 500 in 1985

1951   **Michael Kinsley.** American political commentator, writer and corporate editor

1951   **Billy Freer.** South African tennis player

1955   **Fernando Bujones.** American ballet dancer

1958   **Martin Fry.** American singer with the ABC musical group

1965   **Benito Santiago.** Professional baseball player

March 9 – Events

1074   Pope Gregory VII excommunicated all married Roman Catholic priests.

1152   Frederick I (Barbarossa) was crowned King of Germany at Aix-la-Chapelle.

1776   The British economist Adam Smith published his monumental work, *The Wealth of Nations.*

1796   Napoleon married Josephine de Beauharnais in Paris.

1822   Charles M. Graham of New York was granted a patent for false teeth.

1862   The *Monitor* and the *Merrimack,* in the first naval battle of ironclads, fought to a draw at Hampton Roads, Virginia, in the Civil War.

1864   General U.S. Grant was made commander-in-chief of the Northern armies in the Civil War.

1916   Pancho Villa, the Mexican bandit chieftain, led a raid across the American border, killing 16 people in Columbus, New Mexico.

1954   Newsman Edward R. Murrow, on his TV show, *See It Now,* criticized Senator Joseph R. McCarthy's anti-Communist campaign, helping to bring about McCarthy's later downfall.

1961   *Sputnik IX*, carrying a dog, was launched by Russia.

March 10 – Birthdays

1452   **Ferdinand V.** King of Spain who with his wife, Queen Isabella, financed Columbus's voyage of discovery of America

1503   **Ferdinand I.** Holy Roman Emperor, 1556-1564

1628   **Marcello Malpighi.** Italian anatomist who discovered the capillary blood vessels that carry blood between the arteries and the veins

1730   **George Ross.** Member of the Continental Congress and signer from Pennsylvania of the Declaration of Independence

1768   **Domingos de Sequeira.** Portuguese painter

1772   **Friedrich von Schlegel.** German poet and critic

1776   **Louise of Mecklenburg-Strelitz.** Queen of Prussia who ruled with her husband Frederick William III, 1797-1810, and supplied the backbone to resist Napoleon's attacks on her country

1779   **Fanny Trollope.** English writer and mother of novelist Anthony Trollope, noted in her own right for her controversial book *The Domestic Manners of the Americans* (1832), and for over 30 other works, such as *The Vicar of Wrexhill* (1839) and *The Life and Adventures of a Clever Woman* (1854)

1788   **Joseph Karl B.F. von Eichendorff.** German poet

1810   **Sir Samuel Ferguson.** English poet

1823   **John Bacchus Dykes.** English composer and clergyman, noted for hymns such as "Lead, Kindly Light," "Holy, Holy, Holy! Lord God Almighty" and " Nearer, My God to Thee"

1845   **Alexander III.** Czar of Russia, 1881-1894

1858   **Henry Watson Fowler.** English lexicographer and expert on the English language, noted for his *Dictionary of Modern English Usage* (1926)

1867   **Lillian D. Wald.** American social worker and pacifist who founded the Henry Street Settlement for nurses and who was largely responsible for the American system of public-school nursing

1880   **Mike Jacobs.** Noted American boxing promoter, most famous for his promotion of Joe Louis

1885   **Tamara Karsavina.** Noted Russian ballerina

1886   **Fred Waller.** American inventor noted for cinerama in 1952

1888   **Oscar Gottfried Mayer.** American meat packer who with his brother Oscar F. opened the first Oscar Mayer store, in Chicago in 1883

1888 **Barry Fitzgerald.** Irish-born stage and motion-picture actor and one of Hollywood's prime character actors of the 1940s and 1950s

1892 **Arthur Honegger.** One of the foremost composers of his time, and one of *Les Six,* a famous group of French composers of the 1920s

1898 **Bert Bacharach.** American syndicated columnist and father of songwriter Burt Bacharach

1900 **Peter De Rose.** American composer and pianist noted for songs such as "Wagon Wheels," "Somebody Loves You," "Deep Purple," and "Moonlight Mood"

1909 **Two Ton Tony Galento.** American heavyweight boxer during Joe Louis's reign as champion

1911 **Warner Anderson.** Child star of silent movies and Broadway plays, and a solid supporting player as an adult in motion-pictures and television

1912 **John Fischer.** Professional golfer

1918 **Heywood Hale Broun.** American actor, author, broadcast journalist and son of journalist Heywood Broun

1918 **Pamela Mason.** American motion-picture actress

1920 **Jack Kent.** American artist and writer, and creator in 1950 of the comic strip *King Aroo*

1920 **Kenneth C. "Jethro" Burns.** American country singer who with Homer Haynes formed the "Homer and Jethro" comedy duo specializing in parodies of popular songs

1928 **James Earl Ray.** American assassin convicted of killing Martin Luther King in 1968

1940 **Chuck Norris.** American movie actor and ex-world middleweight karate champion

1940 **David Rabe.** Noted American playwright who won a Tony Award for his first Broadway play, "Sticks and Stones" (1972)

1940 **Leroy Ellis.** Professional basketball player

1941 **Sandra Palmer.** Professional golfer

1947 **Bob Greene.** American newspaper columnist

1948 **Austin Carr.** Professional basketball player

1958 **Sharon Stone.** American motion-picture actress

1958 **Steve Howe.** Professional baseball player

1964 **Prince Edward.** Youngest son of England's Queen Elizabeth II

March 10 – Events

1496 Columbus concluded his second visit to the New World as he left Hispaniola for Spain.

1629 Charles I of England dissolved Parliament. It would not meet again until 1640.

1812 English poet Lord Byron published the first two cantos of *Childe Harold's Pilgrimage,* which immediately established his fame.

1813 King Friedrich Wilhelm III created the Iron Cross, Germany's first and highest decoration for military valor.

1831 The French Foreign Legion, one of the world's most colorful fighting forces, was created by King Louis Philippe for service outside France.

1862 The first paper money was issued by the United States.

1876 Alexander Graham Bell said his famous words, "Mr. Watson, come here. I want you!" It was the first intelligible sentence ever carried on the telephone.

1888 John L. Sullivan and Charlie Mitchell fought 44 rounds to a draw in a boxing match in Apremont, France.

1935 The comic strip *Smokey Stover,* by Bill Holman, first appeared.

1948 Czech foreign minister Jan Masaryk was found dead in Prague. He was either murdered by the Communists or committed suicide in protest of the Communist takeover of Czechoslovakia.

1949 "Axis Sally" (Mildred Gillars) was convicted of treason for her Nazi propaganda broadcasts for the Germans in World War II.

March 11 – Birthdays

1544 **Torquato Tasso.** The greatest Italian poet of the late Renaissance, noted for works such as "Jerusalem Delivered" (1575)

1819 **Sir Henry Tate.** English manufacturer and philanthropist

1885 **Sir Malcolm Campbell.** English automobile racing champion

1887 **Henry Dixon Crowell.** American composer

1887 **Raoul Walsh.** American pioneer motion-picture director and actor who began both careers with D.W. Griffith in 1912 and for 50 years was one of Hollywood's most prolific directors

1890 **Vannevar Bush.** American electrical engineer who was active in U.S. weapons research in World War II and who invented the differential analyzer, an electronic calculating machine, in 1930

1895 **Wanda Gag.** American author and illustrator of children's books, such as *Millions of Cats*

1898 **Dorothy Gish.** American actress with a 60-year career, who with her sister Lillian Gish appeared in such movie classics as *Orphans of the Storm* (1922) and *Hearts of the World* (1918)

1899 **Frederick IX.** King of Denmark, 1947-1972

1903 **Dorothy Schiff.** American editor and publisher of the New York *Post*

1903 **Lawrence Welk.** American bandleader noted for his long-running television show

1914 **Ralph Ellison.** American author best known for his powerful novel *Invisible Man* (1952) and his posthumously-published *Juneteenth* (1999)

1916 **Sir Harold Wilson.** Prime minister of Great Britain, 1964-1970

1923 **Louise Brough.** American tennis player who won four Wimbledon singles titles and was one of the greatest women players of all time

1926 **Ralph Abernathy.** Co-founder with Martin Luther King, Jr., of the Southern Christian Leadership Conference

1931	**Rupert Murdock.** Australian-born newspaper publisher and owner of the Los Angeles Dodgers
1934	**Sam Donaldson.** American broadcast journalist
1936	**Antonin Scalia.** U.S. Supreme Court Justice
1938	**Joseph Brooks.** American songwriter noted for works such as "You Light Up My Life"
1945	**Dock Ellis.** Professional baseball player
1947	**Mark Stein.** American rock singer-musician with Vanilla Fudge
1948	**Cesar Geronimo.** Professional baseball player
1950	**Jerry Zucker.** American motion-picture and television director and screenwriter
1961	**Bruce Watson.** Irish guitarist with the Big Country musical group
1961	**Mike Percy.** British bassist with the Dead or Alive musical group

March 11 – Events

1513	Leo X was elected Roman Catholic pope.
1702	The London *Daily Courant,* the first English daily newspaper, was published by Elizabeth Mallett.
1847	Johnny Appleseed (John Chapman), legendary planter of apple trees along the Ohio River, died at age 72.
1861	The Confederate Congress, meeting in Montgomery, Alabama, adopted the Constitution of the Confederacy.
1888	The famous "Blizzard of '88" struck the northeastern United States, eventually causing the death of some 400 people.
1917	Czar Nicholas II ordered the Duma (the Russian parliamentary body) to disband, but it refused, and the Russian February Revolution continued.
1941	The Lend-Lease Act became law, enabling the U.S. to help Britain in World War II by transferring weapons and equipment to nations fighting the Axis powers.
1942	General Douglas MacArthur left Bataan in World War II and flew to Australia, promising that "I shall return."
1954	The U.S. Army charged that Senator Joseph McCarthy had used pressure to obtain favored treatment for a former consultant to his subcommittee.
1970	Erle Stanley Gardner, American novelist and creator of Perry Mason, died at age 80.

March 12 – Birthdays

1626	**John Aubrey.** English biographer and antiquary
1630	**Andre Le Notre.** French landscape architect who created most of the famous gardens of his day, such as Kensington Gardens in London, Versailles gardens in France, and the Vatican gardens
1685	**George Berkeley.** Irish bishop and philosopher who tried to reconcile the doctrines of Christianity with the science of his day
1710	**Thomas Arne.** English composer who wrote *Rule, Britannia* (1741)
1790	**John Frederic Daniell.** English chemist and inventor of the Daniell battery
1795	**William Lyon Mackenzie.** Canadian politician who led the unsuccessful December Rebellion in upper Canada in 1837
1806	**Jane Means Appleton Pierce.** Wife of President Franklin Pierce
1818	**John L. Worden.** Commander of the Union *Monitor* in 1862 in her famous Civil War battle with the Confederate *Merrimack,* the first between two ironclad ships
1821	**Sir John Joseph Caldwell Abbott.** Prime minister of Canada, 1891-1892
1824	**Gustav Robert Kirchhoff.** German physicist who formulated Kirchhoff's Laws for electric circuits
1831	**Clement Studebaker.** Co-founder with his brother Henry of the Studebaker Brothers Manufacturing Company (1868), which evolved into the automobile company
1832	**Charles Cunningham Boycott.** English land agent in the 1800s who was so harsh with his Irish tenants that his neighbors refused to associate with him, leading to the coining of the word "boycott"
1838	**Sir William Henry Perkin.** English chemist who founded the aniline dye industry
1858	**Adolph Simon Ochs.** American newspaper man who rose from newsboy to become the publisher of the *New York Times*
1863	**Gabriele D'Annunzio.** Italian poet and novelist, noted for works such as *The Flame of Life* (1900), based on his love affair with the famous actress Eleonora Duse
1871	**Ralph Hodgson.** English poet noted for works such as *Time* and *You Old Gypsy Man*
1880	**Kemal Ataturk.** Turkish patriot who founded the Republic of Turkey and served as its president from 1923 until his death in 1938
1894	**Joseph Meyer.** American composer noted for songs such as "California Here I Come" and "If You Knew Susie"
1905	**Allan Roberts.** American composer, author, and pianist, noted for songs such as "You Always Hurt the One You Love," "Into Each Life Some Rain Must Fall," "Good, Good, Good," and "Tampico"
1910	**Masayoshi Ohira.** Post-World War II prime minister of Japan
1912	**Les Brown.** American bandleader of the Big Band Era of the 1940s, whose band was known as the "Band of Renown," and who wrote the popular song "Sentimental Journey"
1912	**Paul Weston.** American composer, author, and conductor, noted for songs such as "Shrimp Boats," "No Other Love," and "Day By Day"
1921	**Gordon MacRae.** American stage and motion-picture actor and singer

1922 **Jack Kerouac.** American poet and novelist, noted for works such as *On the Road* (1956), a novel about the "beat generation," and *Big Sur* (1963)

1922 **Lane Kirkland.** President of the AFL-CIO, who succeeded George Meany

1923 **Walter M. Schirra Jr.** U.S. astronaut who was the command pilot of *Gemini 6* and *Apollo 7*

1925 **Georges Delerue.** French composer and leading cinema scorer, noted for his prolific output

1928 **Edward Albee.** American playwright noted for works such as *The American Dream* (1961) and *Who's Afraid of Virginia Woolf?* (1962)

1930 **Vernon Law.** Professional baseball player

1932 **Andrew Young.** U.S. ambassador to the United Nations under President Carter and Mayor of Atlanta

1941 **Barbara Feldon.** American motion-picture and television actress

1942 **Paul Kantner.** American guitarist with Jefferson Airplane and Jefferson Starship

1946 **Liza Minnelli.** American stage and motion-picture actress and singer, and daughter of actress Judy Garland and director Vincente Minnelli

1948 **Kent Conrad.** U.S. senator

1948 **Mark Moseley.** Professional football player

1953 **Carl Hiaasen.** American journalist and novelist noted for works such as *Native Tongue* (1991)

1956 **Dale Murphy.** Professional baseball superstar

1957 **Marlon Jackson.** American singer with the Jackson 5 musical group

1962 **Darryl Strawberry.** Professional baseball superstar

March 12 – Events

1507 Cesare Borgia, the notorious Italian nobleman and subject of Machiavelli's famous book *The Prince,* was killed in battle at age 32, fighting for the king of Navarre.

1664 New Jersey became a British colony as King Charles II gave the newly-acquired area from Holland to his brother, James, Duke of York.

1912 Juliette Gordon Low founded the Girl Guides, which later became the Girl Scouts of America.

1912 American Army captain Albert Berry made the first parachute jump from an airplane, at Jefferson Barracks, Missouri.

1914 George Westinghouse, the noted American inventor, died at age 67.

1925 The first transatlantic radio broadcast was made.

1933 President Franklin D. Roosevelt broadcast his first "Fireside Chat" on the radio.

1938 German troops crossed the Austrian border after the Austrian government had resigned, accepting Hitler's invasion of the country.

1939 Pius XII was formally installed as Roman Catholic pope.

1940 Finland surrendered to the Soviet Union in the first Russo-Finnish War.

1947 President Harry S. Truman announced the Truman Doctrine, proposing aid to Greece and Turkey against Communist aggression.

1951 The comic strip *Dennis the Menace,* by Hank Ketchum, first appeared.

March 13 – Birthdays

1615 **Innocent XII.** Roman Catholic pope, 1691-1700

1733 **Joseph Priestley.** English clergyman and chemist who shares the credit with Carl Wilhelm Scheele for the discovery of oxygen

1741 **Joseph II.** Holy Roman Emperor and King of Austria

1774 **Pierre-Narcisse Guerin.** French painter

1781 **Johann Rudolph Wyss.** Swiss writer who edited and published *The Swiss Family Robinson,* which was written by his father, Johann David Wyss

1781 **Karl Friedrich Schinkel.** German architect

1798 **Abigail Powers Fillmore.** Wife (and former teacher) of President Millard Fillmore

1855 **Percival Lowell.** American astronomer best known for his belief in the possibility of life on Mars and in the existence of Martian canals

1860 **Hugo Wolf.** Austrian composer who brought the 19th-century German *Lied* to its highest point of development

1870 **William James Glackens.** American painter and illustrator noted for works such as *Chez Mouquin* (1905), and who was one of the original members of The Eight, a group of realistic artists

1884 **Sir Hugh Seymour Walpole.** One of the most popular English novelists of the early 20th century, best known for the *Herries Chronicles* (1930-1933)

1886 **Frank "Home Run" Baker.** Hall of Fame baseball player who, in spite of his nickname, never hit more than 12 home runs in a season

1898 **Henry Hathaway.** American motion-picture director with a 40-year career

1908 **Paul Stewart.** American stage, screen, and television actor

1908 **Walter Annenberg.** American publisher (*TV Guide*) and diplomat

1910 **Sammy Kaye.** American bandleader of the Big Band Era whose "Swing and Sway with Sammy Kaye" music spanned a career of 40 years

1914 **Bob Haggart.** American composer and bass player

1916 **Lindy Boggs.** U.S. congresswoman and wife of Majority Leader Hale Boggs

1930 **Doug Harvey.** Professional hockey player

1931 **Rosalind Elias.** American opera singer

1939 **Neil Sedaka.** American popular singer and songwriter

1948 **James Taylor.** American rock singer and songwriter

1953 **Andy Bean.** Professional golfer

1953 **Deborah Raffin.** American motion-picture and television actress and daughter of actress Trudy Marshall

1960	**Adam Clayton.** Irish bassist of the U2 musical group
1964	**Will Clark.** Professional baseball player

March 13 – Events

1639	Harvard University was named for John Harvard, a Massachusetts clergyman who gave the college its first large gift.
1781	Sir William Herschel, the English astronomer, discovered the planet Uranus, the first planet discovered since prehistoric times.
1791	Thomas Paine's *The Rights of Man* was published in London.
1852	"Uncle Sam" was portrayed in cartoon form representing the United States for the first time, in the New York weekly *Diogenes, Hys Lantern.*
1868	The impeachment trial of President Andrew Johnson began in the U.S. Senate.
1881	Czar Alexander II of Russia, the "czar liberator" who freed the serfs, was assassinated at age 62.
1884	Standard time was established in the United States.
1925	Tennessee's law against teaching evolution in the schools went into effect. It would lead later in the year to the famous Scopes Trial.
1930	The earlier discovery of the planet Pluto (by Clyde W. Tombaugh, an astronomer at the Lowell Observatory in Flagstaff, Arizona) was announced to the world.
1933	Banks in the United States began reopening after a "holiday" declared by President Franklin D. Roosevelt.
1938	Seyss-Inquart, installed by the Nazis as Chancellor of Austria, and his cabinet agreed to the annexation of Austria by Germany.
1969	*Apollo 9* splashed down in the Pacific with astronauts McDivitt, Schweickart, and Scott aboard, after a ten-day flight in space.

March 14 – Birthdays

1681	**Georg Philipp Telemann.** A leading German composer of the late Baroque period, and a contemporary of Johann Sebastian Bach
1782	**Thomas Hart Benton.** U.S. senator and author of *Thirty Years' View* (1854-1856)
1804	**Johann Strauss (the Elder).** Austrian composer of some 250 pieces, such as the "Radetzsky March," and father of the "Waltz King," Johann Strauss, Jr.
1813	**Joseph P. Bradley.** U.S. Supreme Court justice whose vote is generally considered the swing vote in deciding the disputed 1876 presidential election in favor of Rutherford B. Hayes
1820	**Victor Emmanuel II.** King of Sardinia who played a principal role in uniting Italy before becoming its first king, 1861-1878
1844	**Humbert I.** King of Italy, 1878-1900, who was assassinated by a revolutionary

1848	**Theodore A. Metz.** German-born composer, author, and conductor, noted for songs such as "There'll Be a Hot Time in the Old Town Tonight" and "Ta-ra-ra-Boom-de-ree"
1854	**Thomas R. Marshall.** U.S. vice president, 1913-1921 (under President Woodrow Wilson), whose chief claim to fame seems to be his observation that "What this country needs is a good five-cent cigar"
1854	**Paul Ehrlich.** Nobel-prize winning German bacteriologist who founded chemotherapy and in 1910 discovered a remedy for syphilis
1864	**Casey Jones.** American railroad engineer who gave his life to save the lives of his passengers and crew in the famous wreck in Vaughan, Mississippi, in 1900
1865	**Filoteo Alberini.** Italian film pioneer and inventor, noted for the Kinetograph (1894 and 1895)
1871	**Olive Fremstad.** American operatic soprano
1879	**Albert Einstein.** One of the greatest scientists of all time, best known for his theory of relativity (1905), which revolutionized physics and laid the foundation for splitting the atom
1894	**Osa Johnson.** Wife of explorer Martin Johnson, who collaborated with him in his discoveries and documentary filmmaking
1898	**Reginald Marsh.** American artist and illustrator noted for his realistic pictures of American city life
1898	**Richard L. Strout.** American journalist who for nearly 40 years was the author of the noted TRB column in the *New Republic*
1903	**Adolph Gottlieb.** American painter noted for works such as *Thrust* (1959)
1907	**Edward Heyman.** American lyricist and producer, noted for songs such as "You Oughta Be in Pictures," "Body and Soul," and "Boo-Hoo"
1911	**Edward Seiler.** Austrian-born lyricist, noted for songs such as "I Don't Want to Set the World on Fire," "When the Lights Go on Again All Over the World," and "Till Then"
1916	**Horton Foote.** American author and screenwriter noted for *The Trip to Bountiful* (1953)
1919	**Max Shulman.** American humorist
1920	**Hank Ketchum.** American cartoonist and creator of *Dennis the Menace*
1928	**Frank Borman.** American astronaut who commanded the *Apollo 8* space flight that first circled the moon (1968), and who later became an executive with Eastern Air Lines
1929	**Bob Goalby.** Professional golfer
1933	**Michael Caine.** English stage, screen, and television actor
1933	**Quincy Jones.** American jazz musician
1934	**Eugene Andrew Cernan.** American astronaut on the *Gemini 9* (1966) and *Apollo 10* (1969) flights
1942	**Rita Tushingham.** English stage and motion-picture actress
1944	**Clyde Lee.** Professional basketball player
1946	**Wes Unseld.** Professional basketball player and Hall of Famer

1947 **Billy Crystal.** American motion-picture and television actor and comedian
1956 **Butch Wynegar.** Professional baseball player
1958 **Prince Albert Alexander.** Son of Prince Rainier and Princess Grace, and heir to the throne of Monaco
1961 **Kirby Puckett.** Professional baseball player
1965 **Rod Woodson.** Professional football player

March 14 – Events

1743 The first Town Meeting in America was held at Faneuil Hall in Boston.
1794 Eli Whitney patented his cotton gin.
1874 "Taps," the Army's bugle call, was copyrighted by its composers, General Daniel Butterfield and his aide-de-camp, Oliver Wilcox.
1883 Karl Marx, the founder of Communism, died at age 64.
1893 New York's Waldorf Hotel opened on Fifth Avenue and 33rd Street.
1923 Warren G. Harding became the first U.S. President to file an income tax report.
1933 The U.S. Congress approved the sale and manufacture of 3.2 beer.
1938 Adolf Hitler entered Vienna in triumph after the annexation of Austria by Germany.
1951 The United Nations forces recaptured the South Korean capital of Seoul in the Korean War.
1964 A Dallas jury found Jack Ruby guilty of murdering Lee Harvey Oswald, President Kennedy's assassin.
1967 President John F. Kennedy's body was moved to its permanent memorial location in Arlington National Cemetery.

March 15 – Birthdays

1733 **Johann Zoffany.** German-born English painter noted for works such as *Garrick in "The Farmer's Return"* (1762), a portrait of the great actor David Garrick
1767 **Andrew Jackson.** Seventh U.S. president and hero of the Battle of New Orleans in the War of 1812
1779 **William Lamb Melbourne.** British prime minister, 1834-1841
1852 **Lady Isabella Augusta Gregory.** Irish playwright noted for works such as *The Rising of the Moon* and *The Workhouse Ward*
1867 **Lionel Pigot Johnson.** English poet and critic
1874 **Harold L. Ickes.** American social activist and secretary of the interior under Presidents Franklin D. Roosevelt and Harry S. Truman
1877 **Malcolm Whitman.** American tennis player and National Singles Champion in 1898, 1899, and 1890
1887 **Marjorie Merriweather Post.** American businesswoman who inherited the Postum Cereal Co. when her father Charles W. Post committed suicide in 1914

1904 **George Brent.** Irish-American stage and motion-picture actor
1911 **Ivan Allen Jr.** Mayor of Atlanta in the 1970s
1913 **MacDonald Carey.** American stage, screen, and television actor
1913 **Lew Wasserman.** President of MCA, Inc.
1915 **David Schoenbrun.** American news correspondent
1916 **Harry James.** American bandleader of the Big Band Era of the 1940s
1919 **Lawrence Tierney.** American motion-picture actor
1926 **Norman Van Brocklin.** Professional football superstar, coach and Hall of Famer
1932 **Alan L. Bean.** U.S. astronaut who piloted the lunar module *Intrepid* on the *Apollo 12* mission
1933 **Ruth Bader Ginsburg.** U.S. Supreme Court justice
1935 **Judd Hirsch.** American stage, screen, and television actor, noted for the long-running series *Taxi*
1940 **Phil Lesh.** American singer with The Grateful Dead
1941 **Mike Love.** American singer with the Beach Boys musical group
1944 **Sly Stone Stewart.** American rock singer and musician
1944 **William Masters.** Professional football player
1945 **Mark Green.** American lawyer, author, social activist and television commentator
1946 **Bobby Bonds.** Professional baseball player
1949 **Jim Kern.** Professional baseball player
1955 **Mickey Hatcher.** Professional baseball player
1955 **Dee Snider.** American singer with the Twisted Sister musical group
1957 **Park Overall.** American television actress
1957 **Mary Jean Carillo.** American tennis player and sportscaster
1959 **Harold Baines.** Professional baseball player
1959 **Elliott Teltscher.** American tennis player
1961 **Terry Cummings.** Professional basketball player
1962 **Steve Coy.** British drummer with the Dead or Alive musical group

March 15 – Events

44 BC Julius Caesar was stabbed to death by Brutus, Cassius, and a group of Roman aristocrats, as he entered a Senate meeting in Rome. The date was the Ides of March, which reportedly had been predicted as his death date by a soothsayer.
1493 Christopher Columbus arrived in Palos, Spain, completing his first voyage to America. He was aboard the *Nina,* and the *Pinta,* which was feared lost, arrived a few hours later.
1820 Maine was admitted to the Union as the 23rd state.
1836 The U.S. Senate confirmed the nomination of Roger B. Taney as Chief Justice of the Supreme Court.
1875 John McCloskey, the Roman Catholic Archbishop of New York, was named the first American cardinal by Pope Pius IX.

1892	New York became the first state to authorize voting machines.
1913	President Woodrow Wilson held the first regular presidential press conference.
1917	Czar Nicholas II abdicated as a result of the February (by the old calendar) Revolution, and a democratic government was set up in Russia.
1919	The American Legion was founded in Paris by 1,000 veterans of the American Expeditionary Force.
1939	German troops occupied Prague, completing the annexation of Czechoslovakia. Hitler, who arrived in Prague at dusk, proclaimed that "Czechoslovakia has ceased to exist."
1964	Actors Richard Burton and Elizabeth Taylor were married in Montreal. It was her fifth marriage and his second.
1976	Egypt's People's Assembly voted 307 to 2 to end the 1971 treaty of friendship and cooperation with Russia.

March 16 – Birthdays

1568	**Juan Martinez Montanes.** Spanish sculptor
1665	**Giuseppe Maria Crespy.** Italian painter known as La Spagnuolo
1739	**George Clymer.** Signer of the Declaration of Independence from Pennyslvania and member of the first U.S. House of Representatives
1751	**James Madison.** Fourth U.S. president and "Father of the Constitution"
1787	**Georg Simon Ohm.** German physicist who discovered Ohm's Law of electric circuits (1826), and for whom the *ohm,* the unit of electrical resistance, was named
1822	**John Pope.** Union general in the Civil War who commanded the Northern forces in the Second Battle of Bull Run
1822	**Rosa Bonheur.** French painter and sculptor, noted for works such as *The Horse Fair* and *Buffalo Bill*
1839	**Rene François A. Sully-Prudhomme.** French poet noted for works such as "Les Epreuves" (1866) and "Les Solitudes" (1869), and for winning the first Nobel Prize for Literature (1901), defeating Leo Tolstoy, Henrik Ibsen, and Henry James
1846	**Magnus Gosta Mittag-Leffler.** Noted Swedish mathematician
1878	**Reza Shah Pahlavi.** Shah of Iran, 1925-1941, and father of Shah Mohammed Reza Pahlavi
1892	**Cesar Vallejo.** Peruvian poet noted for works such as "The Dark Messengers" (1918) and "Take Thou This Cup from Me" (1940)
1892	**James Caesar Petrillo.** President of the American Federation of Musicians (1940-1958), who forced recording companies in 1942 to pay a royalty to musicians for every record they sold

1897	**Conrad Nagel.** Matinee idol of the American stage and leading man in scores of Hollywood films in the 1920s and 1930s, and a co-founder of the Academy of Motion Picture Arts and Sciences
1903	**Mike Mansfield.** U.S. senator and Majority Leader, 1961-1977, and U.S. Ambassador to Japan in the late 1970s and 1980s
1904	**Buddy Myer.** Professional baseball player
1906	**Lloyd Waner.** Hall of Fame baseball player who hit a record .355 as a rookie
1908	**Robert Rossen.** American motion-picture screenwriter and director noted for works such as *All the King's Men* (1948)
1909	**Don Raye.** American composer, author, and singer, noted for songs such as "Cow Cow Boogie," "Mister Five By Five," "Beat Me Daddy Eight to the Bar," and "Irresistible You"
1912	**Pat Nixon.** Wife of President Richard Nixon
1914	**Oscar Gustave Mayer.** American meat packer and son of one of the founders of the Oscar Mayer company
1915	**Sammy Gallop.** American composer noted for songs such as "Elmer's Tune," "Holiday for Strings," "Count Every Star," and "Vagabond Shoes"
1920	**Leo McKern.** Australian-British stage and motion-picture actor
1926	**Jerry Lewis.** American comedian, actor, and director, with a career of some 40 years
1927	**Daniel Patrick Moynihan.** American educator, expert on urban affairs, and U.S. senator
1932	**R. Walter Cunningham.** U.S. astronaut on the *Apollo 7* flight (1968)
1935	**Teresa Berganza.** Spanish opera and concert singer
1937	**William Armstrong.** U.S. senator
1940	**Bernardo Bertolucci.** Italian film director noted for such works as *The Grim Reaper* (1962) and *Last Tango in Paris* (1972)
1942	**Jerry Jeff Walker.** American country singer and guitarist
1942	**MacArthur Lane.** Professional football player
1949	**Erik Estrada.** American television actor
1951	**Kate Nelligan.** English motion-picture and television actress
1954	**Sammy White.** Professional football player
1954	**Hollis Stacy.** Professional golfer
1954	**Nancy Wilson.** American rock singer with the group Heart

March 16 – Events

1521	Ferdinand Magellan discovered the Philippine Islands on the first around-the-world trip.
1802	The United States Military Academy was founded at West Point, New York.
1850	Nathaniel Hawthorne's great novel *The Scarlet Letter* was first published.

1910	The famous American racer, Barney Oldfield, in a Benz car, set a land speed record of 131.7 miles per hour at Daytona Beach, Florida.
1918	Tallulah Bankhead, the great American actress, made her New York debut in the play *Squab Farm.*
1935	Adolf Hitler effectively scrapped the Treaty of Versailles, proclaiming universal military service and a peacetime German army of 300,000 men.
1945	The U.S. Marines took Iwo Jima after nearly a month of heavy fighting in World War II.
1959	John B. Salling of the Army of the Confederate States of America died at age 113, the oldest age to which a veteran soldier has lived.
1966	U.S. spacecraft *Gemini 8* docked with an *Agena* rocket while in orbit.
1971	Thomas E. Dewey, New York governor and twice unsuccessful candidate for president, died eight days before his 69th birthday.
1999	The Dow Jones Industrial Average crossed 10,000 for the first time in its history, but it failed to hold it at the close until some weeks later.

March 17 – Birthdays

1473	**James IV.** King of Scotland, 1488-1513
1578	**Francesco Albano.** Italian painter
1777	**Roger B. Taney.** Fifth Chief Justice of the U.S. Supreme Court, 1836-1864, best remembered for the controversial Dred Scott Decision
1781	**Ebenezer Elliott.** English poet known as "The Corn-Law Rimester"
1787	**Edmund Kean.** English Shakespearean actor considered the greatest poetic actor of the early 19th century
1804	**Jim Bridger.** One of the greatest American frontiersmen of all time and one of the first white men to see the site of the present Yellowstone National Park
1834	**Gottlieb Daimler.** German engineer who developed the automobile internal-combustion engine and produced the Mercedes automobile (named for his daughter), the forerunner of today's Mercedes-Benz
1846	**Kate Greenaway.** Noted English illustrator of children's books such as *Under the Window* (1879) and *A—Apple Pie* (1886)
1884	**Frank Buck.** American wild animal authority and collector with the motto "Bring 'Em Back Alive," the title of a book he wrote in 1931
1894	**Paul Eliot Green.** American playwright noted for works such as *The Lost Colony* (1937) and the Pulitzer Prize-winning *In Abraham's Bosom* (1926)
1895	**Shemp Howard.** Member of the slapstick vaudeville comedy act that later became the Three Stooges
1899	**Charlie Root.** Professional baseball pitcher who threw the pitch that Babe Ruth hit for a "called" home run in the 1932 World Series

1901	**Alfred Newman.** American composer, conductor, concert pianist, and one of Hollywood's most prolific film scorers, who was associated with some 200 films and won nine Academy Awards
1902	**Bobby Jones.** American golf immortal who won the U.S. Open four times and the British Open three times, and in 1950 was voted "the outstanding golfer of the years 1900 to 1949"
1903	**Marquis Childs.** Noted American newspaper columnist
1907	**John Pastore.** The first person of Italian descent to win election as a state governor (Rhode Island, 1945-1950) and a U.S. senator (1950-1977)
1910	**Bayard Rustin.** American civil rights leader and chief organizer of the 1963 March on Washington
1914	**Sammy Baugh.** One of the greatest quarterbacks in college and professional football history, and member of the Professional Football Hall of Fame
1918	**Mercedes McCambridge.** American stage, screen, and radio actress, called by actor Orson Welles "the world's greatest living radio actress"
1919	**Hank Sauer.** Professional baseball player who hit over 50 home runs in 1952
1919	**Nat King Cole.** Noted American singer and jazz pianist
1920	**Pete Reiser.** Professional baseball player who won the National League batting championship in his rookie year
1930	**James Benson Irwin.** U.S. astronaut who with David R. Scott drove an automobile on the moon in a 66-hour stay in 1971 (*Apollo 15*)
1938	**Rudolf Nureyev.** Noted Russian-born ballet dancer and actor
1944	**John Sebastian.** American singer and guitarist with The Lovin' Spoonful musical group
1949	**Patrick Duffy.** American actor noted for his role in the long-running television series *Dallas*
1951	**Kurt Russell.** American motion-picture and television actor
1953	**Chuck Muncie.** Professional football player
1954	**Lesley-Anne Down.** British motion-picture and television actress
1955	**Gary Sinese.** American motion-picture actor
1959	**Danny Ainge.** Professional basketball player
1964	**Rob Lowe.** American motion-picture actor

March 17 – Events

44 BC	The conspirators in Julius Caesar's murder were granted amnesty in a short-lived reprieve before Mark Antony stirred the people to take revenge on them.
180	Marcus Aurelius, the great Roman emperor, died in Vindobona (now Vienna) at age 58.
461	St. Patrick, the patron saint of Ireland and a saint of the Roman Catholic Church, died in Ireland at an approximate age of 72. The date is celebrated as St. Patrick's Day.

1680 François La Rochefoucauld, the noted French writer, died in Paris at age 66.

1762 New York City had its first St. Patrick's Day parade.

1776 With General George Washington's men occupying Dorchester Heights above the city, British general Howe evacuated Boston in the Revolutionary War.

1861 Italy, previously united by Garibaldi and Cavour, proclaimed itself a kingdom with Victor Emanuel II as the first king.

1871 The National Association of Professional Baseball Players, the forerunner of baseball's National League, was established.

1897 Bob Fitzsimmons defeated Gentleman Jim Corbett in the 14th round in Carson City, Nevada, to win the heavyweight crown.

1905 Franklin D. Roosevelt married Eleanor Roosevelt, his distant cousin and a niece of President Theodore Roosevelt, who gave the bride away.

1906 President Theodore Roosevelt coined the term *muckrake* in a speech to the Gridiron Club in Washington, D.C.

1912 The Camp Fire Girls was founded by Luther Halsey Gulick and his wife, Charlotte, who held many of the first meetings at their summer home in Sebago Lake, Maine.

1941 The National Gallery of Art opened in Washington, D.C.

1942 General Douglas MacArthur arrived in Australia, during World War II, to become supreme commander of the Allied forces in the southwest Pacific.

1958 The United States launched its second earth satellite, *Vanguard II,* which resulted in the discovery that the earth is pear-shaped.

March 18 – Birthdays

1578 **Adam Elsheimer.** German painter and etcher noted for works such as "Flight into Egypt" (1609)

1609 **Frederick III.** King of Norway and Denmark during the 17th century when Norway was a province of Denmark

1690 **Christian Goldbach.** Prussian mathematician noted for Goldbach's conjecture that any even number is the sum of two prime numbers, a conjecture made in 1742 but which is still unproved

1782 **John C. Calhoun.** American statesman, orator, vice president under President Jackson, and the only person to resign the vice presidency other than Spiro Agnew

1796 **Jakob Steiner.** Swiss mathematician noted as one of the founders of synthetic geometry

1813 **Joshua Ballinger Lippincott.** American publisher who founded J.B. Lippincott & Co. in 1835

1837 **Grover Cleveland.** Only U.S. president to serve two nonconsecutive terms (1885-1889 and 1893-1897)

1842 **Stephane Mallarmé.** French poet, essayist, and translator, best known for his dream poem "The Afternoon of a Faun" (1865)

1844 **Nicholas Rimsky-Korsakov.** Russian composer noted for such works as *Scheherazade,* "Song of India," and "Flight of the Bumblebee"

1858 **Rudolf Diesel.** German engineer noted for the diesel engine, which he patented in 1892

1869 **Neville Chamberlain.** British prime minister, 1937-1940, noted for his appeasement policy toward Adolf Hitler, that led, not to "peace in our time," as Chamberlain hoped, but to World War II

1877 **Edgar Cayce.** Noted American psychic who gave spiritual and medical advice to thousands of people

1884 **Joseph A. Burke.** American composer noted for songs such as "Tiptoe Through the Tulips," "Moon Over Miami," "Carolina Moon," and "American Patrol"

1885 **Ed G. Nelson.** American composer, conductor, and pianist, noted for songs such as "I Apologize" and "Auf Wiedersehen, My Dear"

1886 **Edward Everett Horton.** American stage and motion-picture actor in some 150 films

1893 **Wilfred Owen.** British poet who was awarded the Military Cross for gallantry in World War I and was later killed in action at age 25

1897 **Betty Compson.** One of the most popular American movie stars of the Roaring Twenties

1901 **Johnny Cooney.** Professional baseball player

1903 **Count Caleazzo Ciano.** Italian diplomat in the 1930s and 1940s, and son-in-law of Italian dictator Benito Mussolini

1905 **Robert Donat.** English stage and motion-picture actor who won an Academy Award in 1939 for *Goodbye Mr. Chips*

1911 **Smiley Burnette.** American stage and screen actor, and Gene Autry's comic sidekick Frog Milhouse in 81 motion pictures

1915 **Richard Condon.** American author noted for works such as *Prizzi's Honor* (1982)

1916 **Elbie Fletcher.** Professional baseball player

1924 **William Arthur Fredricks.** American composer, author, and singer noted for songs such as "You Can Trust Your Car to the Man Who Wears the Star"

1925 **Peter Graves.** American motion-picture and television actor and brother of actor James Arness

1927 **John Kander.** American composer who with lyricist Fred Ebb is noted for "New York, NY," and the songs from *Cabaret, Chicago,* and *Zorba*

1927 **George Plimpton.** American editor and television personality

1932 **John Updike.** American novelist noted for works such as *The Poorhouse Fair, Rabbit, Run,* and *Couples*

1936 **F.W. DeKlerk.** President of the Union of South Africa who was instrumental in freeing Nelson Mandela and who served later as deputy president under Mandela

1941   **Wilson Pickett.** American soul singer
1942   **Jeff Mullins.** Professional basketball player
1956   **Ingemar Stenmark.** Professional skier
1959   **Irene Cara.** American motion-picture actress and singer
1961   **Curt Warner.** Professional basketball player
1963   **Vanessa Williams.** First black Miss America (1984)
1964   **Bonnie Blair.** American Olympic speedskater and winner of five Olympic gold medals
1970   **Michael Rapaport.** American motion-picture actor

March 18 – Events

1314   Jacques De Molay, the last grand master of the Order of Knights Templars, was burned at the stake in Paris.
1455   Fra Angelico, the famous Italian painter, died in Rome at age 55.
1584   Ivan the Terrible, the first czar of Russia, died at age 53.
1612   Bartholomew Legate became the last person burned in England (at this writing) for his religious beliefs.
1766   The British Parliament repealed the notorious Stamp Act.
1768   Laurence Sterne, the noted English novelist, died of pleurisy in London at age 54.
1902   Enrico Caruso, the great Italian singer, made his first phonograph recording, for the Gramophone Company.
1911   "Alexander's Ragtime Band," by American songwriter Irving Berlin, was published.
1931   Schick, Inc. marketed the world's first electric razor.
1940   Adolf Hitler and Benito Mussolini met at the Brenner Pass in the Tyrol, where Mussolini secretly promised to enter World War II on the side of Germany.
1965   Russian cosmonaut Alexei Leonov became the first man to walk in space.
1974   Seven Arab countries lifted their oil embargo on the United States, in effect since October, 1973.

March 19 – Birthdays

1488   **Johannes Magnus.** Roman Catholic archbishop and historian
1519   **Henry II.** King of France, 1547-1559, who persecuted the Huguenots and took away their land
1593   **Georges de La Tour.** French painter noted for works such as *The Fortune Teller* and *Joseph the Carpenter*
1601   **Alonso Cano.** Spanish painter, sculptor, and architect
1603   **John IV.** Portuguese nobleman, the duke of Braganza, who drove out the Spanish rulers of Portugal in 1640 and became the first king of Portugal of the House of Braganza

1721   **Tobias Smollett.** One of the great early English novelists, best known for his classic novel, *The Expedition of Humphry Clinker* (1771)
1725   **Richard Howe.** British admiral prominent in the American Revolutionary War
1734   **Thomas McKean.** A Delaware signer of the Declaration of Independence, member of the Continental Congress, and governor of Pennsylvania
1813   **David Livingstone.** Famous Scottish missionary and African explorer to whom explorer Henry Morton Stanley said the famous line when they met, "Dr. Livingstone, I presume?"
1821   **Sir Richard Burton.** British explorer, author, and scholar, whose translation of *The Arabian Nights* is a literary classic
1844   **Minna Canth.** Finnish novelist and dramatist
1847   **Albert Pinkham Ryder.** American painter noted for works such as *Toilers of the Sea* (1891)
1848   **Wyatt Earp.** Noted frontiersman and lawman in the American West
1849   **Alfred von Tirpitz.** German naval officer and grand admiral active in building the German Navy prior to and during World War I
1860   **William Jennings Bryan.** American politician and three-time candidate for president
1864   **Charles M. Russell.** American painter, sculptor, and "cowboy artist" who specialized in life of the Old West
1871   **Iron Man Joe McGinnity.** Hall of Fame baseball pitcher who pitched a record 434 innings in 1903
1872   **Sergei Diaghilev.** Russian ballet master and the greatest director in ballet history
1873   **Max Reger.** German composer and organist who wrote over 260 songs
1882   **Gaston Lachaise.** French sculptor noted for rounded, classic figures, which were both robust and delicate, an example of which is *Georgia O'Keeffe* (1927)
1883   **Joseph "Vinegar Joe" Stilwell.** American World War II general who commanded the U.S. forces in the China-Burma-India area
1888   **Josef Albers.** German-born American painter noted for his series of square paintings *Homage to the Square*
1891   **Earl Warren.** U.S. Supreme Court Chief Justice, 1953-1969
1892   **James A. Van Fleet.** American World War II general who trained the armed forces which checked Communist aggression in Greece and Korea
1894   **"Moms" Mabley.** American singer and comedienne
1904   **John J. Sirica.** American judge noted for the Watergate trials
1905   **Albert Speer.** Nazi World War II Minister of Armaments and War Production, and author of *Inside the Third Reich* (1970)
1906   **Adolf Eichmann.** Notorious Nazi who, as commander of Hitler's death camps, sent millions of Jews to their death in World War II

1907 **Kent Smith.** American stage and motion-picture actor

1909 **Louis Hayward.** South African-born stage, screen and television actor

1914 **J. Jay Berwanger.** First winner of the Heisman Trophy, in 1935 (who, however, never played in the NFL)

1916 **Irving Wallace.** American novelist

1919 **Peter Abrahams.** Most prolific of South Africa's black prose writers

1927 **Richie Ashburn.** Professional baseball player

1928 **Patrick McGoohan.** American-born British stage, screen, and television actor and director

1930 **Ornette Coleman.** American avant-garde musician

1932 **Gay Brewer.** Professional golfer

1933 **Philip Roth.** American novelist and short-story writer, noted for works such as *Goodbye, Columbus* (1959) and *Portnoy's Complaint* (1969)

1935 **Phyllis Newman.** American actress and singer

1936 **Ursula Andress.** Swiss-born motion-picture actress

1938 **Joe Kapp.** Professional football player

1943 **Linda Wertheimer.** American radio journalist with National Public Radio

1944 **Lynda Bird Johnson (Robb).** Daughter of President Lyndon B. Johnson and wife of Virginia senator Charles Robb

1946 **Ruth Pointer.** American singer (the Pointer Sisters)

1947 **Glenn Close.** American motion-picture and television actress

1955 **Mike Norris.** Professional baseball player

1955 **Bruce Willis.** American stage, screen, and television actor

1956 **Chris O'Neill.** Australian tennis player

March 19 – Events

235 Maximinus Thrax was proclaimed Emperor of Rome.

1452 Frederick III became the last Holy Roman emperor to be crowned by the pope.

1687 The great French explorer Robert Cavalier, Sieur de La Salle was shot and killed by his own men at the Trinity River in Texas at age 43.

1859 Charles Gounod's opera *Faust* premiered at the Theatre Lyrique in Paris.

1917 The U.S. Supreme Court upheld the eight-hour work day for railroads.

1918 The U.S. Congress approved Daylight Saving Time.

1920 The U.S. Senate rejected the Versailles Treaty providing for a League of Nations.

1931 The Nevada legislature made gambling legal in the state.

1932 The comic strip *Henry,* by Carl Thomas Anderson, first appeared.

1942 All men in the United States between the ages of 45 and 62 were ordered to register for nonmilitary duty during World War II.

1951 Herman Wouk's novel *The Caine Mutiny* was published.

1953 The Academy Awards ceremony was telecast for the first time. The best picture was *The Greatest Show on Earth.*

1979 The U.S. House of Representatives began televising its day-to-day activities.

March 20 – Birthdays

43 BC **Ovid (Publius Ovidius Naso).** The most versatile of the Roman poets, noted for works such as "Metamorphoses" and "Art of Love"

1680 **Emanuele Astorga.** Spanish composer

1741 **Jean Antoine Houdon.** Great French sculptor of the 18th century, noted for statues and busts of Washington, Franklin, Jefferson, and Voltaire, and for the *Diana Nue* in the Louvre Museum

1770 **Friedrich Hölderlin.** German lyric poet

1796 **Edward Gibbon Wakefield.** British statesman who colonized New Zealand

1804 **Neal Dow.** One of the principal leaders in Maine in passing the first prohibition law of any state (1851)

1810 **John Cardinal McCloskey.** Roman Catholic archbishop of New York, 1864-1885, and the first American cardinal (1875)

1811 **George Caleb Bingham.** American painter noted for works such as *Daniel Boone Coming Through the Cumberland Gap* and *Stump Speaking*

1811 **Napoleon II.** King of Rome, Duke of Reichstadt, and only son of Napoleon Bonaparte

1820 **Ned Buntline.** American publisher (born Edward Z.C. Judson) who founded the magazine *Ned Buntline's Own,* and gave the Know-Nothing party its name

1828 **Henrik Ibsen.** Norwegian playwright known as the father of modern drama, who wrote works such as *A Doll's House* (1879), *Hedda Gabler* (1890), and *Peer Gynt* (1867)

1834 **Charles W. Eliot.** American educator, who as its president (1869-1909) made Harvard into one of the great universities of the world

1856 **Frederick Winslow Taylor.** American engineer and efficiency expert for whom "Taylorism," the efficiency movement, was named

1882 **Rene Coty.** Last President of the Fourth French Republic, 1954-1959

1890 **Lauritz Melchior.** Danish operatic tenor noted for his performances in Richard Wagner's operas

1891 **Edmund Goulding.** English motion-picture director noted for works such as *Grand Hotel* (1932) and *Love* (1927), a silent adaptation of *Anna Karenina* starring Greta Garbo

1892 **Stefan Banach.** Ukrainian mathematician and founder of modern functional analysis

1892 **Mort Dixon.** American composer noted for songs such as "That Old Gang of Mine," "Bye, Bye Blackbird," and "I'm Looking Over a Four Leaf Clover"

1900   **Urho Kekkonen.** President of Finland, 1956-1980

1903   **Vincent Richards.** American Hall of Fame tennis player, and youngest player to win a national championship (at age 15)

1906   **Abraham Beame.** Mayor of New York City, 1974-1977

1907   **Ozzie Nelson.** American actor and bandleader, who with his wife Harriet Hilliard starred in *The Adventures of Ozzie and Harriet,* one of television's longest-running hits

1908   **Frank Stanton.** American television broadcaster

1908   **Sir Michael Redgrave.** British stage and screen actor and superstar, and father of actors Corin, Lynn, and Vanessa Redgrave

1914   **Wendell Corey.** American stage and motion-picture actor

1920   **Pamela Harriman.** English-born American government official, wife of Randolph Churchill and Averell Harriman, and ambassador to France

1920   **Werner Klemperer.** German motion-picture and television actor, and son of the famed conductor, Otto Klemperer

1922   **Larry Elgart.** American bandleader

1922   **Ray Goulding.** Ray of the Bob and Ray comedy team

1922   **Carl Reiner.** American comedy writer, actor, producer, director, and father of actor Rob Reiner

1922   **Jack Kruschen.** American stage, screen, and television actor

1925   **John D. Ehrlichman.** Domestic affairs adviser to President Nixon, imprisoned for his role in the Watergate scandal

1928   **Fred M. Rogers.** American television producer and host of *Mr. Rogers' Neighborhood*

1931   **Hal Linden.** American actor and star of the long-running television show *Barney Miller*

1934   **Willie Brown.** American politician and mayor of San Francisco

1937   **Jerry Reed.** American country singer

1939   **Brian Mulroney.** Prime Minister of Canada

1945   **Pat Riley.** Professional basketball player and highly successful coach

1948   **Bobby Orr.** Professional hockey superstar and first defenseman to win the National Hockey League scoring title, with 120 points in 1969-1970

1950   **William Hurt.** American motion-picture actor

1952   **Anand Amritraj.** Indian tennis player

1952   **Rick Langford.** Professional baseball player

1956   **Bill Manson.** American tennis player

1957   **Spike Lee.** American motion-picture director noted for works such as *Malcolm X* (1992)

1958   **Holly Hunter.** American stage, screen and television actor

March 20 – Events

1413   King Henry IV of England, the first king of the House of Lancaster, died in London's Westminster Abbey at age 46.

1727   Sir Isaac Newton, the great English physicist, died at age 84.

1815   King Louis XVIII fled Paris as Napoleon entered the city on his return to power from exile on Elba.

1852   Harriet Beecher Stowe's famous novel, *Uncle Tom's Cabin,* was published for the first time in book form.

1854   A committee was appointed at Ripon, Wisconsin, to form the new Republican Party.

1899   Martha M. Place of New York City was executed at Sing Sing for the murder of her stepdaughter. She was the first woman to be put to death by electrocution.

1940   Edouard Daladier resigned as French premier and was replaced by Paul Reynaud, as the German Armies were positioning themselves for an assault on the West in World War II.

1942   General MacArthur, on his safe arrival in Australia from the Philippines in World War II, vowed that "I shall return."

1969   John Lennon, the noted Beatle, married Yoko Ono in Gibraltar.

March 21 – Birthdays

1685   **Johann Sebastian Bach.** German organist, "greatest genius of 'baroque music','' and one of the two or three greatest composers in world history

1736   **Claude Nicolas Ledoux.** French architect

1763   **Johann Paul Richter.** German writer (known also as John Paul), humorist, and master of satire, noted for works such as *The Invisible Loge* (1793) and *The Titan* (1800-1803)

1768   **Jean Baptiste Joseph Fourier.** French mathematician, noted for, among other things, the Fourier Series

1771   **Thomas Dibdin.** English dramatist and songwriter

1806   **Benito Juarez.** The national hero of Mexico

1821   **Frank Leslie.** English-American publisher noted for *Frank Leslie's Illustrated Weekly*

1839   **Modest Mussorgsky.** Russian composer, noted for the great opera *Boris Godunov* and such other works as *Pictures at an Exhibition*

1869   **Florenz Ziegfeld.** American theatrical producer, noted for the *Ziegfeld Follies* (first produced in 1907)

1880   **Hans Hofmann.** Bavarian-born American abstract painter noted for works such as *The Golden Wall* (1961)

1884   **George David Birkhoff.** One of the foremost American mathematicians of the early 20th century

1887   **Eric Mendelsohn.** German architect, famed for his free and imaginative approach

1893   **Sidney Franklin.** American motion-picture director noted for works such as *Mrs. Miniver* (1942)

1897   **Dorothy M. Stewart.** Australian-born composer, author, and pianist, noted for songs such as "Now Is the Hour"

1897 **Jack Meskill.** American composer and author, noted for songs such as "On the Beach At Bali-Bali" and "Smile, Darn Ya, Smile"

1903 **Edgar Buchanan.** American motion-picture and television actor

1905 **Phyllis McGinley.** American author of children's books and Pulitzer Prize-winning poet

1906 **John D. Rockefeller III.** Head of the Rockefeller Foundation and grandson of philanthropist John D. Rockefeller

1910 **Julio Gallo.** American vintner and one of the Gallo brothers famous for the Gallo Winery

1923 **Mort Lindsey.** American bandleader

1925 **Madison Jones.** American author noted for works such as *A Cry of Absence* (1971)

1929 **James Coco.** American stage, screen, and television actor

1929 **Jules Bergman.** American television newsman

1937 **Tom Flores.** Professional football player and coach who led the Oakland Raiders to two superbowl championships (1984 and 1987)

1939 **Tommy Davis.** Professional baseball player

1944 **Manny Sanguillen.** Professional baseball player

1945 **Charles E. Greene.** Professional sprinter

1946 **Timothy Dalton.** British motion-picture actor

1958 **Gary Oldman.** English motion-picture and television actor

1962 **Rosie O'Donnell.** American comedienne and television talk-show hostess

1962 **Matthew Broderick.** American motion-picture actor

March 21 – Events

47 BC Julius Caesar defeated Ptolemy XII, Cleopatra's brother and rival, at Alexandria, Egypt, thus restoring Cleopatra to the throne.

1556 Archbishop Thomas Cranmer was burned at the stake on orders of the Queen of England, Bloody Mary.

1621 The first Indian treaty by American colonists was made, between Governor Carver of the Plymouth Colony and Massasoit, chief of the Wampanoags.

1790 Thomas Jefferson became the first U.S. secretary of state.

1800 Pius VII was crowned Roman Catholic pope.

1804 The Code Napoleon went into effect in France and its occupied territories.

1918 Germany launched the first of its final offensives of World War I along the Somme.

1945 Seven thousand Allied planes dropped 12,000 tons of explosives on Germany in full daylight in World War II.

1946 The United Nations set up temporary headquarters at Hunter College in New York.

1963 The Alcatraz federal penitentiary in San Francisco Bay was closed after the U.S. government decided it was too expensive to maintain.

1965 The Selma-to-Montgomery civil rights march began in Alabama, led by the Reverend Martin Luther King, Jr.

1972 The U.S. Supreme Court ruled that states could not require a one-year residency for voting eligibility.

March 22 – Birthdays

1459 **Maximilian I.** Holy Roman Emperor, 1493-1519

1517 **Gioseffo Zarlino.** Italian composer and greatest theorist of the mid-16th century

1599 **Sir Anthony Van Dyck.** Most prominent Flemish painter of the 17th century

1797 **Wilhelm I.** King of Prussia and first emperor of modern Germany, 1871-1888

1817 **Braxton Bragg.** Confederate general in the Civil War

1846 **Randolph Caldecott.** English illustrator who began a new era in children's picture books, and for whom the Caldecott Medal, for the year's outstanding children's picture book, was named

1868 **Robert A. Millikan.** American physicist who with his oil drop experiment first measured the charge of an electron

1869 **Emilio Aguinaldo.** Filipino freedom fighter who led the struggle for Philippine independence from Spain and later from the United States

1884 **Arthur H. Vandenburg.** U.S. senator and statesman of the Truman era

1887 **Chico Marx.** American comedian and one of the Marx Brothers comedy group

1907 **James Gavin.** American World War II general

1908 **Maurice Stans.** Secretary of commerce under President Nixon

1908 **Louis L'Amour.** American best-selling author of 86 Western novels

1908 **Jack Crawford.** Australian tennis superstar and Hall of Famer

1910 **Nicholas Monsarrat.** English novelist noted for *The Cruel Sea* (1951) and *The Tribe That Lost Its Head* (1956)

1914 **Karl Malden.** American motion-picture and television actor

1914 **John Stanley.** American comic strip writer and creator of *Little Lulu*

1917 **Ed Furgol.** Professional golfer

1918 **Virginia Grey.** American motion-picture actress

1923 **Marcel Marceau.** Pre-eminent mime of the 20th century

1926 **Billy Goodman.** Professional baseball player

1928 **Ed Macauley.** Professional basketball player with over 11,000 career points

1930 **Stephen Sondheim.** American composer and lyricist noted for works such as *Passion* and the lyrics for *West Side Story* (1957)

1930 **Derek Curtis Bok.** President of Harvard University in the 1960s and 1970s

1930 **Pat Robertson.** American minister and television evangelist

1931	**Burton Richter.** American Nobel Prize-winning physicist
1931	**William Shatner.** American motion-picture and television actor noted for his role as Captain Kirk in the long-running television series *Star Trek*
1934	**Orrin Hatch.** U.S. senator
1935	**Lea Pericoli.** Italian tennis player
1936	**May Britt.** Swedish motion-picture actress
1943	**George Benson.** American singer, guitarist and winner of three Grammy Awards
1946	**Don Chaney.** Professional basketball player
1948	**Andrew Lloyd Webber.** British composer noted for works such as the scores of *Jesus Christ Superstar* (1970), *Cats* (1981), and *Phantom of the Opera* (1986)
1952	**Bob Costas.** American TV sportscaster
1954	**Ross Browner.** Professional football player
1957	**Stephanie Mills.** American singer and actress
1959	**Matthew Modine.** American motion-picture and television actor

March 22 – Events

1622	Indians massacred some 350 colonists at Jamestown, Virginia.
1765	The British Parliament passed the Stamp Act, the first direct tax on the American Colonies.
1794	Congress passed a law prohibiting American ships from supplying slaves to other countries.
1820	Commodore Stephen Decatur was mortally wounded in a duel with Commodore James Barron outside Washington.
1832	Johann Wolfgang von Goethe, the greatest German writer of all time, died in Weimar at age 82.
1882	The U.S. Congress outlawed polygamy.
1894	The first Stanley Cup game was played in Montreal, with Montreal beating Ottawa, 3-1.
1895	The first theater showing of a motion picture took place in Paris, using the cinematographe of inventors Louis and Auguste Lumiere.
1934	The first Master's Golf tournament began, in Augusta, Georgia.
1941	The Grand Coulee Dam on the Columbia River began producing electric power.
1977	Indira Gandhi resigned as prime minister of India after her party's defeat. She returned to power two elections later.
1979	The Israeli Parliament approved the peace treaty with Egypt.

March 23 – Birthdays

1430	**Margaret of Anjou.** Queen consort of England's Henry VI
1736	**Arthur St. Clair.** Scottish-American soldier and statesman and member of the Continental Congress
1749	**Marquis Pierre Simon de Laplace.** French mathematician noted for the Laplace transform
1769	**William Smith.** Father of English geology

1818	**Don Carlos Buell.** Northern Civil War general
1823	**Shuyler Colfax.** U.S. Vice President under President Grant
1835	**Edward Caird.** English philosopher and leader of the Neo-Hegelian school
1857	**Fannie Farmer.** Noted American cooking expert and candy maker
1881	**Roger Martin du gard.** Nobel Prize-winning French novelist noted for *Jean Barois* (1913) and *The World of the Thibaults* (1922-1940)
1887	**Sidney Hillman.** American labor leader and organizer of the Amalgamated Clothing Workers of America
1887	**Juan Gris.** Spanish-born painter and one of the pioneers of cubism
1900	**Erich Fromm.** German psychoanalyst, social philosopher, and author, noted for works such as *Escape from Freedom* (1941)
1903	**Jay W. Johnson.** American composer, author, and entertainer, noted for songs such as "Blue Christmas"
1908	**Joan Crawford.** American stage and motion-picture actress and superstar for nearly 50 years
1911	**Jack Ruby.** American who in 1963 shot Lee Harvey Oswald, President Kennedy's assassin, on live television
1912	**Wernher Von Braun.** German-American rocket and space expert who helped develop the German World War II V-2 rocket and the rockets that sent the first American into space
1917	**John Albert Guarnieri.** American composer, author, and pianist, noted for songs such as "Blue Mood"
1922	**Marty Allen.** American comedian and actor
1927	**Johnny Logan.** Professional baseball player
1929	**Roger Bannister.** British runner who in 1954 became the first man to run the mile in less than four minutes
1937	**Robert Charles Gallo.** American researcher who helped identify the AIDS virus (1984)
1937	**Craig Breedlove.** American automobile racer who set the world land speed record in 1963 at Bonneville Salt Flats in Utah at 407.45 mph, and in 1965 drove a car 600.6 mph at Bonneville
1938	**Maynard Jackson.** First black mayor of Atlanta
1939	**Rosie Darmon.** French tennis player
1943	**Lee May.** Professional baseball player
1945	**David Grisman.** American mandolin player of jazz and bluegrass music
1951	**Ron Jaworski.** Professional football player and superstar
1953	**Chaka Khan.** American rock singer
1955	**Moses Malone.** Professional basketball superstar
1957	**Amanda Plummer.** American stage and screen actress and daughter of actors Christopher Plummer and Tammy Grimes

March 23 – Events

1540	Waltham Abbey, last remaining monastery in England, was dissolved.
1603	Queen Elizabeth I of England died in London at age 69.
1729	English artist William Hogarth eloped with Jane Thornhill, the daughter of his painting teacher, Sir James Thornhill.
1743	Handel's *Messiah* was heard for the first time by a theater audience in London. King George II was in the audience and inaugurated a precedent by rising to his feet to applaud.
1775	In a fiery oration, Patrick Henry said, "Give me liberty or give me death."
1840	The American slang expression "O.K." was first used in print in the New York *New Era*. It came from "Old Kinderhook," a nickname of then President Martin Van Buren.
1842	Stendhal (Marie Henry Beyle), the great French novelist, died in Paris at age 59.
1903	The Wright brothers applied for a patent on their airplane.
1933	The Enabling Act of 1933 passed, establishing Hitler's dictatorship in Germany.
1956	Pakistan became an independent republic within the British Commonwealth.
1973	Watergate burglar James McCord, in testimony to Judge Sirica, implicated higher-ups in the Watergate break-in, which led to the opening up of the case.
1983	Dr. Barney Clark died at the University of Utah Medical Center 112 days after receiving the world's first artificial heart.

March 24 – Birthdays

1490	**Georgius Agricola.** German physician and scientist, known as the father of mineralogy
1688	**John Smibert.** American painter
1693	**John "Longitude" Harrison.** English clockmaker who solved the "longitude problem," the greatest scientific problem of the 1700s, by building five revolutionary clocks that enabled navigators to determine their longitude at sea
1755	**Rufus King.** One of the founding fathers of the United States
1809	**Joseph Liouville.** Noted French mathematician
1820	**Fanny J. Crosby.** Blind American hymn writer noted for such works as "Pass Me Not, O Gentle Savior," "Safe in the Arms of Jesus," "Rescue the Perishing," and over 5,000 other poems and hymns
1834	**William Morris.** English poet, artist, and reformer, who designed the Morris chair and in 1891 founded the Kelmscott Press
1834	**John Wesley Powell.** American geologist who in 1869 was the first to explore the Grand Canyon

1835	**Josef Stefan.** Austrian physicist and co-formulator of the Stefan-Boltzmann Law of radiant heat energy
1855	**Andrew Mellon.** American financier and secretary of the treasury, 1921-1932
1866	**Jack McAuliffe.** American Hall of Fame boxer
1874	**Harry Houdini.** Sensational escape artist and one of the greatest magicians of his time
1885	**Charles Daniels.** America's first great swimmer
1886	**Edward Weston.** One of the most influential 20th-century photographers
1887	**Fatty Arbuckle.** American comic actor, director, and screenwriter
1893	**George Sisler.** Hall of Fame baseball player and one of the game's greatest hitters, with a .340 lifetime batting average
1894	**Al Espinosa.** Professional golfer
1897	**Wilhelm Reich.** German Freudian Marxist psychologist
1899	**Allen Saunders.** American comic strip writer and one of the creators of *Mary Worth*
1902	**Thomas E. Dewey.** Twice candidate for U.S. president, in 1944 and 1948
1903	**Malcolm Muggeridge.** English journalist and television interviewer
1907	**Lauris J. Norstad.** American general and early commander of the Strategic Air Command
1909	**Clyde Barrow.** Notorious American robber and murderer, who with his accomplice Bonnie Parker terrorized the American countryside in the 1930s
1911	**Joseph Barbera.** American animator who with William Hanna created the Tom and Jerry cartoons
1915	**Richard Conte.** American motion-picture actor
1920	**Gene Nelson.** American dancer and actor
1925	**Norman Fell.** American motion-picture and television actor
1928	**Byron Janis.** American concert pianist
1928	**Vanessa Brown.** Austrian-born motion-picture actress
1930	**Steve McQueen.** American motion-picture and television actor
1940	**Bob Mackie.** American fashion designer
1942	**Jesus Alou.** Professional baseball player and brother of baseball players Felipe and Matty Alou
1951	**Patty Bradley.** Professional golfer and Hall of Famer
1951	**Tommy Hilfiger.** American fashion designer
1954	**Donna Pescow.** American television and motion-picture actress
1954	**Robert Carradine.** American motion-picture actor and son of actor John Carradine
1956	**Gary Templeton.** Professional baseball player
1958	**Bruce Hurst.** Professional baseball player
1959	**Renaldo "Skeets" Nehemiah.** Professional football player
1967	**Kathy Rinaldi.** American tennis player

March 24 – Events

1603 James I, the first Stuart king of England, ascended to the throne, succeeding Queen Elizabeth I, who had died the previous day.

1765 England enacted the Quartering Act, requiring American colonists to provide temporary housing to British soldiers.

1882 Professor Robert Koch announced in Berlin his discovery of the pathogenic germs of tuberculosis.

1882 American poet Henry Wadsworth Longfellow died in Cambridge, Massachusetts, at age 75.

1905 Jules Verne, the great French novelist, died in Amiens at age 77.

1934 The United States granted the Philippines its independence, effective July 4, 1946.

1958 Rock and roll singer Elvis Presley was inducted into the U.S. Army in Memphis, Tennessee.

1964 The first U.S. John F. Kennedy half dollars were issued.

1971 The U.S. Senate voted to end sponsorship of the supersonic transport.

1973 Anwar Sadat became president of Egypt.

1989 The Exxon supertanker *Valdez* plowed into a rocky reef off Valdez, Alaska, spilling 240,000 barrels of oil into Prince William Sound, in the worst oil disaster in American waters.

1998 Two school boys, Andrew Golden, age 12, and Mitchell Johnson, age 14, in Jonesboro, Arkansas, opened fire on their classmates and teachers, killing four girls and a teacher.

1999 NATO began a bombing war against Yugoslavia for the stated purpose of preventing Serbian president Slobodan Milosevic from carrying out his plans for "ethnic cleansing" of the people of the province of Kosovo.

March 25 – Birthdays

1133 **Henry II.** King of England, 1154-1189

1252 **Conrad the Younger.** King of Jerusalem and Sicily

1347 **Catherine of Siena.** Patron Saint of Italy

1479 **Vasily III.** Czar of Russia, 1505-33, son of Ivan the Great, and father of Ivan the Terrible

1614 **Juan Carreno de Miranda.** Spanish painter

1771 **Joachim Murat.** Most famous of Napoleon's cavalry commanders

1867 **Arturo Toscanini.** One of the greatest virtuoso conductors of the first half of the twentieth century

1871 **Gutzon Borglum.** American sculptor who planned and began the Mount Rushmore Memorial in South Dakota, which was completed after his death by his son

1879 **William S. Knudsen.** American industrialist who conceived the idea of the conveyer belt in mass producing automobiles, and who directed U.S. war production during World War II

1881 **Bela Bartok.** Hungarian composer and pianist, and one of the giants of the 20th century

1892 **Andy Clyde.** Scottish-born motion-picture and television actor

1900 **Robert B. Reed.** American composer, conductor, and organist, noted for songs such as "Rise Up, O Men of God" and "Let Us Now Praise Famous Men"

1901 **Ed Begley.** American stage, screen, and television actor

1903 **Frankie Carle.** American composer noted for songs such as "Oh What it Seemed to Be" and "Sunrise Serenade" (song of the year in 1938)

1905 **Binnie Barnes.** English-born motion-picture actress

1908 **David Lean.** English motion-picture director

1909 **Jerry Livingston.** American songwriter noted for "Mairzy Doats" (1943)

1909 **Dutch Leonard.** Professional baseball player

1912 **Jean Vilar.** French actor and director

1914 **Aline Saarinen.** American television newswoman

1920 **Howard Cosell.** American television sports announcer

1921 **Simone Signoret.** French motion-picture actress who won an Academy Award for *Room at the Top* (1958)

1925 **Flannery O'Connor.** American novelist and short story writer, noted for such works as *Everything that Rises Must Converge*

1928 **James Arthur Lovell Jr.** U.S. astronaut and participant in the record-breaking 14-day orbit of *Gemini 7* in December 1965

1932 **Wes Santee.** American champion miler

1932 **John Willard Marriott Jr.** American restaurant executive and son of the founder of the Marriott Corporation

1932 **Gene Shalit.** Movie reviewer on NBC's *Today Show*

1934 **Gloria Steinem.** Noted American feminist and editor

1938 **Hoyt Axton.** American singer, actor and songwriter

1940 **Anita Bryant.** American singer and television personality

1942 **Aretha Franklin.** American soul singer

1943 **Paul Michael Glaser.** American actor

1947 **Elton John.** American rock singer and composer

1952 **Bonnie Bedelia.** American stage, screen and television actress

1955 **Lee Mazzilli.** Professional baseball player

1960 **Steve Norman.** British musician with the Spandau Ballet musical group

1965 **Sarah Jessica Parker.** American stage, screen and television actress

1966 **Tom Glavine.** Professional baseball pitcher and Cy Young Award winner in 1998

1967 **Debi Thomas.** American figure skater and Olympic bronze medalist in 1988

1971 **Sheryl Swoopes.** American basketball player and superstar

March 25 – Events

708	Constantine I was elected pope.
1306	Robert Bruce was crowned King of Scotland.
1616	William Shakespeare called in his lawyer, Francis Collins, to revise his will. He died less than a month later.
1634	Lord Baltimore's colonists landed in Maryland.
1668	The first recorded horse race was held in America, at Hempstead, New York.
1776	The Continental Congress conferred the first medal awarded by the colonies upon General George Washington.
1807	The British Parliament abolished slave trade.
1894	Coxey's Army, led by Jacob S. Coxey, started out for Washington, D.C., from Massillon, Ohio, to "save the country" from the Panic of 1893.
1900	The Socialist Party of the United States was organized in Indianapolis.
1911	The Triangle Shirtwaist factory fire occurred in New York City as fire ripped through the building killing 146 people, mostly immigrant seamstresses who were trapped inside by locked doors.
1913	The Palace Theatre, the home of vaudeville, opened in New York City.
1918	Claude Debussy, the French composer, died of cancer in Paris at age 55.
1934	Horton Smith won the first Masters Golf tournament.
1954	RCA began its commercial production of television sets equipped to transmit in color.
1957	The Treaty of Rome established the European Common Market.
1958	Sugar Ray Robinson won the middleweight boxing title for a record fifth time, in a 15-round decision in Chicago over Carmen Basilio.
1964	Britain set aside an acre of land at Runnymede, where the Magna Carta was signed in 1215, as a memorial for John F. Kennedy.
1965	The Reverend Martin Luther King Jr. led 25,000 marchers to the state Capitol in Montgomery, Alabama, completing the Civil Rights march from Selma.
1971	Civil war erupted in East Pakistan, leading to the creation of the independent state of Bangladesh.
1972	Bobby Hull scored his 600th career goal, becoming the only National Hockey League player besides Gordie Howe to reach this mark.
1975	King Faisal of Saudi Arabia was shot to death by a mentally ill nephew.

March 26 – Birthdays

1516	**Konrad Von Gesner.** Pioneer Swiss naturalist known for his five-volume encyclopedic survey, *Historia animalium*
1753	**Sir Benjamin Thompson.** American-born English physicist and statesman who helped found the British Royal Institute in 1800
1850	**Edward Bellamy.** American journalist and author, noted for the novel *Looking Backward* in 1888.
1859	**A.E. Housman.** British poet and scholar, noted for *A Shropshire Lad* in 1896
1868	**Fuad I.** King of Egypt, 1922-1936
1874	**Robert Frost.** The most popular American poet of his time
1874	**Conde Nast.** American publisher and early owner of *Vogue* and *House and Garden* magazines
1879	**Othmar Herman Ammann.** Designer of the Verazano-Narrows Bridge over New York harbor
1880	**Duncan Hines.** American businessman and author, who became an authority on eating and lodging establishments
1893	**James B. Conant.** American scientist and president of Harvard University, 1933-1953
1893	**Palmiro Togliatti.** Leader of the Italian Communist Party after World War II
1904	**Joseph Campbell.** American author known for works such as *The Hero of a Thousand Faces* (1949)
1907	**Leigh Harline.** American composer and conductor, noted for songs such as "When You Wish Upon a Star" and "Jiminy Cricket"
1908	**Betty MacDonald.** American novelist and author of *The Egg and I*
1911	**Tennessee Williams.** American playwright noted for such works as *The Glass Menagerie* and *A Streetcar Named Desire*
1914	**William Westmoreland.** U.S. general in the Vietnam War
1916	**Sterling Hayden.** American actor and writer
1923	**Bob Elliott.** Bob of the Bob and Ray comedy team
1925	**Pierre Boulez.** French composer, pianist, and conductor of the New York Philharmonic
1930	**Sandra Day O'Connor.** First woman appointed to the U.S. Supreme Court
1930	**Gregory Corso.** American poet and member of the Beat movement
1931	**Leonard Nimoy.** American motion-picture and television actor noted for his role as Spock in *Star Trek*
1934	**Alan Arkin.** American motion-picture actor
1934	**Gino Cappelletti.** Professional football player
1937	**Wayne Embry.** Professional basketball player and executive
1939	**James Caan.** American motion-picture actor
1942	**Erica Jong.** American novelist and author of *Fear of Flying*
1943	**Bob Woodward.** American newspaper reporter who with reporter Carl Bernstein helped the *Washington Post* win a Pulitzer Prize for its exposure of the Watergate scandals.
1944	**Diana Ross.** American singer and member of the Supremes singing group
1948	**Steve Tyler.** American rock singer with the Aerosmith band
1949	**Vicki Lawrence.** American actress and comedienne

1950	**Teddy Pendergrass.** American rhythm and blues singer
1950	**Martin Short.** Canadian motion-picture and television actor
1955	**Ann Meyers.** One of the first great female basketball players and Hall of Famer
1956	**Ilano Kloss.** South African tennis player
1957	**Leeza Gibbons.** Television personality and hostess of the *Leeza* show
1960	**Jennifer Grey.** American motion-picture noted for her role in *Dirty Dancing* (1987)
1960	**Marcus Allen.** Professional football player
1962	**John Stockton.** Professional football player

March 26 – Events

1645	Oliver Cromwell's victory at Stowe-on-the-Wold ended the four-year civil war in England.
1804	The Louisiana Purchase was divided into the Territory of Orleans and the District of Louisiana.
1827	Ludwig van Beethoven died in Vienna at age 56. On his death bed the deaf master said, "I shall hear in heaven."
1892	Walt Whitman, the great American poet, died in Camden, New Jersey, five days before his 73rd birthday.
1900	The comic strip, *Happy Hooligan,* by Fred Opper, first appeared.
1918	General Ferdinand Foch of France was appointed commander of all Allied armies in World War I.
1923	Sarah Bernhardt, the noted stage actress, died in Paris at age 81 in the arms of her son Maurice.
1953	Dr. Jonas Salk announced the discovery of the Salk vaccine.
1958	The U.S. Army launched *Explorer Three,* America's third successful satellite.
1971	East Pakistan proclaimed its independence, assuming the name Bangladesh.
1979	Egypt and Israel signed a treaty in Washington ending 31 years of war.

March 27 – Birthdays

1416	**St. Francis of Paola.** Founder of the Minim Friars
1785	**Louis XVII.** Son of the guillotined Louis XVI and King of France who never reigned because he was kept in prison during his two-year tenure as king
1797	**Alfred de Vigny.** French poet, dramatist, and novelist
1813	**Nathaniel Currier.** Senior member of the Currier and Ives print team
1845	**Wilhelm Roentgen.** German physicist who discovered X rays and in 1901 received the first Nobel Prize in physics
1851	**Vincent D'Indy.** French composer, organist, and conductor
1855	**Sir Alfred Ewing.** English physicist who discovered hysteresis
1863	**Sir Henry Royce.** Co-founder of Rolls-Royce, Ltd.

1879	**Edward Steichen.** Pioneer of American photography
1879	**Miller Huggins.** Manager of the great New York Yankee baseball teams of the Babe Ruth era
1886	**Ludwig Mies Van Der Rohe.** A leading German architect of the early 20th century
1892	**Ferde Grofe.** American composer noted for his *Grand Canyon Suite* (1931)
1899	**Gloria Swanson.** American motion-picture actress whose career spanned over 60 years
1901	**Sato Eisaku.** Prime minister of Japan, 1964-1972
1903	**Betty Balfour.** Britain's most popular movie star of the silent film era
1910	**John Robinson Pierce.** American engineer and father of the communications satellite
1912	**James Callaghan.** Prime minister of Britain, 1976-1979
1914	**Budd Schulberg.** American novelist and screen writer
1914	**Snooky Lanson.** American singer
1916	**Albert T. Frisch.** American composer, pianist, and saxophonist, noted for songs such as "Two Different Worlds" and "Come Out Wherever You Are"
1917	**Cyrus Vance.** American secretary of state under President Carter
1922	**Barnaby Conrad.** American bullfighter and author
1924	**Sarah Vaughan.** American jazz singer
1927	**Anthony Lewis.** American newspaper columnist
1931	**David Janssen.** American motion-picture and television actor
1939	**Cale Yarborough.** American automobile racer
1942	**Michael York.** British stage, screen, and television actor
1952	**Maria Schneider.** French stage and motion-picture actress
1953	**Annemarie Proell.** Austrian ski racer
1955	**Chris McCarron.** American Hall of Fame jockey, two-time Kentucky Derby winner and youngest jockey to ride 3,000 winners
1963	**Quentin Tarantino.** American motion-picture actor and director noted for his direction of *Pulp Fiction* (1994)

March 27 – Events

47 BC	Ptolemy XII, King of Egypt and brother of Cleopatra, drowned in the Nile, probably with an assist by Julius Caesar, who thereby made Cleopatra queen.
30	Jesus was condemned to be crucified by Pontius Pilate. The date, which is highly uncertain, is said to have been set down on a copper plate discovered in 1810 in the ancient city of Aquileia.
1513	Ponce de Leon discovered the east coast of Florida in his quest for the fountain of youth. He landed on the island of Bimini and reached the mainland on April 2.
1625	Charles I ascended to the throne of England, Scotland, and Ireland, upon the death of James I.

1794 President Washington signed the act creating the U.S. Navy.

1814 Andrew Jackson defeated the Creek Indians in the Battle of Horseshoe Bend in Alabama.

1836 The first Mormon temple was dedicated in Kirtland, Ohio.

1846 General Winfield Scott took Vera Cruz in the Mexican War.

1884 The first long-distance telephone call was made, between New York and Boston.

1917 The Seattle Metropolitans became the first U.S. team to win the Stanley Cup, defeating the Montreal Canadiens.

1920 Mary Pickford, "America's Sweetheart," married the swashbuckling actor, Douglas Fairbanks.

1958 Nikita Khrushchev became the head of the Soviet government.

1968 Russian cosmonaut Yuri Gagarin, the first man to orbit the earth, was killed in a plane crash.

1977 A KLM Boeing 747 crashed into a Pan Am 747 on a runway on the Canary Island of Tenerife, killing over 580 people, in the worst disaster in aviation history.

1992 Easley Blackwood, the inventor of the Blackwood Convention in bridge, died at age 89.

March 28 – Birthdays

1472 **Fra Bartolommeo.** Italian painter who under the influence of the Florentine preacher Girolamo Savonarola became a member of the Dominican order

1515 **Saint Theresa.** One of the great mystics of the Roman Catholic Church and a patron saint of Spain (also known as St. Theresa of Avila)

1592 **John Amos Comenius.** Czech bishop whose textbook *Orbis Sensualium Pictus* was the first in which pictures were as important as the text

1652 **Samuel Sewall.** Presiding judge who had 20 people put to death in the Salem witch trials in 1692, and who confessed his error five years later

1660 **George I.** First Hanoverian king of England, 1714-1727

1750 **Francisco de Miranda.** A Venezuelan patriot who fought in the American, French, and Spanish-American revolutions

1818 **Wade Hampton.** Confederate general in the Civil War

1836 **Frederick Pabst.** German-American brewer who co-founded Pabst Beer in 1864

1862 **Aristide Briand.** Nobel Peace Prize-winning French statesman who served as Premier of France eleven times and was largely responsible for the peaceful separation of church and state in France

1868 **Maxim Gorki.** Russian novelist and the foremost literary artist of his time in the Soviet Union

1875 **Helen Westley.** American motion-picture actress

1878 **Herbert Henry Lehman.** American philanthropist, governor of New York, and U.S. senator

1890 **Paul Whiteman.** American bandleader and the "King of Jazz"

1893 **Spyros P. Skouras.** Greek motion-picture mogul

1894 **Wallace Carlson.** American cartoonist who with Sol Hess created the comic strip *The Nebbs* (1923-46)

1894 **Octave Blake.** Harness racing Hall of Famer

1899 **August Busch Jr.** Head of the Annheuser Busch beer company and owner of the St. Louis Cardinals baseball team

1902 **Dame Flora Robson.** Superb character actress of the British stage and screen

1903 **Rudolf Serkin.** Czechoslovakian-born pianist and teacher

1906 **Bob Allen.** American stage, screen, and television actor

1907 **Irving "Swifty" Lazar.** Noted American talent agent

1909 **Nelson Algren.** American novelist and author of *The Man with the Golden Arm*

1909 **Lon Warneke.** Professional baseball player and umpire

1914 **Edmund Muskie.** U.S. senator and secretary of state under President Carter

1915 **Jay Livingston.** American composer and lyricist, noted for such songs as "Mona Lisa," "Buttons and Bows," "Silver Bells," and the theme song for the TV show *Bonanza*

1919 **Vic Raschi.** Professional baseball player

1921 **Dirk Bogarde.** English motion-picture actor

1924 **Freddie Bartholomew.** Noted American child actor

1928 **Zbigniew Brzezinski.** National security adviser under President Carter

1933 **Frank Murkowski.** U.S. senator

1937 **Liz Trotta.** American broadcast journalist

1940 **Kevin Loughery.** Professional basketball player and coach

1941 **James Turner.** Professional football player

1941 **Alf H. Clausen.** American composer noted for his music for TV variety shows, comedy shows, and dramatic shows, such as the *Mary Tyler Moore Comedy Hour* and *Charlie's Angels*

1942 **Jerry Sloan.** Professional basketball player

1944 **Rick Barry.** Professional Hall of Fame basketball player and one of the game's superstars

1944 **Ken Howard.** American motion-picture actor

1948 **Sam Lacey.** Professional basketball player

1948 **Dianne Wiest.** American stage and screen actress

1951 **Karen Kain.** Canadian ballerina

1952 **James Scott.** Professional football player

1955 **Reba McEntire.** American country singer

1961 **Glenn Davis.** Professional baseball player

March 28 – Events

193 Roman emperor Publius Helvius Pertinax was murdered by the Praetorian Guard.

1797 Nathaniel Briggs of New Hampshire received a patent for a washing machine.

1834 President Andrew Jackson was censured by the U.S. Senate for removing federal deposits from the U.S. Bank.

1854 Britain and France declared war on Russia, beginning the Crimean War.

1881 Modest Mussorgsky, the Russian composer, died of alcoholism in St. Petersburg at age 42.

1930 The name of Constantinople was officially changed to Istanbul. It had been called Istanbul unofficially since 1453 when the Turks brought down the eastern Roman Empire.

1939 Generalissimo Francisco Franco captured Madrid from the Spanish Loyalists, virtually ending the Spanish Civil War.

1953 Jim Thorpe, one of the greatest athletes of all time, died at age 64.

1969 Ex-President Dwight D. Eisenhower died in Walter Reed Hospital in Washington, D.C. at age 78.

1979 A cooling system malfunctioned at Pennsylvania's Three Mile Island power plant, leaking radioactivity into the air. It was the worst nuclear accident in history at the time.

March 29 – Birthdays

1790 **John Tyler.** Tenth U.S. president and first to succeed to office because of the death of the president

1819 **Edwin Laurentine Drake.** Driller of the first productive United States oil well, at Titusville, Pennsylvania

1840 **Sir John Keltie.** English geographer

1859 **Oscar F. Mayer.** Bavarian-born meat packer who with his brother Oscar Gottfried opened the first Oscar Mayer store, in 1883 in Chicago

1867 **Cy Young.** Winningest pitcher in baseball with a career total of 511 victories, and for whom the Cy Young Award was named

1869 **Sir Edwin Landseer Lutyens.** English architect who designed the British embassy in Washington, D.C., in the 1920s

1875 **Lou Henry Hoover.** Wife of President Herbert Hoover

1878 **Albert Von Tilzer.** American composer noted for songs such as "I'll Be With You In Apple Blossom Time," "Take Me Out To The Ball Game," and "Put Your Arms Around Me, Honey"

1881 **Raymond Mathewson Hood.** Architect of some of America's most striking skyscrapers, such as the Chicago Tribune Tower and Rockefeller Center

1889 **Howard Lindsay.** American playwright, actor, and author of *Life with Father*

1891 **Warner Baxter.** American motion-picture actor

1892 **Josef Cardinal Mindszenty.** Hungarian Roman Catholic Church cardinal who became a symbol of the Hungarian resistance to Communism in the 1948 revolt

1899 **Lavrenty P. Beria.** Head of the Russian secret police under Stalin

1902 **Sir William Walton.** English composer noted for such works as the oratorio *Belshazzar's Feast* and the opera *Troilus and Cressida*

1908 **Arthur O'Connell.** American stage and motion-picture actor

1910 **Bill Dietrich.** Professional baseball player

1911 **Philip Ahn.** American stage, screen, and television actor

1916 **Eugene J. McCarthy.** U.S. senator and opponent of the Vietnam War policy in the 1960s

1917 **Tommy Holmes.** Professional baseball player

1918 **Sam Walton.** American businessman who founded Wal-Mart (1962) and built it into the largest retail chain in the U.S.

1918 **Pearl Bailey.** American singer and actress

1919 **Eileen Heckart.** American stage, motion-picture, and television actress

1921 **Ferris Fain.** Professional baseball player

1937 **Billy Carter.** Brother of President Jimmy Carter

1942 **Larry Pressler.** U.S. senator

1943 **John Major.** British prime minister who succeeded Margaret Thatcher

1943 **Vangelis (Papathanasiou).** Greek composer and pianist

1943 **Eric Idle.** British comedian and actor

1944 **Denny McLain.** Professional baseball pitcher who won 31 games in 1968

1945 **Walt Frazier.** Professional basketball player and Hall of Famer

1949 **Joe Ehrmann.** Professional football player

1950 **Bud Cort.** American motion-picture actor

1955 **Earl Campbell.** Professional football player and Hall of Famer

1956 **Thomas Kurt.** American gynmast and television commentator

1976 **Jennifer Capriati.** American tennis player

March 29 – Events

1461 Edward IV of England defeated ex-King Henry VI at Towton Moor in the War of the Roses. The victory gave Edward the English throne.

1812 The first wedding took place in the White House when Mrs. Lucy Payne Washington, sister of Dolley Madison, married Justice Thomas Todd of the Supreme Court.

1813 Future president John Tyler married Letitia Christian.

1848 Niagara Falls stopped flowing for the first time in recorded history when tons of ice jammed the river near Buffalo. The local residents feared that the world was coming to an end.

1867 The British North America Act was passed, establishing the Dominion of Canada.

1882 The Knights of Columbus was chartered in Connecticut.

1917 The great race horse, Man O' War, was born at Nursery Stud, Kentucky. He went on to win 20 of 21 races before being put out to stud at age four.

1927 Major Henry Segrave drove an automobile 203 miles per hour at Daytona Beach, Florida, the first time a motor-driven vehicle exceeded 200 mph.

1932 Comedian Jack Benny made his radio debut as a guest on the Ed Sullivan program.

1951 Ethel and Julius Rosenberg were found guilty of sabotage. They later became the only convicted spies to be executed by sentence of a U.S. civil court.

1971 First Lieutenant William Calley was found guilty by a U.S. court-martial jury of murdering civilians at My Lai, South Vietnam.

1973 The last American troops left South Vietnam, ending U.S. involvement in the Vietnam War.

March 30 – Birthdays

1135 **Maimonides.** Jewish philosopher who tried to harmonize Judaism with the teachings of Aristotle in his principal work, *The Guide of the Perplexed,* in 1190

1568 **Sir Henry Wotten.** English poet and diplomat

1719 **Sir John Hawkins.** Author of the first history of music in English

1727 **Tommaso Traetta.** Italian composer

1746 **Francisco Goya.** Spanish painter and one of the first masters of modern art, noted for works such as the *Naked Maja* and *The 2nd of May*

1820 **Anna Sewell.** English author noted for *Black Beauty* (1877)

1842 **John Fiske.** American philosopher and historian who helped spread Darwin's theory of evolution

1844 **Paul Verlaine.** French poet of the symbolist movement of the late 19th century

1848 **Don Carlos II.** Claimant to the Spanish throne

1853 **Vincent Van Gogh.** Dutch painter second in importance only to Rembrandt, and noted for works such as *Sunflowers* and *Starry Night*

1858 **De Wolf Hopper.** American actor and singer of the 1880s

1863 **Joseph Caillaux.** French statesman and fiscal expert

1880 **Sean O'Casey.** The greatest Irish playwright of his time

1883 **Jo Davidson.** American portrait sculptor whose greatest works include portraits of General John J. Pershing and Franklin D. Roosevelt

1894 **Sergey Vladimirovich Ilyushin.** Russian aircraft designer

1913 **Richard Helms.** American ambassador and director of the C.I.A. under President Nixon

1913 **Frankie Laine.** American actor, composer, author, and singer, with 16 golden records to his credit

1914 **Sonny Boy Williamson.** American blues musician

1919 **McGeorge Bundy.** Advisor to Presidents Kennedy and Lyndon Johnson

1920 **Turhan Bey.** Austrian-born motion-picture actor

1923 **Dr. Frank Field.** Television weatherman and media superstar

1930 **John Astin.** American stage, screen, and television actor

1937 **Warren Beatty.** American motion-picture actor and producer and brother of actress Shirley MacLaine

1940 **Jerry Lucas.** Professional basketball player and Hall of Famer

1945 **Eric Clapton.** British guitarist and singer

1949 **Ray Magliozzi.** American car repair expert noted with his brother Tom for the radio show *Car Talk*

1957 **Paul Reiser.** American actor, comedian and author

March 30 – Events

317 BC Phocion, the great Athenian general and statesman, died at an approximate age of 85. (He was noted for his frankness, as when he was loudly acclaimed by a crowd, he asked an associate, "What asininity have I uttered that they applaud me so?")

1191 Celestine III was crowned Pope.

1533 Henry VIII of England divorced Catherine of Aragon, his first of six wives.

1842 Dr. Crawford Long became the first physician to use ether as an anesthetic in surgery.

1856 The Treaty of Paris ended the Crimean War.

1858 Hyman Lipman of Philadelphia patented the first pencil equipped with an eraser.

1867 Secretary of State Seward signed the agreement purchasing Alaska from Russia for $7 million—about two cents per acre. Americans roundly condemned the deal as "Seward's Folly."

1870 The Fifteenth Amendment to the Constitution was ratified, guaranteeing the right to vote regardless of race, color, or previous condition of servitude.

1945 Russian troops entered Austria, forcing a Nazi retreat on all fronts in World War II.

1953 Albert Einstein announced his revised Unified Field Theory, aimed at combining gravitational and electromagnetic equations in a single theory.

1981 President Reagan was shot on a Washington, D.C., street by a would-be assassin. Reagan's wound was minor and he became the first president to be shot and survive.

March 31 – Birthdays

1499 **Pius IV.** Roman Catholic Pope, 1559-1563

1596 **Rene Descartes.** French mathematician and "father of modern philosophy," noted for the rectangular, or cartesian coordinate system and for his famous statement "Cogito ergo sum" ("I think, therefore I am")

1621 **Andrew Marvell.** English poet whose works include such classics as "To His Coy Mistress"

1732 **Joseph Haydn.** One of the greatest Austrian composers and "father of the symphony"

1809 **Edward FitzGerald.** English writer and translator of the most famous version of *The Rubaiyat* of *Omar Khayyam*

1809 **Nikolai Gogol.** Russian novelist and dramatist, noted for *The Inspector-General* (1836), perhaps the greatest Russian play, *Dead Souls*, and *The Overcoat* (both in 1842)

1811 **Robert Wilhelm Bunsen.** German chemist who invented the Bunsen burner

1823 **Mary Chesnut.** Preeminent diarist of the Civil War era

1835 **John La Farge.** American painter often called "the father of mural painting in America"

1844 **Andrew Lang.** Scottish poet, historian, and anthropologist, noted for his book *Myth, Ritual, and Religion* (1887)

1870 **James M. Cox.** U.S. presidential candidate in 1920

1878 **Jack Johnson.** First black world heavyweight champion, 1908-1915

1895 **Vardis Fisher.** American novelist known for such works as *The Children of God*, a fictional history of the Mormons published in 1939

1895 **John J. McCloy.** American statesman of the post-World War II era

1903 **Arthur Godfrey.** American television entertainer

1911 **William Golden.** American artist who in 1951 designed the CBS eye trademark

1912 **William Julius Lederer.** American author who co-authored with Eugene Burdick *The Ugly American* (1958)

1915 **Henry Morgan.** American motion-picture and television actor and comedian

1918 **Tommy Bolt.** Professional golfer

1922 **Richard Kiley.** American stage, screen, and television actor

1927 **Cesar Chavez.** U.S. labor leader and president of the United Farm Workers

1928 **Lefty Frizzell.** American Hall of Fame country singer and musician

1928 **Gordie Howe.** Professional hockey player who scored more points than any other player in National Hockey League history until Wayne Gretzky in 1989

1929 **Liz Claiborne.** American fashion designer who founded Liz Claiborne, Inc., in 1976

1931 **Miller Barber.** Professional golfer

1934 **Shirley Jones.** American singer and actress

1935 **Herb Alpert.** American musician and leader of the Tiajuana Brass

1935 **Richard Chamberlain.** American motion-picture and television actor

1936 **John Fowles.** English author noted for works such as *The French Lieutenant's Woman* (1969)

1938 **Jimmy Johnson.** Hall of Fame professional football player and brother of gold medalist Rafer Johnson

1940 **Patrick Leahy.** U.S. senator

1940 **Barney Frank.** U.S. congressman

1945 **Gabe Kaplan.** American television actor

1948 **Rhea Perlman.** American television and motion-picture actress noted for her role in the long-running series *Cheers*

1948 **Albert Gore Jr.** U.S. senator, son of former senator Albert Gore, and vice president under President Clinton

March 31 – Events

1084 Henry VI of Germany, after deposing Pope Gregory VII, was crowned Holy Roman Emperor by Gregory's successor, Pope Clement III.

1631 John Donne, the English poet, died in London at age 59.

1829 Pius VIII was elected Roman Catholic pope.

1837 John Constable, the noted English painter, died in London at age 60.

1854 Commodore Matthew Perry signed a treaty opening Japan to trade with the United States.

1855 Charlotte Brontë, the English novelist, died in Hayworth at age 38.

1870 Thomas Peterson-Mundy of Perth Amboy, New Jersey, became the first black man to vote in America, one day after the 15th Amendment made it possible.

1889 The Eiffel Tower in Paris was officially opened to the public.

1917 The United States took possession of the Virgin Islands by purchase from Denmark.

1931 Knute Rockne, the celebrated Notre Dame football coach, was killed in a plane crash in Kansas.

1932 The Ford Motor Company introduced the V-8 engine in its 1932 models.

1939 Prime Minister Neville Chamberlain pledged British support for Poland in the event of a Nazi invasion.

1943 The great musical *Oklahoma!*, with songs by Richard Rodgers and Oscar Hammerstein II, opened on Broadway.

1973 Ken Norton defeated Muhammad Ali in a 12-round split decision, breaking Ali's jaw in the process.

1979 Iranians voted for a Muslim republic, paving the way for the take-over by Ayatollah Khomeini.

1981 De Witt Wallace, founder of *Reader's Digest,* died at age 91.

4
April

Our fourth month, April, got its name from *Aprilis,* a Latin word meaning *to open,* referring to the opening of leaves and buds during the month. April was the second month in the original Roman calendar, but it became the fourth month with the establishment of the Julian Calendar. April has always had 30 days except for a brief time in the calendar of Numa Pompilius when it had 29.

Special days of April include April Fools' Day (April 1), Pan American Day (April 14) and Patriot's Day, the anniversary of the beginning of the American Revolution in 1775 (April 19). Also, Easter and Good Friday occur most often in April, and the month has given us four Presidents: Thomas Jefferson, James Monroe, James Buchanan and U.S. Grant.

The birthstone of April is the diamond, and the special flowers are the sweet pea and the daisy.

April 1 – Birthdays

1578 **William Harvey.** English physicist who discovered the nature of the circulation of the blood

1697 **Abbe Prevost.** French novelist noted for works such as *Les Memoires d'un homme de qualite*

1755 **Anthelme Brillat-Savarin.** French jurist, writer, and gastronome

1815 **Otto von Bismarck.** Prussian statesman who united the German states into one empire, and became known as the Iron Chancellor of Germany

1834 **Jim Fisk.** American financier known as the "Barnum of Wall Street"

1866 **Ferruccio Benvenuto Busoni.** Italian conductor and composer and one of the greatest pianists since Franz Liszt

1868 **Edmond Rostand.** French dramatist and poet and author of *Cyrano de Bergerac* (1897)

1873 **Sergei Rachmaninoff.** Russian composer and conductor, and one of the greatest pianists of all time

1875 **Edgar Wallace.** English novelist and detective story writer noted for works such as *The Four Just Men* (1905)

1883 **Lon Chaney.** American actor who specialized in macabre characterizations and was known as "The Man of a Thousand Faces"

1886 **Wallace Beery.** American stage and motion-picture actor

1895 **Alberta Hunter.** One of the great ladies of the golden age of jazz

1901 **Johnny Farrell.** Hall of Fame golfer

1909 **Eddie Duchin.** American bandleader and pianist

1915 **Jeff Heath.** Professional baseball player

1920 **Toshiro Mifune.** Japanese motion-picture and television actor

1922 **William Manchester.** American writer and biographer

1928 **Herbert Klein.** Assistant to President Nixon, 1969-1974

1929 **Bo Schembechler.** Highly successful college football coach at the University of Michigan

1929 **Jane Powell.** American singer and actress

1929 **Milan Kundera.** Czech author known for *The Unbearable Lightness of Being*

1931 **Rolf Hochhuth.** German author and playwright noted for *The Deputy* (1963), an attack on Pope Pius XII as a supposed silent accomplice in Hitler's treatment of the Jews

1931 **George Baker.** Bulgarian-born motion-picture and television actor

1932 **Debbie Reynolds.** American motion-picture and television actress and singer

1939 **Rudolph Isley.** American singer with the Isley Brothers

1939 **Ali MacGraw.** American motion-picture actress

1939 **Phil Niekro.** Professional Hall of Fame baseball pitcher who won over 300 career games

1944 **Rusty Staub.** Professional baseball player

1947 **David Eisenhower.** Grandson and biographer of President Eisenhower

1947 **Norm Van Lier.** Professional basketball player

1948 **Willie Montanez.** Professional baseball player

1975 **Magdalena Maleeva.** Bulgarian tennis player and sister of tennis players Manuela and Katerina Maleeva

April 1 – Events

1548 Parliament ordered the *Book of Common Prayer* printed in English.

1564 The French began calling those celebrating April 1 as New Year's (in opposition to the new Gregorian calendar) "April Fools," marking the beginning of April Fool's Day.

1789 The U.S. House of Representatives held its first meeting, in New York City. Frederick A.C. Muhlenberg of Pennsylvania was elected first Speaker of the House.

1885 Swift & Company, one of the world's leading meat-packing companies, was founded by Gustavus Franklin Swift.

1902 Claude Debussy's *Prelude to the Afternoon of a Faun* was played for the first time in America.

1918 The Royal Air Force was founded in Great Britain.

1939 The United States recognized Generalissimo Franco's Nationalist government in Spain, following the end of the Spanish Civil War.

1945 U.S. marines invaded Okinawa in World War II.

1954 The U.S. Congress authorized the establishment of the Air Force Academy.

1960 *Tiros I,* the first satellite to take detailed weather pictures, was launched from Cape Canaveral, Florida.

1972 Major league baseball players struck for the first time in 102 years of organized baseball.

1973 The last of the United States prisoners of war returned home from North Vietnam.

1979 Iran proclaimed itself an Islamic Republic, following the downfall of the Shah.

1998 Judge Susan Webber Wright dismissed the sexual misconduct suit of Paula Jones brought against President Clinton, saying that there were no genuine issues for trial.

April 2 – Birthdays

742 **Charlemagne.** King of the Franks from A.D. 768 to 814, first Holy Roman Emperor, from A.D. 800 to 814, and the greatest ruler of the early Middle Ages

1798 **August Heinrich Hoffman.** Lyricist of "Deutschland, Deutschland, Uber Alles"

1805 **Hans Christian Andersen.** Master of the fairy tale and Denmark's most famous author

1827 **Holman Hunt.** English painter noted for works such as *The Scapegoat* and *The Light of the World*

1834 **Frederic Auguste Bartholdi.** French sculptor who designed the Statue of Liberty

1840 **Emile Zola.** French novelist and critic, noted for such works as *Nana* (1880) and *Germinal* (1885)

1862 **Nicholas Murray Butler.** American educator and political figure, who helped found the Carnegie Endowment for International Peace

1869 **Clifford K. Berryman.** American political cartoonist

1869 **Hugh Jennings.** Professional baseball player and Hall of Famer

1875 **Walter Percy Chrysler.** A founder and first president of Chrysler Corporation

1891 **Max Ernst.** German painter and pioneer in the dada and surrealism movements

1907 **Luke Appling.** Hall of Fame baseball player who once hit a home run at age 75 in an Old Timers game

1908 **Buddy Ebsen.** American dancer and actor

1910 **Arnie Herber.** Hall of Fame professional football player

1912 **Herbert Mills.** American singer and member of the Mills Brothers group

1914 **Sir Alec Guinness.** British stage and motion-picture actor

1920 **Jack Webb.** American actor, producer, and director

1924 **Bobby Avila.** Professional baseball player

1925 **Ernie Stautner.** Hall of Fame professional football player

1926 **Jack Brabham.** Australian automobile racing driver who won the Grand Prix three times

1927 **Billy Pierce.** Professional baseball player

1927 **Carmen Basilio.** World middleweight champion, 1957-1958

1927 **Kenneth Tynan.** English critic and author

1928 **Rita Gam.** American stage, screen and television actress

1939 **Marvin Gaye.** American gospel and rhythm and blues singer

1941 **Leon Russell.** American rock singer and musician

1943 **Larry Coryell.** American jazz guitarist

1945 **Reggie Smith.** Professional baseball player

1945 **Don Sutton.** Professional Hall of Fame baseball pitcher who won over 300 career games

1945 **Linda Hunt.** American stage and motion-picture actress

1947 **Camille Paglia.** American author noted for *Sexual Personae* (1990)

1947 **Emmylou Harris.** American singer, songwriter, and winner of five Grammy music awards

1948 **Roy Gerela.** Professional football player

1949 **Pamela Reed.** American television and motion-picture actress

1952 **David Humm.** Professional football player

1964 **Pete Incaviglia.** Professional baseball player

April 2 – Events

999 Sylvester II was elected pope. He was the first French pope, one of the most learned men of his day (Arabic, mathematics, and science), and was said to have played a major role in popularizing Arabic numerals in the West.

1250 The Seventh Crusade surrendered to the Turks in Egypt and its leader, French King Louis IX, was taken prisoner. He was released after he agreed to pay a huge ransom.

1513 Ponce de Leon landed on the Florida mainland near the present site of St. Augustine, seeking the Fountain of Youth.

1559 The Treaty of Cateau-Cambresis was signed for England. It committed England, Spain, and France to end the war between the late Holy Roman Emperor Charles V and France.

1589 Henry IV, the first Bourbon king, ascended the throne of France.

1792 The United States Mint was established by Congress.

1810 Napoleon married Archduchess Marie Louise of Austria, after divorcing Josephine.

1865 Confederate troops evacuated Richmond and Petersburg in the Civil War. The Confederacy surrendered a week later.

1872 Samuel F.B. Morse, the great American inventor, died in New York at age 80.

1902 Thomas L. Tally opened the first movie theater in Los Angeles.

1917 President Wilson asked Congress to declare war on Germany, saying, "The world must be made safe for democracy."

1956 The television soap operas *As the World Turns* and *The Edge of Night* premiered on CBS.

1963 American satellite *Explorer 17* was launched from Cape Canaveral. It was the first satellite to study the atmosphere.

1980 The U.S. prime interest rate hit a record 20 per cent.

April 3 – Birthdays

1245 **Philip III.** King of France, 1270-1285

1593 **George Herbert.** A leading English poet of the 1600s

1753 **Simon Willard.** American clockmaker and creator of the banjo clock

1778 **Pierre Bretonneau.** First doctor to perform a tracheotomy for croup

1783 **Washington Irving.** First American man of letters and author of such works as *Rip Van Winkle* and *The Legend of Sleepy Hollow*

1822 **Edward Everett Hale.** Author of *The Man Without a Country*

1823 **William Marcy Tweed.** American political boss and head of the infamous "Tweed ring"

1837 **John Burroughs.** American naturalist and writer

1859 **Reginald De Koven.** American composer of light operas and of popular songs such as "Oh, Promise Me"

1863 **Henri Van de Velde.** Belgian architect

1881 **Alcide De Gasperi.** Premier of Italy following World War II

1885 **Allan Dwan.** Motion-picture director credited with over 400 films

1885 **Roger Lewis.** American composer noted for songs such as "One Dozen Roses" and "Down Home Rag"

1885 **Bud Fisher.** American cartoonist and creator of *Mutt and Jeff*

1898 **Henry R. Luce.** Co-founder in 1923 of *Time* magazine and one of the most prominent editors and publishers of his time

1898 **George Jessel.** American singer and actor

1901 **Larry Spier.** American publisher and composer, noted for songs such as "Memory Lane" and "Put Your Little Foot Right Out"

1907 **Iron Eyes Cody.** American Indian actor in many motion-pictures and who is noted for shedding a tear over the destruction of the environment in a TV ecology ad

1916 **Herb Caen.** American newspaper columnist and humorist

1919 **Ervin Drake.** American composer noted for songs such as "I Believe" and "It Was a Very Good Year"

1923 **Jan Sterling.** American stage and motion-picture actress

1924 **Doris Day.** American singer and actress

1924 **Marlon Brando.** American stage and motion-picture actor and superstar

1926 **Virgil I. Grissom.** Second American astronaut to travel in space (January 27, 1967)

1927 **Alex Grammas.** Professional baseball player

1928 **Don Gibson.** English singer and songwriter noted for "Sweet Dreams" and "I Can't Stop Loving You"

1930 **Lawton Chiles.** Governor of Florida

1930 **Helmut Kohl.** President of West Germany in the 1980s

1933 **Rod Funseth.** Professional golfer

1934 **Jim Parker.** Professional football player

1942 **Wayne Newton.** American singer and nightclub performer

1943 **Jan Berry.** Singer of the Jan and Dean duo

1943 **Marsha Mason.** American stage and motion-picture actress

1944 **Tony Orlando.** American singer

1949 **Lyle Alzado.** Professional football player

1952 **Michael C. Moore.** Mississippi attorney general who filed the first successful multi-million dollar lawsuit against the tobacco companies

1954 **Mike Pruitt.** Professional football player

1958 **Alec Baldwin.** American stage, screen and television actor

1959 **David Hyde Pierce.** American actor with the role of Niles Crane on TV's *Frasier*

1961 **Eddie Murphy.** American motion-picture and television actor and comedian

1972 **Jennie Garth.** American television actress

April 3 – Events

1559 The Treaty of Cateau-Cambresis among England, Spain, and France was signed for Spain and France. (England had signed earlier.)

1776 George Washington received an honorary doctor of laws degree from Harvard College.

1800	Congress authorized Martha Washington, widow of George Washington, to send her mail postage free.
1860	The Pony Express postal service was started as two riders simultaneously left St. Joseph, Missouri, and Sacramento, California.
1865	Union forces occupied Richmond, the Confederate capital, during the Civil War.
1882	Jesse James, the notorious outlaw, was shot and killed in St. Joseph, Missouri, by Robert Ford, a member of the James gang.
1897	Johannes Brahms, the great German composer, died in Vienna at age 63.
1936	Bruno Hauptmann was electrocuted in Trenton, New Jersey, for the kidnapping and murder of Charles A. Lindbergh, Jr.
1946	Japanese general Masaharu Homma was executed for ordering the "Death March" of Americans captured in Bataan in World War II.
1948	President Harry S. Truman signed the legislation implementing the Marshall Plan, which provided aid to Western Europe after World War II.
1953	*TV Guide* began publication.
1961	The 23rd Amendment to the U.S. Constitution was proclaimed, giving residents of the District of Columbia the right to vote in presidential elections.
1996	Theodore Kaczynski, the "Unabomber," a notorious killer using letter bombs, was apprehended by the FBI after his brother recognized his ideas expressed in an article sent to the *New York Times*.

April 4 – Birthdays

186	**Caracalla.** Emperor of Rome, A.D. 211-217, whose public baths are among the most splendid of the Roman ruins existing today
1648	**Grinling Gibbons.** English decorative wood carver and sculptor who was noted for much of the beautiful Restoration furniture of the Cromwell era
1752	**Nicola Antonio Zingarelli.** Italian opera composer
1758	**John Hoppner.** English painter
1758	**Pierre-Paul Prud'hon.** French draftsman and painter
1780	**Edward Hicks.** American painter, best known for *The Peaceable Kingdom,* a depiction of the Isaiah prophecy that the lion would lie down with the lamb
1792	**Thaddeus Stevens.** Radical Republican leader during the Reconstruction period who favored harsh treatment for the defeated South
1802	**Dorothea Dix.** American prison and asylum reformer
1821	**Linus Yale.** Designer of the Yale lock
1823	**Sir Wilhelm Siemens.** German-born inventor of a regenerative gas-fired furnace in 1856 that led to the open-hearth steelmaking process
1843	**Hans Richter.** Hungarian-born musician and one of the founders of modern orchestral conducting
1858	**Remy De Gourmont.** French novelist and critic

1875	**Pierre Monteux.** One of the leading 20th-century French-American conductors
1876	**Maurice de Vlaminck.** French painter and leader of the *fauvist* movement of the 1900s
1884	**Isoroku Yamamoto.** Japanese admiral who planned the attack on Pearl Harbor
1888	**Tris Speaker.** One of the greatest outfielders in baseball history, with a graceful fielding form and a .344 lifetime batting average
1895	**Arthur Murray.** American dancing teacher and founder of Arthur Murray Studios
1896	**Robert E. Sherwood.** American playwright, journalist, and biographer, noted for works such as *The Petrified Forest*
1906	**John Cameron Swayze.** American reporter and commercial spokesman
1908	**Anthony Tudor.** One of the most musically sophisticated choreographers in the annals of ballet
1913	**Jerome Weidman.** American author noted for *Fiorello* (1960)
1914	**Frances Langford.** American actress and singer
1915	**Muddy Waters.** American blues musician and singer (born McKinley Morganfield)
1920	**Eric Rohmer.** French writer and film maker
1922	**Elmer Bernstein.** One of Hollywood's most versatile and prolific composers, whose work includes the Oscar-winning original score for the movie *Thoroughly Modern Millie*
1922	**Robert Abplanalp.** American industrialist
1924	**Gil Hodges.** Professional baseball player and manager
1928	**Maya Angelou.** American author and poet noted for works such as *I Know Why the Caged Bird Sings*
1932	**Anthony Perkins.** American motion-picture actor
1932	**Richard G. Lugar.** U.S. senator
1938	**A. Bartlett Giamatti.** Baseball commissioner who succeeded Peter Ueberroth in 1989
1942	**Jim Fregosi.** Professional baseball player and manager
1942	**Kitty Kelley.** American writer noted for "unauthorized" biographies of Nancy Reagan, Frank Sinatra, Elizabeth Taylor and Jackie Onassis
1946	**Craig T. Nelson.** American motion-picture and television actor who played the title role for nine years in *Coach*
1947	**Ray Fosse.** Professional baseball player
1951	**Steve Gatlin.** American country singer with The Gatlin Brothers
1951	**John Hannah.** Professional football player and Hall of Famer
1956	**Tommy Herr.** Professional baseball player

April 4 – Events

| 527 | Justinian I was crowned Emperor of the Byzantine Empire. |
| 1581 | Queen Elizabeth I of England knighted Sir Francis Drake after he had sailed around the world. |

1818 Congress adopted the flag with 13 stripes and one star for each state.

1841 President William Henry Harrison died of pneumonia at age 68, just one month after taking office.

1844 Charles Bulfinch, the great American architect, died in Boston at age 80.

1850 Los Angeles was incorporated as an American city.

1887 Susanna Medora Salter was elected mayor of Argonia, Kansas, becoming the first woman to be elected mayor of any American community.

1914 The first showing of *The Perils of Pauline* took place in New York City.

1932 Professor C.G. King of the University of Pittsburgh became the first to isolate vitamin C.

1949 The North Atlantic Treaty Organization (NATO) was formed as 12 nations signed the treaty in Washington, D.C.

1968 Martin Luther King, Jr., the great civil rights leader, was assassinated in Memphis at age 39.

April 5 – Birthdays

1588 **Thomas Hobbes.** English philosopher and author of the monumental work *Leviathan* in 1651

1649 **Elihu Yale.** English businessman and benefactor of Yale University

1684 **Catherine I.** Wife of Czar Peter I and Empress of Russia, 1725-27

1725 **Giovanni Jacopo Casanova.** Italian writer, soldier, adventurer, and the greatest of romantic lovers

1732 **Jean-Honore Fragonard.** French artist who painted in the highly ornamental style of the Rococo period

1811 **Jules Dupre.** French painter

1827 **Joseph Lister.** English medical scientist and founder of antiseptic surgery

1834 **Frank Richard Stockton.** American author known for his short fairy tales for children and for his short stories such as "The Lady or the Tiger?" (1882)

1837 **Algernon Charles Swinburne.** One of the major English poets of the 1800s, noted for such works as "The Garden of Proserpine"

1856 **Booker T. Washington.** American educator and reformer, noted for his autobiography *Up from Slavery* (1901)

1871 **Pop Warner.** American college football coach with a career of 47 seasons

1900 **Spencer Tracy.** One of Hollywood's greatest actors

1901 **Melvin Douglas.** American stage and motion-picture actor

1901 **Chester Bowles.** American ambassador and statesman

1904 **Richard Eberhart.** American poet who won the Bollingen prize in poetry in 1962 and the Pulitzer Prize in 1966 for his *Selected Poems (1930-1965)*

1908 **Herbert von Karajan.** One of the leading symphony orchestra conductors of the mid-1900s

1908 **Bette Davis.** The "First Lady of the American Screen" and two-time Academy Award winner as the best leading actress

1911 **John Revolta.** Professional golfer

1916 **Gregory Peck.** American motion-picture actor and superstar, who won the best actor Academy Award for *To Kill a Mockingbird* (1962)

1920 **Arthur Hailey.** American novelist and author of *Airport*

1922 **Gale Storm.** American motion-picture and television actress

1923 **Nguyen Van Thieu.** The last president of South Vietnam before the Communist takeover in 1975

1934 **Frank Gorshin.** American actor and impressionist

1937 **Colin L. Powell.** American general and Chairman of the Joint Chiefs of Staff during the Persian Gulf War

1941 **Michael Moriarty.** American stage, screen and television actor

1943 **Max Gail.** American actor (Wojo in the television series *Barney Miller*)

1951 **Brad Van Pelt.** Professional football player

1952 **Sandy Mayer.** American tennis player

1958 **Johann Kriek.** South African-American tennis player

1965 **Robert Downey Jr.** American television and motion-picture actor and son of director Robert Downey

April 5 – Events

1291 A Moslem army attacked Acre in the tiny Latin kingdom of Jerusalem, beginning the end of the history of the Crusader states in the East.

1614 Pocahontas, daughter of Indian chief Powhatan, married the English colonist John Rolfe in Virginia.

1621 The Mayflower left Plymouth on the return trip to England, and though times were very hard, not a single Pilgrim was aboard.

1697 Sweden's great king Charles XII ascended to the throne at the age of 15 upon the death of his father Charles XI.

1768 The first American Chamber of Commerce was founded in New York City.

1792 President George Washington cast his first veto, rejecting a Congressional bill for apportioning representatives among the states.

1818 Chilean troops under Bernardo O'Higgins defeated the Spanish at the Maipo River to win independence for Chile.

1829 Pius VIII was crowned Roman Catholic pope.

1869 The last surviving soldier of the Revolutionary War, Daniel F. Bakeman, died in Freeman, New York, at age 109.

1887 In a letter to Bishop Mandell Creighton, British historian Lord Acton wrote, "Power tends to corrupt and absolute power corrupts absolutely..."

1887 Teacher Anne Sullivan achieved a major break-through with her blind and deaf pupil, Helen Keller, by teaching her the word *water* as spelled out in the Manual Alphabet.

1895 The great Irish writer Oscar Wilde lost his libel suit against the Marquis of Queensberry, and was himself convicted on a morals charge and sent to prison.

1915 Jess Willard knocked out Jack Johnson in the 26th round at Havana, Cuba, to become the world heavyweight champion.

1933 President Franklin D. Roosevelt ordered the surrender of all private stores of gold in the United States.

1955 Sir Winston Churchill resigned as English prime minister at age 81.

1964 General Douglas MacArthur died at age 84.

1976 Howard Hughes, the famous recluse reputed to be the richest man in America, died at age 72.

1980 The world's most valuable stamp, an 1856 British Guiana one-cent magenta, was auctioned in New York to an anonymous buyer for $850,000.

1984 Kareem Abdul-Jabbar scored career point number 31,421, topping Wilt Chamberlain's record and becoming the highest-scoring basketball player in NBA history.

April 6 – Birthdays

1483 **Raphael (Rafaello Sanzio).** Painter, architect, and one of the masters of the Italian Renaissance

1671 **Jean-Baptiste Rousseau.** French dramatist and poet

1773 **James Mill.** English philosopher and statesman and father of the great philosopher and economist John Stuart Mill

1810 **Edmund H. Sears.** Composer of "It Came Upon a Midnight Clear"

1823 **Joseph Medill.** A crusading American editor and publisher of the *Chicago Tribune* from 1855 to 1899

1826 **Gustav Moreau.** French painter noted for works such as *Oedipus and the Sphinx* (1864)

1860 **Rene Lalique.** French jeweler and glassmaker

1866 **Lincoln Steffens.** American journalist, writer, political philosopher, and "muckraker"

1884 **Walter Huston.** American stage and motion-picture performer and brilliant character actor

1890 **Anthony Fokker.** Dutch-German pioneer aircraft manufacturer

1892 **Lowell Thomas.** American news commentator, author, and explorer

1892 **Donald Wills Douglas.** American aircraft designer and founder of Douglas Aircraft Company

1900 **Leo Robin.** American lyricist noted for songs such as "Beyond the Blue Horizon," "Prisoner of Love," "Blue Hawaii," "Thanks for the Memory," "Ebb-Tide," and "Diamonds Are a Girl's Best Friend"

1903 **Charles R. Jackson.** Author of *The Lost Weekend*

1903 **Mickey Cochrane.** Hall of Fame baseball player and one of the greatest catchers in baseball history

1903 **Harold Eugene Edgerton.** American engineer and inventor in 1931of the electronic flash which revolutionized photography

1904 **Kurt Kiesinger.** Chancellor of West Germany, 1966-1969

1905 **Bix Reichner.** American composer and author, noted for songs such as "Stop Beating 'Round the Mulberry Bush" and "Papa Loves Mambo"

1907 **Chon Day.** American Hall of Fame cartoonist

1908 **Ernie Lombardi.** Professional baseball player and Hall of Famer

1909 **Denver Darling.** American composer noted for songs such as "Sioux City Sue" and "Choo Choo Ch-Boogie"

1914 **Ted Mossman.** American lyricist, author, and pianist, noted for songs such as "Till the End of Time" and "Full Moon and Empty Arms"

1925 **Arthur Larson.** American Hall of Fame tennis player

1926 **Alexander Butterfield.** U.S. government official who first revealed to the Watergate committee the existence of the Nixon tapes

1927 **Gerry Mulligan.** American jazz musician

1928 **James Dewey Watson.** American biologist who with Francis H.C. Crick, using research by Maurice H.F. Wilkins, devised the famous Watson-Crick DNA model

1929 **Andre Previn.** German-born composer, arranger, and conductor of the London Symphony Orchestra

1936 **Roy Thinnes.** American motion-picture and television actor

1937 **Merle Haggard.** American country musician, songwriter, and singer

1937 **Billy Dee Williams.** American stage, screen, and television actor

1944 **Michelle Phillips.** American actress and singer with The Mamas and the Papas

1947 **John Ratzenberger.** American actor noted for his role in the television series *Cheers*

1951 **Burt Blyleven.** Professional baseball player

1952 **Marilou Henner.** American stage, screen, and television actress

1953 **Janet Lynn.** American professional figure skater

April 6 – Events

1199 Richard the Lion-Hearted died at age 32 of a crossbow bolt wound.

1520 Raphael, the Italian painter, died in Rome on his 37th birthday.

1528 Albrecht Durer, the German painter, died in Nuremberg at age 56.

1614 El Greco, the Spanish painter, died in Toledo, Spain, at age 73.

1748 The buried city of Pompeii was discovered by an Italian peasant digging in a vineyard.

1830 Joseph Smith founded the Church of Jesus Christ of Latter Day Saints (the Mormons) at Fayette, New York.

1841 John Tyler became U.S. president, the first vice president to succeed to the office. He was shooting marbles with his children when he learned of President Harrison's death.

1862 The Battle of Shiloh (Tennessee) began in the Civil War.

1866 The Grand Army of the Republic (GAR) was organized by Union army veterans at Decatur, Illinois.

1896 The first modern Olympic games were formally opened in Athens, Greece.

1896 Ex-President Benjamin Harrison married his second wife, Mrs. Mary Dimmick.

1909 American explorer Robert Peary reached the North Pole, the first man to do so.

1917 The United States declared war on Germany in World War I by a Senate vote of 82-6.

1917 George M. Cohan wrote his famous World War I song, "Over There."

1936 The comic strip *Mickey Finn,* by Lank Leonard, first appeared.

1941 Germany invaded Yugoslavia and Greece in World War II.

1965 *Early Bird,* the first commercial communications satellite, was launched by the U.S.

April 7 – Birthdays

1613 **Gerard Dou.** Dutch painter

1770 **William Wordsworth.** One of the most important of the English romantic poets

1780 **William Ellery Channing.** American clergyman and founder in 1825 of the American Unitarian Association

1859 **Walter Chauncey Camp.** "Father of American football," who threw the first forward pass and who named the All-America teams from 1889 to 1924

1860 **W.K. Kellogg.** "King of the corn flakes" and founder of the W.K. Kellogg cereal company

1873 **John McGraw.** Professional baseball player and one of the greatest of all major league managers, with 10 pennant winners to his credit

1882 **Kurt Von Schleicher.** One of Hitler's chief political opponents in Germany in 1932-1933

1884 **Bronislaw Malinowski.** Founder of social anthropology

1889 **Gabriela Mistral.** Chilean poet and educator and the first Latin-American writer to win the Nobel Prize for literature

1891 **Sir David Low.** English political cartoonist

1893 **Irene Castle.** Noted American dancer who with her husband Vernon Castle formed the internationally famous ballroom dancing team of the 1910s

1893 **Allen W. Dulles.** Director of the C.I.A. under President Eisenhower

1897 **Walter Winchell.** American newspaper and radio reporter and gossip columnist from the 1930s through the 1960s

1899 **Robert Marcel Casadesus.** French pianist and composer

1908 **Frank Fitzsimmons.** American labor leader who became president of the Teamsters union when Jimmy Hoffa went missing

1908 **Percy Faith.** Canadian bandleader, pianist, and composer

1912 **Jack Lawrence.** American composer and author, noted for songs such as "If I Didn't Care," "All or Nothing At All," "Hold My Hand," "Sunrise Serenade," "Sleepy Lagoon," "Symphony," and "Johnson Rag"

1915 **Billie Holiday.** Outstanding jazz singer of her time

1918 **Bobby Doerr.** Professional baseball player and Hall of Famer

1920 **Ravi Shankar.** Indian sitar virtuoso

1928 **James Garner.** American motion-picture and television actor

1931 **Donald Barthelme.** American short-story writer

1934 **Wayne Rogers.** American television actor who starred as Trapper John in the long-running series *M*A*S*H*

1935 **Hodding Carter III.** American journalist and state department spokesman under President Carter

1936 **Preston Jones.** American playwright and actor

1938 **Edmund "Jerry" Brown, Jr.** Governor of California, 1974-1982

1939 **David Frost.** English television performer and interviewer

1939 **Frances Ford Coppola.** American motion-picture director and screenwriter, noted for films such as *The Godfather*

1954 **Jackie Chan.** Chinese motion-picture actor and amazing stunt performer

1954 **Tony Dorsett.** Professional football player and Hall of Famer

April 7 – Events

30 Christ was crucified on the hill of Calvary, according to his disciple John.

451 Attila the Hun plundered Metz, France.

1449 Felix V, the last antipope, abdicated his office.

1521 Magellan landed at Cebu in the Philippines, where he was later killed. Afterwards his crew completed the first trip around the world that he began.

1739 Dick Turpin, celebrated English robber, was hanged in York for stealing horses.

1827 The first friction matches were sold, in England.

1862 The Battle of Shiloh ended with heavy losses on both sides with the North claiming victory. Confederate general Albert Sydney Johnston was mortally wounded in the battle.

1880 The American Society of Mechanical Engineers was formed.

1927	The first U.S. demonstration of television was given when a New York audience saw Commerce Secretary Herbert Hoover at his desk in Washington, D.C.
1939	Italian troops invaded Albania, a prelude to World War II that was to start in September.
1947	Henry Ford, the great auto pioneer, died in Dearborn, Michigan, at age 83.
1949	The musical play *South Pacific* opened in New York at the Majestic Theater.
1959	The first atomic-generated electricity was produced, in Los Alamos, New Mexico.
1963	Jack Nicklaus won the Masters Gold tournament at age 23, the youngest player ever to win it.

April 8 – Birthdays

1582	**Phineas Fletcher.** English poet
1605	**Philip IV.** King of Spain, 1621-1665
1692	**Giuseppe Tartini.** Great Italian master of the violin, noted composer, and teacher who started the use of thicker strings and lighter bows
1726	**Lewis Morris.** American Revolutionary War general, Continental Congressman, and signer from New York of the Declaration of Independence
1805	**Hugo Von Mohl.** German botanist who coined the word *protoplasm* and helped develop the "Cell Theory"
1842	**Elizabeth Custer.** Wife of the American general, George Custer, who was killed in "Custer's Last Stand"
1869	**Harvey Williams Cushing.** American physician and one of the world's greatest brain surgeons
1875	**Albert I.** King of Belgium, 1909-1934, and a heroic military leader in World War I
1898	**E.Y. "Yip" Harburg.** American playwright and lyricist, noted for songs such as "Over the Rainbow," "April in Paris," "It's Only a Paper Moon," and "Brother Can You Spare a Dime"
1902	**Joseph Krips.** Austrian-born conductor
1905	**Ilka Chase.** American novelist and stage and motion-picture actress
1912	**Sonja Henie.** Norwegian-American actress and world champion figure skater at age 15
1914	**Irving Taylor.** American composer and author, noted for lyrics such as "Mambo Jambo," "Three Little Sisters," and "Onezy-Twozy"
1918	**Betty Ford.** Wife of President Gerald Ford
1919	**Ian Smith.** First native-born prime minister of Rhodesia (now Zimbabwe)
1923	**Franco Corelli.** Italian tenor
1926	**Shecky Greene.** American actor and comedian
1929	**Jacques Brel.** French composer, lyricist, and singer
1932	**Fred Ebb.** American lyricist noted with composer John Kander for works such as "New York, NY" and the songs of *Cabaret, Chicago,* and *Zorba*
1935	**John Gavin.** American motion-picture actor and ambassador to Mexico under President Reagan

1937	**Seymour Hersh.** American investigative reporter and author
1940	**John Havlicek.** Professional Hall of Fame basketball player and one of the game's superstars
1940	**Peggy Lennon.** One of the singing Lennon Sisters
1943	**John Hiller.** Professional baseball player
1944	**Jimmy Walker.** Professional basketball player
1952	**Kim Warwick.** Australian tennis player
1954	**Gary Carter.** Professional baseball player
1955	**Ricky Bell.** Professional football player
1955	**Barbara Kingsolver.** American novelist noted for works such as *Animal Dreams* (1990)
1957	**Fred Smerlas.** Professional football player
1963	**Julian Lennon.** English rock musician and son of Beatle John Lennon and his first wife, Cynthia
1968	**Patricia Arquette.** American motion-picture actress

April 8 – Events

1341	Petrarch was crowned Poet Laureate in Rome.
1378	Urban VI was elected Roman Catholic pope.
1492	Lorenzo the Magnificent, the most famous of the Medicis, died at age 43.
1513	Spanish explorer Ponce de Leon claimed Florida for Spain six days after reaching the mainland.
1730	The first Jewish congregation in the U.S. consecrated its synagogue in New York City.
1865	General Ulysses S. Grant asked General Robert E. Lee to surrender, which he did the following day, ending the Civil War.
1904	The *Entente Cordiale* was signed, establishing a diplomatic partnership between Great Britain and France.
1943	Wendell Willkie's book *One World* was published.
1952	President Truman seized the steel industry to forestall a general strike.
1973	The great painter Pablo Picasso died at his home near Mougins, France, at age 91.
1974	Hank Aaron hit his 715th career home run, breaking Babe Ruth's record of 714.
1981	General Omar Bradley, American World War II hero and first chairman of the Joint Chiefs of Staff, died in New York at age 88.

April 9 – Birthdays

1738	**Rufus Putnam.** Revolutionary War general and founder and father of Ohio
1821	**Charles Baudelaire.** Best known and most widely translated French poet
1835	**Leopold II.** King of Belgium and founder of the Congo Free State
1865	**Charles Proteus Steinmetz.** German-American scientist and one of the world's foremost electrical engineers
1869	**Elie-Joseph Cartan.** Noted French mathematician
1872	**Leon Blum.** French Socialist premier before World War II

1888	**Sol Hurok.** Ukrainian-born international impresario
1889	**Efrem Zimbalist.** Russian-born American violinist
1893	**Mary Pickford.** "America's Sweetheart" of the silent screen
1893	**Charles Ephraim Burchfield.** American painter noted for his landscapes and rural life scenes
1894	**Tommy Manville.** Often-married American heir of the Johns-Manville fortune
1895	**Mance Lipscomb.** American blues musician
1895	**Michel Simon.** French character actor
1898	**Curly Lambeau.** Hall of Fame football player and coach
1898	**Paul Robeson.** American singer and actor
1899	**James Smith McDonnell.** American industrialist and co-founder of McDonnell Douglas Corp. (1967)
1904	**Ward Bond.** American motion-picture and television actor who appeared in some 200 films
1905	**J. William Fulbright.** U.S. senator and initiator of the Fulbright educational program
1909	**Claude Passeau.** Professional baseball player
1910	**Abraham Ribicoff.** U.S. senator of the 1960s and 1970s
1919	**John Presper Eckert.** Co-inventor of the ENIAC, the first electronic computer
1925	**Linda Goodman.** Noted American astrologer and author of the best-selling book *Sun Signs* (1968)
1926	**Hugh Hefner.** Founder of *Playboy* magazine
1928	**Tom Lehrer.** American songwriter, performer, and mathematician, noted for comic songs such as "Be Prepared," "Poisoning Pigeons in the Park," and "The Masochism Tango"
1928	**Paul Arizin.** Professional basketball player who scored over 16,000 career points
1932	**Carl Perkins.** American rockabilly musician
1933	**Jean-Paul Belmondo.** French motion-picture actor
1939	**Michael Learned.** American television actress noted for her role in the long-running series *Little House on the Prairie*
1942	**Brandon De Wilde.** American stage, screen, and television actor
1954	**Dennis Quaid.** American motion-picture actor
1957	**Severiano Ballesteros.** Professional golfer
1963	**Jose Guzman.** Professional baseball player

April 9 – Events

491	Eastern Roman Emperor Zeno died at an approximate age of 65.
1483	King Edward IV of England died at age 40.
1555	Marcellus II was elected pope. He died 22 days later.
1626	Sir Francis Bacon, the great English philosopher, died at Highgate at age 65.
1682	La Salle, the great French explorer, reached the mouth of the Mississippi River and claimed all the land drained by it for France.

1865	General Robert E. Lee surrendered to General U.S. Grant at Appomattox Court House, Virginia, essentially ending the Civil War.
1928	Mae West made her debut in New York in the risque play *Diamond Lil.*
1939	Some 75,000 people gathered at the Lincoln Memorial in Washington, D.C., to hear black singer Marian Anderson perform after the D.A.R. denied her the use of Constitution Hall.
1940	Germany attacked Denmark and Norway in World War II.
1941	The Professional Golfers' Association announced the creation of its Hall of Fame, with the first members selected being Bobby Jones, Francis Ouimet, Walter Hagan, and Gene Sarazen.
1942	U.S. troops on the Bataan peninsula surrendered to the Japanese in World War II.
1945	Dietrich Bonhoeffer, the noted theologian, was executed in a Nazi concentration camp on orders of Heinrich Himmler, only days before he would have been liberated by the Allies.
1959	NASA announced the selection of America's first astronauts: Scott Carpenter, Gordon Cooper, John Glenn, Gus Grissom, Wally Schirra, Alan Shepard, and Donald Slayton.
1959	Frank Lloyd Wright, the great American architect, died in Phoenix at age 89.
1965	The first baseball game, an exhibition between the Houston Astros and the New York Yankees, was played in the newly-built Houston Astrodome.

April 10 – Birthdays

1512	**James V.** King of Scotland, 1513-1542
1583	**Hugo Grotius.** Dutch lawyer, theologian, statesman, poet, and the founder of international law
1647	**John Wilmot.** Second Earl of Rochester and English poet
1755	**Samuel F. Christian Hahnemann.** German physician and founder of homeopathy (the treating of a disease with medicines that produce symptoms of that disease)
1778	**William Hazlitt.** One of the best essayists and critics in English literature
1794	**Matthew C. Perry.** U.S. naval officer who opened trade with Japan, 1853-1854
1827	**Lew Wallace.** American soldier, novelist, and author of *Ben Hur*
1829	**William Booth.** Founder of the Salvation Army
1847	**Joseph Pulitzer.** American newspaper publisher who established the Pulitzer Prizes
1867	**AE (George William Russell).** Irish mystical poet and painter
1868	**George Arliss.** British stage and screen actor
1879	**John Daniel Hertz.** Founder of the Hertz car rental agency
1882	**Frances Perkins.** Secretary of labor under President Franklin D. Roosevelt and the first woman cabinet member in the United States

1885 **Sigmund Gottfried Spaeth.** American musician, author, and authority on opera

1891 **Tim McCoy.** American motion-picture actor and one of Hollywood's most popular Western stars

1894 **Ben Nicholson.** English painter noted for his abstract works which feature geometric forms and pale colors

1903 **Clare Booth Luce.** American playwright, congresswoman, and diplomat

1912 **Roy Hofheinz.** Principal builder of the Houston Astrodome

1912 **W. Clarke Hinkle.** Hall of Fame professional football player

1915 **Harry Morgan.** American motion-picture and television actor

1921 **Chuck Connors.** Professional baseball player and actor

1924 **Kenneth Noland.** American painter of the Abstract Expressionist school

1929 **Max von Sydow.** Swedish stage and motion-picture actor

1932 **Omar Sharif.** Egyptian motion-picture actor and expert bridge player

1932 **Mae Faggs.** One of the world's greatest sprinters who at one time or other held every American sprint record, indoors and outdoors

1934 **David Halberstam.** American correspondent and author

1936 **John Madden.** Professional football coach and sports commentator

1938 **Don Meredith.** Professional football player and sports announcer

1941 **Paul Theroux.** American writer and novelist

1946 **Bob Watson.** Professional baseball player

1949 **Lee Lacy.** Professional baseball player

1950 **Ken Griffey.** Professional baseball player and father of superstar baseball player Ken Griffey, Jr.

1951 **Mike Roth.** American bowler who won 26 professional championships

1952 **Steven Seagal.** American motion-picture actor

April 10 – Events

1606 Sir Walter Raleigh sold his interest in the colony to be established at Jamestown, Virginia.

1790 The United States patent system was created by Congress.

1841 Horace Greeley published the first issue of the New York *Tribune.*

1849 Walter Hunt of New York patented his invention of the safety pin.

1866 The American Society for the Prevention of Cruelty to Animals was chartered in New York.

1912 The luxury liner *Titanic* set sail from Southampton, England, on its ill-fated maiden voyage. (On April 14 it struck an iceberg and sank.)

1938 Austrians voted for annexation to Germany in a plebiscite controlled by Hitler. The percentage for *Anschluss* was 99.73.

1953 The first feature length 3-D movie in color, *House of Wax,* premiered in New York City.

1963 The U.S. nuclear submarine *Thresher* mysteriously sank off Cape Cod, Massachusetts, claiming 129 lives.

1972 The United States, the U.S.S.R., and some 70 other nations signed an agreement banning biological warfare.

April 11 – Birthdays

146 **Lucius Septimius Severus.** Emperor of Rome, A.D. 193-211

1357 **John I.** King of Portugal, 1385-1433, and father of Prince Henry the Navigator

1492 **Marguerite d'Angouleme.** French writer and Queen of Navarre

1586 **Pietro Della Valle.** Italian traveler and writer

1755 **James Parkinson.** Physician and researcher on palsy, or Parkinson's disease

1794 **Edward Everett.** Great American orator and chief speaker at Gettysburg on November 19, 1863, the day Lincoln delivered his famous Gettysburg Address

1857 **John Davidson.** Scottish poet

1862 **Charles Evans Hughes.** U.S. presidential candidate in 1916 and Supreme Court Justice

1869 **Gustav Vigeland.** One of Norway's greatest sculptors and creator of some 150 works in Oslo's Frogner Park

1888 **Francesca Bertini.** Italian stage and motion-picture actress

1893 **Dean Acheson.** American secretary of state under President Truman

1898 **Lou Holtz.** American comedian

1902 **Quentin Reynolds.** American author and reporter

1913 **Oleg Cassini.** French fashion designer

1916 **Alberto Ginastera.** Argentine composer noted for his highly dramatic operas *Don Rodrigo* (1964) and *Bomarzo* (1967)

1916 **Danny Fortmann.** Hall of Fame professional football player

1919 **Hugh Carey.** Governor of New York, 1975-1983

1928 **Ethel Kennedy.** Wife of Senator Robert F. Kennedy

1939 **Louise Lasser.** American television actress known for the title role in *Mary Hartman! Mary Hartman!*

1941 **Ellen Goodman.** American syndicated columnist

1953 **Andrew J. Wiles.** British mathematician who in 1993 proved Fermat's Last Theorem, which mathematicians had been seeking since 1637 when Fermat claimed to prove it but had no room on the page to write it down

1964 **Bret Saberhagen.** Professional baseball player

April 11 – Events

328	The oldest stele (monolith with ornamentations) at Uaxactun, Guatemala, was put in place by the Mayas.
1814	Napoleon abdicated at Fontainbleau and Louis XVIII was crowned King of France. Napoleon returned to power the next year, however, before his final exile.
1865	President Lincoln made his last public speech, addressing a group of citizens at the White House.
1898	President McKinley asked Congress to declare war on Spain.
1921	Iowa became the first state to impose a cigarette tax.
1945	American soldiers of the 8th Division liberated the infamous Nazi concentration camp Buchenwald in eastern Germany near the end of World War II.
1947	Jackie Robinson became the first black major league baseball player, in an exhibition game between the New York Yankees and his team, the Brooklyn Dodgers.
1951	President Truman fired General Douglas MacArthur as U.S. commander in Korea.
1953	Mrs. Oveta Culp Hobby became the first secretary of the Department of Health, Education and Welfare.
1970	*Apollo 13*, the manned lunar flight that had to be aborted, was launched at Cape Kennedy.
1979	Idi Amin was deposed as president of Uganda as rebel forces took control of the capital Kampala.

April 12 – Birthdays

1539	**Garcilaso de la Vega.** One of the greatest Spanish chroniclers of the 16th century
1550	**Edward De Vere.** English lyric poet, 17th Earl of Oxford, and the strongest candidate proposed (next to Shakespeare himself) for the authorship of the plays and sonnets of Shakespeare
1724	**Lyman Hall.** American Revolutionary War statesman and signer of the Declaration of Independence
1744	**François Joseph Belanger.** French architect
1777	**Henry Clay.** American statesman and three-time candidate for president
1791	**Frances P. Blair.** One of the founders of the Republican Party in the 1850s, who, however, returned to the Democratic Party after the Civil War
1857	**John Thomas Underwood.** American merchant who in 1895 founded the Underwood Typewriter Company
1878	**Charles Neil Daniels.** American composer noted for songs such as "Moonlight and Roses," "Yearning," and "Dark Eyes"
1878	**Neil Moret.** American composer and lyricist noted for songs such as "Moonlight and Roses"
1880	**Addie Joss.** Hall of Fame baseball pitcher with a lifetime earned run average of 1.88, the second lowest in baseball history
1883	**Imogen Cunningham.** American photographer
1885	**Robert Delaunay.** French painter
1892	**Johnny Dodds.** American jazz clarinettist
1904	**Lily Pons.** French operatic soprano and actress
1904	**Frankie Masters.** American composer, author, and conductor, noted for songs such as "Scatterbrain" and "Moonlight and You"
1905	**Warren Magnuson.** U.S. senator
1907	**Hardie Gramatky.** American children's author noted for *Little Toot* (1939)
1913	**Lionel Hampton.** American bandleader of the Big Band Era
1918	**Helen Forrest.** American singer with the Harry James band in the 1930s and 40s
1919	**Ann Miller.** American dancer and actress
1922	**Tiny Tim.** American singer (born Herbert B. Khaury) noted for popularizing "Tiptoe through the Tulips"
1926	**Jane Withers.** American stage and motion-picture actress noted for her roles as a child actress
1930	**John Landy.** Australian track star who set a world record of 3 minutes 58 seconds for the mile run in 1954, breaking Roger Bannister's record set a month earlier
1933	**Montserrat Caballe.** Spanish opera singer and recording star
1940	**Herbie Hancock.** American jazz pianist and composer
1944	**John Kay.** Canadian singer with Steppenwolf
1944	**Mike Garrett.** Professional football and baseball player
1947	**David Letterman.** American late-night television host
1949	**Scott Turow.** American author noted for works such as *Presumed Innocent* (1990)
1950	**Jerry Tagge.** Professional football player
1950	**David Cassidy.** American singer and television actor
1965	**Elaine Zayak.** American world champion figure skater
1971	**Shannen Doherty.** American televison actress noted for *Beverly Hills 90210*

April 12 – Events

1204	The Fourth Crusaders captured Constantinople and mercilessly sacked it.
1606	England adopted the Union Jack as its flag.
1633	Galileo was put on trial in Rome by the Inquisition.
1858	The first American billiards championship was played in Detroit.
1861	Confederate troops attacked Fort Sumter, starting the American Civil War.
1877	The first catcher's mask was worn in a baseball game, by James Alexander Tyng, in Lynn, Massachusetts.
1878	William Marcy Tweed, political boss of the notorious Tweed Ring, died in prison.

1922	The trial of Fatty Arbuckle, motion-picture comedian, ended with the jury convicting him of manslaughter in the death of a Hollywood starlet.
1945	President Franklin D. Roosevelt died of a cerebral hemorrhage at age 63 in Warm Springs, Georgia.
1955	The Salk anti-polio vaccine was pronounced effective and safe by the University of Michigan Vaccine Evaluation Center. It was the first effective vaccine against polio.
1961	Yuri Gagarin, sent into orbit in *Vostok I* by the Russians, became the first man in space.
1981	The U.S. space shuttle *Columbia,* with astronauts John Young and Robert Crippen aboard, lifted off at Cape Canaveral.
1981	Joe Louis, the great heavyweight boxing champion, died of a heart attack at age 66.

April 13 – Birthdays

1519	**Catherine De Medicis.** Queen consort of King Henry II of France and mother of three French kings
1721	**John Hanson.** Early American patriot, signer of the Articles of Confederation, and president in 1781 of the Continental Congress
1743	**Thomas Jefferson.** Author of the Declaration of Independence and third United States president
1769	**Sir Thomas Lawrence.** English painter noted for works such as *The Calmady Children* (1823-1824)
1771	**Richard Trevithick.** English inventor and engineer who designed the first high-pressure steam engine
1795	**James Harper.** One of the four Harper brothers who founded the famous publishing house of Harper and Brothers
1852	**F.W. Woolworth.** American merchant who developed the F.W. Woolworth chain of stores
1860	**James Sidney Ensor.** The only modern Belgian painter to acquire an international reputation
1866	**Butch Cassidy.** American cattle rustler and robber of the old West
1873	**Theodore Morse.** American composer noted for songs such as "Keep On the Sunny Side," "M-O-T-H-E-R," and "Hail, Hail, the Gang's All Here"
1892	**Robert Alexander Watson-Watt.** Scottish scientist who invented radar
1899	**Alfred Mosher Butts.** American architect noted for his invention of the famous word game Scrabble
1906	**Samuel Beckett.** Irish-born Nobel Prize-winning playwright and novelist, who often wrote in French and translated his works into English
1907	**Harold Stassen.** Governor of Minnesota and candidate for the Republican nomination for president on numerous occasions
1909	**Eudora Welty.** American short-story writer, novelist, and photographer known for such works as *The Robber Bridegroom* (1942) and *Losing Battles* (1970)

1919	**Madalyn Murray O'Hair.** American atheist whose Supreme Court suit in 1963 resulted in outlawing school prayers
1919	**Howard Keel.** American singer and actor
1927	**Mari Blanchard.** American motion-picture actress
1929	**Marilynn Smith.** Professional golfer
1937	**Lanford Wilson.** American playwright
1939	**Paul Sorvino.** American motion-picture actor
1939	**Christian Kuhnke.** West German tennis player
1942	**Bill Conti.** American composer noted for his work in the films *Rocky* and *The Right Stuff*
1946	**Al Green.** American soul singer
1963	**Gary Kasparov.** Russian chess champion and one of the best of all time
1970	**Ricky Schroeder.** American television actor

April 13 – Events

1436	King Charles VII of France drove the English out of Paris in the Hundred Years' War.
1598	The Edict of Nantes, one of the most famous decrees in history, was signed by Henry IV of France. It gave freedom of worship and equal rights as citizens to the Huguenots.
1605	Boris Godunov, Czar of Russia during "The Time of Troubles," died at age 52.
1759	George Frideric Handel, Anglo-German composer of *The Messiah*, died in London at age 74.
1846	The Pennsylvania Railroad was incorporated by the Pennsylvania legislature.
1941	Russia and Japan signed a five-year neutrality pact.
1943	President Franklin D. Roosevelt dedicated the Thomas Jefferson Memorial in Washington, D.C., as "a shrine to freedom"
1945	Harry S. Truman, still stunned by the death of Franklin D. Roosevelt, making him president the previous day, likened his situation to "a load of hay or a bull" falling on him.
1986	U.S. jets attacked targets in Tripoli and Benghazi, Libya, in retaliation for terrorist attacks on Americans attributed to Libyan strongman Moammar Gadhafi.

April 14 – Birthdays

1527	**Abraham Ortelius.** Belgian map maker and publisher of the first modern atlas
1578	**Philip III.** King of Spain, 1598-1621
1629	**Christian Huygens.** Dutch physicist who discovered the polarization of light, founded the wave theory of light, and invented the hair spring, which made watches possible
1724	**Gabriel de Saint-Aubin.** French printmaker
1810	**Justin S. Morrill.** American legislator noted for the Morrill Act of 1862, which established the Land-Grant Colleges and Universities
1866	**Anne Sullivan.** American teacher famous for teaching Helen Keller

1879 **James Branch Cabell.** American novelist and author of *Jurgen* (1919)

1889 **Arnold Toynbee.** English historian and author of the 12-volume outline of the civilizations of the world, *A Study of History*

1898 **Lee Tracy.** American stage, screen, and television actor, with a 40-year career

1904 **Sir John Gielgud.** One of the greatest British actors of the 20th century

1907 **François "Papa Doc" Duvalier.** Dictator of Haiti in the 1950s and 1960s

1917 **Marvin Julian Miller.** President of the major league baseball players union

1917 **Norman Luboff.** American composer and conductor

1918 **Mary Healy.** American actress and singer, and wife of actor Peter Lind Hayes

1925 **Rod Steiger.** American motion-picture and television actor

1930 **Bradford Dillman.** American motion-picture and television actor

1932 **Loretta Lynn.** American country music singer

1935 **Erich Von Daniken.** Swiss writer noted for *The Ancient Astronauts*

1936 **Bobby Nichols.** Professional golfer

1936 **Frank Serpico.** American police office who was the subject of the 1973 film *Serpico*

1941 **Pete Rose.** Professional baseball superstar, who holds the record of career hits, and who, except for Ty Cobb, is the only player to have over 4,000

1941 **Julie Christie.** English motion-picture actress

1948 **Valerie Martin.** American author noted for *Mary Reilly* (1990)

1949 **Jill Cooper.** English tennis player

1950 **Christine Lahti.** American stage and screen actress

1966 **Greg Maddux.** Professional baseball pitcher and two-time winner of the Cy Young Award

1966 **David Justice.** Professional baseball player

1968 **Anthony Michael Hall.** American motion-picture actor

April 14 – Events

73 After two years of defending the fortress of Masada, the Jews committed mass suicide rather than surrender to the Roman Tenth Legion.

1828 Noah Webster copyrighted the first edition of his great lexicon, *An American Dictionary of the English Language.*

1865 Abraham Lincoln was shot in Ford's Theatre in Washington, D.C., by John Wilkes Booth, while attending a performance of *Our American Cousin.* He died the following day.

1890 The Pan-American Union (now the Organization of American States) was formed by delegates of 18 republics of North, South, and Central America, meeting in Washington, D.C.

1902 J.C. Penney opened his first store, in Kemmerer, Wyoming.

1910 President William Howard Taft started the tradition of throwing out the first ball to open the baseball season.

1912 The British *Titanic,* the largest ship in the world, and considered to be unsinkable, struck an iceberg just before midnight and sank in 2½ hours in the North Atlantic.

1931 The 20 millionth Ford automobile rolled off the assembly line in Detroit.

1968 The Russian linking space vehicle, *Cosmos 212,* was launched.

1969 The Montreal Expos defeated the St. Louis Cardinals, 8-7, at Jarry Park in Montreal in the first major league baseball game ever played outside the U.S.

1981 The U.S. space shuttle *Columbia* landed safely at Edwards Air Force Base, California, after two days in space. It was the first conventional landing by a space vehicle.

April 15 – Birthdays

1452 **Leonardo Da Vinci.** Italian Renaissance painter, sculptor, and scientist, and one of the greatest geniuses of all time

1642 **Suleyman II.** Ottoman sultan, 1687-1691

1707 **Leonhard Euler.** The most prolific mathematician of the 18th century and perhaps of all time (A Swiss society has published 47 volumes of his work but much still remains)

1710 **Marie Camargo.** French opera ballerina

1741 **Charles Willson Peale.** American painter noted for portraits of Revolutionary War heroes

1812 **Theodore Rousseau.** French landscape painter

1814 **John Lothrop Motley.** American historian and diplomat noted for his historical writings on The Netherlands

1843 **Henry James.** One of America's greatest writers, noted for works such as *Portrait of a Lady* and the famous psychological horror tale, *The Turn of the Screw*

1861 **Bliss Carman.** Perhaps Canada's most famous poet, noted for works such as *Low Tide* and *Sappho* (1905)

1873 **Juliette Atkinson.** American Hall of Fame tennis player, three-time U.S. singles champion and four-time U.S. doubles champion

1874 **George Harrison Shull.** American geneticist and father of hybrid corn

1875 **James Jackson Jeffries.** World heavyweight champion, 1899-1905

1888 **Florence Bates.** American motion-picture actress

1889 **A. Philip Randolph.** American labor union leader and civil rights advocate

1889 **Thomas Hart Benton.** American painter of dramatic murals of the American scene, and grandnephew of Sen. Thomas Hart Benton

1890 **Billy De Beck.** American cartoonist and creator of *Barney Google* and *Snuffy Smith*

1895 **Bessie Smith.** American singer and songwriter and one of the finest blues singers in the history of jazz

1897 **Molly McGee.** American actress who was actor Fibber McGee's wife in real life and on the long-running radio show, *Fibber McGee and Molly*

1901 **Rene Pleven.** Twice premier of the French Fourth Republic

1912 **Kim Il Sung.** President of North Korea during the Korean War

1915 **Walter Washington.** Mayor of Washington, D.C.

1916 **Alfred Bloomingdale.** Father of the credit card

1917 **Hans Conreid.** American motion-picture and television actor

1922 **Michael Ansara.** American stage, screen, and television actor

1922 **Harold Washington.** First black mayor of Chicago, 1983-1988

1933 **Roy Clark.** American musician, comedian, and country singer

1933 **Elizabeth Montgomery.** American motion-picture and television actress

1933 **Gloria Caldwell.** American composer noted for songs such as "La Paloma"

1939 **Claudia Cardinale.** Italian motion-picture actress

1940 **Woody Fryman.** Professional baseball player

1944 **Dave Edmunds.** American rock singer and guitarist

1946 **Ted Sizemore.** Professional baseball player

1951 **Heloise (Heloise B. Reese).** American columnist specializing in household hints and information

1957 **Evelyn Ashford.** One of the greatest American track-and-field athletes and winner of one silver and two gold Olympic medals

1959 **Emma Thompson.** British stage, screen and TV actress and winner of the Academy Award for best actress for *Howard's End* (1992)

April 15 – Events

1446 Filippo Brunelleschi, the first important architect of the Italian Renaissance, died in Florence at age 69.

1764 Madame de Pompadour, mistress of King Louis XV of France, died in Versailles at age 42.

1850 The city of San Francisco was incorporated.

1861 President Lincoln issued his first call for troops in the American Civil War.

1865 Abraham Lincoln died in Washington, D.C., at age 56, the day after he was shot by the assassin John Wilkes Booth while attending a play at Ford's Theatre.

1900 Laborers working on the Cornell Dam at Croton, N.Y., went on strike demanding a raise from their current daily wage of $1.25 to $1.50.

1912 The British liner *Titanic* sank in the early morning 2½ hours after striking an iceberg in the North Atlantic the previous night, with 1500 people losing their lives.

1920 A robbery at a shoe company in South Braintree, Mass., resulted in the deaths of two persons, and in the arrest and subsequent execution of anarchists Nicola Sacco and Bartolomeo Vanzetti.

1940 British troops landed in Norway to try to stop the German invaders in World War II.

1945 Franklin D. Roosevelt was buried in the rose garden of his Hyde Park, N.Y., estate.

1947 Jackie Robinson, major league baseball's first black player, appeared in his first game in the majors.

April 16 – Birthdays

1319 **John II.** King of France, 1350-1364, known as "John the Good"

1646 **Jules Hardouin Mansart.** French architect

1815 **Henry Austin Bruce Aberdare.** British statesman

1827 **Octave Cremazie.** Father of French-Canadian poetry, whose "Le Drapeau de Carillon" is today one of the best-loved songs of French Canada

1844 **Anatole France.** Nobel Prize-winning French novelist and author of such works as *Penguin Island*, *The Gods are Athirst*, and *The Revòlt of the Angels*

1850 **Herbert Baxter Adams.** American historian and educator

1854 **Jacob S. Coxey.** American social reformer and leader of Coxey's Army, a group of unemployed men who marched on Washington, D.C., during the depression of the 1890s

1867 **Wilbur Wright.** American inventor who with his brother Orville built and flew the world's first airplane, at Kitty Hawk, North Carolina, on December 17, 1903

1871 **John Millington Synge.** Irish playwright noted for works such as *In the Shadow of the Glen* (1903) and *Riders to the Sea* (1904)

1880 **George A. Norton.** American lyricist and pianist, noted for songs such as "My Melancholy Baby" and "Memphis Blues"

1885 **Leo Weiner.** Austrian composer

1889 **Charlie Chaplin.** Outstanding motion-picture artist and greatest film comedian of all time

1892 **Hubert "Dutch" Leonard.** Professional baseball player

1897 **Milton Cross.** American opera commentator

1903 **Paul Waner.** Hall of Fame baseball player who had 3152 career hits

1904 **Clifford Case.** U.S. senator, 1955-1979

1912 **Garth Montgomery Williams.** American illustrator noted for his work in *Stuart Little* and *Charlotte's Web*

1918 **Spike Milligan.** British comedy star of stage, screen, TV and radio

1920 **Barry Nelson.** American stage, screen and TV actor

1921 **Peter Ustinov.** English motion-picture and television actor and writer

1921 **Clark Mollenhoff.** American journalist and author

1922 **Kingsley Amis.** English novelist and author of *Lucky Jim* (1954)

1924 **Henry Mancini.** American composer and conductor, noted for songs such as "Moon River," "Days of Wine and Roses," and "Two for the Road"

1929 **Edie Adams.** American motion-picture actress

1934 **Robert Stigwood.** Australian-born movie producer noted for works such as *Saturday Night Fever* and *Grease*

1935 **Bobby Vinton.** American singer and musician

1940 **Margrethe II.** Queen of Denmark

1947 **Kareem Abdul-Jabbar.** Professional basketball superstar with the most career points in NBA history (38,387 in regular season play and 5,762 in the playoffs)

1951 **Henry Childs.** Professional football player

1954 **Ellen Barkin.** American stage, screen and television actress

1965 **Jon Cryer.** American stage and screen actor and son of actor David Cryer and songwriter-actress Gretchen Cryer

1972 **Conchita Martinez.** Spanish tennis player and 1994 Wimbledon champion

April 16 – Events

1503 Columbus left Veragua in Central America to start his return home on his fourth and last voyage to America.

1789 President-elect George Washington left Mount Vernon, Va., for New York for his inauguration.

1828 Francisco Goya, the great Spanish painter, died in Bordeaux at age 82.

1859 Alexis de Tocqueville, French historian, died in Cannes at age 53.

1862 President Lincoln signed into law a bill ending slavery in the District of Columbia.

1916 The Chicago Cubs beat the Cincinnati Reds, 7-6, in eleven innings, in the first baseball game played in Chicago's Wrigley Field.

1917 Vladimir Lenin arrived in Petrograd from exile in Germany, receiving a hero's welcome from his Russian supporters.

1935 *Fibber McGee and Molly*, the classic radio comedy show, premiered on NBC.

1938 Britain and Italy signed an agreement recognizing Italian control of Ethiopia in return for the withdrawal from Spain of all Italian "volunteers" in the Spanish Civil War.

1940 Bob Feller pitched an opening-day no hitter as Cleveland beat Chicago, 1 to 0.

1942 The British government presented the entire island of Malta the George Cross for the gallant deed of resisting the German attempts to take the island in World War II.

1947 A French freighter exploded at a dock in Texas City, Texas, causing one of the worst disasters in American history with thousands killed and wounded.

1972 *Apollo 16* was launched on the first manned flight to the mountains of the moon.

April 17 – Birthdays

1622 **Henry Vaughan.** One of the leading English poets of the 1600s

1731 **G.P. Cauvet.** French ornament designer

1741 **Samuel Chase.** U.S. Supreme Court justice who was impeached in 1804 for malfeasance, but acquitted the following year

1806 **William Gilmore Simms.** Outstanding Southern man of letters in the 19th century

1820 **Alexander Joy Cartwright.** New York surveyor who designed the game of baseball almost exactly as it is played today, and who organized the New York Knickerbockers, one of the first professional teams

1837 **J.P. Morgan.** One of the greatest financiers in the history of the United States and founder of the U.S. Steel Corporation

1851 **Cap Anson.** One of the greatest baseball players of all time with a career total of 3524 hits, third only to Ty Cobb and Pete Rose, and a batting average of .421 in 1887

1863 **C.P. Cavafy.** Greek poet

1870 **Ray Stannard Baker.** American editor and historian

1880 **Sir Leonard Woolley.** English archaeologist who excavated the ancient Sumerian city of Ur

1894 **Nikita Khrushchev.** Premier of the Soviet Union, 1958-1964

1897 **Thornton Wilder.** Pulitzer Prize-winning American novelist and playwright, and author of *The Bridge of San Luis Rey* and *Our Town*

1903 **Gregor Piatigorsky.** Famous Russian-born cellist

1905 **Arthur Lake.** American motion-picture actor known for his role as Dagwood Bumstead in the *Blondie* movies of the 1930s and 1940s

1915 **Rebekah Harkness.** American patroness of the dance

1916 **Sirimavo R.D. Bandaranaike.** World's first woman prime minister, of Sri Lanka in 1960

1918 **Anne Shirley.** Child star of silent movies and a leading actress of the talkies

1918 **William Holden.** American motion-picture and television actor

1923 **Harry Reasoner.** American television newscaster

1923 **Lindsay Anderson.** British motion-picture and theatrical director and actor

1941 **Billy Fury.** English rock and ballad singer

1948 **Geoff Petrie.** Professional basketball player

1950 **Kevin Porter.** Professional basketball player

1951 **Pam Teeguarden.** American tennis player

1951 **Delvin Williams.** Professional football player

1951 **Olivia Hussey.** Argentine-born motion-picture and television actress

1961 **Boomer Esiason.** Professional football player

April 17 – Events

1492 Columbus signed a contract with the Spanish sovereigns giving him a commission to seek a westward ocean passage to Asia. He set sail on August 3 of that year.

1521 Martin Luther went before the Diet of Worms to face charges stemming from his religious writing.

1524 Florentine navigator Giovanni da Verrazano discovered the Narrows and New York harbor.

1605 Leo XI was crowned Roman Catholic pope.

1790 Benjamin Franklin died in Philadelphia at age 84. About 20,000 people, almost half the population of the city, honored him at his funeral.

1860 The first world heavyweight championship bout was held at Farnesworth, N.H., between John Heenan and Tom Sayers. The crowd stopped it after 42 rounds because it was so bloody.

1861 Virginia seceded from the Union.

1895 Japan took Formosa from China in the Treaty of Shimonoseki.

1916 Congress issued a charter to the American Academy of Arts and Letters.

1929 Babe Ruth married Claire Hodgson, his second wife, in the Church of St. Gregory the Great in New York City.

1961 The Bay of Pigs invasion by Cuban exiles was crushed by Castro.

April 18 – Birthdays

1480 **Lucretia Borgia.** Italian noblewoman and central figure of the notorious Borgia family

1570 **Thomas Middleton.** English playwright of Shakespeare's time, noted for works such as *The Honest Whore* (with Thomas Dekker) and *A Chaste Maid in Cheapside*

1819 **Franz von Suppe.** Yugoslavian operatic composer

1840 **Palmer Cox.** Canadian-American illustrator and creator of the "Brownies" children's series

1857 **Clarence Darrow.** Famous American lawyer noted for dramatic criminal trials such as the Scopes Trial and the Leopold and Loeb murder trial

1864 **Richard Harding Davis.** American author of romantic novels and the best known reporter of his time

1880 **Sam Crawford.** Hall of Fame baseball player

1881 **Max Weber.** Russian-born American pioneer modern painter noted for works such as *Athletic Contest* (1915)

1882 **Leopold Stokowski.** English-born American virtuoso conductor

1884 **Ludwig Meidner.** German painter

1901 **Al Lewis.** American composer, author, and publisher, noted for songs such as "No! No! A Thousand Times No!" "Blueberry Hill," and "Rose O'Day"

1902 **Harry Owen.** American composer and author, noted for songs such as "Sweet Leilani" and "Down Where the Tradewinds Blow"

1902 **Wynn Bullock.** American photographer

1911 **Huntington Hartford.** American publisher, philanthropist, and heir to the A and P fortune

1912 **Wendy Barrie.** English stage and motion-picture actress

1917 **Frederika.** Queen Mother of Greece

1922 **Barbara Hale.** American motion-picture and television actress noted for her role as Della Street in the long-running TV series *Perry Mason*

1930 **Clive Revill.** British stage, screen and television actor

1936 **Don Ohl.** Professional basketball player with over 10,000 career points

1946 **Hayley Mills.** English motion-picture actress and daughter of actor John Mills

1946 **Catfish Hunter.** Professional baseball pitcher who pitched a perfect game in 1968 (no one reached base)

1947 **James Woods.** American motion-picture and television actor

1956 **Eric Roberts.** American stage and motion-picture actor and brother of actress Julia Roberts

1962 **Jane Leeves.** English motion-picture and television actress known for her role as Daphne Moon in *Frasier*

1963 **Conan O'Brien.** American television talk show host and comedy writer

1967 **Maria Bello.** American motion-picture and TV actress

April 18 – Events

1328 Holy Roman Emperor Louis IV proclaimed Pope John XXII deposed for heresy and "lese majesty." The pope stayed in office, however.

1521 Martin Luther appeared before the Diet of Worms and said, in refusing to retract his teachings, "Here I stand. I can do nothing else. God help me! Amen."

1775 Paul Revere rode across the Massachusetts countryside from Charlestown to Lexington, warning the American colonists that the British were coming.

1906 The San Francisco earthquake occurred, followed by three days of fires. It was the greatest such disaster in U.S. history, with 700 persons killed and 497 blocks of buildings razed.

1923 Yankee Stadium officially opened before 62,281 people, the largest crowd ever to see a baseball game at that time. The Yankees beat Boston on Babe Ruth's three-run home run.

1932 Henry Ford introduced his Ford Model B, the last of the original four-cylinder cars.

1934 The first "Washateria" in the U.S. opened, in Fort Worth, Texas.

1942 U.S. B-25 bombers from the carrier *Hornet* under Major Jimmy Doolittle bombed Tokyo for the first time in World War II.

1945 Ernie Pyle, beloved American war correspondent, was killed by a Japanese bullet in the Ryuku Islands.

1949 The Irish Republic was proclaimed.

1953 Mickey Mantle, New York Yankee superstar, hit a 565-foot home run in Griffith Stadium in Washington, D.C., the longest home run ever measured.

1955 Albert Einstein died in Princeton, New Jersey, at age 76.

1956 Prince Rainier III of Monaco married American actress Grace Kelly in a civil ceremony. A church wedding was performed on the following day.

1981 Tom Seaver of the Cincinnati Reds, and formerly of the New York Mets, struck out his 3,000[th] career batter.

April 19 – Birthdays

1721 **Roger Sherman.** The only man to sign all four of these famous documents: the Articles of Association, the Declaration of Independence, the Articles of Confederation, and the U.S. Constitution

1772 **David Ricardo.** The leading British economist of the early 1800s

1793 **Ferdinand I.** Austrian emperor deposed in the Revolution of 1848

1832 **Lucretia Rudolph Garfield.** Wife of President James A. Garfield

1836 **Augustus Juilliard.** American merchant, philanthropist, and patron of music, who left his fortune to support the Juilliard School in New York City

1883 **Getulio Vargas.** President of Brazil, 1930-1945 and 1950-1954

1887 **John Taylor Arms.** American printmaker

1900 **Constance Talmadge.** American actress, comedienne, and star of the silent film era

1900 **Richard Hughes.** Welsh writer noted for novels such as *A High Wind in Jamaica* (1929)

1903 **Eliot Ness.** FBI specialist who investigated Al Capone's gangsterism

1909 **Bucky Walters.** Professional baseball player

1912 **Glenn Theodore Seaborg.** American nuclear chemist

1915 **Joseph Perkins Greene.** American composer and conductor, noted for songs such as "Across the Alley From the Alamo" and the lyrics for "And Her Tears Flow'd Like Wine"

1925 **Hugh O'Brian.** American motion-picture and television actor

1927 **Don Adams.** American motion-picture and television actor and comedian

1928 **Alexis Korner.** French blues musician

1933 **Jayne Mansfield.** American motion-picture actress

1933 **Dick Sargent.** American actor

1935 **Dudley Moore.** Emglish actor, musician, and composer

1942 **Alan Price.** English singer and songwriter with The Animals musical group

1946 **Tim Curry.** English stage and motion-picture actor

1948 **Rick Miller.** Professional baseball player

1952 **Mark Van Eeghen.** Professional football player

1956 **Sue Barker.** English tennis player

1960 **Frank Viola.** Professional baseball player and Cy Young Award winner in 1988

1960 **R.J. Reynolds.** Professional baseball player

1968 **Ashley Judd.** American stage and screen actress and daughter and half-sister of singers Naomi and Wynonna Judd, respectively

April 19 – Events

1775 The American Revolution began with the Battles of Lexington and Concord.

1782 The Netherlands recognized American independence.

1783 Congress ratified the preliminary peace treaty, ending the Revolutionary War.

1824 George Gordon, Lord Byron, the great English poet, died of fever at Missolonghi, Greece, at age 36.

1827 Rene Caillie, French African explorer, began his trek to Timbuktu.

1865 Funeral services were conducted in the East Room of the White House for Abraham Lincoln.

1891 Herman Melville, the great American writer, finished his novel *Billy Budd.* "End of Book, April 19, 1891," was on the last page of the manuscript, discovered 28 years later.

1892 Charles E. Duryea and his brother Frank completed the prototype of the first commercially successful American automobile, in Springfield, Massachusetts.

1898 The U.S. Congress passed a resolution asserting that Cuba was independent of Spain.

1933 The U.S. abandoned the gold standard by proclamation of President Franklin D. Roosevelt.

1943 Thousands of Jews living in the Warsaw ghetto began their famous fight against Nazi occupation in World War II.

1945 *Carousel*, the noted Rodgers and Hammerstein musical, opened on Broadway.

1951 General MacArthur, addressing Congress after being fired by President Truman, said, "Old soldiers never die; they just fade away."

1981 The Oakland A's won their 11th straight game at the beginning of the season, a major league record at the time. The Atlanta Braves broke the record the following year.

1993 After a 51-day siege by the FBI, 72 people were killed when the headquarters of the Branch Davidian sect near Waco, Texas, burned to the ground. The cult's leader, David Koresh, was among those killed.

1995 The Alfred P. Murrah Federal Building in Oklahoma City was destroyed by a truck bomb killing 168 people. An anti-government domestic terrorist, Timothy McVeigh, was convicted as the ringleader and sentenced to death.

April 20 – Birthdays

1492 **Pietro Aretino.** Italian poet and writer noted for his attacks on the powerful

1494 **Johann Agricola.** Lutheran reformer and advocate of antinomianism

1745 **Philippe Pinel.** French physician and pioneer in the movement for humane treatment for the mentally ill, whose theories became the basis for Freud's psychoanalytic treatment

1805 **Franz Xaver Winterhalter.** German painter who became famous for his royal portraits (Queen Victoria, Louis Philippe, Napoleon III, and others)

1808 **Napoleon III.** Emperor of the French, 1852-1870 (born Charles Louis Napoleon Bonaparte), and the last member of the Bonaparte family to rule France

1850 **Daniel C. French.** American sculptor noted for the statue of Abraham Lincoln in the Lincoln Memorial in Washington, D.C.

1860 **Charles Gordon Curtis.** American inventor who developed the modern steam turbine in the early 1900s, which revolutionized power production

1871 **William Henry Davies.** English poet

1882 **Holland McTeire Smith.** American marine general who led the World War II invasion of Iwo Jima and was known as "the father of modern amphibious warfare"

1889 **Adolf Hitler.** Nazi dictator of Germany, 1933-1945

1891 **Dave Bancroft.** Hall of Fame professional baseball player

1893 **Harold Lloyd.** American motion-picture actor and one of the kings of comedy

1893 **Joan Miro.** Spanish artist and a leader of the Surrealist movement

1897 **Gregory Ratoff.** Russian-born motion-picture actor and director with a 30-year career

1898 **Harvey Firestone, Jr.** President of Firestone Tire and Rubber Company

1905 **Stanley Marcus.** "Merchant Prince of Dallas" and son of the founder of the Neiman-Marcus stores

1910 **Robert F. Wagner.** Mayor of New York City, 1954-1965

1920 **John Paul Stevens.** U.S. Supreme Court justice

1923 **Tito Puente.** American bandleader, composer, and percussionist

1924 **Nina Foch.** Dutch-born motion-picture and television actress

1927 **Phil Hill.** American automobile racing driver

1941 **Ryan O'Neal.** American motion-picture and television actor

1945 **Steve Spurrier.** Professional football player and coach

1949 **Jessica Lange.** American motion-picture actress

1961 **Don Mattingly.** Professional baseball player

April 20 – Events

1534 Jacques Cartier left France on instructions of French king Francis I to explore and claim Canada for France and to find a new sailing route to China.

1653 The Rump Parliament was dissolved by Oliver Cromwell, who entered it at the head of a troop of soldiers.

1812 Vice President George Clinton died in Washington at the age of 73, the first vice president to die in office.

1828 Rene Caillie, French African explorer, arrived in Timbuktu after a long trek across the Sahara Desert.

1861 Robert E. Lee resigned his commission in the U.S. Army in order to join the Confederate forces.

1898 Marie and Pierre Curie discovered the element radium.

1903 Andrew Carnegie presented $ 1.5 million for the construction of the Hague Peace Palace.

1934 Shirley Temple began her career as a child movie star in the film *Stand Up and Cheer.*

1945 The U.S. 7th Army captured the German city of Nuremberg in World War II.

1948 Walter Reuther, president of the United Automobile Workers, was seriously wounded by an unknown assailant with a shotgun.

1962 Russia and China signed a pact of friendship.

1971 The U.S. Supreme Court upheld the use of busing to achieve racial desegregation in the schools.

1972 The U.S. lunar module of *Apollo 16* landed on the moon with astronauts John Young and Charles Duke aboard, while Thomas Mattingly remained in the command module.

1999 Two teenage student gunmen, Eric Harris and Dylan Klebold, went on a shooting rampage at Columbine High School in Littleton, CO, killing 15 students, including themselves, and wounding at least 20.

April 21 – Birthdays

1555 **Lodovico Carracci.** Italian painter and co-founder of the Accademia degli Incamminati in 1582

1671 **John Law.** Scottish financier and gambler, noted for the "Mississippi Scheme," a land speculation deal in colonial Louisiana

1696 **Francesco de Mura.** Italian painter

1782 **Friedrich Froebel.** German educator who founded the kindergarten system in 1837

1816 **Charlotte Brontë.** English novelist whose most famous work, *Jane Eyre,* is one of the great works of world literature

1818 **Josh Billings.** American humorist and cracker barrel philosopher

1828 **Hippolyte Taine.** French historian, critic, and writer, who greatly influenced the naturalist movement in literature

1838 **John Muir.** Scottish-born American naturalist, explorer, writer, and great national park advocate

1846 **William Henry Goodyear.** American art historian, archaeologist, and son of Charles Goodyear, the discoverer of the process of vulcanizing rubber

1857 **Paul Dresser.** American composer noted for songs such as "My Gal Sal" and "On the Banks of the Wabash"

1864 **Max Weber.** German sociologist and political economist, and one of the founders of modern sociology

1869 **Edwin S. Porter.** American motion-picture pioneer director and the most prominent innovator in American cinema during its beginning years

1872 **Billy Bitzer.** American director of photography who photographed D.W. Griffith's famous *The Birth of a Nation* (1915) and many other films

1887 **Joe McCarthy.** One of the greatest professional baseball managers and winner of seven World Series

1898 **Steve Owen.** Professional football player and coach

1899 **Randall Thompson.** American composer

1905 **Edmund "Pat" Brown.** Governor of California, 1958-1966

1909 **Rollo May.** American psychologist and author

1916 **Anthony Quinn.** Mexican-born stage, screen, and television actor

1926 **Elizabeth II.** Queen of Great Britain and head of the British Commonwealth of Nations

1926 **Carolyn Leigh.** American songwriter noted for the lyrics for "Hey, Look Me Over" and "Young at Heart"

1932 **Elaine May.** American comedienne, screenwriter, and director

1935 **Charles Grodin.** American motion-picture and television actor and talk show host

1941 **David Boren.** U.S. senator

1947 **Iggy Pop.** American rock singer, musician and songwriter

1947 **Al Bumbry.** Professional baseball player

1949 **Patti LuPone.** American stage, screen, and television actress, who received a Tony Award for her title role in the Broadway musical *Evita* (1979)

1951 **Tony Danza.** American motion-picture and television actor

1957 **Jesse Orosco.** Professional baseball player

April 21 – Events

753 BC Rome was founded, according to tradition.

1649 The Maryland Toleration Act, providing for freedom of worship for all Christians, was passed by the Maryland Assembly.

1699 Jean Racine, the great French playwright, died at Port-Royal at age 59.

1836 The Texans under General Sam Houston defeated the Mexicans at the Battle of San Jacinto, ending the Texas war of independence.

1910 Mark Twain died in Redding, Connecticut, at age 74.

1918 Manfred von Richthofen, Germany's Red Baron and ace flyer, was shot down and killed in World War I.

1924 The comic strip *Wash Tubbs,* by Roy Crane, first appeared.

1960 Brasilia became the new capital of Brazil, replacing Rio de Janeiro.

1972 *Apollo 16* astronauts John Young and Charles Duke explored the surface of the moon.

April 22 – Birthdays

1451 **Isabella I.** Queen of Castile and Aragon, and sponsor of Columbus in his discovery of America

1707 **Henry Fielding.** English novelist, playwright, and author of *The History of Tom Jones, a Foundling*, one of the world's great novels

1711 **Eleazar Wheelock.** Founder and first president of Dartmouth College

1722 **Christopher Smart.** English poet noted for works such as *A Song to David*

1724 **Immanuel Kant.** One of the greatest philosophers of all time, and author of the *Critique of Pure Reason*

1766 **Madame de Stael.** French political propagandist, conversationalist, and woman of letters

1792 **Uriah Phillips Levy.** U.S. naval officer who in 1836 purchased Monticello, rescued it from ruin, and, with his nephew Jefferson Monroe Levy, in two renovations, restored its grandeur

1840 **Odilon Redon.** French painter, lithographer, and etcher

1866 **Hans von Seeckt.** German general and head of the Reichswehr, 1920-1926

1870 **Vladimir I. Lenin.** Founder of the Russian Communist Party and leader of the Bolshevik Revolution in 1917

1874 **Ellen Glasgow.** American novelist and author of such works as *Barren Ground* and the Pulitzer Prize-winning *In This Our Life*

1876 **Ole Rolvaag.** Norwegian-American novelist and author of *Giants in the Earth*

1881 **Alexander Kerensky.** Premier of the first Russian government after the overthrow of the czar in 1917

1904 **J. Robert Oppenheimer.** American physicist known as the man who built the atomic bomb

1908 **Eddie Albert.** American motion-picture and television actor

1916 **Yehudi Menuhin.** American violin virtuoso

1918 **Mickey Vernon.** Professional baseball player

1923 **Aaron Spelling.** American television producer noted for works such as *Charlie's Angels* and *Dynasty*

1937	**Jack Nicholson.** American motion-picture actor and superstar
1938	**Deane Beman.** Professional golfer
1938	**Glen Campbell.** American musician, singer, and television entertainer
1939	**Jason Miller.** American playwright and actor
1949	**Spencer Haywood.** Professional basketball player
1950	**Peter Frampton.** British singer and guitarist
1951	**Paul Carrack.** English singer and musician with Ace and Squeeze groups
1956	**Moose Haas.** Professional baseball player, who, to the adage "Good pitching beats good hitting," added "And vice-versa"
1959	**Freeman McNeil.** Professional football player

April 22 – Events

960	Basil II was crowned Emperor of the Byzantine Empire.
1445	King Henry VI of England married Margaret of Anjou.
1500	Pedro Alvares Cabral, Portuguese explorer, discovered Brazil.
1509	Henry VII of England died at age 52, and was immediately succeeded by his 17-year-old son Henry VIII.
1836	Texas was granted its independence from Mexico.
1864	Congress authorized the U.S. Mint to use the motto, "In God We Trust," on all coins.
1876	Boston beat Philadelphia, 6-5, in the first National League baseball game.
1889	The Oklahoma Land Rush began when Oklahoma was officially opened for settlement at noon. By evening over 50,000 people had moved in. (Many moved in "sooner," giving rise to the nickname "Sooner state")
1915	The Germans became the first nation to use poison gas in warfare, in the Second Battle of Ypres in World War I.
1944	Allied soldiers invaded New Guinea in World War II.
1945	Russian troops entered Berlin, the first Allied soldiers to do so, in World War II.
1954	The Senate Army-McCarthy hearings began and were shown on television. The result would prove disastrous for Senator McCarthy.
1970	Millions of Americans concerned about the environment observed the first "Earth Day."
1993	Alabama governor Guy Hunt was convicted of an ethics charge and was immediately removed from office.
1994	Richard Nixon died at age 81.

April 23 – Birthdays

1484	**Julius Caesar Scaliger.** French classical scholar and botanist
1500	**Johannes Stumpf.** One of the most important theologians of the Swiss Protestant Reformation
1564	**William Shakespeare.** English dramatist, poet, and the greatest writer of all time
1728	**Samuel Wallis.** English navigator who discovered Easter Island
1775	**Joseph M.W. Turner.** English artist, who ranks with John Constable as one of the two greatest English landscape painters
1791	**James Buchanan.** Fifteenth U.S. president
1813	**Stephen A. Douglas.** American political leader and orator, who participated with Abraham Lincoln in the Lincoln-Douglas Debates in 1858
1818	**James Anthony Froude.** English historian, biographer, and essayist, who wrote the 12-volume *History of England* (1856-1870)
1852	**Edwin Markham.** American poet and lecturer, best known for "The Man with the Hoe" (1899)
1858	**Max Planck.** German theoretical physicist, whose law of radiation laid the foundation for the quantum theory, and for whom Planck's constant was named
1891	**Sergei Prokofiev.** Important Russian composer, best known perhaps for *Peter and the Wolf* (1936)
1893	**Frank Borzage.** American motion-picture director and winner of the 1927 Academy Award for best director for *Seventh Heaven*
1897	**Lester B. Pearson.** Prime minister of Canada, 1963-1968
1897	**Lucius D. Clay.** U.S. World War II general and director of the Berlin Airlift in 1948
1899	**Ngaio Marsh.** New Zealand theatrical producer and prolific mystery story writer
1899	**Vladimir Nabokov.** Russian-born novelist and author of *Lolita* (1955)
1900	**Jim Bottomley.** Hall of Fame baseball player and manager
1904	**Duncan Renaldo.** American motion-picture and television actor
1907	**Dolf Camilli.** Professional baseball player
1921	**Janet Blair.** American motion-picture actress and singer
1921	**Warren Spahn.** Winningest left-handed pitcher in baseball history with 363 career victories
1926	**J.P. Donleavy.** American-born Irish novelist
1928	**Shirley Temple (Black).** Most successful child movie star in Hollywood history
1932	**Jim Fixx.** American writer, editor, and author of a best-selling book on running to keep fit
1932	**Halston.** American fashion designer (born Roy Halston Frowick)
1936	**Roy Orbison.** American rockabilly singer
1937	**Don Massengale.** Professional golfer
1940	**David Birney.** American television actor
1942	**Sandra Dee.** American motion-picture and television actress
1942	**Lee Majors.** American motion-picture and television actor
1943	**Tony Esposito.** Professional hockey player and one of the leading goalkeepers of the 1970s
1943	**Gail Goodrich.** Professional basketball player
1944	**Marty Fleckman.** Professional golfer

1947	**Bernadette Devlin.** Irish civil rights worker
1948	**Vladimir Korotkov.** Russian tennis player
1949	**Joyce De Witt.** American actress
1950	**Joe Ferguson, Jr.** Professional football player
1960	**Valerie Bertinelli.** American television actress
1977	**Andruw Jones.** Professional baseball player

April 23 – Events

1016 Edmund Ironside succeeded his father Ethelred the Unready as king of England.

1349 King Edward III of England instituted the Order of the Garter.

1616 Miguel de Cervantes, the great Spanish novelist, died in Madrid at age 68.

1616 William Shakespeare died in Stratford-upon-Avon on his 52nd birthday.

1789 President-Elect and Mrs. George Washington moved into the first "Presidential Mansion" at the corner of Franklin and Cherry Streets in New York City.

1850 William Wordsworth, the great English poet, died at Rydal Mount at age 80.

1896 Thomas A. Edison presented the first public showing of a motion picture in the United States, at Koster and Bial's Music Hall in New York City.

1946 Ed Head pitched a no-hitter as Brooklyn beat Boston, 5-0.

1964 Ken Johnson pitched a no-hitter but lost as Cincinnati beat Houston, 1-0.

1968 The United Methodist Church was formed as a merger of the Methodist Church and the Evangelical United Brethren Church in a ceremony in Dallas.

1969 Sirhan Sirhan was sentenced to death for the murder of Senator Robert F. Kennedy. The sentence later was reduced to life imprisonment.

April 24 – Birthdays

1743 **Edmund Cartwright.** English inventor and clergyman, who invented a wool combing machine and a steam-powered loom for weaving cotton

1750 **John Trumbull.** American poet and jurist, noted for works such as "The Progress of Dulness," a poetic satire of college education

1766 **Robert Bailey Thomas.** American printer who in 1792 founded the *Farmer's Almanac*

1796 **Karl Leberecht Immerman.** German poet

1815 **Anthony Trollope.** English novelist and author of *The Warden* (1855) and *Barchester Towers* (1857)

1856 **Henri Philippe Petain.** French World War I hero discredited in World War II as a Nazi collaborator

1882 **Tony Sarg.** German puppet maker and showman, whose famous production *The Rose and the Ring* helped revive puppetry in the United States

1889 **Sir Stafford Cripps.** British World War II statesman about whom Churchill said, "There but for the grace of God goes God."

1893 **Leslie Howard.** English stage and screen actor

1894 **Howard Ehmke.** Professional baseball player

1900 **Elizabeth Gouge.** English author noted for *Green Dolphin Street* (1944)

1904 **Willem De Kooning.** Dutch-born abstract expressionist artist, noted for his hectic and violent paintings and swirling patterns

1905 **Robert Penn Warren.** American writer and Pulitzer Prize-winning author of *All the King's Men*

1912 **George Wunder.** American cartoonist who succeeded Milton Caniff as the artist for the strip *Terry and the Pirates* (1947)

1916 **Stanley Kauffmann.** American film and theater critic

1934 **Shirley MacLaine.** American stage and motion-picture actress and sister of actor Warren Beatty

1936 **Jill Ireland.** English motion-picture actress

1940 **Sue Grafton.** American writer noted for her series of novels beginning with *A Is for Alibi* (1982)

1942 **Richard M. Daley.** Mayor of Chicago and son of former mayor Richard J. Daley

1942 **Barbra Streisand.** American singer and actress

1944 **Bill Singer.** Professional baseball player

1949 **Bob Chandler.** Professional football player

1954 **Vince Ferragamo.** Professional football player

April 24 – Events

858 Nicholas I "the Great" was elected Roman Catholic pope.

1585 Sixtus V was elected Roman Catholic pope.

1792 "La Marseillaise," the French national anthem, was composed by French army officer Claude Joseph Rouget de Lisle.

1800 The Library of Congress was established with an appropriation of $5000 and Thomas Jefferson's entire private library.

1814 The British burned Washington, D.C., in the War of 1812.

1877 Federal troops were ordered out of New Orleans, ending the North's post-Civil War rule in the South. The action was widely believed to be the payoff for the South's support of Rutherford B. Hayes in the disputed election of 1876.

1898 Spain declared war on the United States after rejecting America's ultimatum to withdraw from Cuba.

1945 Former senator A.B. "Happy" Chandler of Kentucky was elected baseball commissioner.

1947 Willa Cather, the American novelist, died at age 70.

1953 Winston Churchill was knighted by Queen Elizabeth II. He was made a knight of the Order of the Garter, Britain's highest order of knighthood.

1990 The Hubble Space Telescope was placed in orbit by the United States and, despite a faulty lens discovered after its launch, took pictures of unsurpassed clarity and made measurements of the chemical composition of distant stars.

April 25 – Birthdays

1214	**Louis IX (Saint Louis).** King of France, 1227-1270, noted for his fairness to all his subjects
1284	**Edward II.** King of England, 1307-1327
1533	**William I (the Silent).** Prince of Orange and father of the Dutch Republic
1599	**Oliver Cromwell.** British soldier and statesman of the English Civil War, and ruler of England, 1649-1658
1652	**Giovanni Battista Foggini.** Italian sculptor
1792	**John Keble.** English divine and poet who started the Oxford Movement, a revival in the Church of England in 1833
1822	**James Pierpont.** American composer noted for "Jingle Bells" (1850), one of the two or three most popular songs ever written in the English language
1873	**Walter De la Mare.** English poet and novelist, noted for his poetry of childhood and for his novel, *Memoirs of a Midget*
1873	**Howard R. Garis.** Creator of *Uncle Wiggly*
1874	**Guglielmo Marconi.** Italian physicist and one of the chief developers of the radio
1891	**Sid Richardson.** American oil executive
1898	**Fred Haney.** Professional baseball player and manager
1900	**Wolfgang Pauli.** Austrian physicist and discoverer of the "Pauli exclusion principle" of electron position in an atom
1904	**George Schreiber.** Belgian artist
1906	**William J. Brennan Jr.** U.S. Supreme Court justice
1908	**Edward R. Murrow.** American broadcast journalist of the 1940s and 1950s
1910	**Joseph Hirsch.** American artist
1914	**Marcos Perez Jimenez.** President of Venezuela, 1952-1958
1914	**Bob Russell.** American composer and author, noted for lyrics such as "No Other Love," "Frenesi," "Maria Elena," "Brazil," "Do Nothin' Till You Hear From Me," and "Ballerina"
1916	**Jerry Barber.** Professional golfer
1918	**Ella Fitzgerald.** American singer
1923	**Albert King.** American blues singer and guitarist
1923	**Arnold Miller.** President of the United Mine Workers
1928	**Melissa Hayden.** Canadian ballerina
1930	**Paul Mazursky.** American director, producer, screenwriter and actor, noted for works such as *Bob & Carol & Ted & Alice* (director)
1932	**Meadowlark Lemon.** One of the top stars of the Harlem Globetrotters basketball team
1940	**Al Pacino.** American motion-picture actor
1946	**Talia Shire.** American motion-picture actress
1955	**Christopher Mottram.** English tennis player

April 25 – Events

404 BC	Athens surrendered to Sparta, ending the Peloponnesian War.
1507	"America" was first used for the new world in Martin Waldseemuller's geography book, *Cosmographiae Introductio*.
1719	The first edition of Daniel Defoe's *Robinson Crusoe* was published.
1792	Nicolas-Jacques Pelletier, a highwayman, became the first person under French law to be executed by the guillotine.
1846	Mexican troops crossed the Rio Grande and attacked a small U.S. cavalry group, giving President Polk the opportunity to declare war. War was declared on May 13, 1846.
1859	Construction began on the Suez Canal.
1898	The United States declared war on Spain, beginning the Spanish-American War.
1901	New York became the first state to require automobile license plates. The tax was one dollar.
1915	Allied troops landed on the Gallipolli Peninsula in World War I.
1945	American and Russian troops joined forces at Torgau, on the Elbe, cutting Germany in two in World War II.
1945	A conference of delegates from 50 countries met in San Francisco to organize the United Nations.
1945	Benito Mussolini and his mistress, Clara Petacci, escaped from Milan as U.S. troops entered the city in World War II.
1959	The St. Lawrence Seaway was opened to traffic.
1962	*Ranger IV* became the first U.S. space probe to strike the moon.
1980	The mission to rescue the 52 American hostages in Iran failed because of malfunctioning helicopters.

April 26 – Birthdays

121	**Marcus Aurelius.** Roman Emperor, A.D. 161-180, noted also for his Stoic philosophy contained in his diary, *Meditations,* one of the most influential books ever written by a ruler
1228	**Conrad I.** King of Germany
1573	**Marie de Medicis.** Queen consort of King Henry IV of France
1718	**Esek Hopkins.** First Commodore of the U.S. Navy and the commander of the Continental Navy from 1775 to 1778
1761	**Lady Emma Hamilton.** Beautiful mistress of England's naval hero Lord Horatio Nelson
1785	**John James Audubon.** American naturalist and artist, and one of the first to study and paint the birds of the United States
1787	**Ludwig Uhand.** German poet
1798	**Eugene Delacroix.** French painter, perhaps the illegitimate son of Talleyrand, and the leader of the Romantic movement in French painting

1812 **Alfred Krupp.** German industrialist who developed the Krupp Works in Essen from a firm with four workers to one with 20,000

1812 **Baron Friedrich Von Flotow.** German composer

1822 **Frederick Law Olmstead.** American landscape architect, who helped design New York's Central Park, the first great American park

1834 **Artemus Ward.** American humorist and contemporary of Abraham Lincoln

1875 **Syngman Rhee.** President of South Korea, 1948-1960

1877 **Sir Alliott Verdon-Roe.** First Englishman to design, build, and fly an airplane

1891 **Paul G. Hoffman.** American industrialist and statesman

1893 **Anita Loos.** American screenwriter, playwright, and novelist, best known for *Gentlemen Prefer Blondes* (1925)

1894 **Rudolf Hess.** Adolf Hitler's deputy party leader, who flew to Scotland during World War II to persuade Great Britain to get out of the war

1899 **Guinn "Big Boy" Williams.** American motion-picture actor, who appeared in numerous supporting roles with Tom Mix, Harry Carey, and Roy Rogers

1900 **Hack Wilson.** Hall of Fame baseball player who in 1930 hit 56 home runs and drove in a record 190 runs

1900 **Charles Richter.** American geophysicist and developer of the Richter scale for measuring earthquake intensities

1914 **Bernard Malamud.** American novelist and short story writer noted for works such as *The Fixer* (1966), which won the Pulitzer Prize

1914 **Paul Norris.** American cartoonist and creator of *Power Nelson, Futureman* and *Yank and Doodle*

1916 **Morris West.** Australian novelist

1917 **I.M. Pei.** American architect who designed the glass pyramid addition to the Louve in 1984

1917 **Sal Maglie.** Professional baseball player

1919 **Virgil Trucks.** Professional baseball pitcher who pitched two no-hit games in 1952

1927 **Granny Hamner.** Professional baseball player

1933 **Carol Burnett.** American television and motion-picture comedienne and actress

1937 **Bob Boozer.** Professional basketball player

1944 **Martha Rockwell.** Professional skier

1947 **Amos Otis.** Professional baseball player

1955 **Mike Scott.** Professional baseball player

1960 **Roger Taylor.** Drummer with the Duran Duran musical group

1962 **Michael Damian.** American actor and singer

April 26 – Events

1564 William Shakespeare was baptized at Stratford-on-Avon in the parish church.

1607 John Smith and his colonists reached the Chesapeake Capes after 18 weeks at sea. Eighteen days later they landed at the site they called Jamestown after King James I.

1731 Daniel Defoe, English novelist and author of the famous adventure story *Robinson Crusoe,* died in London at age 70.

1768 England's Royal Academy opened its first art exhibit.

1865 John Wilkes Booth, assassin of Abraham Lincoln, was caught and killed by federal troops near Port Royal, Virginia.

1865 Mrs. Sue Landon Vaughn led a group to decorate Confederate graves in Vicksburg, Miss., causing the day to be celebrated as Confederate Memorial Day.

1910 President William Howard Taft dedicated the Pan-American Union building in Washington, D.C.

1924 Metro-Goldwyn-Mayer was formed in an amalgamation of Metro Picture Corp, Goldwyn Picture Corp. and Louis B. Mayer Pictures.

1937 Nazi planes annihilated the defenseless Basque town of Guernica in the Spanish Civil War, making Guernica a symbol of antifascism and inspiring Pablo Picasso's famous painting.

1954 A nationwide test of the new Salk anti-polio vaccine began in 45 states.

1965 The African nations of Tanganyika and Zanzibar merged to form Tanzania.

1983 The Dow Jones Industrial Average closed above 1,200 for the first time in history.

1986 A power plant reactor caught fire at Chernobyl, near the Soviet city of Kiev, leading to a melt down and the worst nuclear accident in world history.

April 27 – Birthdays

1759 **Mary Wollstonecraft.** English writer noted for her book, *A Vindication of the Rights of Women* (1792)

1791 **Samuel F.B. Morse.** Inventor of the electric telegraph and the Morse code

1820 **Herbert Spencer.** English philosopher and early evolutionist

1822 **Ulysses S. Grant.** U.S. Civil War general and 18th president

1840 **Edward Whymper.** First man to climb the Matterhorn, in 1865

1896 **Rogers Hornsby.** Hall of Fame baseball player and greatest right-handed hitter of all time, with a .358 lifetime batting average

1896 **Wallace H. Carothers.** American chemist whose work led to the invention of synthetic rubber and nylon

1898 **Ludwig Bemelmans.** American humorous writer and painter, who wrote and illustrated books for children and adults

1900 **Walter Lantz.** American animator and cartoon film producer noted especially for his creation of Woody Woodpecker

1904 **Arthur Burns.** American economist and chairman of the Federal Reserve System

1913 **Philip Hauge Abelson.** Noted American physical chemist

1916 **Enos Slaughter.** Professional baseball player and Hall of Famer

1918 **John Scali.** American journalist and diplomat

1922 **Jack Klugman.** American motion-picture and television actor

1927 **Coretta King.** Wife of civil rights leader Martin Luther King Jr.

1931 **Igor Oistrakh.** Russian-born virtuoso violinist

1932 **Anouk Aimee.** French motion-picture actress

1937 **Phil Jones.** American television news correspondent

1937 **Sandy Dennis.** American motion-picture actress

1938 **Earl Anthony.** American bowler, who was Bowler of the Year in 1974, 1975, and 1976

1941 **Judith Blegen.** American operatic soprano

1948 **Georges Goven.** French tennis player

1949 **Guy Walkingstick.** Professional golfer

1951 **Gary Huff.** Professional football player

1952 **George Gervin.** Professional basketball player known as "The Iceman"

1957 **Willie Upshaw.** Professional baseball player

1967 **Prince Willem Alexander.** First male heir to the Dutch throne in three generations

April 27 – Events

1296 Edward I of England defeated the Scots in the Battle of Dunbar, enabling him to seize the Stone of Scone, the symbol of Scottish authority, and make himself king of Scotland.

1509 The city of Venice was excommunicated by Pope Julius II.

1521 Spanish navigator Ferdinand Magellan was killed by tribesmen on the island of Mactan in the Philippines. His crew later completed the first trip around the world.

1667 The great English poet John Milton sold his *Paradise Lost* copyright for 10 English pounds.

1777 Benedict Arnold defeated the British at Ridgefield, Conn., in the American Revolutionary War.

1814 Napoleon was made King of Elba, a tiny island off the coast of Italy, where he supposedly was exiled.

1867 Pi Beta Phi, the first national fraternity for women, was founded at Monmouth College, Monmouth, Illinois.

1882 Ralph Waldo Emerson, the great American philosopher, died in Concord, Massachusetts, at age 78.

1941 German troops occupied Athens in World War II.

1947 "Babe Ruth Day" was observed throughout the United States, honoring the seriously-ill Babe, who died a year later.

1958 The comic strip *Rick O'Shay,* by Stan Lynde, first appeared.

1965 The noted broadcast journalist Edward R. Murrow died in Pawling, New York, at the age of 57.

1968 Jimmy Ellis beat Jerry Quarry in a 15 round decision in Oakland, California, to become heavyweight champion.

April 28 – Birthdays

32 **Marcus Salvius Otho.** Emperor of Rome for less than a year, A.D. 69

1442 **Edward IV.** King of England, 1461-1469 and 1471-1483

1630 **Charles Cotton.** British writer and poet noted for *The Compleat Gamester* (1664)

1753 **Franz Karl Achard.** German chemist who developed in 1793 a process for obtaining sugar from beets

1758 **James Monroe.** Fifth U.S. president

1795 **Charles Stuart.** British explorer of Australia

1838 **Tobias M.C. Asser.** Dutch statesman, author and Nobel Prize winner (1911) for helping form the Permanent Court of Arbitration

1869 **Bertram Grosvenor Goodhue.** American architect noted for his designs of the Rockefeller Chapel at the University of Chicago, numerous New York City churches, and the Nebraska State Capitol building

1874 **Sidney Toler.** American stage and motion-picture actor, who played the title role of the *Charlie Chan* movie series

1878 **Lionel Barrymore.** American stage, radio, and screen actor, and member of the famous Barrymore family of actors

1889 **Antonio de Oliveira Salazar.** Dictator of Portugal, 1932-1968

1892 **John Jacob Niles.** American folksinger

1897 **Felix Bernard.** American composer noted for songs such as "Dardanella," "I'd Rather Be Me," and "Winter Wonderland"

1900 **Jan Hendrik Oort.** Dutch astronomer noted for investigations proving the rotation of the Milky Way

1908 **Oskar Schindler.** German industrialist who saved the lives of hundreds of Jews during World War II by employing them in his factory

1917 **Robert Anderson.** American playwright noted for works such as *Tea and Sympathy* and *I Never Sang for My Father*

1921 **Karl Suessdorf.** American composer and author, noted for songs such as "Moonlight in Vermont," "Key Largo," and "The Good Humor Man"

1921 **Rowland Evans Jr.** Member of the Evans and Novak team of political columnists

1922 **Alistair MacLean.** Scottish author noted for *The Guns of Navarone* (1957)

1924 **Kenneth Kaunda.** Zambian patriot who led the British colony of Northern Rhodesia to independence in 1964 as the Republic of Zambia, and became its first president

1926 **Harper Lee.** American author who won the Pulitzer Prize for her novel, *To Kill a Mockingbird* (1960)

1930 **James A. Baker.** White House Chief of Staff and Secretary of the Treasury under President Reagan and Secretary of State under President Bush

1933 **Carolyn Jones.** American motion-picture and television actress

1937 **Saddam Hussein.** President of Iraq who precipitated the Persian Gulf War by invading Kuwait

1941 **Ann-Margret (Olsson).** Swedish-born motion-picture and television actress

1943 **Ivan Nagy.** Hungarian ballet dancer

1950 **Jay Leno.** American comedian and actor who succeeded Johnny Carson as host of *The Tonight Show*

1964 **Barry Larkin.** Professional baseball player

April 28 – Events

1429 The forces of Joan of Arc entered Orleans in the Hundred Years' War. Orleans was captured from the English five days later.

1521 Hernando Cortes, the Spanish Conquistador, began a 75-day siege of Tenochtitlan, the Aztec city on the site of modern Mexico City.

1788 Maryland became the seventh state of the Union.

1789 The sailors mutinied on the British ship *Bounty* and cast Captain Bligh adrift in a small boat with 18 of his men.

1881 Billy the Kid, the notorious Western outlaw, killed two deputies and escaped from jail, where he was waiting to be hanged.

1945 Benito Mussolini and his mistress Clara Petacci were shot at Lake Como by Italian partisans, and their bodies were taken to Milan and later hung by the heels in front of a garage.

1947 Thor Heyerdahl's *Kon-Tiki* was towed out to sea from Peru in preparation for its departure for Polynesia.

1952 World War II officially ended between the United States and Japan with a treaty signed in San Francisco.

1967 Heavyweight boxing champion Muhammad Ali refused to be inducted into the army.

1969 Charles de Gaulle resigned as president of France.

1988 The Baltimore Orioles lost their 21st straight game, giving them a 0-21 record, the worst start in baseball history.

April 29 – Birthdays

1745 **Oliver Ellsworth.** Third chief justice of the U.S Supreme Court (1796-1800)

1792 **Matthew Vassar.** American brewer who founded Vassar College

1818 **Alexander II.** Czar of Russia, 1855-1881, who liberated the serfs in 1861

1837 **Georges Boulanger.** French general, minister, and politician

1854 **Henri Poincaré.** French mathematician, noted as one of the greatest of modern times

1860 **Lorado Taft.** American sculptor noted for *The Spirit of the Great Lakes* at the Art Institute of Chicago

1863 **William Randolph Hearst.** U.S. newspaper publisher and founder of the Hearst chain

1875 **Rafael Sabatini.** Italian-English novelist noted for works such as *The Sea Hawk* (1915), *Scaramouche* (1921), and *Captain Blood* (1922)

1879 **Sir Thomas Beecham.** Internationally acclaimed British conductor

1885 **Frank Jack Fletcher.** U.S. naval officer known as "Black Jack," who participated in both World Wars

1893 **Harold Urey.** American physicist and discoverer of deuterium

1899 **Duke Ellington.** American composer and jazz orchestra leader

1901 **Hirohito.** Emperor of Japan, 1926-1989

1904 **Russ Morgan.** American composer and bandleader, noted for songs such as "Please Think of Me," "Somebody Else Is Taking My Place," and his theme song, "Does Your Heart Beat for Me?"

1904 **Fletcher Martin.** American artist

1907 **Fred Zinnemann.** American motion-picture director noted for works such as *High Noon, From Here to Eternity,* and *A Man for All Seasons*

1909 **Tom Ewell.** American motion-picture and television actor

1912 **Richard Carlson.** American motion-picture and television actor

1915 **Donald Mills.** American singer and member of the Mills Brothers group

1919 **Celeste Holm.** American stage, screen, and television actress

1921 **Tommy Noonan.** American motion-picture actor

1922 **George Allen.** Professional football player and coach

1933 **Rod McKuen.** American poet and author, noted for songs for films, television, operas, and ballets

1934 **Luis Aparicio.** Hall of Fame baseball player

1936 **Zubin Mehta.** Indian symphony orchestra conductor

1944 **Jim Hart.** Professional football player

1947 **Johnny Miller.** Professional golfer

1947 **Jim Ryun.** American runner who ran the mile in 3:51.1

1948 **James Otis.** Professional football player

1954 **Jerry Seinfeld.** American actor and comedian noted for the long-running television series *Seinfeld*

1955 **Kate Mulgrew.** American television actress noted for her role in *Star Trek*

1957 **Michelle Pfeiffer.** American actress and a leading lady of Hollywood films with four Academy Award nominations

1957 **Daniel Day-Lewis.** English stage and screen actor and son of England's Poet Laureate, Cecil Day-Lewis (C. Day Lewis) and actress Jill Balcon
1966 **Ed Correa.** Professional baseball player
1970 **Uma Thurman.** American motion-picture actress
1970 **Andre Agassi.** American tennis player

April 29 – Events

1770 Captain James Cook discovered Botany Bay in Australia.
1817 The Rush-Bagot Treaty was signed which limited the number of British and American naval forces in the Great Lakes and established a policy of peace along the U.S.-Canadian border.
1862 A Union fleet under Admiral Farragut captured New Orleans in the Civil War.
1894 Coxey's Army, with Jacob S. Coxey at its head, arrived in Washington, D.C., to petition Congress for relief legislation.
1900 Casey Jones brought his Illinois Central *Cannonball* into Memphis the night before the famous wreck.
1913 Gideon Sundback of Hoboken, New Jersey, patented the zipper under the name "separable fastener."
1945 The bodies of Benito Mussolini and his mistress Clara Petacci were hung up by the heels and displayed to the populace in Milan, Italy.
1945 American soldiers in World War II liberated 32,000 prisoners in the notorious Nazi concentration camp in Dachau, Germany, where untold thousands of victims had been killed.
1945 Adolf Hitler and Eva Braun were married in an underground bunker in Berlin, one day before they committed suicide.
1947 Thor Heyerdahl, the Norwegian scientist, left Peru on his raft *Kon-Tiki* to test the theory that pre-Incan Indians had drifted across the ocean to colonize Polynesia.
1974 President Richard Nixon announced the release of transcripts of the Watergate tapes. The transcripts, though edited, were damaging enough to help destroy his presidency.
1981 Steve Carlton, Philadelphia Phillies' pitcher, struck out his 3,000th career batter.
1986 Roger Clemens of the Boston Red Sox struck out a record 20 batters in a nine-inning game, as Boston beat Seattle, 3-1.

April 30 – Birthdays

1309 **Casimir III (The Great).** King of Poland, 1333-1370, who established the first statute of laws in Europe
1504 **Francesco Primaticcio.** Italian painter
1662 **Mary II.** Queen of England, 1689-1694, who with her husband ruled as William and Mary following the Glorious Revolution of 1688

1770 **David Thompson.** British-born explorer, known as "Canada's Greatest Geographer," who was the first to follow the Columbia River from its source to its mouth
1777 **Karl Friedrich Gauss.** German mathematician and physicist, who was perhaps the greatest mathematician of all time
1823 **Henry Oscar Houghton.** American publisher who in 1864 founded Hurd and Houghton, which later became Houghton, Mifflin Company
1845 **Martins Joaquin Pedro de Oliveira.** Portuguese writer
1858 **Mary Dimmick Harrison.** Second wife of President Benjamin Harrison
1870 **Franz Lehar.** Hungarian composer of light operas, noted for such lilting music as *The Merry Widow Waltz*
1877 **Alice B. Toklas.** Companion and secretary of writer Gertrude Stein
1888 **John Crowe Ransom.** American poet, critic and proponent of the New Criticism movement
1893 **Joachim von Ribbentrop.** Adolf Hitler's top diplomatic figure
1901 **Simon Kuznets.** Russian-born American economist and Nobel Prize winner (1971) for studies of national income and business cycles
1904 **John T. Benson Jr.** American composer noted for "Love Lifted Me"
1908 **Eve Arden.** American motion-picture, television, and radio actress and comedienne noted for the title role in the long-running radio series *Our Miss Brooks*
1909 **Juliana.** Queen of The Netherlands, 1948-1980
1916 **Claude E. Shannon.** American mathematician and pioneer in switching and logic whose World War II work contributed to the development of computers
1916 **Robert Shaw.** American choral conductor and one of the most outstanding of his time
1918 **Donald McNeill.** American Hall of Fame tennis player
1924 **Sheldon Harnick.** American lyricist who teamed with composer Jerry Bock to write such songs as "Sunrise, Sunset" from *Fiddler on the Roof*
1925 **Corinne Calvet.** French motion-picture actress
1926 **Cloris Leachman.** American stage, motion-picture, and television actress
1933 **Willie Nelson.** American country singer and composer
1943 **Bobby Vee.** American teen idol singer
1944 **Jill Clayburgh.** American stage and screen actress
1945 **Annie Dillard.** American author noted for *Pilgrim At Tinker Creek* (1975)
1946 **Donald Schollander.** American swimmer who set the 200-meter free style record of 1 minute 54.3 seconds in 1968
1948 **Perry King.** American television and motion-picture actor
1949 **Karl Meiler.** West German tennis player
1961 **Isiah Thomas.** Professional basketball player

1963   **Al Toon.** Professional football player

April 30 – Events

1380   Saint Catherine of Siena, patron saint of nurses, died in Rome at age 33.

1789   George Washington was inaugurated in New York City as the first president of the United States.

1803   The Louisiana Purchase was completed from France by the United States, which with the stroke of a pen doubled the size of the young nation. The treaty was signed by both countries two days later.

1812   Louisiana was admitted to the Union as the 18th state.

1879   Sarah Josepha Hale, author of "Mary Had a Little Lamb," died at age 91.

1883   Edouard Manet, the great French impressionist painter, died in Paris at age 51.

1900   Casey Jones, the "brave engineer" of the famous folk song, was killed at Vaughan, Mississippi, when his Engine 382 collided with a freight train.

1939   The National Broadcasting Company (NBC) began regular television broadcasts.

1945   Adolf Hitler, 56, and his bride of one day, Eva Braun, committed suicide in a bunker 30 feet below the ruins of the Reichchancellery in Berlin. Shortly afterwards the Russians captured the city.

1961   Willie Mays of the San Francisco Giants hit four home runs in a single baseball game.

1970   President Nixon announced the invasion of Cambodia by U.S. forces in Vietnam, for the purpose of clearing out sanctuaries used by the North Vietnamese.

1973   President Nixon announced the resignation of H.R. Haldeman, John Ehrlichman, and Richard Kleindienst, and the firing of John Dean, because of the Watergate scandals.

1974   The White House released edited transcripts of the Watergate tapes, creating shock, dismay, and outrage in Congress and among the people.

1975   The South Vietnamese capital of Saigon fell to Communist forces, as the Vietnam War ended in the unconditional surrender of South Vietnam.

1980   Beatrix became Queen of the Netherlands, succeeding her mother, Juliana, who abdicated in her favor.

1993   Top-ranked woman tennis player Monica Seles was stabbed in the back during a match in Hamburg, Germany, by a man who claimed to be a fan of second-rated Steffi Graf. He was given a suspended sentence and Seles was out of action for a year.

1998   The U.S. Senate voted to approve NATO membership for the Czech Republic, Hungary, and Poland.

5

May

May, the fifth month, was the third month in the early Roman calendar, and it gets its name from the Latin *Maius,* the origin of which is debatable. The most widely accepted story is that the name honored Maia, the Roman goddess of spring and growth, and the mother of Mercury. Many scholars maintain that May was named in tribute to the *majores,* the Latin word for "older men." Thus May would be the month sacred to the majores, as June is to the *juniores* ("younger men"). May was one of the four named months of the calendar of Romulus, at which time it had 30 days, but since then it has always had 31 days.

May Day (May 1) is a special day observed as a festival of spring in many countries. For the ancient Romans it was sacred to Flora, the goddess of flowers, and they celebrated the day with flower-decked parades. In the United States, May 1 is celebrated as Law Day. Other special days of May are Mother's Day, the second Sunday of the month, Armed Forces Day, the third Saturday of the month, and Memorial Day, a federal holiday on the last Monday in May honoring those who died in America's wars. Also, the most famous horse race in the United States, the Kentucky Derby, takes place on the first Saturday of May at Churchill Downs in Louisville, Kentucky.

Two American Presidents, Harry S. Truman and John F. Kennedy, were born in May, as was Queen Victoria of England, whose birthday on May 24 is celebrated in the United Kingdom as Commonwealth Day.

The birthstone for May is the emerald and the flowers are the lily of the valley and the hawthorn.

May 1 – Birthdays

1218   **Rudolf I.** King of Germany, 1254-1273, and founder of the Hapsburg dynasty in Austria, which ruled until 1918

1672   **Joseph Addison.** English essayist, best known for *The Spectator* series published in 1711 and 1712 with Sir Richard Steele

1764   **Benjamin Henry Latrobe.** The first professionally trained architect to practice in the United States, and designer of the south wing of the U.S. capitol after the British burned the original

1769   **Duke of Wellington.** British general (Arthur Wellesley) who conquered Napoleon at the Battle of Waterloo in 1815

1808   **Gerard de Nerval.** French writer whose translation at age 19 of Goethe's *Faust* was praised by Goethe himself

1824   **Alexander William Williamson.** British chemist who described dynamic equilibrium and the role of catalyst

1825   **George Inness.** Noted American landscape painter

1827   **Jules Adolphe Breton.** French painter noted for the famous picture *Return of the Gleaners*

1830   **Mary Harris "Mother" Jones.** Irish-American labor leader who wrote her autobiography at age 95 and whose motto was "Pray for the dead and fight like hell for the living"

1839   **Louis Marie Chardonnet.** French chemist who invented rayon, patented in 1884

1845   **George Harrison Mifflin.** American publisher

1852   **Santiago Ramon y Cajal.** Spanish Nobelist (1906) for research on the nervous system

1852   **Calamity Jane (Martha Jane Canary).** American frontierswoman and companion of Wild Bill Hickok

1862   **Marcel Prevost.** French novelist

1876   **Carl A. Swanson.** Swedish-American businessman who founded the Swanson Co. in 1899 and produced the first frozen "TV dinner" (1954)

1880   **Albert Davis Lasker.** U.S. advertising executive and co-founder of the Albert and Mary Lasker Foundation

1881   **Pierre Teilhard de Chardin.** French Jesuit writer and paleontologist noted for helping discover Peking Man and for his theory that claimed to unify cosmic evolution and Christianity

1887   **Edwin Muir.** Scottish novelist, poet, and critic, noted for works such as *Poor Toni* (1932)

1889   **Alfonso Reyes.** Mexican writer

1895 Leo Sowerby. American composer noted for works such as "Comes Autumn Time"

1896 Mark Clark. U.S. World War II general, who commanded the Fifth Army in Italy

1900 Ignazio Silone. Italian novelist, noted for the intensely human novel *Bread and Wine*

1901 Sterling Brown. American folklorist and author noted for "When the Saints Go Marching Home" (1927)

1904 Valentina. Russian-born American fashion designer

1907 Kate Smith. Noted American popular singer

1910 J. Allen Hynek. American astronomer and UFO authority

1916 Glenn Ford. American motion-picture and television actor and superstar in over 200 movies

1916 Jane Jacobs. American urbanologist and writer

1917 Danielle Darrieux. French stage and motion-picture actress

1917 John Berardino. Professional baseball player and actor

1918 Jack Paar. American television personality and early host of the *Tonight Show*

1919 Dan O'Herlihy. Irish motion-picture actor and brother of director Michael O'Herlihy

1923 Joseph Heller. American novelist and author of *Catch-22* (1961)

1925 M. Scott Carpenter. Second U.S. astronaut to make an orbital space flight, in *Aurora 7* in 1962

1928 Terry Southern. American writer

1929 Sonny James. American singer

1930 Little Walter (Jacobs). American blues musician

1930 Ollie Matson. Professional football player and Hall of Famer

1939 Judy Collins. American folk and pop singer

1939 Frank Beard. Professional golfer

1945 Rita Coolidge. American singer

1954 Ray Parker Jr. American musician and songwriter

1960 Steve Cauthen. American jockey and Kentucky Derby winner when he was a teenager

May 1 – Events

1045 Pope Benedict IX sold the papacy to John Gratianus, Gregory VI.

1316 Edward Bruce was crowned King of Ireland.

1429 Joan of Arc began raising the English siege of Orleans.

1464 King Edward IV of England secretly married Elizabeth Woodville.

1625 King Charles I of England married France's Henrietta Maria by proxy.

1700 John Dryden, the noted English writer, died in London at age 68.

1786 Wolfgang Amadeus Mozart's famous opera *The Marriage of Figaro* premiered in Vienna.

1840 Postage stamps were first sold, in England. They did not carry the name of the country because they were intended for domestic use only.

1851 The London Crystal Palace Exhibition, the first world's fair, opened.

1873 Penny post cards were placed on sale for the first time by the United States Post Office.

1873 The great Scottish explorer David Livingstone was found dead in a village in what is now Zambia. He had apparently died the previous day.

1884 Construction began on the first skyscraper, the Home Insurance Building in Chicago. It had 10 stories and was designed by architect William Le Baron Jenney.

1898 U.S. Commodore George Dewey's Asiatic Squadron of six ships destroyed the entire Spanish fleet in the Battle of Manila Bay in the Spanish-American War.

1931 The Empire State Building was dedicated by New York's former governor Al Smith.

1931 Singer Kate Smith began her long-running radio program on CBS, on her 24th birthday.

1941 The great motion-picture *Citizen Kane,* directed by and starring Orson Welles, premiered in New York City.

1945 Radio Hamburg announced the death of Adolf Hitler, who had committed suicide two days earlier.

1948 Eddie Arcaro became the first jockey to ride four Kentucky Derby winners, winning with Citation.

1960 An American U-2 spy plane was shot down deep inside Russia, and the pilot, Gary Powers, was taken prisoner.

1963 James M. Whittaker of Redmond, Washington, became the first American to conquer Mount Everest.

1991 Nolan Ryan of the Texas Rangers threw his seventh career no-hitter as Texas beat Toronto 3-0.

May 2 – Birthdays

1659 Alessandro Scarlatti. A leading composer of early Italian opera

1729 Catherine II, The Great. Empress of Russia, 1762-1796, who ascended the throne on the death of her husband Peter III

1750 John André. British military officer who was hanged as a spy for colluding with the American traitor Benedict Arnold

1752 Humphrey Repton. English landscape architect whose informal style has become identified with English landscape gardening

1772 Novalis (Friedrich Von Hardenberg). German Romantic poet, noted for such works as *Hymns to the Night* (1800)

1779 John Galt. Scottish novelist

1792 Rufus Porter. Founder of *Scientific American* magazine

1835 **John Heenan.** Hall of Fame boxer

1837 **Henry Martyn Robert.** U.S. Army engineer and author of *Robert's Rules of Order* for parliamentary procedure

1859 **Jerome Klapka Jerome.** British writer and author of *Three Men in a Boat* (1889)

1860 **Theodor Herzl.** Austrian writer who founded the Zionist movement, the aim of which was to set up a Jewish national home in Palestine

1866 **Jesse William Lazear.** U.S. Army surgeon known for his work in controlling yellow fever

1870 **Lewis J. Selznick.** Russian-American film executive, founder of the Selznick Company, and father of film notables David O. and Myron Selznick

1879 **Jimmy Byrnes.** Secretary of State under President Truman

1887 **Eddie Collins.** Hall of Fame baseball player, with 3,313 career hits

1887 **Vernon Castle.** English-born dancer who with his wife Irene Castle formed the internationally famous ballroom dancing team of the 1910s

1892 **Manfred von Richthofen.** Germany's "Red Baron" and top aviator in World War I

1895 **Lorenz Hart.** American lyricist who with Richard Rodgers wrote nearly 400 songs, such as "Blue Moon," "With a Song in My Heart," "You Are Too Beautiful," and "Bewitched, Bothered and Bewildered"

1895 **Peggy Bacon.** American printmaker

1897 **John Frederick "J. Fred" Coots.** American composer noted for songs such as "Santa Claus Is Coming to Town" and "Love Letters in the Sand"

1902 **Brian Aherne.** English-born motion-picture actor

1903 **Dr. Benjamin Spock.** Noted American pediatrician and author

1904 **Bing Crosby.** American singer, actor, and one of the most versatile entertainers in American history

1906 **Aileen Riggin.** Hall of Fame swimmer and diver and the first person to win Olympic medals in both swimming and diving

1924 **Theodore Bikel.** Austrian-born actor and writer

1935 **Faisal II.** King of Iraq, 1953-1958

1945 **Bianca Jagger.** American model and wife of musician Mick Jagger

1946 **Leslie Gore.** American singer

1949 **Larry Gatlin.** American country music singer and songwriter (The Gatlin Brothers)

1952 **John Andrews.** American tennis player

1953 **Jamaal Wilkes.** Professional basketball player

1954 **Keith Moreland.** Professional baseball player

May 2 – Events

1519 Leonardo da Vinci died at the Chateaux de Cloux near Amboise, France, at age 66.

1670 The Hudson Bay Company was chartered by King Charles II of England.

1803 The Louisiana Purchase agreement, completed three days earlier, was formally signed in Paris by American envoys James Monroe and Robert Livingston.

1808 The Spanish populace attacked Napoleon's French guard in the *Dos de Mayo* insurrection in Madrid.

1863 General Stonewall Jackson was shot accidentally by his own soldiers outside Chancellorsville, Virginia. He died eight days later.

1865 The first paid fire department was established, in New York City.

1876 Ross Barnes of the Chicago White Stockings and Baby Jones of the Cincinnati Reds hit the first home runs in major league history, as Chicago won, 15-9.

1885 *Good Housekeeping* magazine was first published by Clark W. Bryan in Holyoke, Massachusetts.

1933 Adolf Hitler abolished labor unions throughout Germany.

1939 Lou Gehrig took himself out of the New York Yankee lineup after a record 2,130 consecutive games, because of the rare paralysis he was stricken with.

1945 The Germans surrendered Berlin to the Russians, and Nazi troops in Italy surrendered unconditionally to the Allies in World War II.

1954 Stan Musial of the St. Louis Cardinals hit a record five home runs in a double-header.

1972 J. Edgar Hoover, first and only FBI director in its first 48-year history, died at age 77.

May 3 – Birthdays

1469 **Niccolo Machiavelli.** Florentine statesman and writer noted for *The Prince,* one of the great works of world literature

1748 **Emmanuel Joseph Sieyes.** French cleric (known as Abbe Sieyes) who helped start the French Revolution with his booklet, *What Is the Third Estate?* (1789)

1761 **August Kotzebue.** German writer whose murder in 1819 as an alleged Russian spy led the Prussian government to issue the repressive Carlsbad Decrees

1849 **Jacob August Riis.** American newspaperman, social reformer, and "America's first photojournalist"

1874 **François Coty.** Noted French perfume manufacturer

1877 **Karl Abraham.** German psychoanalyst

1891 **Eppa Rixey.** Hall of Fame baseball player

1892 **Beulah Bondi.** American stage, screen, and television actress

1897 **V.K. Krishna Menon.** Indian nationalist

1898 **Golda Meir.** Prime minister of Israel, 1969-1974

1902 **Alfred Kastler.** French physicist and Nobel Prize-winner (1966) for his research on the energy level of electrons

1902 **Walter Slezak.** Austrian-born stage and motion-picture actor

1904	**Red Ruffing.** Hall of Fame baseball player
1906	**Mary Astor.** American motion-picture actress
1907	**Earl Wilson.** American columnist on show business activities
1912	**Virgil Fox.** American organist noted for his work at Riverside Church in New York City
1913	**William Inge.** American playwright and screenwriter noted for works such as *Come Back, Little Sheba; Picnic; Bus Stop;* and *The Dark at the Top of the Stairs*
1913	**Earl Blackwell.** American publisher and social arbiter
1915	**Richard Lippold.** American sculptor noted for delicate abstract and geometric work such as *Variation Number 7: Full Moon*
1919	**Betty Comden.** American playwright, lyricist, and songwriter
1919	**Pete Seeger.** American folk protest singer and songwriter
1920	**Sugar Ray Robinson.** Welterweight and six times middleweight world champion and one of the greatest boxers in history
1920	**John Lewis.** American pianist and composer
1921	**Alida Valli.** Italian motion-picture actress
1921	**Goose Tatum.** Basketball star of the Harlem Globetrotters
1927	**Mel Lazarus.** American comic strip artist (with the pseudonym "Mell") noted for *Miss Peach* and *Momma*
1931	**Joe Layton.** American choreographer and director
1936	**James Brown.** American soul singer
1937	**Frankie Valli.** American singer with the Four Seasons
1937	**Englebert Humperdinck.** American singer
1937	**Bobby Driscoll.** American child star of motion-pictures of the 1940s and 1950s
1946	**Davey Lopes.** Professional baseball player
1946	**Greg Gumbel.** American sportscaster and brother of TV personality Bryant Gumbel
1947	**Doug Henning.** Canadian magician noted for the "World of Magic" show and as a coauthor of a book on Houdini
1948	**Garfield Heard.** Professional basketball player
1948	**Peter Oosterhuis.** Professional golfer
1949	**Ron Wyden.** U.S. senator
1963	**Jeff Hornacek.** Professional basketball player

May 3 – Events

1429	Joan of Arc liberated Orleans from the English in the Hundred Years' War.
1471	Edward IV won the Battle of Tewkesbury in the Wars of the Roses to wrest the throne of England from Henry VI.
1765	The first American medical school was established, in the College of Philadelphia, now the University of Pennsylvania.
1802	Washington, D.C., was incorporated as a city.
1810	English poet Lord Byron swam the Hellespont in one hour and 10 minutes.
1921	West Virginia imposed the first state sales tax.
1937	Margaret Mitchell won a Pulitzer Prize for *Gone With the Wind*.
1952	The first big commercial jet plane, the De Havilland Comet, began passenger service in Great Britain.
1979	Margaret Thatcher became the first woman prime minister of England.
1980	Genuine Risk won the Kentucky Derby, becoming the second filly in history to do so. Regret was the first, in 1915.

May 4 – Birthdays

1622	**Juan de Valdes Leal.** Spanish Baroque painter
1655	**Bartolommeo Cristofori.** Italian harpsichord maker who developed the principle of striking a hammer against strings in 1709, which led to the piano
1770	**Charlotte Smith.** English novelist and poet
1770	**Baron François Pascal Simon Gerard.** French painter
1796	**Horace Mann.** Father of American public education
1796	**William Hickling Prescott.** American historian and writer, whose works rank as classics in the study and writing of history
1806	**William F. Cooke.** British electrical engineer who built the first telegraph line in the U.K.
1820	**Julia Gardiner Tyler.** Second wife of President John Tyler
1825	**Thomas Henry Huxley.** British scientist and humanist, who helped advance Darwin's theory of evolution, earning him the nickname, "Darwin's Bulldog," and who coined the words *agnostic* and *biogenesis*
1826	**Frederic Edwin Church.** American artist and one of the best-known landscape painters in the mid-1800s, noted for works such as *Scene in the Catskill Mountains*
1827	**John Hanning Speke.** English African explorer who in 1862 confirmed that Lake Victoria is the source of the Nile
1872	**Harold Bell Wright.** American minister and author, noted for *The Shepherd of the Hills* (1907) and *The Winning of Barbara Worth* (1911)
1886	**Brooks Shelton.** American pianist and composer noted for songs such as "Some of These Days" (1910) and "The Darktown Strutters' Ball" (1915)
1889	**Francis Cardinal Spellman.** Outstanding U.S. leader of the Catholic Church
1896	**Alton Ochsner.** American physician who linked cigarette smoking to lung cancer
1898	**Katharine Burr Blodgett.** American scientist noted for inventing non-reflecting glass
1903	**Elmer Layden.** Football player known as one of the Four Horsemen of Notre Dame

1909	**Howard Da Silva.** American stage and motion-picture actor
1928	**Hosni Mubarak.** Egyptian president who succeeded Anwar Sadat
1928	**Betsy Rawls.** Hall of Fame golfer
1928	**Ferguson Maynard.** Canadian-born virtuoso jazz trumpeter
1929	**Audrey Hepburn.** English stage and motion-picture actress and superstar
1930	**Roberta Peters.** American operatic soprano
1936	**El Cordobes.** Spanish bullfighter (born Manuel Benitez Perez), who was the highest paid in history
1941	**George F. Will.** American newspaper columnist and television commentator
1942	**Tammy Wynette.** American country singer
1942	**Juan Gisbert.** Spanish tennis player
1942	**Nickolas Ashford.** American singer and songwriter
1947	**Butch Beard.** Professional basketball player
1949	**Laura Dupont.** American tennis player
1951	**Jackie Jackson.** American singer and guitarist with the Jackson 5
1956	**Ken Oberkfell.** Professional baseball player
1956	**David Guterson.** American novelist noted for works such as *Snow Falling On Cedars* (1994)
1959	**Randy Travis.** American country singer

May 4 – Events

1328	England recognized Robert Bruce as king of Scotland in the Treaty of Northampton.
1493	Pope Alexander VI drew the Line of Demarcation, dividing the disputed lands of Spain and Portugal.
1494	Columbus discovered the island of Jamaica on his second voyage to America, and named it Santiago.
1626	Peter Minuit, the Dutch colonizer, landed on Manhattan Island, which he later bought from the Indians for $24.
1776	Rhode Island declared its independence from England, the first American colony to do so.
1814	Napoleon arrived on the island of Elba for his first exile.
1863	The Battle of Chancellorsville ended in victory for the South, but they lost their great general Stonewall Jackson, who was shot accidentally by his own men two days earlier.
1886	The Haymarket riot took place in Chicago during a meeting of anarchists to protest police tactics against strikers.
1902	The comic strip *Buster Brown,* by R.F. Outcault, first appeared.
1904	The United States took over the Panama Canal Zone.
1919	The comic strip *Harold Teen,* by Carl Ed, first appeared.
1927	The Academy of Motion Picture Arts and Sciences was formed.
1932	Gangster Al Capone was jailed in Atlanta for income-tax evasion.

1942	The Battle of the Coral Sea began between the United States and Japan in World War II.
1970	Ohio National Guardsmen opened fire on 1,000 Kent State students protesting the Vietnam War, killing four students and wounding eight others.
1980	Marshal Tito (Josip Broz), Yugoslavia's president for 35 years, died three days before his 88th birthday.
1981	Ron Davis, New York Yankees' pitcher, struck out eight straight batters, tying the American League record.
1998	Theodore Kaczynski, the Unabomber, was sentenced to four life sentences plus 30 years.

May 5 – Birthdays

1210	**Alfonso III.** One of the earliest kings of Portugal
1282	**Don Juan Manuel.** Most important prose writer of 14th-century Spain
1747	**Leopold II.** Holy Roman Emperor
1809	**Frederick Augustus Porter Barnard.** American educator and founder of Barnard College (1899)
1813	**Soren Kierkegaard.** Danish philosopher and religious thinker, and one of the founders of existentialism
1818	**Karl Marx.** German sociologist and economist whose ideas formed the basis for Marxism, or Communism
1826	**Eugenie Bonaparte.** Wife of Napoleon III of France
1830	**John Batterson Stetson.** The leading American hat manufacturer in the late 1800s, whose most famous creation was his ten-gallon hat
1846	**Henryk Sienkiewicz.** Popular Polish novelist and author of *A Prophet in His Own Country*
1867	**Nellie Bly.** Newspaper writer famous for an around-the-world race
1882	**Douglas Mawson.** Australian explorer of Antarctica
1883	**Archibald Percival Wavell.** English World War II general
1883	**Chief Bender.** Hall of Fame baseball player
1890	**Christopher Morley.** American literary journalist and author of *Kitty Foyle* (1939)
1895	**Charles MacArthur.** American director, screenwriter, and playwright
1899	**Freeman Gosden.** American actor who played Amos on the *Amos and Andy* radio show
1903	**James Beard.** American gourmet
1911	**Max Frisch.** Swiss author and one of the leading writers of the German-speaking world after World War II
1913	**Tyrone Power.** American motion-picture actor and leading man of the 1930s and 1940s
1915	**Richard Rovere.** American writer and journalist
1915	**Alice Faye.** American stage and motion-picture actress and superstar
1927	**Pat Carroll.** American motion-picture and television actress

1934	**John J. Sweeney.** President of the AFL-CIO, who succeeded Lane Kirkland in 1995
1943	**Michael Palin.** English actor, screenwriter and member of the cast of *Monty Python's Flying Circus*
1944	**Jean-Pierre Leaud.** French motion-picture actor
1947	**Larry Hisle.** Professional baseball player
1949	**Larry Steele.** Professional basketball player
1956	**Ron Oester.** Professional baseball player
1967	**Charles Nagy.** Professional baseball player

May 5 – Events

1645	King Charles I of England surrendered himself to the Scots following the end of the English Civil War.
1821	Napoleon died of cancer at Longwood on the island of Saint Helena at age 51.
1847	The American Medical Association was organized in Philadelphia.
1862	French troops, trying to keep Archduke Maximilian in power in Mexico, were routed by the Mexicans near Puebla. The anniversary is celebrated in Mexico as Cinco De Mayo Day.
1864	The Battle of the Wilderness between generals Lee and Grant began in northern Virginia in the Civil War.
1891	Carnegie Hall (then Music Hall) had its opening night in New York City with a concert that included works conducted by Peter Ilyich Tschaikovsky and Walter Damrosch.
1904	Cy Young, the winningest pitcher in baseball, pitched a perfect game (no man reached base) for the Boston Red Sox against Philadelphia. The Red Sox won, 3-0.
1920	Nicola Sacco and Bartolomeo Vanzetti were arrested for the murder of two payroll guards in South Braintree, Mass. The ensuing trial became one of the most famous in U.S. history.
1925	John T. Scopes was arrested for teaching evolution in Dayton, Tennessee, leading to the famous Scopes trial which tested the right to teach evolution in the schools.
1929	The comic strip *Napoleon,* by Clifford McBride, first appeared.
1936	The Italian army under Marshal Pietro Badoglio captured Addis Ababa, the capitol of Ethiopia.
1956	Jim Bailey ran the mile in 3 minutes 58.6 seconds, the first to run the mile in under 4 minutes in the United States.
1961	Alan B. Shepard in *Freedom 7* made the first U.S. manned space flight.
1973	Secretariat won the Kentucky Derby in the record time of 1 minute, 59 2/5 seconds.

May 6 – Birthdays

| 973 | **Henry II (the Saint).** Emperor of Germany of the Saxon dynasty |

1501	**Marcellus II.** Roman Catholic pope who served for less than a year in 1555
1758	**Maximilien Robespierre.** Most famous and most controversial leader of the French Revolution
1830	**Abraham Jacobi.** Founder of U.S. pediatrics
1856	**Sigmund Freud.** Austrian physician famous as the founder of psychoanalysis
1856	**Robert Edwin Peary.** American Arctic explorer who led the first expedition to the North Pole in 1909
1861	**Rabindranath Tagore.** Indian poet, philosopher, and nationalist
1888	**Perry Jones.** American Hall of Fame tennis player
1888	**Ernst Ludwig Kirchner.** German painter
1895	**Rudolph Valentino.** American motion-picture actor idolized in the 1920s as the "Great Lover"
1898	**Daniel F. Gerber.** American industrialist who invented a strained baby food process and founded Gerber Products (1928)
1902	**Harry Golden.** American publisher and author of *Only in America*
1902	**Max Ophuls.** German-born French motion-picture director
1907	**Weeb Eubank.** The only professional football coach to coach champions in the National Football League, the American Football League, and the Super Bowl
1913	**Stewart Granger.** English motion-picture and television actor
1913	**Carmen Cavallaro.** American bandleader of the Big Band Era of the 1940s
1914	**Randall Jarrell.** American poet and novelist
1915	**Orson Welles.** American actor, director, and writer, noted for his role in the great movie *Citizen Kane* and for scaring an entire nation with his 1938 radio show *War of the Worlds*
1915	**Theodore White.** American editor, novelist and writer, noted for his books on U.S. elections, notably *The Making of the President, 1960*
1916	**Ross Hunter.** American motion-picture producer
1931	**Willie Mays.** Hall of Fame baseball player and second after Babe Ruth to hit 600 career home runs
1933	**Jimmie Rodgers.** American country music singer and guitarist
1951	**Samuel K. Doe.** Head of state of Liberia
1953	**Tony Blair.** British prime minister who succeeded John Major
1953	**Mark Farrell.** English tennis player
1954	**Tom Abernethy.** Professional basketball player

May 6 – Events

1628	The Petition of Right was drawn up by the English Parliament, which declared unconstitutional certain actions of King Charles I.
1835	The New York *Herald* newspaper was first published.
1840	The famous "penny black" stamp was issued in England, the first postage stamp in history.

1851 Dr. John Gorrie of Apalachicola, Florida, received a patent for the manufacture of ice by mechanical means.

1861 Arkansas seceded from the Union.

1862 Henry David Thoreau, American writer and philosopher, died of tuberculosis in Concord, Massachusetts, at age 44.

1864 The Battle of the Wilderness ended indecisively with heavy losses in both Northern and Southern ranks in the Civil War.

1889 The Paris Exposition formally opened, featuring the just-completed Eiffel Tower.

1915 Babe Ruth, a Boston Red Sox pitcher at the time, hit his first major league home run, off New York Yankee pitcher Jack Warhop at the Polo Grounds in New York.

1937 The German zeppelin *Hindenburg* burst into flames and exploded while approaching Lakehurst, New Jersey, killing 36 of the 97 people on board.

1941 Dictator Joseph Stalin dismissed V.M. Molotov and named himself premier of Russia.

1942 American composer Irving Berlin published his classic "White Christmas," which was destined to become the best-selling record of all time.

1942 The U.S. garrison at Corregidor in the Philippines in World War II surrendered to the Japanese.

1953 Bobo Holloman, in his first major league start, pitched a no-hitter, as the St. Louis Browns beat the Philadelphia Athletics, 6-0.

1954 Roger Bannister, British athlete, became the first man to run the mile in less than four minutes (3 minutes 59.4 seconds), at Oxford, England.

1994 The English Channel Tunnel ("Chunnel") was officially opened in a ceremony presided over by Queen Elizabeth II and French President François Mitterand.

1998 Kerry Wood, a Chicago Cubs rookie pitcher, tied the major league record of 20 strikeouts in a nine-inning game as he defeated the Houston Astros in a one-hit, 2-0 victory.

May 7 – Birthdays

1574 **Innocent X.** Roman Catholic pope, 1644-1655

1694 **Pierre Jean Mariette.** French art print publisher

1711 **David Hume.** Scottish philosopher who strongly influenced the development of the philosophical schools of skepticism and empiricism

1812 **Robert Browning.** One of the greatest poets of Victorian England

1826 **Varina Davis.** Second wife of Confederate president Jefferson Davis

1833 **Johannes Brahms.** One of the greatest composers in history, ranking with Bach, Beethoven, and Mozart

1836 **Joseph "Uncle Joe" Cannon.** U.S. Congressman for 46 years and powerful Speaker of the House, 1903-1911

1840 **Peter Ilich Tchaikovsky.** The first Russian composer to gain international fame, and whose works include *Marche Slave, Symphony No. 6* (the *Pathetique*), and the famous *Nutcracker Suite*

1851 **Adolf von Harnack.** German New Testament scholar noted for books such as *The Essence of Christianity* (1904) and *Epistles of Saint Paul* (1926)

1870 **Marcus Loew.** Pioneer American motion-picture theater owner

1885 **George "Gabby" Hayes.** Comic motion-picture sidekick of William Boyd and Roy Rogers who played in over 200 Western movies

1890 **George Archainbaud.** French motion-picture director noted for his many Hopalong Cassidy and Gene Autry films

1892 **Archibald MacLeish.** Pulitzer-prize-winning American poet and playwright noted for works such as "Conquistador" (1932) and *J.B.* (1959)

1892 **Tito (Josip Broz).** Yugoslav World War II hero and head of state, 1945-1980

1896 **Kitty Godfree.** Hall of Fame tennis player who was perhaps Britain's greatest female star

1901 **Gary Cooper.** American motion-picture actor and one of Hollywood's all-time great stars

1909 **Edwin Herbert Land.** American inventor best noted for the Polaroid Land camera

1914 **Jack Elliott.** American composer noted for such songs as "It's So Nice to Have a Man Around the House" and "Sam's Song"

1919 **Eva Peron.** Argentine film actress and wife of President Juan Peron

1922 **Darren McGavin.** American motion-picture and television actor

1923 **Anne Baxter.** American motion-picture actress and granddaughter of noted architect Frank Lloyd Wright

1928 **Dick Williams.** Professional baseball player and manager, who piloted the Oakland Athletics to three consecutive world championships in 1972, 1973, and 1974

1930 **Babe Parilli.** Professional football player

1931 **Teresa Brewer.** American singer

1933 **Johnny Unitas.** One of the greatest professional football quarterbacks in history, who threw at least one touchdown pass in each of 47 consecutive games, 1956-1960

1942 **Bob Weiss.** Professional basketball player

1946 **Marvin Hubbard.** Professional football player

1949 **Bill Lloyd.** Australian tennis player

1950 **Tim Russert.** American broadcast journalist and host of *Meet the Press*

1950 **Janis Ian.** American singer

1955 **Peter McNamara.** Australian tennis player

1969 **Katerina Maleeva.** Bulgarian tennis player and sister of tennis players Manuela and Magdalena Maleeva

May 7 – Events

1536 Archbishop Thomas Cranmer annulled the marriage of King Henry VIII and Anne Boleyn.

1789 The first President's Inaugural Ball was held in honor of George Washington in the Assembly Rooms in New York.

1915 The British passenger liner *Lusitania* sank off the coast of Ireland after it was torpedoed by a German submarine.

1939 Germany and Italy announced the formation of the Rome-Berlin Axis, a prelude to World War II, which was to follow in September.

1943 Tunis and Bizerte surrendered to the Americans in World War II, effectively ending Axis resistance in Africa.

1945 Germany surrendered, ending World War II in Europe after 2,075 days of the bloodiest and costliest war in history.

1954 The Vietminh forces of Ho Chi Minh captured Dien Bien Phu from the French after a 55-day siege.

1977 Seattle Slew won the Kentucky Derby. He went on from there to win horseracing's triple crown.

1999 NATO mistakenly bombed the Chinese Embassy in Belgrade, killing four persons and wounding at least 20 others in its bombing war with Yugoslavia.

May 8 – Birthdays

1668 **Alain Rene Lesage.** French novelist and dramatist, noted for the witty novel *Gil Blas,* a satire on life in Paris

1737 **Edward Gibbon.** The greatest English historian of his century and author of *The History of the Decline and Fall of the Roman Empire*

1753 **Miguel Hidalgo y Costilla.** Mexican priest, called "The Father of Mexican Independence," who rang the church bells in Dolores calling for Mexico to rebel against Spain

1821 **William Henry Vanderbilt.** American philanthropist and son of Cornelius Vanderbilt, the founder of the Vanderbilt fortune

1828 **Jean Henri Dunant.** Swiss banker and founder of the International Red Cross

1847 **Oscar Hammerstein.** German-American theatrical manager, financier, and grandfather of lyricist Oscar Hammerstein II

1855 **John Warne "Bet a Million" Gates.** First of the giant gamblers, who gambled billions of dollars in his lifetime

1858 **Dan Brouthers.** Hall of Fame baseball player

1884 **Harry S. Truman.** 33rd U.S. president

1885 **Thomas B. Costain.** Canadian-American novelist and historian, noted for such works as *The Silver Chalice* (1952)

1892 **Ezio Pinza.** Italian opera singer and star of the long-running play *South Pacific*

1893 **Edd Roush.** Hall of Fame baseball player

1893 **Francis Ouimet.** America's first famous golfer and one of the first three inducted into the Hall of Fame, who shocked the golf world as a 20-year-old ex-caddy by winning the 1913 U.S. Open, defeating a field which included Englishmen Harry Vardon and Ted Ray, two of the greatest golfers of the time

1895 **Edmund Wilson.** American writer and literary and social critic

1895 **Jose Gomez.** One of the greatest matadors of all time

1895 **Fulton J. Sheen.** Roman Catholic bishop and television personality of the 1950s

1903 **Fernandel (Fernand Constandin).** French stage and motion-picture actor

1906 **Roberto Rossellini.** Italian movie director and one-time husband of actress Ingrid Bergman

1913 **Bob Clampett.** American cartoonist and creator of *Looney Tunes*

1919 **Lex Barker.** American motion-picture actor

1920 **Sloan Wilson.** American novelist and author of *The Man in the Gray Flannel Suit*

1926 **Don Rickles.** American comedian and actor

1928 **Theodore Sorenson.** American author and speechwriter for President Kennedy

1930 **Gary Snyder.** American poet of the "Beat" movement

1932 **Sonny Liston.** World heavyweight champion, 1962-1964

1936 **James R. Thompson.** Governor of Illinois

1940 **Rick Nelson.** American actor and singer

1940 **Peter Benchley.** American writer noted for *Jaws* and *The Deep*

1942 **Angel Cordero.** American jockey

1943 **Toni Tennille.** American singer

1945 **Robert Grim.** Professional football player

1951 **Dennis Leonard.** Professional baseball player

1954 **David Keith.** American television and motion-picture actor

1959 **Ronnie Lott.** Professional football player

1964 **Melissa Gilbert.** American television actress

May 8 – Events

1541 Spanish explorer Hernando De Soto discovered the Mississippi River at a point near the present site of Memphis, Tenn.

1660 England's civil war ended as Charles II was proclaimed king.

1823 The famous song "Home, Sweet Home," by John Howard Payne and Sir Henry Bishop, was first sung publicly in the opera *Clari, or The Maid of Milan.*

1846 The first major battle of the Mexican War was fought at Palo Alto, Texas, resulting in victory for American general Zachary Taylor.

1879 George B. Selden of Rochester, New York, filed for the first automobile patent, which led to the famous dispute resulting in the cross-licensing system used by auto makers today.

1880	Gustave Flaubert, French novelist, died at Croisset at age 58.
1886	Coca-Cola first went on sale, at Jacob's Pharmacy in Atlanta. Pharmacist John S. Pemberton had formulated the syrup, which remained unchanged until 1985.
1903	Paul Gauguin, French painter, died in the Marquesas Islands at age 54.
1914	The U.S. Senate approved the observance of Mother's Day annually on the second Sunday in May.
1942	The Battle of the Coral Sea ended in a decisive American victory over Japan in World War II.
1945	The world celebrated V-E Day (Victory in Europe), following the German surrender on the previous day.
1961	The comic strip *Apartment 3-G*, by Nicholas Dallis, Harold Anderson, and Alex Kotzky, appeared for the first time.
1968	Catfish Hunter pitched a perfect game (no man reached base) as Oakland beat Minnesota, 4-0.

May 9 – Birthdays

1439	**Pius III.** Roman Catholic pope, who served less than a year in 1503
1740	**Giovanni Paisiello.** Italian composer who wrote the first version of the opera *The Barber of Seville* in 1782, over 30 years before Rossini's more famous version was created
1800	**John Brown.** Radical abolitionist who led the raid on the United States arsenal at Harpers Ferry on October 16, 1859
1843	**Belle Boyd.** "The Rebel Spy" for the South in the Civil War
1855	**François Pompon.** French sculptor noted for works such as *Polar Bear* (1922)
1860	**Sir James Barrie.** Scottish novelist and playwright, noted for *Peter Pan* (1904)
1870	**Harry Vardon.** The first of the great modern golfers, and winner of the British Open six times between 1896 and 1914
1873	**Howard Carter.** English archaeologist who discovered the tomb of Egyptian king Tutankhamen in 1922
1882	**Henry J. Kaiser.** Noted American shipbuilder during World War II and cofounder of the Kaiser-Frazer automobile corporation
1883	**Jose Ortega y Gasset.** Spanish philosopher
1893	**William Moulton Marston.** Creator of *Wonder Woman*
1895	**Richard Barthelmess.** American motion-picture actor
1904	**Dorothy Clark Wilson.** American author noted for *Climb Every Mountain* (1976)
1905	**Lili D'Alvarez.** Spain's greatest woman tennis player
1908	**Bill Jurges.** Professional baseball player

1909	**Jim Hagerty.** American radio and television executive and press secretary for President Eisenhower
1912	**Pedro Armendariz.** Mexican motion-picture actor
1914	**Carlo Maria Giulini.** Italian-born conductor
1914	**Hank Snow.** American country singer
1918	**Mike Wallace.** American television interviewer and co-host of the *60 Minutes* program
1919	**Betty Jameson.** Hall of Fame golfer
1921	**Daniel Berrigan.** American priest and social activist
1928	**Pancho Gonzales.** American Hall of Fame tennis player, and one of the top players of the post-World War II era
1934	**Alan Bennett.** English dramatist noted for works such as *The Madness of George III* (1991)
1936	**Albert Finney.** English motion-picture actor
1936	**Glenda Jackson.** English stage and motion-picture actress
1937	**David Prater.** American soul singer of the Sam and Dave duo
1939	**Ralph Boston.** Professional long jumper and 1960 Olympic gold medal winner
1939	**Ion Tiriac.** Romanian tennis player and coach
1946	**Candice Bergen.** American motion-picture actress, photojournalist, and daughter of ventriloquist Edgar Bergen
1948	**Calvin Murphy.** Professional basketball player
1948	**John Mahaffey.** Professional golfer
1949	**Billy Joel.** American singer, songwriter, and musician, noted for songs such as "Just the Way You Are"
1951	**Joy Harjo.** American poet noted for the collection *In Mad Love and War* (1990)
1954	**Balazs Taroczy.** Hungarian tennis player
1960	**Tony Gwynn.** Professional baseball player and superstar
1962	**Dave Gahan.** English lead vocalist with the Depeche Mode musical group

May 9 – Events

1502	Christopher Columbus set sail from Cadiz, Spain, on his fourth and last voyage to America.
1754	Benjamin Franklin's famous *Join or Die* cartoon became the first newspaper cartoon in America, appearing in the Pennsylvania *Gazette*.
1864	Union general John Sedgwick, shortly after saying, "They couldn't hit an elephant at this distance," was killed by a Confederate sharpshooter at Spotsylvania, Virginia.
1907	An annual Mother's Day was publicly suggested by Miss Anna Jarvis of Philadelphia.
1926	Admiral Richard E. Byrd and Floyd Bennett became the first men to fly to the North Pole.
1933	The first of the Nazi book burnings took place as 25,000 books were burned in a bonfire in Berlin.
1936	Ethiopia was formally annexed to Italy by Benito Mussolini.

| 1949 | Prince Rainier III became ruler of Monaco. |
| 1974 | Impeachment hearings of the U.S. House Judiciary Committee began against President Nixon. |

May 10 – Birthdays

1760 **Claude Joseph Rouget de Lisle.** French songwriter who in 1792 composed the French national anthem, "La Marseillaise"

1837 **Pinckney Benton Stewart Pinchback.** Only black ever to serve as governor of any state (35 days as governor of Louisiana in 1872) until L. Douglas Wilder of Virginia in 1990

1838 **John Wilkes Booth.** Assassin of Abraham Lincoln

1838 **James Bryce.** British historian, statesman, and author of *The American Commonwealth*

1843 **Benito Perez Galdos.** Spanish novelist and playwright

1850 **Sir Thomas Johnstone Lipton.** Founder of the Lipton tea empire

1868 **Ed Barrow.** Professional baseball general manager who switched Babe Ruth from a pitcher to an outfielder

1885 **Fritz Von Unruh.** German dramatist, poet, and novelist

1886 **Karl Barth.** One of the most influential theologians of the 20th century

1888 **Max Steiner.** Austrian-born composer and conductor, noted for songs such as "A Summer Place," "As Long As I Live," "Sugarfoot," and the score of *Gone With the Wind*

1890 **Clarence Brown.** American motion-picture director noted for films such as *Ah Wilderness* (1935) and *Intruder in the Dust* (1950)

1890 **Alfred Jodl.** Nazi World War II general who signed the terms of Germany's unconditional surrender

1895 **Abe Tuvim.** American lyricist noted for songs such as "A Gay Ranchero" and "Chile Con Conga"

1898 **Ariel Durant.** American historian and wife of Will Durant, with whom she co-authored the last four volumes of the ten-volume series *The Story of Civilization*

1899 **Fred Astaire.** American stage and motion-picture star noted for his graceful, imaginative dancing and acting in over 35 movies in a 50-year career

1902 **David O. Selznick.** American motion-picture producer, whose greatest work was *Gone With the Wind*

1908 **Carl Albert.** U.S. Representative and Speaker of the House, 1971-1977

1910 **Jimmy Demarest.** First professional golfer to win three Masters tournaments

1917 **Margo.** Mexican-born stage and motion-picture actress

1919 **Ella T. Grasso.** Governor of Connecticut, 1975-1980, and first woman to be elected governor who did not follow her husband

1920 **Richard Adams.** English novelist noted for *Watership Down* (1972) and *Shardik* (1974)

1922 **Nancy Walker.** American stage, screen, and television actress

1927 **Mike Souchak.** Professional golfer

1931 **Pat Summerall.** Professional football player and TV sports broadcaster

1936 **Gary Owens.** American comedian and TV personality noted as the comic announcer on the long-running television show, *Laugh In*

1938 **Manuel Santana.** Spanish tennis player

1946 **Donovan (Donovan Leitch).** Scottish folk and pop singer

1955 **Mark David Chapman.** Assassin of the famous singer and Beatle John Lennon

1958 **Rick Santorum.** U.S. senator

May 10 – Events

1508 Michelangelo signed a contract with Pope Julius II to paint the ceiling of the Sistine Chapel.

1774 King Louis XV of France died of smallpox at age 69 and was succeeded by his grandson, the ill-fated Louis XVI.

1775 Ethan Allen and his Green Mountain Boys captured Fort Ticonderoga from the British in the American Revolution.

1818 Paul Revere, the great American Revolutionary War hero, died at age 83.

1857 The Sepoy Rebellion began at Meerut, near Delhi, India, resulting in British rule of India the following year.

1863 Confederate general Stonewall Jackson died after being shot accidentally by his own men on May 2.

1865 Union forces captured Confederate president Jefferson Davis in Irwinville, Georgia, following the end of the Civil War.

1869 The first transcontinental railway in America was completed at Promontory Point, Utah, where the tracks of the Union Pacific and the Central Pacific were joined.

1871 The Treaty of Frankfurt was signed, formally ending the Franco-Prussian War.

1908 The first Mother's Day observance took place during church services in Grafton, West Virginia, and Philadelphia.

1924 J. Edgar Hoover was named the first director of the FBI.

1933 Nazi Storm troopers and students staged a massive book burning in Berlin of works of authors considered offensive to the state.

1940 German troops invaded Belgium and Holland, ending the "phony war" in the West in World War II.

1940 Winston Churchill succeeded Neville Chamberlain as prime minister of Great Britain.

1941 Rudolf Hess, Hitler's second in command, parachuted into Glasgow, Scotland, to "save humanity."

1948 The comic strip *Rex Morgan, M.D.,* by Nicholas Dallis, Frank Edgington, and Marvin Bradley, first appeared.

1954 "Rock Around the Clock," by Bill Haley and the Comets, was released, the first big rock and roll record.

1968 The Vietnam peace talks began in Paris.

1980 The U.S. government gave conditional approval to $1.5 billion in federal loan guarantees to Chrysler Corporation.

May 11 – Birthdays

482 **Justinian I (the Great).** Byzantine (East Roman) emperor, A.D. 527-565, who collected Roman laws under one code, known as the *Justinian Code*

1751 **Ralph Earl.** One of America's finest primitive painters whose greatest work is his portrait of Roger Sherman (1775)

1811 **Chang and Eng Bunker.** The original Siamese twins (so-called because they were born in Meklong, Siam)

1823 **Alfred Stevens.** Belgian painter noted for works such as *After the Ball* (1874)

1852 **Charles W. Fairbanks.** U.S. vice president under Theodore Roosevelt

1854 **Ottmar Mergenthaler.** Inventor of the Linotype typesetting machine

1888 **Irving Berlin.** One of the greatest American popular songwriters, noted for such songs as "White Christmas," "God Bless America," "Alexander's Ragtime Band," and "Always"

1891 **Henry Morgenthau Jr.** Secretary of the Treasury under Franklin D. Roosevelt

1892 **Dame Margaret Rutherford.** English stage and motion-picture actress

1893 **Martha Graham.** American dancer and choreographer, who pioneered the modern dance movement

1894 **Ellsworth Bunker.** American diplomat and last ambassador to South Vietnam

1895 **William Grant Still.** First black to conduct a professional symphony orchestra in the United States

1902 **Bidu Sayao.** Brazilian soprano

1903 **Charlie Gehringer.** Hall of Fame baseball player

1904 **Salvador Dali.** Spanish surrealist painter and one of the most publicized figures in modern art

1907 **Rip Sewell.** Professional baseball player, noted in his latter years for his blooper pitch

1912 **Phil Silvers.** American stage, screen, and television actor and comedian

1912 **Foster Brooks.** American actor and comedian

1920 **Denver Pyle.** American motion-picture and television actor

1921 **Gene Hermanski.** Professional baseball player

1924 **Antony Hewish.** English astronomer who discovered pulsars in 1967

1926 **Mort Sahl.** American comedian and actor

1930 **Stanley Elkin.** American author noted for *The Magic Kingdom* (1985)

1932 **Valentino (Garavani).** Italian dress designer

1933 **Louis Farrakhan.** American political and religious leader and head of the Nation of Islam

1934 **Jack Twyman.** Professional basketball superstar with over 15,000 career points

1935 **Doug McClure.** American motion-picture and television actor

1939 **Milt Pappas.** Professional baseball player

1940 **Butch Hartman.** American auto racer

1941 **Eric Burdon.** Singer with The Animals musical group

1945 **Thomaz Koch.** Brazilian tennis player

1946 **Robert K. Jarvik.** American physician and inventor of the Jarvik heart, the first mechanical heart to be permanently implanted in a human being

1950 **Dane Iorg.** Professional baseball player

1963 **Natasha Richardson.** English stage, screen and television actress, daughter of actress Vanessa Redgrave and granddaughter of actor Sir Michael Redgrave

May 11 – Events

330 Constantinople was dedicated as the new capital of the Roman Empire during the reign of Constantine the Great.

1647 Peter Stuyvesant took over as governor of New Amsterdam.

1792 American explorer Robert Gray discovered the mouth of the Columbia River.

1846 President Polk asked Congress to declare war on Mexico.

1858 Minnesota was admitted to the Union as the 32nd state.

1862 The Confederates scuttled their ironclad, the *Merrimack,* to keep it from being captured by the Union in the Civil War.

1900 Jim Jeffries knocked out Gentleman Jim Corbett in round 23 to retain the heavyweight boxing championship.

1910 Glacier National Park in Montana was established.

1911 The National Health Insurance Bill was introduced in Parliament by Prime Minister Herbert Henry Asquith of Britain.

1943 American forces landed on Japanese-occupied Attu Island in the Aleutians in World War II. The island was retaken three weeks later.

1949 Israel was admitted to the United Nations.

1949 Siam changed its name to Thailand.

May 12 – Birthdays

1496 **Gustavus I.** King of Sweden, 1523-1560, who established the Lutheran faith as Sweden's state religion

1755 **Giovanni Battista Viotti.** Italian violinist and composer, considered by some to be the father of modern violin playing

1812 **Edward Lear.** English landscape painter and writer of nonsense verse, a good example of which is "The Owl and the Pussy-Cat"

1820 **Florence Nightingale.** Founder of the nursing profession and one of the greatest women of England's Victorian Age

1828 **Dante Gabriel Rossetti.** One of England's most famous poets and painters of the 1800s

1842 **Jules Massenet.** French composer noted for his operas, the best known of which is *Manon* (1884)

1845 **Gabriel Fauré.** French composer and organist, who played one of the biggest roles in freeing French music from German influences

1850 **Henry Cabot Lodge.** U.S. senator, 1893-1924, who led the fight against America's joining the League of Nations

1880 **Lincoln Ellsworth.** American Arctic and Antarctic explorer, who with Roald Amundsen made the first aerial crossing of the vast North Polar Basin in 1925

1895 **Harold Olsen.** Hall of Fame basketball player and coach

1897 **Jumping Joe Dugan.** Professional baseball player who played on the great New York Yankee team of 1927

1902 **Philip Wylie.** American writer and author of *Generation of Vipers* (1942)

1903 **Wilfred Hyde-White.** English character actor with a motion-picture career of 50 years

1907 **Katharine Hepburn.** American stage and motion-picture superstar for over 50 years, and the only actress to win three Academy Awards for leading roles

1910 **Gordon Hill Jenkins.** American composer and author, noted for songs such as "San Fernando Valley"

1914 **Howard K. Smith.** American newscaster and commentator

1918 **Mary Kay Ash.** Company executive and founder of Mary Kay Cosmetics

1918 **Julius Rosenberg.** U.S. citizen who with his wife Ethel was the first to be executed for espionage by the sentence of a civil court

1925 **John Simon.** American writer and critic

1925 **Yogi Berra.** Hall of Fame baseball player and one of the three or four greatest catchers in history

1929 **Burt Bacharach.** American composer noted for songs such as "Raindrops Keep Falling on My Head" and "What the World Needs Now"

1935 **Felipe Alou.** Professional baseball player and manager and brother of baseball players Matty and Jesus Alou

1936 **Tom Snyder.** American television talk show host

1936 **Frank Stella.** American artist

1938 **George Carlin.** American comedian and author

1939 **Ron Ziegler.** Press secretary for President Nixon

1941 **Susan Hampshire.** English motion-picture and television actress

1948 **Steve Winwood.** English singer, musician, and songwriter with the Traffic group

1950 **Gabriel Byrne.** Irish-born actor and leading man of stage and screen

1950 **Billy Squier.** American singer and guitarist

1953 **Kevin Grevey.** Professional basketball player

1955 **Colin Dowdeswell.** Zimbabwean tennis player

1957 **Lou Whitaker.** Professional baseball player

1959 **Kevin Bass.** Professional baseball player

1962 **Emilio Estevez.** American motion-picture actor and son of actor Martin Sheen

1965 **Steve Finley.** Professional baseball player

1969 **Kim Fields.** American stage, screen and TV actress

May 12 – Events

1621 The first wedding took place in Plymouth Colony, Massachusetts, as Edward Winslow married Susanna White.

1780 An entire Continental Army of 2,500 soldiers surrendered to the British at Charleston, South Carolina, in the American Revolution.

1789 The Society of Tammany was formed in New York City by William Mooney.

1875 The first shut-out in major league baseball occurred, as Chicago beat St. Louis, 1-0, in the National Association of Professional Baseball Players, later the National League.

1926 Roald Amundsen and Lincoln Ellsworth crossed the North Pole by dirigible, only a few days after Admiral Byrd's historic flight.

1932 Charles A. Lindbergh's kidnapped baby son was found dead in Hopewell, New Jersey.

1937 George VI was crowned King of England in Westminster Abbey, succeeding Edward VIII, who had abdicated.

1943 The last organized Axis army force in Africa in World War II surrendered in southern Tunisia.

1949 The Russians called off the Berlin blockade after 328 days, during which time the United States and Britain supplied the city by means of the Berlin Airlift.

May 13 – Birthdays

1655 **Innocent XIII.** Roman Catholic pope, 1721-1724

1717 **Maria Theresa.** Empress, Archduchess of Austria, Queen of Hungary, and mother of French queen Marie Antoinette

1729 **Henry William Stiegel.** Early American iron and glass manufacturer, best known for *Stiegel glass,* considered by many experts today as the most beautiful glass ever blown

1792 **Pius IX.** Roman Catholic pope, 1846-1878, who had the longest reign in papal history

1840 **Alphonse Daudet.** French novelist sometimes called the "French Dickens"

1842   **Sir Arthur Sullivan.** One of the most famous English composers of his day and co-composer with Sir William Gilbert of the Gilbert and Sullivan operettas

1877   **Joseph Stella.** American painter

1882   **Georges Braque.** French artist, who, with Pablo Picasso, led the development of cubism in the early 1900s

1907   **Daphne Du Maurier.** English writer of popular romantic novels, such as *Rebecca* and *Jamaica Inn*

1911   **Robert Middleton.** American stage and motion-picture actor

1913   **William R. Tolbert Jr..** President of Liberia, 1937-1980

1914   **Joe Louis.** Heavyweight boxing champion, 1937-1949, and one of the all-time greats of the ring

1922   **Gladys Heldman.** Hall of Fame tennis player and founder of *World Tennis* magazine

1926   **Bea Arthur.** American television actress

1927   **Fred Hellerman.** American singer, guitarist, and songwriter, with The Weavers musical group

1927   **Clive Barnes.** American drama critic

1927   **Herbert Ross.** American director and choreographer noted for films such as *Carmen Jones* and *Funny Girl*

1941   **Jody Conradt.** Hall of Fame basketball player and winningest women's basketball coach in NCAA history (654 wins at the University of Texas as of 1995)

1941   **Harvey Keitel.** American stage and screen actor

1941   **Marshall Field V.** American newspaper publisher

1949   **Franklin Ajaye.** American actor

1950   **Stevie Wonder.** American blind-from-birth pop rock musician, singer, and composer, noted for songs such as "You Are the Sunshine of My Life" and "Living for the City"

1953   **Pat Gregg.** Australian tennis player

1961   **Dennis Rodman.** Professional basketball player

1965   **Jose Rijo.** Professional baseball player

May 13 – Events

1783   Society of the Cincinnati, the oldest military organization in the United States, was founded, with George Washington as its first president.

1787   British captain Arthur Phillip sailed from Portsmouth, England, with 11 ships and a cargo of convicts bound for settlement in Australia.

1846   The Mexican War began, as Congress declared war.

1854   The first American billiard match of importance was held at Malcolm Hall in Syracuse, N.Y., as Joseph N. White defeated George Smith for the $200 purse by a score of 500 to 484.

1867   Jefferson Davis, the ex-Confederate president, was released from prison in Ft. Monroe, Virginia, where he had been held for two years awaiting trial.

1917   Three peasant children reported seeing near Fatima, Portugal, a vision of the Virgin Mary, since known as Our Lady of Fatima.

1918   The first United States air mail stamps were issued.

1940   Winston Churchill made his first speech as British prime minister, saying, "I have nothing to offer but blood, toil, tears, and sweat."

1954   President Dwight D. Eisenhower signed the bill authorizing construction of the St. Lawrence Seaway.

1981   Pope John Paul II was shot twice in an assassination attempt in Rome. He later fully recovered.

May 14 – Birthdays

1686   **Gabriel Daniel Fahrenheit.** German physicist who developed the Fahrenheit temperature scale

1710   **Adolf Frederick.** King of Sweden, 1751-1771

1727   **Thomas Gainsborough.** One of the greatest English painters of all time, whose most famous work is *The Blue Boy*

1752   **Timothy Dwight.** American religious leader during the Jeffersonian era

1771   **Thomas Wedgwood.** The first person to conceive the basic process of modern photography, and the son of Josiah Wedgwood, the famous English pottery designer

1771   **Robert Owen.** Welsh-born social reformer who set up the famous New Harmony community in Indiana in 1825

1852   **Alton B. Parker.** U.S. presidential candidate in 1904

1853   **Sir Thomas Henry Hall Caine.** English novelist

1880   **Bertie Forbes.** Scottish-born journalist and founder of *Forbes* magazine (1916)

1881   **Ed Walsh.** Hall of Fame baseball pitcher who pitched a record 464 innings in one season

1885   **Otto Klemperer.** Famous German conductor and composer, who directed the Kroll Opera in Berlin, the Los Angeles Philharmonic Orchestra, and the New York Philharmonic Orchestra

1891   **Grant Clarke.** American composer noted for songs such as "Ragtime Cowboy Joe" and "I Hate to Lose You"

1899   **Earle Combs.** Hall of Fame baseball player, who with Babe Ruth and Bob Meusel constituted the great 1927 New York Yankees' "perfect outfield"

1900   **Billie Dove.** "The American Beauty" of the silent and early sound screen

1907   **Mohammad Ayab Khan.** President of Pakistan, 1958-1969

1925   **Patrice Munsel.** American operatic soprano

1925   **Les Moss.** Professional baseball player

1936   **Bobby Darin.** American songwriter and actor

1937   **Dick Howser.** Professional baseball player and manager

1942   **Byron Dorgan.** U.S. senator

1942   **Tony Perez.** Professional baseball player

1943   **Jack Bruce.** Bassist and singer with the musical group Cream

1944   **George Lucas.** American motion-picture director and writer noted for films such as *American Graffiti* and *Star Wars*

1944   **Francesca Annis.** English stage, screen and television actress

1955   **Dennis Martinez.** Professional baseball player

May 14 – Events

1607   Captain James Smith and his colonists landed at Jamestown, Virginia, and established the first permanent English colony in America.

1610   Henry IV, the great king of France who issued the Edict of Nantes, was murdered at age 56 by the fanatic François Ravaillac.

1643   Louis XIV, the "Grand Monarch" of France, became king upon the death of his father Louis XIII.

1787   Delegates began gathering in Philadelphia for the convention to draw up the U.S. Constitution.

1796   Edward Jenner, the great English physician, performed the first vaccination against smallpox, on an eight-year-old boy.

1804   Meriwether Lewis and William Clark left St. Louis on their journey to explore the Northwest, the famous Lewis and Clark Expedition.

1851   Gail Borden, of Brooklyn, New York, applied for a patent for condensed milk.

1874   The first real football game with rules similar to those of the modern game was played between Harvard and McGill Universities.

1904   The first Olympic games to be held in the United States opened in St. Louis.

1940   The Dutch armies surrendered to the Germans in World War II.

1942   Congress established the WAACs, the Women's Auxiliary Army Corps.

1948   Great Britain ended its 31-year rule in Palestine, followed immediately by a proclamation in Tel Aviv of the birth of the state of Israel.

1965   The John F. Kennedy Memorial was dedicated at Runnymede, England.

1973   *Skylab I* was launched, the first American manned space station.

1975   U.S. forces recaptured the American merchant ship *Mayaguez* in a raid off the Cambodian island of Koh Tang.

1998   Legendary crooner Frank Sinatra died of a heart attack at age 82 in California.

May 15 – Birthdays

1265   **Dante (Alighieri).** Italy's greatest poet, whose epic work, the *Divine Comedy,* ranks among the greatest works of world literature

1625   **Carlo Maratti.** Italian painter

1773   **Prince Klemens von Metternich.** Austrian statesman who helped defeat Napoleon and reshape Europe after 1815

1788   **James Gadsden.** U.S. minister to Mexico who negotiated the Gadsden Purchase from Mexico of the land along the southern bank of the Gila River

1813   **Stephen Heller.** Hungarian pianist and composer

1845   **Elie Metchnikoff.** Noted Russian biologist and 1908 Nobel Prize winner for his studies of the white blood cells

1856   **Lyman Frank Baum.** American writer and author of *The Wonderful Wizard of Oz* (1900)

1859   **Pierre Curie.** French physicist and co-discoverer, with his wife Marie Curie, of the element radium

1860   **Ellen Louise Axson Wilson.** First wife of President Woodrow Wilson

1862   **Arthur Schnitzler.** Austrian playwright and novelist, whose best-known story is the short novel *Leutnant Gustl* (1901)

1890   **Katherine Anne Porter.** American novelist and short-story writer, noted for her Pulitzer Prize-winning *Collected Short Stories* (1965) and *Ship of Fools* (1962)

1902   **Richard J. Daley.** Mayor of Chicago, 1955-1976

1904   **Clifton Fadiman.** American critic, author, and radio and television master of ceremonies

1905   **Joseph Cotten.** American stage and motion-picture actor

1909   **James Mason.** English stage and motion-picture actor

1910   **Constance Cummings.** American stage and motion-picture actress

1914   **Turk Broda.** Hall of Fame hockey player

1914   **Tenzing Norgay.** Nepalese mountain climber who climbed Mt. Everest with Edmund Hillary (1953)

1915   **Paul Samuelson.** American Nobel Prize-winning economist, writer, and author in 1948 of the best-selling economics textbook in the world

1918   **Eddy Arnold.** American country music singer

1923   **Richard Avedon.** A leading 20th century photographer

1926   **Peter Levin Shaffer.** English playwright noted for *Amadeus* (1981)

1930   **Jasper Johns.** American "pop artist"

1931   **Ken Venturi.** Professional golfer

1931   **Joseph Califano Jr..** Secretary of Health, Education, and Welfare under President Carter

1936   **Anna Maria Alberghetti.** Italian actress and singer

1937   **Trini Lopez.** American musician, actor, and bandleader

1937   **Madeleine Albright.** Secretary of state under President Clinton

1940   **Roger Ailes.** Communications consultant and advisor to George Bush in the 1988 presidential election

1940   **Don Nelson.** Professional basketball player

1948   **Brian Eno.** Avant garde rock musician

1953   **George Brett.** Professional baseball player and Hall of Famer

1967   **Omar Vizquel.** Professional baseball player

1967 John Smoltz. Professional baseball player and superstar

May 15 – Events

1485 Ferdinand, King of Aragon, captured Rondo (Spain) from the Moors.

1602 Bartholomew Gosnold, the English navigator, discovered Cape Cod.

1862 Congress created the Department of Agriculture.

1885 Canadian rebel Louis Riel surrendered to Canadian government forces, ending the *metis* rebellion, or the Riel Rebellion. He was later hanged.

1886 Emily Dickinson, the great American poet, died in Amherst, Massachusetts, at age 55.

1917 General Ferdinand Foch was named chief of staff of the French Army in World War I.

1918 The U.S. Post Office launched the first air mail service, between Washington, Philadelphia, and New York.

1930 United Air Lines hired the first flight attendant in airlines history, Ellen Church, who served on a flight between San Francisco and Cheyenne, Wyoming.

1941 Joe DiMaggio, the great New York Yankee baseball player, singled off Chicago White Sox pitcher Ed Smith to begin his famous 56-game hitting streak.

1948 The new state of Israel was attacked by Egyptian planes and invaded in the north and east by troops from Lebanon and Transjordan.

1953 Rocky Marciano knocked out Jersey Joe Walcott in the first round to retain his heavyweight championship.

1972 Alabama governor George C. Wallace was shot and left paralyzed in Laurel, Md., while campaigning for president. The would-be assassin, Arthur Bremer, was later sent to prison.

1981 Len Barker pitched a perfect game (no one reached base) as Cleveland beat Toronto, 3-0.

May 16 – Birthdays

1763 Louis-Nicholas Vauquelin. French chemist who discovered the elements chromium and beryllium

1782 John Sell Cotman. English landscape painter and etcher, noted for works such as *Greta Bridge* (1805)

1801 William H. Seward. U.S. secretary of state, 1862-1869, noted for promoting the purchase of Alaska from Russia in 1867

1804 Elizabeth Peabody. Founder of one of the first U.S. kindergartens, in Boston in 1860

1821 Pafnuty Lvovich Chebyshev. Russian mathematician noted for the Chebyshev polynomials

1824 Levi Parsons Morton. Vice President under President Benjamin Harrison

1827 Norman Jay Colman. First U.S. Secretary of Agriculture (1889)

1831 Edward David Hughes. American scientist who invented the first real microphone, in 1878

1832 Philip Danforth Armour. Co-founder of Armour and Company

1905 Henry Fonda. American stage, motion-picture, and television actor, and top-ranking star for over 50 years

1911 Margaret Sullavan. American stage and motion-picture actress, and first wife of actor Henry Fonda

1912 Studs Terkel. American journalist and author noted for works such as *Hard Times* (1970)

1913 Woody Herman. American saxophone player and bandleader

1919 Liberace. American pianist and television performer

1920 Dave Philley. Professional baseball player

1921 Harry Carey Jr. American motion-picture actor

1924 Frank Mankiewicz. American columnist and author

1928 Billy Martin. Professional baseball player and manager

1929 John Conyers Jr. U.S. congressman

1931 Lowell Weicker. U.S. senator

1940 Lainie Kazan. American nightclub and television singer

1943 Donny Anderson. Professional football player

1943 Dan Coats. U.S. senator

1944 Billy Cobham. American jazz drummer

1948 Jim Langer. Hall of Fame professional football player

1949 Rick Reuschel. Professional baseball player

1952 Pierce Brosnan. American television and motion-picture actor, noted for his title role in the series *Remington Steele*

1953 Rick Rhoden. Professional baseball player

1955 Olga Korbut. Russian gymnast

1955 Jack Morris. Professional baseball player

1960 Yannick Noah. French tennis player

1970 Gabriela Sabatini. Argentine tennis player

May 16 – Events

1532 Sir Thomas More resigned as Lord Chancellor because of his disapproval of Henry VIII's plan to marry Anne Boleyn.

1605 Paul V was elected pope of the Roman Catholic Church.

1770 The future king of France (Louis XVI), at age 16, married Marie Antoinette, the 15-year-old daughter of Maria Theresa of Austria.

1866 Congress authorized the first U.S. five-cent piece, first called the half-dime and later referred to as the nickel because of its content of 25% nickel and 75% copper.

1868 The U.S. Senate failed by one vote to convict President Andrew Johnson on the first count in his impeachment trial. Ten days later the votes on the other two counts failed.

1903 George A. Wyman left San Francisco for New York City. Two months later he completed the trip, becoming the first person to cross the North American continent by motorcycle.

1920 Joan of Arc was canonized as a saint by Pope Benedict XV.

1927 The Supreme Court ruled that bootleggers must file income tax returns.

1929 The first Oscars were awarded by the Motion Picture Academy. Winners were Janet Gaynor, best actress, Emil Jannings, best actor, and *Wings* was the best picture.

1940 German units penetrated the northwest extension of France's Maginot Line in World War II.

May 17 – Birthdays

1740 **John Penn.** A North Carolina delegate to the Continental Congress and a signer of the Declaration of Independence

1749 **Edward Jenner.** British physician and discoverer of vaccination as a means of preventing smallpox

1768 **Caroline.** Wife of King George IV of England

1803 **Robert Smith Surtees.** English novelist

1860 **Schuyler Skaats Wheeler.** American inventor who in 1886 made the first electric fan

1866 **Erik Satie.** French composer and pianist whose bold harmonies influenced Maurice Ravel and several other composers

1868 **Horace Elgin Dodge.** One of the Dodge brothers who developed the Dodge automobile

1875 **Jean Angelo.** French stage and motion-picture actor

1886 **Alfonso XIII.** The last king of Spain, 1902-1931, before the Spanish Civil War

1899 **Del Webb.** American builder and baseball executive with the New York Yankees during their glory years of the 1950s

1903 **Cool Papa Bell.** Hall of Fame baseball player

1906 **Zinka Milanov.** Yugoslav soprano

1911 **Maureen O'Sullivan.** Irish-born motion-picture actress

1911 **Clark Kerr.** Noted American educator

1912 **Archibald Cox.** American law professor and first Watergate special prosecutor

1914 **Stewart Alsop.** American newspaper columnist

1916 **Richard W. Bolling.** U.S. congressman

1918 **Birgit Nilsson.** Swedish dramatic soprano and one of the finest singers of heroic roles in the operas of Richard Wagner

1919 **Merle Miller.** American writer and biographer, noted for *Plain Speaking* (1973), an oral biography of Harry S. Truman

1920 **Harriet Van Horne.** American columnist and author

1921 **Bob Merrill.** American composer noted for songs such as "Honeycomb," "Love Makes the World Go Round," "How Much Is That Doggie In the Window?" and "If I Knew You Were Coming I'da Baked a Cake"

1932 **Billy Hoeft.** Professional baseball player

1934 **Earl Morrall.** Professional football player

1936 **Dennis Hopper.** American motion-picture actor and director, noted for *Easy Rider* (1969)

1938 **Paolo Bortoluzzi.** Italian ballet dancer

1941 **Ronald Tavel.** American writer

1945 **Tony Roche.** Australian tennis player and superstar

1950 **Wendy Paish.** Australian tennis player

1955 **Debra Winger.** American motion-picture actress

1956 **Sugar Ray Leonard.** Welterweight boxing champion

1957 **Linda Mottram.** English tennis player

1957 **Pascual Perez.** Professional baseball player

May 17 – Events

352 Liberius became pope of the Roman Catholic Church.

885 Stephen V became pope of the Roman Catholic Church. He was Stephen VI at the time, but in 1961 Stephen II was dropped from the list of popes.

1510 Sandro Botticelli, the great Italian painter, died in Florence at age 65.

1792 The New York Stock Exchange had its real beginning in a meeting of 24 brokers under a buttonwood tree on the present site of 68 Wall Street.

1814 Norway adopted its present constitution, which was accepted by Sweden, but the Swedes refused to grant Norway its independence and continued to rule the country until 1905.

1827 Andrew Johnson married Eliza McCardle.

1875 The first Kentucky Derby was run, at Churchill Downs in Louisville. The winner was Aristides and the purse was $2,850.

1939 King George VI visited Canada, the first reigning British monarch to do so.

1940 The Germans occupied Brussels in World War II.

1954 The U.S. Supreme Court ruled unanimously that racial segregation in the public schools was unconstitutional, and ordered it ended with "all deliberate speed."

1969 The Russian space vehicle *Venera 6* landed on Venus.

1973 The Senate Select Committee opened hearings on the Watergate affair under the chairmanship of Senator Sam Ervin.

1998 David Wells of the New York Yankees pitched a perfect game, beating the Minnesota Twins, 4-0.

May 18 – Birthdays

1610 **Stefano della Bella.** Italian printmaker

1742 **Lionel Luken.** Inventor of lifeboats

1836 **Wilhelm Steinitz.** World chess champion who reigned from 1866 to 1885

1846 **Peter Carl Faberge.** Russian jeweler and one of the world's greatest goldsmiths and designers, noted espcially for his imperial Easter eggs, which were the delight of the Russian czars

1850 **Oliver Heaviside.** English physicist and mathematician

1862 **Josephus Daniels.** U.S. Secretary of the Navy during World War I

1868 **Nicholas II.** The last czar of Russia, who was executed in 1918 by the Bolsheviks

1872 **Bertrand Russell.** English mathematician and philosopher and coauthor with Alfred North White-head of the monumental work *Principia Mathematica*

1883 **Walter Gropius.** German architect and founder of the famous Bauhaus school of design in Germany

1889 **Thomas Midgley Jr.** American chemist who first discovered lead as an anti-knock additive to gasoline

1897 **Frank Capra.** Italian-born motion-picture director, noted for the classic *It Happened One Night,* which won the Academy Awards for Best Actor, Best Actress, and Best Picture

1902 **Meredith Willson.** American composer, author, and flutist, noted for songs such as "76 Trombones," "Iowa," "May the Good Lord Bless and Keep You," and "It's Beginning to Look a Lot Like Christmas"

1904 **Jacob Javits.** U.S. senator in the 1960s and 1970s

1909 **Fred Perry.** British Hall of Fame tennis player and Wimbledon singles champion, 1934-1936

1912 **Dan Topping.** American baseball executive and principal owner of the New York Yankees during their glory years of the 1950s

1912 **Perry Como.** American singer and actor with a career of over 40 years as a star

1912 **Richard Brooks.** American screenwriter and motion-picture director, noted for such films as *The Blackboard Jungle* (1955), *The Brothers Karamazov* (1958), and *Elmer Gantry* (1960)

1914 **Pierre Balmain.** French fashion designer

1919 **Dame Margot Fonteyn.** England's leading ballerina of the 20th century, and one of the first English dancers to achieve an international reputation

1920 **John Paul II.** Roman Catholic pope

1921 **Patrick Dennis.** American writer and author of *Auntie Mame*

1924 **"Choo Choo" Charlie Justice.** Professional football player

1930 **Pernell Roberts.** American television actor

1930 **Warren Rudman.** U.S. Senator

1931 **Robert Morse.** American motion-picture actor

1934 **Dwayne Hickman.** American motion-picture and television actor

1937 **Brooks Robinson.** Hall of Fame baseball player

1946 **Reggie Jackson.** Hall of Fame baseball player who hit 563 career homeruns

1951 **Jim Sundberg.** Professional baseball player

1952 **George Strait.** American country music singer

May 18 – Events

1291 The Crusaders abandoned Tyre to the Moslems, the prelude to the end of the final Crusade.

1642 Montreal, Canada, was founded by a small Roman Catholic missionary group headed by Paul de Chomedey, Sieur de Maison-neuve.

1643 The Battle of Rocroi was won by the great French commander, the Prince de Conde, over the Spanish, destroying the myth of the "invincible Spanish infantry."

1804 Napoleon Bonaparte was proclaimed Emperor of France by the French senate.

1852 Massachusetts became the first state to make school attendance compulsory.

1860 Abraham Lincoln was nominated for president on the third ballot by the Republican convention in Chicago.

1863 General U.S. Grant began the siege of Vicksburg in the Civil War. The siege lasted until July 4, when the defenders surrendered.

1910 Halley's Comet neared the earth, after passing over the sun in late April, frightening hundreds of thousands of people in the U.S., who thought the world was coming to an end.

1933 The Tennessee Valley Authority was created by Congress.

1940 Nazi forces in Belgium broke through toward the coast, capturing Antwerp in World War II.

1953 American aviator Jacqueline Cochran became the first woman to fly faster than the speed of sound, in an F-86 sabrejet at 652.3 miles per hour.

1974 India joined the nuclear club by exploding its first atomic bomb.

1980 The Mount Saint Helens volcano in Washington State erupted, killing 60 persons and dumping 600,000 tons of ash on the surrounding area.

May 19 – Birthdays

1593 **Claude Vignon.** French painter

1593 **Jacob Jordaens.** Flemish painter

1611 **Innocent XI.** Pope of the Roman Catholic Church, 1676-1689

1762 **Johann Gottlieb Fichte.** German philosopher, who strongly influenced German nationalism in the late 18th and early 19th centuries

1795 **Johns Hopkins.** American financier and philanthropist, who financed the founding of Johns Hopkins University and Johns Hopkins Hospital

1860 **Vittorio Emanuele Orlando.** Italian World War I prime minister

1861 **Dame Nellie Melba.** Australian soprano for whom Peach Melba was named, and who was said to have had "as many lovers as she gave encores"

1890 Ho Chi Minh. President of North Vietnam, 1954-1969, and leader in North Vietnam's successful fight for independence from France

1897 Lady Astor (Nancy Langhorne). First woman to serve in the British Parliament

1909 Bruce Bennett. American actor and Olympic shot-putter

1925 Malcolm X (Malcolm Little). Leader of the Black Muslims in the 1950s and 1960s

1928 Dolph Schayes. Professional basketball player with over 19,000 career points

1928 Pol Pot. Ruthless communist dictator of Cambodia, 1976-1979

1929 Curt Simmons. Professional baseball player

1929 Gil McDougald. Professional baseball player

1934 Jim Lehrer. American television newsman and commentator on the *McNeil-Lehrer Report*

1935 David Hartman. American actor and television host

1939 Nancy Kwan. Eurasian motion-picture actress

1941 Nora Ephron. American writer

1942 Frank Froehling III. American tennis player

1945 Pete Townshend. British guitarist and songwriter for The Who musical group

1949 Archie Manning. Professional football player and superstar

1950 Patrick Caddell. American public opinion analyst and pollster

1952 Joey Ramone. American musician with The Ramones musical group

1952 Dan Ford. Professional baseball player

1955 Ed Whitson. Professional baseball player

1959 Nicole Brown Simpson. American woman whose ex-husband, football legend O.J. Simpson, was acquitted of her 1994 murder in the criminal trial and found guilty in the civil trial

May 19 – Events

715 Gregory II (Saint Gregory) was elected Roman Catholic pope.

1342 Clement VI was crowned Roman Catholic pope. He was one of the French popes who resided at Avignon.

1536 Anne Boleyn, the second queen of England's King Henry VIII, was beheaded on Henry's orders on charges of adultery.

1571 Manila was founded by Spanish conquistador Miguel Lopez de Legazpe.

1643 Massachusetts, Plymouth, Connecticut, and New Haven formed the "United Colonies of New England."

1649 The Commonwealth of England was established following the overthrow of King Charles I.

1795 James Boswell, Dr. Samuel Johnson's famous biographer, died in London at age 54.

1864 Nathaniel Hawthorne, the noted American writer, died in Plymouth, New Hampshire, at age 59.

1884 The five Ringling Brothers founded their famous circus, in Baraboo, Wisconsin.

1935 Lawrence of Arabia (T.E. Lawrence) was killed in a motorcycle accident at Clouds Hill, Dorset, at age 46.

1940 General Maxime Weygand was appointed commander-in-chief of Allied forces in World War II, replacing General Gamelin, in the face of advancing Nazi forces in France.

1945 Four hundred U.S. Superfortress bombers attacked Tokyo in World War II.

1994 Jacqueline Kennedy Onassis died at age 64 in New York City.

1994 The English Channel Tunnel ("Chunnel") was opened to traffic when shuttle trains carrying trucks and their drivers began operating. The construction, begun in December, 1987, thus took over seven years.

May 20 – Birthdays

1364 Sir Henry Percy. English rebel who led an uprising against King Henry IV

1663 William Bradford. American printer who established New York's first newspaper, the New York *Gazette*

1764 Johann Gottfried Schadow. German sculptor

1768 Dolley Payne Madison. Wife of President James Madison

1772 Sir William Congreve. English artillery officer, who invented the rocket used by British troops against Napoleon, and those whose "rockets' red glare" was referred to in "The Star-Spangled Banner"

1799 Honoré de Balzac. French writer and one of the most important novelists of the 1800s, noted for works such as *Pere Goriot* and *Eugenie Grandet*

1806 John Stuart Mill. English philosopher and economist, noted for his *System of Logic* (1843), which ranks with Aristotle's works on logic

1808 Thomas Dartmouth Rice. Father of the U.S. minstrel show

1818 William George Fargo. Co-founder of the gold-rush express company of Wells, Fargo & Company

1851 Emile Berliner. American inventor of the practical telephone transmitter in 1877 and the "lateral-cut" recording disc in 1887

1856 Henri Edmond Cross. French painter

1882 Sigrid Undset. Nobel Prize-winning Norwegian novelist, noted for the epic trilogy *Kristin Lavransdatter* (1920-1922)

1899 John Marshall Harlan. U.S. Supreme Court justice, 1955-1971

1908 Jimmy Stewart. American stage, screen, and television actor, and star performer for some 50 years

1915 Moshe Dayan. Israeli soldier and statesman, who commanded the Israeli forces in the Arab-Israeli war of 1956 and the six-day war against Egypt, Jordan, and Syria in 1967

1919 **George Gobel.** American comedian and television performer

1921 **Hal Newhouser.** Hall of Fame baseball pitcher who won 29 games in 1945

1927 **Bud Grant.** Professional football player and coach

1931 **Ken Boyer.** Professional baseball player and manager

1936 **Anthony Zerbe.** American motion-picture actor

1937 **Dave Hill.** Professional golfer

1940 **Sadaharu Oh.** Japanese baseball player with over 800 career home runs in Japan

1940 **Stan Mikita.** Professional hockey player who won the National Hockey League trophies for most valuable player, leading scorer, and sportsmanship in 1966-1967 and 1967-1968

1942 **Frew McMillan.** South African tennis player noted for his doubles play with Bob Hewitt

1944 **Joe Cocker.** British rock singer

1946 **Cher (Cherilyn Sakisian).** American singer, television performer, and motion-picture actress

1946 **Bobby Murcer.** Professional baseball player, who toward the end of his career, joked that "If I hit a home run this year, they'll expect me to hit one next year"

1951 **Cullen Bryant.** Professional football player

1952 **Rickie Upchurch.** Professional football player

1954 **Jimmy Henderson.** American rock musician

1958 **Ron Reagan.** American dancer and son of President Reagan

1959 **Bronson Pinchot.** American motion-picture and television actor

1963 **David Wells.** Professional baseball pitcher who pitched a perfect game for the New York Yankees (no one reached base) in 1998

1965 **Todd Stottlemyre.** Professional baseball player and son of baseball player Mel Stottlemyre

May 20 – Events

1498 Vasco da Gama anchored at Calicut, India, after his historic voyage around the Cape of Good Hope.

1506 Christopher Columbus died in Valladolid, Spain, at age 54. The "Discoverer of America and Admiral of the Ocean Sea" died in a humble dwelling in poverty.

1536 King Henry VIII of England married Jane Seymour one day after he had beheaded his first wife, Anne Boleyn.

1830 The first railroad timetable was published, in the newspaper *Baltimore American.*

1861 The capital of the Confederacy was moved from Montgomery, Alabama, to Richmond, Virginia.

1861 North Carolina seceded from the Union. It was among the last of the southern states to do so.

1862 President Lincoln signed the Homestead Act, opening millions of acres of Western land to settlers.

1882 The Triple Alliance was formed in Vienna between Germany, Austria, and Italy.

1927 Charles A. Lindbergh left New York's Roosevelt Field in his *Spirit of St. Louis* on the first nonstop solo trip across the Atlantic. He landed in Paris the next day.

1932 Amelia Earhart began the first solo flight by a woman across the Atlantic Ocean. She made the trip from Newfoundland to Londonderry in 15 hours.

1939 The Pan American Airways *Yankee Clipper* took off from Port Washington, N.Y., for Europe, inaugurating regular transatlantic air service.

1941 German paratroops invaded Crete in World War II.

1998 Because of unrest due to the collapsing economy, Suharto resigned as president of Indonesia after 32 years in office.

May 21 – Birthdays

1471 **Albrecht Durer.** German painter, engraver, and designer, and one of the foremost artists of his country during the Renaissance

1527 **Philip II.** King of Spain, 1556-1598, during whose reign Spain conquered Portugal, but was defeated by the English in the destruction of Spain's Invincible Armada in 1588

1688 **Alexander Pope.** Great English poet and brilliant satirist whose works are the most often quoted of any English author except Shakespeare

1780 **Elizabeth Gurney Fry.** Pioneer British prison reformer, who was among the first to insist that prisoners need help rather than punishment in becoming good citizens

1792 **Gustave-Gaspard Coriolis.** French mathematician noted for analyzing the Coriolis force on moving objects due to the earth's rotation

1844 **Henri Rousseau.** French "primitive" painter whose works, such as *The Dream* (1910), strongly influenced the surrealism movement of the 1920s

1873 **Richard Bennett.** American stage and screen actor, leading matinee idol of his day, and father of actresses Barbara, Constance, and Joan Bennett

1878 **Glenn Curtiss.** American inventor and pioneer in the development of aircraft

1884 **Sir Claude Auchinleck.** British World War II field marshal

1889 **Mario Bonnard.** Italian motion-picture actor and director

1890 **Harry Austin Tierney.** Australian-born composer and pianist, noted for songs such as "Alice Blue Gown" (with lyricist Joseph McCarthy)

1898 **Armand Hammer.** American financier, manufacturer, and art collector

1902 **Earl Averill.** Professional baseball player who hit the ball that injured Dizzy Dean's toe and ultimately ended his career

1904 **Robert Montgomery.** American motion-picture actor and director

1904 **Fats Waller.** American pianist, composer, and jazz musician

1909 **Berta Hummel.** German nun and artist whose drawings were the inspiration for the famous Hummel figurines

1912 **Monty Stratton.** Professional baseball player

1913 **Irving Shulman.** American novelist and author of *The Amboy Dukes* (1947)

1916 **Harold Robbins.** Highly popular American novelist

1917 **Raymond Burr.** American television and motion-picture actor noted for the long-running series *Perry Mason*

1917 **Dennis Day.** American singer and actor

1921 **Andrei Dmitriyevich Sakharov.** Russian physicist and noted dissident who shared the 1958 Nobel Prize in physics

1923 **Ara Parseghian.** American football coach and sportscaster

1925 **Peggy Cass.** American stage and television actress

1926 **Kay Kendall.** English stage and motion-picture actress

1926 **Robert Creeley.** American poet and founder of the "Black Mountain" movement of the 1950s

1941 **Ronald Isley.** American singer with the Isley Brothers

1944 **Mary Robinson.** Irish politician and first woman elected president of Ireland (1990)

1944 **Peter Banaszak.** Professional football player

1948 **Jurgen Fassbender.** West German tennis player

1951 **Al Franken.** American actor, comedian and author of *Rush Limbaugh Is a Big Fat Idiot and Other Observations* (1995)

1960 **Kent Hrbek.** Professional baseball player

1961 **Tim Lever.** British keyboardist and saxophonist with the Dead or Alive musical group

May 21 – Events

1542 Hernando de Soto, the Spanish explorer, died and was buried in the Mississippi River, which he had discovered the previous year.

1819 The first bicycle was ridden on the streets of New York. It was considered such a hazard that a city law was passed forbidding "velocipedes in public places."

1832 The first Democratic National Convention was held, in Baltimore. President Andrew Jackson was nominated for a second term.

1854 Lawrence, Kansas, was sacked by pro-slavery "border ruffians."

1881 Clara Barton founded the American Association of the Red Cross, which later became the American Red Cross.

1924 Fourteen-year-old Bobby Franks was murdered by two students, Nathan Leopold Jr. and Richard Loeb, resulting later in the famous Leopold-Loeb trial.

1927 Charles A. Lindbergh arrived at Le Bourget Field near Paris, France, completing the first solo nonstop flight across the Atlantic Ocean.

1932 Amelia Earhart landed in Londonderry, Ireland, completing the first woman's solo nonstop transatlantic flight.

1940 Berlin Radio claimed the annihilation of the French Ninth Army in World War II.

1972 Michelangelo's *Pieta,* one of the world's sculptural masterpieces, was severely damaged in St. Peter's Basilica by Lazlo Toth, a Hungarian emigre.

1977 Seattle Slew won the Preakness Stakes at Pimlico on his way to the Triple Crown of horseracing.

May 22 – Birthdays

1620 **Comte Frontenac, Louis de Buade.** French courtier and Governor-general of New France (1672-1682 and 1689-1698)

1733 **Hubert Robert.** French painter

1783 **William Sturgeon.** English electrical engineer who devised the first electromagnet capable of supporting more than its own weight

1813 **Richard Wagner.** One of the world's four or five greatest composers

1820 **Worthington Whittredge.** American landscape painter

1845 **Mary Cassatt.** One of America's greatest women painters, noted for works such as *The Cup of Tea, The Bath,* and *Woman and Child Driving*

1859 **Sir Arthur Conan Doyle.** British writer and creator of Sherlock Holmes, the world's best-known detective

1860 **Willem Einthoven.** Dutch physiologist who developed the electrocardiogram (1895)

1891 **Edwin B. Edwards.** American composer, violinist, and trombonist, noted for such songs as "Tiger Rag"

1902 **Al Simmons.** Hall of Fame baseball player

1907 **Sir Laurence Olivier.** One of the most exciting and versatile actors in the English-speaking world

1908 **Horton Smith.** Hall of Fame golfer, and first to win the Masters Tournament (in 1934)

1914 **Vance Packard.** American writer and author of *The Hidden Persuaders*

1915 **George Baker.** American cartoonist and creator of *The Sad Sack*

1922 **Judith Crist.** American film critic

1924 **Charles Aznavour.** French lyric writer, singer, and actor

1928 **T. Boone Pickens Jr.** American business executive and "corporate raider," noted for his takeover attempts of U.S. corporations

1930 **Marisol.** American sculptor

1934 **Garry Wills.** American writer and author of political biography

1934 **Peter Nero.** American pianist

1938 **Susan Strasberg.** American stage and motion-picture actress and daughter of actor and director Lee Strasberg

1938 **Richard Benjamin.** American motion-picture actor

1940 **Bernard Shaw.** American television journalist and anchor/reporter with CNN

1940 **Michael Sarrazin.** Canadian television and motion-picture actor

1941 **Paul Edward Winfield.** American motion-picture and television actor

1942 **Barbara Parkins.** Canadian-born television and motion-picture actress

1942 **Theodore Kaczynski.** The "Unabomber," a former mathematics professor and notorious killer who dispatched his victims with letter bombs over a period of some 20 years before being apprehended in 1998

1943 **Tommy John.** Professional baseball player

1947 **Chuck Baltazar.** American jockey

1955 **Nancy Yeargin.** American tennis player

May 22 – Events

337 Roman emperor Constantine the Great died at age 49, after being baptized a Christian on his deathbed.

1819 The U.S.S. *Savannah* set out from Savannah, Georgia, on the first successful transatlantic voyage by a steamship. It docked in Liverpool, England, on June 20.

1849 Abraham Lincoln was granted a patent titled "Buoying Vessels over Shoals," making him the only president of the United States to hold a patent.

1885 Victor Hugo, the great French novelist, died in Paris at age 83.

1906 Wilbur and Orville Wright were granted a patent on their airplane.

1923 The comic strip *The Nebbs,* by Sol Hess, first appeared.

1939 Adolf Hitler and Benito Mussolini concluded their "Pact of Steel," allying Germany and Italy in a prelude to World War II.

1960 The world's strongest assessable earthquake, 9.5 on the Richter scale, occurred south of Concepcion, Chile.

1972 President Nixon arrived in Moscow, the first U.S. president to visit the Russian capital.

1979 Joseph Clark was elected the youngest prime minister in the history of Canada.

1992 Johnny Carson hosted *The Tonight Show* for the last time, ending a 30-year career as its host.

May 23 – Birthdays

1707 **Carolus Linnaeus.** Swedish botanist who established the modern scientific method of naming plants and animals by their genus (group) and species (kind)

1734 **Franz Mesmer.** Austrian physician who pioneered in the practice of hypnotism, and for whom the word *mesmerism* (animal magnetism) was named

1799 **Thomas Hood.** English poet and humorist, who excused himself for working so hard by punning, "So that I may earn my livelihood I have to be a lively Hood"

1810 **Margaret Fuller.** American journalist, social reformer, and a leader of the philosophical movement called transcendentalism

1820 **James Buchanan Eads.** American engineer and inventor, who designed and built the steel-arch Eads Bridge in St. Louis

1824 **Ambrose Everett Burnside.** Civil War Union general whose whiskers on the side of his face gave rise to the term *burnsides,* which later became sideburns

1828 **Edward Hitchcock.** First professor of physical education in the United States, in 1861 at Amhurst

1850 **Virginia Knight Logan.** American composer and author (songs such as "A Song for You and Me," "Rose of My Heart," and "Moonlight Waltz"), and mother of composer Frederick Logan

1883 **Douglas Fairbanks.** American stage and motion-picture actor and one of the superstars of Hollywood in the 1920s

1886 **James Gleason.** American stage and screen actor in over 100 films

1888 **Zack Wheat.** Hall of Fame baseball player

1890 **Herbert Marshall.** English stage and motion-picture actor

1898 **Frank McHugh.** American stage, screen, and television actor in over 100 movies

1908 **Max Abramovitz.** American architect

1908 **John Bardeen.** American physicist and co-inventor of the transistor

1910 **Scatman Crothers.** American singer, drummer, guitarist and actor

1910 **Franz Kline.** American abstract painter noted for his large black-and-white paintings

1910 **Artie Shaw.** American bandleader of the big band era of the 1930s and 1940s

1911 **Betty Nuthall.** English Hall of Fame tennis player and one of the youngest women to play in the U.S. Open (in 1927 at age 15)

1912 **John Payne.** American motion-picture and television actor

1919 **Betty Garrett.** American stage, screen and television actor

1921 **Helen O'Connell.** American singer with the Jimmy Dorsey band

1921 **James Benjamin Blish.** American author noted for his books about *Star Trek*

1928 **Rosemary Clooney.** American actress and singer

1929 **Marvin Chomsky.** American television director noted for such shows as *Star Trek* and *Gunsmoke*

1933 **John Browning.** American pianist

1933 **Joan Collins.** English motion-picture and television actress and writer

1934 **Robert A. Moog.** Inventor of the Moog electronic synthesizer

1934 **Mason Rudolph.** Professional golfer

1944	**John Newcombe.** Australian tennis player and Wimbledon singles champion, 1970-1971
1946	**David Graham.** Professional golfer
1949	**James Braxton.** Professional football player
1951	**Anatoly Karpov.** Russian grand master of chess
1952	**Marvin Hagler.** Middleweight boxing champion known as Marvelous Marvin

May 23 – Events

1430 Joan of Arc was captured by the Burgundians at Compiegne and sold to the English for the equivalent of $3,000.

1498 Girolamo Savonarola, Italian friar and fiery religious reformer, was hanged and his body burned for heresy on orders of Pope Alexander VI.

1533 Archbishop Thomas Cranmer divorced King Henry VIII of England from Catherine of Aragon so that Henry's earlier secret marriage to Anne Boleyn would have validity.

1618 The "Defenestration of Prague" occurred, in which prominent Protestant leaders in Prague were seized and thrown out of a castle window, marking the start of the Thirty Years' War.

1701 Captain William Kidd was hanged in London for piracy and murder.

1785 Benjamin Franklin, in a letter to George Whatley, first described the bifocal eyeglasses he had just invented.

1788 South Carolina entered the Union as the eighth state.

1873 The Royal Canadian Mounted Police was established.

1906 Henrik Ibsen, the great Norwegian playwright, died in Oslo at age 78.

1911 The New York Public Library building at Fifth Avenue and 42nd Street was dedicated by President William Howard Taft.

1915 Italy declared war on Austria-Hungary, thus entering World War I on the side of the Allies.

1922 *Abie's Irish Rose*, a new comedy by Anne Nichols, opened at the Fulton Theater in New York.

1934 Clyde Barrow and Bonnie Parker, the notorious outlaws, were killed in a hail of bullets near Shreveport, Louisiana.

1945 Heinrich Himmler, the notorious Nazi Gestapo chief, died by biting a cyanide capsule hidden in his mouth, three days after his capture by British troops.

1951 The Chinese Communists annexed Tibet.

May 24 – Birthdays

1494	**Jacopa Da Pontormo.** Italian painter
1544	**William Gilbert.** English physician and pioneer researcher in electricity and magnetism
1616	**John Maitland.** Scottish statesman and Duke of Lauderdale
1693	**Georg Raphael Donner.** Austrian sculptor
1743	**Jean Paul Marat.** One of the most radical leaders of the French Revolution, who, with Danton and Robespierre, was responsible for the Reign of Terror
1816	**Emanuel Gottlieb Leutze.** German painter known for his American historical works, such as his masterpiece, *Washington Crossing the Delaware*
1819	**Victoria.** Queen of England, 1837-1901, and one of the greatest rulers in English history
1854	**Richard Mansfield.** One of the best-known actors in the United States during the 1890s
1870	**Jan Christiaan Smuts.** South African soldier, scholar, and World War II prime minister
1878	**Harry Emerson Fosdick.** One of the best known Protestant ministers in the United States in the first half of the 20th century
1895	**Samuel I. Newhouse.** American newspaper publisher
1899	**Suzanne Lenglen.** French tennis player, six times Wimbledon singles champion, and one of the greatest women players in history
1903	**Dwight B. Latham.** American composer, author, and singer, noted for songs such as "MacNamara's Band" and "I'm My Own Grandpaw"
1909	**Wilbur Mills.** U.S. congressman prominent during the 1950s and 1960s
1914	**Lilli Palmer.** German-born stage and motion-picture actress
1918	**Coleman Young.** Mayor of Detroit
1925	**Mai Zetterling.** Swedish motion-picture and television actress
1927	**John B. Kelly Jr..** U.S. olympic champion and brother of Princess Grace of Monaco
1934	**Jane M. Byrne.** Mayor of Chicago who succeeded Richard J. Daley
1941	**Bob Dylan.** American folk singer, musician, and composer, noted for songs such as "Blowin' in the Wind" (1962), "The Times They Are A-changin'" (1964), and "Like a Rolling Stone" (1965)
1943	**Gary Burghoff.** American television actor noted for his role as Radar on the long-running series M*A*S*H
1945	**Priscilla Presley.** American actress and wife of singer Elvis Presley
1946	**Francisco "Pancho" Guzman.** Ecuadorian tennis player
1947	**Cecilia Martinez.** American tennis player
1950	**Jo Ann Washam.** Professional golfer
1953	**Michael Strachan.** Professional football player

May 24 – Events

1626 Peter Minuit, the Dutch colonial governor, bought the island of Manhattan from the Indians for the equivalent of $24.

1738 John Wesley was given "saving faith" during a Moravian meeting in Aldersgate Street, London, which eventually led him to establish Methodism.

1830   The first division of the Baltimore & Ohio Railroad was completed, a 13-mile link from Baltimore to Ellicott Mills.

1844   "What hath God wrought!" was sent by Samuel F.B. Morse from the Supreme Court room in the Capitol to Baltimore, as the first public telegraph message.

1859   "Ave Maria," by Charles Gounod, was sung for the first time at a concert in Paris.

1883   The Brooklyn Bridge was opened to traffic, linking Brooklyn and Manhattan.

1935   The first major league night baseball game was played, at Crosley Field in Cincinnati, with the Reds defeating the Philadelphia Phillies, 2-1.

1940   Adolf Hitler ordered the German armored units to halt mop-up operations and head toward Paris in World War II. This move saved 380,000 British soldiers trapped at Dunkerque.

1941   The British H.M.S. *Hood,* the world's largest warship at the time, was sunk by the German battleship *Bismarck* between Iceland and Greenland in World War II.

1950   Sweetwater Clifton joined the New York Knickerbockers, becoming the first black National Basketball Association player.

1962   U.S. astronaut Scott Carpenter made a three-orbit flight in *Aurora 7,* the second orbital flight by an American.

May 25 – Birthdays

1616   **Carlo Dolci.** Italian painter

1803   **Ralph Waldo Emerson.** American poet and essayist and a leading figure in the thought and literature of American civilization

1803   **Edward George Bulwer-Lytton.** English historical novelist and playwright, best known for his major novel, *The Last Days of Pompeii* (1834)

1818   **Jakob Burckhardt.** Swiss historian, art critic, and author of the four-volume work, *A Cultural History of Greece* (1898-1902)

1825   **Daniel Baird Wesson.** American firearms manufacturer and co-founder with Horace Smith of Smith and Wesson Revolver Company

1845   **Lip Pike.** Baseball's first professional player

1878   **Bojangles Robinson.** American dancer and actor of vaudeville, the musical stage, and motion-pictures

1886   **Philip Murray.** American labor leader and second president of the CIO, 1940-1952

1889   **Igor Sikorsky.** Russian-born pioneer in aircraft design, who produced the world's first four-engine airplane in 1913

1894   **Joe Judge.** Professional baseball player

1897   **Gene Tunney.** World heavyweight champion, 1926-1928, who defeated Jack Dempsey for the crown

1898   **Bennett Cerf.** American publisher and television personality

1905   **Joseph Harsch.** American journalist and commentator

1908   **Theodore Roethke.** American poet who received the Pulitzer Prize in 1954 for *The Waking: Poems 1933-1953*

1908   **Robert Morley.** English actor and playwright

1912   **Augie Galan.** Professional baseball player

1916   **Lindsey Nelson.** American sportscaster

1916   **Ginny Simms.** American singer and radio performer

1917   **Steve Cochran.** American stage and motion-picture actor

1917   **Theodore Hesburgh.** American priest, president of the University of Notre Dame, and civil rights champion

1918   **Claude Akins.** American stage, screen, and television actor

1921   **Hal David.** American songwriter and lyricist who collaborated with Burt Bacharach on such songs as "Raindrops Keep Falling on My Head" and "What the World Needs Now"

1923   **John Weitz.** German-American fashion designer, author, and sportsman, who served as a World War II spy for the United States

1925   **Jeanne Crain.** American motion-picture actress

1926   **Miles Davis.** American trumpeter and pioneer of cool jazz

1926   **Bill Sharman.** Greatest free thrower in the history of professional basketball, and Hall of Famer

1927   **Robert Ludlum.** American novelist noted for works such as *The Icarus Agenda, The Bourne Supremacy,* and *The Osterman Weekend*

1929   **Beverly Sills.** American operatic soprano

1932   **K. C. Jones.** Professional Hall of Fame basketball player and coach

1934   **Ron Nesson.** American newsman and press secretary for President Ford

1935   **Cookie Gilchrist.** Professional football player

1936   **Tom T. Hall.** American singer and songwriter

1939   **Sir Ian McKellen.** British stage, screen, and television actor and superstar

1939   **Dixie Carter.** American actress noted for the long-running TV show *Designing Women* (1987-1993)

1943   **Leslie Uggams.** American singer and actress

1947   **Jessi Colter.** American country singer

1947   **Karen Valentine.** American television actress

1950   **John Montefusco.** Professional baseball player

1954   **Bob Knepper.** Professional baseball player

1969   **Anne Heche.** American motion-picture actress

May 25 – Events

1539   Spanish explorer Hernando De Soto landed in the Tampa Bay area and claimed Florida for Spain. (Ponce de Leon had already claimed Florida for Spain in 1513, however.)

1787   The Constitutional Convention opened in Independence Hall in Philadelphia to draft a constitution for the United States.

1810 Buenos Aires overthrew Spanish authority and set up its own self-government. The rest of Argentina declared its independence eight years later.

1878 The world premiere of Gilbert and Sullivan's operetta *H.M.S. Pinafore* was held in London.

1914 The Irish Home Rule Bill was passed by the British Parliament.

1927 Henry Ford announced the discontinuance of the Model T and plans to replace it with the Model A.

1935 Jesse Owens, America's future Olympic star, broke five world's records and tied a sixth at the Big Ten Championships at Ann Arbor, Mich. He did all six in 45 minutes.

1935 Babe Ruth hit the last home run of his career, number 714, at Forbes Field in Pittsburgh.

1938 The Soviet ambassador to the U.S. declared that Moscow was "ready to defend Czechoslovakia in the event of aggression" by Adolf Hitler. England and France, however, declined to live up to their agreements to do likewise.

1943 Franklin D. Roosevelt and Winston Churchill concluded their Washington *Trident* conference after agreeing on the future strategies of World War II.

1945 The U.S. Chiefs of Staff set November 1 as the date for the launching of Operation Olympic, the invasion of Japan in World War II.

1961 President John F. Kennedy called for the nation to put a man on the moon by the end of the 1960s.

1979 A DC-10 jet crashed in Chicago, killing all 272 persons aboard, in the worst disaster in the history of American aviation.

1985 A hurricane roared in from the Bay of Bengal and devastated Bangladesh coastal communities, leaving some 20,000 dead.

May 26 – Birthdays

1602 **Philippe de Champaigne.** French painter

1650 **Duke of Marlborough.** One of England's greatest generals

1667 **Abraham De Moivre.** Noted French mathematician best known for De Moivre's Theorem for extracting roots of any number, real or complex

1822 **Edmond de Goncourt.** French novelist, art critic, and diarist, who with his brother Jules provided the basis for the realist and naturalist literary movements in France

1837 **Washington Augustus Roebling.** American engineer who completed the Brooklyn Bridge after the death of his father John Augustus Roebling, who designed the bridge and began its construction

1886 **Al Jolson.** American singer, actor, and most popular recording artist of his time

1894 **Paul Lukas.** Hungarian stage and motion-picture actor whose career spanned over 50 years

1895 **Dorothea Lange.** Depression-era American photographer noted for the famous photo "Migrant Mother" of Florence Thompson, a pea picker in California

1897 **Norma Talmadge.** One of the most popular idols of the American screen in the 1920s, who appeared in over 200 silent films

1907 **John Wayne.** American motion-picture actor and superstar who appeared in some 250 films in a career of over 40 years

1910 **Laurance Rockefeller.** American millionaire and conservationist

1910 **Adolfo Lopez Mateos.** President of Mexico, 1958-1964

1911 **Ben Alexander.** American motion-picture and television actor

1912 **Janos Kadar.** Premier of Hungary after the Hungarian Revolt of 1956

1913 **Peter Cushing.** English stage and motion picture actor in some 75 horror films

1919 **Jay Silverheels.** Canadian-born actor who played Tonto in *The Lone Ranger*

1920 **Peggy Lee.** American singer and actress

1923 **James Arness.** American motion-picture actor and star of television's long-running series, *Gunsmoke*

1923 **Roy Dotrice.** English stage, screen, and television actor, and Tony award winner for *A Moon for the Misbegotten* (2000)

1927 **Jacques Bergerac.** French motion-picture actor

1928 **Jack Kevorkian.** American physician noted for his assisted suicides

1932 **Ranan R. Lurie.** American cartoonist and most widely syndicated columnist in the world

1937 **Jack R. Murphy.** Noted American jewel thief known as "Murph the Surf"

1941 **Cliff Drysdale.** South African tennis player and sportscaster

1947 **Darrell Evans.** Professional baseball player

1948 **Stevie Nicks.** American singer and songwriter with Fleetwood Mac

1949 **Hank Williams Jr.** American country singer and son of one of the great country singers of the time

1949 **Dan Pastorini.** Professional football player

1951 **Sally Ride.** First American woman astronaut

1966 **Helena Bonham Carter.** English stage, screen, and television actress, and great granddaughter of British prime minister Herbert Asquith

May 26 – Events

735 The Venerable Bede, the learned English writer, died at an age of approximately 63.

1521 The Diet of Worms, a special meeting of princes, nobles, and clergymen, outlawed Martin Luther and his followers, after Luther refused to retract his teachings.

1583 Susanna, the first child of William Shakespeare and Anne Hathaway, was baptized.

1703 Samuel Pepys, the noted English diarist, died in London at age 70.

1865 General Edmund Kirby-Smith surrendered the last Confederate army still in the field, finally ending the Civil War fighting.

1927 The Ford Motor Company turned out its 15 millionth car.

1940 British prime minister Winston Churchill made the decision to evacuate Dunkerque in Operation Dynamo in World War II.

1954 The funeral ship of the Egyptian pharoah Cheops was unearthed in a limestone chamber near the Great Pyramid of Giza.

1959 Harvey Haddix pitched 12 perfect innings but lost in the 13th as Milwaukee beat Pittsburgh, 1-0.

1991 Rick Mears won the Indianapolis 500 for the fourth time, tying the records of A.J. Foyt and Al Unser.

May 27 – Birthdays

1626 **William II.** Prince of Orange

1629 **Pierre Legros.** French sculptor

1699 **Giovanni Antonio Guardi.** Italian painter

1794 **Cornelius Vanderbilt.** American shipping and railroad magnate and founder of the Vanderbilt fortune, one of the greatest in America

1818 **Amelia Jenks Bloomer.** American temperance reformer and women's rights advocate, who, because of her famous "Turkish pantaloons," caused the word *bloomers* to be added to the language

1819 **Julia Ward Howe.** American poet and social reformer who wrote "The Battle Hymn of the Republic"

1836 **Jay Gould.** American financier and founder of the Gould fortune

1837 **James Butler "Wild Bill" Hickok.** American frontier scout and peace officer in the West

1867 **Arnold Bennett.** English novelist and playwright, best known for *The Old Wives' Tale* (1908)

1871 **Georges Rouault.** French painter, printmaker, and ceramicist, noted for such works as *The Old King* and *Miserere*

1878 **Isadora Duncan.** American dancer who greatly influenced dancing in the 1900s

1894 **Dashiell Hammett.** American detective fiction writer and creator of Sam Spade (in *The Maltese Falcon*) and Nick and Nora Charles (*The Thin Man*)

1894 **Louis Ferdinand Celine.** French novelist noted for works such as *Journey to the End of the Night* (1932)

1902 **Peter Marshall.** American religious leader who was the subject of *A Man Called Peter* by his wife Catherine

1907 **Rachel Carson.** American marine biologist and science writer, and author of *The Sea Around Us* (1951) and *Silent Spring* (1962)

1908 **Harold Jacob Rome.** American composer and author, noted for lyrics such as "All of a Sudden My Heart Sings" and "On the Avenue"

1909 **Pinky Higgins.** Professional baseball player

1911 **Hubert H. Humphrey.** U.S. Vice President, 1965-1969, and presidential candidate in 1968

1911 **Vincent Price.** American motion-picture actor

1912 **Sam Snead.** Professional golfer who won over 130 tournaments

1912 **John Cheever.** American novelist and short-story writer

1915 **Fred Wise.** American lyricist noted for songs such as "A-You're Adorable" and "Let Me Go, Lover"

1915 **Herman Wouk.** American novelist who won a Pulitzer Prize in 1952 for *The Caine Mutiny*

1923 **Sumner Redstone.** American entertainment industry executive (Viacom, MTV and Nickelodeon)

1923 **Henry Kissinger.** U.S. secretary of state under Presidents Nixon and Ford

1925 **Tony Hillerman.** American mystery writer noted for works such as *A Thief of Time* (1988) and *Talking God* (1989)

1928 **Thea Musgrave.** Scottish composer and conductor

1930 **John Barth.** Highly original American novelist, whose best known work is *The Sot-Weed Factor* (1960)

1935 **Lee Meriweather.** American television actress

1936 **Louis Gosset Jr.** American stage, screen, and television actor

1941 **Allan Carr.** American show business producer noted for *La Cage aux Folles*

1944 **Christopher Dodd.** U.S. senator and son of Senator Thomas Dodd

1950 **Michael Siani.** Professional football player

1954 **Catherine Carr.** Professional swimmer

1956 **Mark Clear.** Professional baseball player

1965 **Pat Cash.** Australian tennis player who won the men's singles championship at Wimbledon in 1987

1968 **Jeff Bagwell.** Professional baseball player and superstar

May 27 – Events

1564 John Calvin, the great Swiss religious leader, died in Geneva at age 57.

1679 The Act of Habeas Corpus, one of the basic guarantees of personal freedom in English and American law, was passed by the English Parliament.

1703 The construction of St. Petersburg, Russia, was begun by Peter the Great.

1840 Niccolo Paganini, the great Italian violinist, died of cancer at age 57, after a legendary deathbed performance on his Guarnerius violin.

1905 The naval battle of Tsushima Strait between Japan's island of Kyushu and Korea began in the Russo-Japanese War. The result was the near annihilation of the Russian fleet.

1929 Charles A. Lindbergh, the hero of the first solo Atlantic flight, married Anne Morrow.

1935 The U.S. Supreme Court ruled the National Industrial Recovery Act unconstitutional.

1936 The Cunard Line's *Queen Mary* began its transatlantic maiden voyage.

1937 The Golden Gate Bridge was opened to the public.

1941 The British navy sank the powerful German battleship *Bismarck* off the coast of France, in one of the most important naval actions of World War II.

1942 Reinhard Heydrich, the "Hangman of Czechoslovakia," was murdered by patriots in Prague during World War II. In revenge the Nazis destroyed the town of Lidice.

1949 Robert Leroy Ripley, founder of Ripley's *Believe It or Not,* died at age 55.

1964 Jawaharlal Nehru, India's first prime minister, died at the age of 74.

1997 The Supreme Court ruled that Paula Jones's sexual harassment suit against President Clinton must not be delayed until after Clinton's term, since the suit was "highly unlikely to occupy any substantial amount [of the president's] time." (It took up nearly two more years of his time and led to his impeachment by the House and trial by the Senate.)

May 28 – Birthdays

1738 **Joseph Guillotin.** French physician and inventor of the guillotine in 1792

1743 **Louis Jean Desprez.** French architect

1759 **William Pitt (the Younger).** British prime minister, 1783-1801 and 1804-1806, and the youngest person ever to hold the post

1779 **Thomas Moore.** Irish poet, satirist, and composer of "Believe Me If All Those Endearing Young Charms"

1807 **Louis Agassiz.** Swiss-born naturalist, geologist, and educator

1818 **Pierre G.T. Beauregard.** Confederate general who directed the bombardment of Fort Sumter, which started the Civil War, and who also fought at the first Battle of Bull Run and at Shiloh

1853 **Carl Larsson.** Swedish illustrator

1884 **Eduard Benes.** Co-founder of Czechoslovakia in 1918 and president at the time of the Nazi takeover in 1938

1888 **Ward L. Lambert.** Hall of Fame professional basketball player and coach who introduced the fast break

1888 **Jim Thorpe.** One of the most accomplished all-around athletes in history and member of the Professional Football Hall of Fame

1895 **Warren Giles.** President of baseball's National League in the 1950s and 1960s

1896 **Dick Sanford.** American author and singer, noted for lyrics such as "Purple Shadows," "The Singing Hills," and "Mention My Name in Sheboygan"

1900 **Jack Little.** English-born composer, author, and producer, noted for songs such as "A Shanty in Old Shanty Town"

1908 **Ian Fleming.** English novelist and creator of James Bond

1912 **David Barbour.** American composer noted for songs such as "Manana" and "It's A Good Day"

1916 **Walker Percy.** American novelist and essayist noted for works such as *Love in the Ruins*

1917 **Barry Commoner.** American biologist, environmentalist, and presidential candidate in 1980

1925 **Dietrich Fischer-Dieskau.** German baritone

1931 **Stephen Birmingham.** American writer and novelist

1931 **Carroll Baker.** American motion-picture actress

1934 **Dionne quintuplets.** Annette, Cecille, Emilie, Marie, and Yvonne Dionne, the first quintuplets to survive infancy

1938 **Jerry West.** Professional basketball superstar and Hall of Famer

1944 **Gladys Knight.** American singer

1944 **Rudolph Giuliani.** Mayor of New York City who took office in 1994

1945 **John Fogerty.** American singer, songwriter, and guitarist with Creedence Clearwater Revival

1947 **Beth Howland.** American actress

1947 **Sondra Locke.** American actress

1957 **Kirk Gibson.** Professional baseball player

1958 **Bill Doran.** Professional baseball player

May 28 – Events

1291 Acre, in the Kingdom of Jerusalem, fell to the Moslems, ending the Crusades.

1533 Archbishop Thomas Cranmer pronounced King Henry VIII's marriage to Anne Boleyn valid.

1628 The English Parliament presented the Petition of Right to King Charles I, declaring unconstitutional certain actions of the king.

1863 The first black regiment from the North left Boston to fight in the Civil War.

1892 The Sierra Club, dedicated to the cause of conservation and preserving nature, was organized in San Francisco.

1905 Japan completed the destruction of the Russian fleet begun the previous day in Tsushima Strait in the Russo-Japanese War.

1918 Units of the U.S. First Division launched the first American offensive in France in World War I, capturing Cantigny from the Germans.

1929 The first color movie, *On With the Show,* was released by Warner Brothers.

1934 The Dionne quintuplets, the first in history to survive infancy, were born in Callender, Ontario, Canada.

1935 Twentieth Century Fox was born as Darryl F. Zanuck merged 20th Century Pictures with Fox.

1937 Neville Chamberlain became prime minister of Britain.

1940 King Leopold III surrendered the 300,000-man Belgian army to the Nazis in World War II, and in turn was disowned by his cabinet.

1972 The Duke of Windsor, formerly King Edward VIII of England, died at age 77.

May 29 – Birthdays

1630 **Charles II.** King of England, 1660-1685, and the first of the restored Stuart line after the end of the Commonwealth

1698 **Edme Bouchardon.** French sculptor

1736 **Patrick Henry.** American orator and revolutionary, who said, "Give me liberty or give me death" in 1775 before the Virginia Provincial Convention

1826 **Ebenezer Butterick.** Inventor of paper patterns for clothing

1860 **Isaac Manuel Francisco Albeniz.** Spanish pianist and composer and founder of contemporary Spanish music

1874 **G.K. Chesterton.** English critic and author, known as "The Prince of Paradox"

1880 **Oswald Spengler.** German philosopher of history noted for *The Decline of the West* (1918-1922)

1892 **Max Brand.** American writer of Western novels such as *Destry Rides Again*, who in his prime turned out roughly two books per month

1894 **Josef von Sternberg.** Austrian-American motion-picture director and one of the great masters of the American screen

1898 **Beatrice Lillie.** English actress and one of the brightest and most natural comediennes of her time

1900 **Jack Palmer.** American composer and author, noted for songs such as "Jumpin' Jive" and "Sentimental Baby"

1903 **Bob Hope.** American stage, screen, and television actor, and one of America's top comedians for 60 years

1906 **T.H. White.** English novelist and satirist, noted for works such as *The Sword in the Stone* (1939), published as part of the trilogy, *The Once and Future King* (1958)

1913 **Iris Adrian.** American motion-picture actress in some 100 films

1913 **Tony Zale.** Middleweight boxing champion, 1940-1947 and 1948

1917 **John F. Kennedy.** 35th U.S. president

1918 **Herb Shriner.** American humorist and television personality in the 1950s

1928 **Felix Rohatyn.** American financier who helped rescue New York City from bankruptcy in the 1970s

1932 **Richie Guerin.** Professional basketball player with over 14,000 career points

1932 **Paul Ehrlich.** American population biologist and author of *The Population Bomb*

1938 **Fay Vincent.** Baseball commissioner who succeeded A. Bartlett Giamatti

1939 **Al Unser.** American racing car driver who won the Indianapolis 500 four times

1944 **Helmut Berger.** Austrian motion-picture actor

1950 **Lesley Hunt.** Australian tennis player

1953 **Danny Elfman.** American songwriter, composer and member of the group Oingo Bingo

1955 **John W. Hinckley Jr.** Attempted assassin of President Reagan in 1981

1958 **Annette Bening.** American stage, screen and television actress

1961 **Melissa Etheridge.** American singer, songwriter and guitarist

1962 **Eric Davis.** Professional baseball player

May 29 – Events

1453 Constantinople fell to the Turkish sultan Mohammed II, marking the end of the Eastern Roman Empire or, as it was then called, the Byzantine Empire.

1649 England was declared a Commonwealth with Oliver Cromwell as Lord Protector.

1660 Charles II entered London, achieving the Restoration of the Stuart monarchy in England after Oliver Cromwell's death.

1724 Benedict XIII was elected pope of the Roman Catholic Church.

1765 Patrick Henry made his famous speech to the Virginia House of Burgesses, in which he said, "If this be treason, make the most of it."

1790 Rhode Island became the last of the original 13 colonies to ratify the U.S. Constitution and thus became the 13th state.

1848 Wisconsin was admitted to the Union as the 30th state.

1867 The Austrian Compromise was forced upon Emperor Francis Joseph I, creating the Dual Monarchy of Austria-Hungary.

1911 Sir William Gilbert, the great English composer of Gilbert and Sullivan fame, died at Harrow Weald, Middlesex, at age 74.

1932 World War I veterans known as the "bonus army" began arriving in Washington to demand cash bonuses then that they were promised to receive at the later date of 1945.

1940 The British began the evacuation of Dunkerque in World War II, an operation in which 336,000 soldiers were rescued.

1953 Edmund Hillary of New Zealand and Tenzing Norgay of Nepal became the first men to climb Mt. Everest, the world's highest mountain.

1977 A.J. Foyt won the Indianapolis 500 for a record fourth time.

May 30 – Birthdays

1867 **Arthur Vining Davis.** American businessman and founder of Alcoa

1871 **Amos Rusie.** Hall of Fame professional baseball player

1875 **Giovanni Gentile.** "Philosopher of Fascism"

1885 **Karl Behr.** American Hall of Fame tennis player

1887 **Alexander Archipenko.** Russian-born sculptor noted for using solids and hollows in portraying the human form

1888 **James A. Farley.** Franklin D. Roosevelt's campaign manager in 1932 and 1936, and postmaster general of the United States, 1933-1940

1891 **Ben Bernie.** American composer and violinist noted for "Sweet Georgia Brown"

1896 **Howard Hawks.** American motion-picture director and screenwriter, who directed such films as *The Road to Glory, Sergeant York,* and *The Big Sleep*

1899 **Irving Thalberg.** American motion-picture director and "Boy Wonder of Hollywood" in the 1920s

1901 **Cornelia Otis Skinner.** American stage actress and writer

1902 **Stepin Fetchit.** First black actor to receive featured billing in American motion pictures

1906 **Norris Goff.** American actor who played Abner Peabody on the radio program, *Lum and Abner,* of the 1930s and 1940s

1908 **Mel Blanc.** American actor and voice specialist, who supplied the voice of numerous cartoon characters

1909 **Benny Goodman.** American bandleader whose career spanned the Big Band Era of the 1930s and 1940s to the 1980s

1912 **Joseph Stein.** American dramatist noted for *Fiddler on the Roof* (1965)

1913 **Pee Wee Erwin.** American trumpeter and composer

1915 **Frank Blair.** Television newscaster who spent 20 years on the *Today* show

1920 **Franklin Schaffner Jr..** American motion-picture and television director who won the 1970 Academy Award for best director for *Patton*

1920 **George London.** American bass-baritone famous for his strong, masculine voice

1926 **Christine Jorgensen.** Noted American transsexual

1927 **Clint Walker.** American motion-picture and television actor

1934 **Aleksei Leonov.** Russian cosmonaut and first man to walk in space

1936 **Keir Dullea.** American stage, screen, and television actor

1939 **Michael J. Pollard.** American stage and motion-picture actor

1943 **Gale Sayers.** Professional Hall of Fame football superstar

1946 **Candy Lightner.** American reformer who in 1980 founded Mothers Against Drunk Driving (MADD)

1949 **Lydell Mitchell.** Professional football player

1964 **Wynonna Judd.** American country singer who with her mother, Naomi, formed the singing Judds duo until Naomi retired, at which point the daughter shortened her name to Wynonna

May 30 – Events

1431 Joan of Arc was burned at the stake in the Old Market Square of Rouen by the English.

1498 Christopher Columbus departed from Sanlucar, Spain, on his third voyage to America.

1588 The Spanish Armada of 130 ships, commanded by the Duke of Medina Sidonia, sailed from Lisbon to prepare to engage the English.

1593 Christopher Marlowe, the great English playwright, was killed in a tavern brawl in Deptford at age 29.

1640 Peter Paul Rubens, the noted Flemish painter, died in Antwerp at age 62.

1744 Alexander Pope, the great English poet, died at Twickenham, outside London, at age 56.

1778 Voltaire, the greatest French philosopher of all time, died in Paris at age 83.

1878 The great French artist, Henri Toulouse-Lautrec, fell at age 13 and broke his leg. A year later he broke the other leg, stunting his growth.

1894 Robert Lowe of the Boston Red Sox hit four home runs in four consecutive times at bat.

1896 The first automobile accident occurred, in New York City.

1911 The first Indianapolis 500 auto race was held; it was won by Ray Harroun driving a 1911 Marmon Wasp at an average speed of 74.59 miles per hour.

1922 The Lincoln Memorial was dedicated in Washington, D.C., by Chief Justice William Howard Taft.

1942 Cologne, Germany, was raided by the RAF in the first 1,000-bomber attack.

1961 Rafael Trujillo, the tyrannical dictator of the Dominican Republic, was assassinated, ending 31 years of harsh and severe rule.

1971 The U.S. Martian probe, *Mariner 9,* was launched.

May 31 – Birthdays

1443 **Margaret Beaufort.** Mother of King Henry VII of England and founder of St. John's and Christ's Colleges, Cambridge

1469 **Manuel I (the Fortunate).** King of Portugal, 1495-1521, who was in power when Portuguese heroes Vasco da Gama sailed around the Cape of Good Hope to India and Pedro Alvares Cabral discovered Brazil

1557 **Feodor I.** Czar of Russia, 1584-98, and son of Ivan the Terrible

1622 **Jan Abrahamsz Beerstraaten.** Dutch painter noted for works such as *Skating at Slooten*

1773 **Ludwig Tieck.** German writer

1810 **Horatio Seymour.** Democratic presidential candidate who lost to U.S. Grant in 1868

1819 **Walt Whitman.** American poet and essayist whose *Leaves of Grass* is considered one of the world's major literary works

1819 **William Worrall Mayo.** Founder with his two sons of the Mayo Clinic in 1889 at St. Mary's Hospital in Rochester, Minnesota

1857 **Pius XI.** Roman Catholic pope, 1922-1939, who settled the "Roman Question" with Italy, whereby the pope was granted temporal sovereignty over Vatican City

1860 **Walter Richard Sickert.** Most important of the British Impressionist painters

1883 **Frances Alda.** New Zealand soprano

1888 **Jack Holt.** American motion-picture hero of some 100 Hollywood silents and talkies, and father of actors Jennifer, Tim, and David Holt

1894 **Fred Allen.** American comedian and actor

1898 **Norman Vincent Peale.** American minister noted also for his books (such as *The Power of Positive Thinking*) and radio and television programs

1903 **Honey Russell.** Hall of Fame basketball player and coach

1908 **Don Ameche.** American motion-picture and television actor, and leading man in more than 40 films

1909 **Art Coulter.** Hall of Fame professional hockey player

1912 **Henry Jackson.** U.S. senator from the 1960s to the early 1980s

1920 **Edward Bennett Williams.** American lawyer and defender of controversial clients

1923 **Rainier III.** Prince of Monaco and husband of actress Grace Kelly

1923 **Ellsworth Kelly.** American painter

1924 **Patricia Harris.** Secretary of Housing and Urban Development under President Carter

1930 **Clint Eastwood.** American television and motion-picture actor and director

1933 **Shirley Verrett.** American mezzo-soprano

1938 **Peter Yarrow.** American singer and guitarist with the Peter, Paul, and Mary musical group

1941 **Johnny Paycheck.** American singer best noted for popularizing David Allan Coe's hit song, "Take This Job and Shove It"

1943 **Sharon Gless.** American television actress (*Cagney and Lacy*)

1943 **Joe Namath.** Professional Hall of Fame football superstar and actor

1947 **John Bonham.** British drummer with the Led Zeppelin musical group

1950 **Tippy Martinez.** Professional baseball player

1955 **Laura Baugh.** Professional golfer and LPGA Rookie of the Year in 1975

1965 **Brooke Shields.** American motion-picture and television actress

May 31 – Events

1594 Tintoretto, the great Venetian painter of the Italian Renaissance, died in Venice at age 76.

1669 Samuel Pepys, the great English writer, ended his famous *Diary*.

1740 Frederick the Great ascended the Prussian throne.

1790 The U.S. copyright law was enacted by Congress.

1809 Franz Joseph Haydn, the great Austrian composer, died in Vienna at age 77.

1889 Johnstown, Pennsylvania, suffered a disastrous flood after heavy rains caused the Conemaugh Dam to burst. More than 2,000 people were killed in its wake.

1902 The Treaty of Vereeniging ended the Boer War, with the two defeated republics, the Orange Free State and the South African Republic (the Transvaal), becoming British colonies.

1907 A flotilla of "taximeter cabs" arrived in New York from Paris, the first taxis to be seen in any American city.

1910 The Union of South Africa was founded.

1913 Amendment 17 to the Constitution went into effect, providing for the direct election of U.S. senators.

1916 The Battle of Jutland, the greatest naval battle of World War I, began in the North Sea.

1927 The last Model T Ford was produced, to make way for Henry Ford's new Model A. Over 15 million of the *Tin Lizzies* had been built since their introduction in 1908.

1961 South Africa became an independent republic.

1962 Adolf Eichmann was hanged by Israel for World War II crimes against humanity.

1979 Rhodesia got black-majority rule and changed its name to Zimbabwe-Rhodesia, which later became Zimbabwe.

1983 Jack Dempsey, the legendary boxing great, died in New York City at age 78.

1989 Representative Jim Wright resigned his post as Speaker of the House under the cloud of ethics charges, becoming the first speaker in U.S. history to quit in mid-term.

6

June

June, our sixth month, was originally the fourth month in the ancient Roman calendar, and has always had 30 days, except for a brief time under Numa Pompilius, when it had 29. Most scholars believe that its Latin name *Junius* was chosen to honor the young men of Rome (the *juniores*). Other authorities believe that June was named for Juno, the patron goddess of marriage. Both beliefs have some credibility, since it is known that the Romans dedicated the month to the young men of Rome, and for centuries June has been known as a favorable month for marriages.

The United States celebrates Flag Day on June 14, commemorating the day in 1777 when the Stars and Stripes was adopted as the official flag. Another special June day is Father's Day, celebrated on the third Sunday. President George Bush was born in June, and June is also the birth month of Jefferson Davis, the President of the Confederacy, and Amerigo Vespucci, for whom the American continents were named.

The birthstones for June are the pearl, the moonstone and the alexandrite. Its special flowers are the rose and the honeysuckle.

June 1 – Birthdays

1503   **Wilhelm Von Grumbach.** German knight and adventurer

1637   **Jacques (Father) Marquette.** French missionary and North American explorer, who, with Louis Joliet, discovered that the Mississippi River flowed into the Gulf of Mexico

1780   **Carl von Clausewitz.** Influential Prussian military strategist and author of *On War*, one of the most important books on military matters

1793   **Henry Francis Lyte.** British clergyman and hymnalist remembered for "Abide With Me" and "Jesus, I My Cross Have Taken"

1801   **Brigham Young.** Head of the Church of Jesus Christ of Latter-day Saints, who, after succeeding Joseph Smith as head, led the Mormons to Utah and established their church in the Great Salt Lake valley

1804   **Mikhail Ivanovich Glinka.** The first important Russian composer, and the founder of a distinctly Russian type of music

1831   **John B. Hood.** Confederate general in the Civil War

1833   **John Marshall Harlan.** Noted U.S. Supreme Court justice, 1877-1911

1849   **Francis Edgar Stanley.** American automobile manufacturer who with his twin brother Freelan built the Stanley Steamer (1897)

1849   **Freelan O. Stanley.** American automobile manufacturer who with his twin brother Francis built the Stanley Steamer (1897)

1878   **John Masefield.** English writer and 16th poet laureate of England, 1930-1967

1882   **John Drinkwater.** English playwright, poet, and biographer, and author of *Abraham Lincoln* and *Robert E. Lee*

1887   **Clive Brook.** English stage and motion-picture actor with a 40-year career

1890   **Frank Morgan.** American stage and motion-picture actor in over 100 films

1905   **Robert Newton.** English motion-picture and television actor

1907   **Sir Frank Whittle.** English pioneer developer of the turbojet engine, whose Whittle engine powered the first British jet plane in 1941 and was the model for the first U.S. turbojets

1908   **Billy Werber.** Professional baseball player

1921   **Nelson Riddle.** American composer and musician

1922   **Joan Caulfield.** American stage, screen, and television actress

1926   **Richard S. Schweiker.** U.S. senator and secretary of Health and Human Services under President Reagan

1926   **Marilyn Monroe.** American actress and sex symbol of the 1950s

1926   **Andy Griffith.** American motion-picture and television actor

1930   **Edward Woodward.** English stage, screen, and television actor

1933	**Alan "The Horse" Ameche.** Hall of Fame football player and superstar
1934	**Pat Boone.** American singer, actor, and author
1937	**Red Grooms.** American artist
1937	**Morgan Freeman.** American stage, screen and television actor
1937	**Colleen McCullough.** Australian novelist noted for works such as *The Thorn Birds* (1977)
1939	**Cleavon Little.** American stage and screen actor
1940	**René Auberjonois.** American stage, screen and television actor
1947	**Ron Wood.** British rock guitarist with the Rolling Stones
1947	**Jonathan Pryce.** British stage and screen actor
1953	**David Berkowitz.** American murderer who left the message "Son of Sam" with each of his victims
1963	**Alan Wilder.** British keyboardist and songwriter with the Depeche Mode musical group

June 1 – Events

1789	President George Washington signed the first act of Congress, concerning the administration of oaths.
1792	Kentucky was admitted to the Union as the 15th state.
1796	Tennessee was admitted to the Union as the 16th state.
1812	President James Madison asked Congress to declare war on Great Britain.
1813	Captain James Lawrence was mortally wounded in a sea battle in the War of 1812, and uttered the famous words that would become the U.S. Navy's password: "Don't give up the ship!"
1868	Ex-President James Buchanan died in Lancaster, Pennsylvania, at age 77.
1916	The Battle of Jutland ended in a draw with Britain losing 14 ships and Germany 11. But British sea supremacy endured, and the German fleet was inactive for the rest of World War I.
1925	Lou Gehrig, the great New York Yankees' first baseman, began his record string of playing in 2,130 consecutive games.
1925	The comic strip *Ella Cinders,* by Bill Conselman and Charlie Plumb, first appeared.
1958	General Charles de Gaulle became premier of France.
1968	Helen Keller, the great blind and deaf writer, died at age 87.
1980	Cable News Network (CNN) made its debut as television's first all-news service.

June 2 – Birthdays

1535	**Leo XI.** Roman Catholic pope (1605)
1731	**Martha Custis Washington.** Wife of George Washington
1740	**Marquis De Sade.** French author of erotic writings, whose use of torture gave to the language the term *sadism*
1773	**John Randolph.** American statesman, whose biting tongue made him the most feared orator of his time
1788	**Solomon Willard.** American architect
1835	**Pius X.** Roman Catholic pope, 1903-1914, who was beatified in 1951 and canonized in 1954
1840	**Thomas Hardy.** English novelist and poet, known for such works as *Far from the Madding Crowd, The Return of the Native,* and *Jude the Obscure*
1845	**Arthur MacArthur.** American general and father of General Douglas MacArthur
1849	**Albert Besnard.** French painter
1852	**Charles B. Lawlor.** Irish-born composer and singer, noted for songs such as "The Sidewalks of New York"
1857	**Sir Edward Elgar.** British composer, best known for *Pomp and Circumstance,* a set of five marches
1863	**Wilbert Robinson.** Hall of Fame baseball player and manager
1875	**Charles Stewart Mott.** American automotive pioneer and early executive in the General Motors Corporation
1887	**Howard E. Johnson.** American lyricist noted for songs such as "M-O-T-H-E-R" and "When the Moon Comes Over the Mountain"
1890	**Hedda Hopper.** American gossip columnist and actress
1895	**Alex Gerber.** American composer and author, noted for songs such as "My Home Town Is a One-Horse Town"
1899	**Edwin Way Teale.** American naturalist, writer, and photographer
1904	**Johnny Weissmuller.** American swimmer and actor who played the motion-picture role of Tarzan from 1932 to 1948
1907	**Dorothy West.** American author noted for *Living It Easy* (1948)
1929	**Ken McGregor.** American tennis player
1930	**Charles Conrad Jr..** U.S. astronaut and commander of the *Apollo 12* flight to the moon in 1969
1938	**Gene Michael.** Professional baseball player and manager
1938	**Sally Kellerman.** American motion-picture actress
1940	**Constantine II.** King of Greece, 1964-1967
1940	**Jim Maloney.** Professional baseball pitcher who pitched two no-hit games in 1965
1941	**Charlie Watts.** British drummer with the Rolling Stones
1941	**Stacy Keach.** American stage and motion-picture actor
1944	**Marvin Hamlisch.** American composer and pianist, who won a record three oscars in one night—one for the score of *The Sting* and two (for the score and for the title song) for *The Way We Were*
1944	**Garo Yepremian.** Professional football player
1947	**Clarence Page.** American syndicated columnist
1950	**Lawrence McCutcheon.** Professional football player

1950   **Joanna Gleasson.** Canadian stage and motion-picture actress

1953   **Craig Stadler.** Professional golfer

1955   **Dana Carvey.** American comedian and motion-picture and TV actor (*Saturday Night Live*, 1986-1993)

1962   **Paula Newby-Fraser.** Perhaps the most successful female triathlete in history, who placed first in seven Ironman Triathlon World Championships

June 2 – Events

597   Saxon King Ethelbert was converted to Christianity and baptized by St. Augustine of Canterbury.

1420   King Henry V of England married Catherine, the daughter of King Charles VI of France.

1851   Maine passed the first prohibition law in United States history. It stayed on the books until 1934.

1875   Alexander Graham Bell discovered the secret of the telephone in an attic electrical workshop in Boston.

1886   Grover Cleveland married Frances Folsom in the White House, the first time that a U.S. president had married in the executive mansion.

1896   Guglielmo Marconi patented his wireless telegraphy in Great Britain.

1924   Congress conferred citizenship upon all American Indians.

1941   Lou Gehrig, the New York Yankees' great first baseman, died at age 37, of a rare form of paralysis now known as Lou Gehrig's disease.

1953   Queen Elizabeth II of England was crowned in Westminster Abbey in London.

1997   Timothy McVeigh was found guilty of bombing the Murrah Building in Oklahoma City, and was sentenced to death.

June 3 – Birthdays

1736   **Augustin de Saint-Aubin.** French printmaker

1771   **Sydney Smith.** English clergyman, gourmet, wit, and one of the foremost preachers of his day

1808   **Jefferson Davis.** President of the Confederate States of America during the Civil War

1819   **Johan Barthold Jongkind.** Dutch painter and etcher

1844   **Garret A. Hobart.** U.S. vice president in President McKinley's first term

1864   **Ransom Eli Olds.** American pioneer automobile inventor and manufacturer for whom the Oldsmobile and the Reo (his initials) were named

1865   **George V.** King of England, 1910-1936

1877   **Raoul Dufy.** French artist best known for his lively, decorative paintings, of which *Le Haras du Pin* is is a good example

1883   **Harold F. Orlob.** American composer and author, noted for songs such as "I Wonder Who's Kissing Her Now"

1887   **Roland Hayes.** American lyric tenor, winner of the 1924 Spingarn medal, and first black singer to appear at New York's Carnegie Hall

1891   **Mary K. Browne.** Professional golfer and tennis champion

1901   **Maurice Evans.** English stage, screen, and television actor with a career of some 50 years

1904   **Jan Peerce.** One of the most successful American opera and concert tenors of the 20th century

1906   **Josephine Baker.** American singer, motion-picture actress, and night club entertainer

1911   **Paulette Goddard.** American motion-picture actress

1913   **Ellen Corby.** American motion-picture and television actress

1915   **Leo Gorcey.** American stage and motion-picture actor who starred in the movies the *Dead End Kids* and the *Bowery Boys*

1923   **Charles Sifford.** Professional golfer

1925   **Tony Curtis.** American stage, screen, and television actor

1926   **Colleen Dewhurst.** Canadian stage and motion-picture actress

1926   **Allen Ginsberg.** American poet of the Beat generation

1931   **Raul Castro.** First Cuban vice premier and brother of Cuban revolutionary leader Fidel Castro

1931   **Bert Lance.** Budget director under President Carter

1936   **Larry Jeff McMurtry.** American author noted for works such as *Lonesome Dove* and *Terms of Endearment*

1942   **Curtis Mayfield.** American soul singer

1943   **Billy Cunningham.** Hall of Fame professional basketball player and coach

1945   **Hale Irwin.** Professional golfer

1946   **Jaime Fillol.** Chilean tennis player

1952   **Lief Johansson.** Swedish tennis player

1954   **Sue Stap.** American tennis player

June 3 – Events

1621   The Dutch West India Company received a charter for New Netherlands, now known as New York.

1864   General Lee held off General Grant with heavy losses in the Battle of Cold Harbor in the Civil War. Grant lost 6,000 men in one hour, forcing him to withdraw and change his tactics.

1871   Jesse James robbed the newly-opened Obocock Bank in Corydon, Iowa, escaping with $15,000.

1875   Georges Bizet, the noted French composer, died at Bougival, France, at age 36, exactly three months after the first performance of his great opera *Carmen*.

1888   "Casey at the Bat," the immortal baseball classic written by Ernest L. Thayer, was published for the first time, in the San Francisco *Examiner*.

1899   Johann Strauss, Jr., the "Waltz King," died in Vienna at age 73.

1924 Franz Kafka, the noted Austrian writer, died of tuberculosis in Klosterneuberg, Austria, at age 40.

1932 Lou Gehrig of the New York Yankees hit four home runs in one game against the Philadelphia Athletics.

1935 The French liner *Normandie* set a record on its maiden voyage, crossing the Atlantic in less than four days and 12 hours.

1937 The Duke of Windsor, formerly King Edward VIII of England, married Mrs. Wallis Warfield Simpson in Monts, France. He had abdicated the English throne in order to marry her.

1948 The world's largest telescope, the 200-inch Hale reflector, was dedicated at Mount Palomar Observatory, California.

1963 Pope John XXIII died in Rome at age 81.

1965 Astronaut Edward White spent 21 minutes outside his spacecraft, *Gemini 4,* becoming the first American to walk in space.

1989 Chinese soldiers stormed Tiananmen Square in Beijing and crushed a three-week student sit-in for democracy, firing machine guns and killing 500 to 2,000 people.

June 4 – Birthdays

1738 **George III.** King of England, 1760-1820, who reigned during the American Revolutionary War.

1862 **Bob Fitzsimmons.** World middleweight champion, 1891-1897, heavyweight champion, 1897-1899, and light-heavyweight champion, 1903-1905

1867 **Carl Gustav Mannerheim.** Finnish World War II general, and one of the founders of the Republic of Finland in 1919

1880 **Clara Blandick.** American motion-picture actress who played Judy Garland's aunt in *The Wizard of Oz*

1881 **Nathalie Gontcharova.** Russian painter

1891 **Erno Rapee.** Hungarian-born composer and conductor, noted for songs such as "Charmaine" and "Rockettes on Parade"

1903 **Luther Adler.** American stage and screen actor

1904 **Alvah Bessie.** American novelist and screenwriter noted for works such as *One for My Baby*

1908 **Rosalind Russell.** American stage and motion-picture actress

1916 **Gaylord Nelson.** U.S. senator in the 1960s and 1970s

1917 **Howard Metzenbaum.** U.S. senator

1917 **Charles Collingwood.** American television news reporter

1919 **Robert Merrill.** Noted American baritone

1920 **Russell Errol Train.** Noted American conservationist

1922 **Samuel Lea Gravely Jr.** First black admiral in the history of the U.S. Navy

1924 **Dennis Weaver.** American motion-picture and television actor, who played Chester in the long-running series *Gunsmoke*

1936 **Bruce Dern.** American motion-picture and television actor

1937 **Freddy Fender.** American country music singer

1937 **Robert Fulghum.** American author noted for *All I Really Need to Know I Learned in Kindergarten* (1989)

1943 **Sandra Haynie.** Hall of Fame professional golfer

1946 **Bettina Gregory.** American broadcast journalist

1948 **Sandra Post.** Professional golfer

1952 **Parker Stevenson.** American motion-picture and television actor

1953 **Mike Barber.** Professional football player

1956 **Terry Kennedy.** Professional baseball player

1957 **Tony Pena.** Professional baseball player

1965 **Andrea Jaeger.** American tennis player

June 4 – Events

1070 The process of making Roquefort cheese was discovered by an anonymous shepherd in a cave near Roquefort, France.

1260 Kublai Khan, the grandson of Genghis Khan, became the leader of the Mongol dynasty that ruled China for a century.

1543 The second of the New Laws of Spain was passed to prevent the establishment of a Spanish-American nobility in America.

1658 English and French troops defeated a Spanish relief force in the Battle of the Dunes, resulting in the surrender of Dunkerque to the English after a long siege.

1798 Giovanni Jacopo Casanova, the greatest of romantic lovers, died in Bohemia at age 73.

1800 The White House, though as yet unfinished, was declared ready for occupancy by President and Mrs. John Adams.

1893 The Anti-Saloon League of America was organized in Ohio.

1896 Henry Ford drove the first Ford car out of a brick shed at 58 Bagley Avenue, Detroit, and conducted a trial run around the city.

1940 The evacuation of Dunkerque was completed, with 336,000 Allied soldiers rescued by the British Navy in World War II.

1942 The Battle of Midway, one of the most decisive naval battles in history, began between the United States and Japan in World War II.

1944 The Allies captured Rome, which became the first Axis capital to fall in World War II.

1970 Sonny Tufts, the American motion-picture actor, died at age 58.

June 5 – Birthdays

1718 **Thomas Chippendale.** The most famous English cabinetmaker of his time

1723 **Adam Smith.** Scottish social philosopher, author of *The Wealth of Nations* (1776), and the founder of modern economics

1771 **Asher Benjamin.** American architect

1819 **John Couch Adams.** Co-predictor with Urbain J.J. Leverrier of the position of the planet Neptune (1845)

1850 **Pat Garrett.** American lawman noted for killing the notorious outlaw Billy the Kid (1881)

1874 **Jack Chesbro.** Hall of Fame baseball pitcher who won 41 games in 1904

1877 **John Henry Breck.** American businessman who founded Breck, Inc. (1929)

1877 **Pancho Villa.** Mexican revolutionary and bandit chieftain, who sought unsuccessfully to control Mexico after the fall of President Profirio Diaz in 1910

1883 **John Maynard Keynes.** Father of Keynesian economics and one of the most important economists of all time

1897 **Madame Chiang Kai-shek.** Wife of Chinese premier Chiang Kai-shek, the leader of mainland China from 1926 to 1949

1898 **William Boyd.** American actor, producer, and title role star of 54 Hopalong Cassidy episodes

1898 **Frederico Garcia Lorca.** One of the greatest Spanish poets, who with Miguel de Cervantes is the most widely translated Spanish author

1900 **Dennis Gabor.** Hungarian electrical engineer who invented the hologram (a three-dimensional photographic image)

1901 **Anastasia Romanov.** Daughter of Czar Nicholas II thought to have survived the execution of the Romanov family, which was never proven (DNA testing in the 1990s indicated that she had not)

1911 **George Vaughn Horton.** American composer, author, and arranger, noted for songs such as "Mockin' Bird Hill" and "Choo Choo Ch' Boogie"

1915 **Alfred Kazin.** Russian-born writer, critic, and educator

1921 **Cornelius Ryan.** Irish-born American author

1929 **Robert Lansing.** American motion-picture and television actor

1934 **Bill Moyers.** American broadcast journalist

1939 **Charles Joseph "Joe" Clark.** Youngest prime minister in Canada's history (1979-1980)

1942 **Nelson Burton Jr.** Hall of Fame professional bowler

1949 **Ken Follett.** Welsh author noted for works such as *On Wings of Eagles* (1983)

1954 **Ernie Ewart.** Australian tennis player

June 5 – Events

1294 Saint Celestine V was elected Roman Catholic pope. He was unhappy, however, with the office, and abdicated before the year was out.

1783 The brothers Jacques and Joseph Montgolfier sent up the first balloon, a large smoke-filled cloth bag, at Annonay, France.

1884 General William T. Sherman refused the Republican nomination for president, saying, "I will not accept if nominated and will not serve if elected."

1917 More than nine million American men, between the ages of 21 and 30, registered for the draft under the Selective Military Conscription Act.

1933 President Franklin D. Roosevelt signed the bill taking the United States off the gold standard.

1940 The Germans began the Battle of France in World War II.

1947 The Marshall Plan for saving Western Europe's economy was described by Secretary of State George C. Marshall at the commencement exercises at Harvard University.

1967 The Six-Day War began as Israeli planes launched a lightning attack on airfields in Egypt, Jordan, and Syria, almost completely destroying the Arab air forces.

1968 Senator Robert F. Kennedy was shot in Los Angeles after a campaign speech. He died the following day.

1975 Egypt reopened the Suez Canal to shipping exactly eight years after it was closed during the Six-Day War.

1993 Julie Krone became the first woman jockey to ride a winner in a Triple Crown race with Colonel Affair in the 125th Belmont Stakes.

June 6 – Birthdays

1436 **Regiomontanus (Johann Muller).** German astronomer responsible in the 1490s for the revival of trigonometry in Europe

1599 **Diego Velazquez.** The major Spanish painter of the 17th century

1606 **Pierre Corneille.** Father of French classical tragedy and the founder of French heroic comedy

1625 **Domenico Guidi.** Italian sculptor

1714 **Joseph I.** A minor king of Portugal in the 18th century

1755 **Nathan Hale.** American Revolutionary War officer who immortalized the words, "I only regret that I have but one life to give for my country," before being hanged by the British as a spy

1756 **John Trumbull.** American painter, best known for his small, dramatic paintings of Revolutionary War scenes

1799 **Alexander Pushkin.** Russia's most celebrated poet, novelist, and dramatist, noted for such works as the poem "Eugene Onegin" and the play *Boris Godunov*

1804 **Louis Antoine Godey.** Founder in 1830 of *Godey's Lady's Book,* the first woman's magazine in the United States

1850 **Karl Ferdinand Braun.** German physicist who invented the oscillograph in 1897

1872 **Alexandra.** Empress of Russia and wife of Russian czar Nicholas II, the last of the Russian czars

1875   **Thomas Mann.** German-American novelist and 1929 Nobel Prize winner, noted for such works as *Buddenbrooks* (1901) and *The Magic Mountain* (1924)

1886   **Paul Dudley White.** Heart specialist and personal physician of President Dwight D. Eisenhower

1894   **Harry Greb.** American Hall of Fame boxer and the only fighter to defeat Gene Tunney (1922)

1898   **Walter Abel.** American stage and motion-picture actor

1901   **Sukarno.** First president of Indonesia and leader of the Indonesian independence movement

1902   **Jimmy Lunceford.** American jazz musician and bandleader of the Big Band Era

1903   **Aram Khachaturian.** Russian composer, noted for the ballet *Gayne,* which includes the famous "Sabre Dance"

1907   **Bill Dickey.** Hall of Fame baseball player and manager, and one of the two or three greatest catchers in the history of baseball

1909   **Sir Isaiah Berlin.** Noted English political scientist and writer, noted for works such as *Karl Marx* and *The Hedgehog and the Fox*

1917   **Kirk Kerkorian.** American corporation executive and chairman of Metro Goldwyn Mayer

1926   **T.K. (Tom) Ryan.** American cartoonist and creator of *Tumbleweeds*

1932   **Billie Whitelaw.** British stage, screen, and television actress

1932   **David R. Scott.** U.S. astronaut who with astronaut James B. Irwin drove the moon car Rover on the surface of the moon on the *Apollo 15* mission

1934   **Roy Innis.** American civil rights leader and national director of CORE

1939   **Gary U.S. Bonds.** American singer and songwriter

1955   **Sandra Bernhard.** American motion-picture and television actress and comedienne

1956   **Bjorn Borg.** Swedish tennis player, winner of five straight Wimbledon singles titles, and one of the greatest players in history

1959   **Amanda Pays.** British motion-picture and television actress

June 6 – Events

1660   The Peace of Copenhagen ended the Danish-Swedish War, resulting in Sweden's taking all the Danish territory in what is now Sweden.

1844   The Young Men's Christian Association (YMCA) was founded in London by George Williams.

1918   The World War I Battle of Belleau Wood began. It would end in victory for the U.S. Marines over the Germans 19 days later.

1925   The Chrysler Corporation was created by Walter Chrysler, by a reorganization of the Maxwell Motor Company.

1933   The first motion-picture drive-in theater opened, in Camden, New Jersey.

1934   The Securities and Exchange Commission was established.

1941   Louis Chevrolet, organizer of the Chevrolet Motor Company in 1911, died at age 63.

1942   The Battle of Midway ended in disaster for Japan. It also ended Japanese threats to Hawaii and the United States.

1944   The largest air, sea, and land operation in history was carried out on D Day, as the Americans and British invaded the beaches of Normandy in France in World War II.

1956   Elvis Presley, the rock singer, appeared on television for the first time, on the *Ed Sullivan Show.*

1968   Senator Robert F. Kennedy died in Los Angeles from a gunshot wound inflicted by the assassin Sirhan Sirhan the previous day.

1974   The White House admitted that President Nixon was named an unindicted co-conspirator in the Watergate case by the grand jury.

1978   California voters approved Proposition 13, cutting property taxes 57%.

June 7 – Birthdays

1502   **Gregory XIII.** Roman Catholic pope, 1572-1585, who in 1582 established the Gregorian calendar, which is still in use today

1778   **Beau Brummell.** English dandy and fashion leader in the early 1800s

1825   **Richard Doddridge Blackmore.** English author noted for *Lorna Doone* (1869)

1848   **Paul Gauguin.** French painter noted for his colorful and decorative style, and for his paintings of the South Sea Island people

1868   **Charles Rennie Mackintosh.** Scottish architect

1879   **Knud Rasmussen.** Danish Arctic explorer and writer, who in 1910 founded the trading station of Thule in Greenland

1894   **Alexander De Seversky.** Russian-American pilot, aircraft designer, and military authority, who founded the Seversky Aero Corporation in 1922

1896   **Imre Nagy.** Premier of Hungary at the time of the 1956 Hungarian revolt against the Russians

1908   **Lew Quadling.** American composer and author, noted for songs such as "Sam's Song"

1909   **Peter Rodino.** U.S. congressman and chairman of the committee investigating charges against President Nixon in the Watergate affair in 1973-1974

1909   **Jessica Tandy.** English stage and motion-picture actress

1917   **Gwendolyn Brooks.** American poet who won the 1950 Pulitzer Prize for *Annie Allen,* her second collection of poems

1917   **Dean Martin.** American motion-picture and television singer and actor

1922   **Rocky Graziano.** World middleweight champion, 1947-1948

1928 **James Ivory.** American motion-picture director who with producer Ismail Merchant created films such as *Howard's End* (1992)
1933 **Herb Score.** Professional baseball player
1934 **Philippe Entremont.** French pianist and conductor
1940 **Tom Jones.** Welch-American singer whose earliest hit was "The Green, Green Grass of Home"
1944 **Cazzie Russell.** Professional basketball player
1946 **Bill Kreutzmann.** American musician with The Grateful Dead
1947 **Thurman Munson.** Professional baseball player
1947 **Don Money.** Professional baseball player
1947 **David Lundstrom.** Professional golfer
1959 **Prince.** American rock and roll soul singer
1977 **Kerry Wood.** Professional baseball pitcher who in his rookie season struck out a record-tying 20 men (5-6-1998) in defeating the Houston Astros 2-0
1981 **Anna Kournikova.** Russian tennis player

June 7 – Events

1576 Martin Frobisher, the English navigator, left England on his first trip to seek a Northwest Passage to India. He never succeeded, but he discovered Frobisher Bay on Baffin Island.
1628 King Charles I of England formally accepted the Petition of Right from Parliament. He continued his autocratic rule, however, until it led to his execution in 1649.
1769 Daniel Boone first set eyes on Kentucky. The date is now celebrated as Boone Day by the Kentucky State Historical Society.
1776 Richard Henry Lee of Virginia introduced in the Continental Congress the resolution calling for the declaration of independence from England.
1832 The Reform Act of 1832 was passed by the British Parliament, giving most men of the middle class the right to vote.
1864 Abraham Lincoln was renominated for president at his party's convention in Baltimore.
1909 Mary Pickford, the great American movie star, made her debut in the film, *The Violin Maker of Cremona.*
1917 The International Association of Lions Clubs was founded in Chicago.
1937 Jean Harlow, the famous American motion-picture actress, died of cerebral edema at age 26.
1940 After 62 days of bitter fighting, the Germans finally drove the Allies out and completed their occupation of Norway in World War II.
1948 President Eduard Benes of Czechoslovakia resigned rather than sign a new Communist-dictated constitution for his country.
1981 Israeli planes destroyed a nuclear power plant in Iraq.

June 8 – Birthdays

1687 **Giuseppe Antonio Guarneri.** Famous Italian violinmaker whose uncle Andrea Guarneri studied with Stradivari in the workshop of Amati
1772 **Robert Stevenson.** Scottish engineer and noted lighthouse builder, who invented the flashing light used in lighthouses
1810 **Robert Schumann.** Noted German composer and pianist who ranks with Franz Liszt and Frederic Chopin in developing the techniques of romantic piano music
1814 **Charles Reade.** English novelist and author of *The Cloister and the Hearth* (1861), considered by some to be the greatest historical novel in English
1829 **Sir John Everett Millais.** English painter and a founder of the Pre-Raphaelite Brotherhood in 1848
1847 **Ida Saxton McKinley.** Wife of President William McKinley
1867 **Frank Lloyd Wright.** One of America's greatest and most influential architects, noted for his Prairie Style of buildings and for such projects as New York's Guggenheim Museum
1876 **Richard H. Gerard.** American composer noted for songs such as "Sweet Adeline"
1903 **Ralph Yarborough.** U.S. senator in the 1960s
1911 **Van Lingle Mungo.** Professional baseball player
1916 **Francis H.C. Crick.** Nobel Prize-winning British biologist who helped build the Watson-Crick model of the molecular structure of DNA, the substance that transmits genetic information
1917 **Byron R. "Whizzer" White.** American football player and U.S. Supreme Court justice
1918 **Robert Preston.** American motion-picture and stage actor
1921 **Suharto.** Second president of Indonesia, after Sukarno
1921 **Alexis Smith.** Canadian-born motion-picture actress
1923 **Malcolm Boyd.** American priest, author and Freedom Rider
1924 **Lyn Nofziger.** Republican Party strategist
1925 **Barbara Pierce Bush.** Wife of President George Bush
1925 **Del Ennis.** Professional baseball player
1927 **LeRoy Neiman.** Highly popular American artist
1930 **Dana Wynter.** English motion-picture and television actress
1933 **Joan Rivers.** American comedienne
1936 **James Darren.** American motion-picture and television actor
1939 **Herb Adderley.** Professional football player and Hall of Famer
1940 **Nancy Sinatra.** American singer and actress and daughter of singer Frank Sinatra
1943 **Willie Davenport.** American Olympic champion hurdler
1944 **Mark Belanger.** Professional baseball player

1950	**Kathy Baker.** American stage and motion-picture actress
1952	**Dave Jennings.** Professional football player
1955	**Griffin Dunne.** American motion-picture actor and son of producer Dominick Dunne
1955	**Tim Berners-Lee.** English computer scientist who in 1990 created the World Wide Web, which in 1991 became a part of the Advanced Research Projects Agency, or ARPAnet, or Internet, and was the instrument for making the Internet easier to use and thus more popular
1962	**Nick Rhodes.** Keyboardist with the Duran Duran musical group
1966	**Sandy Alomar Jr.** Professional baseball player and son of baseball player Sandy Alomar

June 8 – Events

632	The prophet Mohammed, the founder of the Islamic religion, died in Medina at age 63.
1191	Richard the Lion-Hearted of England arrived at the port of Acre in the Holy Land during the third Crusade. He captured Acre, but could not recapture Jerusalem from the Turks.
1504	Michelangelo's statue of David was set in place in the Palazzo in Florence.
1809	Thomas Paine, the great American Revolutionary patriot, died in New Rochelle, New York, at age 72.
1830	The USS *Vincennes* returned to New York, becoming the first warship to circumnavigate the globe.
1845	Andrew Jackson died at the Hermitage at age 78.
1861	Tennessee became the last state to secede from the Union.
1869	Ives W. McGaffey of Chicago patented the vacuum cleaner, described by him as a "sweeping machine."
1915	Secretary of State William Jennings Bryan resigned, protesting the firm notes of President Wilson to the Germans in connection with the sinking of the *Lusitania*.
1953	The Supreme Court ruled that restaurants in the District of Columbia could not refuse to serve blacks.
1965	The Russian moon shot *Luna 6* was launched.
1966	The merger of the National and American football leagues was announced, to take effect in 1970. The new league would be the National Football League with American and National Football Conferences.
1967	The Israelis occupied the Gaza Strip, the Sinai Peninsula, and Jordanian territory west of the River Jordan in the Six-Day War.

June 9 – Birthdays

1595	**Wladyslaw IV Vasa.** Swedish nobleman of the House of Vasa, chosen by the ruling Polish *szlachta* to be king of Poland, 1632-1648

1597	**Pieter Jansz Saenredam.** Dutch pioneer of the "church portrait"
1672	**Peter the Great.** Czar of Russia, 1682-1725, who founded the city of St. Petersburg and started Russia on the path of modernization
1768	**Samuel Slater.** Founder of the U.S. cotton textile industry, who began operating the first successful cotton mill in America on December 11, 1790, in Pawtucket, RI.
1781	**George Stephenson.** English inventor known as the "Founder of Railways" and "engine Doctor" because of the many locomotives and railroads he built
1785	**Sylvanus Thayer.** American army officer known as the father of West Point because of his long service as superintendent of the United States Military Academy
1791	**John Howard Payne.** American playwright, actor, and diplomat, who wrote the lyrics for the famous song, "Home, Sweet Home"
1865	**Carl August Nielsen.** Danish composer best known for six symphonies and the comic opera *Maskarade* (1906)
1891	**Cole Porter.** American composer of popular music, noted for such songs as "Begin the Beguine," "Night and Day," "Wunderbar," and "I've Got You Under My Skin"
1893	**Irish Meusel.** Professional baseball player and brother of baseball player Bob Meusel
1900	**Fred Waring.** American bandleader of the big band era of the 1930s and 1940s
1911	**Frank McCormick.** Professional baseball player
1912	**Buddy Feyne.** American composer noted for songs such as "Tuxedo Junction," "Jersey Bounce," and "The Shadow Knows"
1916	**Robert S. McNamara.** U.S. secretary of defense, 1961-1968, and president of the World Bank
1922	**George Axelrod.** American novelist and playwright, noted for works such as *The Seven-Year Itch*
1923	**Les Paul.** American singer and electric guitar and recording pioneer
1926	**Mona Freeman.** American motion-picture and television actress
1930	**Marvin Kalb.** American broadcast journalist
1931	**Bill Virdon.** Professional baseball player and manager
1934	**Jackie Mason.** American comedian and actor
1938	**Barry Phillips-Moore.** Australian tennis player
1951	**Dave Parker.** Professional baseball player
1961	**Michael J. Fox.** Canadian-born motion picture and television actor
1964	**Wayman Tisdale.** Professional basketball player

June 9 – Events

68	Roman emperor Nero committed suicide at age 31 after being sentenced to death by the Senate.

1156	Frederick Barbarossa, King of Germany and Holy Roman Emperor, married Beatrix of Upper Burgundy.
1534	Jacques Cartier, the French explorer, sailed into the St. Lawrence River, so named by him because he discovered it on St. Lawrence's feast day.
1815	The Vienna Settlement, under the leadership of Austria's Prince Metternich, reshaped Europe after the final defeat of Napoleon.
1870	Charles Dickens, the great English novelist, died of a stroke at Gadshill, Kent, at age 58.
1899	Jim Jeffries knocked out Bob Fitzsimmons at Coney Island, New York, to win the heavyweight boxing championship.
1940	Norway surrendered to the Nazis in World War II.
1943	Congress passed the "Pay-As-You-Go" income tax deduction law, authorizing employers to withhold income taxes.
1954	Attorney Joseph Welch, in the Army-McCarthy hearings, helped end Senator Joseph McCarthy's career, by asking him, "Have you no sense of decency, sir? At long last, have you left no sense of decency?"
1959	The *George Washington,* the first ballistic-missile submarine, was launched by the United States.
1960	Bing Crosby was awarded the first ever platinum disc for selling two hundred million records.
1973	Secretariat won the Belmont Stakes in New York to become horse racing's first Triple Crown winner since Citation in 1948.
1978	One of the 21 known complete copies of the Gutenberg Bible was sold in London for 2.4 million dollars, a record price for a printed book.

June 10 – Birthdays

1741	**Joseph Warren.** American patriot who sent Paul Revere on his famous ride to alert the countryside that the British were coming
1819	**Gustave Courbet.** French painter famous for his efforts to develop realism in French painting in the 1800s
1832	**Nikolaus August Otto.** German engineer who, with Eugen Langen, built the world's first four-stroke internal combustion engine
1854	**François Curel.** French dramatist and novelist
1875	**James MacDermid.** American composer and organist, noted for songs such as "My Love Is Like the Red Red Rose"
1880	**André Derain.** French artist, and one of the leaders of the *fauves,* a noted group of painters of the early 1900s
1887	**Harry Flood Byrd.** Powerful United States senator from Virginia, 1933-1965
1889	**Sessue Hayakawa.** Japanese motion-picture actor noted for his role in *The Bridge Over the River Kwai*
1895	**Hattie McDaniel.** American motion-picture actress and Academy Award winner in 1939 for best supporting actress in *Gone With the Wind*
1904	**Frederick Loewe.** Austrian-American composer, who, with lyricist Alan Jay Lerner, wrote the hits for such Broadway musicals as *My Fair Lady, Camelot, Gigi,* and *Paint Your Wagon*
1908	**Robert "Bob" Cummings.** American motion-picture and television actor
1910	**Howlin' Wolf (Chester Burnett).** American blues guitarist
1911	**Sir Terrance Mervyn Rattigan.** English playwright noted for *Separate Tables* (1954)
1913	**Wilbur Cohen.** American educator who helped draft the Social Security Act and who held the first Social Security card
1915	**Saul Bellow.** Canadian-American novelist noted for works such as *Dangling Man, The Victim, Humboldt's Gift,* and *Mr. Sammler's Planet*
1921	**Prince Philip, Duke of Edinburgh.** Duke of Edinburgh and husband of Queen Elizabeth II of England
1922	**Judy Garland.** American singer, actress, and superstar
1925	**Nat Hentoff.** American newspaper columnist
1926	**June Haver.** American stage, screen, and television actress
1928	**Maurice Sendak.** American illustrator and writer of children's books, the best known of which is *Where the Wild Things Are*
1929	**James A. McDivitt.** U.S. astronaut on the flight of *Gemini 4* in 1965
1933	**F. Lee Bailey.** Noted American trial lawyer
1943	**Jeff Greenfield.** American broadcast commentator and newspaper columnist
1943	**Jon McGlocklin.** Professional basketball player
1947	**Ken Singleton.** Professional baseball player
1950	**John Gianelli.** Professional basketball player
1951	**Danny Fouts.** Professional football player and Hall of Famer
1951	**Jackie Fayter.** English tennis player
1953	**Dean Joubert.** South African tennis player
1955	**Floyd Bannister.** Professional baseball player
1963	**Elizabeth Shue.** American motion-picture and television actress
1967	**Nicole Kidman.** American motion-picture actress
1982	**Tara Lipinski.** Youngest world champion (in 1997) in the history of women's figure skating

June 10 – Events

1190	Holy Roman Emperor Frederick Barbarossa drowned at age 67 while crossing the River Calycadnus in Citica during the Third Crusade.
1610	The first Dutch settlers arrived on Manhattan Island.
1692	Bridget Bishop became the first of the Salem, Massachusetts, "witches" to be hanged.

1801 Tripoli declared war on the United States to force the payment of more tribute money for the protection of American shipping.

1847 The *Chicago Tribune* began publication.

1865 The world premiere of Richard Wagner's *Tristan und Isolde* took place in Munich.

1935 Alcoholics Anonymous was founded by Bill Wilson, a stockbroker, and Bob Smith, a physician.

1940 With the French on the verge of collapse in World War II, Italian premier Mussolini declared war and invaded France from the south. (He was afraid the war would be over before he could get in, but Winston Churchill assured him that he would have plenty of war.)

1942 In retaliation for the assassination of Nazi "Hangman" Reinhard Heydrich, the Germans burned the Czech town of Lidice, shot its 173 males, and imprisoned its women and children.

1959 Rocky Colavito of the Cleveland Indians hit four home runs in one game.

1967 The Israelis captured Syria's Golan Heights in the Six-Day War.

1983 The Northern and Southern branches of the Presbyterian Church reunited after being separated since the Civil War began in 1861.

June 11 – Birthdays

1555 **Ludovico Zacconi.** Italian Renaissance writer on music

1572 **Ben Jonson.** English dramatist and poet of the Elizabethan era, noted for such works as *The Alchemist* and the famous song "Drink to Me Only With Thine Eyes"

1758 **Kamehameha I.** King and founder of the Kingdom of Hawaii

1769 **Anne Newport Royall.** America's first female crusading journalist

1776 **John Constable.** One of the greatest English landscape artists

1815 **Julia Margaret Cameron.** One of the greatest portrait photographers of the 19th century

1838 **Mariano Fortuny y Carbo.** Spanish painter

1864 **Richard Strauss.** German composer and conductor, noted for such works as *Der Rosenkavalier* (1910) and *Capriccio* (1941)

1867 **Charles Fabry.** French physicist who discovered the earth's ozone layer

1867 **Edward Bradford Fitchener.** Co-founder of experimental psychology in the United States

1879 **Roger Bresnahan.** Hall of Fame baseball player

1880 **Jeannette Rankin.** First woman to be elected to the U.S. Congress, and the only member of the House to vote against America's entering World War II (She also opposed entering World War I.)

1883 **Frank King.** American comic strip cartoonist and creator of *Gasoline Alley*

1895 **Nikolai Bulganin.** Russian premier, 1955-1958

1895 **Jacques Brugnon.** French Hall of Fame tennis player, who with Rene Lacoste, Jean Borotra, and Henri Cochet, formed the Four Musketeers and dominated French tennis in the 1920s and 30s

1900 **Lawrence Spivak.** Longtime moderator of the radio and television program *Meet the Press*

1905 **Richard A. Loeb.** American who with Nathan Leopold killed young Bobby Franks for thrills in "The Crime of the Century" (1924)

1910 **Jacques-Yves Cousteau.** Noted French undersea explorer and writer

1912 **James Algar.** Director and screenwriter with Walt Disney Productions

1913 **Rise Stevens.** American operatic soprano

1913 **Vince Lombardi.** Noted professional football coach, who led the Green Bay Packers to five National Football League titles

1919 **Richard Todd.** Irish stage and motion-picture actor

1925 **William Styron.** American novelist and 1968 Pulitzer Prize winner for *The Confessions of Nat Turner*

1929 **Frank Thomas.** Professional baseball player

1930 **Charles Rangel.** U.S. representative

1935 **Gene Wilder.** American actor, scriptwriter, and director

1936 **Chad Everett.** American motion-picture and television actor

1939 **Jackie Stewart.** Most successful Grand Prix driver in history, with a record total of 27 career wins

1945 **Adrienne Barbeau.** American stage, screen and television actress

1954 **Gary Fencik.** Professional football player

1956 **Joe Montana.** Professional football player and superstar

June 11 – Events

1509 King Henry VIII of England married Catherine of Aragon, the first of his six wives.

1580 Buenos Aires was founded by Spanish conquistador Juan de Garay.

1770 Captain James Cook discovered the Great Barrier Reef off Australia.

1776 The Continental Congress appointed a committee to draft a declaration of independence, consisting of John Adams, Benjamin Franklin, Thomas Jefferson, Robert Livingston, and Roger Sherman. Jefferson was given the task of preparing the draft.

1861 A convention met in Wheeling to protest Virginia's seceding from the Union and to form the new state of West Virginia. Its final name, however, was not chosen until 1862.

1895 The Duryea brothers Charles and Frank were granted a patent on the first successful gasoline-powered automobile in the United States.

1919 Sir Barton won the Belmont States, becoming horse racing's first Triple Crown winner.

1927 President Coolidge presented the first Distinguished Flying Cross to Charles A. Lindbergh.

1934	The comic strip *Mandrake the Magician,* by Lee Falk and Phil Davis, first appeared.
1938	Johnny Vander Meer pitched the first of two consecutive no-hitters, as Cincinnati beat Boston, 3-0.
1940	The French cabinet withdrew to Tours as German troops neared Paris in World War II.
1950	Ben Hogan won the U.S. Open golf championship in a miraculous comeback after suffering near-fatal injuries in an earlier car accident.
1977	Seattle Slew won the Belmont Stakes, becoming the first horse to win the triple crown since Citation in 1948.
1989	Michael Chang defeated Stefan Edberg in five sets to become at 17 the youngest man ever to win the French Open tennis title and the first American to do so since 1955.

June 12 – Birthdays

1512	**Paulus Manutius.** Founder of the Aldine press in Venice
1720	**Isaac Pinto.** Translator of the first Jewish prayer-book published in America
1733	**Alessandro Longhi.** Italian painter
1806	**John Augustus Roebling.** American civil engineer who designed the Brooklyn Bridge
1819	**Charles Kingsley.** English novelist, clergyman, and author of *Westward Ho!* (1855)
1827	**Johanna Spyri.** Swiss author of children's stories, best known for *Heidi* (1881)
1851	**Sir Oliver Joseph Lodge.** English physicist whose electric wave research helped in developing the radio
1851	**Pol Plancon.** French bass
1874	**Charles McNary.** U.S. senator and vice presidential candidate with Wendell Willkie in 1940
1876	**Thomas Clark Hinkle.** American author of children's books
1897	**Anthony Eden.** Prime minister of Great Britain, 1955-1957
1899	**Anni Albers.** American textile designer
1912	**Russell Hayden.** American Western movie actor and television director
1912	**Dick Manning.** Russian-born composer and author, noted for songs such as "Takes Two to Tango," "Allegheny Moon," and "Papa Loves Mambo"
1915	**David Rockefeller.** Chairman of the board of Chase Manhattan Bank
1919	**Uta Hagen.** American stage and screen actress and teacher
1924	**George Herbert Walker Bush.** U.S. 41st President and vice president under President Reagan
1928	**Richard Morton Sherman.** American composer noted for the score of *Mary Poppins*
1928	**Vic Damone.** American singer and actor
1929	**Anne Frank.** German-Jewish girl who wrote a vivid diary while hiding from the Nazis during World War II

1933	**Jim Nabors.** American singer and actor
1935	**Nicole Berger.** French motion-picture actress
1960	**Mark Calcavecchia.** Professional golfer
1967	**Sherry Springfield.** American stage and television actress
1971	**Kristi Yamaguchi.** American figure skater and Olympic gold medalist

June 12 – Events

1381	Wat Tyler's Rebellion occurred as Wat Tyler led a march on London to protest forced labor, heavy taxation, and serfdom. King Richard III, 14 years old at the time, agreed to the demands.
1458	The College of St. Mary Magdalen was founded at Oxford, England.
1775	The American sloop *Unity* captured the British schooner *Margaretta* in the first naval battle of the Revolutionary War.
1776	George Mason drafted the Virginia Bill of Rights, as part of the new Virginia constitution.
1839	Abner Doubleday, an American army officer, allegedly invented the game of baseball at Cooperstown, N.Y. (Others give the credit to Alexander Joy Cartwright, who established the early rules.)
1864	Emperor Maximilian arrived in Mexico City from France to take over the Mexican government.
1878	William Cullen Bryant, America's first important poet, died in New York at age 83.
1880	John Richmond pitched the first perfect game (not a runner reached base) in major league history, as Worcester beat Cleveland, 1-0.
1917	The Secret Service extended its protection of the president to his family as well.
1930	Max Schmeling won the heavyweight championship, defeating Jack Sharkey in four rounds in New York.
1939	The Baseball Hall of Fame was established at Cooperstown, New York, with the enshrinement of 26 players chosen in three previous elections.
1964	Black African dissident Nelson Mandela was sentenced to life imprisonment for conspiring to overthrow the South African government.
1979	Bryan Allen, a 26-year-old cyclist, flew a man-powered aircraft, the *Gossamer Albatross,* across the English Channel.
1981	Major league baseball players went on strike for the first time in history during a regular season.
1994	Nicole Brown Simpson, ex-wife of football legend O.J. Simpson, and a friend, Ronald Goldman, were stabbed to death at her condo in Los Angeles. Simpson was charged with the murders but acquitted.

June 13 – Birthdays

37	**Gnaeus Julius Agricola.** Roman general noted for conquering all of England and part of Scotland from A.D. 77 to 84

823 **Charles I (the Bald).** Grandson of Charlemagne who with his two half brothers divided Charlemagne's empire into three parts, with Charles becoming the first king of France, A.D. 843-877

1692 **Joseph Highmore.** English portrait painter

1752 **Fanny Burney.** English novelist and diarist noted for *Evelina, or the History of a Young Girl's Entry into the World* (1778), where she coined the phrase "I'd do it as soon as say Jack Robinson"

1786 **Winfield Scott.** American general and hero of the Mexican War, officer in the War of 1812 and briefly in the Civil War, and presidential candidate in 1852

1854 **Sir Charles Algernon Parsons.** English engineer and inventor of the first marine steam turbine

1865 **William Butler Yeats.** Irish poet and dramatist thought by some to be the greatest poet of his time

1879 **Robert Elkington Wood.** American businessman who from 1928 to 1954 made Sears Roebuck and Company into the world's largest merchandising firm

1880 **Vincent Rose.** Italian-born composer, conductor, and pianist, noted for songs such as "Avalon," "Whispering," "Linger Awhile," and "Blueberry Hill"

1884 **Burrill Bernard Crohn.** American physician known for his research on Crohn's disease

1892 **Basil Rathbone.** British stage and motion-picture actor with a 50 year career

1892 **Richard M. Jones.** American composer, author, and conductor, noted for songs such as "Trouble in Mind" and "Red Wagon"

1894 **Watson Washburn.** American Hall of Fame tennis player

1894 **Mark Van Doren.** American poet, writer, and teacher, who won the Pulitzer Prize in 1940 for his *Collected Poems*

1897 **Paavo Nurmi.** Finnish track star who dominated long-distance running in the 1920s

1899 **Carlos Chavez.** Mexican composer and conductor, noted for such works as *Sinfonia India* (1936)

1903 **Red Grange.** The "Galloping Ghost" of football, and one of the greatest football players of all time

1908 **Marie Vieira da Silva.** Portuguese painter

1911 **Luis Alvarez.** American nuclear physicist who won the 1968 Nobel Prize for contributions to the knowledge of subatomic particles

1913 **Ralph Edwards.** Host of the television show *This Is Your Life*

1915 **Don Budge.** American Hall of Fame tennis player, and the first man in history to win the Grand Slam (1938)

1920 **Ben Johnson.** American motion-picture actor

1922 **Mel Parnell.** Professional baseball player

1926 **Paul Lynde.** American motion-picture and television actor and comedian

1931 **Jay Macpherson.** Canadian lyric poet

1935 **Christo (Javacheff).** Bulgarian artist

1936 **Larry Adams.** American jockey

1947 **Zeljko Franulovic.** Yugoslavian tennis player

1948 **Brian Fairlie.** New Zealand tennis player

1951 **Richard Thomas.** American stage, screen, and television actor

1951 **Fred Saunders.** Professional basketball player

1953 **Tim Allen.** American television and motion-picture actor noted for the long-running series *Home Improvement*

1962 **Ally Sheedy.** American motion-picture actress

1963 **Bettina Bunge.** German tennis player

June 13 – Events

323 BC Alexander the Great died of a fever in Babylon at age 33.

49 Pope Leo I, The Great, presented his *Tome*, affirming the reality of the two natures of Christ (human and divine) to Flavian, the Bishop of Constantinople.

1231 Saint Anthony of Padua, the noted Franciscan scholar, died in Vercelli, Italy, at age 36.

1877 The last Russo-Turkish War began.

1927 Charles A. Lindbergh was honored for his historic transatlantic flight in a ticker tape parade in New York City.

1935 Senator Huey Long of Louisiana spoke 15 hours and 35 minutes on the Senate floor, setting a filibuster record.

1935 Jim Braddock won the heavyweight boxing title from Max Baer in a 15-round decision at Long Island City, New York.

1940 The French army abandoned Paris in World War II in the face of advancing German troops.

1944 Germany's World War II "secret weapon," the V-1 rocket, or flying bomb, was dropped on London for the first time.

1955 The worst accident in the history of auto racing occurred at LeMans, France, as 77 spectators and a driver were killed by an out-of-control car.

1966 The Supreme Court issued its landmark *Miranda v. Arizona* decision, saying that an accused cannot be questioned without his consent and he must be advised of his rights.

1967 President Lyndon B. Johnson nominated Thurgood Marshall to become the first black justice on the U.S. Supreme Court.

1971 The *New York Times* began publication of "The Pentagon Papers," based on secret Pentagon studies of the Vietnam War.

1983 The U.S. space probe *Pioneer 10* crossed Neptune's orbit and left the solar system for parts unknown.

June 14 – Birthdays

1716 **Peter Harrison.** American architect

1736 **Charles Augustin de Coulomb.** French physicist known for Coulomb's Law of force between two electrical charges

1811 **Harriet Beecher Stowe.** American author noted for *Uncle Tom's Cabin,* one of the most famous novels in American history

1820 **John Bartlett.** American publisher known chiefly for the book *Familiar Quotations*

1850 **Horatio Herbert Kitchener.** Noted English field marshal who distinguished himself as governor-general of the Sudan, commander of the Egyptian army, and victorious commander in the Boer War

1855 **Robert M. La Follette.** U.S. senator and leader of the progressive movement of the first quarter of the 20th century

1856 **Andrey Andreyevich Markov.** Russian mathematician noted for the theory of stochastic processes and Markov chains

1874 **"Major" (Edward) Bowes.** American radio broadcaster and master of ceremonies of the 1930s and 1940s

1895 **May Allison.** American motion-picture actress and a leading star of Hollywood silent films

1906 **Margaret Bourke-White.** American photographer and writer who was the first accredited woman correspondent to go overseas in World War II

1908 **John Scott Trotter.** American composer and conductor, who recorded the fantastically successful "White Christmas" record with Bing Crosby

1909 **Burl Ives.** American actor and folk singer

1912 **E. Cuyler Hammond.** American medical researcher and the first to link cigarette smoking and lung cancer (1952)

1914 **Yuri Andropov.** Soviet Communist party chairman and premier who succeeded Leonid Brezhnev in 1983

1918 **Dorothy McGuire.** American stage and motion-picture actress

1919 **Sam Wanamaker.** American motion-picture actor and director

1921 **Gene Barry.** American motion-picture and television actor

1922 **Kevin Roche.** American architect

1925 **Pierre Salinger.** American journalist and press secretary for President John Kennedy

1926 **Don Newcombe.** Professional baseball player

1928 **Ernesto "Che" Guevara.** Cuban revolutionary and second most powerful man in Fidel Castro's Cuban government

1929 **Cy Coleman.** American songwriter noted for works such as "If My Friends Could See Me Now"

1933 **Jerzy Kosinski.** American novelist noted for works like *Being There* (1971)

1946 **Marla Gibbs.** American actress

1946 **Donald Trump.** American businessman and real estate tycoon

1950 **Fred Hemmes.** Dutch tennis player

1952 **Pat Summitt.** Hall of Fame women's basketball player and highly successful coach

1952 **Eddie Mekka.** American actor

1955 **Laurie Rowley.** American tennis player

1955 **Vince Evans.** Professional football player

1958 **Eric Heiden.** American speed skater and winner of five gold medals in the 1980 Olympics

1968 **Yasmine Bleeth.** American stage, screen and television actress

1969 **Steffi Graf.** German tennis player who won the grand slam (all four of the major tournaments) in 1988

June 14 – Events

1645 Oliver Cromwell defeated the forces of Charles I at the Battle of Naseby.

1775 The U.S. Army was founded by the Continental Congress.

1777 The Continental Congress adopted the Stars and Stripes as the official flag of the United States.

1800 After a famous march across the Alps, Napoleon defeated the Austrians at Marengo, Italy, consolidating his political position in France.

1807 Napoleon routed the Russian armies at Friedland, forcing Czar Alexander I to make peace.

1825 Pierre Charles L'Enfant, designer of the United States capital, died in Green Hill, Maryland, at age 70.

1846 California was proclaimed a republic, as the Bear Flag was hoisted at Sonoma.

1866 The Seven Weeks' War began between Austria and Prussia. It was engineered by Otto von Bismarck, chancellor of Prussia, to make Prussia the dominant power in Germany.

1917 American general John J. Pershing and his staff arrived in Paris, symbolizing America's entry into World War I. The American Expeditionary Forces arrived on June 26.

1919 John Alcock and Arthur Whitten-Brown left St. Johns, Newfoundland, in a twin-engine Vickers on the first transatlantic flight. They landed in Ireland the next day.

1922 President Warren G. Harding made the first presidential radio broadcast, on Baltimore station WEAR, dedicating the Francis Scott Key memorial at Ft. McHenry.

1934 Max Baer knocked out Primo Carnera in the 11th round in Long Island City, New York, to win the heavyweight championship.

1936 G.K. Chesterton, the noted English writer, died in Beaconsfield, Buckinghamshire, at age 62.

1940 The Germans occupied Paris in World War II.

1963 The Russian manned space flight *Vostok 5* was launched.

1982 Argentine forces on the Falkland Islands surrendered to the British, ending the war over the islands.

1985 Lebanese Shiite hijackers seized an Athens-to-Rome TWA plane and took the 153 people aboard hostage. The last of them were finally released 17 days later.

1998 The Chicago Bulls won the NBA title for the third consecutive year, beating the Utah Jazz four games to two.

June 15 – Birthdays

1330   **Edward, the Black Prince.** One of the most famous warriors in English history, noted for his exploits in the Hundred Years' War

1605   **Thomas Randolph.** English poet and dramatist

1728   **Shah Alam.** Ruler of the Mogul Empire in India

1767   **Rachel Donelson Jackson.** Wife of President Andrew Jackson

1843   **Edvard Grieg.** Norwegian composer, pianist, and conductor, noted for works such as *Concerto in A minor* and *Peer Gynt*

1861   **Ernestine Schumann-Heink.** Greatly admired Czechoslovakian contralto

1870   **Maud Barger-Wallach.** American Hall of Fame tennis player

1880   **Osami Nagano.** Japanese naval officer who planned and carried out the attack on Pearl Harbor in 1941

1887   **Malvina Hoffman.** American sculptor

1892   **Tex Owens.** American composer, author, and singer, noted for works such as Eddy Arnold's theme song, "Cattle Call"

1896   **Walter L. Jacobs.** American businessman and founder of Hertz Rent-a-Car (1954)

1900   **Otto Luening.** American composer, conductor, and flutist

1910   **David Rose.** English songwriter noted for "Holiday for Strings"

1912   **Babe Dahlgren.** New York Yankee first baseman who replaced Lou Gehrig at the end of Gehrig's famous streak of 2,130 consecutive games

1914   **Saul Steinberg.** Romanian-American cartoonist and illustrator noted for his small-scale pen-and-ink drawings

1920   **Amy Clampitt.** American poet, noted for the collection, *The Kingfisher* (1983)

1921   **Erroll Garner.** American jazz pianist and composer, noted for such songs as "Misty" and "Gaslight"

1922   **Morris Udall.** U.S. congressman

1932   **Mario Cuomo.** Governor of New York, 1983-95

1937   **Waylon Jennings.** American country singer

1938   **Billy Williams.** Hall of Fame Professional baseball player and superstar

1941   **Harry Nilsson.** American singer and songwriter

1949   **Dusty Baker.** Professional baseball player and manager

1954   **Jim Belushi.** American television and movie actor and brother of actor John Belushi

1955   **Julie Hagerty.** American stage and screen actress

1956   **Lance Parrish.** Professional baseball player

1958   **Wade Boggs.** Professional baseball player and superstar

1963   **Helen Hunt.** American motion-picture and television actress and 1997 Academy Award winner for *As Good As It Gets*

June 15 – Events

1094   El Cid, the great Spanish national hero, captured Valencia from the Moors.

1215   The Magna Carta was approved at Runnymede by King John of England.

1521   Pope Leo X denounced Martin Luther's writings and ordered Luther to recant.

1752   Benjamin Franklin demonstrated the relationship between electricity and lightning when he launched a kite at Philadelphia during a summer storm.

1775   The Continental Congress appointed George Washington commander in chief of the colonial forces.

1836   Arkansas was admitted to the Union as the 25th state.

1844   Charles Goodyear was granted a patent for rubber vulcanization.

1846   The United States and Great Britain signed the Oregon Treaty setting the boundary between Canada and the U.S. at the 49th parallel.

1846   The English Parliament repealed the Corn Law, which had severely restricted the import of corn and other grain.

1849   James K. Polk died in Nashville, Tennessee, at age 53.

1853   Stephen Foster's famous song "My Old Kentucky Home, Good Night" made its debut.

1864   Secretary of War Edwin Stanton signed an order establishing a military burial ground, which became Arlington National Cemetery.

1903   Barney Oldfield, the great American automobile racer, became the first to drive an automobile a mile a minute, in Indianapolis.

1919   John Alcock and Arthur Whitten-Brown landed near Clifden, Ireland, completing the world's first transatlantic flight.

1938   Johnny Vander Meer pitched his second consecutive no-hitter, a fantastic feat, as Cincinnati beat Brooklyn, 6-0.

1944   American troops invaded Saipan in the Mariana Islands in World War II.

1992   Vice President Dan Quayle, relying on a faulty flash card, instructed a Trenton, NJ, elementary school student to spell potato "potatoe" during a spelling bee.

June 16 – Birthdays

1514   **Sir John Cheke.** English humanist

1762   **Giuseppe Bernardino Bison.** Italian painter

1858   **Gustavus V.** King of Sweden, 1907-1950

1890   **Stan Laurel.** Member of the Laurel and Hardy comedy team, the most successful comedy duo in screen history

1895   **Lew Pollack.** American composer, author, and singer, noted for songs such as "Charmaine" and "The Right Somebody to Love"

1903   **Helen Traubel.** American operatic singer

1907	**Jack Albertson.** American character actor of stage, screen and television
1910	**Ilona Massey.** Hungarian-born actress and singer
1916	**Hank Luisetti.** Hall of Fame professional basketball player
1917	**Katherine Graham.** Publisher of the *Washington Post,* 1969-1979
1917	**Irving Penn.** Influential American photographer
1935	**Jim Dine.** American artist
1937	**Erich Segal.** American writer noted for *Love Story* and *Oliver's Story*
1938	**Joyce Carol Oates.** American novelist, poet, and short-story writer
1946	**Derek Sanderson.** Professional hockey player
1946	**Ivan Molina.** Colombian tennis player
1951	**Roberto Duran.** World welterweight champion in 1980
1952	**Ron LeFlore.** Professional baseball player
1962	**Wally Joyner.** Professional baseball player

June 16 – Events

1464	Roger van der Weyden, the famous Flemish painter who helped found the Flemish movement in painting, died in Brussels at age 64.
1845	The Congress of the Republic of Texas agreed to annexation by the United States.
1845	The American premiere of Gioacchino Rossini's famous opera *William Tell* took place in New York City.
1846	Pius IX was elected Roman Catholic pope. He served for 32 years, the longest reign in papal history.
1858	Abraham Lincoln made his famous speech which included the line: "A house divided against itself cannot stand."
1903	The Ford Motor Company was founded by Henry Ford.
1940	Marshal Henri Philippe Petain replaced Paul Reynaud as premier of France, as the Germans pierced the Maginot Line and were poised to overrun France in World War II.
1963	The Russians launched the first woman cosmonaut, Valentina Tereshkova, into space in *Vostok VI.*

June 17 – Birthdays

1239	**Edward I.** King of England, 1272-1307, of the Plantagenet line, and son of King Henry III
1682	**Charles XII.** One of the greatest kings and military leaders in Sweden's history, reigning from 1697, at age 15, until he was killed in battle in 1718
1703	**John Wesley.** English religious leader and founder of the Methodist Church
1818	**Charles Gounod.** French composer, whose best known work is the opera *Faust* (1859, revised in 1869), noted for its familiar "Soldiers' Chorus"

1832	**Sir William Crookes.** English chemist noted for the invention of the Crookes tube and for the discovery of the element thallium
1867	**John Robert Gregg.** American inventor noted for the Gregg system of shorthand
1882	**Igor Stravinsky.** Russian composer noted for such works as *The Firebird* (1910) and *The Rite of Spring* (1913)
1888	**Heinz Guderian.** One of the greatest German generals of World War II, and the architect of *Blitzkrieg,* which was so successful in the early stages of the war
1900	**Martin Bormann.** High Nazi official close to Hitler who disappeared after World War II and whose fate was unknown for years, but is now believed to have died shortly after Hitler did
1902	**Sammy Fain.** American composer, singer, and pianist noted for songs such as "Let a Smile Be Your Umbrella," "Secret Love," "Love Is a Many Splendored Thing," and "I'll Be Seeing You"
1904	**Ralph Bellamy.** American stage, screen, and television actor
1907	**Charles Eames.** American designer
1910	**Red Foley.** American country singer and musician
1914	**John Hersey.** American Pulitzer Prize-winning novelist, noted for such works as *A Bell for Adano* (1945) and *Hiroshima* (1946)
1919	**Kingman Brewster Jr.** President of Yale and U.S. ambassador to Great Britain
1923	**Elroy "Crazylegs" Hirsch.** Professional football player and Hall of Famer
1929	**Tigran Vartanovich Petrosyan.** Russian chess master and world champion, 1966-1969
1943	**Newt Gingrich.** U.S. congressman and controversial Speaker of the House (1995-1999)
1944	**Chris Spedding.** British session guitarist
1946	**Barry Manilow.** American pop singer and songwriter
1948	**Dave Concepcion.** Professional baseball player
1951	**Joe Piscapo.** American comedian and television and motion-picture actor
1980	**Venus Williams.** American tennis player

June 17 – Events

1673	Father Jacques Marquette and Louis Joliet began exploring the Mississippi River.
1682	The city of Philadelphia was founded by William Penn.
1775	The British won the Battle of Bunker Hill, with heavy losses due to American Col. William Prescott's order, "Don't fire until you see the whites of their eyes."
1794	Fifty-four people were guillotined in the "Reign of Terror" of the final stages of the French Revolution.
1856	The first Republican National Convention was held, in Philadelphia. John C. Fremont was nominated as the party's first candidate for president.

1880 John M. "Monte" Ward pitched the second perfect game (not a runner reached base) in major league history, as Providence beat Buffalo, 5-0.

1939 Eugen Weidmann, a French murderer, became the last person to be publicly guillotined.

1940 Russia invaded Estonia, Latvia, and Lithuania in a prelude to World War II.

1940 Marshal Henri Petain, who had just taken over as head of the French government, agreed to surrender to Germany in World War II.

1942 The term "G.I. Joe" first appeared, in Dave Breger's comic strip in *Yank*.

1944 Iceland officially gained independence from Denmark, and the Republic of Iceland was founded. The date is celebrated as Independence Day for Iceland.

1953 East Germans rebelled against Russian rule, but German rock throwers were no match for Soviet tanks, and the revolt was quickly crushed.

1954 Rocky Marciano retained his heavyweight title, defeating former champion Ezzard Charles.

1963 The Supreme Court prohibited the reading of biblical verses and the recitation of the Lord's Prayer in public schools.

1967 Communist China exploded its first hydrogen bomb.

1972 Five men were arrested by Washington, D.C., police in the Watergate Hotel break-in that led ultimately to the destruction of the Nixon presidency.

June 18 – Birthdays

1618 **Jean Lepautre.** French designer

1621 **Allart van Everdingen.** Dutch painter

1716 **Joseph Vien.** French painter

1803 **Robert W. Weir.** American painter

1812 **Ivan Alexandrovich Goncharov.** Russian novelist noted for works such as *Fregat Pallada* (1858) and *Oblomov* (1859)

1854 **Edward Wyllis Scripps.** Famous American newspaper publisher who started the first newspaper chain and founded the United Press Associations, now United Press International

1857 **Henry Clay Folger.** Founder in 1930 of the Folger Shakespeare Library in Washington, D.C.

1877 **James Montgomery Flagg.** Illustrator of the World War I recruiting poster with Uncle Sam saying, "I want you"

1884 **Edouard Daladier.** French premier at the beginning of World War II

1891 **Con Conrad.** American songwriter noted for "Margie" (1920)

1895 **Blanche Sweet.** American stage and screen actress and a favorite D.W. Griffith leading lady of the silent period

1901 **Jeanette MacDonald.** American singer and actress, especially noted for the films she made with Nelson Eddy in the most successful singing partnership in musical film history

1901 **Jimmy Dale.** American composer noted for songs such as "I Hate to See the Evening Sun Go Down"

1903 **Raymond Radiguet.** French poet and novelist

1904 **Gordon Buehrig.** American car designer noted for the Duesenberg, Cord, and Auburn designs

1904 **Keye Luke.** Chinese-American stage, screen, and television actor, noted for his role as the "Number One Son" in the *Charlie Chan* movies

1906 **Kay Kyser.** American musician and bandleader of the Big Band Era

1908 **Sam Martin.** American composer and author, noted for songs such as "You Call Everybody Darling"

1910 **E.G. Marshall.** American motion-picture and television actor

1910 **Ray McKinley.** American composer, author, and bandleader, noted for lyrics such as "Beat Me Daddy, Eight to the Bar"

1913 **Sylvia Porter.** American financial columnist and writer

1913 **Sammy Cahn.** American lyricist noted for such songs as "Three Coins in the Fountain," "I'll Walk Alone," "Let It Snow, Let It Snow, Let It Snow," and "High Hopes"

1916 **Richard Boone.** American motion-picture and television actor

1924 **George Mikan.** Professional Hall of Fame basketball player who dominated the game in the 1940s and 1950s

1926 **Eva Bartok.** Hungarian motion-picture actress

1926 **Tom Wicker.** American journalist and author

1935 **Al Michaels.** American sportscaster

1937 **John D. "Jay" Rockefeller IV.** Governor of West Virginia and U.S. senator

1939 **Lou Brock.** Hall of Fame baseball player who stole a record 118 bases in 1974 and broke Ty Cobb's career record of 892 in 1977

1942 **Roger Ebert.** American motion-picture critic and co-author with Gene Siskel of a movie review column

1942 **Paul McCartney.** Member of the Beatles musical group

1952 **Carol Kane.** American stage and motion-picture actress

1952 **Isabella Rossellini.** Italian-born motion-picture actress and daughter of actress Ingrid Bergman and director Roberto Rossellini

1956 **Kathy May.** American tennis player

1961 **Allison "Alf" Moyet.** British vocalist with the Yaz musical group

1961 **Andres Galarraga.** Professional baseball player

June 18 – Events

1155 Frederick Barbarossa was crowned Holy Roman Emperor.

1778 American forces occupied Philadelphia as the British withdrew in the Revolutionary War.

1798 Concluding a toast to John Marshall at O'Eller's Tavern in Philadelphia, U.S. Representative Robert Goodloe Harper said, "Millions for defense, but not one cent for tribute!" (The reference was to the XYZ Affair in which France was demanding tribute from the United States.)

1812 Congress declared war on Great Britain, marking the beginning of the War of 1812.

1815 In one of history's most decisive battles, Napoleon was defeated in the Battle of Waterloo by an allied army under the Duke of Wellington, ending Napoleon's remarkable career.

1873 Susan B. Anthony, the noted American suffragist, was fined $100 for trying to vote in Rochester, New York, in the 1872 presidential election.

1902 Samuel Butler, the noted English novelist, died in London at age 66.

1928 Amelia Earhart became the first female passenger on a transatlantic flight, from Newfoundland to Burry Port, Wales, in a plane piloted by Wilmer Stultz.

1940 On the eve of the Battle of Britain, Winston Churchill said, "If the British Empire and its Commonwealth last for a thousand years, men will still say, 'This was their finest hour.'"

1941 Joe Louis knocked out Billy Conn in the 13th round in New York to retain his heavyweight title. Conn was ahead on points and would have won had he avoided a knockout.

1963 Russian cosmonaut Valentina Tereshkova, the first woman in space, completed her flight.

1979 President Jimmy Carter and Russian president Leonid Brezhnev signed the SALT II treaty in Vienna. The U.S. Senate, however, failed to ratify it.

1983 Sally Ride became America's first woman astronaut in space as she and four colleagues blasted off aboard the space shuttle *Challenger*.

1986 Pitcher Don Sutton won his 300th career game, as California defeated Texas, 5-1.

June 19 – Birthdays

1507 **Annibale Caro.** Italian poet noted for translating Virgil's *Aeneid*

1566 **James I.** The first Stuart king of England, 1603-1625, successor to Queen Elizabeth I, and the king who sponsored the translation known as the King James Version of the Bible

1623 **Blaise Pascal.** French philosopher, mathematician, scientist, and author, noted for the great work *Pensees*

1783 **Thomas Sully.** One of the finest U.S. portrait painters of the 19th century

1856 **Elbert Green Hubbard.** American author, biographer, and publisher, who died in the sinking of the *Lusitania* in in 1915

1861 **Douglas Haig.** Commander in chief of the British forces in France in World War I, who directed the attack that broke Germany's Hindenburg Line and led to the end of the war

1865 **Dame May Whitty.** English stage and motion-picture actress with a career of over 60 years

1877 **Charles Coburn.** American stage and motion-picture actor in nearly 100 films

1881 **Jimmy Walker.** Mayor of New York City, 1926-1932

1884 **Eddie Cicotte.** One of the top baseball pitchers of his day, and one of the Chicago White Sox players banned from baseball in the 1919 "Black Sox" scandal

1896 **Wallis Warfield Simpson.** The Duchess of Windsor and wife of former King Edward VIII of England, who abdicated his throne to marry her

1897 **Moe Howard.** American comedian and actor and one of the original Three Stooges

1900 **Laura Zametkin Hobson.** American novelist noted for *Gentleman's Agreement* (1947)

1902 **Guy Lombardo.** American bandleader of the Big Band Era, whose career extended into the 1980s

1903 **Lou Gehrig.** One of baseball's all-time greatest players, and "Iron Horse," who played in a record 2,130 consecutive games, a record which stood for more than 50 years

1908 **Quentin Burdick.** U.S. senator

1908 **Mildred Natwick.** Gifted character actress of the American stage and screen, whose career spanned 45 years

1909 **Osamu Dazai.** Foremost Japanese novelist of his day

1910 **Abe Fortas.** Supreme Court justice, 1965-1969

1912 **Martin Gabel.** American stage, screen, and television actor

1914 **Alan Cranston.** U.S. senator

1919 **Pauline Kael.** Noted American movie critic and author

1919 **Louis Jourdan.** French motion-picture actor

1921 **Howell Heflin.** U.S. senator

1928 **Nancy Marchand.** American stage, screen, and television actress

1932 **Pier Angeli.** Italian-born motion-picture and twin sister of actress Marisa Pavan

1932 **Marisa Pavan.** Italian-born motion-picture actress and twin sister of actress Pier Angeli

1934 **Gena Rowlands.** American stage, screen, and television actress

1940 **Shirley Muldowney.** American pioneer drag racer and first woman to drive a Top Fuel dragster professionally

1941 **Harold Elschenbroich.** West German tennis player

1943 **Malcolm McDowell.** English motion-picture actor

1947 **Salman Rushdie.** British author sentenced to death, since rescinded, by Iranian ruler Ayatollah Khomeini for his novel *The Satanic Verses* (1989)

1948 **Felicia Rashad.** American television actress (*The Cosby Show*)

1949	**Jerry Reuss.** Professional baseball player
1954	**Kathleen Turner.** American stage and screen actress
1954	**Johnnie LeMaster.** Professional baseball player
1955	**Bruce Harper.** Professional football player
1963	**Paula Abdul.** Noted singer, dancer, and choreographer

June 19 – Events

1215 The articles of the Magna Carta, agreed to by King John four days earlier, were written out in legal form, or engrossed, as a royal charter.

1586 English colonists left Roanoke Island, N.C., for home, after failing to establish the first permanent English colony in America.

1588 The Spanish Armada anchored at Corunna, Spain, to pick up provisions and regroup after a violent storm on the Portuguese coast, before proceeding to engage the English fleet.

1846 Alexander Joy Cartwright brought the New York Knickerbockers and the New York Nine to Hoboken, N.J., to play the first game of baseball. The Nine won, 23-1.

1856 The Republicans adjourned their first National Convention after nominating John C. Fremont as their first presidential candidate.

1865 Word finally reached the piney woods of East Texas that the slaves were freed. The date was thereafter celebrated as Freedom Day, or *Juneteenth,* by African Americans.

1867 Maximilian, the usurper Emperor of Mexico, was executed by a firing squad of troops of the Mexican Republic.

1886 William Howard Taft married Helen Herron.

1910 Father's Day was first observed. It was started by Mrs. John Bruce Dodd of Spokane, Washington.

1912 The U.S. government adopted the eight-hour work day for its employees.

1923 The comic strip, *Moon Mullins,* by Frank Willard, first appeared.

1934 The Federal Communications Commission was created.

1936 Max Schmeling knocked out Joe Louis in the 12th round at New York's Yankee Stadium.

1944 The Battle of the Philippine Sea began between the United States and Japan in World War II. It ended decisively in the Americans' favor on the following day. The result was so one-sided (402 Japanese planes lost to 27 American) that the battle was also nicknamed "The Marianas Turkey Shoot."

1953 Ethel and Julius Rosenberg were executed for spying for the Russians. They were the first Americans given a death sentence for espionage by a United States civilian court.

1978 The comic strip *Garfield,* by Jim Davis, first appeared.

June 20 – Birthdays

1566 **Sigismund III.** King of Poland, 1587-1632, of the House of Vasa

1615 **Salvator Rosa.** Italian painter noted for works such as *Prometheus* (1635) and *L'Umana Fragilita* (1656)

1674 **Nicholas Rowe.** English poet and playwright, noted for *Tamerlane* (1701) and *The Fair Penitent* (1703), in which he created the "gay Lothario," whose name has come down to us as a charming seducer

1819 **Jacques Offenbach.** French composer best known for his opera, the *Tales of Hoffmann*

1858 **Charles W. Chesnutt.** First important black American novelist

1858 **Medardo Rosso.** Italian sculptor

1873 **Alberto Santos-Dumont.** Brazilian-born French aviation pioneer in both lighter-than-air and heavier-than-air machines

1891 **John Costello.** Prime minister of the Republic of Ireland, 1948-1951 and 1954-1957

1894 **George Delacorte.** American publisher and philanthropist

1903 **Glenna Collett Vare.** Sportswoman who dominated U.S. women's golf in the 1920s and 1930s

1905 **Lillian Hellman.** America's foremost woman playwright, noted for such works as *The Children's Hour* (1934) and *The Little Foxes* (1939)

1909 **Errol Flynn.** Tasmanian-born motion-picture actor and dashing hero of the 1940s

1911 **Gail Patrick.** American actress and producer

1921 **Pancho Segura.** Ecuadorian tennis player noted for his two-handed grip

1924 **Chet Atkins.** American guitarist

1924 **Audie Murphy.** American World War II hero and motion-picture actor

1925 **Doris Hart.** American Hall of Fame tennis player, who ranked in the top ten for 14 consecutive years, 1942-1955

1928 **Martin Landau.** American stage, screen, and television actor

1931 **Olympia Dukakis.** American stage and screen actress who won an Academy Award for *Moonstruck* (1987)

1933 **Danny Aiello.** American stage, screen, and television actor

1934 **Rossanna Podesta.** Italian motion-picture actress

1935 **Len Dawson.** Professional football player and Hall of Famer

1940 **John Mahoney.** English-American stage, screen and television actor noted for his role in TV's *Fraser*

1942 **Brian Wilson.** American singer and composer with the Beach Boys musical group

1945 **Anne Murray.** Canadian singer who was named Canada's Top Female Vocalist, 1970-86

1946 **Bob Vila.** American TV personality and expert on home repairs and historic houses

1946	**Andre Watts.** American pianist
1947	**Candy Clark.** American motion-picture actress
1949	**Lionel Richie.** American singer who won five Grammy Awards
1952	**John Goodman.** American stage, screen, and television actor, noted as the wisecracking husband in *Roseanne*
1953	**Paul Ramirez.** Mexican tennis player
1953	**Cyndi Lauper.** American rock singer
1958	**Dickie Thon.** Professional baseball player
1960	**John Taylor.** Bassist of the Duran Duran musical group
1969	**Mali-vai Washington.** American tennis player

June 20 – Events

404	The first Cathedral of Santa Sophia in Constantinople was burned to the ground by rioters.
1389	The Turks defeated the Serbs on the Kossovo Plain, destroying the Serbian Empire and resulting in Turkish rule of Serbia for 400 years.
1530	The Diet of Augsburg opened. It was called by Holy Roman Emperor Henry V to end the quarrels between Catholics and Protestants.
1632	The second Lord Baltimore received a grant from the king of England for the tract of land on which he founded the colony of Maryland.
1756	The Black Hole of Calcutta, a suffocating dungeon, got its name, when a number of British prisoners were locked in it overnight and died of suffocation.
1782	Congress adopted the Great Seal of the United States.
1789	The Tennis Court Oath pledging the Third Estate to a new constitution was taken, marking the beginning of the French Revolution.
1793	Eli Whitney applied for a patent on his cotton gin.
1837	Queen Victoria of England began her 64-year reign.
1863	West Virginia was admitted to the Union as the 35th state.
1893	Lizzie Borden was found not guilty of murdering her father and stepmother, who were hacked to death in Fall River, Massachusetts, on August 4, 1892.
1910	Fannie Brice made her debut in the Ziegfeld Follies of 1910.
1944	The Battle of the Philippine Sea ended with a decisive U.S. victory over Japan in World War II. The Americans lost 27 planes while the Japanese lost 402.
1948	Ed Sullivan's television variety show, *Toast of the Town,* made its debut. It ran for nearly 23 years.
1960	Floyd Patterson regained the heavyweight boxing title, knocking out Ingemar Johansson in the fifth round in New York.

June 21 – Birthdays

1002	**Leo IX.** Roman Catholic pope, 1049-1054, known as Saint Leo
1639	**Increase Mather.** Puritan minister and scholar of colonial Massachusetts, and father of Puritan minister Cotton Mather
1640	**Abraham Mignon.** German painter
1676	**Anthony Collins.** English deist and freethinker
1774	**Daniel D. Tompkins.** U.S. vice president under President Monroe
1781	**Simeon-Denis Poisson.** Noted French mathematician
1839	**Joaquim Maria Machado de Assis.** The greatest figure in Brazilian literature, and the founder in 1897 of the Brazilian Academy of Letters
1850	**Daniel Carter Beard.** American naturalist and illustrator, and an early pioneer in shaping the Boy Scouts of America
1859	**Henry Ossawa Tanner.** American painter noted for works such as *Daniel in the Lions' Den* (1896)
1863	**Max Wolf.** German astronomer and discoverer of 228 asteroids
1879	**Henry Creamer.** American composer noted for songs such as "Way Down Yonder in New Orleans" and "After You've Gone"
1880	**Arnold Gesell.** American physician who founded the Gesell Institute of Child Development
1882	**Rockwell Kent.** American painter, illustrator, printmaker, and author
1892	**Reinhold Niebuhr.** One of the most important American theologians of the 20th century
1903	**Al Hirschfield.** American cartoonist and artist
1904	**Mack Gordon.** Polish-American composer noted for songs such as "I've Got a Gal in Kalamazoo," "Chattanooga Choo-Choo," "You'll Never Know," "Mam'selle," and "I Can't Begin to Tell You"
1905	**Jean-Paul Sartre.** French existential philosopher, novelist, and playwright
1906	**Harold Spina.** American composer and author, noted for songs such as "It's So Nice to Have a Man Around the House"
1912	**Mary McCarthy.** American novelist, critic, essayist, and author of *The Group* (1963)
1913	**Willie Mosconi.** Noted American billiard player, and 15 times world pocket billiards open champion
1918	**Eddie Lopat.** Professional baseball player and manager
1919	**Paolo Soleri.** Italian architect, designer, and city planner
1921	**Gower Champion.** American dancer, director, and choreographer
1921	**Jane Russell.** American motion-picture and television actress
1922	**Judy Holliday.** American motion-picture actress
1925	**Maureen Stapleton.** American stage, screen, and television actress
1931	**Margaret Heckler.** American congresswoman and secretary of Health and Human Services under President Reagan
1935	**Françoise Sagan.** French novelist and author of *Bonjour Tristesse* (1954)

1938   **Ron Ely.** American motion-picture actor and the screen's 15th Tarzan

1941   **Mariette Hartley.** American motion-picture and television actress and morning show host

1944   **Ray Davies.** British singer and guitarist with The Kinks musical group

1947   **Meredith Baxter.** American television actress

1947   **Michael Gross.** American television actor

1949   **Duane Thomas.** Professional football player

1951   **Nils Lofgren.** American musician and songwriter with E Street Band

1953   **Charlie Moore.** Professional baseball player

1956   **Rick Sutcliffe.** Professional baseball player

1957   **Berke Breathed.** American cartoonist and creator of *Bloom County* (1980-1989)

1957   **Mark Brzezicki.** Irish drummer with the Big Country musical group

1959   **Tom Chambers.** Professional football player

1973   **Juliette Lewis.** American motion-picture actress

1982   **Prince William.** Prince of Wales, and son of Prince Charles and Lady Diana of England

June 21 – Events

1631   John Smith, one of the founders of Jamestown, Virginia, died at age 51.

1788   New Hampshire ratified the U.S. Constitution, the ninth state to do so, which made it operative.

1810   Zachary Taylor married Margaret Mackall Smith.

1834   Cyrus Hall McCormick was granted a patent for an improved version of his reaper, originally invented in 1831.

1879   F.W. Woolworth opened his first five-and-ten-cent store, in Lancaster, Pennsylvania.

1932   Jack Sharkey won the heavyweight title from Max Schmeling in 15 rounds in Long Island City, New York.

1939   Baseball fans were saddened as they learned that Lou Gehrig had a rare type of paralysis, later dubbed Lou Gehrig's Disease, and would never play again.

1940   Richard Nixon married Pat Ryan.

1945   The U.S. marines took Okinawa in World War II after nearly three months of fighting.

1948   CBS demonstrated the first long-playing 33 1/3 rpm records. Two of the first releases were Mendelssohn's *Violin Concerto* and Tchaikovsky's *Fourth Symphony.*

1954   John Landry of Australia established a new world's record in running the mile in 3 minutes, 58 seconds, in Turku, Finland.

1963   Paul VI became Roman Catholic pope.

1964   Jim Bunning pitched a perfect game (no man reached base) as the Philadelphia Phillies beat the New York Mets, 6-0.

1982   John Hinckley Jr. was found innocent by reason of insanity for attempting to assassinate President Reagan.

June 22 – Birthdays

1555   **Francisco Ribalta.** Spanish painter

1758   **George Vancouver.** British navigator and explorer for whom Vancouver, Canada, was named

1805   **Giuseppe Mazzini.** Italian patriot and pioneer in the struggle to unite Italy in the 1830s and 1840s

1844   **Margaret Sidney.** Author of *The Five Little Peppers and How They Grew*

1856   **Sir Henry Rider Haggard.** Highly successful English writer of the late 1800s and author of *King Solomon's Mines* (1885) and *She* (1887)

1869   **Hendrikus Colijn.** Dutch prime minister during the Great Depression

1882   **William M. Scholl.** American medical school graduate and former shoemaker who developed Dr. Scholl's arch support and promoted corn and bunion pads to ease aching feet

1887   **Julian Huxley.** British biologist, writer, and grandson of the famous zoologist, T.H. Huxley

1898   **Erich Maria Remarque.** German-American novelist and author of *All Quiet on the Western Front* (1929), one of the most famous war stories of all time

1903   **John Dillinger.** Notorious American criminal of the Depression era

1903   **Carl Hubbell.** Hall of Fame baseball pitcher who won 16 consecutive games in 1936

1906   **Billy Wilder.** Austrian-born motion-picture director, noted for such films as *Stalag 17* (1953) and *Witness for the Prosecution* (1958)

1906   **Anne Morrow Lindbergh.** American poet and wife of aviator hero Charles A. Lindbergh, and author of such works as *Gift from the Sea* (1955)

1907   **Michael Todd.** American motion-picture producer and showman, noted for such shows as *Oklahoma!* (1955) and *Around the World in 80 Days* (1956)

1909   **Buddy Adler.** American motion-picture producer who won an Academy Award in 1953 for *From Here to Eternity*

1915   **Cornelius Warmerdam.** American athlete and the first man to pole vault 15 feet (15 feet 1 1/8 inches in 1940)

1921   **Joseph Papp.** One of Broadway's greatest producers, noted for some 100 plays, among which are *Electra* (1964), *Hair* (1967), *A Chorus Line* (1975), and *The Pirates of Penzance* (1980)

1922   **Bill Blass.** American fashion designer

1928   **Ralph Waite.** American television actor noted for his role as the father in the long-running series *The Waltons*

1933   **Dianne Feinstein.** Mayor of San Francisco and U.S. senator

1937   **Kris Kristofferson.** American singer and motion-picture actor

1941   **Ed Bradley.** American television personality, noted as a regular on the long-running show *60 Minutes*

1947   **Robert Douglass.** Professional football player

1947	**Pete Maravich.** Professional basketball player and Hall of Famer
1948	**Todd Rundgren.** American rock musician
1949	**Meryl Streep.** American stage, screen, and television actress, who won Academy Awards for best actress in *Sophie's Choice* and *Kramer versus Kramer*
1949	**Lindsay Wagner.** American motion-picture and television actress
1954	**Freddie Prinze.** American television actor and comedian
1962	**Clyde Drexler.** Professional basketball player
1964	**Amy Brenneman.** American stage, screen, and television actress

June 22 – Events

1527	Niccolo Machiavelli, the great Italian writer, died in Florence at age 58.
1611	The famous explorer Henry Hudson, his son, and seven loyal sailors were set adrift in a small boat in Hudson Bay by mutineers and were never heard of again.
1633	Galileo was forced by the Court of Inquisition to confess the "falsehood" of the Copernican theory of planetary motion.
1812	Napoleon crossed the Nieman River with his *Grande Armee* of 600,000 men, opening his campaign against Russia.
1815	After his defeat at the Battle of Waterloo, Napoleon abdicated for the second and last time.
1846	Adolphe Sax patented the saxophone, his invention of a few years earlier.
1870	Congress created the Department of Justice.
1937	Joe Louis knocked out Jim Braddock in the eighth round at Comiskey Park in Chicago to become heavyweight champion of the world.
1938	Joe Louis knocked out Max Schmeling in the first round to retain his heavyweight championship. The victory avenged an earlier loss to Schmeling, the only loss Louis had in his prime.
1940	France surrendered to Germany in World War II.
1941	More than 150 German and other Axis divisions invaded Russia in *Operation Barbarossa* in World War II.
1944	The GI Bill of Rights became law, under which more than 7,800,000 World War II veterans studied or trained.
1949	Ezzard Charles defeated Joe Walcott in a 15 round decision to become heavyweight champion.
1969	Judy Garland, the noted American actress, was found dead at age 47.
1973	The *Skylab 1* astronauts returned to earth after 28 days in space.
1981	Mark David Chapman pleaded guilty to killing John Lennon outside the rock star's New York City apartment building.

June 23 – Birthdays

1625	**John Fell.** English clergyman and scholar
1763	**Josephine de Beauharnais.** Wife of Napoleon Bonaparte
1859	**Edouard Michelin.** Co-founder of the Michelin Tire Company
1875	**Carl Wilhelm Emil Milles.** Swedish-American sculptor, noted for fountains such as *Meeting of the Waters* in St. Louis
1876	**Irvin S. Cobb.** American journalist, humorist, and actor
1889	**Anna Akhmatova.** The greatest woman poet in Russian literature
1894	**Alfred Charles Kinsey.** American physician and student of human sexual behavior, whose books on the subject were considered sensational in the 1940s
1894	**Edward VIII.** King of England, who abdicated his throne in 1936 (to marry Wallis Simpson, "the woman he loved") and subsequently became the Duke of Windsor
1895	**Norman R. Raine.** Creator of *Tugboat Annie*
1895	**George Weiss.** Professional baseball general manager, whose tenure with the New York Yankees produced their great teams of the 1950s and 1960s
1898	**Charles Francis Kenny.** American composer and author, noted for such songs as "Love Letters in the Sand" and "There's a Gold Mine in the Sky"
1910	**Edward P. Morgan.** American broadcast journalist
1910	**Jean Anouilh.** Popular French playwright known for his polished dramas
1912	**Alan M. Turing.** English mathematician, who developed the Turing machine (1937) and played a significant part in breaking the German World War II "Enigma" codes
1913	**William Rogers.** U.S. secretary of state under President Nixon
1915	**Dennis Price.** English stage and motion-picture actor
1927	**Bob Fosse.** American dancer, choreographer, and director, noted for such hits as *Damn Yankees* and *Cabaret*
1929	**June Carter Cash.** American country singer and wife of singer Johnny Cash
1933	**Dave Bristol.** Professional baseball player and manager
1936	**Richard David Bach.** American writer noted for *Jonathan Livingston Seagull*
1940	**Wilma Rudolph.** American sprinter and winner of three gold medals in the 1960 Olympic Games
1948	**Clarence Thomas.** U.S. Supreme Court justice
1956	**Tony Hill.** Professional football player

June 23 – Events

1483 King Edward V of England, age 12, and his younger brother, the Duke of York, were murdered in the Tower of London, probably on orders of their uncle, the future Richard III.

1683 William Penn signed a friendship treaty with the Leni-Lenape Indians on the Delaware River, shortly after he arrived in the Pennsylvania region.

1713 Queen Anne of England ordered French descendants in Nova Scotia to take an oath of allegiance to England within a year, or leave.

1860 The United States Secret Service was established, for the purpose of protecting the president and his family.

1863 French historian Ernest Renan published his *Life of Jesus.*

1868 Christopher Latham Sholes, Carlos Glidden, and Samuel W. Soule patented their *Type-Writer,* the first such machine that was practical.

1931 Aviators Wiley Post and Harold Gatty took off from New York on the first flight around the world in a single-engine plane.

1931 Spanish tennis player Lili de Alvarez showed up for her Wimbledon match wearing shorts, which opened the door for women to wear practical dress instead of the usual skirts and stockings.

1947 Congress overrode President Truman's veto to enact the Taft-Hartley Act.

1967 Jim Ryun, the United States runner, ran the mile in a record 3 minutes, 51.1 seconds.

1967 President Lyndon Johnson met Russia's premier Aleksei Kosygin at the Glassboro, New Jersey, summit conference.

1972 President Nixon and H.R. Haldeman agreed to use the CIA to obstruct the FBI's Watergate investigations. This was the subject of the "smoking gun" tape on which Nixon told Haldeman, "Have them stay the hell out."

1999 Fernando Tatis of the St. Louis Cardinals hit two bases-loaded homeruns in one inning, a feat never before accomplished, as the Cardinals beat the Los Angeles Dodgers, 12-5.

June 24 – Birthdays

1450 **John Cabot.** Italian navigator, who, sailing under the English flag to North America in 1497, landed on either Newfoundland or Nova Scotia

1542 **John of the Cross.** Spanish poet, born Juan de Yepes y Alvarez

1616 **Ferdinand Bol.** Dutch painter

1693 **Michael Rysbrack.** English sculptor

1771 **E.I. Du Pont.** French-American industrialist who founded the powder works in 1802 in Delaware that formed the beginning of the Du Pont Company

1795 **Ernst Heinrich Weber.** German anatomist and physiologist

1813 **Henry Ward Beecher.** Noted Congregational minister and Protestant spokesman, and brother of Harriet Beecher Stowe, the author of *Uncle Tom's Cabin*

1839 **Gustavus Franklin Swift.** American industrialist who in 1885 founded Swift & Company

1842 **Ambrose Bierce.** American misanthropic writer and journalist, and author of *Can Such Things Be?* (1893) and *The Devil's Dictionary* (1911)

1848 **Brooks Adams.** American historian, critic of capitalism, and grandson of John Quincy Adams

1850 **William Stryker Gummere.** American football pioneer who helped set up the rules for the first game (1869)

1852 **Victor Adler.** Creator of the Austrian Socialist Party

1879 **Agrippina Vaganova.** Russian ballerina and teacher

1895 **Jack Dempsey.** One of the most popular world heavyweight boxing champions of all time (1919-1926)

1906 **Phil Harris.** American actor and musician

1907 **Rollie Hemsley.** Professional baseball player

1911 **Juan-Manuel Fangio.** World champion automobile racer who won the Grand Prix five times, four times in succession (1954-1957)

1912 **Norman Cousins.** Editor of *The Saturday Review* for 32 years

1915 **Sir Fred Hoyle.** English mathematician, astronomer, and proponent of the "steady-state" theory of the universe (holding that matter is being created at a rate fast enough to keep the universe at a constant mean density)

1916 **John Ciardi.** American poet and long-time poetry editor of *The Saturday Review*

1923 **Jack Carter.** American comedian

1928 **Larry Foust.** Professional basketball player

1930 **Claude Chabrol.** French motion-picture director

1931 **Billy Casper.** Professional golfer

1933 **Sam Jones.** Professional Hall of Fame basketball superstar with over 14,000 career points

1933 **Doug Sanders.** Professional golfer

1935 **Pete Hamill.** American newspaper columnist

1942 **Mick Fleetwood.** English rock musician of the Fleetwood Mac musical group

1944 **Jeff Beck.** British rock and jazz guitarist

1944 **Arthur Brown.** British rock singer

1945 **George Pataki.** Governor of New York who succeeded Mario Cuomo in 1995

1945 **Betty Stove.** Dutch tennis player

1946 **Robert B. Reich.** Labor secretary under President Clinton

1948 **Steve Patterson.** Professional basketball player

1950 **Nancy Allen.** American motion-picture actress

1957 **Doug Jones.** Professional baseball player

1960 **Juli Inkster.** Only golfer to win two Ladies Professional Gold Association tournaments in her rookie year

1961 **Ralph Reed.** Executive director of the "Christian Coalition" in the 1990s

June 24 – Events

217 Hannibal defeated the Romans at Lago di Trasimeno in the Second Punic War.

451 Attila the Hun raised his siege of Orleans, France, in a prelude to his being pushed out of France by a combined army of Romans and barbarians.

1314 The Battle of Bannockburn was fought in which Scotland's Robert Bruce defeated England's King Edward II, taking Stirling Castle, the last English foothold in Scotland.

1497 John Cabot completed his historic voyage for England to the new world, landing on the North American coast at what is believed to be either Newfoundland or Nova Scotia.

1519 Lucretia Borgia, the central figure in the notorious Borgia family, died at age 39.

1540 Henry VIII of England divorced his fourth wife, Anne of Cleves.

1665 Thomas Willett, the first mayor of New York City, was installed in office.

1885 Woodrow Wilson married his first wife, Ellen Louise Axson.

1898 The United States defeated the Spanish in the Battle of Las Guasimas, Cuba, the first land engagement of the Spanish-American War.

1908 Grover Cleveland died in Princeton, New Jersey, at age 71.

1948 The Russians initiated the Berlin Blockade, stopping all rail, water, and highway routes to West Berlin.

1956 Dean Martin and Jerry Lewis broke up their comedy team after ten years and 16 films.

June 25 – Birthdays

1852 **Antonio Gaudi.** Spanish architect noted for Barcelona's Casa Mila, completed in 1910

1865 **Robert Henri.** American painter and art teacher, and the guiding spirit of The Eight, an informal association of painters in the early 20th century

1874 **Rose Cecil O'Neill.** American author, illustrator and creator in 1909 of the Kewpie doll

1886 **Henry H. "Hap" Arnold.** American general who developed the small U.S. Army Air Corps into the powerful U.S. Air Force of World War II, and the only man to serve as both general of the Army and Air Force

1887 **George Abbott.** American playwright, director, producer, and screenwriter who wrote, directed, or produced more than 120 Broadway plays and was active at age 100

1900 **Lord Louis Mountbatten.** English naval leader and statesman, and the last viceroy of India before its independence in 1947

1903 **George Orwell.** British writer and author of *Animal Farm* (1945) and *1984* (1949)

1906 **Roger Livesey.** English stage, screen, and television actor

1906 **Joe Kuhel.** Professional baseball player

1913 **Adele Girard Marsala.** American composer and harpist, noted for songs such as "Little Sir Echo"

1915 **Peter Lind Hayes.** American actor, composer, and author

1918 **Sid Tepper.** American composer and author, noted for songs such as "Red Roses for a Blue Lady," "The Naughty Lady of Shady Lane," and "Say Something Sweet to Your Sweetheart"

1923 **Dorothy Gilman.** American author and creator of Mrs. Pollifax

1923 **Sam Francis.** American painter

1924 **Sidney Lumet.** American motion-picture director, noted for such films as *Murder on the Orient Express* (1974), *Dog Day Afternoon* (1975), and *Network* (1976)

1925 **June Lockhart.** American motion-picture and television actress

1933 **James Meredith.** American civil rights advocate and first black graduate of the University of Mississippi

1942 **Willis Reed.** Professional basketball player and Hall of Famer

1945 **Carly Simon.** American pop rock singer

1949 **Phyllis George.** American television personality and former Miss America

1963 **George Michael.** British singer, composer, musician, and founder of the Wham! musical group

June 25 – Events

1503 Two of Columbus's ships were beached in Jamaica, where he was marooned for a year on the return trip of his fourth voyage to America.

1630 Governor John Winthrop of the Massachusetts Bay Colony introduced the fork to America.

1788 Virginia ratified the Constitution, becoming the 10th state.

1876 The Battle of the Little Bighorn began between U.S. General Custer and Chief Crazy Horse. The battle, known as "Custer's Last Stand," ended in disaster for Custer the next day.

1886 Arturo Toscanini, a 19-year-old cellist, conducted the orchestra in a Rio de Janeiro performance of *Aida* so successfully that he became a conductor, the greatest of his time.

1916 Thomas Eakins, the American painter, died in Philadelphia at age 71.

1918 United States marines captured Belleau Wood in World War I.

1938 The Fair Labor Standards Act became law.

1950 The North Koreans invaded South Korea, starting the Korean War.

1951   The first commercial color telecast took place as CBS transmitted a one-hour special from New York to four other cities.

1962   The U.S. Supreme Court declared prayer in the public schools unconstitutional.

1973   John Dean testified before the Select Senate Committee that President Nixon knew about the Watergate break-in as early as September 15, 1972.

June 26 – Birthdays

1742   **Arthur Middleton.** American Revolutionary War leader and one of the South Carolina signers of the Delcaration of Independence

1763   **George Morland.** English painter

1819   **Abner Doubleday.** Alleged Inventor of baseball, who laid out the first diamond-shaped field in Cooperstown, New York, in 1839, and coined the word *baseball*

1824   **Lord Kelvin (William Thomson).** One of the greatest British physicists of the 1800s, and for whom the Kelvin temperature scale is named

1853   **Frederick Henry Evans.** English photographer

1854   **Sir Robert L. Borden.** Prime minister of Canada, 1911-1920, and one of the greatest of all time

1891   **Sidney Coe Howard.** American playwright noted for works such as *They Knew What They Wanted* (1924) and *Alien Corn* (1933)

1892   **Pearl Buck.** Nobel Prize-winning American author noted for novels of life in China, such as *The Good Earth* (1932)

1893   **Big Bill Broonzy.** American musician and one of the great blues singers

1894   **Clarence Lovejoy.** Founder of the college guides

1894   **Jeanne Eagels.** American stage and motion-picture actress

1897   **Hans Barth.** German painter and composer

1898   **Willy Messerschmitt.** German aircraft designer

1901   **Stuart Symington.** U.S. senator in the 1950s, 1960s, and 1970s

1902   **Bill Lear.** Father of the Lear jet plane

1903   **Babe Herman.** Professional baseball player

1904   **Peter Lorre.** Hungarian-American motion-picture actor

1906   **Al Stillman.** American lyricist noted for songs such as "I Believe," "The Breeze and I," "Chances Are," "It's Not for Me to Say," "In Spain They Say 'Si Si'," and "Jukebox Saturday Night"

1908   **Debs Garms.** Professional baseball player who won the National League batting championship in 1940

1914   **Mildred "Babe" Didrikson Zaharias.** One of the greatest woman athletes in history, who excelled in basketball, baseball, and tennis, and won 17 major women's golf tournaments in a row

1921   **Howie Pollet.** Professional baseball player

1922   **Eleanor Parker.** American motion-picture and television actress

1934   **John Tunney.** U.S. senator and son of boxing great Gene Tunney

1936   **Hal Greer.** Professional basketball superstar with over 15,000 career points

1939   **Charles Robb.** Governor of Virginia, U.S. senator, and son-in-law of President Lyndon B. Johnson

1940   **Billy Davis Jr..** Member of the Fifth Dimension singing group

1961   **Greg LeMond.** American cyclist and three-time winner of the Tour de France cycling race

1974   **Derek Jeter.** Professional baseball player

June 26 – Events

363   Emperor Julian, the last Roman emperor to oppose Christianity, died in Mesopotamia at age 32, while fighting the Persians.

1284   The Pied Piper of Hamelin, Germany, according to legend, lured 130 children of the town into oblivion.

1483   Richard III, the last Plantagenet king of England, assumed the throne.

1541   Spanish explorer Francisco Pizarro, the conquerer of Peru, was killed by a group of his enemies, who burst into his house while he was entertaining guests at dinner.

1844   John Tyler married his second wife, Julia Gardiner, becoming the first president to marry while in office.

1876   The Battle of the Little Bighorn ended with Crazy Horse wiping out General George Custer and his entire column of 208 men.

1906   The first French Grand Prix auto race began at Le Mans. It was completed the following day.

1916   The Cleveland Indians, in a game with the Chicago White Sox, appeared on the field with numbers on their uniforms, the first time numbers were used to identify baseball players.

1917   The first U.S. troops landed in France in World War I, under the command of General John J. Pershing.

1945   The United Nations Charter was signed by all 50 nations present at the San Francisco Conference.

1948   The United States announced the Berlin Airlift to fly cargo to West Berlin and nullify the Russian blockade.

1959   Ingemar Johansson knocked out Floyd Patterson in the third round in New York City to win the heavyweight championship.

1963   "Ich bin ein Berliner," President John F. Kennedy said to a cheering crowd in West Berlin.

June 27 – Birthdays

1462   **Louis XII.** King of France, 1498-1515, known as "The Father of His People"

1550   **Charles IX.** King of France, 1560-1574

1806   **Augustus De Morgan.** English mathematician, noted for *De Morgan's Theorems* of logic

1835 **Fred Harvey.** American restaurateur who opened "Harvey House" restaurants in railroad depots in the Southwestern U.S.

1846 **Charles Stewart Parnell.** Irish Nationalist leader of the 1870s and 1880s

1850 **Lafcadio Hearn.** American author noted for works such as *Chita: A Memory of Last Island* (1889) and *In Ghostly Japan* (1899)

1859 **Mildred J. Hill.** American composer, author, and pianist, noted for songs such as "Good Morning to All" and the most popular English language song of all time, "Happy Birthday to You"

1872 **Paul Laurence Dunbar.** American novelist and poet, and one of the earliest U.S. black writers

1874 **John Golden.** American playwright and songwriter

1880 **Helen Keller.** Outstanding American author and educator who was blind and deaf

1895 **Joseph Patrick McEvoy.** American novelist and creator of the comic strip *Dixie Dugan*

1897 **Maceo Pinkard.** American composer and author, noted for songs such as "Sweet Georgia Brown" and "Gimme a Little Kiss, Will Ya Huh?"

1900 **Otto E. Passman.** U.S. congressman, 1947-1977

1907 **John McIntire.** American motion-picture and television actor

1913 **Philip Guston.** American painter noted for his melancholy city scenes such as *Martial Memory* (1940-1941)

1922 **Bob Keeshan.** American television actor who played Captain Kangeroo for 30 years (October 1955 to December 1984)

1923 **Gus Zernial.** Professional baseball player

1929 **Peter Maas.** American author

1930 **H. Ross Perot.** American millionaire, philanthropist, and candidate for president in 1992 and 1996

1933 **Gary Crosby.** American singer and son of singer Bing Crosby

1936 **John Shalikashvili.** U.S. army general and Chairman of the Joint Chiefs of Staff under President Clinton

1938 **Bruce Edward Babbitt.** Governor of Arizona

1941 **Errol Mann.** Professional football player

1943 **Rico Petrocelli.** Professional baseball player and sports announcer

1944 **Bruce Johnston.** American musician with the Beach Boys musical group

1945 **Catherine Lacoste.** Professional golfer

June 27 – Events

1787 Edward Gibbon, the great English historian, completed his monumental work, *The Decline and Fall of the Roman Empire,* at his house in Lausanne, Switzerland.

1844 Joseph Smith, founder of the Mormon Church, was murdered by a mob in Carthage, Illinois.

1847 New York and Boston were first linked by telegraph wires.

1861 The Central Pacific Railroad was organized in California.

1864 Confederate troops won the Battle of Kenesaw Mountain, Georgia, in the Civil War.

1921 The New York Curb Exchange became an indoor securities market as it opened its first building in New York City.

1941 The U.S. Army's four-engined B-19, the largest bomber in the world at the time, passed its first test flight in California.

1944 The Allies captured Cherbourg in World War II, giving them an excellent harbor for the upcoming liberation of France.

1947 Automobile workers received the first pension in automotive history as the Ford Motor Company agreed to finance their pension plan.

1950 President Harry S. Truman ordered the U.S. air and naval forces under General Douglas MacArthur to help repel the North Korean invaders of South Korea.

1985 Tennis player Anne White appeared at Wimbledon in white leotards. She was allowed to play but was warned not to wear such dress again.

June 28 – Birthdays

1476 **Paul IV.** Roman Catholic pope, 1555-1559

1491 **Henry VIII.** King of England, 1509-1547, noted for establishing the Reformation in England and for his six wives

1503 **Giovanni Della Casa.** Italian bishop, poet, and translator

1577 **Peter Paul Rubens.** The greatest Flemish painter of the 1600s and the most important baroque painter of northern Europe

1712 **Jean Jacques Rousseau.** French philosopher, who was the most important writer of the Enlightenment movement of the 1700s, and whose political philosophy was the inspiration for the French Revolution

1795 **Lambert Hitchcock.** American chairmaker

1858 **Otis Skinner.** Distinguished American stage actor of the late 19th and early 20th centuries, and father of actress Cornelia Otis Skinner

1867 **Luigi Pirandello.** Nobel Prize-winning Italian dramatist noted for his philosophic plays

1874 **Oley Speaks.** American composer and singer, noted for songs such as "On the Road to Mandalay" and "Now the Day Is Over"

1875 **Henri Leon Lebesgue.** Distinguished French mathematician, noted for the Lebesgue integral

1883 **Pierre Laval.** French politician who collaborated with the Nazis in World War II and served as premier in their puppet Vichy French regime

1894 **Francis Townsend Hunter.** American Hall of Fame tennis player

1902 **Richard Rodgers.** One of the greatest American composers of popular music, who wrote nearly 400 songs and composed the music for such hits as *Oklahoma!, South Pacific,* and *The Sound of Music*

1905 **Ashley Montagu.** English anthropologist and writer

1909 **Eric Ambler.** English author noted for his mystery novels of intrigue and international adventure

1914 **Lester Raymond Flatt.** American guitarist and singer who with Earl Scruggs formed the Flatt and Scruggs musical duo

1915 **Leonard C. McKenzie Jr..** American composer and author, noted for songs such as "Chiquita Banana"

1926 **Mel Brooks.** American comedian, actor, and motion-picture director

1933 **Pat Morita.** American motion-picture and television actor

1936 **Tom Magliozzi.** American car repair expert noted with his brother Ray for the radio show *Car Talk*

1946 **Gilda Radner.** American motion-picture and television actress

1948 **Kathy Bates.** American stage and screen actress and Academy Award winner as best actress in *Misery* (1990)

1948 **Raymond Chester.** Professional football player

1949 **Don Baylor.** Professional baseball player

1949 **Clarence Davis.** Professional football player

1949 **Don Nottingham.** Professional football player

1950 **Chris Speier.** Professional baseball player

1952 **Joe Sambito.** Professional baseball player

1954 **Mark Edmondson.** Australian tennis player

1955 **Matt Robinson.** Professional football player

1964 **Mark Grace.** Professional baseball player

1966 **John Cusack.** American motion-picture actor and brother of actress Joan Cusack

1966 **Mary Stuart Masterson.** American motion-picture actress and daughter of actor-director Peter Masterson and actress Carlin Glynn

1969 **Danielle Brisebois.** American television actress

June 28 – Events

1461 King Edward IV of England was crowned at Westminster Abbey.

1519 Charles I of Spain became Charles V, Holy Roman Emperor, creating overnight a vast empire larger than any since ancient Rome.

1709 Peter the Great of Russia destroyed Sweden as a major power in the Battle of Poltava in the Great Northern War, one of the greatest military battles in history.

1778 Molly Pitcher took her mortally wounded husband's place at a cannon in the Battle of Monmouth, New Jersey, in the American Revolutionary War.

1836 James Madison died at Montpelier, his country estate in Virginia, at age 85.

1838 Queen Victoria was crowned at Westminster Abbey a year after she ascended the English throne.

1894 Congress made Labor Day a national holiday, designating it as the first Monday in September.

1907 New York catcher Branch Rickey, the future great baseball executive, in a game with the Washington Senators, allowed 13 stolen bases, an all-time record.

1914 Archduke Francis Ferdinand, heir to the throne of Austria-Hungary, and his wife, Sophie, were assassinated in Sarajevo, in the Austrian province of Bosnia, triggering World War I.

1919 Harry S. Truman married Elizabeth Virginia "Bess" Wallace.

1919 The Treaty of Versailles was signed in the Hall of Mirrors of the Palace of Versailles, near Paris, ending World War I and establishing the League of Nations.

1948 The Communist Party Cominform denounced Marshal Tito of Yugoslavia for his anti-Soviet opinions.

1950 The North Koreans captured Seoul, South Korea's capital, in the Korean War.

1978 The U.S. Supreme Court ruled in the Bakke case that the University of California Medical School must admit Allan P. Bakke. Bakke, a white man, had charged "reverse discrimination."

June 29 – Birthdays

1798 **Count Giacomo Leopardi.** Italian lyric poet and essayist of the early 19th century

1805 **Hiram Powers.** The greatest American sculptor of the mid-1800s, noted for his statues of George Washington and Benjamin Franklin, and for his most famous work, *Greek Slave*

1830 **J.Q.A. Ward.** American sculptor

1858 **George Washington Goethals.** American civil engineer and army officer who directed the completion of the Panama Canal

1861 **William James Mayo.** American physician who, with his father and brother, founded the Mayo Clinic in Rochester, Minnesota, in 1889

1865 **William E. Borah.** One of the leaders of the U.S. senate for almost 33 years

1868 **George E. Hale.** American astronomer who founded the three largest U.S. observatories— Yerkes (1895), Mount Wilson (1904), and Palomar (dedicated in 1948)

1871 **Luisa Tetrazzini.** Italian operatic soprano noted for her remarkable vocal agility in coloratura roles

1885 **John Storrs.** American sculptor

1900 **Antoine de Saint-Exupery.** French aviator and writer, who was the chief influence in the creation of the literature of aviation

1901 **Nelson Eddy.** American singer and actor, who joined with Jeanette MacDonald to become the most popular screen duo of their day

1908 **Joan Davis.** American stage and motion-picture actress and comedienne

1908　**Leroy Anderson.** American songwriter, conductor, and composer of "The Blue Tango" (1952)

1910　**Frank Loesser.** American composer and author, noted for songs such as "Heart and Soul," "Let's Get Lost," "On a Slow Boat to China," "Two Sleepy People," "Baby, It's Cold Outside," and "Thumbelina"

1911　**Prince Bernhard.** Husband of Queen Juliana of Holland

1912　**John Willard Toland.** American journalist, historian, and author, noted for books such as *The Rising Sun* and *Adolf Hitler*

1915　**Ruth Warrick.** American stage, screen, and television actress and star of the television soap opera *All My Children*

1915　**Dizzy Trout.** Professional baseball player

1919　**Slim Pickens.** American motion-picture and television actor

1934　**Carl Levin.** U.S. senator

1936　**Harmon Killebrew.** Hall of Fame baseball player who had 573 career home runs

1944　**Gary Busey.** American motion-picture and television actor

1948　**Fred Grandy.** American television actor and U.S. representative

1949　**Valerie Ziegenfuss.** American tennis player

1949　**Dan Dierdorf.** Professional football player and Hall of Famer

1955　**Jimmy Rogers.** Professional football player

1956　**Pedro Guerrero.** Professional baseball player

1962　**Sharon Lawrence.** American stage and television actress

June 29 – Events

64　Saint Peter, the leading apostle of Jesus Christ, was executed in the gardens of Nero at the foot of Vatican Hill (traditional date). He was crucified head downward at his own request.

67　Saint Paul, one of the greatest preachers and organizers of the Christian Church, was executed on the Via Ostia three miles from Rome(date uncertain).

1312　Henry VII of Germany was crowned Holy Roman Emperor in Rome.

1408　The Council of Cardinals met to end the Great Schism in the Roman Catholic Church.

1504　Columbus sailed from Jamaica for home on his fourth and last voyage to America.

1767　The British Parliament approved the Townshend Revenue Acts which imposed duties on glass, lead, paint, paper, and tea shipped to America, and which ultimately led to the American Revolution.

1776　The Virginia state constitution was adopted, and Patrick Henry was elected as the first governor.

1852　Henry Clay, U.S. senator and secretary of state, died at age 75.

1861　Elizabeth Barrett Browning, the English poet, died in Florence at age 55.

1916　The Western Pacific Railroad was incorporated.

1933　Primo Carnero knocked out Jack Sharkey in the sixth round in Long Island City, New York, to win the heavyweight title.

1934　Zaro Agha died in Istanbul at age 164. He was alleged to be the oldest man in the world.

1949　South Africa began its racial segregation program of apartheid.

1972　The U.S. Supreme Court ruled the death penalty, as it was being meted out, could constitute cruel and unusual punishment.

June 30 – Birthdays

1685　**Dominikus Zimmerman.** German architect

1685　**John Gay.** English playwright and poet, best known for *The Beggar's Opera* (1728)

1768　**Elizabeth Kortright Monroe.** Wife of President James Monroe

1771　**Joseph Short.** American cabinetmaker

1789　**Horace Vernet.** French painter

1819　**William A. Wheeler.** U.S. vice president under President Hayes.

1879　**Walter Hampden.** American stage, screen, radio, and television actor with a career that spanned over 50 years

1884　**Georges Duhamel.** French scientist, mathematician, and author

1893　**Harold Laski.** English political scientist and educator

1893　**Walter Ulbricht.** Premier of East Germany after World War II

1900　**Madge Bellamy.** American motion-picture and stage actress

1901　**Willie Sutton.** Famous American bank robber who, when asked why he robbed banks, said, "Because that's where the money is"

1905　**William Zeckendorf.** American real estate empire builder

1906　**John William Van Ryn.** One of the greatest doubles tennis players of the 1930s

1908　**Grady Watts.** American composer and author, noted for songs such as "Blue Champagne" and "Daddy's Boy"

1915　**Harry M. Weese.** American architect

1917　**Lena Horne.** American singer and actress

1917　**Buddy Rich.** American drummer

1918　**Susan Hayward.** American motion-picture actress, who had five Oscar nominations and won for Best Actress in *I Want to Live* (1958)

1927　**Shirley Fry Irvin.** American Hall of Fame tennis player who ranked in the top ten from 1944 through 1956

1938　**Geoffrey Moss.** American cartoonist and illustrator

1942　**Robert Ballard.** American scientist and author, who discovered the sunken *Titanic*

1966　**Mike Tyson.** World heavyweight champion

June 30 – Events

1604 King James I of England approved a list of 54 scholars to revise the Bible. Under the leadership of Richard Bancroft, they produced the King James Version seven years later.

1859 French acrobat Emile Blondin made the first tight-rope crossing of Niagara Falls, a distance of 1,100 feet, as 5,000 people watched, 160 feet below him.

1882 Charles Guiteau was hanged for the assassination of President James A. Garfield.

1906 The Federal Food and Drug Act of 1906 was signed into law by President Theodore Roosevelt.

1918 Eugene V. Debs, U.S. socialist leader, was arrested for interference with army and navy recruiting. He subsequently served nearly 3 years of a 10-year jail sentence.

1924 The Teapot Dome scandals of the Harding Administration resulted in the indictment of Secretary of the Interior Albert Fall and two oilmen.

1934 On orders of Adolf Hitler, the Nazis exterminated their enemies in Germany on the "Night of the Long Knives."

1936 Margaret Mitchell published her famous novel, *Gone With the Wind*.

1940 The comic strip *Brenda Starr,* by Dale Messick, appeared for the first time.

1950 President Harry S. Truman ordered U.S. ground forces into the Korean War.

1963 Paul VI was crowned as the 262nd pope of the Roman Catholic Church.

1971 The 26th Amendment to the U.S. Constitution was ratified, making 18 years the minimum age for voting.

1971 Three Russian cosmonauts, who set a 24-day endurance record in orbit, became the first men to die in space, as their *Soyuz 11* vehicle burned on entering the earth's atmosphere.

7

July

July, the seventh month of the year, was originally the fifth month of the ancient Roman calendar. As such it was appropriately named *Quintilis,* the Latin word for *fifth.* To honor Julius Caesar, who gave the world the Julian Calendar, the name of the month was changed to *Julius,* or July. In the first calendar of Romulus, July had 30 days, but from the time of Numa Pompilius, it has had 31 days.

July 4 is Independence Day in the United States, commemorating the day in 1776 when the Declaration of Independence was adopted. Bastille Day, the French Independence Day, occurs on July 14, and Canada celebrates July 1 as Dominion Day, marking the anniversary of the establishment of the Dominion of Canada in 1867. The Philippines, Venezuela, Argentina, Peru, Belgium and The Netherlands all celebrate their Independence Day in July, as well. One other special day is Moon Day (July 20), the anniversary of the first landing on the moon in 1969. Four American Presidents, John Quincy Adams, James Garfield, Calvin Coolidge and Gerald Ford, were born in July, as was Caesar, himself, on July 12, 100 B.C.

The birthstone for July is the ruby, and the flowers are the water lily and the larkspur.

July 1 – Birthdays

1506 **Louis II.** King of Hungary and Bohemia (1516-1526)

1646 **Gottfried Wilhelm Leibnitz.** German mathematician and scholar who shares with Isaac Newton the distinction of inventing the calculus

1725 **Jean Baptiste Rochambeau.** French general who helped the Americans in the Revolutionary War

1742 **Georg Christoph Lichtenberg.** German physicist and satirist

1802 **Gideon Welles.** Secretary of the Navy under Presidents Lincoln and Andrew Johnson

1804 **George Sand.** Highly popular French novelist of the 1800s, known also for her love affairs with the composer Frederic Chopin and the poet Alfred de Musset

1807 **Thomas G. Clemson.** American mining engineer, for whom Clemson University was named

1857 **Roger Connor.** Hall of Fame baseball player with a lifetime batting average of .325

1861 **John Clarkson.** Hall of Fame baseball pitcher who won 53 games in 1885 and 49 games in 1889

1872 **Louis Bleriot.** French aviation pioneer, who made the first flight across the English Channel in 1909

1892 **James M. Cain.** American novelist noted for such works as *The Postman Always Rings Twice*

1893 **Walter White.** American writer and executive secretary of the NAACP, 1931-1955

1899 **Charles Laughton.** English stage and motion-picture actor, and master performer for 40 years

1902 **William Wyler.** German-American motion-picture director, who won Academy Awards for *Mrs. Miniver* (1942), *The Best Years of Our Lives* (1946), and *Ben-Hur* (1959)

1907 **Bill Stern.** Colorful American sports announcer

1907 **Ilya Bolotowsky.** American painter and sculptor noted for the geometric style

1909 **Madge Evans.** American child actress of the silent films from age five, who made the transition to leading lady roles in Hollywood and on Broadway

1912 **David Brower.** American conservationist and president of Friends of the Earth

1916 **Olivia De Havilland.** One of Hollywood's leading dramatic actresses of the 1930s and 1940s, whose film career spanned over 40 years and resulted in two Academy Awards for best actress

1925 **Farley Granger.** American stage, screen, and television actor

1929 **Nell Jackson.** Hall of Fame track and field player and first black head coach of a U.S. Olympic team (1956)

1931 **Leslie Caron.** French dancer and motion-picture actress

1931 **Tab Hunter.** American motion-picture actor

1934 **Sydney Pollack.** American motion-picture director and actor, and Academy Award-winning director for *Out of Africa* (1985)

1934	**Jean Marsh.** English motion-picture and television actor and writer
1934	**Kirsten Simone.** Prima ballerina of Denmark
1936	**Jamie Farr.** American actor who played the role of Klinger in the long-running television show M*A*S*H
1941	**Twyla Tharp.** American choreographer and dancer
1941	**Sally Quinn.** American journalist
1942	**Karen Black.** American stage and motion-picture actress
1942	**Genevieve Bujold.** Canadian stage and motion-picture actress
1946	**Debbie Harry.** American rock singer for the Blondie musical group
1952	**Dan Akroyd.** American motion-picture and television actor and comedian
1952	**Roger Carr.** Professional football player
1958	**Nancy Lieberman.** Hall of Famer and one of the greatest players in women's basketball
1959	**Ann Smith.** American tennis player
1961	**Carl Lewis.** American track-and-field athlete and Olympic medalist in 1984, 1988 and 1996
1961	**Princess Diana.** English noblewoman (Lady Diana Spencer), who became the wife of Prince Charles, the heir to the English throne

July 1 – Events

1535	Sir Thomas More, the noted English writer, was convicted of high treason against King Henry VIII on perjured evidence, and was condemned to death. He was executed on July 6.
1642	Londoners revolted against King Charles I, marking the beginning of the English Civil War.
1847	The first U.S. adhesive postage stamps went on sale in the form of Benjamin Franklin 5-cent stamps and George Washington 10-cent stamps.
1862	The Battle of the Seven Days ended in General Robert E. Lee's saving Richmond from the Union forces in the Civil War.
1863	The Battle of Gettysburg, the greatest ever fought in the Western hemisphere, began in Gettysburg, Pennsylvania, in the Civil War.
1867	The British North America Act went into effect, creating the Dominion of Canada.
1867	"On the Beautiful Blue Danube," the famous waltz of Johann Strauss Jr., was played in America for the first time, at a New York City concert.
1896	Harriet Beecher Stowe, author of *Uncle Tom's Cabin,* died in Hartford, Connecticut, at age 85.
1898	Theodore Roosevelt and his "Rough Riders" occupied San Juan Hill in Cuba in the Spanish-American War.
1916	British troops attacked the Germans on the Somme front to relieve pressure on Verdun in World War I.
1916	Dwight D. Eisenhower married Mamie Geneva Doud.
1932	Franklin D. Roosevelt was nominated for president at the Democratic Convention in Chicago.

1943	The "pay-as-you-go" system of income tax withholding began for American wage earners.
1944	Delegates from 44 countries began a conference at Bretton Woods, NH, where they agreed to establish the International Monetary Fund and the world bank.
1966	Medicare went into effect in the United States.
1971	The 182-year-old U.S. Post Office Department was replaced by the U.S. Postal Service.
1980	"O Canada" was officially proclaimed the Canadian national anthem.
1983	Buckminster Fuller, the inventor of the geodesic dome, died at age 87.
1997	China resumed sovereignty over Hong Kong, ending 156 years of British rule.

July 2 – Birthdays

419	**Valentinian III.** Emperor of Rome, AD 425-455, who was crowned at the age of 6
1486	**Jacopo Sansovino.** Florentine sculptor and architect
1489	**Thomas Cranmer.** First Protestant archbishop of Canterbury, and supporter of King Henry VIII in his successful attempt to divorce his first wife, Catherine of Aragon
1714	**Christoph Willibald Gluck.** German composer who reformed opera in the 1700s by achieving a balance between the music and the dramatic parts
1796	**Michael Thonet.** Austrian furniture designer
1855	**Clarence W. Barron.** Founder of *Barron's Financial Weekly*
1862	**Sir William Bragg.** British physicist who shared the 1915 Nobel Prize for research on the structure of crystals
1877	**Hermann Hesse.** German novelist, poet, and 1946 Nobel Prize winner, noted for works such as *Steppenwolf* (1927)
1879	**Bob Zuppke.** One of the most famous coaches in college football, who introduced the offensive huddle in the early 1930s
1898	**Anthony C. McAuliffe.** U.S. World War II general who said "Nuts!" to the Nazi ultimatum to surrender in the Battle of the Bulge
1903	**Sir Alexander Douglas-Home.** British prime minister, 1963-1964
1903	**Olav V.** King of Norway, who succeeded his father Haakon VII in 1957
1905	**Rene Lacoste.** French tennis player and one of the greatest of the 1920s and 1930s, who won two Wimbledon titles, two U.S. titles, and three French titles (Lacoste, Jean Borotra, Jacques Brugnon and Henri Cochet were known as the Four Musketeers)
1908	**Thurgood Marshall.** The first black justice of the U.S. Supreme Court
1922	**Dan Rowan.** American comedian and co-star of television's long-running *Laugh-in*
1925	**Medger Evers.** American civil rights leader
1925	**Patrice Lumumba.** First prime minister of Zaire

| 1931 | **Larry Costello.** Professional basketball player |

1931 **Larry Costello.** Professional basketball player
1932 **Dave Thomas.** American restaurateur and founder of the Wendy's chain (1969)
1935 **Ed Bullins.** American playwright
1937 **Polly Holliday.** American actress who played Flo in the long-running television series *Alice*
1937 **Richard Petty.** Most successful Grand National stock car driver in the U.S. in the 1970s and 1980s
1947 **Luci Baines Johnson.** Daughter of President Lyndon B. Johnson
1949 **Curtis Rowe.** Professional basketball player
1954 **Victor Amaya.** American tennis player
1961 **Jimmy McNichol.** American motion-picture actor
1964 **Jose Canseco.** Professional baseball player and first to hit 40 home runs and steal 40 bases in one season (1988)
1968 **Ronald Goldman.** Famous American murder victim who happened to be present and was killed in 1994 along with Nicole Brown Simpson, the wife of football great O.J. Simpson

July 2 – Events

1566 Nostradamus, the French astrologer, physician, and prophet, died in Salon at age 63.
1644 Oliver Cromwell defeated the Royalists in the Battle of Marston Moor in the English Civil War.
1776 The Continental Congress approved the Declaration of Independence, to be signed two days later.
1778 Jean Jacques Rousseau, the great French writer, died at Ermenonville, France, at age 66.
1881 President James A. Garfield was shot by the assassin Charles Guiteau. Garfield lived for over two months before dying on September 19.
1890 The Sherman Anti-Trust Act was passed by Congress, outlawing monopolies that hindered trade.
1903 Ed Delahanty, one of the greatest baseball players of all time, was swept over Niagara Falls and killed at age 35, in the prime of his career.
1904 Anton Chekhov, the great Russian playwright, died of tuberculosis in the German resort of Badenweiler at age 44.
1926 The United States Army Air Corps was established by Congress.
1932 Franklin D. Roosevelt accepted the Democratic Party's nomination for president, pledging "a new deal for the American people."
1937 Amelia Earhart, the noted American aviator, was lost in the Pacific Ocean. Her disappearance is still an unsolved mystery.
1941 Joe DiMaggio, the great Yankee outfielder, hit a home run to extend his hitting streak to 45 games, breaking the old record of 44 set by Wee Willie Keeler in 1897.
1955 *The Lawrence Welk Show* premiered on ABC television. It was to air for over 40 years.
1961 Ernest Hemingway, the noted American writer, committed suicide by shooting himself at Ketchum, Idaho, at age 58.

1964 President Lyndon Johnson signed the Civil Rights Act of 1964 into law. It was the strongest civil rights law in United States history.
1976 North and South Vietnam were officially reunited.

July 3 – Birthdays

1423 **Louis XI.** King of France, 1461-1483, known as the "terrible king"
1567 **Samuel de Champlain.** French explorer who founded Quebec and was called the "Father of New France"
1683 **Edward Young.** English poet and essayist
1728 **Robert Adam.** Scottish architect and furniture designer famous with his brother James for the *Adam style* of architecture
1731 **Samuel Huntington.** Connecticut signer of the Declaration of Independence
1738 **John Singleton Copley.** The greatest portrait painter in colonial America
1746 **Henry Grattan.** Irish statesman
1789 **Johann Friedrich Overbeck.** German painter of Christian religious subjects
1881 **Leon Errol.** Australian-born stage and screen actor and comedian
1883 **Franz Kafka.** Czechoslovakian-born Austrian novelist, noted for such works as *The Trial* and *In the Penal Colony*
1901 **Jean Dubuffet.** French painter noted for works such as *M. Plume, Portrait of Henri Michaux* (1947), *Corps de Dame* (1950), and *Les Vagabonds* (1954)
1903 **Dick Robertson.** American composer, author, and singer, noted for songs such as "A Little on the Lonely Side" and "Goodnight, Wherever You Are"
1905 **Frank Layton Ryerson.** American composer and author, noted for songs such as "Blue Champagne," and "The Boston Tea Party"
1906 **George Sanders.** British stage and motion-picture actor
1908 **M.F.K. Fisher.** American writer, noted for her essays on gastronomy, such as *How to Cook a Wolf* (1942)
1909 **Earl Butz.** Secretary of agriculture in the Nixon-Ford administration
1909 **Stavros Niarchos.** Greek shipowner and tycoon
1913 **Dorothy Kilgallen.** American journalist and television entertainer
1927 **Ken Russell.** English motion-picture director
1930 **Pete Fountain.** American jazz musician
1937 **Tom Stoppard.** Czech-born British author and playwright noted for *Rosencrantz and Guildenstern Are Dead* (1967) and *Shakespeare in Love* (1998)
1940 **John Patrick Sears.** American lawyer and political campaign manager
1947 **Betty Buckley.** American actress
1952 **Adriano Panatta.** Italian tennis player
1953 **Frank Tanana.** Professional baseball player
1955 **Matt Keough.** Professional baseball player

1956 **Montel B. Williams.** American television personality and host of *The Montel Williams Show*
1957 **Laura Branigan.** American singer
1962 **Tom Cruise.** American motion-picture actor
1965 **Greg Vaughn.** Professional baseball player
1966 **Moises Alou.** Professional baseball player and son of baseball player Felipe Alou

July 3 – Events

1608 French explorer Samuel de Champlain founded Quebec and gave it its name.
1775 General George Washington formally took command of the Continental Army at Cambridge, Massachusetts.
1863 The Battle of Gettysburg ended in General Lee's defeat and marked the turning point in the Civil War. General Pickett led his famous charge on this last day of the battle.
1890 Idaho was admitted to the Union as the 43rd state.
1898 The Spanish fleet in Santiago Bay, Cuba, was destroyed by U.S. Commodore Winfield Schley in the Spanish-American War.
1945 The first post-World War II civilian automobile left the Ford Motor Company assembly line.
1950 U.S. soldiers engaged the North Koreans for the first time in the Korean War.
1962 Algeria became independent after 132 years of French rule.
1976 Israeli commandos, in a daring raid, rescued 103 hostages being held by terrorists at Uganda's Entebbe Airport.
1988 The *U.S.S. Vincennes* shot down an Iranian jetliner over the Persian Gulf, killing all 290 passengers and crew after the Americans erroneously identified the plane as an Iranian F-14 fighter.

July 4 – Birthdays

1477 **Aventinus (Johannes Turmair).** Bavarian humanist and historian
1756 **William Rush.** American sculptor noted as the finest of the early wood carvers
1804 **Nathaniel Hawthorne.** One of America's greatest writers and author of *The Scarlet Letter* (1850), a masterpiece of American literature
1807 **Giuseppe Garibaldi.** Italian military hero and one of the principal leaders in the unification of Italy into a single kingdom
1816 **Hiram Walker.** American distiller who founded Hiram Walker's Distillery in 1857
1819 **E.R. Squibb.** American pharmacist who founded the forerunner of the pharmaceutical firm of E.R. Squibb and Sons in 1858
1826 **Stephen Foster.** One of America's best-loved composers, who wrote over 200 songs, such as "Swanee River," "My Old Kentucky Home, Good Night," "Oh Susanna," and "Jeanie with the Light Brown Hair"

1837 **Carolus-Duran.** French painter
1847 **James A. Bailey.** Partner with P.T. Barnum in the Barnum and Bailey Circus
1859 **Mickey Welch.** Hall of Fame professional baseball pitcher with 308 wins in 13 seasons
1872 **Calvin Coolidge.** 30th U.S. president
1878 **George M. Cohan.** American actor, songwriter, and playwright, noted for "Give My Regards to Broadway" and "You're a Grand Old Flag," among others (His real birthday was July 3, but he claimed July 4.)
1883 **Rube Goldberg.** American cartoonist known for his complicated mechanical contrivances for accomplishing simple tasks and for his creation of the cartoon character Boob McNutt
1885 **Louis B. Mayer.** Russian-born movie executive who in the 1930s developed Metro-Goldwyn-Mayer into one of the greatest Hollywood studios, with "more stars than there are in the heavens"
1889 **Joseph Young.** American lyricist noted for songs such as "Rockabye Your Baby With a Dixie Melody," "Dinah," "I'm Sitting on Top of the World," and "In a Shanty in Old Shanty Town"
1895 **Irving Caesar.** American composer noted for songs such as "Swanee," "Tea for Two," "Animal Crackers in My Soup," and "Is It True What They Say About Dixie"
1898 **Gertrude Lawrence.** Noted British stage and screen actress and comedienne
1900 **Louis Armstrong.** American singer, musician, and bandleader, and one of the world's leading jazz performers, whose career spanned over half a century
1902 **George Murphy.** American dancer, actor, and U.S. senator
1902 **Meyer Lansky.** American mobster of the 1930s
1903 **Abe Saperstein.** Professional basketball coach who founded the Harlem Globetrotters
1905 **Lionel Trilling.** American writer, scholar, and critic
1911 **Mitch Miller.** American oboist and conductor
1912 **Virginia Graham.** American television talk show hostess
1916 **Tokyo Rose (Iva Toguri D'Aquino).** American World War II traitor who broadcast pro-Japanese propaganda during the war to American troops
1918 **Ann Landers.** American newspaper advice columnist and twin sister of columnist Abigail Van Buren
1918 **Abigail Van Buren.** American newspaper advice columnist and twin sister of columnist Ann Landers
1920 **Leona Helmsley.** American hotel executive and wife of businessman Harry Helmsley
1924 **Eva Marie Saint.** American stage, motion-picture, and television actress
1927 **Neil Simon.** American playwright and screenwriter, noted for such works as *Come Blow Your Horn* (1961) and *Barefoot in the Park* (1967)
1928 **Gina Lollobrigida.** Italian motion-picture actress
1928 **Stephen Boyd.** Irish motion-picture actor

1929 **Chuck Tanner.** Professional baseball player and manager

1930 **George Steinbrenner.** American industrialist and owner of the New York Yankees baseball team

1938 **Bill Withers.** American singer and songwriter

1940 **Bob Carmichael.** Australian tennis player

1943 **Emerson Boozer.** Professional football player and sportscaster

1943 **Geraldo Rivera.** American broadcast journalist

1948 **Clamma Dale.** American soprano

1948 **Wayne Nordhagen.** Professional baseball player

1951 **John Alexander.** Australian tennis player

1955 **John Waite.** English singer and songwriter

1962 **Pam Shriver.** American tennis player

1963 **Henri LeConte.** French tennis player

July 4 – Events

1623 William Byrd, the noted English composer, died at Stondon Massey, Essex, at age 80.

1776 The Declaration of Independence was adopted in Independence Hall in Philadelphia, and signed by John Hancock "by order and in behalf of Congress."

1778 George Rogers Clark and his frontiersmen, the "Big Knives," captured the supply base of Kaskaskia in Illinois from the British during the Revolutionary War.

1798 George Washington was commissioned as "Lieutenant General and Commander in Chief of the Armies" by President John Adams.

1802 The United States Military Academy opened at West Point, New York.

1826 John Adams died in Quincy, Mass., at age 90. His last words were "Thomas Jefferson still survives." By a remarkable coincidence, however, Jefferson died also that day, at age 83.

1831 James Monroe died in New York City at age 73. He was the third ex-President to die on Independence Day, five years after the deaths of John Adams and Thomas Jefferson.

1848 François Rene de Chateaubriand, the great French novelist, died in Paris at age 79.

1863 Vicksburg surrendered, after a long siege, to General U.S. Grant's Union army in the Civil War.

1884 The Statue of Liberty was presented to the United States by France in a Paris ceremony.

1895 The verses of "America the Beautiful," by Katherine Lee Bates, appeared for the first time, in *The Congregationalist,* a Boston magazine.

1917 "Lafayette, we are here!" announced Colonel Charles Stanton after U.S. troops arrived in France in World War I.

1919 Jack Dempsey won the heavyweight championship, knocking out Jess Willard in the third round in Toledo, Ohio.

1939 Baseball immortal Lou Gehrig said farewell to New York fans at Yankee Stadium honoring him on his special day.

1946 The Republic of the Philippines was established as an independent nation.

1976 The U.S. celebrated its 200th birthday throughout the land. In New York harbor President Ford struck the ship's bell of the USS *Forrestal* once for each original colony.

1984 Phil Niekro got career strikeout number 3,000, as he pitched the New York Yankees to a 5-0 win over the Texas Rangers. He was only the ninth pitcher in history to strike out 3,000 men.

July 5 – Birthdays

1709 **Etienne de Silhouette.** French minister of finance for whom the silhouette was named because of his reputation for stinginess

1753 **Jonathan Carter Hornblower.** Inventor of the double-beat valve

1755 **Sarah Siddons.** The greatest of English tragic actresses, whose striking beauty made her a subject of poets and painters

1801 **David Farragut.** U.S. admiral who at the Civil War battle of Mobile Bay said, "Damn the torpedoes. Full steam ahead!"

1803 **George Borrow.** English linguist, writer, and traveler

1810 **P.T. Barnum.** The world's most famous showman, and founder in 1871 of the circus "The Greatest Show on Earth"

1820 **William John Macquorn Rankine.** Scottish engineer and a founder of thermodynamics, noted for the Rankine cycle

1853 **Cecil Rhodes.** British diamond king, statesman, and empire builder, largely responsible for the development of the British Empire in Africa

1879 **Dwight Filley Davis.** American statesman and tennis enthusiast, who in 1900 established the Davis Cup, an annual award for the world champion tennis team

1879 **Wanda Landowska.** Noted Polish harpsichordist, pianist, and composer

1880 **Beatrix Hoyt.** Noted professional golfer

1889 **Jean Cocteau.** French playwright, novelist, artist, and avant garde writer, noted for such works as *Les Enfants Terribles* (1929) and *Orpheus* (1950)

1902 **Henry Cabot Lodge.** U.S. ambassador to the United Nations under President Eisenhower and vice presidential candidate in 1960

1904 **Milburn Stone.** American motion-picture and television actor who played Doc Adams in the long-running television series *Gunsmoke*

1911 **Georges Pompidou.** President of France, 1969-1974, who succeeded General de Gaulle

1912 **Mack David.** American lyricist noted for some 100 songs such as "Candy," "I Don't Care If the Sun Don't Shine," and "La Vie En Rose"

1917 **Manolete (Manuel L.R. Sanchez).** One of the greatest Spanish matadors in history

1923 John McKay. Noted college and professional football coach

1928 Warren Oates. American motion-picture and television actor

1937 Shirley Knight. American stage and motion-picture actress

1943 Mark Cox. English tennis player

1948 Julie Nixon Eisenhower. Daughter of President Richard Nixon and wife of David Eisenhower

1950 Gary Matthews. Professional baseball player

1951 Goose Gossage. Professional baseball player

1956 James Lofton. Professional football player

July 5 – Events

1632 Sir Anthony Van Dyck, the famous Flemish painter, was knighted by King Charles I in London.

1811 Venezuela declared its independence from Spain, the first of the South American countries to do so.

1865 William Booth, a former Methodist minister, founded in the slums of London the organization that in 1878 became the Salvation Army.

1935 The National Labor Relations Act was signed into law by President Franklin D. Roosevelt.

1940 Great Britain broke diplomatic relations with Vichy France during World War II.

1943 The Battle of Kursk, the greatest tank battle of all time, began between the Russians and Germans in World War II. It involved 6,000 tanks and 4,000 planes, and was one of the turning points of the war. The Germans never mounted another offensive on the central front.

1945 General Douglas MacArthur announced the liberation of the Philippines in World War II.

1945 The Labor Party, in a great surprise, defeated the Conservative Party, resulting in British prime minister Winston Churchill's being replaced by Clement Attlee 21 days later.

1946 The Bikini, the shocking new bathing suit of designer Louis Reard, was first modeled at a Paris fashion show.

1947 Larry Doby signed a contract with the Cleveland Indians, becoming the American League's first black player.

1948 England adopted the National Health Service Act, providing free medical service for all.

1971 The 26th Amendment to the Constitution was certified, lowering the voting age to 18.

July 6 – Birthdays

1739 Georges Jacob. French cabinetmaker

1747 John Paul Jones. American Revolutionary War hero and the "Father of the American Navy"

1755 John Flaxman. English sculptor and illustrator, and one of the leaders of the neoclassical movement of the late 1700s

1796 Nicholas I. Czar of Russia, 1825-1855, noted for his harsh rule and for putting down the Decembrist revolution in 1825

1832 Maximilian. Archduke of Austria and Emperor of Mexico, 1864-1867

1884 Harold Stirling Vanderbilt. American yachtsman, grandson of Cornelius Vanderbilt and inventor of contract bridge (1925)

1891 Steve O'Neill. Professional baseball player and manager

1892 Jack Yellen. Polish-born composer noted for songs such as "Are You From Dixie," "Ain't She Sweet," "Happy Days are Here Again" (campaign song of FDR), and "Wonder What's Become of Sally"

1899 Mignon Eberhart. American author of popular mystery novels

1909 Andrei Gromyko. Russian foreign minister during the Cold War

1913 Gwyn Thomas. English novelist

1913 Eleanor Clark. American writer

1915 La Verne Andrews. American singer and member of the Andrews Sisters singing group, a highly popular trio in the 1940s

1918 Sebastian Cabot. English-born motion-picture and television actor

1919 Dorothy Kirsten. American operatic soprano

1921 Nancy Reagan. American actress and wife of President Ronald Reagan

1921 Bill Haley. American pioneer rock and roll musician, noted for the first rock and roll record, "Rock Around the Clock"

1924 Darrell Royal. Famous football head coach at the University of Texas, 1957-1977

1925 Merv Griffin. American television talk show host

1927 Pat Paulson. American comedian

1927 Janet Leigh. American motion-picture actress

1932 Della Reese. American singer and actress

1935 Dalai Lama. Religious leader (the 14th Incarnate Dalai Lama) and, until the Chinese invaded his country in 1950, the supreme ruler of Tibet

1937 Ned Beatty. American motion-picture actor

1946 George W. Bush. Governor of Texas (elected in 1994) and son of former president George Bush

1946 Sylvester Stallone. American motion-picture actor and screenwriter noted for his roles in the *Rocky* and *Rambo* movies

1946 James Wyeth. American painter and son of painter Andrew Wyeth

1948 Fred Dryer. Professional football player and actor

1948 Brad Park. Professional hockey player

1952 Shelley Hack. American model and actress

1952 Grant Goodeve. American actor

1954 Louise Erdrich. American author known for works such as *The Beet Queen* (1987)

1954 Jason Thompson. Professional baseball player

1954 Willie Randolph. Professional baseball player

1956 Billy Taylor. Professional football player

July 6 – Events

1189 King Henry II of England died at age 55 and was succeeded by his son, Richard I, The Lion-Hearted.

1415 John Huss, whose teachings were forerunners of those of Martin Luther, was burned at the stake on a charge of heresy.

1535 Sir Thomas More, the great English writer, was beheaded in London at age 57 on orders of King Henry VIII.

1553 Mary I (Bloody Mary) became queen of England upon the death of her brother, Edward VI.

1701 Captain Kidd (William Kidd) was hanged in England for piracy.

1777 British troops captured Fort Ticonderoga from the Americans in the Revolutionary War.

1854 The delegates formally adopted the name *Republican* for their new party, at a party meeting in Jackson, Michigan.

1865 *The Nation*, a liberal weekly magazine, was founded in New York.

1885 Louis Pasteur innoculated the first person, Joseph Moister, who had been bitten by a rabid dog. Moister consequently survived.

1928 A preview of the first all-talking motion picture, *Lights of New York*, took place at the Strand Theater in New York.

1933 Baseball's first All-Star game was played in Chicago, with the American League beating the National League, 4-2, on Babe Ruth's two-run home run.

1957 Althea Gibson became the first black tennis player to win a Wimbledon singles title, defeating fellow American Darlene Hard, 6-3, 6-2.

1979 Martina Navratilova won the Wimbledon women's singles title for the second straight year.

1980 Bjorn Borg won the Wimbledon men's singles championship for the fifth straight year, an unprecedented feat.

1985 Martina Navratilova defeated Chris Evert Lloyd for her fourth consecutive Wimbledon singles championship.

July 7 – Birthdays

1586 **Thomas Hooker.** Congregational preacher and a founder of Connecticut

1752 **Joseph Marie Jacquard.** French inventer who perfected the automatic pattern, or Jacquard, loom

1833 **Felicien Rops.** Belgian painter

1884 **Lion Feuchtwanger.** American novelist and playwright

1887 **Raymond Hatten.** American stage and screen actor with a 50-year career

1887 **Marc Chagall.** Russian-born French painter and designer, noted for his dreamlike, fanciful paintings

1899 **George Cukor.** American motion-picture director whose entertainment career spanned 60 years

1902 **Vittorio De Sica.** Italian motion-picture actor and director

1906 **Satchell Paige.** Professional baseball pitcher thought by some to have been the greatest of all time

1907 **Robert Anson Heinlein.** American author noted for works such as *The Moon is a Harsh Mistress* (1966)

1909 **Billy Herman.** Professional baseball player

1911 **Gian Carlo Menotti.** Italian-American opera composer, noted for such works as *Amahl and the Night Visitors* (1951), *The Consul* (1950), and *The Saint of Bleecker Street* (1954)

1917 **Lawrence F. O'Brien.** Political strategist for President Kennedy and commissioner of the American Basketball Association

1919 **William Kunstler.** Crusading American lawyer

1921 **Ezzard Charles.** World heavyweight champion, 1950-1951

1922 **Pierre Cardin.** French fashion designer

1924 **Mary Ford.** American singer and musician (Les Paul and Mary Ford duo)

1927 **Doc Severinsen.** American trumpeter and bandleader on the *Tonight Show* with Johnny Carson

1933 **David McCullough.** American historian and author known for works such as *Truman* (1992)

1940 **Richard Armey.** U.S. congressman and Minority Leader

1940 **Ringo Starr.** Member of the Beatles musical group

1944 **Ian Wilmut.** British embryologist who headed the team that cloned the sheep Dolly, the first mammal produced from the nonreproductive tissue of an adult

1944 **Tony Jacklin.** Professional golfer

1946 **Tadeusz Nowicki.** Polish tennis player

1948 **Fred Brown.** Professional basketball player

1949 **Shelley Duvall.** American motion-picture actress

1955 **Len Barker.** Professional baseball pitcher who pitched a perfect game in 1981

1960 **Ralph Lee Sampson.** Professional basketball superstar

1968 **Chuck Knoblauch.** Professional baseball player

1980 **Michelle Kwan.** U.S. national champion and world champion figure skater (both 1996)

July 7 – Events

1307 King Edward I of England died at age 68 on his way to subdue the new Scottish king, Robert Bruce.

1754 King's College (later Columbia University) in New York City was chartered.

1846 Monterey, California, was captured from the Mexicans by a band of American settlers and proclaimed to be annexed to the United States.

1898 Hawaii was annexed by the United States.

1923 Warren G. Harding became the first U.S. president to visit Alaska.

1930 Sir Arthur Conan Doyle, the British novelist, died at Crowborough, Essex, at age 71.

1937	The Japanese staged an "incident" near Peiping (Beijing) as an excuse for starting war with China.
1946	Jimmy Carter married Rosalynn Smith of Plains, Georgia.
1979	Bjorn Borg won his fourth straight Wimbledon singles title.
1984	Martina Navratilova won her third straight Wimbledon singles championship and her fifth in seven years.
1985	Boris Becker, a 17-year-old German, defeated Kevin Curren to win the Wimbledon singles championship, becoming the youngest player ever to win this or any Grand Slam tournament.

July 8 – Birthdays

1478	**Giangiorgio Trissino.** Italian philologist, dramatist, and poet
1621	**Jean de La Fontaine.** French poet famous for his *Fables* (1668-1694) and a collection of racy stories called *Contes* (1664-1666)
1790	**Fitz-Greene Halleck.** American poet
1837	**William Quantrill.** Confederate guerrilla band captain in the Civil War
1838	**Ferdinand von Zeppelin.** Famous German pioneer in lighter-than-air vehicles, and the first large-scale builder of dirigible balloons, which became known as zeppelins
1839	**John D. Rockefeller.** American industrialist, founder of the Standard Oil Company, and at one time the world's richest man
1867	**Kathe Kollwitz.** German painter, sculptor, and printmaker, noted for violent images of common people and for becoming, in 1919, the first woman elected to the Berlin Academy
1869	**William Vaughn Moody.** American poet, dramatist, teacher, and literary historian, noted for his landmark drama, *The Great Divide* (1906)
1872	**Harry Von Tilzer.** American composer noted for songs such as "A Bird in a Gilded Cage," "On a Sunday Afternoon," and "I Want a Girl Just Like the Girl That Married Dear Old Dad"
1882	**Percy Grainger.** Australian-American composer, pianist, and conductor, noted as a leading interpreter of Edvard Grieg's piano music and for his own works such as "Marching Song of Democracy" (1917)
1890	**Stanton MacDonald-Wright.** American painter
1892	**J. Russel Robinson.** American composer and author, noted for songs such as "Mary Lou," "Singin' the Blues," "Margie," and "Memphis Blues"
1898	**Alec Waugh.** English novelist and travel writer, noted for such works as *The Loom of Youth* (1917)
1906	**Philip Johnson.** American architect
1907	**George Romney.** Governor of Michigan, 1963-1969, and secretary of housing and urban development under President Nixon

1908	**Nelson Rockefeller.** Governor of New York, 1958-1974, and U.S. vice president under President Ford
1914	**Billy Eckstine.** American singer
1917	**Fay Emerson.** American motion-picture and television actress
1918	**Craig Stevens.** American motion-picture and television actor
1918	**Irwin Hasen.** American cartoonist and creator of *The Green Hornet* and *Green Lantern*
1926	**Elisabeth Kubler-Ross.** Swiss-born psychiatrist and author of *On Death and Dying*
1926	**George H. Weyerhaeuser.** President of Weyerhaeuser Company
1931	**Roone Arledge.** American television producer and executive
1935	**John David Crow.** Heisman Trophy winner (1957) and professional football superstar
1935	**Steve Lawrence.** American singer and actor
1942	**Phil Gramm.** U.S. senator
1946	**Cynthia Gregory.** American ballet dancer
1947	**Kim Darby.** American motion-picture and television actress
1951	**Alan Ashby.** Professional baseball player
1952	**Jack Lambert.** Hall of Fame professional football player
1953	**Anna Quindlen.** American author noted for *Object Lessons* (1991)
1956	**Terry Puhl.** Professional baseball player
1958	**Kevin Bacon.** American stage, screen and television actor
1961	**Andy Fletcher.** British keyboardist with the Depeche Mode musical group

July 8 – Events

49 BC	The city of Paris, France, was founded by the Parisii, a Celtic tribe of fishermen.
1497	Vasco da Gama, the Portuguese navigator, left Lisbon on the voyage that would make him the first man to sail around the Cape of Good Hope to India.
1663	King Charles II of England granted Rhode Island its second charter, which remained the law of the colony and state until 1843.
1776	The Liberty Bell rang out in Philadelphia to announce the adoption of the Declaration of Independence.
1822	Percy Bysshe Shelley, the great English poet, died in a sailing accident in the Gulf of Spezia, near Leghorn, Italy, at age 29.
1835	The famous crack in the Liberty Bell appeared as the bell was being rung during the funeral of Chief Justice John Marshall.
1889	The *Wall Street Journal* was first published.
1889	John L. Sullivan fought the last bare-knuckle heavyweight championship fight, defeating Jake Kilrain in the 75th round to retain his title.
1891	Warren G. Harding married Florence Kling DeWolfe.

1896	William Jennings Bryan made his famous "Cross of Gold" speech at the Democratic National Convention in Chicago.
1907	The first *Ziegfeld Follies* was staged on the roof garden of the New York Theater.
1919	The comic strip *Toots and Casper,* by Jimmy Murphy, first appeared.
1950	General Douglas MacArthur was appointed United Nations commander in Korea.
1978	Bjorn Borg, the Swedish tennis star, won his third consecutive Wimbledon singles title.
1984	John McEnroe became the first American since Don Budge in 1938 to win two consecutive Wimbledon singles championships.

July 9 – Birthdays

1562	**Orazio Gentileschi.** Italian painter
1764	**Ann Radcliffe.** English Gothic novelist whose best known work is *The Mysteries of Udolpho* (1794)
1819	**Elias Howe.** American inventor, noted for his invention of the sewing machine, which he patented in 1846
1835	**Tomas Estrada Palma.** First president of Cuba, 1902-1906
1856	**Nikola Tesla.** Hungarian-born engineer who invented the alternating-current induction motor and played the major role in establishing 60-hertz power in the U.S.
1856	**Daniel Guggenheim.** American industrialist and philanthropist, who in 1924 set up the Daniel and Florence Guggenheim Foundation to promote "the well-being of mankind"
1878	**H.V. Kaltenborn.** American radio commentator recognized as the "father" of his profession
1879	**Ottorino Respighi.** One of the best-known Italian composers of the early 1900s, and composer of "The Fountains of Rome" (1917) and "The Pines of Rome" (1924)
1887	**Samuel Eliot Morison.** American rear admiral, historian, and Pulitzer Prize winner in 1943 for his *Admiral of the Ocean Sea,* a biography of Columbus, and in 1960 for *John Paul Jones*
1890	**Walter Henry "Hy" Heath.** American composer and author, noted for songs such as "Mule Train"
1894	**Percy LeBaron Spencer.** American inventor noted for the microwave oven (1946)
1894	**Dorothy Thompson.** Noted American journalist and wife of the famous novelist Sinclair Lewis
1897	**Albert Wedemeyer.** American World War II general
1901	**Barbara Cartland.** World's all-time best selling author of romantic fiction, with over 250 books that have sold over 100 million copies
1908	**Minor White.** American photographer
1916	**Edward Heath.** British prime minister, 1970-1974
1927	**Ed Ames.** American singer and actor
1928	**Vince Edwards.** American stage, screen, and television actor

1928	**Donald Joyce Hall.** Chief executive officer of Hallmark Cards and son of its founder, Joyce Clyde Hall
1933	**Oliver Sacks.** American physician and author noted for *Awakenings* (1973)
1933	**Hedrick Smith.** American journalist
1937	**David Hockney.** English painter noted for works such as *Mt. Fuji and Flowers* (1972)
1938	**Brian Dennehy.** American stage, screen, and television actor
1945	**Dean Koontz.** American author of horror novels such as *Watchers* (1987) and *Midnight* (1989)
1945	**Mike Riordan.** Professional basketball player
1947	**O.J. Simpson.** Professional Hall of Fame football player and superstar
1951	**Anjelica Huston.** American stage, screen, and television actress and daughter of director John Huston
1952	**John Tesh.** American composer, TV anchorman, reporter and host (*Entertainment Tonight*)
1954	**Debbie Sledge.** American singer, member of Sister Sledge, noted for their 1979 hit, "We Are Family"
1955	**Jimmy Smits.** American actor noted for the TV shows *LA Law* and *NYPD Blue*
1955	**Willie Wilson.** Professional baseball player
1956	**Tom Hanks.** American motion-picture actor and winner of back-to-back Academy Awards for *Philadelphia* (1993) and *Forrest Gump* (1994)
1957	**Kelly McGillis.** American motion-picture actress
1965	**Courtney Love.** American singer, songwriter and guitarist

July 9 – Events

1540	The English Parliament declared the marriage of Henry VIII and Anne of Cleves null and void.
1755	English general George Braddock was decisively defeated by the French at Fort Duquesne in the French and Indian War in a battle in which his assistant, Colonel George Washington, distinguished himself. Braddock later died of wounds received in the battle.
1776	The Declaration of Independence was read aloud to General George Washington's troops in New York.
1797	Edmund Burke, the great British statesman, died at Beaconsfield at age 68.
1816	Argentina declared its independence of Spain, following the lead of Buenos Aires, which had been independent since 1810.
1850	President Zachary Taylor died in the White House at age 65 of a typhus infection.
1877	The world's first telephone company, the Bell Telephone Company, was founded.
1918	Congress authorized the Distinguished Service Medal.
1924	The Democrats nominated John W. Davis for president on the 103rd ballot, an all-time record number.

1963   The comic strip *Fred Basset,* by Alex Graham, first appeared.

July 10 – Birthdays

1509   **John Calvin.** One of the chief leaders of the Protestant Reformation and the founder of the Presbyterian Church

1723   **Sir William Blackstone.** English jurist whose *Commentaries on the Laws of England* became the most influential book in the history of English law

1792   **George Mifflin Dallas.** U.S. vice president under President Polk, for whom the city of Dallas, Texas, was named

1792   **Frederick Marryat.** English author whose novels about life at sea were widely read in the 1800s

1824   **Richard King.** American cattleman who founded the famous King Ranch in Texas

1830   **Camille Pissarro.** French impressionist painter, and perhaps the most popular and respected member of the impressionist group

1834   **James McNeill Whistler.** The most original American artist of the 1800s, best known for his *Arrangement in Grey and Black,* commonly known as *Whistler's Mother*

1852   **William James Chalmers.** American manufacturer and co-founder in 1901 of the Allis-Chalmers Co.

1861   **Albert Bigelow Paine.** American writer

1867   **Finley Peter Dunne.** American writer, humorist, and creator of *Mr. Dooley*

1868   **Bobby "Link" Lowe.** First major league baseball player to hit four home runs in one game (May 30, 1894)

1871   **Marcel Proust.** French novelist and author of the seven-part novel and masterpiece of world literature *Remembrance of Things Past,* which contains *Swann's Way* (1913) and six other novels

1882   **Ima Hogg.** Noted American philanthropist

1885   **Mary O'Hara.** American writer and author of *My Friend Flicka* (1941)

1888   **Giorgio de Chirico.** Italian painter and founder of the Metaphysical School of painting

1889   **Noble Sissle.** American author and conductor, noted for songs such as "I'm Just Wild About Harry" and "You Were Meant for Me"

1891   **Rexford Guy Tugwell.** Assistant secretary of agriculture under Franklin D. Roosevelt and one of Roosevelt's original brain trusters

1892   **Slim Summerville.** American comedian of the silent films and character actor of the talkies

1894   **Jimmy McHugh.** American composer, noted for songs such as "I'm in the Mood for Love," "On the Sunny Side of the Street," "It's a Most Unusual Day," "Let's Get Lost," and "How Blue the Night"

1895   **John Gilbert.** American actor and great screen idol of the silent movies, who teamed with Greta Garbo in a number of scorching screen romances, but was unable to make a successful transition to the talkies

1900   **Mitchell Parish.** Prolific American songwriter who wrote the lyrics to "Stars Fell on Alabama," "Star Dust," "Deep Purple," "Moonlight Serenade," and some 600 other popular songs

1903   **Horace Stoneham.** American baseball owner who moved the New York Giants to San Francisco after the 1957 season

1908   **H.J. Heinz II.** Chairman of the board of the H.J. Heinz company

1914   **Joe Shuster.** American comic book artist and co-creator with Jerry Siegel of *Superman*

1918   **Jack Easton.** American composer, author, and pianist, noted for scores of numerous Broadway plays and for the NBC Peacock Theme

1920   **David Brinkley.** American television newscaster and commentator

1920   **Owen Chamberlain.** American physicist noted for co-discovering the antiproton

1921   **Jeff Donnell.** American motion-picture actress

1921   **Jake LaMotta.** Middleweight boxing champion, 1949-1951

1923   **Jean Kerr.** American writer, author of *Please Don't Eat the Daisies,* and wife of writer Walter Kerr

1923   **Earl Henry Hamner Jr.** American author noted for the television story *The Waltons*

1926   **Fred Gwynne.** American actor noted for his role in the long-running television show *The Munsters*

1926   **Carleton Carpenter.** American motion-picture actor, singer, and dancer

1927   **David Dinkins.** Mayor of New York City, 1990-1994

1931   **Nick Adams.** American motion-picture actor

1931   **Del Insko.** Professional harness racer

1933   **Jan De Gaetani.** American singer

1933   **Jerry Herman.** American popular songwriter, noted for works such as "Hello Dolly!" (which won the 1965 Grammy Award) and "Mame"

1933   **Richard Gordon Hatcher.** One of the first black men to be elected mayor of a major U.S. city (Gary, Indiana, in 1967)

1940   **Gene Alley.** Professional baseball player

1943   **Arthur Ashe.** American tennis player and Wimbledon singles champion in 1975, for whom Arthur Ashe Stadium at the U.S. Open was named

1945   **Ron Glass.** American actor noted for his role on the long-running TV show *Barney Miller*

1945   **Toni Fritsch.** Professional football player

1945   **Virginia Wade.** English tennis player who won the Wimbledon singles title in 1977

1946   **Hal McRae.** Professional baseball player

1947   **Arlo Guthrie.** American guitarist, singer, songwriter, and son of singer Woody Guthrie

1949   **James Montgomery.** Professional football player

1954   **Andre Dawson.** Professional baseball player

July 10 – Events

138   Roman emperor Hadrian died at Baiae at age 62.

1460 The Duke of York defeated King Henry VI at Northampton, but Henry survived on the throne of England until the following year.

1850 Millard Fillmore became the 13th U.S. president, succeeding Zachary Taylor, who had died the previous day.

1890 Wyoming was admitted to the Union as the 44th state.

1923 Benito Mussolini secured his fascist dictatorship by dissolving Italy's nonfascist parties.

1925 The Scopes Trial began in Dayton, Tenn., with John T. Scopes accused of teaching evolution in a public school. The opposing lawyers were Clarence Darrow and William Jennings Bryan.

1929 Congress made official the current size of U.S. paper money.

1936 Chuck Klein of the Philadelphia Phillies hit four home runs in a ten-inning baseball game.

1940 The Battle of Britain began, as the German *Luftwaffe* started the great World War II air raids on the British Isles that would continue until October 31.

1943 British, American, and Canadian troops invaded Sicily in World War II.

1951 Armistice talks began at Kaesong, aimed at ending the Korean War.

1962 The communications satellite *Telstar I* was launched by the United States in Cape Canaveral, Florida, to relay TV and telephone signals between America and Europe.

July 11 – Birthdays

1274 **Robert Bruce.** King of Scotland, 1328-1329, who spent most of his life in a gallant struggle to free his country from English rule

1657 **Frederick I.** First king of Prussia, 1701-1713, and son of the "great elector" of Brandenburg, Frederick William

1767 **John Quincy Adams.** Sixth U.S. president and son of President John Adams

1819 **Susan Warner.** American novelist, noted for *The Wide, Wide World* (1850), considered by many to be the first U.S. best seller

1838 **John Wanamaker.** American merchant and philanthropist and founder of John Wanamaker & Company, one of the largest department stores in the United States

1849 **Harry Keller.** American magician, "dean of magic," regarded by many of his time as the "most beloved magician in history"

1854 **Dr. Thomas Bowdler.** Self-appointed cleanser of literature, whose "cleaned-up" version of Shakespeare gave to the language the new word *bowdlerize* (expurgate)

1857 **Alfred Binet.** French psychologist who designed the first standard intelligence test

1861 **George W. Norris.** American statesman, U.S. senator, and advocate of public ownership of hydroelectric power plants, such as TVA

1885 **Roger de La Fresnaye.** French painter noted for works such as *The Artillery* (1912)

1890 **Theodora "Dolly" Morse.** American lyricist noted for songs such as "Three O'Clock in the Morning," "Hail, Hail, the Gang's All Here," and "Siboney"

1890 **Arthur William Tedder.** Marshal of the RAF and deputy supreme commander to General Dwight D. Eisenhower in World War II

1892 **Thomas Mitchell.** American stage, screen, and television actor, and one of the screen's greatest character actors

1894 **Walter Wanger.** American motion-picture producer

1897 **Johnny Marvin.** American composer, author, and singer, who wrote such songs as "Goodbye Little Darlin'" for many Gene Autry films

1899 **E.B. White.** American writer and author of *Stuart Little* (1945) and *Charlotte's Web* (1952)

1906 **Harry Von Zell.** American actor and television announcer for shows such as Burns and Allen

1910 **Sally Blane.** American motion-picture actress and sister of actress Loretta Young

1915 **Cecil Isbell.** Professional football superstar and member of the great Isbell to Hutson passing combination

1922 **Gene Evans.** American motion-picture and television actor

1944 **Lou Hudson.** Professional basketball player

1953 **Leon Spinks.** Heavyweight boxing champion, who won the title from Muhammad Ali in 1977

1957 **Peter Murphy.** British rock musician with the Bauhaus musical group

1959 **Suzanne Vega.** American rock and jazz singer and songwriter

July 11 – Events

1533 King Henry VIII of England was excommunicated by Pope Clement VII for marrying Anne Boleyn.

1598 San Juan de Los Caballeros, the first settlement in New Mexico, was founded by Juan de Onate.

1798 The Marine Corps was re-created as a separate military service by an act of Congress.

1804 Alexander Hamilton was mortally wounded at age 49 in a duel with Vice President Aaron Burr at Weehawken, New Jersey. He died the following day.

1864 Confederate General Jubal Early invaded the outskirts of Washington. Lincoln watched the battle from a parapet, becoming the only president under enemy fire while in office.

1916 The Second Battle of the Somme began in World War I.

1936 Adolf Hitler guaranteed Austria's frontier in a treaty with the Austrians. (Two years later he annexed the country.)

1937 George Gershwin, the noted American composer, died in Hollywood at age 38.

1955 The U.S. Air Force Academy was dedicated at Lowry Air Base, Colorado. The academy moved to its permanent site near Colorado Springs in 1958.

1962 The first U.S. television programs were broadcast by the BBC via satellite.

1979 The doomed spaceship *Skylab* plummeted to earth after six years and 34,981 orbits in space.

1985 Nolan Ryan struck out his 4,000[th] career batter, becoming the first pitcher ever to reach that plateau.

July 12 – Birthdays

100 BC **Julius Caesar.** Roman general and statesman, and one of the greatest men in the history of the world

1730 **Josiah Wedgwood.** England's greatest potter and one of the most famous pottery designers of all time

1817 **Henry David Thoreau.** American essayist, poet, celebrated practical philosopher, and the author of *Walden,* one of the world's great books

1824 **Eugene Louis Boudin.** French painter

1849 **Sir William Osler.** Canadian physician and one of the greatest medical teachers

1854 **George Eastman.** American inventor and manufacturer, who founded the Eastman Kodak Company

1863 **Albert Calmette.** Bacteriologist and developer of a tuberculosis vaccine

1868 **Stefan George.** German poet and a major representative of the European symbolism movement in poetry

1884 **Amedeo Modigliani.** One of the greatest Italian artists of the 1900s

1886 **Jean Hersholt.** Danish radio and motion-picture actor and "elder statesman" of the film community

1889 **Max Friedman.** Hall of Fame basketball player

1895 **Buckminster Fuller.** American writer and designer of automobiles, cities, and geodesic domes

1895 **Kirsten Flagstad.** Norwegian operatic soprano, and the greatest Wagnerian soprano of the mid-20th century

1895 **Oscar Hammerstein II.** American lyricist and collaborator with composers Jerome Kern, George Gershwin, and Richard Rogers, best known perhaps for "Ol' Man River"

1908 **Milton Berle.** American motion-picture and television actor and comedian, known as "Mr. Television" in the 1950s

1910 **Edward Johnson.** American composer, trombonist, and arranger, noted for songs such as "The Jersey Bounce"

1915 **Yul Brynner.** American motion-picture and television actor

1917 **Andrew Wyeth.** The most popular American painter of his time

1919 **Vera Ralston.** Czechoslovakian motion-picture actress

1920 **Keith Andes.** American motion-picture and television actor

1922 **Mark Hatfield.** U.S. senator

1934 **Van Cliburn.** American pianist who in 1958 won the International Tchaikovsky Competition in Moscow

1937 **Bill Cosby.** American actor and comedian noted for his television role in *The Bill Cosby Show,* one of the most popular of the 1980s

1938 **Ron Fairly.** Professional baseball player

1943 **Paul Silas.** Professional basketball player

1943 **Christine Perfect McVie.** English singer and musician with the Fleetwood Mac musical group

1948 **Richard Simmons.** American fitness guru

1951 **Jamey Sheridan.** American stage, screen and television actor

1951 **Cheryl Ladd.** American motion-picture and television actress

1953 **Tony Armas.** Professional baseball player

1956 **Mario Soto.** Professional baseball player

July 12 – Events

526 Saint Felix IV became Roman Catholic pope.

1153 Anastasius IV was crowned Roman Catholic pope.

1536 Desiderius Erasmus, the great Dutch humanist, died in Basel, Switzerland, at an approximate age of 70.

1543 King Henry VIII of England married his sixth wife, Catherine Parr.

1690 England's William III defeated James II, the Catholic pretender, in the Battle of the Boyne, completing the Protestant conquest of Ireland.

1691 Innocent XII was elected Roman Catholic pope.

1730 Clement XII was elected Roman Catholic pope.

1812 General William Hull's American army of 2,000 men invaded Canada at a point near Detroit in the War of 1812.

1862 Congress authorized the Medal of Honor (sometimes called the Congressional Medal of Honor) and designated it as the United States' highest military award.

1863 General Jubal Early's Confederate army, which had bombarded the outskirts of Washington, D.C., was thrown back by Union forces in the Civil War.

1870 John Wesley Hyatt, an American printer, patented Celluloid, which he had invented the previous year.

1912 *Queen Elizabeth*, starring Sarah Bernhardt, became the first foreign film shown in America.

1933 The minimum wage in the United States was set at 40 cents an hour.

1941 German armies cracked the Stalin Line in Russia in World War II, and marched toward Moscow. They eventually penetrated its suburbs, but were never able to take it.

1961 Weather satellite *Tiros 3* was launched, which discovered Hurricane Esther over the Atlantic Ocean.

1984 Democratic candidate for president Walter Mondale announced his choice of Congresswoman Geraldine Ferraro as the first woman to run for vice president on a major party ticket.

July 13 – Birthdays

1590 **Clement X.** Roman Catholic pope, 1670-1676

1607 **Wenceslaus Hollar.** English printmaker

1608 **Ferdinand III.** Holy Roman emperor who signed the Peace of Westphalia, ending the Thirty Years' War

1793 **John Clare.** English poet noted for works such as *Rural Muse* (1827) and for his best known verse, written in an asylum, "I am: yet what I am, who knows or cares?"

1821 **Nathan Bedford Forrest.** Confederate general in the Civil War, whose motto was "Git thar fustest with the mostest men"

1841 **Otto Wagner.** Austrian architect

1859 **Sidney Webb.** British economist and influential Fabian Socialist of the late 1800s and early 1900s

1863 **Mary Emma Woolley.** American educator and first woman to receive a bachelor's degree from Brown University

1886 **Father Edward Joseph Flanagan.** American priest who founded Boys Town in Nebraska in 1917

1889 **Stan Coveleski.** Hall of Fame baseball player

1892 **Punch Broadbent.** Hall of Fame hockey player

1895 **Sidney Blackmer.** American stage and motion-picture actor whose career spanned over 50 years

1901 **Mickey Walker.** World welterweight champion, 1922-1926, and middleweight champion, 1926-1931

1908 **Dorothy Round.** Hall of Famer who dominated British tennis in the 1930s and who was in the top ten in the world in 1933 through 1937

1913 **Dave Garroway.** Original host of television's *Today Show*

1918 **Marcia Joan Brown.** American children's artist, illustrator and winner of two Caldecott medals

1928 **Bob Crane.** American motion-picture and television actor

1928 **Sven Davidson.** Swedish tennis player

1931 **Frank Ramsey.** Professional basketball player

1934 **Wole Soyinka.** Nigerian dramatist, Nobel Prize winner (1986), and perhaps the foremost English language poet and playwright of black Africa

1935 **Jack Kemp.** Professional football player, U.S. congressman, Secretary of Human Services under President Bush, and candidate for Vice President in 1996

1937 **Charles Coody.** Professional golfer

1940 **Patrick Stewart.** English theater and television actor, noted for his role in *Star Trek—The Next Generation*

1940 **Paul Prudhomme.** American cajun chef and author

1942 **Roger McGuinn.** American guitarist, singer, and founder of The Byrds musical group

1942 **Harrison Ford.** American motion-picture actor noted for his roles as Indiana Jones, among others

1944 **Erno Rubik.** Hungarian educator who created the Rubik's cube in 1974

1946 **Richard Anthony "Cheech" Marin.** American writer, actor, and member with Tommy Chong of the Cheech and Chong musical duo

1961 **Anders Jarryd.** Swedish tennis player

July 13 – Events

1787 Congress passed the Northwest Ordnance, one of the most important laws ever adopted, providing for the governing of the Northwest Territory and subsequently all the U.S. territories.

1793 Jean Paul Marat, the notorious French revolutionary, was stabbed to death while sitting in his bathtub, by a young French girl, Charlotte Corday.

1798 William Wordsworth wrote his famous poem "Tintern Abbey."

1837 Buckingham Palace in London's West End became the official residence of British royalty, as Queen Victoria became the first British monarch to occupy it.

1863 Rioting against the Civil War military draft erupted in New York City, resulting in the death of over 1,000 people over the next three days.

1865 In an editorial in *The New Yorker,* Horace Greeley gave the famous advice, "Go West, young man, go West and grow up with the country."

1870 The "Ems Telegram" was sent to Otto von Bismarck, who condensed it deliberately to infuriate the French, leading, as he had hoped it would, to the Franco-Prussian War.

1896 Ed Delahanty of the Philadelphia Phillies hit four home runs in one game.

1900 Allied troops took Tientsin, China, in the Boxer Rebellion.

1972 The Paris peace talks on the Vietnam War resumed after a ten-week suspension.

1985 President Reagan underwent surgery to remove a large intestinal polyp. Vice President Bush was given unprecedented acting temporary powers under the 25th Amendment.

July 14 – Birthdays

1454 **Angelo Poliziano.** The best known of the brilliant group of writers gathered at the court of Lorenzo de Medici, who revived Italian literature in the second half of the 15th century

1602 **Jules Cardinal Mazarin.** French statesman, clergyman, and chief minister of France after the death of Cardinal Richelieu in 1642

1658 **Camillo Rusconi.** Italian sculptor

1750 **Aaron Arrowsmith.** English geographer and cartographer

1794	**John Gibson Lockhart.** Scottish writer
1852	**Dr. James Dwight.** Father of American lawn tennis and early tennis great
1858	**Emmeline Goulden Pankhurst.** English suffragette who was one of the foremost leaders in securing equal voting privileges for women in England
1860	**Owen Wister.** American novelist, best known for *The Virginian* (1902)
1862	**Gustav Klimt.** Austrian painter
1883	**Monte Carlo.** Danish-born composer noted for songs such as "Tangerine"
1890	**Ossip Zadkine.** Russian sculptor
1894	**Ted Koehler.** American lyricist noted for songs such as "Between the Devil and the Deep Blue Sea," "I Love a Parade," "Stormy Weather," "Let's Fall in Love," and "Animal Crackers in My Soup"
1894	**Dave Fleischer.** American animator who with his brother Max created the animated cartoons of *Betty Boop* and *Popeye the Sailor*
1899	**William J. "Billy" Hill.** American composer noted for songs such as "Empty Saddles," "Have You Ever Been Lonely," "The Last Round-Up," "In the Chapel in the Moonlight," and "The Old Spinning Wheel"
1902	**Harry Haenigsen.** American cartoonist and creator of the comic strips *Our Bill* and *Penny*
1903	**Irving Stone.** American novelist and biographer, noted for *Lust for Life* (1934), a novel about Vincent Van Gogh, and for *The Agony and the Ecstasy* (1961), a biography of Michelangelo
1904	**Isaac Bashevis Singer.** Polish-born Yiddish writer noted for works such as *Satan in Goray* and *Yentl*
1908	**Johnny Murphy.** Professional baseball player
1909	**Annabella (Suzanne Charpentier).** French dancer and actress
1910	**William Hanna.** American cartoonist and animator, noted with Joseph Barbera and Fred Quimby for creating the Tom and Jerry cartoons
1911	**Terry-Thomas.** English stage, screen, and television actor and comedian
1912	**Woody Guthrie.** Influential American folk singer and composer, who wrote more than 1,000 songs, including "This Land Is Your Land" and "So Long, It's Been Good to Know You"
1912	**Willard Francis Motley.** American novelist noted for *Knock On Any Door* and his posthumously published *Juneteenth*
1913	**Gerald R. Ford.** 38th U.S. president
1916	**Claude Harmon.** Professional golfer
1918	**Ingmar Bergman.** Internationally-known Swedish motion-picture director
1923	**Dale Robertson.** American motion-picture actor
1927	**Peggy Parish.** American children's author and creator of *Amelia Bedelia*
1927	**John Chancellor.** American television newscaster
1929	**Bob Purkey.** Professional baseball player
1930	**Polly Bergen.** American motion-picture and television actress

1932	**Roosevelt Grier.** Professional football player and actor
1934	**Lee Elder.** Professional golfer
1938	**Moshe Safdie.** Israeli architect who designed the master plan of Expo 67
1938	**Jerry Rubin.** American political activist
1943	**Bob Unger.** Professional golfer
1947	**Steve Stone.** Professional baseball player and broadcaster
1948	**Kenneth Burrough.** Professional football player
1961	**Boy George O'Dowd.** Lead singer with the British musical group Culture Club

July 14 – Events

1789	Parisians stormed the Bastille prison, marking the start of the French Revolution. The date has since been known as Bastille Day, the great national holiday of France.
1806	Meriwether Lewis and William Clark, of the Lewis and Clark Expedition, became the first white men in history to enter what is now Washington state from the east.
1830	Emma Hart Willard wrote "Rocked in the Cradle of the Deep" while at sea.
1853	Commodore Matthew C. Perry was received by the Lord of Toda on his mission to open trade between the U.S. and Japan.
1865	Edward Whymper became the first man to climb the Matterhorn, one of Europe's most ferocious peaks.
1881	Billy the Kid was killed in Fort Sumner, New Mexico, by Sheriff Pat Garrett.
1908	D.W. Griffith's first picture, *The Adventures of Dollie,* was released and shown for the first time, at Keith & Proctor's Union Square Theater in New York.
1921	Nicola Sacco and Bartolomeo Vanzetti were convicted of murder in the famous Sacco-Vanzetti trial.
1965	Adlai E. Stevenson, twice a presidential candidate, died of a heart attack in London at age 65.

July 15 – Birthdays

1573	**Inigo Jones.** First major architect of the English Renaissance
1606	**Rembrandt (Harmenszoon van Rijn).** The Netherlands' greatest artist
1631	**Richard Cumberland.** Father of English Utilitarianism
1704	**August Gottlieb Spangenberg.** American bishop and founder of the Moravian Church of America
1779	**Clement Clarke Moore.** American poet who in 1822 wrote the most popular of American Christmas poems, "A Visit from St. Nicholas," also known as "'Twas the Night Before Christmas"
1796	**Thomas Bulfinch.** American historian and author of *Bulfinch's Mythology,* a collection of works such as *The Age of Fable* and *The Age of Chivalry*

1833 **Thomas Collier Platt.** U.S. senator and New York political boss

1895 **Jane "Ginny" Bunford.** Tallest woman in the world at 7 feet 11 inches, reduced to 7 feet 7 inches, because of a spine curvature disease

1903 **Walter D. Edmonds.** American author, noted for novels such as *Drums Along the Mohawk* (1936)

1905 **Dorothy Fields.** American lyricist noted for such songs as "The Way You Look Tonight," "I Can't Give You Anything But Love, Baby," "I'm in the Mood for Love," and "On the Sunny Side of the Street"

1906 **Richard Armour.** American author and humorist noted for works such as *Light Armour* (1954), *The Classics Reclassified* (1960), and *The Academic Bestiary* (1974)

1919 **Iris Murdoch.** British novelist noted for her complex and witty works, such as *A Fairly Honourable Defeat* (1970)

1933 **Julian Bream.** English classical guitarist

1935 **Alex Karras.** Professional football player, sportscaster, and actor

1939 **Patrick Wayne.** American actor and son of actor John Wayne

1941 **Archie Clark.** Professional basketball player

1944 **Jan-Michael Vincent.** American motion-picture and television actor

1946 **Laura Rossouw.** South African tennis player

1946 **Linda Ronstadt.** American country rock singer

1948 **Tom Leonard.** American tennis player

1950 **Arianna Huffington.** Greek-American writer and commentator

1951 **Jesse Ventura.** American politician and wrestler (known as "The Body"), who was elected governor of Minnesota in 1998

1952 **Charles Lesley.** English tennis player

July 15 – Events

971 Saint Swithin, the Bishop of Winchester, was reburied inside his cathedral. The day is celebrated in England as Saint Swithin's Day.

1099 The Crusaders captured Jerusalem, slaughtering 40,000 people and burning the mosques.

1870 Georgia became the last of the Confederate states to be readmitted to the Union.

1876 George Washington Bradley of the Washington baseball team pitched the first no-hit game in major league history, defeating Hartford, 2-0.

1883 Tom Thumb (Charles S. Stratton), 40 inch-tall midget in P.T. Barnum's circus, died at age 45.

1912 Jim Thorpe sparked the U.S. team to victory in the 1912 Olympics. He won 15 events and was called "the most wonderful athlete in the world" by Sweden's King Gustav.

1916 William Boeing founded the Boeing Company (then known as Pacific Aero Products) in Seattle.

1918 Germany launched its last offensive on the Marne in World War I.

1948 President Harry S. Truman was nominated for reelection by the Democrats in their convention in Philadelphia, in spite of widespread doubts that he could win in November.

1958 U.S. marines landed in Lebanon to prevent a Communist takeover.

1965 American scientists displayed close-up pictures of the planet Mars taken by the *Mariner 4* spacecraft.

1971 President Nixon announced that he would make a historic trip to Peking to confer with officials of the People's Republic of China.

1973 Nolan Ryan pitched his second no-hitter of the season as California beat Detroit, 6-0.

1985 His doctors announced that President Reagan had cancer in a portion of his large intestine that had been removed, and they were optimistic that he would recover completely.

July 16 – Birthdays

1486 **Andrea del Sarto.** Outstanding painter of the Italian Renaissance, noted for works such as *The Madonna of the Harpies' with Saints Francis and John the Evangelist*

1661 **Pierre le Moyne Sieur d' Iberville.** French-Canadian explorer and founder of the province of Louisiana

1723 **Sir Joshua Reynolds.** One of the greatest English portrait painters of all time

1796 **Jean-Baptiste Camille Corot.** French landscape and figure painter and one of the leaders of the Barbizon school

1821 **Mary Baker Eddy.** Founder of Christian Science and the Church of Christ, Scientist

1848 **Eben Rexford.** Composer of "Silver Threads Among the Gold"

1872 **Roald Amundsen.** Norwegian explorer who discovered the South Pole in December of 1911

1880 **Kathleen Norris.** American writer whose novels (such as *Mother*) were serialized in women's magazines for more than 30 years

1883 **Charles Sheeler.** American painter and photographer noted for paintings that blend realism with cubism

1887 **Shoeless Joe Jackson.** Professional baseball player with a .356 lifetime batting average, who was banished from baseball because of the 1919 "Black Sox" scandal

1888 **Percy Kilbride.** American actor and co-star with Marjorie Main of the *Ma and Pa Kettle* films

1896 **Trygve Lie.** First United Nations secretary-general

1903 **Carmen Lombardo.** Canadian-born singer, brother of bandleader Guy Lombardo, and composer, noted for songs such as "Coquette," "Boo Hoo," and "Seems Like Old Times"

1904 **Mabel Wayne.** American composer and vocalist noted for songs such as "Ramona" and "It Happened in Monterey"

1907 **Barbara Stanwyck.** American stage, screen, and television actress, and one of the top stars of the 1930s and 1940s

1911 **Sonny Tufts.** American stage and motion-picture actor, whose name and statistics became favorites of trivia buffs

1911 **Ginger Rogers.** American dancer and actress with a 40-year career, who won an Academy Award for her performance in *Kitty Foyle* (1940)

1915 **Bernard Hughes.** American motion-picture and television actor

1920 **Jose Lopez Portillo.** President of Mexico in the 1970s

1924 **Bess Myerson.** American television personality and consumer official

1932 **Richard Thornburgh.** Attorney General under Presidents Reagan and Bush

1942 **Margaret Smith Court.** Australian tennis superstar and the second woman (after Maureen Connolly) to win the grand slam of tennis (1970)

1943 **Jimmy Johnson.** American football coach and first to win both a national college title (with the University of Miami) and a Super Bowl (with the Dallas Cowboys)

1948 **Marianne Kindler.** Swiss tennis player

1948 **Pinchas Zukerman.** Israeli-born violin virtuoso

1952 **Stewart Copeland.** American musician and drummer for The Police musical group

July 16 – Events

622 Mohammed made his famous flight, or *Hegira,* from Mecca to Medina, marking the beginning of the Moslem calendar.

1054 Michael Cerularius, Patriarch of Constantinople, was excommunicated by delegates of Pope Leo IX, precipitating the schism between the Churches of Rome and Constantinople.

1769 The first mission in California was established in San Diego by Father Junipero Serra.

1790 The District of Columbia was established by Congress.

1862 David G. Farragut became the first rear admiral in the U.S. Navy.

1918 Ex-Czar Nicholas II of Russia and his family were murdered by the Bolsheviks in a cellar in Ekaterinburg (now Sverdlovsk).

1935 The first parking meters were installed, in Oklahoma City.

1941 New York Yankee superstar Joe DiMaggio set his amazing record of hitting safely in 56 consecutive games, going 3 for 4 against Cleveland.

1945 The first atomic bomb was exploded, near Alamogordo, New Mexico. It produced the equivalent of 17,000 tons of TNT.

1969 *Apollo 11* lifted off from Cape Kennedy, bound for the moon, with astronauts Armstrong, Aldrin, and Collins on board. Four days later it put the first men on the moon.

1973 White House aide Alexander Butterfield publicly revealed the existence of President Nixon's taping system in the White House.

1981 Singer Harry Chapin was killed when his car was struck by a tractor-trailer on New York's Long Island Expressway.

1999 John F. Kennedy Jr. was killed at age 38, along with his wife Carolyn and her sister Lauren Bissette, when his private plane crashed into the Atlantic Ocean just west of Martha's Vineyard, Massachusetts.

July 17 – Birthdays

1674 **Isaac Watts.** English clergyman, noted for composing 761 hymns and psalms, including such classics as "Joy to the World" and "O God, Our Help in Ages Past"

1744 **Elbridge Gerry.** Massachusetts governor for whom *gerrymander* was named, because he went to such lengths to redistrict the state, one district looked like a salamander, or *gerrymander*

1763 **John Jacob Astor.** American fur magnate and founder of the famous Astor fortune

1827 **Sir Frederick Augustus Abel.** British chemist and explosive expert

1860 **Gustav Mahler.** Bohemian composer (ten symphonies and works such as *Das Lied von der Erde*), who was also regarded as the greatest conductor of his time.

1871 **Lyonel Feininger.** Internationally-known American satirical cartoonist and painter, noted for works such as *The Market Church in Halle*

1876 **Maxim Litvinov.** Russian diplomat who negotiated the recognition of Russia by the United States in 1933

1877 **Edward Madden.** American lyricist noted for songs such as "By the Light of the Silvery Moon," "Moonlight Bay," and "Silver Bell"

1878 **Harold Hackett.** American Hall of Fame tennis player, who, with Fred Alexander, formed one of the most famous doubles teams of the early 1900s

1888 **Shmuel Yosef Agnon.** Hebrew novelist and short story writer, who shared the Nobel Prize for literature in 1966

1889 **Erle Stanley Gardner.** American author, noted for the Perry Mason mystery novels

1889 **Max Fleischer.** American strip and film cartoonist who with his brother Dave created the cartoon character *Betty Boop* and popularized the film versions of E.C. Segar's *Popeye the Sailor*

1895 **Machine Gun Kelly.** Notorious American criminal

1899 **James Cagney.** American stage and motion-picture superstar, with a career spanning 60 years

1900 **Marcell Dalio.** French motion-picture actor with a 40-year career

1905 **William Gargan.** American stage and motion-picture actor

1905 **John Carroll.** American actor and singer

1909	**Hardy Amies.** English fashion designer
1912	**Art Linkletter.** American television personality and writer
1915	**Cass Daley.** American actress, singer, and comedienne
1917	**Lou Boudreau.** Hall of Fame baseball player and manager
1917	**Phyllis Diller.** American comedienne and actress
1930	**Roy McMillan.** Professional baseball player
1934	**Donald Sutherland.** Canadian stage and motion-picture actor
1935	**Peter Schickele.** American composer
1935	**Benjamin R. Civiletti.** Attorney general under President Carter
1935	**Diahann Carroll.** American singer and motion-picture actress
1941	**Daryle Lamonica.** Professional football player
1942	**Connie Hawkins.** Professional basketball player
1951	**Lucie Arnaz.** American television actress and daughter of actors Lucille Ball and Desi Arnaz
1953	**Mike Thomas.** Professional football player

July 17 – Events

1453	The Hundred Years' War ended with the defeat of the English by the French at Castillon.
1821	Spain transferred Florida to the United States.
1841	*Punch*, the English humor periodical, published its first issue in London.
1861	The first U.S. paper money, or "greenbacks," was issued.
1898	U.S. troops captured Santiago, Cuba, in the Spanish-American War.
1903	James McNeill Whistler, the American painter, died in London at age 69.
1938	"Wrong Way" Corrigan left Floyd Bennett Field, New York, for California and wound up the next day in Ireland.
1941	Joe DiMaggio's famous hitting streak was finally stopped at 56 consecutive games, as he went hitless against Cleveland's Al Smith and Jim Bagby Jr.
1955	Disneyland opened in California.
1975	U.S. astronauts and Soviet cosmonauts joined hands after linking their *Apollo* and *Soyuz* spacecrafts.
1987	The Dow Jones Industrial Average closed at 2510.04, the first time in history it had closed above 2500.

July 18 – Birthdays

1635	**Robert Hooke.** English physicist who discovered the law of elasticity
1659	**Hyacinthe Rigaud.** French painter famous for the 1701 full-length portrait of Louis XIV in all his royal robes and splendor
1811	**William Makepeace Thackeray.** English Victorian novelist and author of *Vanity Fair,* one of the great books of world literature
1843	**Virgil W. Earp.** American lawman of the old West and brother of Marshall Wyatt Earp
1845	**Tristan Corbiere.** French poet
1852	**Gertrude Kasebier.** American photographer
1853	**Henrik Antoon Lorentz.** Dutch physicist noted for the electron theory of matter
1867	**Molly Brown.** American activist in social and political causes, who gained the nickname "Unsinkable Molly Brown" from her survival of the sinking of the *Titanic*
1882	**Hermann Hagedorn.** American author and poet
1882	**Manuel Galvez.** Argentine novelist and biographer
1887	**Vidkun Quisling.** Norwegian army officer whose collaboration with the Nazis in World War II established his name as a synonym for traitor
1891	**Gene Lockhart.** American stage, screen, and television actor with a 60-year career
1893	**M.K. Jerome.** American composer and publisher, noted for songs such as "My Wild Irish Rose," "Just a Baby's Prayer at Twilight," and "Sweet Dreams, Sweetheart"
1894	**Richard Dix.** American stage and motion-picture actor
1902	**Jessamyn West.** American writer and novelist, best known for *Friendly Persuasion* (1945)
1903	**Chill Wills.** American vaudeville and motion-picture actor with a screen career of over 40 years
1906	**Clifford Odets.** Leading American dramatist of the theater of social protest of the 1930s, noted for works such as *The Golden Boy* (1937)
1906	**S.I. Hayakawa.** American university president and U.S. senator
1911	**Hume Cronyn.** Canadian stage and motion-picture actor with a career of over 60 years
1913	**Red Skelton.** American comedian and actor
1913	**Walter Kerr.** American newspaper columnist and writer, noted for works such as *Pieces at Eight* and *The Silent Clowns*
1914	**Harriet Hilliard.** American motion-picture and television actress, singer and wife of actor Ozzie Nelson
1921	**John Glenn Jr.** First U.S. astronaut to orbit the earth (February 20, 1962), and U.S. senator
1929	**Screamin' Jay Hawkins.** American singer and pioneer of rock theatrics
1929	**Dick Button.** American champion figure skater
1940	**James Brolin.** American motion-picture and television actor
1940	**Joe Torre.** Professional baseball player and manager who led the New York Yankees to a record 125 victories (counting the post season) in 1998
1943	**Calvin Peete.** Professional golfer
1944	**Rudy May.** Professional baseball player
1947	**Malcolm "Steve" Forbes Jr.** American magazine publisher, politician, and son of publisher Malcolm Forbes
1949	**Wally Carter Bryson.** American musician with The Raspberries
1954	**Ricky Skaggs.** American singer and musician

1957   **Nick Faldo.** English professional golfer
1961   **Elizabeth McGovern.** American stage and screen actress
1963   **Bruce Smith.** Professional football player
1963   **Mike Greenwell.** Professional baseball player

July 18 – Events

64   Two-thirds of Rome burned while Emperor Nero allegedly fiddled.

1374   Petrarch, the great Italian poet, died in Arqua, Italy, two days before his 70th birthday.

1610   Michelangelo Caravaggio, the Italian painter, died at Port Ercole at age 36.

1817   Jane Austen, the great English novelist, died in Winchester, England, at age 41.

1872   Britain introduced the concept of voting by secret ballot.

1918   France opened the Second Battle of the Marne in World War I.

1927   Baseball superstar Ty Cobb got his 4,000th base hit, becoming the only player to reach that total until Pete Rose did it 58 years later.

1936   The Spanish Civil War began as army chiefs in Spanish Morocco headed by General Francisco Franco start a revolt against the Madrid government.

1938   "Wrong Way" Corrigan, who had left New York for California, arrived at Baldonnel Airport in Dublin, Ireland.

1940   President Franklin D. Roosevelt was nominated for an unprecedented third term by the Democratic convention in Chicago.

1944   Allied troops captured St. Lô in World War II, opening the way for General Omar Bradley's U.S. First Army to break out of the Normandy peninsula and sweep across France.

1948   Pat Seerey of the Chicago White Sox hit four home runs in an 11-inning game.

1951   Jersey Joe Walcott knocked out Ezzard Charles in seven rounds in Pittsburgh to win the heavyweight championship.

1969   *Apollo 11* entered the moon's gravitational sphere two days before its occupants became the first men on the moon.

1969   A car driven by Senator Edward Kennedy plunged off a bridge on Chappaquiddick Island, resulting in the drowning of Mary Jo Kopechne, a young campaign worker for Kennedy.

1984   In the worst one-day massacre in American history, 21 people were shot to death in a McDonald's restaurant in San Ysidro, California, by James Oliver Huberty, an unemployed laborer.

1999   David Cone pitched a perfect game (no batter reached base) as the New York Yankees defeated the Montreal Expos, 6-0.

July 19 – Birthdays

1789   **John Martin.** English painter noted for vast canvases teeming with people, such as *Belshazzar's Feast* (1821) and *The Deluge* (1826)

1814   **Samuel Colt.** American inventor, known for the Colt revolver, the first successful repeating pistol

1834   **Edgar Degas.** Noted French impressionist painter, famous for showing his figures in awkward or informal positions

1846   **Edward Charles Pickering.** American astronomer who invented a meridian photometer to measure the brightness of the stars

1860   **Lizzie Borden.** Alleged American murderess who according to the poem, "took an axe and gave her mother forty whacks...," and then applied the same treatment to her father (She was later acquitted, however.)

1865   **Charles Horace Mayo.** American physician and one of the founders of the Mayo Clinic in Rochester, Minnesota

1893   **Vladimir Vladimirovich Mayakovsky.** Russian poet and playwright

1896   **Bob Meusel.** Professional baseball player and member of the New York Yankees' 1927 "perfect outfield" of Babe Ruth, Earle Combs, and Meusel

1896   **A.J. Cronin.** British physician and novelist, noted for such works as *The Citadel* (1937) and *The Keys to the Kingdom* (1942)

1898   **Herbert Marcuse.** American philosopher and writer, noted for *One Dimensional Man* (1964)

1904   **Robert Todd Lincoln Beckwith.** Great grandson and last descendent of Abraham Lincoln

1916   **Phil Cavaretta.** Professional baseball player

1917   **William Scranton.** Governor of Pennsylvania, 1963-1967

1922   **George S. McGovern.** U.S. senator and presidential candidate of the Democratic Party in 1972

1923   **Pat Hingle.** American motion-picture and television actor

1942   **Vicki Carr.** American singer

1943   **Dennis Cole.** American television actor noted for *Felony Squad*

1946   **Ilie Nastase.** Romanian tennis player

1947   **Maria Nasuelli.** Italian tennis player

1949   **Mike Estep.** American tennis player

1954   **Alvan Adams.** Professional basketball player

July 19 – Events

1318   Austria recognized the Three Forest Cantons, marking the beginning of modern Switzerland.

1553   Lady Jane Grey was deposed, and King Henry VIII's daughter Mary was proclaimed Queen of England.

1692   Rebecca Nurse was hanged on Gallows Hill in Salem, Mass., for witchcraft, one of the first victims of the frenzy stirred up by the preacher Cotton Mather.

1842 The SS *Great Britain* was launched, the first of the screw-propelled steamships.

1848 The first Women's Rights Convention was held, in Seneca Falls, New York.

1870 France declared war on Prussia, starting the Franco-Prussian War.

1918 German armies began a general retreat across the Marne River in France, after their last great World War I offensive failed.

1941 Winston Churchill launched his "V for Victory" campaign in World War II.

1942 Arturo Toscanini conducted the NBC Symphony Orchestra in the first American performance of the *Seventh Symphony* by Dmitri Shostakovich.

1969 *Apollo 11* went into orbit around the moon, one day before it landed the first men on the moon.

1970 The Russian space vehicle *Soyuz 9* landed after a record 268 orbits around the earth.

1973 Both Republican and Democratic senior counsels to the House Judiciary Committee urged the panel to recommend that President Nixon be impeached.

1984 The Democratic Convention nominated Geraldine Ferraro to run for vice president with Walter Mondale. She was the first woman candidate for the office on a major party ticket.

July 20 – Birthdays

1304 **Petrarch (Francisco Petracco).** Great Italian poet, scholar, and humanist

1519 **Innocent IX.** Roman Catholic pope who served for less than a year in 1591

1785 **Mahmud II.** Ottoman sultan, 1808-1839

1844 **Marquis of Queensberry.** British sportsman (John Sholto Douglas) who drew up the modern boxing code, the Marquis of Queensberry Rules, in 1867, and who prosecuted Oscar Wilde on a morality charge causing Wilde to be sent to prison

1847 **Max Liebermann.** German painter known for works such as *Women Plucking Geese*

1890 **Theda Bara.** Early silent film star, known as The Vamp because of her sensational role in *A Fool There Was* (1915), based on Kipling's poem "The Vampire"

1890 **Giorgio Morandi.** Italian painter

1894 **E(rrett) L(obban) Cord.** American automobile manufacturer who at one time or another owned the Auburn, Cord, Duesenberg, and Checker Motors auto companies, and whose Model J Duesenberg is considered to be the finest American car ever built, giving rise to the expression, "It's a doozie"

1895 **Lazlo Moholy-Nagy.** Hungarian artist

1901 **Heinie Manush.** Hall of Fame baseball player

1909 **William "Fish Bait" Miller.** U.S. Congressional doorkeeper

1919 **Benson Ford.** American industrialist and grandson of noted automobile maker Henry Ford

1919 **Sir Edmund Percival Hillary.** New Zealand mountain climber who was the first to climb Mt. Everest (1953)

1920 **Elliot Richardson.** Holder of three cabinet posts under President Nixon

1921 **Fred Schroeder.** American Hall of Fame tennis player and 1949 Wimbledon singles champion

1925 **Lola Albright.** American motion-picture and television actress

1930 **Sally Ann Howes.** English stage, screen, and television actress

1936 **Barbara Mikulski.** U.S. senator

1938 **Natalie Wood.** American motion-picture actress who made the transition from child star to adult star

1938 **Diana Rigg.** English motion-picture and television actress

1939 **Judy Chicago.** American artist

1940 **Tony Oliva.** Professional baseball player

1947 **James L. Harris.** Professional football player

1947 **Carlos Santana.** Mexican rock and jazz guitarist

1950 **Nick Weatherspoon.** Professional football player

1955 **Jim Smith.** Professional football player

1956 **Mima Jausovec.** Yugoslavian tennis player

1960 **Mike Witt.** Professional baseball player

1964 **Chris Cornell.** American singer and songwriter

July 20 – Events

1402 The Mongol conqueror Tamerlane completely destroyed the Ottoman army sent against him in Ankara.

1605 French explorer Samuel de Champlain reached Cape Cod during one of his eleven trips to Canada.

1796 Explorer Mungo Park first saw the River Niger in Africa.

1881 Indian chief Sitting Bull surrendered to the United States government and was put on a reservation for two years.

1917 Alexander Kerensky was named premier of Russia by the provisional government. His government lasted only a few months until Lenin and his Bolsheviks seized power.

1925 Clarence Darrow cross-examined William Jennings Bryan as an expert witness on the Bible in the Scopes Trial in Dayton, Tennessee. The result was a disaster for Bryan.

1942 The first detachment of WAACs started their basic training at Fort Des Moines, Iowa, in World War II.

1944 Adolf Hitler was seriously injured and narrowly escaped death when a time bomb planted by German officer Claus von Stauffenberg exploded in Hitler's headquarters.

1945 The U.S. flag was raised over Berlin, as the first American troops prepared to participate in the occupation government following World War II.

1969   *Eagle*, of the *Apollo 11* mission, landed on the Sea of Tranquility, and Neil Armstrong became the first man to set foot on the moon. He was followed shortly by Edwin Aldrin Jr. Armstrong's first words as he reached the moon's surface were, "One small step for man, one giant leap for mankind."

1976   U.S. space vehicle *Viking 1* landed on Mars and relayed crisp surface photographs to the earth.

July 21 – Birthdays

1414   **Sixtus IV.** Roman Catholic pope, 1471-1484

1664   **Matthew Prior.** English poet noted for *The Story of the Country-Mouse and the City-Mouse* and the famous line from *Hans Carvel,* "The end must justify the means" (1700)

1673   **John Weaver.** English dancer and ballet master

1816   **Paul Julius Reuter.** Founder of the first news agency, which still bears his name

1817   **Sir John Gilbert.** English Romantic painter

1858   **Chauncey Olcott.** American composer, author, and actor, noted for songs such as "My Wild Irish Rose," "When Irish Eyes Are Smiling," and "Mother Machree"

1863   **Sir C. Aubrey Smith.** British stage and motion-picture actor in nearly 70 movies, best known for his memorable character roles

1864   **Frances Folsom Cleveland.** Wife of President Grover Cleveland

1878   **Ernest R. Ball.** American composer noted for songs such as "Let the Rest of the World Go By," "Mother Machree," and "When Irish Eyes Are Smiling" (last two with Chauncey Olcott)

1881   **Johnny Evers.** Hall of Fame baseball player and member of the famous Tinker-to-Evers-to-Chance double play combination

1885   **Frances Parkinson Keyes.** American novelist

1895   **Ken Maynard.** One of Hollywood's most popular cowboy actors

1899   **Ernest Hemingway.** One of the most influential and most famous American writers of his time, noted for works such as *The Sun Also Rises* (1926) and *For Whom the Bell Tolls* (1940)

1899   **Hart Crane.** American poet, best known for "The Bridge"

1901   **Allyn Joslyn.** American stage and motion-picture character actor and comedian

1905   **David M. Kennedy.** U.S. secretary of the treasury under President Nixon

1905   **Diana Trilling.** American novelist

1911   **Marshall McLuhan.** Canadian communications theorist and writer, noted for *Understanding Media* (1964) and *The Medium Is the Massage* (1967)

1920   **Isaac Stern.** Russian-born violin virtuoso

1922   **Kay Starr.** American singer

1924   **Don Knotts.** American motion-picture and television actor

1926   **Norman Jewison.** Canadian-born movie director and producer, noted for works such as *In the Heat of the Night* (1967), *Fiddler on the Roof* (1971), and *Moonstruck* (1987)

1926   **Paul Burke.** American motion-picture and television actor

1930   **Gene Littler.** Professional golfer

1933   **John Gardner.** American novelist

1938   **Janet Reno.** Attorney General under President Clinton

1944   **Paul David Wellstone.** U.S. senator

1946   **Kenneth Starr.** American lawyer who, as a special prosecutor, investigated President Clinton for most of his two terms

1947   **Yusuf Islam.** English singer and songwriter, noted for "Morning Has Broken" (formerly known as Cat Stevens)

1949   **Al Hrabosky.** Professional baseball player

1952   **Robin Williams.** American motion-picture and television actor and comedian

1957   **Jon Lovitz.** American actor and comedian

July 21 – Events

365   A great earthquake struck the eastern Mediterranean and destroyed the Roman city of Kourion on the island of Cyprus.

1796   Robert Burns, the great Scottish poet, died in Dumfries at age 47.

1831   Leopold I was proclaimed King of the Belgians, as Belgium became independent of Holland.

1861   Northern troops retreated in disorder after the first Battle of Bull Run, at which Confederate general Thomas J. Jackson gained his nickname "Stonewall."

1873   Jesse James carried out the world's first train robbery, holding up the Rock Island Express at Adair, Iowa.

1918   Allied troops captured Chateau-Thierry in World War I.

1925   The Scopes Trial ended in Dayton, Tennessee, as John Scopes was found guilty and fined $100 for teaching evolution in the public schools.

1944   Franklin D. Roosevelt was renominated for an unprecedented fourth term at the Democratic Convention in Chicago.

1954   The Indochinese War between France and Vietnam ended with a treaty granting North Vietnam its independence.

1959   The United States launched the *Savannah,* the world's first nuclear-powered merchant ship.

1961   U.S. astronaut Virgil Grissom became the second American in space, as *Liberty Bell Seven* was launched for a suborbital flight of 16 minutes.

1969   Astronauts Neil Armstrong and Edwin Aldrin Jr. returned from the moon to the command module, rejoining astronaut Michael Collins.

July 22 – Birthdays

1478 Philip the Handsome. Archduke of Austria who became king of Spain by marrying Juana of Castile

1596 Michael Romanov. First of the Romanov czars of Russia, a dynasty which lasted until 1917

1713 Jacques Germain Soufflot. French architect

1784 Friedrich Wilhelm Bessel. German astronomer and mathematician, noted for Bessel's equation and its solutions, the Bessel functions

1822 Gregor Johann Mendel. Austrian botanist who discovered the principles of heredity

1833 Benjamin R. Hanby. Composer of "Darling Nellie Gray"

1844 William Archibald Spooner. British clergyman noted for slips of the tongue, or "spoonerisms," causing syllables to be transposed, such as "Work is the curse of the drinking class"

1849 Emma Lazarus. American poet who wrote the sonnet inscribed on the pedestal of the Statue of Liberty that begins with "Give me your tired, your poor..."

1860 Frederick William Rolfe. English writer

1870 Tom Pendergast. Democratic party boss of Kansas City and leader of one of the largest political machines in the U.S. in the 1930s and 1940s

1881 Margery Williams Bianco. American childrens' author noted for works such as *The Velveteen Rabbit* (1922)

1882 Edward Hopper. American painter who produced some of the finest realistic works of his time

1888 Floretta McCutcheon. Hall of Fame bowler with ten perfect games and an average score of 201 in over 8,000 career games

1890 Rose Fitzgerald Kennedy. Mother of President John F. Kennedy

1891 Ely Culbertson. American bridge player who was an expert in auction bridge and was the world's top player in contract bridge in the 1930s

1892 Arthur Seyss-Inquart. Austrian Nazi leader during the Austrian *anschluss* engineered by Adolf Hitler in 1937

1893 Karl Menninger. American psychiatrist whose ideas widely influenced public attitudes toward mental illness

1893 Jesse Haines. Hall of Fame baseball player

1898 Alexander Calder. One of the first American sculptors of international significance, and one of the best-known American artists of the mid-20th century

1898 Stephen Vincent Benet. American poet, novelist, and short-story writer, noted for such works as *By the Waters of Babylon* and *John Brown's Body*

1901 Charles Weidman. Major innovator of the U.S. modern dance

1905 Doc Cramer. Professional baseball player

1908 Amy Vanderbilt. American expert on etiquette

1913 Licia Albanese. American soprano

1917 Adam Malik. Indonesian diplomat and president of the 26th U.N. General Assembly

1921 William Roth. U.S. senator who was the prime mover behind the Roth IRA

1923 Robert Dole. U.S. senator, Minority Leader, Majority Leader, and Republican candidate for president in 1996

1928 Orson Bean. American actor and comedian

1932 Oscar De la Renta. American fashion designer

1934 Louise Fletcher. American motion-picture and television actress, who won the Academy Award for best actress in *One Flew Over the Cuckoo's Nest* (1975)

1940 Alex Trebek. Game show host on television's *Jeopardy*

1941 Susie Maxwell Berning. Professional golfer

1943 Kay Bailey Hutchison. U.S. senator

1944 Sparky Lyle. Professional baseball player

1944 Joyce Hume. English tennis player

1947 Albert Brooks. American motion-picture and television actor and comic

1947 Danny Glover. American stage and motion-picture actor

1947 Cliff Johnson. Professional baseball player

1951 Ron Turcotte. American jockey

1955 Willem Dafoe. American actor and leading man of stage and films

1956 Scott Sanderson. Professional baseball player

1957 Dave Stieb. Professional baseball player

1965 David Spade. American stage and motion-picture actor and comedian

1966 Tim Brown. Professional football player

July 22 – Events

1587 The second "Lost Colony" was established on Roanoke Island, off the North Carolina coast. It, too, like the first one, disappeared.

1588 After a month of regrouping at Corunna, Spain, the Spanish Armada headed toward the English Channel to engage the English fleet.

1613 Michael, the first Romanov Czar of Russia, was crowned. Sixteen more Romanov czars followed him to the Russian throne.

1796 Cleveland, Ohio, was founded by Moses Cleaveland, a surveyor, and a group of Connecticut settlers.

1871 The notorious "Tweed Ring," headed by New York boss William Marcy Tweed, was exposed by the *New York Times*.

1893 Wellesley professor Katharine Lee Bates wrote the original version of her poem "America the Beautiful" in Colorado Springs.

1933 American aviator Wiley Post in his plane, the *Winnie Mae*, completed the first round-the-world solo flight.

1934 John Dillinger, "Public Enemy Number One," was shot and killed by FBI agents as he left the Biograph Theater in Chicago.

1967 Carl Sandburg, the great American biographer and poet, died in Flat Rock, North Carolina, at age 89.

1969 *Apollo 11* left the moon's atmosphere bound for home, after placing the first men on the moon.

1975 Congress voted to restore the American citizenship of Confederate General Robert E. Lee.

1995 Alan Hale and Thomas Bopp discovered independently the "Hale-Bopp Comet," which made its closest approach to earth in March 1997.

July 23 – Birthdays

1339 **Louis I.** Duke of Anjou

1477 **Francesco Granacci.** Italian painter noted for works such as *Scenes from the Life of Saint John the Baptist* (around 1510)

1777 **Philipp Otto Runge.** German painter

1816 **Charlotte Saunders Cushman.** First native-born American stage star

1823 **Coventry Patmore.** English poet

1864 **F. Holland Day.** American photographer

1883 **Alanbrooke (Alan Francis Brooke).** British World War II field marshal

1884 **Emil Jannings.** Swiss-born motion-picture actor who was the first to win the Academy Award for best actor, in 1927-1928 for *The Last Command* and *The Way of All Flesh*

1884 **Albert Warner.** One of the Warner Brothers who founded the motion-picture company of the same name

1888 **Gluyas Williams.** American cartoonist, primarily for *The New Yorker* magazine

1888 **Raymond Chandler.** American novelist, creator of detective Philip Marlowe, and author of *The Big Sleep* (1939)

1891 **Harry Cohn.** American film executive who co-founded Columbia Pictures (1924)

1892 **Haile Selassie.** Emperor of Ethiopia, 1930-1974

1894 **Arthur Treacher.** English stage, screen, and television actor

1895 **Aileen Pringle.** American leading lady of Hollywood silents and early talkies

1908 **Ival Goodman.** Professional baseball player

1918 **Pee Wee Reese.** Hall of Fame baseball player

1923 **Ray Boone.** Professional baseball player

1924 **Gloria DeHaven.** American stage, screen, and television actress

1926 **Johnny Groth.** Professional baseball player

1930 **Moon Landrieu.** Mayor of New Orleans and secretary of Health and Human Services under President Carter

1934 **Bert Convy.** American television host and actor

1936 **Anthony McLeod Kennedy.** U.S. Supreme Court justice

1936 **Don Drysdale.** Hall of Fame baseball player and sports announcer

1940 **Don Imus.** American radio talk show host

1947 **David Essex.** English singer and drummer

1950 **Belinda J. Montgomery.** American actress

1961 **Woody Harrelson.** American television (*Cheers*) and motion-picture actor

1961 **Martin Gore.** British keyboardist with the Depeche Mode musical group

1971 **Alison Krauss.** American fiddler and country singer

July 23 – Events

685 John V became Roman Catholic pope.

1803 Robert Emmett, Irish patriot, led an unsuccessful insurrection against the British in Ireland.

1829 William A. Burt of Mount Vernon, Michigan, patented his "typographer," claimed by many to be the first typewriter.

1904 The ice cream cone was invented by Charles E. Menches of St. Louis.

1914 Austria-Hungary issued an ultimatum to Serbia, demanding that Austrian officials participate in the trial of those accused of murdering Archduke Francis Ferdinand.

1942 The best seller *See Here, Private Hargrove*, by Marion Hargrove, was first published.

1944 The Russians crossed the Curzon Line into Poland in World War II.

1945 Marshal Henri Philippe Petain, the French collaborator with the Nazis in World War II, went on trial for treason in Paris.

1951 Marshal Petain died in prison at age 95.

1984 Vanessa Williams became the first Miss America to give up her title, after nude pictures of her appeared in *Penthouse* magazine.

July 24 – Birthdays

1686 **Bennedetto Marcello.** Venetian composer and writer

1725 **John Newton.** English clergyman and lyricist, in 1779, of "Amazing Grace"

1783 **Simon Bolivar.** The great South American general who won independence from Spain for Bolivia, Colombia, Ecuador, Peru, and Venezuela

1802 **Alexandre Dumas.** French novelist (known also as Dumas *pere* to distinguish him from his son, Dumas *fils*), noted for *The Three Musketeers* (1844) and *The Count of Monte Cristo* (1845), two of the most popular historical novels in world literature

1803 **Alexander Jackson Davis.** American architect

1803 **Adolphe Charles Adam.** Composer of "Holy Night"

1843 **Sir William de Wivelealie Abney.** British specialist in the chemistry of photography

1864 **Frank Wedekind.** German playwright, noted for *Spring's Awakening* (1890-1891) and *Pandora's Box* (1894)

1871 **Giacomo Balla.** Italian painter and sculptor

1878 **Lord Dunsany.** Irish writer (born Edward John Plunkett), noted for his tales and for such plays as *The Gods of the Mountain* (1911)

1880 **Ernest Bloch.** Swiss-American composer, noted for the opera *Macbeth* (1910) and the rhapsody "America" (1928)

1895 **Robert Graves.** English author, poet, and translator, noted for works such as *I, Claudius* (1934), *The White Goddess* (1948), and 136 other novels and books of poetry

1897 **Amelia Earhart.** American aviator and first woman to fly alone over the Atlantic Ocean

1900 **Zelda (Sayre) Fitzgerald.** American writer and wife of novelist F. Scott Fitzgerald

1916 **Bob Eberle.** American singer with the Dorsey Brothers of the Big Band Era, and brother of singer Ray Eberle

1916 **John D. MacDonald.** The "General Motors of American novelists," noted for some 75 books such as *The Executioners* (1958) and *Condominium* (1977)

1920 **Bella Abzug.** U.S. congresswoman and advocate of women's rights

1921 **Billy Taylor.** American pianist, composer, and conductor

1922 **Charles McC. Mathias Jr.** U.S. senator

1927 **Alex Katz.** American painter

1932 **William D. Ruckelshaus.** Director of the Environmental Protection Agency under Presidents Nixon and Reagan

1935 **Patrick Bruce Oliphant.** American political cartoonist

1936 **Ruth Buzzi.** American comedienne

1942 **Chris Sarandon.** American stage and screen actor

1948 **Mack Herron.** Professional football player

1951 **Lynda Carter.** American actress and singer

1953 **Steve Grogan.** Professional football player

1963 **Julie Krone.** American jockey and first woman to win a Triple Crown race (Belmont Stakes, 1993)

1963 **Karl Malone.** Professional basketball player and superstar

1964 **Barry Bonds.** Professional baseball player, Most Valuable Player in 1990 and 1992, and son of professional baseball player Bobby Bonds

July 24 – Events

1680 New Hampshire became a royal colony of the British crown.

1704 British naval forces captured Gibralter from Spain, and have retained it to the present.

1847 Brigham Young and his Mormon followers settled Salt Lake City, Utah.

1862 Martin Van Buren died in Kinderhook, New York, at age 79.

1866 Tennessee became the first state of the Confederacy to be readmitted to the Union.

1945 The Potsdam Conference opened at Potsdam, near Berlin, following Germany's defeat in World War II. Attending were Harry S. Truman, Winston Churchill, and Joseph Stalin.

1946 The United States made the first underwater test of an atomic bomb, at Bikini Atoll in the Pacific Ocean.

1959 Vice President Richard Nixon and Russian Premier Nikita Khrushchev engaged in their "Kitchen Debate" at a U.S. exhibition in Moscow.

1969 The *Apollo 11* mission, placing the first men on the moon, ended with a successful splashdown in the Pacific Ocean.

1974 The Supreme Court ruled 8-0 that President Nixon must produce the subpoenaed Watergate tapes.

July 25 – Birthdays

1654 **Agostino Steffani.** Italian composer and singer

1750 **Henry Knox.** American Revolutionary War general, who directed Washington's troops when they crossed the Delaware, and who became the first U.S. secretary of war

1775 **Anna Symmes Harrison.** Wife of President William Henry Harrison

1799 **Charles Coffin Little.** American publisher who with James Brown founded Little, Brown & Co. in 1837

1844 **Thomas Eakins.** One of the greatest American realist painters of the 1800s

1848 **Arthur James Balfour.** British prime minister, 1902-1905, noted for the Balfour Declaration of 1917, favoring the establishment of a national Jewish home in Palestine

1854 **David Belasco.** American actor, playwright, and a leading theatrical producer for nearly 40 years

1857 **Frank Julian Sprague.** American electrical engineer and inventor who in 1887 built the first large electric railway system ever attempted, in Richmond, VA

1870 **Maxfield Parrish.** American painter and illustrator noted for Maxfield Parrish blue, the unusual shade of blue used in many of his paintings

1874 **Joaquin Torres-Garcia.** Uruguayan painter

1889 **J. Warren Kerrigan.** American movie actor and leading star of the silent screen

1894 **Walter Brennan.** American motion-picture and television actor, and first to win three Academy Awards

1902 **Eric Hoffer.** American writer and political scientist

1907 **Johnny Hodges.** American composer and saxophonist, noted for songs such as "I'm Beginning to See the Light," "Wanderlust," and "Wonder of You"

1919 **Jack Gilford.** American stage, screen, and television actor

1924 **Frank Church.** U.S. senator in the 1960s and 1970s

1926 **Whitey Lockman.** Professional baseball player

1927 **Stanley Dancer.** American harness-racing driver

1929 **Peter Farb.** American author and editor

1940 **John Pennel.** American pole vaulter who set the world's record of 17 feet 10½ inches in 1969

1941   **Nate Thurmond.** Professional football player and Hall of Famer

1943   **Janet Margolin.** American stage and screen actress

1945   **Donna Theodore.** American singer

1954   **Walter Payton.** Professional Hall of Fame football player and superstar who broke Jimmy Brown's career rushing record in 1984 and ended his own career with 16,726 total yards

1955   **Iman.** Somali-born American model and actress

1957   **Ray Billingsly.** American cartoonist and creator of the comic strip *Curtis*

1957   **Gordon Jones.** Professional football player

July 25 – Events

44   Saint James, the brother of John and the son of Zebedee, and one of the 12 apostles, became the first of the apostles to be martyred when he was killed on orders of Herod Agrippa I.

1215   Frederick II, called *Stupor Mundi* (The Amazement of the World), was crowned Holy Roman Emperor at Aix-la-Chapelle.

1593   King Henry IV of France, a Protestant, converted to Roman Catholicism in order to end the religious wars in his country.

1814   George Stephenson, the great British engineer, first successfully demonstrated a steam locomotive. His engine, *Puffing Billy,* pulled heavy loads of coal for years.

1834   Samuel Taylor Coleridge, the famous English poet, died in London at age 61.

1866   Ulysses S. Grant was named General of the Army, the first officer to hold that rank.

1909   French aviator Louis Bleriot made the first airplane flight across the English Channel.

1934   Chancellor Englebert Dollfus of Austria was murdered by the Nazis because he tried to prevent Adolf Hitler from taking over Austria.

1943   Benito Mussolini, the Fascist dictator of Italy, resigned and Marshal Badoglio took over as Italian chief of state, following Italy's collapse in World War II.

1944   U.S. forces broke out of Normandy and began the sweep across France in World War II.

1952   Puerto Rico became a self-governing commonwealth.

1956   The luxury liner *Andrea Doria* and the steamer *Stockholm* collided 45 miles off Nantucket Island, resulting in 54 deaths.

1963   The United States, Russia, and Britain signed the test-ban treaty, prohibiting nuclear testing in the atmosphere, in space, or underwater.

1978   The world's first test tube baby (conceived outside a woman's womb) was born to John and Lesley Brown in Oldham, England.

July 26 – Birthdays

1739   **George Clinton.** Governor of New York and U.S. vice president, 1805-1812

1796   **George Catlin.** American painter and student of Indian life

1799   **Isaac Babbit.** American inventor, known for special alloys called Babbit metals, used to reduce friction in moving parts

1856   **George Bernard Shaw.** Most significant British playwright since the 17th century

1858   **Colonel Edward M. House.** Confidential adviser to President Woodrow Wilson

1874   **Serge Koussevitzky.** Russian-born conductor and foremost double bass player of his time, known primarily for conducting the Boston Symphony Orchestra from 1924 to 1949

1875   **Carl Jung.** Swiss psychologist and psychiatrist who invented the terms *introvert* and *extrovert* to describe personalities

1875   **Antonio Marchado y Ruiz.** Spanish poet

1885   **Andre Maurois.** French biographer and novelist, noted for such works as *Ariel* (1923), *The Life of Disraeli* (1927), and *The Titans* (1957)

1892   **Sad Sam Jones.** Professional baseball player

1893   **George Grosz.** German painter and graphic artist

1894   **Aldous Huxley.** English novelist, poet, essayist, and author of *Brave New World* (1932) and *Point Counter Point* (1928)

1897   **Paul Gallico.** American novelist and essayist

1902   **Gracie Allen.** American comedienne who teamed with her husband, George Burns, to form the Burns and Allen comedy duo

1903   **Estes Kefauver.** U.S. senator and vice presidential candidate in 1956 with Adlai Stevenson

1904   **Edwin Albert Link.** American inventor who developed the mechanical trainer, a machine that simulates flying conditions on the ground

1908   **Salvador Allende.** Marxist president of Chile in the early 1970s

1912   **Vivian Vance.** American actress noted for her role as Ethel Mertz in TV's *I Love Lucy*

1914   **Erskine Hawkins.** American trumpeter and bandleader

1914   **Ralph Blane Hunsecker.** American composer noted for songs such as "Buckle Down, Winsocki!" "Have Yourself a Merry Little Christmas," "Skip to My Lou," "The Trolley Song," and "Pass That Peace Pipe"

1920   **Bob Waterfield.** Professional football player and Hall of Famer

1922   **Jason Robards Jr.** American motion-picture and television actor

1922   **Blake Edwards.** American motion-picture producer and author

1923   **Hoyt Wilhelm.** Hall of Fame baseball pitcher who pitched in a record number of games and retired at age 49

1928	**Stanley Kubrick.** American motion-picture director, noted for such films as *2001: A Space Odyssey* (1968) and *A Clockwork Orange* (1971)
1929	**Alexis Weissenberg.** Bulgarian-born French pianist
1939	**Bob Lilly.** Hall of Fame professional football player
1943	**Mick Jagger.** British singer with The Rolling Stones musical group
1945	**Helen Mirren.** Celebrated British classical actress of stage, screen, and television
1950	**Charlie Smith.** Professional football player
1950	**Susan George.** English motion-picture and television actress
1951	**Bobby Wadkins.** Professional golfer
1954	**Vitus Gerulaitis.** American tennis player
1956	**Dorothy Hamil.** American ice-skating champion
1957	**Wayne Grady.** Australian professional golfer
1959	**Kevin Spacey.** American stage and motion-picture actor

July 26 – Events

1581	The Netherlands declared its independence from Spain.
1775	Benjamin Franklin became Postmaster General.
1788	New York ratified the Constitution, becoming the 11th state.
1847	Liberia was proclaimed an independent republic.
1908	The investigative agency which later became the F.B.I. was created on orders of U.S. Attorney General Charles J. Bonaparte.
1925	William Jennings Bryan died of a stroke in Dayton, Tenn., five days after his participation in the Scopes Trial.
1945	The Potsdam conferees issued an ultimatum demanding the unconditional surrender of Japan in World War II.
1945	Clement Attlee replaced Winston Churchill as prime minister after the Labor Party's unexpected defeat of the Conservative Party in the English elections of July 5.
1947	President Harry S. Truman signed the National Security Act, consolidating the Department of Defense.
1956	Egypt's president Gamal Abdel Nasser seized the Suez Canal from its British and French owners.
1971	*Apollo 15*, with three astronauts aboard, was launched from Cape Kennedy, and headed for the moon.

July 27 – Birthdays

1672	**Gilles Marie Oppenord.** French architect
1768	**Charlotte Corday.** Young French girl who stabbed French revolutionary Jean-Paul Marat to death while he was sitting in his bathtub
1835	**Giosue Carducci.** Italian poet and critic
1842	**Hugo Henneberg.** Austrian photographer
1861	**Louis Vivin.** French painter
1870	**Hilaire Belloc.** British poet, novelist, and essayist, who wrote more than 150 books
1880	**Donald Crisp.** Scottish-born motion-picture actor who appeared in 364 films in a 55-year career
1880	**Joe Tinker.** Hall of Fame baseball player and member of the famed Tinker-to-Evers-to-Chance double play combination
1904	**Anton Dolin.** First internationally famous English male dancer
1906	**Leo Durocher.** Professional baseball player and highly successful manager
1916	**Elizabeth Hardwick.** American writer and editor
1916	**Keenan Wynn.** American stage and motion-picture actor and son of actor Ed Wynn
1918	**Leonard Ross.** American violincellist
1920	**Henry Doyle "Homer" Haynes.** American country singer who with Jethro Burns formed the "Homer and Jethro" comedy duo specializing in parodies of popular songs
1922	**Norman Lear.** American television producer, noted for the long-running comedy *All in the Family*
1939	**Irv Cross.** Professional football player and sportscaster
1942	**Dennis Ralston.** American tennis player
1944	**Bobbie Gentry.** American country singer and songwriter, noted for songs such as "Ode to Billy Joe"
1946	**Haven Moses.** Professional football player
1948	**Peggy Fleming.** American ice figure skater and Olympic champion
1948	**Betty Thomas.** American actress
1948	**Mack Calvin.** Professional basketball player
1949	**Maureen McGovern.** American singer and actress
1952	**Melvin Barnes.** Professional basketball player
1952	**Bump Wills.** Professional baseball player and son of baseball great Maury Wills
1975	**Alex Rodriguez.** Professional baseball player

July 27 – Events

1694	The Bank of England was founded in London.
1789	The U.S. Department of Foreign Affairs, the forerunner of the Department of State, was established by Congress, and made an executive agency under the President.
1866	The first permanent Atlantic cable was laid by Cyrus W. Field, stretching from Valencia, Ireland, to Hearts Content, Newfoundland.
1909	Orville Wright set a record by staying aloft in an airplane for 1 hour, 12 minutes, and 40 seconds.
1921	Insulin was isolated for the first time by Dr. Frederick Banting and his assistant, Charles Best, at the University of Toronto Medical School.
1940	The cartoon character Bugs Bunny made his debut as Warner Brothers released the animated short *A Wild Hare*.

1953   The Korean War ended with a truce agreement between the U.N. and North Korea.

1974   The U.S. House Judiciary Committee passed its first article of impeachment against President Richard Nixon.

July 28 – Birthdays

1618   **Abraham Cowley.** English poet and essayist whose first volume of verse, *Poetical Blossoms,* was published when he was 15

1746   **Thomas Heywood Jr.** American patriot, statesman, and soldier, and a South Carolina signer of the Declaration of Independence

1844   **Gerard Manley Hopkins.** One of the major poets of Victorian England

1857   **Ballington Booth.** Founder of the Volunteers of America and son of William Booth, the founder of the Salvation Army

1866   **Beatrix Potter.** British author and illustrator, who created the *Peter Rabbit* children's books, known all over the world

1887   **Marcel Duchamp.** French painter of the cubist school, who was later influential in the Dada movement

1891   **Carl Spaatz.** First chief of staff of the U.S. Air Force

1892   **Joe E. Brown.** American actor and comedian

1898   **Charles William Mayo.** American surgeon and son of Charles Horace Mayo, a founder of the Mayo Clinic

1901   **Freddie Fitzsimmons.** Professional baseball player

1901   **Rudy Vallee.** American actor, national radio singing idol of the 1920s, and composer, noted for songs such as "I'm Just a Vagabond Lover" and "There Is a Tavern in the Town"

1909   **Malcolm Lowry.** English novelist and author of *Under the Volcano*

1910   **Richard Lewine.** American composer, author, and producer, noted for songs such as "Love Makes the World Go Round"

1929   **Jacqueline Kennedy Onassis.** Wife of President John F. Kennedy

1934   **Jacques D'Amboise.** American ballet dancer and leading member of the New York City Ballet

1937   **Peter Duchin.** American pianist and bandleader

1941   **Ricardo Muti.** Italian conductor who succeeded Eugene Ormandy as director of the Philadelphia Orchestra in 1980

1943   **Mike Bloomfield.** American blues musician

1943   **Bill Bradley.** Professional Hall of Fame basketball superstar, U.S. senator, and candidate for the Democratic nomination for president in 2000

1945   **Jim Davis.** American cartoonist and creator of *Garfield*

1945   **Rick Wright.** English keyboardist for the Pink Floyd musical group

1948   **Sally Struthers.** American actress and one of the stars of the long-running television comedy *All in the Family*

1949   **Vida Blue.** Professional baseball player

1951   **Doug Collins.** Professional basketball player

1957   **Charles Alexander.** Professional football player

1960   **John Elway.** Professional football superstar who quarterbacked the Denver Broncos to two consecutive Super Bowl victories in 1997 and 1998

July 28 – Events

1402   Mongol leader Tamerlane defeated the Turks at the Battle of Angora in Anatolia.

1540   King Henry VIII of England secretly married his fifth wife, Catherine Howard.

1540   Thomas Cromwell, chief minister of King Henry VIII of England, was beheaded.

1750   Johann Sebastian Bach, the great composer, died in Leipzig at age 65.

1794   Maximilien Robespierre, the notorious French Revolutionary leader, was guillotined in Paris at age 36.

1821   Peru declared its independence from Spain.

1868   The 14th Amendment to the Constitution was ratified, extending citizenship to all persons born or naturalized in the United States.

1896   Miami, Florida, with 269 inhabitants, was incorporated.

1914   Austria-Hungary declared war on Serbia to begin World War I.

1932   The Bonus Marchers, a 15,000-man "army" of World War I veterans, were dispersed with tanks, cavalry, and infantry by General Douglas MacArthur in Washington, D.C.

1973   *Skylab 3* was launched, beginning a 59-day mission plagued with defects that required emergency repairs by the astronauts themselves.

1976   Earthquakes rocked northern China, killing 655,000 people.

July 29 – Birthdays

1580   **Francesco Mochi.** Italian sculptor

1605   **Simon Dach.** German poet of the early Baroque movement

1794   **Thomas Corwin.** U.S. senator and author of Corwin's Law: "If you would succeed in life, you must be solemn, solemn as an ass."

1796   **Walter Hunt.** American inventor noted for the safety pin and the fountain pen

1805   **Alexis de Tocqueville.** French statesman and political philosopher, known for his book *Democracy in America* (1835-1840)

1824   **Alexandre Dumas (the Younger).** French novelist, playwright, son of novelist Alexandre Dumas, and author of *La Dame aux Camelias* (1852)

1824   **Eastman Johnson.** American painter

1869 **Booth Tarkington.** Pulitzer Prize-winning American novelist and dramatist, and author of *Monsieur Beaucaire* (1900) and *The Magnificent Ambersons* (1919)

1877 **William Beebe.** American naturalist and writer, noted for his vivid accounts of tropical jungles, undersea explorations, and studies of birds

1878 **Donald Perry "Don" Marquis.** American writer and newspaper columnist who created Archy, the cockroach, and Mehitabel, the cat

1883 **Benito Mussolini.** Italian Fascist dictator, 1922-1943

1887 **Sigmund Romberg.** Noted Hungarian-American composer of operettas, such as *The Student Prince* and *Blossom Time*

1889 **Ernst Reuter.** Mayor of post-World War II West Berlin

1892 **William Powell.** Smooth villain of Hollywood silents and leading man of the talkies, especially noted for the *Thin Man* series of movies with actress Myrna Loy

1900 **Don Redman.** American saxophonist, composer and jazz orchestra pioneer

1900 **Owen Lattimore.** American author and China expert

1905 **Thelma Todd.** Vivacious American motion-picture actress and comedienne

1905 **Dag Hammarskjold.** Swedish statesman and second U.N. secretary general

1907 **Melvin Belli.** Noted American trial lawyer

1914 **Marcel Bich.** French industrialist who invented Bic pens, razors and lighters

1916 **Charlie Christian.** American musician and guitarist who pioneed the use of electrical amplification

1918 **Edwin O'Connor.** American novelist and author of *The Last Hurrah*

1921 **Richard Egan.** American motion-picture actor

1924 **Mark Ethridge Jr..** Noted American publisher

1926 **Don Carter.** Noted professional American bowler

1930 **Paul Taylor.** American modern dancer and choreographer

1932 **Nancy Landon Kassebaum Baker.** U.S. senator, daughter of presidential candidate Alf Landon, and wife of former senator Howard Baker

1933 **Randy Sparks.** American composer and author noted for film and television songs, such as "The Singing Nun"

1936 **Elizabeth Dole.** Member of the Cabinet under Presidents Reagan and Bush, and wife of U.S. Senator Robert Dole

1938 **Peter Jennings.** Canadian-born American television news correspondent and anchorman

1948 **Neal Walk.** Professional basketball player

1949 **Marilyn Quayle.** Wife of former vice president Dan Quayle

1951 **Dan Driessen.** Professional baseball player

1952 **Scott Wedman.** Professional basketball player

1953 **Ken Burns.** American documentary filmmaker, noted for his TV masterpieces, *The Civil War* (1990) and *Baseball* (1994)

1954 **Flo Hyman.** American Hall of Fame volleyball player

July 29 – Events

1030 King Olaf II, the patron saint of Norway, was killed in battle.

1565 Mary, Queen of Scots, married Henry Stuart, Lord Darnley.

1588 "We have time enough to finish the game and beat the Spaniards, too," said Sir Francis Drake during a game of bowls when told the Spanish Armada had been sighted near the Scilly Isles.

1703 Daniel Defoe, author of *Robinson Crusoe,* was put in a pillory for a political pamphlet he wrote.

1754 The first international boxing match in history took place as the British champion Jack Slack knocked out the French contender Jean Petit.

1778 The French fleet arrived at Rhode Island to help the American colonists in the Revolutionary War.

1830 The July Revolution in Paris ended with the overthrow of Charles X and the call to power of Louis Philippe, the Duke of Orleans.

1856 Robert Schumann, the great German composer, died at Endenich, near Bonn, at age 46.

1890 Vincent van Gogh, the famous Dutch painter, died in Auers, France, after shooting himself two days earlier. He was 37 years old.

1914 Transcontinental telephone service began with the first phone conversation, between New York and San Francisco.

1945 An armada of U.S. B-29 bombers dropped 3,500 tons of fire bombs on six Japanese cities in World War II.

1957 Jack Paar made his debut as host of NBC's *Tonight Show.*

1958 President Eisenhower signed the National Aeronautics and Space Act, which created NASA.

1968 Pope Paul VI issued his edict against artificial birth control.

1974 The U.S. House Judiciary Committee passed its second article of impeachment against President Nixon.

1981 Prince Charles, heir to the English throne, and Lady Diana Spencer were married in St. Paul's Cathedral in London.

July 30 – Birthdays

1511 **Giorgio Vasari.** Florentine Mannerist painter and writer best remembered for *The Lives of the Artists* (1550), a book of biographies of Italian painters

1763 **Samuel Rogers.** English poet

1818 **Emily Brontë.** English novelist and author of *Wuthering Heights* (1847), a masterpiece of world literature

1857   **Thorstein Veblen.** One of the most original and creative thinkers in the history of American economics, and author of the famous work *The Theory of the Leisure Class* (1899)

1863   **Henry Ford.** American pioneer automobile industrialist, founder of the Ford Motor Company, and developer of the Model T and Model A automobiles

1880   **Robert R. McCormick.** Editor of the *Chicago Tribune,* 1925-1955, who made it one of the nation's most important newspapers

1889   **Vladimir Zworykin.** Russian-born American physicist, who invented the iconoscope and is sometimes called "the father of television"

1889   **Emanuel Haldeman-Julius.** American publisher and founder of the E. Haldeman-Julius company noted for its Little Blue Books

1890   **Casey Stengel.** Hall of Fame baseball player and one of the most successful managers in history, who managed the New York Yankees to ten pennants in 12 years

1898   **Henry Moore.** Enclish sculptor, noted for such works as *King and Queen* (1953) and *Reclining Figure* (1965)

1922   **Henry Bloch.** American businessman and co-founder of H & R Block

1928   **Joe Nuxhall.** Professional baseball player who began his major league career at age 15

1934   **Bud Selig.** Baseball commissioner first elected in 1991

1939   **Peter Bogdanovich.** American motion-picture director, producer, and screenwriter

1940   **Patricia Schroeder.** U.S. Congresswoman who labeled Ronald Reagan "the Teflon President"

1941   **Paul Anka.** Canadian-born singer, actor, and songwriter

1944   **Pat Kelly.** Professional baseball player

1945   **David Sanborn.** American saxophonist and composer

1947   **William Atherton.** American stage and motion-picture actor

1947   **Arnold Schwarzenegger.** Austrian-born bodybuilder, holder of Mr. World and Mr. Universe male physique titles, and actor

1948   **Jim Mandrich.** Professional football player

1951   **Efren Herrera.** Professional football player

1954   **Ellis Valentine.** Professional baseball player

1956   **Anita Hill.** American lawyer, educator and accuser of Supreme Court justice Clarence Thomas' having sexually harrassed her

1956   **Delta Burke.** American television actress noted for her role in the long-running comedy *Designing Women*

1957   **Eddie Lee Ivery.** Professional football player

1957   **Steve Trout.** Professional baseball player and son of baseball player Dizzy Trout

1974   **Hilary Swank.** American motion-picture and television actress

July 30 – Events

1502   Christopher Columbus reached the Bay Islands off the coast of Honduras on his fourth voyage to America.

1588   The Spanish Armada entered the English Channel and had its first engagement with the English fleet on the following day.

1619   The House of Burgesses of Virginia, the first representative legislative body in America, met for the first time, in Jamestown.

1729   Baltimore Town, which later became Baltimore, was founded by the Maryland colonial government.

1771   Thomas Gray, the noted English poet, died at age 54.

1862   The term *Copperhead,* meaning a Northerner sympathetic to the South, first appeared, in the Cincinnati *Gazette.*

1898   Otto von Bismarck, Germany's Iron Chancellor, died at Friedrichsruh at age 83.

1918   Sergeant Joyce Kilmer, American poet and author noted for the famous poem "Trees," was killed in action in France in World War I.

1932   Vice President Charles Curtis officially opened the 1932 Summer Olympic Games in Los Angeles.

1942   President Franklin D. Roosevelt signed the bill creating the WAVES, the women's branch of the U.S. Navy.

1947   Thor Heyerdahl, on his raft *Kon-Tiki,* sighted Puka Island in eastern Polynesia, after a journey from Peru.

1965   President Lyndon B. Johnson signed the Medicare bill into law.

1974   The U.S. House Judiciary Committee passed its third article of impeachment against President Nixon.

July 31 – Birthdays

1396   **Philip the Good.** Duke of Burgundy, 1419-1467, who presided over a magnificent medieval court and founded the Order of the Golden Fleece (1429)

1689   **Samuel Richardson.** English publisher, one of the founding fathers of the novel, and author of *Pamela; or Virtue Rewarded* (1740)

1803   **John Ericsson.** Swedish-American engineer who invented the screw propeller and designed and built the *Monitor,* the famous ironclad warship of the Union in the Civil War

1867   **Sebastian Spering Kresge.** American merchant and founder of S.S. Kresge's, which later became K-Mart

1875   **Jacques Villon.** French painter

1883   **Erich Heckel.** German painter

1900   **Elmo Roper.** American marketing consultant and founder of the Roper Poll

1912   **Irv Kupcinet.** American journalist and television host, noted for *Kup's Show*

1912 **Milton Friedman.** American economist, columnist, and author of *Capitalism and Freedom*, in which he advocated a "negative income tax"

1916 **William Selden Todman.** American television producer noted for his shows with Mark Goodson

1919 **Curt Gowdy.** American television sportscaster

1920 **Ndabaningi Sithole.** Clergyman and nationalist leader in Zimbabwe's struggle against white rule

1921 **Whitney M. Young Jr.** American civil rights leader and head of the National Urban League, 1961-1971

1922 **Hank Bauer.** Professional baseball player and manager

1929 **Don Murray.** American stage and motion-picture actor

1939 **Norman Snead.** Professional football player

1939 **France Nuyen.** French motion-picture actress

1943 **Edward Herrmann.** American stage, screen and television actor

1943 **Susan Flannery.** American actress

1944 **Geraldine Chaplin.** American actress and daughter of comedian Charlie Chaplin and granddaughter of playwright Eugene O'Neill

1946 **Bob Welch.** American rock musician with the Fleetwood Mac musical group

1951 **Evonne Goolagong Cawley.** Australian tennis player and twice Wimbledon singles champion

1957 **Leon Durham.** Professional baseball player

1966 **Dean Cain.** American actor who played Clark in TV's *Lois and Clark: The New Adventures of Superman* (1993-1997)

July 31 – Events

432 Saint Sixtus III was elected Roman Catholic pope.

1485 William Caxton, the first English printer, published his version of Sir Thomas Malory's great romance of knighthood, *Morte D'Arthur.*

1498 Christopher Columbus discovered Trinidad on his third voyage to America.

1556 Saint Ignatius Loyola, founder of the Jesuits, died in Rome at age 65.

1588 The Spanish Armada made its first contact with the English, commanded by Lord Howard of Effingham. The first contact was a probing action, the actual battle beginning on the next day.

1777 The Marquis de Lafayette of France was commissioned a major general in the Continental Army in the Revolutionary War.

1790 The first United States patent was issued, for potash manufacture.

1875 Andrew Johnson died in Carter Station, Tennessee, at age 66.

1945 The French World War II traitor Pierre Laval surrendered to U.S. occupation authorities in Linz, Austria.

1948 New York's Idlewild Airport (now John F. Kennedy Airport) was dedicated by President Harry S. Truman.

1950 Joe Adcock of the Milwaukee Braves hit four home runs and a double in a single game.

1964 U.S. space probe *Ranger 7* landed on the moon and televised 4,308 pictures of the moon to the earth.

1972 Vice-presidential candidate Thomas Eagleton withdrew from Senator George McGovern's ticket following disclosures that Eagleton had once undergone psychiatric treatment.

1975 Teamsters ex-president Jimmy Hoffa was reported missing. He was never found.

1981 The seven-week major league baseball strike came to an end.

1988 The last Playboy Club in the U.S. closed, in Lansing, Michigan.

8
August

August, the eighth month of the year, was the sixth month of the ancient Roman calendar, and was appropriately called *Sextilis,* the Latin word for *sixth.* In the original calendar of Romulus, August had 30 days. This was changed to 29 by Numa Pompilius and changed again to 30 in the Julian Calendar. In 8 B.C. the Roman Senate changed the name of the month to *Augustus* (August) to honor the emperor Augustus. He had been born in September, but he chose Sextilis for his month because during it so many fortunate events had happened to him, such as his election as one of the two consuls, the conquest of Egypt, and the cessation of the civil wars. According to legend, Augustus took one day from February and added it to August, giving it its present total of 31 days. He wanted his month to have as many days as July, the month of his great uncle Julius Caesar.

Bolivia, Ecuador, India, and Switzerland celebrate their national independence days in August, and V-J Day on August 14 marks the Allied victory over Japan in World War II in 1945. Three United States Presidents, Herbert Hoover, Lyndon B. Johnson, and Bill Clinton, were born in August, and Christopher Columbus set sail from Palos, Spain, on August 3, 1492, to discover the new world.

The birthstones for August are the sardonyx and the peridot, and the August flowers are the poppy and the gladiolus.

August 1 – Birthdays

10 BC   **Claudius I.** Emperor of Rome, A.D. 41-54, who built Rome's harbor at Ostia, and conquered parts of England and Thrace (now the Balkans)

126   **Publius Helvius Pertinax.** Emperor of Rome who served for less than one year (A.D. 193)

1495   **Jan van Scorel.** Dutch painter

1520   **Sigismund II Augustus.** King of Poland, 1548-1572

1714   **Richard Wilson.** British landscape painter

1744   **Chevalier de Lamarck.** French naturalist who introduced the term "biology" and was noted for being one of the first to propose a theory of biological evolution

1770   **William Clark.** American explorer, who with Meriwether Lewis led the famous Lewis and Clark exploration of the U.S. northwest territory from 1804 to 1806

1779   **Francis Scott Key.** American lawyer and poet who wrote the words to "The Star-Spangled Banner" during the War of 1812

1815   **Richard Henry Dana.** American novelist and author of *Two Years Before the Mast* (1840)

1818   **Maria Mitchell.** American astronomer noted for her studies of sunspots and as the first woman member of the American Academy of Arts and Sciences

1819   **Herman Melville.** One of America's greatest writers, and author of *Moby Dick* (1851), one of the great novels in literature, and *Billy Budd* (published in 1924 after Melville's death)

1843   **Robert Todd Lincoln.** Eldest son of Abraham Lincoln and the only son of Lincoln's to survive to manhood

1883   **Jonathan M. Wainwright.** American World War II general and hero of Bataan and Corregidor

1891   **Edward Streeter.** American author noted for works such as *Father of the Bride* (1949)

1898   **Morris Stoloff.** American composer, conductor, and violinist, noted for songs such as "A Song to Remember," and scores for movies such as *Cover Girl, The Jolson Story,* and *Song Without End*

1898   **William B. Ziff.** American publisher

1899   **William Steinberg.** Noted American conductor of the Pittsburgh Symphony and the Boston Symphony orchestras

1914   **Lloyd Mangrum.** Professional golfer and winner of the U.S. Open in 1946

1921   **Jack Kramer.** One of the great all-time tennis players

1922   **C. Peter McColough.** Chairman of Xerox Corporation

1922   **Arthur Hill.** Canadian stage and motion-picture actor

1929 **Ralph Kessler.** American composer noted for the background music of such TV shows as *Buck Rogers, Quincy,* and *Barnaby Jones*

1930 **Geoffrey Holder.** Trinidad-born choreographer and costume designer

1931 **Tom Wilson.** American cartoonist and creator of *Ziggy*

1933 **Dom De Luise.** American actor and comedian

1936 **Yves Saint-Laurent.** French dress designer

1937 **Alfonse D'Amato.** U.S. senator, 1981-1999

1939 **Robert James Waller.** American author noted for *The Bridges of Madison County* (1991)

1941 **Lionel Bart.** English composer, lyricist and dramatist noted for his work in *Oliver* (1963) and *La Strada* (1969)

1941 **Ron Brown.** Secretary of Commerce under President Clinton

1942 **Jerry Garcia.** American guitarist with The Grateful Dead musical group

1942 **Giancarlo Giannini.** Italian motion-picture actor

1948 **Cliff Branch.** Professional football player

1950 **Milt May.** Professional baseball player

1952 **Greg Gross.** Professional baseball player

1973 **Tempestt Bledsoe.** American television actress noted for her role in the *Bill Cosby Show*

August 1 – Events

1137 Louis VI, the Fat, King of France, died of dysentery.

1291 The three Swiss cantons signed the Perpetual Covenant, establishing the Swiss Confederation, which became known later as Switzerland.

1423 The English defeated the French at Crevant in the Hundred Years' War.

1498 Christopher Columbus, on his third voyage to America, sailed across the Gulf of Paria to the mainland of Venezuela. He did not actually land until August 5.

1588 The first day's battle between the Spanish Armada and the English fleet was indecisive, with both sides exchanging long-range gunfire.

1589 King Henry III of France was stabbed to death while sitting on the privy, by a fanatic monk, Jacques Clement.

1774 British scientist Joseph Priestley succeeded in isolating oxygen from air. He shares credit for the discovery of oxygen with Carl Wilhelm Scheele of Sweden whose work was independent of Priestley's.

1788 Thomas Gainsborough, the great English painter, died in London at age 61.

1790 The first U.S. census was completed, showing a population of 3,929,214 in 17 states.

1794 The Whiskey Rebellion began in Pennsylvania, in protest of the excise tax on alcoholic beverages.

1798 British admiral Horatio Nelson in the Battle of the Nile almost destroyed the French fleet, ending Napoleon's hopes of a vast Eastern conquest.

1876 Colorado was admitted to the Union as the 38th state.

1907 The U.S. Army established an Aeronautical Division, the forerunner of the U.S. Air Force.

1914 Germany declared war on Russia in World War I.

1933 Carl Hubbell, the New York Giants' ace pitcher, pitched his 44th consecutive scoreless inning, a record.

1944 An uprising broke out in the Warsaw ghetto against the Nazis in World War II. The revolt lasted two months before the Germans brutally crushed it, while the Russian army watched nearby.

1946 The U.S. Atomic Energy Commission was established.

1966 Charles Joseph Whitman killed 15 people from a tower on the campus of the University of Texas at Austin, before he was killed by the police.

1972 Nate Colbert of the San Diego Padres hit five home runs in a doubleheader.

August 2 – Birthdays

1696 **Mahmud I.** Ottoman sultan, 1730-1754

1754 **Pierre Charles L'Enfant.** French engineer and architect, who planned the design of Washington, D.C.

1820 **John Tyndall.** English physicist and natural philosopher, who first demonstrated the Tyndall effect, explaining why the sky is blue

1835 **Elisha Gray.** American inventor, who claimed to have invented the telephone before Alexander Graham Bell, and who was a founder of the Western Electric Company

1865 **Irving Babbitt.** American critic, teacher, and leader of the "new humanism" movement

1867 **Ernest Dowson.** English poet and outstanding representative of the Aesthetic Movement, best known for "Cynara" (1891) and "The Days of Wine and Roses" (1896)

1868 **Constantine I.** King of Greece, 1913-1917 and 1920-1923

1871 **John French Sloan.** American painter and etcher, and member of the Eight, an association of painters in the early 20th century

1880 **Arthur Garfield Dove.** American painter, whose paintings were among the earliest abstract works painted in America

1892 **Jack Warner.** American motion-picture producer and co-founder of Warner Brothers in 1923

1892 **John Kieran.** American columnist and radio performer

1894 **Westbrook Pegler.** American journalist

1905 **Myrna Loy.** American motion-picture actress, known especially for her starring roles opposite William Powell in *The Thin Man* series of movies

1915 **Gary Merrill.** American stage and motion-picture actor

1918   **Beatrice Straight.** American motion-picture and television actress
1922   **Paul Laxalt.** U.S. senator
1924   **James Baldwin.** American novelist, essayist, and playwright, noted for *The Fire Next Time* (1963) and *Another Country* (1962)
1925   **Carroll O'Connor.** American stage, screen, and television actor, and star of the long-running television comedy *All in the Family*
1932   **Leo Joseph Boivin.** Professional hockey player and Hall of Famer
1932   **Peter O'Toole.** English motion-picture actor with a career of over 40 years
1932   **Lamar Hunt.** American sports franchise owner and son of billionaire H.L. Hunt
1937   **Billy Cannon.** Heisman Trophy winner (1959) and professional football player
1944   **Joanna Cassidy.** American motion-picture and television actress
1946   **Bob Beamon.** American long jumper who set the world's record of 29 feet 2¼ inches in 1968
1949   **Wes Craven.** American motion-picture and television director noted for works such as *A Nightmare on Elm Street* (1984)
1952   **Mike Ivie.** Professional baseball player
1963   **Cynthia Stevenson.** American stage, screen and television actress
1967   **Aaron Krickstein.** American tennis player

August 2 – Events

216 BC   The great Carthaginian general Hannibal and his elephants routed the Romans in the Battle of Cannae, a battle famous for Hannibal's use of "double envelopment," still used today.
47 BC   Upon defeating Pharnaces, King of Pontus, Julius Caesar said, "I came, I saw, I conquered."
1776   Members of the Continental Congress began the process of signing the Declaration of Independence. Fifty members signed on this day.
1824   New York City's Fifth Avenue was opened.
1832   The U.S. defeated Chief Black Hawk and his Sauk and Fox Indians in the Battle of Bad Axe, effectively ending the Black Hawk War.
1858   The first street letter boxes were set up, in Boston.
1867   President Andrew Johnson suspended Secretary of War Stanton, testing the Tenure of Office Act, recently enacted by Congress. The suspension resulted in Johnson's impeachment by the House.
1876   Wild Bill Hickok was murdered at age 39 while playing poker and holding two aces and two eights, known ever since as a "dead man's hand."
1909   The first Lincoln pennies were issued.
1923   President Warren G. Harding died suddenly in San Francisco at age 57. He was succeeded the next day by Vice President Calvin Coolidge.
1927   "I do not choose to run," said President Calvin Coolidge, taking himself out of the 1928 presidential race.

1934   German president Paul von Hindenburg died, leaving Adolf Hitler free to consolidate his dictatorship.
1936   Jesse Owens, the great American athlete, set a new world's record for the 100-meter run in the Olympic Games in Berlin.
1939   The Hatch Act was passed by Congress, forbidding federal civil service employees from taking an active part in political campaigns.
1943   Navy Lieutenant John F. Kennedy rescued the members of his boat, *PT-109*, after it was sheared in two by a Japanese destroyer in the South Pacific.
1945   The Potsdam Conference ended with President Truman, Premier Stalin, and Prime Minister Attlee, who had replaced Churchill, calling for Germany's disarmament and Japan's surrender.
1956   Albert Woolson, the last Union veteran of the Civil War, died at age 109.
1978   The movie *Star Wars* surpassed *Jaws* as the all-time high money maker.
1983   The House of Representatives voted overwhelmingly to make Dr. Martin Luther King Jr.'s birthday, January 15, a national holiday.
1990   Iraqi dictator Saddam Hussein seized Kuwait, announcing that it was a part of Iraq, and triggering the Persian Gulf War.

August 3 – Birthdays

1746   **James Wyatt.** English architect
1770   **Frederick William III.** King of Prussia, 1797-1840, who was defeated by Napoleon at the Battles of Jena and Auerstadt in 1806
1801   **Joseph Paxton.** English architect noted for his design of the Crystal Palace of the 1851 London Exhibition, one of the first buildings to have prefabricated parts made in factories
1811   **Elisha Graves Otis.** American inventor, who built the first elevator protected by safety devices against accidentally falling
1841   **Julianna Horatia Ewing.** English children's author noted for the classic tale *Jackanapes* (1884)
1867   **Stanley Baldwin.** Three times British prime minister, 1923-1924, 1924-1929, and 1935-1937
1872   **Haakon VII.** First king of Norway after it gained its independence from Sweden in 1905
1886   **Russ Westover.** American comic strip writer, and creator of *Tillie the Toiler* in 1921
1887   **Rupert Brooke.** English poet, noted primarily for his sonnet-sequence "1914"
1894   **Harry Heilmann.** Hall of Fame baseball player who hit .403 in 1923
1900   **Ernie Pyle.** Beloved American World War II war correspondent who was killed on Okinawa in 1945
1901   **John C. Stennis.** U.S. senator
1905   **Dolores Del Rio.** Glamorous Mexican motion-picture actress, and one of the most beautiful women ever to grace the American screen
1905   **Maggie Kuhn.** Founder of the Gray Panthers

1909 **Walter van Tilburg Clark.** American author noted for *The Ox-Bow Incident* (1940)

1918 **James MacGregor Burns.** American historian and writer, and author of *Roosevelt: The Lion and the Fox* (1956)

1920 **P.D. James.** English author noted for works such as *The Black Tower* (1975)

1920 **George C. Cory Jr.** American composer noted for songs such as "I Left My Heart in San Francisco" (with Ernest Altschuler)

1920 **Jim Hegan.** Professional baseball player

1921 **Richard Adler.** American songwriter who teamed with Jerry Ross to write songs such as "Hey There," "Whatever Lola Wants," and "Hernando's Hideaway"

1921 **Marilyn Maxwell.** American actress and singer

1923 **Jean Hagen.** American motion-picture and television actress

1924 **Leon Uris.** American novelist and author of *Exodus* (1958)

1926 **Tony Bennett.** American singer with a career of some 40 years

1931 **Alex Cord.** American motion-picture actor

1935 **Richard Lamm.** Governor of Colorado

1940 **Lance Alworth.** Professional football player

1940 **Martin Sheen.** American stage, screen, and television actor

1941 **Martha Stewart.** American expert on lifestyles, author, and host of her own television show

1951 **Paulo Bertolucci.** Italian tennis player

1960 **Sid Bream.** Professional baseball player

1960 **Tim Mayotte.** American tennis player

1964 **Kevin Elster.** Professional baseball player

August 3 – Events

30 BC Mark Antony committed suicide in Alexandria, Egypt, to which he had been pursued by Octavian after the Battle of Actium.

1291 The Crusaders abandoned Tortosa to the Moslems.

1422 King Henry V of England died of dysentery in France at age 34, after having won the entire northern half of France in the Hundred Years' War.

1492 Christopher Columbus sailed from Palos, Spain, on his first voyage to America, with a fleet of three ships—the *Santa Maria*, the *Pinta*, and the *Nina*—and 90 men.

1610 Henry Hudson, the great British sea captain and adventurer, discovered Hudson Bay in Canada.

1778 Milan's world-famous opera house, La Scala, opened for its first performance.

1858 John Hanning Speke, the English African explorer, discovered Lake Victoria.

1914 Germany declared war on France in World War I.

1923 Calvin Coolidge became president of the United States upon the death of President Harding. He was sworn in at 2:45 A.M. by the light of a kerosene lamp by his father, a notary public.

1924 Joseph Conrad, the great Polish-English novelist, died in Bishopsbourne, England, at age 66.

1948 Whittaker Chambers, the admitted ex-Communist, accused Alger Hiss of being a member of the Communist underground.

1949 The National Basketball Association was formed with 17 teams in three divisions.

1958 The U.S. atomic submarine *Nautilus* crossed the North Pole under the Arctic ice.

August 4 – Birthdays

1521 **Urban VII.** Roman Catholic pope, who served for less than one year in 1590

1755 **Nicholas Jacques Conte.** French developer in 1795 of the pencil-making process that is still used in the manufacture of modern pencils

1792 **Percy Bysshe Shelley.** One of the greatest English Romantic poets, noted for such poems as "Ode to the West Wind" (1819) and *Adonais* (1821), an elegy for John Keats

1816 **Russell Sage.** American banker and philanthropist whose widow, Margaret, incorporated the Russell Sage Foundation to help remove the causes of poverty

1839 **Walter Horatio Pater.** English essayist and critic, and author of *Marius the Epicurean* (1885)

1841 **William Henry Hudson.** British author and naturalist, best noted for the novel *Green Mansions* (1904)

1853 **John Henry Twachtman.** One of the first U.S. Impressionist painters

1859 **Knut Hamsun.** Nobel Prize-winning Norwegian novelist, best known for *The Growth of the Soil* (1917)

1861 **Jesse W. Reno.** American inventor noted for the invention of the escalator

1870 **Sir Harry Lauder.** Scottish comedian, ballad singer, and "Scotland's Goodwill Ambassador," who became one of the world's most beloved entertainers

1890 **Dolf Luque.** Professional baseball player

1900 **Queen Mother Elizabeth.** Wife of George VI and mother of Elizabeth II of England (born Elizabeth Bowes-Lyon)

1910 **William Howard Schuman.** American composer and administrator, who won the Pulitzer Prize in 1943

1913 **Wesley Addy.** American stage and screen actor

1920 **Helen Thomas.** American journalist

1934 **Dallas Green.** Professional baseball player, manager, and executive

1948 **John Grubb.** Professional baseball player

1949 **John Riggins.** Professional football superstar and Hall of Famer

1958 **Mary Decker Slaney.** Noted American world champion runner

1962   **Roger Clemens.** Professional baseball pitcher who struck out a record 20 batters in a nine-inning game (April 29, 1986) and won both the Cy Young and Most Valuable Player Awards in 1986

1964   **B.J. Surhoff.** Professional baseball player

August 4 – Events

1060   Philip I became king of France at age eight.

1578   Sebastian I of Portugal was killed and his army utterly defeated at Al-Kasr al-Kebir in Northwest Africa, ending for a time European excursions into Africa.

1735   John Peter Zenger won an acquittal of libel charges intended to censor his attacks on the Crown. The case established freedom of the press in America.

1790   Congress established the Revenue Cutter Service, later known as the United States Coast Guard.

1821   The weekly magazine *Saturday Evening Post* was founded.

1875   Hans Christian Andersen, the great Danish fairy tale writer, died in Copenhagen at age 70.

1892   Lizzie Borden's parents were murdered with an axe in Fall River, Massachusetts. It seemed obvious that "Lizzie Borden took an axe...," but she was later acquitted.

1903   Pius X was elected Roman Catholic pope.

1914   Germany invaded neutral Belgium and Great Britain declared war on Germany in World War I.

1916   Denmark and the United States signed a treaty transferring control of the Virgin Islands to the United States.

1944   Anne Frank and her family were betrayed to the Gestapo in Amsterdam, after two years of hiding, during which time she wrote her famous diary.

1985   Baseball greats Tom Seaver and Rod Carew reached career milestones, as Seaver won his 300th game and Carew got his 3,000th base hit.

August 5 – Birthdays

1540   **Joseph Justus Scaliger.** French philosopher and historian

1604   **John Eliot.** English clergyman and "Apostle to the Indians," and the first minister to teach the Christian religion to the Indians of New England

1694   **Leonardo Leo.** Italian composer and teacher

1749   **Thomas Lynch Jr.** South Carolina signer of the Declaration of Independence

1802   **Niels Heinrich Abel.** One of the greatest Norwegian mathematicians of all time

1813   **Ivar Aasen.** Norwegian language scholar

1827   **Manoel Deodoro da Fonseca.** First president of Brazil, who ruled for a few months in 1891

1850   **Guy De Maupassant.** French author and one of the world's great short-story writers

1889   **Conrad Aiken.** American poet, novelist, and critic, whose *Selected Poems* won the Pulitzer Prize in 1930

1890   **Naum Gabo.** Russian-born sculptor

1906   **John Huston.** Noted American motion-picture actor and director, and son of actor Walter Huston, who directed such films as *The Treasure of Sierra Madre* (1948) and *The African Queen* (1952)

1908   **Harold Edward Holt.** Australian Prime Minister who mysteriously drowned while in office in Port Philip Bay, Australia

1911   **Robert Taylor.** American motion-picture and television actor, and one of Hollywood's top stars for 30 years

1914   **David Brian.** American stage and motion-picture actor

1918   **Tom Drake.** American motion-picture actor

1920   **George Tooker.** American painter noted for works such as *Government Bureau* (1956)

1923   **Richard Kleindienst.** Attorney-general under President Nixon

1930   **Neil Armstrong.** U.S. astronaut and first man to set foot on the moon (July 20, 1969)

1933   **Tom Skerritt.** American motion-picture and television actor

1935   **John Saxon.** American stage, screen and television actor

1940   **Roman Gabriel.** Professional football player and superstar

1943   **Nelson Briles.** Professional baseball player and announcer

1945   **Loni Anderson.** American television actress

1950   **Holly Palance.** American actress and daughter of actor Jack Palance

1950   **Bob McKinley.** American tennis player

1952   **Freddie Scott.** Professional football player

1953   **Samantha Sang.** Australian singer

1953   **Rick Mahler.** Professional baseball player

1962   **Patrick Ewing.** Professional basketball superstar

1968   **John Olerud.** Professional baseball player and National League batting champion in 1993

1970   **Josie Bissett.** American motion-picture and television actress

August 5 – Events

1498   Columbus landed on the Paria Peninsula in Venezuela on his third voyage, and wrote in his log, "I believe that this is a very great continent which until today has been unknown."

1858   The first transatlantic cable was completed, between Trinity Bay, Newfoundland, and Valentia, Ireland. It failed, however, after only four weeks of service.

1861   Congress abolished flogging in the U.S. Army.

1864   Union admiral David Farragut won the Battle of Mobile Bay in the Civil War, after giving the order, "Damn the torpedoes! Full steam ahead!"

1886   The Republic of Colombia was founded.

1912 The newly-formed Progressive Party met to select a presidential candidate for the 1912 campaign. They ultimately chose Theodore Roosevelt, leading to a three-way race with Woodrow Wilson and incumbent president William Howard Taft.

1924 The comic strip *Little Orphan Annie,* by Harold Gray, first appeared.

1957 The comic strip *Andy Capp,* by Reginald Smythe, first appeared.

1962 Marilyn Monroe, the glamorous American actress, died in her bedroom from acute barbiturate poisoning.

1974 President Nixon released the "smoking gun" tape, showing him guilty of the Watergate coverup. On the June 23, 1972 tape he ordered the FBI "to stay the hell out of this."

August 6 – Birthdays

1644 **Louise de la Valliere.** Mistress of King Louis XIV of France

1651 **François de La Mothe Fenelon.** French writer and archbishop, whose best known work is the novel *Telemachus* (1699)

1697 **Charles VII.** The first Holy Roman emperor (1742-1745) in 300 years who was not a member of the Hapsburg family

1809 **Alfred Lord Tennyson.** One of the most important English poets of the 1800s and one of the supreme craftsmen in the English language, noted for works such as *In Memorium* and *Locksley Hall*

1828 **Andrew Taylor Still.** American physician and founder of osteopathy

1851 **John Robertson Reid.** English painter

1868 **Paul Claudel.** One of the foremost French poets and playwrights of the 1900s

1876 **Miller Hutchinson.** Inventor of the Dictograph and the Klaxon horn

1880 **Leo Carrillo.** American motion-picture and television actor

1881 **Alexander Fleming.** British bacteriologist who discovered penicillin in 1929

1888 **Arthur Fields.** American composer noted for songs such as "And the Angels Sing" and "Aba Daba Honeymoon"

1892 **Hoot Gibson.** American actor and "World's All-Around Champion Cowboy" in 1912

1893 **Wright Patman.** U.S. congressman

1893 **Louella Parsons.** American Hollywood gossip columnist

1896 **Ray Blades.** Professional baseball player and manager

1900 **Nat Simon.** American composer, author, and conductor, noted for songs such as "Poinciana," "No Can Do," and "The Old Lamplighter"

1900 **Dutch Schulz.** American gangster and Prohibition era bootlegger

1906 **Ken Strong.** Hall of Fame professional football player

1908 **Helen Hull Jacobs.** One of the greatest women tennis players in history and winner of the U.S. singles title four years in a row (1932-1935)

1911 **Lucille Ball.** American comedienne, actress, and star of television's long-running comedy *I Love Lucy*

1917 **Robert Mitchum.** American motion-picture actor and veteran of more than 60 films

1919 **Pauline Betz.** American tennis player who dominated the game during the middle 1940s

1922 **Sir Frederick A. Laker.** Owner and founder of Laker Airways

1922 **Doug Ford.** Professional golfer

1930 **Abbey Lincoln.** American jazz singer and motion-picture actress

1938 **Bert Yancey.** Professional golfer

1945 **Andy Messersmith.** Professional baseball player

1953 **Janet Newberry.** American tennis player

1955 **Ron Davis.** Professional baseball player

1957 **Bob Horner.** Professional baseball player

August 6 – Events

1338 The Diet of Frankfurt issued the decree *Licet Juris,* marking the beginning of the papacy's exclusion from Imperial affairs.

1497 John Cabot landed in Bristol on his return from his North American voyage.

1588 The Spanish Armada anchored at Calais after an inconclusive six-day battle with the English. It remained there for two days before being attacked again by the English.

1623 Anne Hathaway, wife of William Shakespeare, died at age 67.

1637 Ben Jonson, English dramatist and poet, died in London at age 65.

1660 Diego Velazquez, the great Spanish painter, died in Madrid at age 61.

1806 The Holy Roman Empire came to an end, precipitated by the armies of Napoleon.

1825 Bolivia became independent of Spain and Peru.

1890 New York became the first state to electrocute a criminal, as William Kemmler was electrocuted for murder in Auburn, New York.

1890 Cy Young, baseball's winningest pitcher, appeared in his first major league game.

1926 Harry Houdini, the great American escape artist, remained under water for 91 minutes in an airtight case and survived.

1926 Gertrude Ederle, a 20-year-old New Yorker, became the first woman to swim the English Channel.

1926 The first talking pictures were shown, at the Warner Theater in New York City.

1940 Estonia was annexed as one of the republics of the Soviet Union.

1945 The first atomic bomb was dropped, on Hiroshima, Japan, by the *Enola Gay,* a high-flying U.S. B-29 bomber.

1945 Jamaica became independent of Great Britain.

1973   Vice President Spiro Agnew acknowledged he was being investigated for law violations. As a result he later became the second vice president to resign the office. (John C. Calhoun was the first.)

1978   Pope Paul VI died in the 15th year of his reign.

1999   Berlin became the functioning capital of the united German state once again.

August 7 – Birthdays

317   **Flavius Julius Constantius.** Roman emperor, A.D. 337-361

1742   **Nathanael Greene.** American Revolutionary War general, ranked second only to George Washington as a military leader

1779   **Karl Ritter.** German geographer and co-founder of modern geographical science

1783   **John Heathcoat.** English inventor who developed a machine for making a kind of lace known as bobbinet

1867   **Emil Nolde.** German impressionist painter noted for works such as *Harvest Day* (1904) and *The Life of Christ* (1912)

1876   **Mata Hari.** French dancer (Margaret Gertrude Zelle) who was executed as a German spy during World War I, and whose name has become a synonym for the seductive female spy

1881   **François Darlan.** French World War II admiral

1885   **Billie Burke.** American stage, screen, and television actress, with a 60-year career

1886   **Bill McKechnie.** Professional baseball player and manager

1893   **C. Luckeyth "Luckey" Roberts.** American composer, conductor, and pianist, noted for songs such as "Moonlight Cocktail"

1901   **Ann Harding.** American stage and motion-picture actress, who was a leading lady in the 1930s and a veteran character actor in the 1940s and 1950s

1903   **Louis S.B. Leakey.** English anthropologist and paleontologist, who discovered fossil remains in Africa of Homo erectus and others, ranging in age up to 1,750,000 years

1904   **Ralph Bunche.** American United Nations diplomat

1910   **Freddie Slack.** American composer, author, and bandleader, noted for songs such as "Cow Cow Boogie," "Beat Me Daddy Eight to the Bar," and "O Sole Mio"

1925   **Felice Bryant.** American songwriter noted with her husband Boudleaux for works such as "Bye Bye Love" and "Wake Up Little Susie"

1926   **Stan Freberg.** American composer, author, and comedian

1927   **Edwin Edwards.** Three-term Governor of Louisiana in the 1970s,1980s, and 1990s

1929   **Don Larson.** Professional baseball pitcher who pitched a perfect game (no one reached base) in the 1956 World Series as the New York Yankees defeated the Brooklyn Dodgers, 2-0

1942   **Garrison Keillor.** American humorist noted for the long-running radio program *A Prairie Home Companion*

1944   **Lana Cantrell.** Australian-born singer

1947   **Kerry Melville Reid.** Australian tennis player

1950   **David James Wottle.** American mile runner

1951   **Gary Hall.** American swimmer who set the world record 400-Meter individual medley of four minutes 31 seconds in 1970

1954   **Steve Kemp.** Professional baseball player

1960   **David Duchovny.** American actor and star of TV's *The X-Files*

1975   **Charlize Theron.** South African motion-picture actress

August 7 – Events

1782   The Badge of Military Merit, which in 1932 became the Purple Heart, was established by George Washington.

1789   Congress created the United States War Department.

1882   The famous Hatfield-McCoy feud in West Virginia and eastern Kentucky broke out, leading eventually to 100 men, women, and children killed or wounded.

1912   The Progressive Party nominated Theodore Roosevelt for president, leading to the three-way race with Woodrow Wilson and President William Howard Taft.

1928   The comic strip *Alley Oop*, by V.T. Hamlin, made its first appearance.

1928   New American dollars were issued in a size one-third smaller than the previous bills.

1942   U.S. troops landed on Guadalcanal in the Solomon Islands in World War II.

1947   Thor Heyerdahl, on the raft *Kon-Tiki,* landed in Tuamotu Archipelago in Polynesia, having drifted 4,000 miles from Peru in 15 weeks.

1954   Dr. Roger Bannister defeated John Landy, as both ran the mile in less than four minutes. Bannister's time was 3 minutes 58.8 seconds and Landy's was 3 minutes 59.6 seconds.

1964   The Gulf of Tonkin resolution was passed by Congress, giving the president powers to repel attacks on U.S. armed forces.

1971   *Apollo 15* splashed down in the Pacific Ocean after exploring the moon's surface.

August 8 – Birthdays

1646   **Sir Godfrey Kneller.** Anglo-German portrait painter

1763   **Charles Bulfinch.** The greatest architect in New England history

1799   **Nathaniel Brown Palmer.** American sea captain believed to be the first explorer to sight Antarctica, in 1820

1819 **Charles A. Dana.** American editor who built the New York *Sun* into one of the most important newspapers of its time

1866 **Matthew Henson.** Only black member of Admiral Robert E. Peary's North Pole expedition

1879 **Dr. Bob (Robert Holbrook Smith).** American physician (Robert Holbrook Smith) who with Bill W. co-founded Alcoholics Anonymous in 1935

1879 **Emiliano Zapata.** Mexican Indian leader of the Mexican Revolution in 1910

1884 **Sara Teasdale.** American poet and author of "Flame and Shadow" (1920)

1896 **Marjorie Kinnan Rawlings.** American novelist and author of *The Yearling* (1939)

1900 **Victor Young.** American composer, conductor, and violinist, noted for songs such as "Sweet Sue, Just You," "Stella By Starlight," "I Don't Stand a Ghost of a Chance With You," and "Golden Earrings"

1901 **Ernest Orlando Lawrence.** American Nobel Prize-winning atomic physicist, who helped develop the cyclotron

1902 **Paul A.M. Dirac.** British Nobel Prize-winning physicist noted for his prediction of the existence of the positive electron, or positron

1908 **Arthur Goldberg.** U.S. Supreme Court justice and U.N. ambassador under President Lyndon Johnson

1910 **Sylvia Sidney.** American stage and motion-picture actress and one of the most popular leading ladies of the 1930s

1913 **Axel Stordahl.** American composer, conductor, and arranger of the Big Band Era

1913 **Robert Stafford.** U.S. senator

1919 **Dino De Laurentiis.** Italian motion-picture producer noted for works such as *Bitter Rice* (1948) and *La Strada* (1954)

1922 **Rudi Gernreich.** American fashion designer, noted for women's topless bathing suits and miniskirts

1923 **Esther Williams.** American swimming star and motion-picture actress

1923 **Rory Calhoun.** American motion-picture and television actor

1926 **Webb Pierce.** American country singer

1926 **Richard Anderson.** American motion-picture and television actor

1927 **Andy Warhol.** American film maker and pop artist

1930 **Jerry Tarkanian.** College basketball coach

1930 **Joan Adams Mondale.** Wife of Vice President Walter Mondale

1932 **Mel Tillis.** American country singer and songwriter

1936 **Frank Howard.** Professional baseball player and manager

1937 **Dustin Hoffman.** American motion-picture actor who won Academy Awards for best actor in *Kramer versus Kramer* (1979) and *Rainman* (1989)

1938 **Vada Pinson.** Professional baseball player

1938 **Connie Stevens.** American singer and actress

1942 **Tory Ann Fretz.** American tennis player

1947 **Jose Cruz.** Professional baseball player

1949 **Brian Sipe.** Professional football player

1949 **Keith Carradine.** American actor and son of the great character actor John Carradine

1958 **Deborah Norville.** American television and radio personality

1968 **Suzy Hamilton.** American runner with nine NCAA championships and 23 Big Ten Athletic Conference titles

August 8 – Events

117 Roman emperor Trajan died at Selinus at age 63.

1588 The English sent 8 burning ships into Calais harbor, driving the Spanish Armada out to sea, where it was badly defeated, with only 67 of its original 130 ships returning to Spain.

1815 Napoleon Bonaparte set sail for St. Helena to spend the rest of his days in exile.

1844 Brigham Young was chosen to lead the Mormon Church, following the murder of Joseph Smith.

1900 The first Davis Cup Tennis Tournament began, in Massachusetts.

1911 The membership of the House of Representatives was fixed at 435.

1918 The British broke the German line at Amiens in World War I.

1936 Jesse Owens won his fourth gold medal in the Berlin Olympics as the U.S. took first place in the 400-meter relay.

1945 Russia declared war on Japan in World War II, and invaded Manchuria.

1950 Florence Chadwick swam the English Channel in 13 hours, 28 minutes, a new record for women.

1973 Vice President Spiro Agnew called reports that he had taken kickbacks from government contracts "damned lies." He was later forced to resign because they did not seem to be.

1974 President Nixon announced that he would resign at noon on the following day.

August 9 – Birthdays

1593 **Izaak Walton.** English author and critic, known for his classic on fishing, *The Compleat Angler* (1653)

1757 **Thomas Telford.** Scottish civil engineer, noted for the Telford road construction method of using large flat stones for road foundations

1776 **Amedeo Avogadro.** Italian physicist known for Avogadro's Law of gases, and for the table of atomic weights

1819 **William Thomas Green Morton.** American dentist, who introduced ether as an anesthetic for painless dentistry

1832 **Nathaniel Pitt Langford.** Co-discoverer of the geysers at Yellowstone Park

1836 **James Norris Gamble.** American manufacturer and partner in Proctor and Gamble Co.

1839 **Gaston Paris.** The greatest French philologist of his time

1880   **Ramon Perez de Ayala.** One of the greatest Spanish novelists of the 20th century

1896   **Jean Piaget.** Swiss philosopher and psychologist who developed "genetic epistemology," the study of how a child acquires and modifies abstract ideas

1899   **P.L. Travers.** British writer noted for *Mary Poppins*

1899   **Paul Kelly.** American stage and motion-picture actor in over 60 films

1901   **Charles Farrell.** American silent film, talkies, and television actor

1905   **Leo Genn.** English stage and screen actor

1905   **Zino Francescatti.** French violinist noted for his concert performances in Europe and America

1913   **Herman Talmadge.** Governor of Georgia, U.S. senator, and son of Georgia governor Eugene Talmadge

1919   **Ralph Houk.** Professional baseball player and manager with a career spanning over 40 years

1921   **J. James Exon.** U.S. senator

1927   **Robert Shaw.** English stage and motion-picture actor and novelist

1928   **Harold Johnson.** American Hall of Fame boxer and lightweight champion, 1954-1963

1928   **Bob Cousy.** One of the greatest all-around players in professional basketball history, who led the Boston Celtics to six world championships

1931   **Hurricane Jackson.** American professional boxer

1938   **Rod Laver.** One of the greatest tennis players of all time, and the first to win the Grand Slam twice

1939   **Claude Osteen.** Professional baseball player

1942   **David Steinberg.** American comedian, actor, and writer

1942   **Tommie Agee.** Professional baseball player

1944   **Sam Elliott.** American motion-picture and television actor

1945   **Ken Norton.** American boxer

1946   **Jim Kiick.** Professional football player

1949   **Ted Simmons.** Professional baseball player

1952   **John Cappelletti.** Professional football player

1954   **Henry Marshall.** Professional football player

1955   **Doug Williams.** Professional football player

1957   **Melanie Griffith.** American motion-picture actress and daughter of actress Tippi Hedron

1963   **Whitney Houston.** American actress, singer and superstar

1964   **Brett Hull.** Professional hockey player

1967   **Deion Sanders.** Professional football and baseball player

August 9 – Events

48 BC   Julius Caesar defeated Pompey in the Battle of Pharsalus, in Greece, but Pompey escaped to Egypt, where he was later murdered.

117   Hadrian succeeded Trajan as Emperor of Rome.

1638   Jonas Bronck became the first European settler in what is now the Bronx, New York, which was named for his family, the Broncks.

1842   The Webster-Ashburton Treaty was signed in Washington, D.C., fixing the boundary between Canada and Maine, and settling other minor disputes.

1854   Henry David Thoreau published *Walden,* one of the world's great books.

1901   The coronation of Edward VII as King of England took place in London. Edward had become king following the death of his mother, Queen Victoria, in January.

1921   Franklin D. Roosevelt was stricken with polio on Campobello Island, off New Brunswick, Canada.

1937   Japanese troops captured Nanking, the capital of China, in the Sino-Japanese War.

1945   The American bomber *Bock's Car* dropped the second atomic bomb used in warfare, on Nagasaki, Japan.

1965   Singapore became independent of the Malaysian Federation.

1969   Actress Sharon Tate and four others were found brutally murdered in Bel Air, California. Charles Manson and others of the "Manson family" were later convicted of the crime.

1974   Richard M. Nixon became the first president in history to resign. He was succeeded by Vice President Gerald Ford.

August 10 – Birthdays

1729   **William Howe.** British general who ordered the hanging of Nathan Hale in the American Revolutionary War

1753   **Edmond Randolph.** General George Washington's aide-de-camp during the Revolutionary War and one of the framers of the U.S. Constitution

1798   **Minard Lafever.** American architect

1810   **Camillo Benso di Cavour.** Italian count and statesman who played a principal role in uniting Italy under a single kingdom in 1861

1848   **William Harnett.** The leading American still-life painter of the late 1800s

1865   **Alexander Konstantinovich Glazunov.** Russian composer

1874   **Herbert Hoover.** 31st U.S. president

1895   **Harry Richman.** American composer, author, and singer, noted for songs such as "Walking My Baby Back Home" and "Cherie"

1897   **Larry Shay.** American composer and conductor, noted for songs such as "When You're Smiling (The Whole World Smiles With You)," "Everywhere You Go," and "Highways Are Happy Ways"

1897   **Reuben Nakian.** American sculptor

1898   **Walter Lang.** American motion-picture and stage director noted for works such as *The King and I* (1956)

1899   **Jack Haley.** American stage and screen actor noted for his role as the Tin Man in *The Wizard of Oz* (1939)

1900 **Norma Shearer.** "First Lady of Hollywood" in the 1920s and 1930s

1908 **Claude Thornhill.** American composer, pianist, and bandleader of the Big Band Era

1909 **Leo Fender.** American manufacturer who developed the Stratocruiser electric guitar

1914 **Ken Annakin.** English motion-picture director noted for films such as *The Longest Day*

1914 **Jeff Corey.** American motion-picture and television actor

1915 **Noah Beery Jr.** American motion-picture and television actor

1916 **Buddy Lewis.** Professional baseball player

1920 **Red Holzman.** Hall of Fame basketball coach

1923 **Rhonda Fleming.** American motion-picture actress

1924 **Martha Hyer.** American motion-picture actress

1928 **Jimmy Dean.** American singer and actor

1928 **Eddie Fisher.** American singer

1933 **Rocky Colavito.** Professional baseball player

1942 **Betsey Johnson.** American fashion designer

1942 **Heide Orth.** West German tennis player

1947 **Ian Anderson.** Scottish singer, flutist, and songwriter for the Jethro Tull musical group

1956 **Gerald Small.** Professional football player

1956 **Dianne Fromholtz.** Australian tennis player

1956 **Rosanna Arquette.** American motion-picture actress

1962 **Jon Farriss.** Australian drummer with the INXS musical group

1967 **Riddick Bowe.** American boxer and heavyweight champion

August 10 – Events

1471 Sixtus IV was elected Roman Catholic pope.

1776 A committee of Benjamin Franklin, John Adams, and Thomas Jefferson suggested *E Pluribus Unum* as the motto for the Great Seal of the United States.

1790 The *Columbia*, piloted by Captain Robert Gray, returned to Boston Harbor after a three-year voyage, becoming the first ship to carry the American flag around the world.

1792 Paris rioters stormed the Tuileries, where King Louis XVI was under house arrest, and killed the king's famous Swiss Guard.

1821 Missouri was admitted to the Union as the 24th state.

1833 Chicago, with a population of 200, was incorporated as a town.

1846 Congress established the Smithsonian Institution, naming it for James Smithson, who bequeathed his fortune for its establishment.

1897 Chemist Felix Hoffmann of Bayer, Germany, discovered aspirin, by synthesizing a shelf-stable form of acetyl-salicylic acid.

1943 The Quebec Conference in World War II between President Roosevelt and Prime Minister Churchill began in the Citadel in Quebec.

1945 Japan offered to surrender in World War II if the emperor could keep his throne.

August 11 – Birthdays

1657 **Pierre Etienne Monnot.** French sculptor

1743 **David Roentgen.** German cabinetmaker

1778 **Friedrich Ludwig Jahn.** German teacher who invented gymnastics

1819 **Martin Johnson Heade.** American painter

1833 **Robert G. Ingersoll.** American politician, lawyer, and writer, noted for his oratory and agnosticism

1837 **Sadi Carnot.** French engineer noted for the Carnot cycle theory of heat engines

1861 **James Bryan Herrick.** American physician who discovered sickle-cell anemia

1862 **Carrie Jacobs Bond.** American songwriter, noted for "I Love You Truly" (1906) and "A Perfect Day" (1910)

1865 **Gifford Pinchot.** American statesman and pioneer of U.S. forestry and conservation

1867 **Hobart Bosworth.** American stage and motion-picture actor with a career of nearly 70 years

1891 **Helen Broderick.** American actress, star of the first Ziegfield Follies (1907), and mother of actor Broderick Crawford

1900 **Alan Dunn.** American cartoonist with the *New Yorker* magazine for over 40 years

1902 **Lloyd Nolan.** American stage, screen, and television actor with a career of over 50 years

1907 **Bobo Newsom.** Professional baseball player who played with half of the 16 major league teams of his time

1912 **Jean Parker.** Leading lady of the 1930s and 1940s Hollywood films

1914 **Hugh Martin.** American composer, author, and singer, noted for songs such as "Buckle Down Winsocki," "The Trolley Song," "Have Yourself a Merry Little Christmas," and, with Ralph Blane, "Meet Me in St. Louis"

1918 **Dik Browne.** American cartoonist and creator of *Hagar the Horrible,* one of the most popular comic strips of the 1980s

1921 **Alex Haley.** American writer and author of *Roots*

1924 **Arlene Dahl.** American stage and motion-picture actress

1925 **Carl Thomas Rowan.** American newspaper columnist

1925 **Mike Douglas.** American television talk show host

1926 **Claus von Bulow.** Danish-born businessman who was acquitted in two sensational trials of attempted murder of his wife, heiress Sunny von Bulow

1933 **Jerry Falwell.** American television clergyman

1941 **William Munson.** Professional football player

1941 **Elizabeth Holtzman.** American congresswoman and state attorney-general (New York)

1942 **Otis Taylor Jr.** Professional football player

1944 **Clem Haskins.** Professional basketball player

1946 **Marilyn vos Savant.** American journalist noted for her IQ of 228 and her column "Ask Marilyn" in *Parade* magazine

1949 **Eric Carmen.** American singer and musician with The Raspberries

1953 **Hulk Hogan.** American professional wrestler

August 11 – Events

1492 Rodrigo Borgia, the head of the notorious Borgia family of Italy, was elected Roman Catholic pope, and crowned as Alexander VI.

1596 Hamnet, son of William Shakespeare and Anne Hathaway, died at age 11.

1834 The minstrel song "Old Zip Coon" was introduced at the Bowery Theater in New York City.

1862 Sarah Bernhardt, the great French actress, made her debut at the Comedie-Francaise in Jean Racine's play *Iphigenie.*

1902 Oliver Wendell Holmes was appointed associate justice of the U.S. Supreme Court by President Theodore Roosevelt.

1909 The first radio SOS in history was sent when the liner *Araphoe* asked for help off Cape Hatteras, North Carolina.

1919 The Weimar Constitution was adopted at Weimar, creating a republican Germany.

1924 A newsreel motion-picture short was made of the presidential candidates for the first time in history. They were Calvin Coolidge, John W. Davis, and Robert M. LaFollette.

1945 The Allies agreed for Emperor Hirohito to keep his throne in return for the surrender of Japan in World War II.

1952 Hussein I became King of Jordan.

1954 A formal peace announcement ended the Indo-China War between the victorious Vietminh and the French.

1956 Jackson Pollack, the great American artist, was killed in an automobile accident on Long Island, New York, at age 44.

1964 Pope Paul VI became the first Roman Catholic pope to ride in a helicopter.

1984 Carl Lewis, American runner, won his fourth gold medal in the Olympic games in Los Angeles. The four events he won were the same ones won by Jesse Owens in the Olympics of 1936.

August 12 – Birthdays

1753 **Thomas Bewick.** English printmaker

1762 **George IV.** King of England, 1820-1830

1774 **Robert Southey.** English poet laureate during the time of Keats, Shelley, and Byron, and who popularized the fairy tale "The Three Bears"

1781 **Robert Mills.** Early American architect and engineer, noted for his design of the Washington Monument

1849 **Abbott Thayer.** American painter

1856 **Diamond Jim Brady.** Famous American gambler and gourmet

1862 **Julius Rosenwald.** American philanthropist, who was president of Sears, Roebuck and Company, 1909-1924, and who gave over $63 million to worthy causes

1876 **Mary Roberts Rinehart.** American novelist and playwright, noted for works such as *The Circular Staircase* (1908)

1880 **Christy Mathewson.** One of the first five players chosen for the Baseball Hall of Fame, and winner of 373 career games as a pitcher

1881 **Cecil B. DeMille.** American giant of the motion-picture industry, noted for directing over 200 films in a 60-year career, a notable example of which is *The Ten Commandments* (1923 and 1956)

1882 **George Wesley Bellows.** A leading American artist of the early 1900s

1887 **Erwin Schrodinger.** Austrian physicist noted for contributions to quantum mechanics, such as Schrodinger's equation

1892 **Ray Schalk.** Hall of Fame baseball player

1897 **Charles O'Flynn.** American lyricist noted for songs such as "Smile, Darn Ya, Smile"

1898 **Oscar Homolka.** Austrian stage and motion-picture actor

1904 **Frank Ervin.** Professional harness racer

1905 **Marion William Isbell.** American hotel executive and founder of Ramada Inns (1929)

1907 **Joe Besser.** American comedian and one of the later members of the Three Stooges group

1911 **Jane Wyatt.** American stage, screen, and television actress

1911 **Cantinflas (Mario Moreno Reyes).** Mexican actor and comedian with a 40-year career

1918 **Roy C. Bennett.** American composer noted for songs such as "Red Roses for a Blue Lady" and "Naughty Lady of Shady Lane"

1919 **Fred Hutchinson.** Professional baseball player and manager

1921 **Marjorie Reynolds.** American motion-picture actress

1925 **Dale Bumpers.** Governor of Arkansas and U.S. senator

1926 **John Derek.** American motion-picture actor and director

1927 **Porter Wagoner.** American country music singer

1929 **Buck Owens.** American guitarist and television actor

1930 **George Soros.** Hungarian-born financier and philanthropist

1931 **William Goldman.** American novelist and playwright noted for works such as *Marathan Man*

1933 **Parnelli Jones.** American automobile racing driver

1936 **John Poindexter.** American admiral and National Security Adviser under President Reagan who claimed to act for the president without his knowledge in the Iran-Contra scandal of 1987

1939 **George Hamilton.** American motion-picture actor

1946	**Robert Maud.** South African tennis player
1949	**Mark Knopfler.** British guitarist with the Dire Straits musical group
1950	**George McGinnis.** Professional basketball player
1971	**Pete Sampras.** American tennis superstar and youngest U.S. Open champion (1990)

August 12 – Events

1492	Christopher Columbus reached San Sebastian in the Canary Islands on his first voyage to America. He stayed there until September 6 before resuming his voyage.
1588	The English turned away, allowing the stricken Spanish Armada to sail North and eventually West around the British Isles back to Spain.
1658	The first police force in America was organized by the Dutch in New Amsterdam.
1676	King Philip, chief of the Wampanoag Indians, was killed by English colonists near Mt. Hope, R.I., ending King Philip's War, the most destructive Indian war in New England history.
1827	William Blake, the English poet, died in London at age 69.
1851	American inventor Isaac Singer put his sewing machine into production and organized his company.
1877	Thomas A. Edison, the great American inventor, invented the phonograph, one of the most original of all the world's inventions.
1898	The United States annexed the Hawaiian Islands.
1898	The U.S. and Spain signed an armistice, ending the Spanish-American War.
1937	Edith Wharton, the noted American novelist, died at St. Brice-sous-Foret, France, at age 75.
1941	President Franklin D. Roosevelt and Prime Minister Winston Churchill signed the Atlantic Charter on a cruiser off the coast of Newfoundland. It was made public two days later.
1953	The Russians exploded their first hydrogen bomb.
1955	Thomas Mann, the German writer, died in Zurich at age 80.

August 13 – Birthdays

1422	**William Caxton.** English merchant who introduced printing into England with *The Dictes or Sayings of the Philosophers* (1477), the first book printed in England
1655	**Johann Christoph Denner.** German oboe maker
1757	**James Gillray.** English illustrator
1814	**Anders Jonas Angstrom.** Swedish physicist for whom the Angstrom unit of wave length was named
1818	**Lucy Stone.** American pioneer in the women's rights movement, and perhaps the first married woman to keep her maiden name.
1819	**Sir George Gabriel Stokes.** Noted English physicist and mathematician

1820	**Sir George Grove.** English writer of music and bible dictionaries
1851	**Felix Adler.** American educator, reformer, and founder of the first free kindergarten in New York City
1860	**Annie Oakley.** American markswoman who starred in Buffalo Bill's Wild West Show for 17 years
1867	**George Luks.** American painter and illustrator and one of the original members of the group of realistic painters called *The Eight*
1871	**Fielder Jones.** Professional baseball player and manager
1895	**Bert Lahr.** American stage and motion-picture actor and comedian, who played the Cowardly Lion in *The Wizard of Oz*
1898	**Jean Borotra.** One of France's famous Four Musketeers of tennis, who dominated the game in the late 1920s and early 1930s (The other Musketeers were Rene Lacoste, Jacques Brugnon and Henri Cochet.)
1899	**Alfred Hitchcock.** English-American motion-picture director and master of suspense, noted for such films as *The Man Who Knew Too Much* (1934), *Psycho* (1960), and *The Birds* (1963)
1902	**Felix Wankel.** Inventor of the Wankel engine
1904	**Buddy Rogers.** American motion-picture actor and second husband of the great actress Mary Pickford (from 1937 until her death in 1979)
1908	**Gene Raymond.** American motion-picture and television actor and leading man of the 1930s
1909	**John Beal.** American motion-picture actor with a 40-year career
1910	**Lou Finney.** Professional baseball player
1912	**Ben Hogan.** One of the all-time great golfers, who won the U.S. Open four times and the Masters Tournament twice
1912	**Salvador Luria.** Nobel Prize-winning Italian-American biologist
1913	**Archbishop Makarios.** Religious and political leader of Cyprus, and its first president after gaining independence from Great Britain
1917	**Sid Gordon.** Professional baseball player
1919	**Rex Humbard.** American evangelist
1919	**George Shearing.** Blind English pianist
1921	**Neville Brand.** American motion-picture and television actor
1926	**Fidel Castro.** Guerrilla leader and premier of Cuba after the overthrow of the Batista regime in 1959
1929	**Pat Harrington Jr.** American motion-picture and television actor noted for his role in the long-running series *One Day At a Time*
1930	**Don Ho.** American singer
1933	**Joycelyn Elders.** First surgeon general under President Clinton
1935	**Mudcat Grant.** Professional baseball player
1949	**Andre Thornton.** Professional baseball player
1949	**Bobby Clarke.** Professional hockey player

1951 **Dan Fogelberg.** American singer and composer noted for "Leader of the Band" (1982)
1955 **Betsy King.** American Hall of Fame golfer
1964 **Jay Buhner.** Professional baseball player

August 13 – Events

523   John I was elected Roman Catholic pope.
1099 Paschal II was elected Roman Catholic pope.
1521 Hernando Cortes, the Spanish conquistador, completed his conquest of Mexico with the surrender of Tenochtitlan (the present site of Mexico City) by Aztec ruler Montezuma.
1624 French King Louis XIII named Cardinal Richelieu his first minister.
1704 England's Duke of Marlborough routed the French, destroying their reputation for invincibility, in the Battle of Blenheim, one of the most decisive battles in European history.
1792 French revolutionaries imprisoned King Louis XVI and his family.
1863 Eugene Delacroix, the great French painter, died in Paris at age 65.
1923 Mustafa Kemal Ataturk was elected the first president of the new Republic of Turkey.
1928 The comic strip *Tim Tyler's Luck,* by Lyman Young, first appeared.
1930 Frank Hawks, an American flier, set a new speed record by flying from Los Angeles to New York City in 12 hours, 25 minutes.
1946 H.G. Wells, the great English writer, died in London at age 79.
1960 The first two-way telephone conversation by satellite took place, using the first passive communications satellite, *Echo I.*
1961 East German police started building the Berlin Wall, sealing off the East-West boundary of the two Germanys.
1995 Mickey Mantle, one of the greatest baseball players of all time, died after a liver transplant at age 63.

August 14 – Birthdays

1714 **Joseph Vernet.** French landscape and marine artist
1734 **Thomas Sumter.** American Revolutionary War officer, nicknamed the "Gamecock"
1734 **Pius VII.** Roman Catholic pope, 1800-1823
1777 **Hans Christian Oersted.** Danish physicist who discovered electromagnetism
1810 **Samuel Sebastian Wesley.** English composer, organist, and son of noted composer Samuel Wesley
1860 **Ernest Thompson Seton.** English-American naturalist, popular writer and illustrator, and an active participant in founding the Boy Scouts of America
1863 **Ernest L. Thayer.** American author noted for the famous poem "Casey at the Bat" (1888)
1867 **John Galsworthy.** English novelist and playwright, noted for *The Forsythe Saga* (1906-1921)

1880 **Fred Alexander.** American Hall of Fame tennis player, who, with Harold Hackett, formed one of the most famous doubles teams of the early 1900s
1886 **Arthur Jeffrey Dempster.** American physicist who in 1935 discovered Uranium 235, the rare isotope of the element uranium
1903 **John Ringling North.** American circus showman
1913 **Paul "Daffy" Dean.** Professional baseball pitcher who with his famous brother Dizzy won over 50 games in 1934 to spark the St. Louis Cardinals "Gas House Gang" to the world championship
1919 **Ted Kroll.** Professional golfer
1920 **Nehemiah Persoff.** American stage, screen and television actor
1925 **Russell Baker.** American newspaper columnist and host of public television's Masterpiece Theater
1926 **Buddy Greco.** American singer
1930 **Earl Weaver.** Highly successful professional baseball manager and sportscaster
1935 **John Brodie.** Professional football superstar, sportscaster and Hall of Famer
1940 **Dash Crofts.** American singer and songwriter (Seals and Crofts)
1940 **Arthur Laffer.** U.S. economist and supply-side theoretician
1941 **David Crosby.** American singer and guitarist with the Crosby, Stills, Nash, and Young musical group
1944 **Robyn Smith.** First female jockey at a major track
1946 **Susan St. James.** American motion-picture and television actress
1947 **Danielle Steel.** American author of romantic bestsellers such as *The Promise* (1979)
1948 **Steve Martin.** American motion-picture and television actor and comedian
1950 **Gary Larson.** American cartoonist and creator of *The Far Side* (1979)
1952 **Debbie Meyer.** American freestyle swimmer and 1968 Olympic champion
1959 **Magic Johnson.** Professional basketball player and superstar

August 14 – Events

1040 Duncan, King of Scots, was murdered by Macbeth, who became king.
1281 A Mongol armada with 150,000 men was destroyed by a typhoon, which ended 53 days of fighting with the Japanese.
1457 The *Mainz Psalter* was published, the first book printed in Europe to bear the name of its printers—Johann Fust and Peter Schoffer. (It was due, however, to Johannes Gutenberg).
1756 American frontiersman Daniel Boone, at age 21, married 16-year-old Rebecca Bryan. Their marriage lasted 56 years and produced ten children.
1900 U.S. marines captured Peking, China, ending the Boxer Rebellion.
1917 China declared war on Germany and Austria in World War I.

1923	The comic strip *Felix the Cat,* by Pat Sullivan, first appeared.
1935	The U.S. Social Security Act was passed by Congress.
1945	V-J Day finally arrived, as Japan accepted the Allies' World War II surrender terms, ending the greatest war in the history of the world.
1947	Pakistan became independent of India.
1973	The United States ended the bombing of Cambodia, officially terminating its involvement in Indochina.

August 15 – Birthdays

1702	**Francesco Zuccarelli.** Italian painter
1769	**Napoleon Bonaparte.** Emperor of the French, 1804-1815, the greatest military genius of his time, and one of the most celebrated personages in the history of the West
1771	**Sir Walter Scott.** Scottish romantic writer and author of *The Lady of the Lake* (1810) and *Ivanhoe* (1819)
1785	**Thomas De Quincey.** English essayist, noted for *Confessions of an English Opium-Eater* (1821)
1810	**Louise Colet.** French poet and novelist
1845	**Walter Crane.** English illustrator noted for works such as *Beauty and the Beast* (1874)
1859	**Charles A. Comiskey.** Professional baseball player and early owner of the Chicago White Sox
1860	**Florence Kling DeWolfe Harding.** Wife of President Warren G. Harding
1875	**Samuel Coleridge-Taylor.** English composer
1879	**Ethel Barrymore.** "First Lady" of the American theater, and member of the famous Barrymore family of actors
1881	**Ted Snyder.** American composer and pianist, noted for songs such as "The Sheik of Araby" and "Who's Sorry Now?"
1885	**Edna Ferber.** American novelist and playwright, noted for such works as *Cimarron, Show Boat,* and *Giant*
1886	**Francis C.C. Yeats-Brown.** English author and army officer noted for *Lives of a Bengal Lancer* (1930)
1888	**Lawrence of Arabia.** English soldier and writer, born Thomas Edward Lawrence, and one of the most adventurous personalities of World War I
1888	**Albert Spalding.** One of the leading American violinists of his day
1890	**Jacques Ibert.** French composer noted for the orchestral suite *Escales* or *Ports of Call* (1922)
1892	**Louis Victor de Broglie.** French theoretical physicist noted for his discovery of the wave nature of the electron
1892	**Sidney Clare.** American composer noted for songs such as "Ma, He's Making Eyes at Me," "On the Good Ship Lollipop," and "Polly Wolly Doodle"
1894	**Harry Akst.** American composer noted for songs such as "Baby Face" and "Guilty"

1898	**Charles Tobias.** American composer noted for songs such as "Rose O'Day," "The Old Lamplighter," "No Can Do," "As Long As I Live," and "Get Out and Get Under the Moon"
1898	**Lillian Carter.** Mother of President Jimmy Carter
1901	**Ned Washington.** American lyricist noted for songs such as "I'm Getting Sentimental Over You," "La Cucaracha," "When You Wish Upon a Star," "High Noon," and "The Nearness of You"
1903	**Joseph C. Garland.** American composer noted for songs such as "In the Mood"
1904	**Bill Baird.** American puppeteer
1909	**Hugo Winterhalter.** American bandleader of the 1950s
1909	**Johnny Lange.** American composer and author, noted for songs such as "Mule Train" and "Someone's In the Kitchen With Dinah"
1912	**Dame Wendy Hiller.** English stage, screen, and television actress, with a career of over 50 years
1912	**Julia Child.** American cooking expert and television performer
1915	**Signe Hasso.** Swedish stage, screen, and television actress
1916	**Debra Messing.** American motion-picture and television actress
1924	**Phyllis Schlafly.** American writer and political activist
1924	**Robert Bolt.** English playwright noted for works such as *A Man for All Seasons* (1960)
1925	**Mike Connors.** American television actor
1925	**Oscar Peterson.** Canadian jazz pianist and singer
1930	**Tom Mboya.** Major political figure in Kenya's early days of independence
1933	**Lori Nelson.** American motion-picture actress
1935	**Vernon Jordan.** American civil rights leader and president of the National Urban League
1935	**Jim Dale.** English stage and screen actor and composer, noted for the lyrics to "Georgy Girl"
1938	**Stephen G. Breyer.** U.S. Supreme Court justice
1944	**Linda Ellerbee.** American author and journalist
1946	**Jim Webb.** American contemporary music composer
1950	**Samuel Cunningham Jr..** Professional football player
1950	**Princess Anne.** Daughter of Queen Elizabeth II of England
1958	**Joe Cowley.** Professional baseball player
1959	**Pete Burns.** British rock singer with the Dead or Alive musical group

August 15 – Events

1057	Macbeth, King of Scots, was killed by Malcolm Canmore, son of ex-king Duncan, while fleeing from the Battle of Dunsinane.
1237	Berlin was founded by fishermen and traders.
1534	Ignatius of Loyola founded the Jesuits (Society of Jesus) in Paris.

1812	Indian allies of the British massacred the soldiers and settlers of Fort Dearborn, near the present site of Chicago.
1914	The Panama Canal officially opened, as the S.S. *Ancon* went through.
1918	The United States and Russia broke diplomatic relations.
1920	The comic strip *Peter Rabbit,* adapted by Harrison Cady, first appeared.
1935	Humorist Will Rogers and aviator Wiley Post were killed in a plane crash near Point Barrow, Alaska.
1944	U.S. and British troops invaded southern France in World War II, landing near Toulon.
1947	India became independent of Great Britain.
1948	The independent Republic of Korea was proclaimed with Seoul as its capital.
1960	The Congo became independent of Belgium.
1969	The Woodstock rock-music festival was staged near Bethel, New York, with some 500,000 fans attending.

August 16 – Birthdays

1557	**Agostino Carracci.** Italian painter
1645	**Jean de La Bruyere.** French satirist noted for ridiculing the injustice and hypocrisy he saw in French life, as exemplified by his best-known work, *Les Caracteres ou les Moeurs de ce Siecle*
1795	**Heinrich August Marschner.** German composer
1798	**Mirabeau Buonaparte Lamar.** Texan independence fighter and second president of the Texas Republic, 1838-1841
1831	**Henry Timken.** Pioneer developer of differential gearing in the United States
1845	**Gabriel Jonas Lippmann.** French physicist who developed color photography
1860	**Jules Laforgue.** French writer
1861	**Arthur Cayley.** English mathematician noted for his work in invariants and matrices, and as a giant in the Victorian era
1861	**Edith Carow Roosevelt.** Second wife of President Theodore Roosevelt
1862	**Amos Alonzo Stagg.** U.S. college football coach who had a 71-year career
1868	**Bernarr Macfadden.** American physical culturist who founded *Physical Culture* and *True Story* magazines and once opened a New York restaurant at which most items sold for one cent
1877	**Karl Hoschna.** Bohemian-American composer and oboist, noted for songs such as "Cuddle Up a Little Closer, Lovey Mine" and "Girl of My Dreams"
1884	**George Whiting.** American singer and lyricist, noted for songs such as "My Blue Heaven" and "Strolling Through the Park One Day"
1888	**Armand John Piron.** American composer and author, noted for songs such as "Day by Day" and "I Wish I Could Shimmy Like My Sister Kate"
1892	**Otto Messmer.** American cartoonist and creator of *Felix the Cat* (1914)

1892	**Harold Foster.** American cartoonist and creator of *Prince Valiant*
1894	**George Meany.** President of the AFL-CIO, 1955-1979
1898	**Jerome Irving Rodale.** American author and publisher who founded *Prevention* magazine in 1950
1899	**Glenn Strange.** American actor who played Frankenstein's monster in several films and the bartender Sam in the long-running television series *Gunsmoke*
1907	**Mae Clarke.** Early motion-picture leading lady, noted as the recipient of the grapefruit in her face from James Cagney in *The Public Enemy* (1931)
1910	**Glenn J. Spencer.** American composer, author, and conductor, noted for such works as the TV theme of *Gunsmoke*
1913	**Menachem Begin.** Israeli prime minister in the late 1970s and early 1980s
1913	**Osie Penman Hawkins Jr.** American operatic baritone
1914	**Joseph J. Lilley.** American composer, author, and director, noted for songs such as "Jingle Jangle Jingle"
1922	**Gene Woodling.** Professional baseball player
1922	**William Alfred.** American playwright and educator
1923	**Shimon Peres.** Israeli Labor Party leader and premier
1926	**Fess Parker.** American motion-picture and television actor
1927	**Neil Edward Strawser.** American broadcast journalist
1928	**Ann Blyth.** American motion-picture actress
1930	**Tony Trabert.** American Hall of Fame tennis player and sportscaster
1930	**Robert Culp.** American motion-picture and television actor
1930	**Frank Gifford.** Professional football superstar, sportscaster, and Hall of Famer
1932	**Betsy Von Furstenberg.** German-born stage and motion-picture actress
1932	**Eydie Gorme.** American singer
1933	**Stuart A. Roosa.** American astronaut and participant in the *Apollo 14* moon exploration mission
1935	**Julie Newmar.** American stage, screen, and television actress
1945	**Joaquin Loro-Mayo.** Mexican tennis player
1946	**Marie Pinterova.** Czechoslovakian tennis player
1946	**Lesley Ann Warren.** American motion-picture and television actress
1953	**Kathy Lee Gifford.** Paris-born American actress and talk show hostess
1958	**Angela Bassett.** American stage and motion-picture actress
1958	**Jose Luis Clerc.** Argentine tennis player
1958	**Tim Farriss.** Australian guitarist with the INXS musical group
1958	**Madonna.** American rock singer

| 1960 | **Laura Innes.** American television actress (*ER, Wings*) |
| 1960 | **Timothy Hutton.** American motion-picture actor |

August 16 – Events

1513	King Henry VIII of England defeated the French in the Battle of the Spurs at Guinegatte.
1777	The Americans defeated the British in the Battle of Bennington in the Revolutionary War. The British had 900 casualties as compared to the Americans' 80.
1780	General Cornwallis almost completely destroyed the American army of General Horatio Gates in the Battle of Camden in the Revolutionary War.
1812	British and Indian forces captured Detroit in the War of 1812.
1858	"England and America are united by telegraphy. Glory to God in the highest..." was the first transatlantic message, sent by Queen Victoria to President Buchanan over Cyrus Field's cable.
1903	Lt. General Samuel B.M. Young became the first U.S. Army chief of staff.
1923	Carnegie Steel Corporation established the eight-hour work day for its employees.
1948	Babe Ruth, perhaps baseball's greatest player, died in New York at age 53.
1962	The Beatles fired their drummer, Pete Best, and replaced him with Ringo Starr.
1963	Ralph Briggs Fuller, American cartoonist and creator of *Oaky Doaks,* died in Boothbay Harbour, Maine, at age 73.
1974	President Ford ordered all of President Nixon's White House tape recordings and other documents held in custody until the Watergate legal issues were settled.
1977	Elvis Presley, the rock and roll idol, died in Memphis at age 42.

August 17 – Birthdays

1601	**Pierre de Fermat.** French mathematician who was noted for his work in the development of number theory, analytic geometry, and calculus, but was best known for Fermat's "Last Theorem," which took mathematicians 350 years to prove
1786	**Davy Crockett.** Soldier, Congressman, and one of the most famous frontiersmen in United States history
1888	**Monty Woolley.** American stage and motion-picture actor and director
1890	**Harry L. Hopkins.** Closest personal advisor of President Franklin D. Roosevelt
1892	**Mae West.** American vaudeville and motion-picture actress and one of the movies' true greats
1896	**Leslie Groves.** U.S. army officer who directed the Manhattan Project in which the atomic bomb was developed during World War II

1899	**Stephan Weiss.** Austrian-born composer and author, noted for songs such as "Put Your Dreams Away" and "Sentimental Me"
1904	**John Hay Whitney.** U.S. ambassador and publisher
1906	**Hazel Bishop.** Noted American cosmetics manufacturer
1909	**Larry Clinton.** American composer noted for songs such as "The Dipsy Doodle" and "My Reverie"
1913	**Rudy York.** Professional baseball player
1914	**Franklin D. Roosevelt Jr.** U.S. congressman and son of President Roosevelt
1920	**Maureen O'Hara.** Irish motion-picture actress and superstar of the 1940s and '50s
1920	**Evelyn Ankers.** English stage and motion-picture actress
1923	**Larry Rivers.** American painter whose works suggest the speed and diversity of modern life by including seemingly unfinished parts
1926	**Jiang Zemin.** President of China who succeeded Deng Xiaoping
1929	**Francis Gary Powers.** American U2 pilot captured on a reconaissance mission deep inside Russia in 1960
1930	**Ted Hughes.** British poet
1932	**Red Kerr.** Professional basketball superstar with over 12,000 career points
1933	**Jim Davenport.** Professional baseball player
1941	**Boog Powell.** Professional baseball player
1943	**Robert De Niro.** American stage and motion-picture actor who won the Academy Award for best actor in *Raging Bull* (1980)
1952	**Guillermo Vilas.** Argentine tennis player
1960	**Sean Penn.** American motion-picture actor
1970	**Jim Courier.** American tennis player

August 17 – Events

1498	Cesare Borgia, a Cardinal at age 18 by appointment of his father, Pope Alexander VI, renounced his great office to marry a French princess.
1590	John White, the leader of the second expedition of English settlers to Roanoke Island, returned from a trip to England to find that the entire colony had vanished.
1786	Prussia's Frederick the Great died at Sans-Souci in Potsdam at age 74.
1807	Robert Fulton's famous steamboat, the *Clermont,* made its first run up the Hudson River from New York City to Albany.
1877	Billy the Kid, the notorious Western outlaw, killed his first man, F.P. Cahill, who earlier in the day had humiliated Billy by wrestling him to the floor in a saloon.
1896	Gold was discovered in the Klondike at Bonanza Creek, Alaska, by George W. Carmack and his Indian wife Kate.

1933 Lou Gehrig, New York Yankee baseball great, broke the record of consecutive games played when he appeared in his 1,308th game. He went on eventually to 2,130.

1940 The United States and Canada made formal arrangements for a joint defense of North America during World War II.

1942 U.S. bombers made their first independent raid on Europe in World War II, attacking Rouen, France.

1945 Indonesia proclaimed its independence from The Netherlands.

1969 The Woodstock rock-music festival in Woodstock, New York, ended after three days.

1969 Hurricane Camille slammed into the Mississippi Gulf Coast, claiming more than 250 lives.

1978 The first transatlantic balloon crossing was successfully completed when the *Eagle II* landed in Normandy, after a five-day trip from the U.S.

1998 President Clinton, in an address to the nation, admitted that the "improper relation" he had with White House intern Monica Lewinsky "was wrong."

1999 A giant earthquake, one of the most powerful recorded in the twentieth century, hit the Turkish town of Golcuk, 80 miles southeast of Istanbul, killing over 12,000 people and injuring tens of thousands.

August 18 – Birthdays

1587 **Virginia Dare.** The first English child born in America (on Roanoke Island, the Lost Colony off the coast of what is now North Carolina)

1685 **Brook Taylor.** English mathematician noted for Taylor's series

1774 **Meriwether Lewis.** American explorer, who with William Clark, led the Lewis and Clark Expedition that explored the Pacific Northwest, 1804-1806

1807 **Charles Francis Adams.** Son of President John Quincy Adams, and an American diplomat considered second only to Benjamin Franklin

1830 **Francis Joseph I.** Emperor of Austria and later of Austria-Hungary, 1848-1916, and member of the ancient ruling family of Hapsburg

1835 **Marshall Field.** American merchant who developed the world-famous Marshall Field & Company department store in Chicago

1873 **Otto Abels Harbach.** American lyricist noted for songs such as "Rose-Marie," "No, No, Nanette," "Cuddle Up a Little Closer, Lovey Mine," "I Won't Dance," and "Smoke Gets in Your Eyes"

1879 **Gus Edwards.** German-American composer noted for songs such as "By the Light of the Silvery Moon," "In My Merry Oldsmobile," and "Jimmy Valentine"

1893 **Burleigh Grimes.** Hall of Fame baseball player, and the last of the legal National League spitball pitchers before the pitch was banned

1896 **Alan Mowbray.** English-born motion-picture actor who appeared in nearly 200 films

1897 **Stanley Marshall Rinehart Jr.** American book publisher

1915 **Max Lanier.** Professional baseball player

1917 **Caspar Weinberger.** Secretary of defense under President Reagan

1919 **Walter Joseph Hickel.** Secretary of the Interior under President Nixon

1922 **Shelley Winters.** American stage and motion-picture actress

1927 **Rosalynn Smith Carter.** Wife of President Jimmy Carter

1933 **Roman Polanski.** Polish motion-picture director and actor, who directed such films as *Rosemary's Baby* (1968) and *Chinatown* (1974)

1934 **Vincent Bugliosi.** American lawyer and author who prosecuted the notorious Charles Manson and wrote the books *Helter-Skelter* (1974) and *No Island of Sanity* (1998)

1934 **Roberto Clemente.** Hall of Fame baseball player

1935 **Gail Fisher.** American television actress in the long-running drama *Mannix*

1935 **Rafer Johnson.** Professional football superstar and motion-picture actor

1937 **Robert Redford.** American motion-picture actor and director, and highly popular star of the 1970s and 1980s

1939 **Johnny Preston.** American singer

1941 **Christopher Jones.** American actor and singer

1943 **Martin Mull.** American motion-picture and television actor and comedian

1945 **Nona Hendryx.** American singer

1950 **Nadine Strossen.** American educator and President of the American Civil Liberties Union

1951 **Gregory Pruitt.** Professional football player

1955 **Patrick Swayze.** American motion-picture and television actor

1955 **Bruce Benedict.** Professional baseball player

1958 **Madeleine Stowe.** American theater and motion-picture actress

1968 **Zac Maloy.** Rock singer-musician with The Nixons

1969 **Christian Slater.** American stage, screen and television actor

August 18 – Events

328 Saint Helena, the mother of Roman Emperor Constantine the Great, died at age 82.

1227 Genghis Khan, the great Mongol conqueror, died at age 60.

1503 Pope Alexander VI died accidentally of poison, probably intended for a guest and probably administered from habit by one of his notorious children, Cesare or Lucretia Borgia.

1678 Andrew Marvell, the English poet, died in London at age 57.

1786 Reykjavik, Iceland, was founded.

1846 U.S. Brigadier General Stephen W. Kearny captured Santa Fe, New Mexico, in the Mexican War.

1850 Honore de Balzac, the great French novelist, died in Paris at age 51.

1856 Gail Borden patented the first successful milk-condensing process.

1880 Work began on the Washington Monument after the first false start in 1848.

1902 The first unassisted triple play in baseball was made by Henry O'Hagen.

1914 President Woodrow Wilson issued his Proclamation of Neutrality, aimed at keeping the U.S. out of World War I.

1919 The Anti-Cigarette League of America was organized in Chicago.

1923 Helen Wills, 18-year-old Californian and future superstar, won the Women's National Tennis Championship at Forest Hills, New York.

1963 James Meredith became the first black graduate of the University of Mississippi.

1991 Mikhail Gorbachev was ousted as president of the USSR and replaced by a committee headed by Vice President Gennady Yanayev. The coup failed three days later when Boris Yeltsin led a counter revolt.

August 19 – Birthdays

1398 **Inigo Lopez de Mendoza Santillana.** Spanish poet and literary patron

1631 **John Dryden.** The outstanding English writer of the Restoration period (the second half of the 17th century)

1646 **John Flamsteed.** "Astronomer royal" (director of the Royal Greenwich Observatory), 1675-1719, whose discoveries helped Isaac Newton formulate the laws of gravitation

1785 **Seth Thomas.** Pioneer American clock maker

1796 **Agnes Strickland.** English biographer

1843 **Charles Montagu Doughty.** English writer and traveler

1851 **Charles E. Hires.** American manufacturer who in 1876 invented root beer

1856 **Harold Frederic.** American journalist and novelist, noted for *The Damnation of Theron Ware* (1896)

1858 **Edith Nesbit.** English writer of children's stories and a founding member of the Fabian Society

1870 **Bernard Baruch.** American financier and adviser to every U.S. president from Woodrow Wilson to Dwight D. Eisenhower

1871 **Orville Wright.** One of the Wright brothers who made the world's first controlled airplane flight in 1903

1878 **Manuel Quezon.** Philippine statesman and first president of the Philippine Commonwealth, 1935-1944

1881 **Georges Enesco.** Romanian violinist and composer noted for the opera *Oedipe* (1936)

1883 **Gabrielle "Coco" Chanel.** Parisian high-fashion dress designer

1889 **Stoddard King.** American lyricist noted for songs such as "Listen to the Mocking Bird" and "There's a Long, Long Trail A-Winding"

1892 **Alfred Lunt.** American stage and motion-picture actor, who with his wife, Lynn Fontanne, formed one of the most celebrated acting teams in the history of the theater

1898 **Eleanor Boardman.** American leading lady and Kodak Gir of the silent movies of the 1920s

1899 **Bradley Walker Tomlin.** American abstract expressionist painter

1900 **Colleen Moore.** American star of the Hollywood silents and early talkies, who "created the flapper" of the 1920s

1902 **Ogden Nash.** American writer of humorous poetry, found in such books as *I'm a Stranger Here Myself* (1938)

1903 **Claude Dauphin.** French stage and motion-picture actor

1903 **James Gould Cozzens.** Pulitzer Prize-winning American novelist, and author of *By Love Possessed* (1957)

1906 **Philo T. Farnsworth.** American developer of the image dissector, one of the pioneering inventions that led to television

1910 **Atley Donald.** Professional baseball pitcher with a lifetime won-loss percentage of .663

1913 **Harry Mills.** American singer and member of the Mills Brothers group

1915 **Ring Lardner Jr.** American writer and son of the famous author and sports reporter

1919 **Malcolm S. Forbes.** Editor-in-chief of *Forbes Magazine*

1921 **Gene Roddenberry.** American television producer noted for the long-running show *Star Trek*

1926 **Robert Schakne.** American journalist

1931 **Willie Shoemaker.** American jockey with over 6,000 winners

1933 **Debra Paget.** American motion-picture actress

1934 **Renee Richards.** American dentist and tennis player

1939 **Ginger Baker.** English drummer with the Cream rock music group

1940 **Jill St. John.** American motion-picture and television actress

1940 **Johnny Nash.** American singer, recording artist, and composer, noted for songs such as "My Merry Go Round" and "I Can See Clearly Now"

1946 **Bill Clinton.** 42nd U.S. president

1948 **Tipper Gore.** Wife of Vice President Al Gore

1948 **Gerald McRaney.** American television actor (*Major Dad*)

1953 **Mary Matalin.** American political consultant and commentator and wife of political consultant James Carville

1960 **Ron Darling.** Professional baseball player

1965 **Kyra Sedgwick.** American motion-picture and television actress

1967 **Tabitha Soren.** American broadcast journalist

1971   **Mary Jo Fernandez.** American tennis player

August 19 – Events

480 BC The Battle of Thermopylae was won by the Persians under Xerxes. The main Greek force escaped, however, and they eventually won the war.

14   Roman emperor Augustus died at Nola at age 76 after a 41-year reign.

312   Roman emperor Constantine the Great supposedly saw a vision of a cross and the words, "In this sign conquer," causing him to eventually embrace Christianity.

1580   Andrea Palladio, the great Italian Renaissance architect, died in Venice at age 71.

1662   Blaise Pascal, the great French philosopher, died in Paris at age 39.

1692   Martha Carrier was hanged on Gallows Hill in Salem, Mass., for witchcraft. She was accused by little children, including her own.

1700   Peter the Great of Russia declared war on Sweden, marking the beginning of the Great Northern War which destroyed Sweden as one of the world's major powers.

1812   The U.S. frigate *Constitution* defeated the British frigate *Guerriere* in a famous battle of the War of 1812, in which the *Constitution* won its nickname "Old Ironsides"

1819   James Watt, the inventor of the steam engine, died at age 83.

1862   The Second Battle of Bull Run began in the Civil War. The battle lasted two days and resulted in the South's regaining nearly all of Virginia.

1890   The Daughters of the American Revolution was founded in Washington, D.C.

1934   Germany voted almost 10 to 1 for Adolf Hitler to succeed the late President Hindenburg in an election overseen by Hitler's Nazis.

1942   Canadian, British, and American commandos tried out invasion tactics in a suicidal raid on the Nazi forces in Dieppe, France, in World War II.

1944   The U.S. Third Army under General George S. Patton reached the River Seine in France in World War II.

1945   Lieutenant General Jonathan Wainwright, hero of the Battle of Corregidor, was liberated from a Japanese World War II prison in Sian, Manchuria.

1951   Eddie Gaedel, a 3 feet 7 inch midget, pinch hit and was walked for the St. Louis Browns against the Detroit Tigers.

1953   Premier Mohammed Mossadegh of Iran was ousted in a revolt that brought the Shah back to power.

1960   Gary Powers, pilot of a United States U2 reconnaissance plane downed deep inside Russia, was convicted of espionage by the Russians.

1977   American comedian Groucho Marx died at age 86, but his own epitaph was not used: "Here lies Groucho Marx, and lies, and lies, and lies."

1991   Boris Yeltsin mounted a tank in Moscow and denounced the coup that had toppled Mikhail Gorbachev, defying the would-be coup-makers.

August 20 – Birthdays

1561   **Jacopo Peri.** Italian composer

1745   **Francis Asbury.** Early American circuit rider and the most important Methodist leader in America during the late 1700s and early 1800s

1778   **Bernardo O'Higgins.** Liberator of Chile from Spain

1785   **Oliver Hazard Perry.** U.S. naval officer, who after capturing the British fleet on Lake Erie in the War of 1812, reported, "We have met the enemy and they are ours."

1795   **Robert F. Stockton.** U.S. naval officer who helped conquer California in the Mexican War

1807   **Narcisse Diaz de la Pena.** French painter

1833   **Benjamin Harrison.** 23rd U.S. president

1860   **Raymond Poincare.** French prime minister before World War I

1873   **Eliel Saarinen.** Finnish-born architect noted for works such as the famous Helsinki railroad station and, with his son Eero, the Tabernacle Church of Christ in Columbus, Indiana

1881   **Edgar Guest.** English-born American poet, noted for "A Heap o' Living" (1916) and "Life's Highway" (1933)

1886   **Paul Tillich.** Noted German-American theologian

1890   **H.P. Lovecraft.** American horror story writer and 20th century master of the Gothic tale, noted for works such as *The Dunwich Horror* and *At the Mountains of Madness*

1905   **Jack Teagarden.** American trombonist and first successful non-black blues singer

1908   **Al Lopez.** Professional baseball player and highly successful manager

1910   **Eero Saarinen.** Noted Finnish-American architect, and designer of the Gateway Arch along the Mississippi River in St. Louis

1913   **Donald Yetter Gardner.** American composer noted for songs such as "All I Want for Christmas Is My Two Front Teeth"

1920   **Ralph Mallory Kovel.** American columnist and antique authority

1923   **Jim Reeves.** American country music singer

1926   **Jacqueline Susann.** American writer and author of *Valley of the Dolls*

1933   **George Mitchell.** U.S. senator and Senate Majority Leader, 1989-1995

1942   **Fred Norman.** Professional baseball player

1942   **Isaac Hayes.** American popular songwriter

1944   **Graig Nettles.** Professional baseball player

1944   **Rajiv Gandhi.** Prime minister of India who succeeded his mother, Indira Gandhi, after her assassination in 1984

1946   **Connie Chung.** American television newscaster

1947 **Robert Plant.** British singer with the Led Zeppelin musical group

1954 **Al Roker.** American weather forecaster on TV's *Today Show*

1956 **Joan Allen.** American motion picture and stage actress

1960 **Tom Brunansky.** Professional baseball player

August 20 – Events

1741 Vitus Bering, a Danish sea captain commissioned by Peter the Great of Russia to probe for a land connection between Asia and North America, discovered Alaska, landing on Kayak Island.

1794 General Anthony Wayne defeated the Indians in the Battle of Fallen Timbers, ending 20 years of Indian warfare on the American frontier.

1837 Queen Victoria ascended the throne of England immediately following the death of her Uncle, King William IV.

1914 The Germans occupied Brussels in World War I.

1923 The comic strip *Just Kids,* by Clare Briggs, appeared for the first time.

1934 The comic strip *Li'l Abner,* by Al Capp, first appeared.

1940 "Never in the field of human conflict was so much owed by so many to so few," said Winston Churchill in praising the RAF to the House of Commons during World War II.

1940 Leon Trotsky, exiled Soviet Bolshevist and arch rival of Joseph Stalin, was stabbed with an ice pick in Mexico by one of Stalin's agents. He died the following day.

1968 Russian and Russian satellite troops invaded Czechoslovakia to suppress a bold Czech move for more freedom.

1974 President Gerald Ford nominated former New York governor Nelson Rockefeller to be vice president.

August 21 – Birthdays

1165 **Philip II (Philip Augustus).** The first great king of the Capetian dynasty in France

1725 **Jean Baptiste Greuze.** French painter whose works were highly popular from 1750 to the French Revolution

1765 **William IV.** King of England, 1830-1837, and son of King George III

1789 **Augustin Louis Cauchy.** Famous French mathematician who published nearly 800 papers on algebra, geometry, mechanics, optics, and astronomy

1796 **Asher B. Durand.** American painter and engraver

1798 **Jules Michelet.** French historian

1865 **Charles B. Ward.** English-born composer and singer noted for "Strike Up the Band" and "The Band Played On"

1872 **Aubrey Vincent Beardsley.** English artist who illustrated stories and plays with elegant black and white line drawings

1892 **F. Dudleigh Vernor.** American composer and organist, noted for songs such as "Sweetheart of Sigma Chi"

1893 **Theresa Weld Blanchard.** Hall of Fame skater and first American woman to win a medal at the Winter Olympics

1895 **Benny Davis.** American composer noted for songs such as "Margie," "Baby Face," "Yearning," "Carolina Moon," and "Make Believe"

1896 **Roark Bradford.** American playwright and author of *Green Pastures* (1930)

1904 **Count Basie.** American pianist, composer, and jazz band leader

1906 **Friz Frelong.** American director, producer and creator of Bugs Bunny, Porky Pig, and the Pink Panther

1907 **Hy Zaret.** American composer and author, noted for songs such as "Unchained Melody" and "So Long for Awhile" (theme song of the *Hit Parade*)

1908 **Ray Berres.** Professional baseball player

1916 **Murry Dickson.** Professional baseball player

1920 **Gerry Staley.** Professional baseball player

1924 **Chris Schenkel.** American sportscaster with a 50-year career

1929 **Herman Badillo.** Puerto Rican-born lawyer and congressman

1930 **Princess Margaret.** Sister of Queen Elizabeth II of England

1936 **Mart Crowley.** American writer and author of *The Boys in the Band*

1936 **Wilt Chamberlain.** One of the greatest offensive players in the history of professional basketball, who once made 100 points in a single game (in 1962)

1938 **Kenny Rogers.** American country music singer

1945 **Patty McCormack.** American motion-picture and television actress

1950 **Arthur Bremer.** American attempted assassin who shot presidential candidate George C. Wallace in 1972, paralyzing him for life

1950 **Ray Wersching.** Professional football player

1951 **Harry Smith.** American television reporter and co-anchor of the CBS *This Morning* show

1954 **Archie Griffin.** Professional football player and only player to win the Heisman Trophy twice (1974 and 1975)

1957 **Kim Sledge.** American musician with Sister Sledge, noted for their 1979 hit "We Are Family"

August 21 – Events

1621 "1 Widow and 11 Maides" were sent from London to the Jamestown, Virginia, colony to be sold to wife-seeking bachelors for 120 pounds of tobacco apiece.

1680 The Pueblo Indians, in revolt under their leader Pope, took possession of Santa Fe, New Mexico, after driving out the Spanish.

1745   Czar Peter III of Russia married Catherine the Great (as she became), who upon Peter's death became empress of Russia.

1831   Nat Turner's Rebellion, the largest slave revolt in American history, occurred near Jerusalem, Virginia. Fifty-one whites were killed and Nat Turner was captured and hanged.

1858   The first of the great Lincoln-Douglas debates was held at Ottawa, Illinois.

1887   Dan Casey of the New York Giants struck out in the ninth inning, providing Ernest L. Thayer with the inspiration for his famous poem "Casey at the Bat."

1911   The priceless *Mona Lisa* painting of Leonardo da Vinci was stolen from the Louve Museum in Paris by Vicenzo Peruggia. He was arrested and the painting was returned two years later.

1940   Leon Trotsky, the Russian revolutionary leader and arch rival of Joseph Stalin, died of wounds inflicted by an assassin the previous day in Mexico City.

1951   The U.S. ordered construction of the first atomic-powered submarine. The program resulted in 1955 in the *Nautilus,* the world's first nuclear-powered warship.

1959   Hawaii was admitted to the Union as the 50th state.

1968   The Russians seized Alexander Dubcek, Czechoslovakia's liberal Communist leader, putting an end to the Czech revolt.

1991   The coup that toppled Mikhail Gorbachev crumbled as a result of Boris Yeltsin's activism, and the would-be coup-makers were arrested.

August 22 – Birthdays

1764   **Charles Percier.** French architect

1769   **Leo XII.** Roman Catholic pope, 1823-1819

1834   **Samuel Pierpont Langley.** American astronomer, physicist, and pioneer in aeronautics, for whom Langley Air Force Base in Virginia is named

1851   **Daniel Frohman.** American theatrical manager identified with the theater for over 60 years

1862   **Claude Debussy.** One of the greatest French composers of the late 1800s

1880   **George Herriman.** American cartoonist and creator of Krazy Kat

1890   **Urban Shocker.** Professional baseball player and key pitcher with the New York Yankees' great 1927 team

1891   **Jacques Lipchitz.** Polish-American sculptor and modern artist

1893   **Dorothy Parker.** American short-story writer and poet, and one of the great humorists of her time

1897   **Max Rich.** American composer, author, and pianist, noted for songs such as "Smile, Darn Ya, Smile"

1901   **Vernon B. Stouffer.** American restaurateur who founded the Stouffer Lunch (1924), which grew into a restaurant chain and a food services business

1902   **Leni Riefenstahl.** German motion-picture actress and director, noted for her films dramatizing the Nazi movement

1904   **Xiaoping Deng.** Chinese premier in the 1990s who brought capitalism to China

1917   **John Lee Hooker.** One of the early American blues musicians

1918   **Mary McGrory.** American syndicated columnist

1920   **Denton A. Cooley.** American surgeon noted as a pioneer in heart transplant operations

1920   **Ray Bradbury.** Science fiction writer and television and movie scriptwriter noted for books such as *Fahrenheit 451*

1921   **Ira George Corn Jr.** American bridge player who organized "The Aces," the first U.S. professional bridge team

1928   **F. Ray Marshall.** Secretary of Labor under President Carter

1929   **Honor Blackman.** American motion-picture actress

1934   **H. Norman Schwartzkopf Jr.** American commanding general who defeated the Iraqis in the Persian Gulf War

1934   **Diana Sands.** American motion-picture actress

1935   **E. Annie Proulx.** American writer and novelist, noted for works such as *The Shipping News* (1993)

1935   **Morton Dean.** American broadcast journalist

1939   **Carl Yastrzemski.** Hall of Fame baseball player

1940   **Valerie Harper.** American motion-picture and television actress

1941   **Bill Parcells.** Noted professional football coach with the New York Jets

1942   **Kathy Lennon.** One of the singing Lennon Sisters

1945   **Steve Kroft.** American broadcast journalist (*60 Minutes*)

1947   **Cindy Williams.** American motion-picture and television actress

1949   **Diana Nyad.** American world marathon swimming champion and world record holder for the longest swim in history (102.5 miles, 1979)

1950   **Steven Brill.** American journalist, media executive and founder of *Brill's Content*

1955   **Ann Kiyomura.** American tennis player

1955   **Carrie Meyer.** American tennis player

1956   **Wes Chandler.** Professional football player

1956   **Paul Molitor.** Professional baseball player

1964   **Mats Wilander.** Swedish tennis player

1966   **John Wetteland.** Professional baseball pitcher noted for his ability as a closer

August 22 – Events

1485   Henry Tudor (later Henry VII) killed Richard III at Bosworth Field, the last battle of the Wars of the Roses, to become the first Tudor king of England.

1762   Ann Franklin became America's first newspaper editor, with the Newport (Rhode Island) *Mercury*.

1787   John Fitch successfully demonstrated his side-paddled steamboat on the Delaware River.

1818 The U.S.S. *Savannah* was launched. The next year it was to become the first steamship to cross the Atlantic Ocean.

1848 U.S. Grant married Julia Dent.

1851 The U.S. yacht *America* won the America's Cup for the first time. An American yacht won every America's Cup race since then until 1984.

1903 Theodore Roosevelt became the first American president to ride in an automobile, in Hartford, Connecticut.

1903 Barney Dreyfuss, an American sportsman, proposed that baseball organize a World Series, resulting in the first World Series in October 1903 between Pittsburgh and Boston.

1942 "We are attacking Stalingrad and we shall take it," Hitler announced in the Sportpalast in Berlin. He did attack, but the Battle of Stalingrad was an eventual disaster for him.

1968 Pope Paul VI arrived in Bogota, Colombia, for the start of the first papal visit in history to Latin America.

August 23 – Birthdays

1754 **Louis XVI.** King of France, 1774-1793, who was on the throne at the beginning of the French Revolution, and who was beheaded in 1793 by the revolutionaries

1769 **Baron de Cuvier.** French naturalist and founder of comparative anatomy

1849 **William Ernest Henley.** English poet and critic, and author of "Invictus"

1869 **Edgar Lee Masters.** American poet, novelist, and author of *Spoon River Anthology* (1915)

1882 **Will Hough.** American lyricist noted for songs such as "I Wonder Who's Kissing Her Now" (with Joseph Edgar Howard)

1884 **Will Cuppy.** American humorist and author of *The Decline and Fall of Practically Everybody* (1950)

1894 **Sholom Secunda.** Russian-born composer and conductor, noted for songs such as "Bei Mir Bist Du Schon" and "Dana, Dana, Dana"

1895 **Florence Vidor.** Popular star of Hollywood silents and wife of director King Vidor

1896 **Wendell Woods Hall.** American composer and singer, noted for songs such as "It Ain't Gonna Rain No Mo'"

1904 **William Primrose.** Scottish violinist and teacher

1905 **Ernie Bushmiller.** American cartoonist and creator of *Fritzi Ritz* and *Nancy*

1908 **Arthur Adamov.** One of the founders of the Theater of the Absurd

1912 **Gene Kelly.** American dancer and motion-picture actor and director

1913 **Bob Crosby.** American bandleader and brother of singer Bing Crosby

1922 **George Kell.** Hall of Fame baseball player

1924 **Sherman Lollar.** Professional baseball player

1929 **Vera Miles.** American motion-picture and television actress

1932 **Mark Russell.** American political satirist and comedian

1932 **Howard B. Johnson.** President of Howard Johnson's Restaurant chain and son of the founder

1933 **Pete Wilson.** Governor of California (1991-1999)

1934 **Barbara Eden.** American motion-picture and television actress

1934 **Sonny Jurgenson.** Professional football player and sportscaster

1942 **Nancy Richey Gunter.** American tennis player

1946 **Keith Moon.** British drummer for musical group The Who

1948 **Ron Blomberg.** Professional baseball player and first to bat as a designated hitter (1973)

1949 **Rick Springfield.** American singer

1949 **Shelley Long.** American motion-picture and television actress (*Cheers*)

1949 **Stephanie Beacham.** British motion-picture and television actress

1951 **Queen Noor.** Wife of King Hussein of Jordan

1957 **Mike Boddicker.** Professional baseball player

1970 **River Phoenix.** American motion-picture actor

August 23 – Events

1500 Because of discontent and troubles among the Spanish settlers on Hispaniola, Columbus was put in chains and ordered back to Spain. He was later released by the king and queen.

1775 King George III of England declared all the colonies to be in rebellion, and ordered a naval blockade of the colonies.

1777 King Louis XVI of France finally consummated his seven-year marriage to Marie Antoinette, after undergoing surgery for a phimosis condition.

1838 Mount Holyoke Female Seminary in South Hadley, Mass., the first college for women, graduated its first students.

1902 Fannie Farmer opened her School of Cookery in Boston.

1914 Japan declared war on Germany in World War I.

1926 Hundreds of thousands of women mourned the death of Rudolph Valentino, the screen's "Great Lover"

1927 Nicola Sacco and Bartolomeo Vanzetti, the principals in the famous anarchist case, were executed in the Charlestown, Massachusetts, prison.

1939 German foreign minister Joachim von Ribbentrop flew to Moscow to conclude a nonaggression pact with Joseph Stalin.

1947 Margaret Truman, daughter of President Harry Truman, gave her first public concert in the Hollywood Bowl.

1948 The World Council of Churches was founded in Amsterdam.

1970 Mark Spitz, American swimmer, broke the 100-meter free style record with a time of 51.9 seconds.

1998 Barry Bonds of the San Francisco Giants hit a home run against the Florida Marlins making him the first player in history to hit 400 home runs and steal 400 bases.

August 24 – Birthdays

1113 **Geoffrey Plantagenet.** Count of Anjou and ancestor of the Plantagenet kings of England

1580 **John Taylor.** English novelist and poet

1591 **Robert Herrick.** English "Cavalier" poet who wrote the famous line "Gather ye Rosebuds while ye may," in his well-known poem "To the Virgins"

1724 **George Stubbs.** English painter noted for works such as *Mares and Foals* (1762)

1759 **William Wilberforce.** A leader in the fight to abolish slavery in the British Empire

1772 **William I.** First king of the present-day kingdom of the Netherlands, 1815-1840

1784 **Joseph Emerson Worcester.** American lexicographer

1847 **Charles Follen McKim.** American architect who helped design the Boston Public Library and the Pennsylvania Railway Station in New York City

1852 **Jim O'Rourke.** Hall of Fame baseball player and manager

1872 **Sir Max Beerbohm.** British writer and caricaturist, and author of *Zuleika Dobson* (1911)

1886 **William Francis Gibbs.** Director of mass production of U.S. World War II cargo ships

1887 **Harry Hooper.** Hall of Fame professional baseball player

1895 **Tuanku Abdul Rahman.** First chief of state of the Federation of Malaya

1895 **Richard Cardinal Cushing.** American Roman Catholic cardinal

1897 **Fred Rose.** American composer, author, and singer, noted for songs such as "Roly Poly," "Hang Your Head In Shame," and "Be Honest With Me"

1898 **Malcolm Cowley.** American writer

1899 **Jorge Luis Borges.** Argentine essayist, poet, and master of the short story, noted for works such as *Ficciones* (1944)

1903 **Graham Vivian Sutherland.** English painter noted for his surrealistic landscapes

1912 **Durward Kirby.** American television comedian noted for his work on the *Carol Burnett Show*

1917 **Dennis James.** American television host

1924 **Louis Teicher.** American pianist and composer with the musical team of Ferrante and Teicher

1942 **Max Cleland.** U.S. senator

1946 **Ray Moore.** South African tennis player

1949 **Michael Richards.** American actor noted for the role of Kramer in *Seinfeld*

1956 **Antonio "Garcia" Bernazard.** Professional baseball player

1956 **Gerry Cooney.** American heavyweight boxer

1958 **Steve Guttenberg.** American stage, screen and television actor

1960 **Cal Ripken Jr.** Professional baseball player who broke Lou Gehrig's record of 2,130 consecutive games played.

1965 **Marlee Matlin.** Deaf American actress who won the Academy Award for best actress in *Children of a Lesser God* (1986)

1965 **Reggie Miller.** Professional basketball player

August 24 – Events

79 Mount Vesuvius erupted violently and buried the Roman cities of Pompeii and Herculaneum. Pliny the Elder died of asphyxiation at age 56 while witnessing the scene from the coast.

410 Alaric, leader of the Visigoths, sacked Rome, but spared its churches.

1215 Pope Innocent III, on an appeal from King John of England, issued a bull annulling the Magna Charta, which, however, remained in effect.

1313 Henry VII, Holy Roman emperor, died at age 44.

1572 The Massacre of St. Bartholomew's Day began in Paris, in which thousands of French Huguenots (Protestants) were killed.

1814 British troops captured Washington, D.C., and burned the White House in the War of 1812.

1932 Amelia Earhart became the first woman to make a non-stop flight across the United States, flying from Los Angeles to Newark in just over 19 hours.

1939 The Nazi-Soviet nonaggression pact was announced to the world, which reacted in disbelief.

1949 The North Atlantic Treaty went into effect, organizing the U.S. and Western Europe in NATO to defend themselves against aggression.

1954 President Getulio Vargas of Brazil killed himself after his regime was overthrown by federal troops.

1959 Daniel K. Inouye was sworn in as the first Japanese-American U.S. congressman and Hiram L. Fong was sworn in as the first Chinese-American U.S. senator. Both were from Hawaii.

1968 France tested its first hydrogen bomb, in the South Pacific.

1989 Pete Rose, baseball superstar, was banished from baseball by Baseball Commissioner A. Bartlett Giamatti for betting on the games.

1992 Hurricane Andrew hit southern Florida destroying a wide swath across the state including the town of Homestead. The storm caused some $30 billion damage, the worst in U.S. history.

August 25 – Birthdays

1530 **Ivan IV (The Terrible).** Czar of Russia (1533-1584) who conquered Siberia, made Moscow the capital of the country, and who ranks second to Peter the Great as the greatest Russian czar

1678 **Jacques Caffieri.** French sculptor

1744 **Johann Gottfried von Herder.** One of the most original and versatile German writers and philosophers, who inspired the great German writer Goethe and the other writers of the *Sturm und Drang* movement

1819 **Allan Pinkerton.** American detective and founder in 1850 of the Pinkerton detective agency

1836 **Bret Harte.** One of the greatest American story writers, noted for *The Luck of Roaring Camp* and *The Outcasts of Poker Flat*

1837 **Jacob Maris.** Dutch painter

1850 **Bill Nye.** American humorist who wrote comic histories, such as *Bill Nye's History of the United States* (1894)

1860 **George Fawcett.** Character actor of the silent screen in nearly 100 roles

1884 **Vincent Auriol.** First president of the Fourth French Republic

1901 **Kjeld Abell.** Danish dramatist and social critic

1905 **Clara Bow.** American actress and "It" girl of the Roaring '20s

1909 **Michael Rennie.** English motion-picture actor

1909 **Ruby Keeler.** Canadian motion-picture actress, dancer, and singer

1912 **Theodore Key.** American cartoonist and author, especially noted for his work in the *New Yorker* magazine

1913 **Walt Kelly.** American cartoonist and creator of *Pogo*

1913 **Jill Jackson.** American composer, author, and publisher, noted for lyrics such as "Let There Be Peace on Earth (and Let It Begin With Me)"

1916 **Van Johnson.** American motion-picture actor and leading man of the 1940s and 1950s

1917 **Don Defore.** American motion-picture and television actor

1917 **Mel Ferrer.** American motion-picture actor and director

1918 **Leonard Bernstein.** American conductor, composer, and pianist, who wrote the music for *On the Waterfront* (1954) and *West Side Story* (1957)

1919 **George C. Wallace.** Governor of Alabama and candidate for president in 1968 and 1972

1923 **Monty Hall.** Canadian-born television game show host

1927 **Althea Gibson.** American Hall of Fame tennis player, and Wimbledon singles champion in 1957 and 1958

1930 **Sean Connery.** British actor and original star of the James Bond series of movies

1933 **Regis Philbin.** American television host

1938 **Frederick Forsyth.** English author noted for *The Day of the Jackal* (1971)

1942 **Margaret Murdock.** One of the greatest shooters in history and the first woman in any sport to break a men's world record (at the 1967 Pan American Games with a score of 391)

1946 **Rollie Fingers.** Professional baseball player

1948 **Anne Archer.** American motion-picture actress

1949 **Gene Simmons.** American rock singer, actor and co-founder in 1972 of the group *Kiss*

1953 **Bob Lacey.** Professional baseball player

1954 **Elvis Costello.** English rock singer and songwriter

1961 **Billy Ray Cyrus.** American singer with the smash hit "Achy Breaky Heart" (1992)

August 25 – Events

608 Boniface IV became Roman Catholic pope.

1270 King Louis IX of France (Saint Louis) died in northern Africa while leading the Eighth Crusade.

1572 The Massacre of St. Bartholomew's Day in Paris ended, but not before thousands of Huguenots were killed.

1580 Spain gained control of Portugal by winning the Battle of Alcantara near Lisbon.

1718 New Orleans, Louisiana, was founded by French governor Jean Baptiste le Moyne, Sieur de Bienville, and named in honor of the Duke of Orleans.

1825 Uruguay declared its independence from Brazil.

1835 Ann Rutledge, reportedly Abraham Lincoln's only true love, died in New Salem, Illinois, at age 22.

1867 Michael Faraday, the great English physicist, died at age 75.

1875 Matthew Webb became the first person to swim the English Channel, swimming from Dover to Cap Gris-Nez, France, in 21 hours.

1916 The National Park Service was established within the Department of the Interior.

1921 The United States signed a peace treaty with Germany, formally ending World War I hostilities between the two nations.

1928 Admiral Richard E. Byrd's first Antarctic expedition left New York.

1939 Great Britain signed a treaty to support Poland in case of a German attack.

1944 U.S. and French troops liberated Paris in World War II after four years of Nazi occupation.

1950 President Harry S. Truman ordered the Army to seize the nation's railroads to avert a strike.

1952 Virgil Trucks pitched his second no-hit game of the season as Detroit beat New York, 1-0.

August 26 – Birthdays

1676 **Robert Walpole.** The most influential politician in England during the first half of the 18th century, and the first man to serve as prime minister

1740 **Joseph Michel Montgolfier.** French balloonist who with his brother Jacques invented the first balloons to carry men into the air

1743 **Antoine Laurent Lavoisier.** French chemist, considered the father of modern chemistry, noted for the law of conservation of matter, the present-day system of chemical names, and for the first modern textbook

1819	**Prince Albert.** Prince of Saxe-Coburg-Gotha and husband of Queen Victoria of England
1869	**Jacques Emile Ruhlmann.** French cabinetmaker
1873	**Lee De Forest.** American inventor, noted for the triode vacuum tube that made radio possible
1874	**Andrew B. Sterling.** American lyricist noted for songs such as "Wait Till the Sun Shines, Nellie," "Meet Me in St. Louis, Louis," "On a Sunday Afternoon," and "Strike Up the Band"
1875	**John Buchan.** Scottish Baron, author and statesman, who wrote such novels as *Prester John* (1910) and *The 39 Steps* (1915), and served as governor general of Canada
1880	**Guillaume Apollinaire.** French poet and art critic, who coined the word *surrealism* in 1917
1884	**Earl Biggers.** American author and creator of the fictional detective "Charlie Chan"
1885	**Jules Romains.** French novelist, dramatist, and poet, best known for the satirical play *Dr. Knock* (1923) and the novels published under the general title of *Men of Good Will* (1913-1946)
1892	**Ruth Roland.** Queen of Hollywood silent serials, billed when she was a child star on stage as *Baby Ruth*
1895	**Earl K. Long.** Three-times governor of Louisiana, and brother of the noted Louisiana political boss, Huey P. Long
1901	**Maxwell D. Taylor.** American general in World War II and Vietnam
1904	**Christopher Isherwood.** English-American novelist noted for works such as *Goodbye to Berlin* (1939)
1906	**Albert Sabin.** Russian-American developer of the Sabin polio vaccine approved for use in 1961
1915	**Jim Davis.** American motion-picture and television actor
1920	**Brant Parker.** American cartoonist who with Johnny Hart created *The Wizard of Id*
1921	**Benjamin Bradlee.** American journalist and author
1922	**Irving R. Levine.** American broadcast journalist
1931	**Guy Vander Jagt.** U.S. congressman
1933	**Ben J. Wattenberg.** American writer, author, and social observer, noted for *The Good News Is the Bad News Is Wrong* (1984)
1934	**Tom Heinsohn.** Professional Hall of Fame basketball player, coach, and sportscaster
1935	**Geraldine Ferraro.** Democratic vice presidential candidate in 1984, and the first woman to run for the office on a major party ticket
1939	**Al Green.** Professional golfer
1941	**Barbara Ehrenreich.** American journalist, writer and social critic
1952	**Will Shortz.** American puzzle maker, puzzle editor and enigmatologist
1952	**Donnie Shell.** Professional football player
1980	**Macauley Culkin.** American motion-picture child actor noted for *Home Alone* (1990)

August 26 – Events

55 BC	Julius Caesar and his Roman Legions invaded what is now Great Britain.
1346	The Battle of Crecy in the Hundred Years' War established England as a great power. The hero was Edward, the Black Prince, 16-year-old son of Edward III of England.
1382	Moscow was burned by the Mongols.
1498	Michelangelo was commissioned to make the *Pieta,* which is now in St. Peter's Church in Rome, and is one of his most enduring works.
1666	Franz Hals, the great Dutch painter, died in Haarlem, The Netherlands, at age 86.
1797	John Quincy Adams married Louisa Catherine Johnson.
1801	Robert Morris, the financer of the American Revolution, was released after two years from debtor's prison.
1847	Liberia was proclaimed an independent republic.
1884	Ottmar Mergenthaler, the German-American inventor, received a patent for the Linotype machine.
1888	Peter Tchaikovsky, the great Russian composer, completed his *Fifth Symphony,* one of his finest works.
1918	In World War I Germany began a general retreat to the Hindenburg Line, making this "the Black Day" in the history of the German army, according to German general Wilhelm Ludendorff.
1920	The 19th Amendment to the Constitution was proclaimed, giving women the right to vote.
1939	The first televised major league baseball games were shown, on an experimental station. The occasion was a double-header between the Brooklyn Dodgers and the Cincinnati Reds.
1948	Axis Sally (Mildred Elizabeth Gillars) was flown to the U.S. to face charges of treason for her wartime propaganda broadcasts for the Nazis in World War II.
1974	Russian cosmonaut Lev Demin became the first grandfather in space, when *Soyuz 15* was launched by the Soviets.
1978	John Paul I was elected Roman Catholic pope.

August 27 – Birthdays

550 BC	**Confucius.** Famous wise man of China whose teachings formed the basis for Confucianism (date uncertain)
1545	**Allesandro Farnese.** Spanish Duke of Parma, whose failure to link up his forces with those of the Spanish Armada contributed to the Armada's defeat by the English
1725	**Charles Townshend.** British chancellor of the exchequer whose taxation policies helped cause the American Revolution
1770	**Georg Wilhelm Friedrich Hegel.** German idealist philosopher and one of the most influential thinkers of recent times

1809	**Hannibal Hamlin.** U.S. vice president in President Lincoln's first term
1825	**William Balfour Baikie.** British explorer and philologist
1858	**Giuseppe Peano.** Italian mathematician and a founder of symbolic logic
1865	**Charles G. Dawes.** U.S. vice president under President Coolidge
1871	**Theodore Dreiser.** Foremost American novelist in the "naturalism movement," and author of *Sister Carrie* (1900) and *An American Tragedy* (1925)
1877	**Charles Stewart Rolls.** English automobile manufacturer who with Frederick Henry Royce founded the Rolls-Royce company in 1906
1882	**Samuel Goldwyn.** Pioneer American filmmaker who with Edgar Selwyn formed the Goldwyn company, and who was noted for unintentionally funny sayings like "Include me out"
1890	**Man Ray.** American painter and photographer and one of the founders of New York's Societe Anonyme, Inc., in 1920
1893	**Victor Heerman.** American motion-picture director noted for *Animal Crackers* (1930), starring the Marx Brothers
1896	**Morris Ankrum.** American stage and motion-picture actor
1899	**C.S. Forester.** English novelist who won fame for his fictional creation of Horatio Hornblower
1905	**Mary Jane Ward.** American author noted for *The Snake Pit* (1946)
1908	**Frank Leahy.** Highly successful coach of the Notre Dame football team during the World War II era
1908	**Lyndon B. Johnson.** 36th U.S. president
1909	**Don George.** American composer noted for such lyrics as "I'm Beginning to See the Light" and "The Wonder of You"
1909	**Pres Young.** American saxophonist and jazz musician
1910	**Mother Teresa.** Noted humanitarian and Nobel Peace Laureate
1915	**Walter Heller.** American economist and adviser to Presidents Kennedy and Johnson
1916	**Martha Raye.** American motion-picture actress and comedienne
1929	**Ira Levin.** American novelist noted for works such as *Rosemary's Baby* and *The Stepford Wives*
1937	**Tommy Sands.** American rock-and-roll singer and guitarist
1943	**Bob Kerrey.** U.S. senator
1943	**Tuesday Weld.** American motion-picture and television actress
1951	**Buddy Bell.** Professional baseball player
1954	**John Lloyd.** English tennis player
1955	**Diana Scarwid.** American stage, screen and television actress
1970	**Jim Thome.** Professional baseball player

August 27 – Events

1576	Titian, the great Italian painter, died in Venice at an age of approximately 99.
1660	English poet John Milton's books were burned in London because of his attacks on King Charles II.
1665	The first play, *Ye Bare and Ye Cubb,* was performed in the North American colonies, at Accomac, Virginia. Three local residents were fined for acting in it.
1776	The British defeated George Washington's patriots in the Battle of Long Island in the Revolutionary War.
1783	French physicist J.A.C. Charles sent up the first hydrogen balloon, in Paris. It climbed to about three thousand feet and remained in view for an hour.
1789	The Declaration of the Rights of Man was accepted by the French National Assembly.
1859	Edwin L. Drake struck oil in Titusville, Pennsylvania, marking the beginning of the oil industry.
1883	The island volcano Krakatoa blew up, causing tidal waves that claimed 36,000 lives in Java and Sumatra.
1904	The first automobile driver to be jailed for speeding was given a five-day sentence in Newport County, Rhode Island.
1912	*Tarzan,* Edgar Rice Burroughs' famous novel, first appeared, in a magazine. (It appeared as a comic strip in 1929.)
1928	The Kellogg-Briand Pact was signed by 15 nations in Paris, condemning the use of war and calling for the peaceful settlement of disputes.
1945	Admiral William F. "Bull" Halsey led the U.S. Third Fleet into Sagami Bay near Tokyo in preparation for the signing by General MacArthur of the peace treaty with Japan, ending World War II.
1975	Haile Selassie, Ethiopia's last emperor, died in Addis Ababa at age 83, almost a year after his overthrow in a military coup.

August 28 – Birthdays

1749	**Johann Wolfgang von Goethe.** German author and one of the greatest writers of all time, whose masterpiece is the verse play *Faust*
1774	**Elizabeth Ann Bayley Seton.** American religious leader known as Mother Seton who founded the Sisters of Charity in the United States and became the first person born in the U.S. to be canonized
1810	**Constant Troyon.** French painter
1831	**Lucy Ware Webb Hayes.** Wife of President Rutherford B. Hayes, who gained the nickname "Lemonade Lucy" because she refused to serve alcoholic beverages in the White House
1833	**Sir Edward Coley Burne-Jones.** English painter and designer

1886 **Byron Gay.** American composer and musician, noted for songs such as "The Vamp" and "Little Ford Rambled Right Along"

1894 **Karl Boehm.** Austrian-born conductor

1897 **Charles Boyer.** French-American motion-picture actor and "great lover" of the 1930s and 1940s

1898 **Charlie Grimm.** Professional baseball player and manager

1906 **Sir John Betjeman.** England's most popular 20th century poet, noted for works such as *Summoned by Bells* (1960)

1907 **Sam Levene.** American stage, screen, and television actor

1910 **Morris Graves.** American painter noted for paintings that show the influence of oriental mysticism

1913 **Richard Tucker.** The outstanding American operatic tenor of his time

1916 **C. Wright Mills.** American sociologist and writer

1917 **Jack Kirby.** American comic book artist and creator of *Captain America*

1921 **Nancy Kulp.** American motion-picture and television actress noted for her role in the long-running TV series, *The Beverly Hillbillies*

1925 **Donald O'Connor.** American actor, singer, and dancer

1930 **Ben Gazzara.** American motion-picture and television actor

1936 **Tony Gonzalez.** Professional baseball player

1939 **Catherine Mackin.** American broadcast journalist

1940 **William Cohen.** U.S. congressman, senator, and Secretary of Defense under President Clinton

1943 **Lou Pinella.** Professional baseball player, manager, and executive

1946 **Mike Torrez.** Professional baseball player

1950 **Ron Guidry.** Professional baseball player

1958 **Scott Hamilton.** American skater who won the gold medal in men's figure skating in the 1984 Winter Olympics

1971 **Janet Evans.** First American woman to win four Olympic gold medals in swimming (1988, 1992)

August 28 – Events

430 Saint Augustine, the great Christian theologian, died at age 75.

476 The western Roman Empire founded by Augustus in 27 BC ended at Ravenna, where Emperor Romulus Augustulus was deposed by the barbarian leader Odovacar (Odoacer).

1565 Spanish explorers, led by Don Pedro Menendez, founded St. Augustine, Florida, the oldest city in the United States.

1609 Henry Hudson discovered Delaware Bay.

1811 English poet Percy Bysshe Shelley eloped with 16-year-old Harriet Westbrook.

1830 The first American-built locomotive, the *Tom Thumb,* by Peter Cooper, lost its famous race to a horse-drawn stagecoach at the last minute when a pulley belt slipped.

1833 Slavery was abolished in the British colonies by Parliament.

1850 Richard Wagner's famous opera *Lohengrin* was first performed, in Weimar, Germany.

1922 The first radio commercial was aired, an ad for the Queensboro Realty Company of Jackson Heights, New York, on station WEAF in New York.

1941 Japanese ambassador Kichisaburo Nomura delivered a note to President Franklin D. Roosevelt declaring Japan's peaceful intentions.

1963 Some 200,000 persons staged a "Freedom March" on Washington, D.C., to demonstrate demands for civil rights. The highlight of the gathering was Dr. Martin Luther King, Jr.'s "I have a dream" speech at the Lincoln Memorial.

1968 Police clashed with anti-war demonstrators in the streets of Chicago as the Democratic National Convention nominated Vice President Hubert H. Humphrey for president.

August 29 – Birthdays

1609 **Sassoferrato.** Italian painter

1619 **Jean Baptiste Colbert.** French minister of finance to King Louis XIV for 22 years

1632 **John Locke.** One of the greatest English philosophers of all time, whose work had a profound influence on Thomas Jefferson in writing the Declaration of Independence

1780 **Jean Laffite.** French pirate and smuggler who fought for the U.S. in the War of 1812

1780 **Jean Auguste Dominique Ingres.** French painter and the leading neoclassical painter of the early 1800s

1809 **Oliver Wendell Holmes.** American physician, poet, and humorist

1862 **Maurice Maeterlinck.** Belgian poet and dramatist who won the Nobel Prize for literature in 1911

1871 **Jack Butler Yeats.** The leading Irish painter of the 20th century

1876 **Charles F. Kettering.** American inventor who developed automobile self-starters, leaded gasoline, a diesel engine for trains, and a high-compression automobile engine

1879 **Harry Williams.** American lyricist noted for songs such as "In the Shade of the Old Apple Tree," "Good Night, Ladies," and "Mickey"

1891 **Joyce Clyde Hall.** American businessman who founded Hallmark Greeting Cards

1898 **Preston Sturges.** American motion-picture director and playwright

1899 **Lyman L. Lemnitzer.** American general and chairman of the Joint Chiefs of Staff, 1960-1962

1909 **George Macready.** American stage, screen, and television actor

1912 **Barry Sullivan.** American stage, screen, and television actor

1915 **Ingrid Bergman.** Swedish motion-picture actress and a superstar for 40 years

1916   **George Montgomery.** American motion-picture actor

1920   **Charlie Parker.** American alto saxophonist and jazz musician

1923   **Richard Attenborough.** English motion-picture actor and director noted for his direction of the Academy Award-winning picture *Gandhi* (1983)

1927   **Gary Gabelich.** American racing car driver, who set a record speed of 631 miles per hour in 1970

1934   **David Pryer.** U.S. senator

1936   **John McCain.** U.S. senator

1938   **Robert E. Rubin.** Secretary of the Treasury under President Clinton

1938   **Elliott Gould.** American motion-picture and television actor

1939   **William Friedkin.** American motion-picture director noted for works such as *The Exorcist* (1973)

1940   **James Brady.** White House press secretary who was shot in the attempt on President Reagan's life

1941   **Robin Leach.** English-born reporter, columnist, and founder of *Go Magazine,* and the genius behind the TV shows *Lifestyles of the Rich and Famous* and *Entertainment Tonight*

1947   **Bob Lutz.** American tennis player

1950   **Doug De Cinces.** Professional baseball player

1958   **Michael Jackson.** American singer who started out with the Jackson 5 musical group

August 29 – Events

28   John the Baptist was beheaded by Herod at the request of his stepdaughter Salome.

1261   Urban IV was elected Roman Catholic pope.

1484   Innocent VIII was elected Roman Catholic pope.

1526   The Battle of Mohacs (Hungary) ended in the victory of the Turks over the Hungarians, which destroyed the medieval kingdom of Hungary.

1533   Atahualpa, last ruler of the Inca Empire in Peru, was executed by Spanish conquistador Francisco Pizarro, after Atahualpa had purchased his freedom with a huge treasure.

1825   Portugal recognized Brazil's independence, completing without bloodshed the three-year transition from a colony to an independent nation.

1831   Michael Faraday, the great English physicist, discovered induction, the principle on which electric generators and motors operate.

1842   The Treaty of Nanking ended the Opium War in China.

1852   Brigham Young proclaimed the "celestial law of marriage," signifying approval of polygamy among Mormons.

1877   Brigham Young, Mormon pioneer leader, died in Salt Lake City at age 76.

1896   Chop suey was first concocted and served, not in China but in the U.S., by the chef of the visiting Chinese statesman Li Hung-Chang.

1910   Japan annexed Korea and made the Korean emperor a prince.

1944   Paris celebrated its liberation from the Nazis as 15,000 American troops marched down the Champs-Elysees in World War II.

1949   The Soviet Union tested its first atomic bomb.

1966   The Beatles played their last live show before a paying audience, in Candlestick Park, San Francisco.

August 30 – Birthdays

1334   **Pedro the Cruel.** King of Castile and Leon

1494   **Correggio (Antonio Allegri).** Italian artist who at the peak of the Renaissance ranked with Michelangelo and Titian

1609   **Artus Quellinus I.** Flemish sculptor

1748   **Jacques Louis David.** The most celebrated French artist during the French Revolution and the Napoleonic era

1794   **Stephen Watts Kearny.** American general who helped win California during the Mexican War

1797   **Mary Wollstonecraft Shelley.** Author of the famous horror novel *Frankenstein* (1818), and second wife of the English poet Percy Bysshe Shelley

1820   **George Frederick Root.** American composer noted for songs such as "The Battle Cry of Freedom" and "Tramp, Tramp, Tramp, the Boys Are Marching"

1837   **Ellen Lewis Herndon Arthur.** Wife of President Chester A. Arthur

1871   **Lord Rutherford.** English physicist (born Ernest Rutherford), the "father of nuclear science," who worked out the nuclear theory of the atom and discovered alpha and beta rays and protons

1892   **George Aiken.** U.S. senator, 1940-1976, and "father of food stamps"

1893   **Huey P. Long.** Founder of the Long political dynasty in Louisiana that began in the late 1920s and lasted until the 1960s

1896   **Raymond Massey.** Canadian-born motion-picture actor who appeared in more than 60 films

1899   **Kiki Cuyler.** Hall of Fame baseball player

1901   **John Gunther.** American journalist and author of a series of nonfiction books such as *Inside Europe* (1936) and *Inside Asia* (1939)

1901   **Roy Wilkins.** American civil rights advocate and NAACP executive director, 1965-1977

1907   **Shirley Booth.** American stage, motion-picture, and television actress

1907   **John W. Mauchly.** Co-inventor of ENIAC, the first electronic computer, in 1946

1908   **Fred MacMurray.** American stage, screen, and television star, with a career of over 45 years

1912   **Joan Blondell.** American motion-picture actress

1912   **Edward Mills Purcell.** American physicist who shared the 1952 Nobel Prize for developing a method for determining the magnetic properties of nuclei

1914   **Julie Bishop.** American motion-picture actress

1918   **Ted Williams.** Hall of Fame baseball player who hit .406 in 1941 and was one of the greatest hitters of all time

1919   **Kitty Wells.** American country singer

1923   **Vic Seixas.** American Hall of Fame tennis player and 1953 Wimbledon singles champion

1927   **Geoffrey Beene.** American fashion designer

1930   **Warren Buffett.** American businessman and one of the two richest men in the country, with a legendary ability to buy and sell stocks

1931   **John L. Swigert Jr.** U.S. astronaut and participant in the *Apollo 13* mission

1935   **John Phillips.** American singer with The Mamas and the Papas

1937   **Bruce McLaren.** Automobile racing driver

1939   **Elizabeth Ashley.** American motion-picture actress and author

1943   **Jean-Claude Killy.** French dare-devil skier

1943   **Robert Crumb.** American cartoonist and creator of *Felix the Cat,* a con man cat not to be confused with the earlier comic strip of the same name

1944   **Tug McGraw.** Professional baseball player

1950   **Timothy Bottoms.** American motion-picture actor

1952   **Wojek Fibak.** Polish tennis player

1953   **Robert L. Parish.** Professional basketball player

1953   **Jose Moreno.** Spanish tennis player

1955   **Marvin Powell.** Professional football player

1972   **Cameron Diaz.** American motion-picture actress

August 30 – Events

257   Sixtus III became Roman Catholic pope.

1462   Paul II was elected Roman Catholic pope.

1483   Louis XI of France, the "terrible king," died at age 60.

1637   Anne Hutchinson was banished from Massachusetts for "traducing the ministers and the ministry."

1682   William Penn sailed from England for America, to take over and open for settlement the land granted to him by the king, which was named Pennsylvania, meaning Penn's Woods.

1780   Benedict Arnold, the American Revolutionary War traitor, first conspired with the British to surrender the American fort at West Point.

1862   Generals Robert E. Lee and Stonewall Jackson led the Southern troops to victory in the second Battle of Bull Run in the Civil War.

1905   Ty Cobb, one of the greatest baseball players of all time, made his first major league appearance, hitting a double and driving in two runs for the Detroit Tigers.

1932   Hermann Goering, one of Hitler's underlings, was elected president of the German Reichstag, enabling him to frustrate democratic procedures and help Hitler gain power.

1941   The siege of Leningrad by German troops began during World War II.

1945   General Douglas MacArthur arrived in Yokohama to set up headquarters for the U.S. occupation of Japan following World War II.

1967   The U.S. Senate confirmed the appointment of Thurgood Marshall as the first black justice on the Supreme Court.

1968   The English musical group the Beatles released "Hey Jude," the first single on their own Apple record label.

1983   The U.S. shuttle Challenger blasted off from Cape Canaveral, Fla., with Guion S. Bluford, Jr., the first black American astronaut to go into space, and four others aboard.

1984   U.S. space shuttle Discovery was launched at Cape Canaveral, Florida.

August 31 – Birthdays

12   **Caligula.** Emperor of Rome, A.D. 37-41, noted for his cruelty and insanity

161   **Commodus.** Emperor of Rome, A.D. 180-192 (born Lucius Aelius Aurelius)

1740   **Johann Friedrich Oberlin.** Lutheran pastor for whom Oberlin College was named

1806   **Charles James Lever.** Irish novelist noted for works such as *Charles O'Malley* (1840)

1811   **Theophile Gautier.** French poet, novelist, and critic, noted for *Enamels and Cameos* (1852)

1821   **Hermann von Helmholtz.** Noted German physicist who helped prove the law of conservation of energy

1870   **Maria Montessori.** Italian educator, who developed the special method of teaching young children known as the Montessori Method

1875   **Eddie Plank.** Hall of Fame baseball pitcher and winner of 327 career games

1879   **Yoshihito.** Emperor of Japan, 1912-1926, and father of Emperor Hirohito

1880   **Wilhelmina.** Queen of the Netherlands, 1890-1948

1885   **DuBose Heyward.** American novelist and poet, best known for the novel *Porgy* (1925), which George Gershwin used later as the basis for his opera *Porgy and Bess*

1886   **L. Wolfe Gilbert.** Russian-born composer and author, noted for songs such as "Waiting for the Robert E. Lee," "Green Eyes," "Lily of the Valley," and "Down Yonder"

1897   **Fredric March.** American stage and screen star and winner of two Academy Awards for Best Actor

1905   **Dore Schary.** American motion-picture director and playwright, who shared an Academy Award for *Boys Town* (1938)

1907   **Ramon Magsaysay.** President of the Philippines, 1953-1957

1908   **William Saroyan.** American playwright and novelist, noted for such works as *The Daring Young Man on the Flying Trapeze* (1934) and *The Time of Your Life* (1939)

1910   **Jack Howard.** President of the Scripps-Howard newspaper chain

1914	**Richard Basehart.** American stage and motion-picture actor with a 40-year career
1916	**Daniel Schorr.** American television news commentator
1918	**Alan Jay Lerner.** American playwright and lyricist, who with Frederick Loewe composed the hits for *Brigadoon, My Fair Lady,* and *Camelot*
1924	**Buddy Hackett.** American comedian and actor
1928	**James Coburn.** American motion-picture actor
1931	**Jean Beliveau.** Professional hockey player
1935	**Eldridge Cleaver.** American civil rights activist
1935	**Frank Robinson.** Hall of Fame baseball player and manager, who won the most valuable player award in each major league
1937	**Warren Berlinger.** American motion-picture actor
1945	**Itzhak Perlman.** Highly popular Israeli violinist
1945	**Van Morrison.** Irish rock singer
1948	**Howard Porter.** Professional basketball player
1949	**Richard Gere.** American stage and motion-picture actor
1954	**Claudell Washington.** Professional baseball player
1958	**Von Hayes.** Professional baseball player

August 31 – Events

30 BC	Cleopatra, the famous queen of Egypt, killed herself, supposedly by clasping an asp to her breast.
1688	John Bunyan, the noted English writer and preacher, died at age 59.
1867	Charles Baudelaire, the great French poet, died in Paris at age 46.
1881	The U.S. Lawn Tennis Association held its first championship tournament, in Newport, R.I.
1886	The most disastrous American earthquake to occur east of the Mississippi River hit Charleston, South Carolina, killing 100 people.
1907	The Triple Entente was agreed to by Great Britain, France, and Russia.
1914	The Germans, under Paul von Hindenburg, crushed the Russian Second Army in the Battle of Tannenberg in World War I.
1939	Adolf Hitler promised peace if Poland would accept sixteen conditions. Poland refused and World War II began the following day.
1949	The last meeting of the Grand Army of the Republic was held at Indianapolis with six of the surviving Civil War veterans attending.
1950	Gil Hodges of the Brooklyn Dodgers hit four home runs in a single game.
1969	Rocky Marciano, ex-heavyweight champion, was killed in a plane crash one day before his 46th birthday.
1976	Mexico floated the peso which immediately dropped 40% in value.
1980	Polish labor leaders signed agreements with the Communist government establishing the right to strike. The result was the Solidarity labor federation.
1997	Diana, Princess of Wales, was killed in an automobile crash in Paris at age 36.

9

September

September, the ninth month of the year, was originally the seventh month in the ancient Roman calendar, accounting for its Latin name *Septembris,* meaning *seventh.* It originally had 30 days in the calendar of Romulus, but its length was reduced to 29 days by Numa Pompilius. The Julian Calendar increased its number of days to 31, and the emperor Augustus reduced it to its present number of 30 when he made several changes in order to increase his month, August, to one of 31 days.

Labor Day, the first Monday in September, is the only legal holiday to occur in the month, but the Jewish holidays of Rosh Hashanah, or New Year, and Yom Kippur, the Day of Atonement, also often fall in September. Another special day is Constitution Day on September 17, commemorating the signing of the Constitution on that date in 1787. Also, one United States President, William Howard Taft, was born in September.

The birthstone for September is the sapphire and the special flowers are the aster and the morning glory.

September 1 – Birthdays

1529 **Taddeo Zuccaro.** Italian painter and leader of the Mannerist school

1549 **Duke of Medina Sidonia.** Commander (born Alonzo Perez de Guzman) of the ill-fated Spanish Armada in its defeat by England in 1588 in the English Channel

1566 **Edward Alleyn.** One of the greatest actors of the Elizabethan stage

1854 **Englebert Humperdinck.** German composer noted for his opera *Hansel and Gretel* (1893)

1868 **Frank McKinney "Kin" Hubbard.** American humorist, journalist, cartoonist, and creator of *Abe Martin*

1875 **Edgar Rice Burroughs.** American author and creator of *Tarzan of the Apes* (1914), one of the most famous characters in fiction

1888 **Clement Wood.** American lyricist noted for songs such as "Short'nin Bread" and "De Glory Road"

1893 **Betty Blythe.** American stage and motion-picture actress

1898 **Jimmy Hatlo.** American cartoonist noted for his daily panel, *They'll Do It Everytime*

1899 **Richard Arlen.** American motion-picture actor with a career of over 40 years

1904 **Johnny Mack Brown.** Rose Bowl football hero and motion-picture actor in nearly 200 films

1907 **Walter Reuther.** American labor leader and president of the United Auto Workers, 1946-1970

1910 **Jack Hawkins.** British stage and motion-picture actor

1920 **Liz Carpenter.** American journalist and press secretary for Mrs. Lyndon Johnson

1920 **Richard Farnsworth.** American motion-picture actor with a career of 60 years

1922 **Melvin Laird.** U.S. congressman and secretary of defense under President Nixon

1922 **Yvonne De Carlo.** Canadian-born motion-picture and television actress

1922 **Vittorio Gassman.** Italian motion-picture actor

1923 **Rocky Marciano.** World heavyweight boxing champion, 1952-1956, who retired with 49 wins and no losses

1927 **Lloyd M. Bucher.** Commander of the U.S.S. *Pueblo* when it was seized by the North Koreans in 1968

1933 **Ann Richards.** Governor of Texas in the 1990s

1933 **Conway Twitty.** American country music singer

1935 **Guy Rodgers.** Professional basketball player

1935 **Seiji Ozawa.** Japanese-American conductor with the Boston Symphony Orchestra, New York Philharmonic, and the San Francisco Symphony Orchestra

1937 **Ron O'Neal.** American stage, screen, and television actor

1937 **Don Stroud.** American motion-picture actor

1937 **Al Geiberger.** Professional golfer

1938 **Alan Dershowitz.** Noted American lawyer, writer, and professor

1938 **George Maharis.** American motion-picture and television actor

1939	**Lily Tomlin.** American motion-picture and television actress
1941	**Rico Carty.** Professional baseball player
1944	**Archie Bell.** American singer
1947	**Edward Podolak.** Professional football player
1949	**Gary Maddox.** Professional baseball player
1954	**Patrick DuPre.** American tennis player
1957	**Gloria Estefan.** Cuban-born singer and songwriter
1961	**Dee Dee Myers.** White House press secretary under President Clinton
1961	**James Boney.** Jazz musician
1970	**Spigg Nice.** Rapper with Lost Boyz
1975	**Scott Speedman.** American motion-picture actor

September 1 – Events

1181	Lucius III became Roman Catholic pope.
1271	Gregory X was elected Roman Catholic pope.
1715	Louis XIV, the great French king, died in Paris four days before his 77th birthday.
1878	The first woman telephone operator, Miss Emma Nutt, was hired by the Telephone Dispatch Company in Boston.
1923	Japan suffered the worst earthquake in its history in which 143,000 persons were killed.
1939	World War II began at 5 A.M., as German troops smashed into Poland.
1972	Bobby Fischer became America's first world chess champion, defeating Russia's Boris Spassky in Reykjavik, Iceland.
1979	American space probe *Pioneer 11* flew past Saturn sending back information on two newly-discovered rings.
1983	A Korean Air Lines Boeing 747 was shot down over the Sea of Japan by a Russian jet fighter, killing all 269 people on board.
1985	The Titanic was discovered by a team of French and American scientists on the ocean floor 13,000 feet below the surface and 400 miles south of Newfoundland.

September 2 – Birthdays

1838	**Liliuokalani.** Last Queen of Hawaii, 1891-1893
1839	**Henry George.** American social reformer, who first proposed the "single tax," and who wrote the classic book *Progress and Poverty* (1879)
1840	**Giovanni Verga.** Highly influential Italian novelist, playwright, and short story writer
1850	**Albert G. Spalding.** Professional baseball player and manager, and sporting goods executive
1850	**Eugene Field.** American poet and humorist, noted for "Little Boy Blue" and "Wynken, Blynken, and Nod"
1864	**Louis Seraphine.** French painter
1866	**Hiram Johnson.** American politician and candidate for vice president on Theodore Roosevelt's Progressive Party ticket in 1912

1901	**Adolph Rupp.** Longtime basketball coach at the University of Kentucky
1905	**Vera Vague.** American actress and comedienne
1911	**Bill Harrah.** American gambler, businessman and founder of Harrah's Casino (1937)
1914	**Romare Bearden.** American painter
1917	**Cleveland Amory.** American writer and columnist
1918	**Martha Mitchell.** Wife of attorney-general and Watergate figure John Mitchell
1918	**Allen Drury.** American editor and writer, who won the Pulitzer Prize in 1960 for his novel *Advise and Consent*
1921	**Marge Champion.** American dancer and actress
1936	**Andrew Grove.** American businessman who developed Intel Corporation into a major company
1937	**Peter Ueberroth.** Commissioner of Baseball, 1984-1989
1938	**C. Wilson Markle.** Canadian engineer who invented the computerized film colorization process
1941	**John Thompson.** American basketball coach (at Georgetown University)
1948	**Nate Archibald.** Professional basketball player and Hall of Famer
1948	**Terry Bradshaw.** Professional football superstar and Hall of Famer
1950	**Lamar Johnson.** Professional baseball player
1951	**Mark Harmon.** American motion-picture and television actor and son of football great Tom Harmon and actress Elyse Knox
1952	**Jimmy Connors.** American tennis player, 1974 Wimbledon singles champion, and the first man to win 100 singles titles
1960	**Eric Dickerson.** Professional football player and superstar
1965	**Keanu Reeves.** Canadian motion-picture actor

September 2 – Events

44 BC	Cicero delivered his *First Philippic,* an attack on Mark Antony, in the Roman senate.
31 BC	Octavian's general, Agrippa, defeated the combined fleets of Antony and Cleopatra in the Battle of Actium, establishing Octavian as the ruler of the entire Roman world.
1666	The Great Fire of London broke out and within a week destroyed four fifths of the city.
1789	The U.S. Department of the Treasury was established.
1864	Union troops under General Sherman entered Atlanta before continuing their "March to the Sea," in the Civil War.
1870	Napoleon III and his 80,000 troops surrendered to the Germans at Sedan in the Franco-Prussian War.
1901	Theodore Roosevelt, then vice president, said at the Minnesota State Fair, "Speak softly and carry a big stick; you will go far."
1930	The first nonstop flight from Europe to the United States was completed by French aviators Dieudonne Coste and Maurice Bellonte.

1945 The Allies and Japan signed the World War II surrender agreement on board the battleship *Missouri* in Tokyo Bay. President Truman proclaimed it V-J (Victory over Japan) Day.

September 3 – Birthdays

1499 **Diane de Poitiers.** Duchess of Valentinois and mistress of King Henry II of France

1734 **Joseph Wright (Wright of Derby).** English painter

1814 **James Joseph Sylvester.** Noted English mathematician and one of the greatest of the Victorian era

1849 **Sarah Orne Jewett.** American novelist and short-story writer, noted for *The Country of the Pointed Firs* (1896)

1856 **Louis Henri Sullivan.** One of America's greatest architects, and the pioneer of the skyscraper

1860 **Edward Albert Filene.** American merchant and founder of the Twentieth Century Fund to study major economic problems

1878 **Dorothea Lambert Chambers.** English tennis player, seven-time Wimbledon champion and first great intense competitor in women's tennis

1891 **Bessie Delany.** American dentist and writer, noted for *Having Our Say: The Delany Sisters' First 100 Years* (1993)

1900 **Sally Benson.** American author noted for works such as *Meet Me in St. Louis* (1942)

1907 **Loren Eiseley.** American anthropologist and writer

1910 **Dorothy Maynor.** American operatic soprano

1913 **Alan Ladd.** American motion-picture actor in over 50 leading roles and especially noted for *Shane*

1914 **Dixy Lee Ray.** Governor of Washington

1915 **Kitty Carlisle.** American stage, screen, and television actress

1916 **Eddie Stanky.** Professional baseball player and manager

1916 **Doug Bentley.** Professional hockey player and Hall of Famer

1920 **Marguerite Higgins.** American journalist during the Korean and Vietnam Wars

1923 **Mort Walker.** American cartoonist and creator of *Beetle Bailey*

1925 **Hank Thompson.** American singer, guitarist, and bandleader

1926 **Irene Papas.** Greek stage and screen actress and dancer

1926 **Anne Jackson.** American stage, screen, and television actress

1927 **Hugh Sidey.** Contributing editor for *Time* magazine

1935 **Bob Ussery.** American jockey

1935 **Eileen Brennan.** American stage, screen, and television actress

1942 **Al Jardine.** Guitarist with the Beach Boys musical group

1943 **Dave Eichelberger.** Professional golfer

1944 **Valerie Perrine.** American television and movie actress

1952 **Natalie Fuchs.** French tennis player

1965 **Charlie Sheen.** American motion-picture actor and son of actor Martin Sheen

September 3 – Events

1189 Richard the Lion-Hearted was crowned King of England.

1651 Oliver Cromwell, the English Commonwealth ruler, defeated the Royalists at Worcester, but Charles II, whom they were trying to restore to the throne, escaped to France.

1658 Oliver Cromwell, English Lord Protector, died at age 58.

1783 The Treaty of Paris recognized the independence of the 13 American colonies, and established the boundaries of the new United States.

1826 The U.S.S. *Vincennes* left New York Harbor to circumnavigate the globe, the first warship to accomplish that feat.

1883 Ivan Turgenev, the great Russian writer, died in Bougival, near Paris, at age 64.

1894 The first Labor Day was celebrated as a legal holiday.

1914 Benedict XV was elected Roman Catholic pope.

1939 Great Britain and France declared war on Germany in World War II, two days after German dictator Adolf Hitler had attacked Poland.

1943 The Allies invaded the Italian mainland in World War II, landing at Calabria in southern Italy. The Italians signed an armistice later in the day.

1944 Canadian and British troops liberated Brussels in World War II.

1950 The comic strip *Beetle Bailey,* by Mort Walker first appeared, on Walker's 27th birthday.

1951 The long-running TV soap opera *Search for Tomorrow* made its debut.

1969 Ho Chi Minh, North Vietnamese president, died at age 79.

1972 Mark Spitz, American swimmer, won the sixth of his seven gold medals in the 1972 Olympics in Munich, by winning the 100-meter free-style.

1976 U.S. spacecraft *Viking 2* landed on Mars and began relaying to earth the first close-up, color photographs of the Martian surface.

September 4 – Birthdays

1768 **François Rene de Chateaubriand.** One of the most important figures in French romantic literature, noted for works such as the autobiographical *Memoires d'Outre-Tombe*

1802 **Marcus Whitman.** American pioneer, doctor, and missionary among the Indians

1804 **Thomas Ustick Walter.** American architect who added the Senate and House wings and the large cast-iron dome to the United States Capitol

1824 **Anton Bruckner.** Austrian composer and organist, best known for his nine symphonies

1824 **Phoebe Cary.** American poet

1846 **Daniel Hudson Burnham.** American architect who built the Railway Exchange Building in Chicago, one of the first skyscrapers in the U.S.

1848 **R.R. Bowker.** American publisher, editor, and author

1882 **Luther Knerr.** American cartoonist who took over the *The Katzenjammer Kids* in 1914 from its creator Rudolph Dirks

1888 **Peck Griffin.** American Hall of Fame tennis player

1892 **Darius Milhaud.** French-born composer noted for his works for the stage, such as *The Creation of the World* and *Christophe Colomb*

1893 **Frank Warshauer.** American composer, author, and conductor, noted for songs such as "It Isn't Fair" and "Rainy Day Blues"

1895 **Nigel Bruce.** Mexican-born motion-picture actor

1905 **Mary Renault.** English novelist noted for works such as *The Last of the Wine* (1956), *The King Must Die* (1958), and *The Bull from the Sea* (1962)

1908 **Richard Wright.** American novelist, short-story writer, and author of *Native Son* (1940) and *Black Boy* (1945)

1915 **Richard Thomas Goldhahn.** American composer noted for songs such as "Sioux City Sue" and "Esmereldy"

1917 **Henry Ford II.** President of the Ford Motor Company and grandson of Ford founder Henry Ford

1918 **Paul Harvey.** American television commentator

1918 **Bill Talbert.** One of the world's outstanding doubles tennis players, ranking in the top ten for 13 years

1919 **Howard Morris.** American stage, screen and television actor and comedian-writer

1920 **Craig Claiborne.** American cooking expert

1926 **Donald Petersen.** Chairman and Chief Executive Office of Ford Motor Company

1929 **Thomas Eagleton.** U.S. senator and 1972 candidate for vice president whose place was taken by Sargent Schriver because of Eagleton's history of mental treatment

1930 **Mitzi Gaynor.** American actress and dancer

1933 **Richard Castellano.** American stage, screen, and television actor

1942 **Ray Floyd.** Professional golfer

1944 **Jennifer Salt.** American motion-picture actress and daughter of screenwriter Waldo Salt

1949 **Tom Watson.** Professional golfer and one of the game's superstars of the 1970s and 1980s

1950 **Doyle Alexander.** Professional baseball player

1950 **Frank White.** Professional baseball player

1951 **Judith Ivey.** American stage, screen, and television actress

1968 **Mike Piazza.** Professional baseball player and superstar

September 4 – Events

1609 Henry Hudson, the famous British sea captain, discovered Manhattan Island.

1781 Los Angeles was founded by Felipe de Neve, the Spanish governor of Upper California.

1870 Revolutionists overthrew the Empire of Napoleon III and proclaimed the Third Republic in France, two days after Napolean surrendered at Sedan in the Franco-Prussian War.

1882 America's first steam electric-power plant, the Pearl Street Station, built by Thomas A. Edison, went into operation in New York City.

1886 The famous Apache chief Geronimo surrendered to U.S. General Nelson Miles at Skeleton Canyon in Arizona.

1888 George Eastman patented the first hand-held roll-film camera, which he called a Kodak.

1929 The *Graf Zeppelin* completed the only round-the-world trip by an airship.

1939 The U.S. Navy received orders to shoot on sight any vessel that threatened American ships, as World War II raged in Europe.

1944 The Allies liberated Antwerp from Germany in World War II.

1948 After celebrating her Golden Jubilee in August, Queen Wilhelmina abdicated, making her daughter Juliana Queen of The Netherlands.

1957 The school integration crisis began in Little Rock, Arkansas, resulting eventually in President Eisenhower's sending in Federal troops to enforce the court integration orders.

1957 Ford Motor Company introduced the Edsel automobile, which was subsequently so unpopular its name became synonymous with failure.

1965 Albert Schweitzer, the great German philosopher, physician, and musician, died at age 90.

1972 American swimmer Mark Spitz won a record seventh Olympic gold medal in the 400-meter relay at the Munich Olympic Games.

September 5 – Birthdays

1187 **Louis VIII.** Capetian king of France, 1223-1226

1568 **Tommaso Campanella.** Italian Platonic philosopher, poet, and writer, best known for his socialistic work *The City of the Sun* (1602)

1638 **Louis XIV.** The "Sun King" of France, 1643-1715, who ruled in one of France's most brilliant periods

1735 **Johann Christian Bach.** German composer and youngest son of Johann Sebastian Bach

1774 **Kaspar David Friedrich.** German painter

1791 **Giacomo Meyerbeer.** German composer who was one of the most popular opera composers of his day

1817 **Aleksey Konstantinovich Tolstoy.** Russian poet and novelist (no relation to the famous novelist Leo Tolstoy)

1847 **Jesse James.** Notorious outlaw of the American West, who specialized in robbing trains and banks

1875 **Napoleon Lajoie.** Hall of Fame baseball player, who hit .422 in 1901 and had 3,251 career hits

1897 **Arthur C. Nielsen.** Founder of the Nielsen system of rating television shows

1897 **Morris Carnovsky.** American stage and motion-picture actor with a career of over 55 years

1901 **Florence Eldridge.** American stage and motion-picture actress with a career of over 40 years

1902 **Darryl F. Zanuck.** Flamboyant picture maker of Hollywood's Golden Age, who produced such classics as *The Grapes of Wrath* (1940) and *Tobacco Road* (1941)

1905 **Arthur Koestler.** Yugoslavian novelist and essayist, noted for *Darkness at Noon* (1941)

1910 **Clyde D. Sandgren.** American composer and author, noted for songs such as "Near You," "Little Girl," and "I'm Pretending"

1912 **John Cage.** Highly original and controversial modern American composer, noted for seeking new sounds, such as by inserting objects between some of the piano strings

1913 **John Mitchell.** U.S. attorney general, Watergate figure, and the first member of any president's cabinet to be imprisoned

1916 **Frank Yerby.** American novelist and author of works such as *The Foxes of Harrow*

1921 **Jack Valenti.** President of the Motion Picture Association of America

1927 **Paul A. Volcker Jr.** Chairman of the board of governors of the Federal Reserve System under Presidents Carter and Reagan

1929 **Bob Newhart.** American comedian and actor

1932 **Carol Lawrence.** American actress and dancer

1933 **Katherine Helmond.** American actress

1936 **Bill Mazeroski.** Professional baseball player who hit the last pitch of the 1960 World Series for a home run to give the Pittsburgh Pirates the victory over the New York Yankees

1936 **John Danforth.** U.S. senator

1939 **John Stewart.** American singer and songwriter noted for "Daydream Believer" (1967)

1939 **Bill Kilmer.** Professional football superstar

1939 **William Devane.** American stage, screen, and television actor

1940 **Raquel Welch.** American motion-picture actress

1946 **Buddy Miles.** American rock drummer

1950 **Cathy Lee Guisewite.** American cartoonist and creator of the comic strip *Cathy*

1960 **Candy Maldonado.** Professional baseball player

1969 **Dweezil Zappa.** American musician, actor and son of musician Frank Zappa

September 5 – Events

1316 John XXII, the second Roman Catholic pope to reside in Avignon, France, rather than Rome, was crowned.

1569 Pieter Bruegel the Elder, the great Flemish painter, died at age 44.

1698 Russian czar Peter the Great imposed a tax on beards.

1755 Six thousand Acadians were expelled by the British from Nova Scotia, providing the inspiration for Longfellow's famous poem "Evangeline"

1774 The First Continental Congress met at Philadelphia, with 56 delegates, representing 12 colonies, attending.

1791 Wolfgang Amadeus Mozart, the great composer, died in Vienna at age 35.

1836 Sam Houston was elected as first president of the Republic of Texas.

1882 Workers staged the first Labor Day parade, in New York City.

1885 Jake D. Gumper of Fort Wayne, Indiana, bought the first gasoline pump manufactured in the United States.

1905 The Treaty of Portsmouth ended the Russo-Japanese War.

1972 Arab terrorists killed two Israeli Olympic players and held nine others hostage in Munich. The hostages and the terrorists were later killed in a police shoot-out.

1975 President Gerald Ford escaped assassination in Sacramento, California, when a Secret Service agent deflected a gun pointed at him by a woman named Squeaky Fromme.

1984 Space shuttle *Discovery* safely completed its flight as it landed at Edwards Air Force Base, California.

1991 The deputies of the Soviet parliament voted to replace the Soviet Union by a loose confederation of republics, thus ending the 74-year-old USSR.

September 6 – Birthdays

1475 **Sebastiano Serlio.** Italian Mannerist architect and painter

1666 **Ivan V.** Czar of Russia, 1682-1689, and weak-minded half brother of Peter the Great

1757 **Marquis de Lafayette.** French soldier and statesman who fought with the Americans in the Revolutionary War

1766 **John Dalton.** English chemist who in 1802 formulated Dalton's Law, the law of partial pressures in gases

1805 **Horatio Greenough.** American sculptor noted for the famous statue of George Washington (1840) that stands in the Smithsonian Institution in Washington, D.C.

1835 **Justin Louis Emile Combes.** French premier during the Dreyfus Affair

1860 **Jane Addams.** American social worker and humanitarian, who founded Hull House in Chicago and shared the 1931 Nobel Peace prize

1873 **Howard Earle Coffin.** American car designer and co-founder of the Hudson Motor Car Co. (1909)

1876 **John J.R. MacLeod.** Scottish physician who co-discovered insulin, with Frederick Banting

1876 **Boardman Robinson.** American artist, mural painter, and illustrator, noted for his illustrations for Fyodor Dostoevsky's novel *The Brothers Karamazov*

1885 **Otto Kruger.** American stage and motion-picture actor with a 50-year career

1888 **Joseph P. Kennedy.** American ambassador, financier, and father of President John F. Kennedy

1888 **Red Faber.** Hall of Fame baseball player

1890 **Claire L. Chennault.** American aviator, USAF general, and leader of the *Flying Tigers* in China in World War II

1893 **John W. Bricker.** U.S. senator and vice presidential candidate in 1944

1895 **Ida Fuller.** American social reformer who received the first U.S. social security check (1940)

1899 **Billy Rose.** American theatrical impresario and pop song composer, noted for songs such as "Me and My Shadow," "The Night Is Young and You're So Beautiful," and "It's Only a Paper Moon"

1903 **"Slapsie" Maxie Rosenbloom.** American professional boxer and character comedian of Hollywood films

1908 **Raymond Firestone.** Chairman of the board of Firestone Tire and Rubber Company

1924 **John Melcher.** U.S. senator

1929 **Dow Finsterwald.** Professional golfer

1937 **Jo Ann Worley.** American actress and comedienne

1939 **David Allan Coe.** American singer and songwriter noted for "Take This Job and Shove It" (1978)

1944 **Roger Waters.** Bass player for the Pink Floyd rock group

1944 **Swoosie Kurtz.** American stage, screen, and television actress

1947 **Jane Curtin.** American actress and comedienne

1958 **Jeff Foxworthy.** American actor and comedian (*The Jeff Foxworthy Show*)

1973 **Greg Rusedski.** British tennis player

September 6 – Events

1492 Christopher Columbus left San Sebastian in the Canary Islands, resuming his first voyage westward to America.

1522 The *Victoria,* the last surviving ship of Magellan's fleet, commanded by Sebastian del Cano, arrived in Sanlucar, Spain, completing the first trip around the world.

1628 The Massachusetts Bay Colony was established in Salem, Massachusetts, by a group of 100 English Puritans led by John Endecott.

1628 The Massachusetts Bay Colony was established in Salem, Massachusetts, by a group of 100 English Puritans led by John Endecott.

1898 Queen Wilhelmina was crowned Queen of The Netherlands. She had been queen since 1890 with her mother, Queen Emma, ruling as regent until 1898.

1901 President William McKinley was shot by the assassin Leon Czolgosz at the Pan-American Exposition in Buffalo. He died eight days later.

1914 The First Battle of the Marne began in France in World War I.

1948 The coronation of Queen Juliana of The Netherlands took place in Amsterdam.

1978 Camp David summit talks began between Egypt's President Anwar Sadat, Israel's President Menachem Begin, and President Jimmy Carter.

1991 The Kremlin's new leadership granted independence to Lithuania, Latvia and Estonia, ending more than 50 years of Soviet rule.

1995 Cal Ripken, the great Baltimore shortstop, played in his 2,131st consecutive game, breaking the iron man record of Lou Gehrig.

September 7 – Birthdays

1492 **Giacoma Aconcio.** Italian protestant leader of the Reformation era

1533 **Elizabeth I.** Queen of England, 1558-1603, during one of the most glorious periods in English history, and one of the greatest monarchs of all time

1707 **Georges-Louis Leclerc de Buffon.** French naturalist and writer, and one of the forerunners of Charles Darwin in considering the facts of evolution

1819 **Thomas A. Hendricks.** U.S. vice president in President Cleveland's first term

1831 **Victorien Sardou.** One of the most successful French playwrights of his time, whose *La Tosca* became the basis of Giacomo Puccini's noted opera of the same name

1840 **Luther Childs Crowell.** American inventor noted for the machine to make square-bottomed paper bags

1860 **Grandma Moses.** American primitive painter, born Anna Mary Robertson Moses, who started painting at age 76 and painted 25 pictures after her 100th birthday

1867 **J.P. Morgan Jr.** American financier who succeeded his father as chairman of the board of U.S. Steel Corporation

1885 **Elinor Wylie.** American poet, noted for "Jennifer Lorn" (1923)

1887 **Dame Edith Sitwell.** English poet and literary critic

1897 **Al Sherman.** Russian-born composer and author, noted for songs such as "On the Beach at Bali-Bali," "For Sentimental Reasons," and "No! No! A Thousand Times No!"

1900 **Taylor Caldwell.** English-born American novelist noted for works such as *Dynasty of Death* (1938) and *This Side of Innocence* (1946)

1903 **Margaret Landon.** Author of *Anna and the King of Siam*

1905 **Ivy Baker Priest.** Treasurer of the United States under President Eisenhower

1908 **Paul Brown.** Professional football player and coach, noted for his work with the Cleveland Browns (the only professional football team ever named for its coach)

1908 **Michael Ellis De Bakey.** American heart surgeon noted for his pioneering work in the treatment of cardiovascular disease

1909 **Elia Kazan.** Turkish-born American motion-picture director, noted for films such as *Gentlemen's Agreement* (1947), *On the Waterfront* (1954), and *East of Eden* (1955)

1912 **David Packard.** American businessman and co-founder of Hewlett-Packard Corp. in 1939

1913 **Anthony Quayle.** British motion-picture and television actor

1914 **James A. Van Allen.** American physicist, who in 1958 discovered the Van Allen radiation belts that circle the earth

1923 **Peter Lawford.** American motion-picture actor

1923 **Louise Suggs.** Professional golfer

1924 **Daniel Inouye.** First U.S. senator of Oriental descent

1929 **Clyde Lovellette.** Professional Hall of Fame basketball player with 12,000 career points

1930 **Baudouin.** King of Belgium who assumed the throne in 1951 when his father, Leopold III, abdicated

1930 **Sonny Rollins.** American saxophonist

1936 **Buddy Holly.** American singer, guitarist, and songwriter

1937 **John Phillip Law.** American motion-picture actor

1942 **Richard Roundtree.** American motion-picture actor

1946 **Joe Rudi.** Professional baseball player

1948 **John Brockington.** Professional football player

1951 **Julie Kavner.** American motion-picture and television actress (the voice of Marge Simpson on *The Simpsons*)

1951 **Bert Jones.** Professional football player

1955 **Corbin Bernsen.** American motion-picture and television actor noted for his role in the popular series *L.A. Law*

September 7 – Events

70 The Romans sacked Jerusalem, leaving only the "Wailing Wall" intact.

1502 Amerigo Vespucci, the Italian traveler for whom America was named, returned to Lisbon after his third trip to America.

1812 Napoleon defeated the Russians, led by Marshal Mikhail I. Kutuzov, in the Battle of Borodino, and subsequently captured Moscow. In the process, however, his French Grande Armee was decimated.

1822 Brazil declared its independence from Portugal. The break was accomplished without bloodshed.

1825 The French hero of the American Revolution, the Marquis de Lafayette, gave his last farewell to President John Quincy Adams at the White House while on his famous U.S. tour.

1876 Jesse James and the Younger Brothers attempted to rob the First National Bank of Northfield, Minnesota, in a bungled holdup that destroyed the notorious James-Younger gang.

1892 Gentleman Jim Corbett knocked out John L. Sullivan in the 21st round of the first major prize fight fought under the Marquis of Queensberry rules.

1921 The first American beauty contest ever held, the first Miss America contest in Atlantic City, New Jersey, was won by Margaret Gorham.

1940 German planes blasted London, marking the beginning of the London blitz in World War II in which the city was bombed 82 out of 85 nights.

1963 The Professional Football Hall of Fame in Canton, Ohio, opened as 17 players were enshrined, including Jim Thorpe, Sammy Baugh, Red Grange, George Halas, Don Hutson and Dutch Clark.

1977 President Jimmy Carter and General Omar Torrijos Herrera, Panama's chief of government, signed the Panama Canal treaties providing for eventual return of the canal to Panama.

September 8 – Birthdays

1157 **Richard the Lion-Hearted.** King of England, 1189-1199 (known also as Richard I), who was the second of the Plantagenet dynasty, after his father Henry II

1474 **Ludovico Ariosto.** Italian Renaissance poet, noted for the long narrative poem *Orlando Furioso* (1516), which influenced the works of Byron, Milton, and Shakespeare

1767 **August Wilhelm von Schlegel.** German writer and critic, and translator of Shakespeare's plays

1804 **Eduard Morike.** German lyric poet and novelist

1830 **Frederic Mistral.** French Nobel Prize-winning poet, noted for works such as "Mireille" and "Song of the Rhine"

1841 **Antonin Dvorak.** Czechoslovakian composer best known for his symphony *From the New World*

1844 **Charles Guiteau.** American assassin who shot President Garfield (1881) and was himself hanged in 1882

1886 **Siegfried Sassoon.** English poet and writer

1889 **Robert A. Taft.** U.S. senator, 1939-1953, and son of President William Howard Taft

1896 **Howard Dietz.** American songwriter and publicity executive, who created the MGM trademark, Leo the Lion, and its Latin motto, *Ars Gratia Artis,* and who is noted for songs such as "Dancing in the Dark" and "Something to Remember You By"

1896 **Frank Silver.** American conductor, author, and drummer, noted for songs such as "Yes, We Have No Bananas"

1897 **Jimmy Rodgers.** American composer, author, and singer, noted for songs such as "In the Jailhouse Now" and "Mississippi Moon"

1900 **Claude Pepper.** U.S. senator who served also in Congress and was a strong advocate for the elderly until his death in 1989

1901 **Hendrik F. Verwoerd.** Prime minister of the Republic of South Africa, 1958-1966

1907 **Buck Leonard.** Hall of Fame baseball player

1911 **Euell Gibbons.** American writer and nutritional expert

1912 **Jacques Fath.** French clothing designer

1912 **Leo Cherne.** American author, sculptor, and diplomat

1915 **Duffy Daugherty.** Noted American football coach

1916 **Hillary Brooke.** American stage and motion-picture actress

1922 **Sid Caesar.** American comedian and actor

1924 **Grace Metalious.** American writer and author of *Peyton Place*

1924 **Wendell Ford.** U.S. senator

1925 **Peter Sellers.** English comedian and motion-picture actor

1930 **Nguyen Cao Ky.** South Vietnamese military and political leader

1932 **Patsy Cline.** American country singer with hits like "Crazy"

1938 **Sam Nunn.** U.S. senator

1946 **Ken Forsch.** Professional baseball player

1946 **Ron "Pigpen" McKernan.** American rock musician with The Grateful Dead

1946 **Patrick Hombergen.** Belgian tennis player

1960 **Daniel Steele.** American pop musician with the Fine Young Cannibals

1971 **Henry Thomas.** American motion-picture actor who was a child star in *E.T., The Extra-Terrestrial* (1982)

September 8 – Events

1380 Dmitri Donskoi, the Prince of Moscow, defeated the Mongols in the Battle of Kulikovo.

1565 Spanish explorer Pedro Menendez de Aviles founded St. Augustine, Florida, the oldest city in the United States.

1664 Peter Stuyvesant surrendered New Amsterdam to the British fleet sent by the Duke of York. The British renamed the city New York.

1892 The earliest version of "The Pledge of Allegiance" appeared in *The Youth's Companion.*

1935 Senator Huey Long of Louisiana, the founder of the famous Long dynasty, was shot in the state capitol in Baton Rouge by Dr. Carl Weiss. He died two days later.

1941 Twenty-three German armies surrounded Leningrad and began a 17-month siege in World War II.

1943 Italy's unconditional surrender to the Allies in World War II, signed five days earlier by Marshal Badoglio, was announced by General Dwight D. Eisenhower.

1944 The Germans fired the first of their V-12 rockets into London.

1950 United Nations forces stopped the Communist advance at the Pusan Peninsula in southeastern Korea in the Korean War.

1968 Saundra Williams was chosen the first "Miss Black America."

1974 President Gerald Ford granted a "full, free, and absolute" pardon to former President Richard Nixon for all crimes he committed "or may have committed" while president.

1998 Mark McGwire of the St. Louis Cardinals broke Roger Maris's single-season home run record by hitting his 62nd home run against the Chicago Cubs.

September 9 – Birthdays

1585 **Cardinal Richelieu.** One of the ablest of French statesmen, who as chief minister to King Louis XIII was the actual ruler of France from 1624 to 1642

1711 **Thomas Hutchinson.** The last royal governor of the Massachusetts Bay colony, who precipitated the Boston Tea Party by refusing to let the tea ships leave Boston Harbor

1737 **Luigi Galvani.** Italian pioneer in the study of electricity and its relation to living organisms

1754 **William Bligh.** English captain of the H.M.S. *Bounty* at the time of the famous mutiny in 1789

1828 **Leo Tolstoy.** One of Russia's greatest writers, and the author of *War and Peace* (1865-1869) and *Anna Karenina* (1875-1877), two of the great books of world literature

1852 **John Henry Poynting.** English physicist for whom the Poynting vector was named

1873 **Max Reinhardt.** Austrian-American theatrical producer and director, noted for his spectacular productions

1877 **Frank Chance.** Hall of Fame baseball player and member of the famed Tinker-to-Evers-to-Chance double play combination

1887 **Alfred M. Landon.** U.S. presidential candidate in 1936

1890 **Colonel Harland Sanders.** Founder of the Kentucky Fried Chicken restaurant chain

1894 **Arthur Freed.** American lyricist and producer, noted for songs such as "You Were Meant for Me," "Singin' in the Rain," and "Temptation"

1898 **Frank Frisch.** Hall of Fame baseball player and manager

1899 **Waite Hoyt.** Hall of Fame baseball player

1900 **James Hilton.** English novelist, noted for *Lost Horizon* (1933), in which the name Shangri-La was coined to denote a remote utopian land, and *Goodbye, Mr. Chips* (1934)

1905   **Joseph E. Levine.** American motion-picture producer, noted for films such as *The Graduate* (1967) and *The Lion in Winter* (1968)

1917   **Frank Robbins.** American cartoonist noted for *Johnny Hazard* (1944)

1919   **Jimmy "The Greek" Snyder.** American oddsmaker and sportscaster

1924   **Jane Greer.** American motion-picture actress

1925   **Cliff Robertson.** American stage and motion-picture actor

1932   **Sylvia Miles.** American stage and motion-picture actress

1941   **Otis Redding.** American soul singer

1949   **John Curry.** British-born ice skating virtuoso

1949   **Joe Theismann.** Professional football player

1951   **Michael Keaton.** American television and motion-picture actor

1952   **Jerry Mumphrey.** Professional baseball player

1962   **Kristy McNichol.** American motion-picture and television actress

September 9 – Events

1087   William the Conqueror died in Rouen at age 59 after an accident while riding his horse.

1492   Columbus and his men lost sight of land, three days after leaving the Canary Islands. They would not see land again until October 12, when the new world was discovered.

1499   Vasco da Gama, the great Portuguese navigator, returned to Lisbon after becoming the first man to reach India by sailing around the Cape of Good Hope.

1689   Peter the Great took power in Russia when he was 17 by deposing his sister Sophia, who had seized the regency when Peter was 10.

1776   The Continental Congress made the name *United States* official.

1850   California was admitted to the Union as the 31st state.

1901   Henri Toulouse-Lautrec, the great French painter, died at Chateau de Malrome at age 36.

1914   The Allies stopped the Germans, as the First Battle of the Marne ended in World War I.

1926   The National Broadcasting Company (NBC) was organized with 25 radio stations.

1934   The comic strip *The Little King,* by Otto Soglow, first appeared.

1943   The U.S. Fifth Army under General Mark Clark invaded Italy at Salerno in World War II.

1965   Sandy Koufax pitched a perfect game (no runner reached base), as Los Angeles beat Chicago, 1-0. It was Koufax's fourth career no-hit game.

1965   Bert Campaneris of the Kansas City A's became the first major-league baseball player to play each of the nine field positions in a single game.

1971   The John F. Kennedy Center for the Performing Arts opened in Washington, D.C., with a performance of Leonard Bernstein's *Mass.*

1976   Chairman Mao Tse-tung of China died at 82.

September 10 – Birthdays

1487   **Julius III.** Roman Catholic pope, 1550-1555

1624   **Thomas Sydenham.** English physician and one of the best of his time

1638   **Marie-Therese.** Queen consort of Louis XIV, the great "Sun King" of France

1736   **Carter Braxton.** American Revolutionary War statesman, member of the Continental Congress, and signer of the Declaration of Independence

1753   **Sir John Soane.** English architect

1771   **Mungo Park.** Scottish explorer of the Niger River in Africa

1836   **Joseph Wheeler.** American soldier who served as a general in the Confederate Army and who returned to the American Army after the Civil War

1839   **Isaac K. Funk.** Co-publisher of Funk and Wagnalls' dictionary

1873   **Charles Talbut Onions.** British lexicographer

1885   **Carl Van Doren.** American writer and winner of the 1939 Nobel Prize in biography for *Benjamin Franklin*

1886   **Hilda Doolittle.** American poet, leader of the imagist movement, and author of "Sea Garden" (1916)

1890   **Elsa Schiaparelli.** French clothing designer

1890   **Franz Werfel.** Austrian novelist, playwright, and poet, noted for works such as *The Song of Bernadette* (1941)

1892   **Arthur H. Compton.** American physicist who headed one of the groups that produced the atomic bomb, and shared the 1927 Nobel Prize for his discovery of the Compton effect

1895   **George "Highpockets" Kelly.** Professional baseball player

1898   **Bessie Love.** One of the greatest actresses of the D.W. Griffith era, whose career spanned 60 years

1900   **Francis Craig.** American composer and pianist, noted for songs such as "Near You" and "Beg Your Pardon"

1902   **Jim Crowley.** American football player and one of the Four Horseman of Notre Dame

1903   **Cyril Connolly.** English novelist and editor of *Horizon*

1906   **Leonard Lyons.** American newspaper columnist

1914   **Robert Wise.** American director and film editor noted as the editor of the great classic *Citizen Kane* and the Academy Award-winning director of *The Sound of Music*

1915   **Edmond O'Brien.** American motion-picture and television actor

1924   **Ted Kluszewski.** Professional baseball player and coach

1927   **Yma Sumac.** South American singer

1929 **Arnold Palmer.** One of the world's greatest golfers, who dominated the game in the 1950s and 1960s, and became the first professional to win $1 million in tournament prize money

1934 **Roger Maris.** Professional baseball player who hit a record 61 home runs in 1961

1934 **Charles Kuralt.** American broadcast journalist and host of the television shows *On the Road with Charles Kuralt* and *Sunday Morning*

1940 **Buck Buchanan.** Hall of Fame football player

1944 **John Alec Entwistle.** English musician and singer with The Who musical group

1945 **Jose Feliciano.** Blind-from-birth Puerto Rican singer and guitarist

1945 **Marlin Briscoe.** Professional football player

1948 **Bob Lanier.** Hall of Fame professional basketball player

1951 **Gary Danielson.** Professional football player

1953 **Amy Irving.** American stage and motion-picture actress

1958 **Jennifer Tilly.** Canadian-American stage, screen and television actress and sister of actress Meg Tilly

1963 **Randy Johnson.** Professional baseball player and superstar

September 10 – Events

422 Saint Celestine I was elected Roman Catholic pope.

1419 John the Fearless, Duke of Burgundy, was assassinated by followers of the Orleanists, or Armagnacs, in retaliation for the murder of the Duke of Orleans by John.

1533 Future Queen Elizabeth I of England was christened.

1608 John Smith was elected president of the colony council of Jamestown, Virginia.

1742 Faneuil Hall, the "Cradle of Liberty" in Boston, was completed.

1813 Commodore Oliver Hazard Perry defeated the British in the Battle of Lake Erie in the War of 1812, and sent the message: "We have met the enemy and they are ours."

1846 Elias Howe patented his sewing machine.

1938 The comic strip *The Lone Ranger,* by Ed Kressy, first appeared.

1939 Canada declared war on Germany, the first time in history that Canada had declared war independently.

1944 The U.S. First Army fired the first American shells to reach German soil, near Aachen, in World War II.

1955 The television show *Gunsmoke* began its weekly run that lasted nearly 20 years.

1967 Gibraltar residents voted to remain British rather than join Spain.

1988 Steffi Graf of West Germany won the U.S. Open women's final to become the first Grand Slam winner of tennis since Margaret Court in 1970.

September 11 – Birthdays

1524 **Pierre de Ronsard.** French Renaissance poet, known as the "Prince of Poets," who led the influential group of poets called the Pleiade

1556 **St. Joseph Calasanctius.** Spanish priest and teacher

1611 **Henri D'Auvergne Turenne.** French marshal who led the Frondeurs in an unsuccessful uprising against Jules Cardinal Mazarin

1700 **James Thomson.** The most celebrated Scottish poet of the 1700s until Robert Burns

1743 **Nicolai Abraham Abildgaard.** The most renowned Danish painter of the late 18th century

1744 **Sarah Franklin Bache.** The only daughter of Benjamin Franklin

1854 **William Holabird.** American architect

1862 **O. Henry.** American writer (born William Sydney Porter) and master of the short story, noted for works such as *Cabbages and Kings* (1904), *The Gentle Grafter* (1908), and the short story "The Gift of the Magi"

1877 **Sir James Jeans.** English physicist and mathematician, noted for his contributions to the kinetic theory of gases

1885 **D.H. Lawrence.** Influential English novelist, noted for works such as *The Rainbow* (1915), *Women in Love* (1920), and *Lady Chatterly's Lover* (1928)

1885 **Herbert Stothart.** American composer, conductor, and pianist, noted for songs such as "I Wanna Be Loved By You" and "The Donkey Serenade"

1899 **Jimmie H. Davis.** Twice-elected governor of Louisiana (1944 and 1960), singer, and songwriter, noted for *You Are My Sunshine*

1911 **Ramez Idriss.** American composer, author, and musician, noted for songs such as "The Woody Woodpecker Song"

1913 **Paul "Bear" Bryant.** The winningest college football coach in history, with 323 career victories

1917 **Jessica Mitford.** British-born polemicist and muckraker best known for her 1963 book, *The American Way of Death*

1917 **Ferdinand Marcos.** President of the Philippines

1922 **Charles Evers.** American civil rights leader

1924 **Tom Landry.** Highly successful professional football coach

1928 **Reuben Askew.** Governor of Florida

1928 **Earl Holliman.** American motion-picture and television actor

1932 **Bob Packwood.** U.S. senator

1935 **Gherman Stepanovich Titov.** Russian cosmonaut on the first manned space flight of more than a single orbit, in *Vostok 2* in 1961

1940 **Brian De Palma.** American motion-picture director noted for *The Bonfire of the Vanities* (1990) and *Mission Impossible* (1996)

1943 **Mickey Hart.** American singer and musician with The Grateful Dead

1944 **Dave Roberts.** Professional baseball player

1947 **Larry Cox.** Professional baseball player

1958 **Don Slaught.** Professional baseball player

1964 **Ellis Burks.** Professional baseball player

1967 **Harry Connick Jr.** American musician, songwriter and actor

September 11 – Events

814 Louis I, the Pious, succeeded his father, the great French king Charlemagne, as King of the Franks and Emperor of the Romans.

1777 General William Howe defeated George Washington at the Battle of Brandywine, enabling the British to occupy Philadelphia in the Revolutionary War.

1789 Alexander Hamilton was appointed America's first Secretary of the Treasury.

1814 American commander Thomas Macdonough defeated the British on Lake Champlain in the War of 1812, in one of the most decisive battles ever fought by the U.S. Navy.

1847 Stephen Foster's "Oh! Susanna" was first sung publicly, in Andrew's Eagle Ice Cream Saloon in Pittsburgh.

1850 Jenny Lind, "The Swedish Nightingale," opened her American concert series at Castle Garden in New York.

1941 President Franklin D. Roosevelt ordered the U.S. Navy to shoot on sight German U-boats threatening American ships.

1944 Prime Minister Churchill and President Roosevelt held their second Quebec Conference in World War II.

1945 Former Japanese premier Hideki Tojo attempted suicide in Tokyo. He was hospitalized and lived to be executed for war crimes.

1971 Nikita Khrushchev, the former Soviet premier, died at age 77.

1973 Chilean President Salvador Allende Gossens was deposed in a military coup, and, according to the new leaders, he committed suicide.

1985 Pete Rose broke Ty Cobb's long-standing record as he made his 4,192nd career base hit.

1998 The House of Representatives, on a party line vote, released to the public the report by Special Prosecutor Kenneth Starr outlining the grounds for possible impeachment of President Clinton.

September 12 – Birthdays

1310 **Niccolo Acciaiuoli.** Italian statesman and soldier

1494 **Francis I.** King of France, 1515-1547, great patron of the Renaissance in France, and pleasure lover, whose self-proclaimed pastime was to "go a-whoring"

1575 **Henry Hudson.** British sea captain who in his famous ship, the *Half Moon,* explored the Hudson River, the Hudson Bay, and Hudson Strait (date of birth uncertain)

1788 **Alexander Campbell.** American religious leader, who was a co-founder in the early 1800s of the Christian Church (Disciples of Christ)

1812 **Richard March Hoe.** American inventor and manufacturer, who in 1846 invented the rotary press used in modern newspaper printing

1818 **Richard Jordan Gatling.** American inventor, best known for the invention of the Gatling gun, the first practical, quick-firing machine gun developed in the United States

1829 **Anselm Feuerbach.** German painter

1852 **Herbert Henry Asquith.** Prime minister of Great Britain, 1908-1916, during whose administration the Old Age Pension Act and the National Insurance Act were passed

1880 **H.L. Mencken.** American journalist, author, and pungent critic, who greatly influenced American writing in the 1920s

1888 **Maurice Chevalier.** French musical comedy actor, singer, and dancer, with a 60-year career

1892 **Alfred A. Knopf.** American publisher and founder of Alfred A. Knopf, Inc.

1893 **Lewis B. Hershey.** American army general who headed the national draft board in World War II and the Korean War

1898 **Ben Shahn.** Lithuanian-born American artist, noted for his realistic paintings and drawings

1901 **Ben Blue.** Canadian comic actor, deadpan mine, and dancer of the American stage, screen and television

1902 **Juscelino Kubitschek.** President of Brazil who pushed through construction of the new capital of Brasilia

1907 **Spud Chandler.** Professional baseball pitcher with a career win-loss percentage of .717

1909 **Agnes DeMille.** American choreographer, dancer, and author

1913 **Jesse Owens.** American athlete, who in one day set three world track records and tied another, and who was the hero of the 1936 Olympics in Berlin

1914 **Eddy Howard.** American composer, conductor, and guitarist, noted for songs such as "Lonesome Tonight"

1916 **Charlie Keller.** Professional baseball player

1938 **Tatiana Troyanos.** American mezzo-soprano

1940 **Mickey Lolich.** Professional baseball player

1942 **Linda Gray.** American actress noted for her role as Sue Ellen in the long-running television series *Dallas*

September 12 – Events

1185 Byzantine emperor Andronicus I was tortured and executed by the Greek nobility, led by Isaac Angelus, during a war between the Byzantines and Norman invaders of the empire.

1609 Henry Hudson, the famous British sea captain, discovered the Hudson River.

1687 John Alden, the last surviving member of the Pilgrims who came to America on the *Mayflower,* died at age 88.

1759 British troops scaled the heights below the Plains of Abraham before Quebec. The next morning they were there ready to face the startled French defenders of the city in the French and Indian War.

1846 Robert Browning and Elizabeth Barrett, the noted English poets, were married secretly because Elizabeth's father violently opposed the wedding.

1847 American general Winfield Scott attacked Chapultepec, a fortified hill guarding the gates to Mexico City in the Mexican War.

1848 The Swiss Confederation was formed with the adoption of a new constitution.

1908 Winston Churchill married Clementine Hozier.

1928 Katharine Hepburn, the great American actress, made her New York debut in the play *Night Hostess.*

1943 Benito Mussolini was rescued by German paratroopers from a hotel in Lake Bracciano, Italy, where he was held captive by the Italian government.

1944 General Courtney Hodge's First Army became the first American troops to enter Germany in World War II, as they smashed across the German border near Trier.

1953 John F. Kennedy married Jacqueline Lee Bouvier.

1959 Russia launched *Luna 2,* the first man-made object to reach the moon.

1960 Democratic presidential candidate John F. Kennedy told the Houston Ministerial Association: "I believe in an America where the separation of church and state is absolute."

1974 Emperor Haile Selassie I of Ethiopia was deposed by military leaders, after 58 years as absolute ruler.

September 13 – Birthdays

1813 **Daniel Macmillan.** Co-founder of Macmillan and Company publishers

1819 **Clara Schumann.** German pianist and wife of composer Robert Schumann

1826 **Anthony Joseph Drexel.** American financier and philanthropist, who in 1891 founded Drexel Institute of Technology

1851 **Walter Reed.** U.S. Army pathologist who proved that yellow fever is transmitted by the bite of a mosquito

1857 **Milton Snavely Hershey.** American industrialist who founded the Hershey Chocolate Corporation

1860 **John J. Pershing.** American general who commanded the American Expeditionary Forces in Europe during World War I

1863 **Cyrus Adler.** American scholar, educator, and editor

1873 **Constantin Caratheodory.** Noted Greek mathematician

1874 **Arnold Schoenberg.** Austrian composer

1876 **Sherwood Anderson.** American short-story writer and novelist, noted for works such as *Winesburg, Ohio* (1919)

1894 **John Boynton Priestley.** English novelist, playwright, and journalist, noted for such works as *The Good Companions* (1929) and *Lost Empires* (1965)

1905 **Claudette Colbert.** French-born American stage and motion-picture actress, who won the 1934 Academy Award for best actress in *It Happened One Night*

1906 **Thornton Lee.** Professional baseball player

1911 **Bill Monroe.** American singer, songwriter and "Father of Bluegrass"

1916 **Roald Dahl.** English writer noted for works such as *The Gremlins* (1943) and *Charlie and the Chocolate Factory* (1964)

1916 **Dick Haymes.** American singer and actor

1924 **Scott Brady.** American motion-picture and television actor

1924 **Maurice Jarre.** French composer who won Academy Awards for the scores of *Lawrence of Arabia* (1962) and *Dr. Zhivago* (1965)

1925 **Mel Torme.** American composer, author, and singer, noted for songs such as "Stranger in Town," "The Christmas Song," and "Born to Be Blue"

1937 **Fred Silverman.** American television broadcasting executive

1938 **Judith Martin.** American journalist noted for the "Miss Manners" column

1941 **Pierre Barthes.** French tennis player

1944 **Jacqueline Bisset.** English-born motion-picture actress

1945 **Rick Wise.** Professional baseball player

1948 **Nell Carter.** American television actress and comedienne

1948 **Perry Curtis.** Professional basketball player

1949 **Jim Cleamons.** Professional basketball player

1949 **Rick Dempsey.** Professional baseball player

1956 **Joni Sledge.** American singer and member of Sister Sledge, noted for their 1979 hit, "We Are Family"

1968 **Bernie Williams.** Professional baseball player and American League batting champion in 1998

1968 **Denny Neagle.** Professional baseball player

1971 **Goran Ivanisevic.** Bosnian tennis player and superstar

September 13 – Events

81 Roman emperor Titus, who was on the throne when Pompeii was destroyed by the eruption of Mount Vesuvius, died in Rome at age 40.

604	Sabinianus was elected Roman Catholic pope.
1592	Michel Eyquem de Montaigne, the great French writer, died at Chateau de Montaigne, near Bordeaux, at age 59.
1759	The British defeated the French in the Battle of Quebec, in the French and Indian War. Both generals Wolfe and Montcalm were killed, and as a result of the battle the French lost their American empire.
1788	The U.S. Constitutional Convention authorized the first national election in the United States.
1847	U.S. general Winfield Scott defeated the Mexicans in the Battle of Chapultepec, near Mexico City, one of the last engagements of the Mexican War.
1922	The temperature hit 136.4 degrees Fahrenheit in Al'azizyah, Libya, the highest recorded in history.
1931	The song "Life is Just a Bowl of Cherries" was introduced by singer Rudy Vallee in a musical revue in New York.
1943	Chiang Kai-shek became president of China.
1993	Israeli prime minister Yitzhak Rabin and PLO chairman Yasser Arafat, with prompting from President Clinton, signed a historic agreement promising self-government for the Palestinians in return for their recognition of the Israeli state.
1998	Chicago Cubs slugger Sammy Sosa hit his 62nd home run of the season bettering Roger Maris's record which Mark McGwire had broken five days earlier. Sosa went on to hit 66, second only to McGwire's 70 for the season.

September 14 – Birthdays

1547	**Jan Van Oldenbarneveldt.** Dutch prime minister and one of the foremost statesmen of his time
1618	**Sir Peter Lely.** Dutch-English painter noted for works such as the *Beauties* of King Charles II's entourage
1645	**Jeremiah Dummer.** American silversmith
1742	**James Wilson.** Pennsylvania signer of the Declaration of Independence and the United States Constitution
1760	**Luigi Cherubini.** Italian-French composer of some 30 operas and 11 masses, best known for *Requiem in C minor* (1816), which commemorated King Louis XVI
1769	**Alexander von Humboldt.** German scientist and geographer, who helped found modern geography and was a pioneer in climatology
1782	**Christian Magnus Falsen.** Author of the Norwegian constitution
1846	**George B. Selden.** American inventor who developed the gasoline engine
1859	**Janis Cakste.** First president of the Republic of Latvia
1860	**Hamlin Garland.** American author, noted for *Main-Travelled Roads* (1891)
1867	**Charles Dana Gibson.** American illustrator who drew the famous *Gibson Girl* in the 1890s and early 1900s

1869	**Kid Nichols.** Hall of Fame professional baseball pitcher with 360 career wins
1883	**Margaret Sanger.** American nurse who led the birth-control movement in the United States and founded the Planned Parenthood Federation of America
1886	**Jan Masaryk.** Czechoslovakian statesman and son of Tomas Masaryk, the co-founder of Czechoslovakia
1887	**Karl Taylor Compton.** American physicist and specialist in the field of electrical discharge in gases, and chairman of the board that evaluated the Bikini atomic bomb tests in 1946
1891	**John H. Striebel.** American cartoonist who, with J.P. McEvoy, created the comic strip *Dixie Dugan*
1896	**John Robert Powers.** Founder of the famous Powers modeling agency
1899	**Hal B. Wallis.** American motion-picture producer of over 400 films
1914	**Clayton Moore.** American motion-picture and television actor, best known for his role as the Lone Ranger in the long-running television series
1921	**Hughes Rudd.** American television news correspondent
1923	**Bud Palmer.** American sports commentator
1924	**Jerry Coleman.** Professional baseball player and manager
1933	**Zoe Caldwell.** Australian stage actress and teacher
1934	**Kate Millett.** American sculptor, feminist, and author of *Sexual Politics*
1940	**Larry Brown.** Professional basketball coach
1944	**Joey Heatherton.** American motion-picture and television actress
1958	**Tim Wallach.** Professional baseball player
1959	**Mary Frances Crosby.** American actress and daughter of actor-singer Bing Crosby and actress Kathryn Grant

September 14 – Events

1321	Dante Alighieri, the great Italian poet, died in Ravenna at age 56.
1638	Clergyman John Harvard died in Massachusetts and left half of his estate to the "seminary" that was to become Harvard University.
1741	George Frederck Handel finished his great *Messiah*, just 24 days after starting it.
1752	Great Britain and the American colonies formally made the switch to the Gregorian calendar by changing this day from September 3 to September 14, 1752.
1812	Napoleon occupied Moscow, and found himself in a deserted city. The next day he moved into the Kremlin and waited for Czar Alexander to sue for peace, which never happened.
1814	Francis Scott Key wrote "The Star Spangled Banner" while witnessing the bombardment of Fort McHenry in Baltimore harbor by the British in the War of 1812.

1847 General Winfield Scott's American army occupied Mexico City, marking the end of hostilities in the Mexican War.

1851 James Fenimore Cooper, America's first important novelist, died one day before his 62nd birthday.

1852 The Duke of Wellington, the English general who conquered Napoleon at Waterloo, died at age 83.

1901 Theodore Roosevelt became president upon the death of President William McKinley, eight days after McKinley had been shot by an assassin.

1923 Jack Dempsey defeated Luis Angel Firpo, the "Wild Bull of the Pampas," in the second round after being knocked clear out of the ring by Firpo in the first round.

1927 The great modern dance pioneer Isadora Duncan was killed in France when her scarf became entangled in the wheel of an open car.

1940 Congress passed the Selective Service Act, providing for the first peacetime draft in U.S. history.

1963 The first U.S. quintuplets, four girls and a boy, to survive early infancy were born to parents Andrew James and Mary Ann Fischer in Aberdeen, South Dakota.

1964 The third session of the ecumenical council Vatican II of the Roman Catholic Church opened in Rome.

1965 The fourth and final session of the ecumenical council Vatican II opened in Rome.

1975 Elizabeth Ann Seton was proclaimed the first U.S.-born saint of the Roman Catholic Church.

1982 Grace Kelly (Princess Grace of Monaco) died at age 52 of injuries suffered in a car crash the day before.

1994 Baseball Commissioner Bud Selig announced that the rest of the baseball season would be canceled and there would be no World Series for the first time in 90 years because of the baseball strike.

September 15 – Birthdays

53 **Trajan.** Emperor of Rome, A.D. 98-117, who reigned during one of the empire's most prosperous periods

1613 **François de La Rochefoucauld.** French writer famous for his *Maxims* (1665), a collection of some 500 sayings that expose the vanity and hypocrisy in human behavior

1789 **James Fenimore Cooper.** America's first important novelist, noted for *The Leatherstocking Tales,* which include, among others, *The Last of the Mohicans* (1826) and *The Deerslayer* (1841)

1795 **Zachariah Allen.** Inventor of the first home hot-air furnace

1795 **Antoine Louis Barye.** French sculptor and painter noted for his portrayals of animals

1830 **Porfirio Diaz.** President of Mexico, 1877-1880 and 1884-1911, and a hero of the war against the French invaders from 1863 to 1867

1855 **Adam Geibel.** German-American composer, organist, and conductor, noted for such songs as "Stand Up, Stand Up for Jesus"

1857 **William Howard Taft.** 27th U.S. president, and the only man in history to serve first as president, then as Chief Justice of the Supreme Court

1870 **Mabel Caroline Bragg.** American children's author noted for works such as *The Little Engine That Could* (1930)

1876 **Bruno Walter.** One of the leading symphony orchestra and opera conductors of the 1900s

1881 **Ettore Arco Isidoro Bugatti.** Italian builder of the famous Bugatti automobile

1889 **Robert Benchley.** American humorist, journalist, critic, writer, and actor, who won an Academy Award in 1936 for writing and starring in the picture *How to Sleep*

1890 **Dame Agatha Christie.** English detective novelist, and author of over 60 popular works, such as *The Murder of Roger Ackroyd* (1926) and *Witness for the Prosecution* (1953)

1894 **Jean Renoir.** Son of the famous French painter Auguste Renoir, and distinguished motion-picture director with a career of some 50 years

1898 **Eddie Gottlieb.** American Hall of Fame basketball coach and executive, who was one of the founders of the NBA

1899 **Milton Eisenhower.** American statesman and brother of President Dwight D. Eisenhower

1903 **Roy Acuff.** Noted American country music singer and musician

1904 **Umberto II.** Son of Victor Emmanuel III and King of Italy for two months in 1946 before the Italians voted to abolish the monarchy

1907 **Fay Wray.** Canadian-born actress who appeared in nearly 50 motion pictures including the original *King Kong*

1908 **Penny Singleton.** American motion-picture actress noted for her portrayal of Blondie in the Blondie and Dagwood movies

1911 **Luther L. Terry.** American physician who was the first U.S. Surgeon-General to warn that cigarette smoking causes cancer and who first promoted the idea of seatbelts in automobiles

1912 **Ray Gilbert.** American composer noted for songs such as "The Three Caballeros," "You Belong to My Heart," "Zip-a-Dee-Doo-Dah," "Two Silhouettes" (lyrics), and "Casey at the Bat"

1914 **Creighton Adams.** U.S. general and Army chief of staff

1916 **Margaret Lockwood.** English stage and motion-picture actress

1920 **William Joseph Zellerbach.** American paper industry executive

1921 **Jackie Cooper.** American motion-picture actor, director, and executive, who at first was a famous child star and successfully made the transition to adult roles

1924 **Bobby Short.** American singer, pianist and actor

1927	**Norm Crosby.** American comedian noted for his deliberate misuse of words
1928	**Julian "Cannonball" Adderly.** American saxophonist and cool jazz musician
1938	**Gaylord Perry.** Hall of Fame professional baseball pitcher who won the Cy Young Award in each of the two major leagues, and had over 300 career wins
1940	**Merlin Olsen.** Professional Hall of Fame football player and actor
1945	**Jessye Norman.** American opera singer and superstar
1946	**Tommy Lee Jones.** American stage, screen and television actor
1946	**Oliver Stone.** American motion-picture director, writer and producer, noted for films such as *Platoon* (1986) and *JFK* (1991)
1961	**Dan Marino.** Professional football player

September 15 – Events

1159	Alexander III was crowned Roman Catholic pope.
1776	The British occupied New York City in the Revolutionary War, forcing George Washington, who fought desperately, to retreat to Harlem Heights.
1789	Congress changed the name of the Department of Foreign Affairs to the Department of State.
1794	James Madison married Dolley Payne Todd.
1810	Miguel Hidalgo y Costilla, the "Father of Mexican Independence," rang the church bells in the village of Dolores and demanded Mexico's independence from Spain.
1812	On Napoleon's first full day of occupation of Moscow, the city mysteriously began to burn. In four days two thirds of Moscow had been destroyed.
1882	The British army occupied Cairo and took control of Egypt, ending the bloody revolt of the Egyptians to free the government of non-Egyptian influence.
1916	The comic strip *Mutt and Jeff,* by Bud Fisher, first appeared under that title.
1916	The British army introduced a new weapon, the tank, in the Battle of Flers-Courcelette in World War I.
1917	Russia was proclaimed a republic by Alexander Kerensky, the head of the provisional government that came to power after the abdication of Czar Nicholas II.
1930	The comic strip *Blondie,* by Chic Young, appeared for the first time.
1938	Prime Minister Neville Chamberlain of England met with Adolf Hitler at Berchtesgaden, and conceded the right of the Sudeten Germans in Czechoslovakia to self determination.
1938	Thomas Wolfe, the great American novelist, died of tuberculosis of the brain in Baltimore at age 37.
1940	The RAF had their greatest day in the Battle of Britain in World War II, destroying 185 German planes.

1942	German armies attacked Stalingrad in World War II.
1949	*The Lone Ranger* premiered on television with Clayton Moore as the masked hero and Jay Silverheels as Tonto.
1949	Konrad Adenauer became the first chancellor of the German Federal Republic.
1950	In a surprise move that changed the course of the Korean War, U.S. troops made an amphibious landing behind enemy lines at Inchon.
1963	Four children were killed when a bomb exploded in a black Baptist church in Birmingham, Alabama, during the racial unrest of the 1960s.
1969	Pitcher Steve Carlton of the St. Louis Cardinals struck out a record 19 batters in a game with the New York Mets.
1978	Muhammad Ali won the heavyweight boxing title for an unprecedented third time, defeating Leon Spinks at the Superdome in New Orleans.

September 16 – Birthdays

1387	**Henry V.** King of England, 1413-1422, who defeated the French in the Battle of Agincourt (1415), one of the most famous victories in English history
1462	**Pietro Pomponazzi.** Italian Renaissance philosopher
1745	**Mikhail Kutuzov.** Russian general who defended Moscow against Napoleon in the Battle of Borodino in 1812
1823	**Francis Parkman.** One of America's greatest historians
1838	**James J. Hill.** American railroad operator and "Empire Builder," who constructed the Great Northern Railway from Lake Superior to Puget Sound, Washington
1875	**J.C. Penney.** American merchant and founder of the J.C. Penney Company
1877	**Jacob Schick.** American industrialist who invented the first practical electric shaver in 1923 and founded the Schick Dry Razor company in 1930
1880	**Alfred Noyes.** English poet noted for "The Highwayman"
1887	**Hans Arp.** French sculptor and painter (known also as Jean Arp), who helped found the Dada movement in Zurich
1888	**Walter Owen Bentley.** English automobile manufacturer and builder of the Bentley car, merged later into the Rolls-Royce Co.
1891	**Karl Doenitz.** German World War II admiral who succeeded Adolf Hitler as German head of state
1911	**Jerry Wald.** American motion-picture producer and screenwriter
1914	**Allen Funt.** American television performer and star of the long-running show *Candid Camera*
1922	**Janis Paige.** American singer and actress
1924	**Lauren Bacall.** American stage and motion-picture actress and star for over 50 years
1925	**Charlie Byrd.** American guitarist

1925	**Charles J. Haughey.** Prime minister of Ireland
1925	**B.B. King.** American blues singer and guitarist
1926	**Robert Schuller.** American clergyman, author, and television evangelist
1927	**Peter Falk.** American motion-picture and television actor
1930	**Anne Francis.** American motion-picture and television actress
1934	**Elgin Baylor.** Professional Hall of Fame basketball player and one of the game's superstars
1934	**George Chakiris.** American motion-picture actor, singer, and dancer
1940	**Earl Buchholz.** American tennis player
1940	**Jim McManus.** American tennis player
1943	**Dennis Conner.** American yachtsman and winner of the America's Cup for the U.S.
1948	**Kenny Jones.** English musician with The Who
1948	**Rosemary Casals.** American tennis player
1949	**Ed Begley Jr.** American actor and son of the noted character actor Ed Begley
1953	**Bob Knapp.** Professional baseball player
1953	**Jerry Pate.** Professional golfer
1954	**Wilbert Montgomery.** Professional football player
1955	**Robin Yount.** Professional baseball player and Hall of Famer
1956	**David Copperfield.** American magician
1958	**Orel Hershiser.** Professional baseball pitcher who won the Cy Young Award in 1988 and pitched a record 59 consecutive scoreless innings
1959	**Tim Raines.** Professional baseball player and superstar

September 16 – Events

335 BC	Alexander the Great destroyed every building in Thebes, Egypt, except the temples and the house of the poet Pindar.
1485	The Beefeaters, or Yeoman Warders, were established in London as the bodyguard of the king or queen by King Henry VII.
1492	Christopher Columbus and his men saw the first patches of seaweed in mid-ocean on the first voyage to America.
1620	The *Mayflower* left Plymouth, England, with 102 Pilgrims bound for America.
1630	The village of Shawmut, Massachusetts, changed its name to Boston.
1810	The Mexican revolution against Spain began, the day after Hidalgo y Costilla rang the church bells in Dolores, demanding Mexican independence.
1893	The Cherokee Strip was opened in Oklahoma to homesteaders. Over 100,000 homesteaders claimed six million acres from the U.S. government.
1908	The General Motors Company, which in 1916 became the General Motors Corporation of today, was incorporated in New Jersey.
1919	Congress granted a national charter to the American Legion.

1940	The Selective Service Act was signed into law by President Franklin D. Roosevelt.
1941	Mohammed Reza Pahlavi became Shah of Iran when the British and Russian occupiers of Iran forced his father Reza Khan to abdicate.
1942	German forces entered Stalingrad in World War II. They were never able to take the city, however.
1945	The British retook Hong Kong from the Japanese after World War II.
1953	*The Robe,* the first movie filmed in CinemaScope, had its world premiere at the Roxy Theater in New York.
1966	The Metropolitan Opera opened in its new opera house at New York's Lincoln Center with the premiere of *Antony and Cleopatra,* by Samuel Barber.

September 17 – Birthdays

1271	**Wenceslas II.** King of Poland, 1300-1305
1550	**Paul V.** Roman Catholic pope, 1605-1621
1676	**Louis Juchereau de Saint Denis.** French founder in 1714 of Natchitoches, Louisiana, the oldest city in the Louisiana Purchase
1730	**Baron von Steuben.** German soldier who helped the Americans in the Revolutionary War
1743	**Marquis de Condorcet.** French mathematician and philosopher, who was one of the leaders of the "Age of Reason" of the late 1700s
1826	**Georg Friedrich Riemann.** German mathematician and one of the most creative of the 19th century, noted for, among other things, the Riemann integral
1855	**David Dunbar Buick.** Pioneer American automobile manufacturer who in 1902 founded the Buick Manufacturing Company
1874	**Ben Turpin.** Slapstick American comedian of the silent screen
1883	**William Carlos Williams.** American physician and poet, who won the 1963 Pulitzer Prize for "Pictures from Breughel"
1890	**Gabriel Heatter.** American radio news broadcaster, noted particularly for his optimistic newscasts during World War II
1900	**John Willard Marriott.** American restaurant entrepreneur, who in 1927 founded the Hot Shoppe chain in Washington, D.C., which in 45 years grew into the Marriott Corporation
1905	**Jerry Colonna.** American comic actor in motion-pictures and on radio
1905	**Dolores Costello.** American motion-picture star of the 1920s, 1930s, and 1940s, and daughter of the famous actor Maurice Costello
1907	**Warren Burger.** U.S. Supreme Court chief justice
1918	**Chaim Herzog.** Israeli statesman and ambassador to the United States
1923	**Charlie Conerly.** Professional football player and superstar

1923   **Hank Williams.** American country and western singer and composer, noted for songs such as "Your Cheating Heart," "Jambalaya," and "Cold, Cold Heart"

1927   **George Blanda.** Professional Hall of Fame football superstar who scored 2,002 points in a 26-year career

1928   **Roddy McDowall.** English-born stage, screen, and television actor

1929   **Stirling Moss.** English automobile racing driver, considered to be one of the world's best

1930   **Edgar D. Mitchell.** U.S. astronaut and member of the *Apollo 14* mission which explored the moon in 1971

1930   **Thomas P. Stafford.** U.S. astronaut and commander of the *Apollo 10* mission

1931   **Anne Bancroft.** American television and motion-picture actress

1933   **Charles E. Grassley.** U.S. senator

1933   **Dorothy Loudon.** American singer and actress

1934   **Maureen Connolly.** First woman to win the grand slam of tennis (1953), and one of the greatest women players of all time

1935   **Ken Kesey.** American writer and author of *One Flew Over the Cuckoo's Nest*

1937   **Lamonte McLemore.** Member of the Fifth Dimension singing group

1939   **David Hackett Souter.** U.S. Supreme Court justice

1940   **Roger Stewart Nichols.** American composer noted for songs such as "We've Only Just Begun"

1944   **Reinhold Messner.** South Tyrolean alpinist and one of the world's greatest mountain climbers

1945   **Phil Jackson.** Professional basketball player and coach

1947   **Jeff MacNelly.** American cartoonist noted for the comic strip *Shoe*

1948   **John Ritter.** American motion-picture and television actor, and son of cowboy actor and singer Tex Ritter

1950   **Fee Waybill.** American singer (*The Tubes*)

1951   **Kermit Washington.** Professional basketball player

1952   **Harold Solomon.** American tennis player

1957   **Earl Cooper.** Professional football player

1960   **Anthony Calvin Carter.** Professional football player

September 17 – Events

1156   The Bavarian East Mark became the Duchy of Austria with a charter from the German emperor, Frederick I Barbarossa.

1771   Tobias Smollett, the noted English novelist, died near Leghorn at age 50.

1787   The Constitutional Convention delegates completed and signed the new Constitution of the United States.

1862   Northern troops under General George B. McClellan defeated General Robert E. Lee in the Battle of Antietam, one of the bloodiest of the Civil War.

1920   The American Professional Football Association, a precursor of the NFL, was formed in Canton, Ohio.

1935   Manuel Quezon was elected as the first president of the Commonwealth of the Philippines.

1939   Russia invaded Poland in World War II, as had been secretly agreed on earlier in the Nazi-Soviet pact.

1940   Adolf Hitler indefinitely postponed Operation Sea Lion, the projected German invasion of the British Isles in World War II.

1946   The first postwar television sets went on sale in the United States.

1947   James V. Forrestal was sworn in as the first U.S. secretary of defense.

1948   Count Folke Bernadotte, U.N. mediator in the war between Israel and the Arab countries, was murdered near Jerusalem.

1972   The comedy-drama series *M*A*S*H* premiered on CBS TV.

1978   Egyptian President Anwar Sadat and Israeli Prime Minister Menachem Begin concluded their summit meeting with President Carter by signing the Camp David agreement for peace.

1983   Vanessa Williams became the first black contestant to be crowned Miss America.

September 18 – Birthdays

1596   **James Shirley.** English playwright and poet who wrote over 40 plays, including works such as *The Maid's Revenge* and *The Gamester*

1709   **Samuel Johnson.** One of the greatest English writers of his day and the subject of James Boswell's famous biography, one of the great works of world literature

1733   **George Read.** Signer of the Declaration of Independence from Delaware, member of the Continental Congress, and member of the Constitutional Convention

1752   **Adrien Marie Legendre.** French mathematician who was an expert in number theory and differential equations, and for whom the Legendre polynomials are named.

1765   **Gregory XVI.** Roman Catholic pope, 1831-1846

1819   **Jean Foucault.** French physicist who measured the speed of light in different media, and discovered the existence of eddy currents in a conductor moving in a magnetic field

1869   **Ellen Hansell.** Hall of Fame tennis player and first U.S. female champion (1887)

1883   **Elmer Henry Maytag.** American manufacturer who developed the modern washing machine and founded the Maytag Co.

1889   **Heinie Groh.** Professional baseball player and manager

1895 **John Diefenbaker.** Prime minister of Canada, 1957-1963

1897 **Sam H. Stept.** Russian-born composer and conductor, noted for songs such as "That's My Weakness Now," "Don't Sit Under the Apple Tree," and "Please Don't Talk About Me When I'm Gone"

1898 **George Uhle.** Professional baseball pitcher with 200 career wins

1901 **Harold Clurman.** American theatrical director and drama critic

1905 **Greta Garbo.** Swedish film actress and one of the screen's greatest stars

1905 **Eddie Anderson.** American actor who played Rochester on the *Jack Benny Show*

1907 **Edwin Mattison McMillan.** American physicist and co-discoverer in 1940 of the elements neptunium and plutonium

1912 **Sarah Palfrey Danzig.** American Hall of Fame tennis player and "sweetheart of tennis"

1916 **Rossano Brazzi.** Italian stage and motion-picture actor with a 50-year career

1916 **John J. Rhodes.** U.S. congressman and minority leader

1920 **Jack Warden.** American stage, screen, and television actor

1925 **Harvey Haddix.** Professional baseball pitcher, who in 1959 pitched 12 perfect innings (no man reached base), only to lose the game in the 13th inning

1929 **Phyllis Kirk.** American motion-picture and television actress

1933 **Mark Di Suvero.** American sculptor

1934 **Robert Blake.** American motion-picture and television actor

1939 **Frankie Avalon.** American singer and actor

1944 **Dick Crealy.** Australian tennis player

1950 **Isabel Fernandez.** Colombian tennis player

1954 **Dennis Johnson.** Professional basketball player and superstar

1955 **Billy Sims.** Professional football player

1959 **Ryne Sandberg.** Professional baseball player

September 18 – Events

96 Marcus Nerva became emperor of Rome after Emperor Domitian was stabbed to death with his wife's help.

1759 The British captured Quebec in the French and Indian War, five days after defeating the French on the Plains of Abraham before the city.

1793 President George Washington laid the cornerstone of the U.S. Capitol in Washington, D.C.

1810 Chile declared its independence from Spain.

1850 Congress passed a new Fugitive Slave Law imposing heavy penalties on persons who aided a slave's escape or interfered with his recovery.

1851 The *New York Times* began publication under the leadership of Henry J. Raymond and two associates.

1927 The Columbia Broadcasting System (CBS) first went on the air with a network of 16 radio stations.

1931 The Japanese invaded Manchuria, marking the beginning of the Sino-Japanese War.

1947 The United States Air Force was created as a separate department.

1949 The British devalued the pound from $4.03 to $2.80.

1961 Dag Hammarskjold, secretary-general of the United Nations, was killed in a plane crash in Africa.

1975 Patricia Hearst, the newspaper heiress, was rescued by the FBI 19 months after being kidnapped by a terrorist organization, and arrested for collaborating with her captors.

September 19 – Birthdays

1551 **Henry III.** King of France, 1574-1589, and the last of the Valois kings

1730 **Augustin Pajou.** French sculptor and decorator

1737 **Charles Carroll.** American lawyer, member of the Continental Congress, and the last surviving signer of the Declaration of Independence

1739 **Andrew Pickens.** American frontiersman and Revolutionary War soldier

1796 **Hartley Coleridge.** English poet and son of the famous poet Samuel Taylor Coleridge

1802 **Lajos Kossuth.** Hungarian national hero of the rebellion of 1848-1849 against Austria

1839 **George Cadbury.** Co-founder of the Cadbury Brothers chocolate manufacturing enterprise

1867 **Arthur Rackham.** English artist and illustrator noted for his work for children's books such as *Peter Pan, Grimm's Fairy Tales,* and *Aesop's Fables*

1889 **Sadie Delany.** American educator and writer, noted for *Having Our Say: The Delany Sisters' First 100 Years* (1993)

1900 **Ferdinand Porsche.** Austrian automotive engineer and son of Ferdinand Porsche, the designer of the German Volkswagen

1902 **James Van Alen.** American Hall of Fame tennis player who developed the Van Alen Simplified Scoring System, and who, with a variation by Peter John, developed the tie-break, in universal use today

1904 **Bergen Evans.** American language expert and television personality

1905 **Leon Jaworski.** Second special prosecutor in the Watergate Case

1907 **Lewis Powell.** U.S. Supreme Court justice

1911 **William Golding.** English novelist noted for *Lord of the Flies* (1954)

1912 **Clifton Daniel.** *New York Times* managing editor and husband of Margaret Truman

1913 **Frances Farmer.** American motion-picture and stage actress

1922 **Willie Pep.** World featherweight champion, 1946-1948 and 1949-1950

1926	**Lurleen Wallace.** Governor of Alabama, 1967-1970, and wife of Alabama governor George C. Wallace

1926   **Lurleen Wallace.** Governor of Alabama, 1967-1970, and wife of Alabama governor George C. Wallace

1926   **Duke Snider.** Hall of Fame baseball player who had 407 career home runs

1927   **Harold Brown.** Secretary of defense under President Carter

1928   **Adam West.** American actor and star of television's *Batman* series

1930   **Bob Turley.** Professional baseball player

1932   **Mike Royko.** American newspaper columnist

1933   **David McCallum.** Scottish motion-picture and television actor

1934   **Brian Epstein.** Manager of The Beatles, 1962-1967

1937   **Orlando Cepeda.** Professional baseball player and Hall of Famer

1940   **Paul Williams.** American singer, composer, and actor, noted for songs such as "We've Only Just Begun," "An Old Fashioned Love Song," "Family of Man," and "Let Me Be the One"

1941   **Cass Elliot.** American singer and member of The Mamas and the Papas

1943   **Joe Morgan.** Professional baseball player and Hall of Famer

1945   **Jane Blalock.** Professional golfer

1946   **Joe Ferguson.** Professional baseball player

1947   **Larry Brown.** Professional football player

1948   **Jeremy Irons.** British stage, screen, and television actor who won the Academy Award for best actor in *Reversal of Fortune* (1990)

1949   **Kerry Harris.** Australian tennis player

1949   **Sidney Wicks.** Professional basketball player

1949   **Twiggy.** English model and motion-picture actress

1950   **Joan Lunden.** Hostess of the television program *Good Morning America*

1951   **Nathaniel Moore.** Professional football player

September 19 – Events

1356   Edward, the Black Prince of England, defeated the French in the Battle of Poitiers, and captured King John II of France, in the Hundred Years' War.

1777   The First Battle of Freeman's Farm near Saratoga, New York, began, in the Revolutionary War. The series of battles ended a month later with the surrender of the British army.

1783   Etienne Montgolfier sent a sheep, a duck, and a rooster up a height of one mile in a balloon in Versailles, France, the first time animals had gone aloft in a manmade craft.

1796   President George Washington's Farewell Address first appeared in print, in the *American Daily Advertiser*, a Philadelphia newspaper.

1846   English poets Robert Browning and Elizabeth Barrett eloped to Pisa a week after their secret marriage, during which time they had seen each other only a few minutes.

1859   The Confederate war song "Dixie" was sung for the first time, by its composer, actor Daniel Decatur Emmett, in a New York minstrel show.

1863   The Civil War Battle of Chickamauga began between Union general Rosecrans and Confederate general Bragg. It ended the following day in victory for the South.

1881   President James A. Garfield died of a gun shot inflicted by an assassin on July 2, 1881.

1928   Walt Disney's Mickey Mouse first appeared, in the animated cartoon *Steamboat Willie,* at the Colony Theater in New York.

1934   Bruno Richard Hauptmann was arrested in New York and charged with kidnapping and killing the baby son of Charles A. Lindbergh in 1932.

1955   Juan Peron was deposed as president of Argentina.

1991   The "iceman," the body of a 5,300 year-old Stone Age wanderer, was found in the melting Similaun glacier high in the Alps near the Austrian-Italian border by a German tourist, Helmut Simon. The iceman was the most ancient human being ever found virtually intact.

September 20 – Birthdays

356 BC   **Alexander The Great.** King of Macedonia and one of the greatest generals in history

1762   **Pierre Leonard Fontaine.** French architect

1819   **Theodore Chasseriau.** French painter

1833   **Petroleum Nasby.** American humorist (born David Ross Locke) of the Civil War era, whose humor was especially enjoyed by President Lincoln

1872   **Maurice Gamelin.** French World War II general and chief of staff of the French army, whose endless delays in fighting contributed to the success of the Nazi blitzkrieg in France in 1940

1873   **Robert Duffield Wrenn.** American Hall of Fame tennis player and four times National Singles Champion

1878   **Upton Sinclair.** American writer and "muckraker," best known for his novel *The Jungle* (1906), which exposed conditions in the meat packing industry and resulted in the first pure food laws

1885   **Ferdinand "Jelly Roll" Morton.** American jazz and blues pianist and bandleader noted for "The Jelly Roll Blues"

1886   **Sister Elizabeth Kenny.** Noted Australian nurse who developed a special method of treating poliomyelitis

1892   **Roy Turk.** American lyricist noted for songs such as "Where the Blue of the Night Meets the Gold of the Day," "Gimme a Little Kiss, Will Ya Huh?" "Walkin' My Baby Back Home," and "I'll Get By"

1898   **Chuck Dressen.** Professional baseball player and manager

1901   **Gus Edson.** American cartoonist, creator of the comic strip *Dondi,* and continuer of the comic strip *The Gumps,* after the death of its creator, Sidney Smith

1908   **Zeke Bonura.** Professional baseball player
1911   **Frank De Vol.** American composer, conductor, and arranger
1917   **Fernando Rey.** Spanish motion-picture actor
1917   **Red Auerbach.** Longtime coach of the Boston Celtics basketball team
1924   **Anne Meara.** American comedienne and actress
1924   **Gogi Grant.** American singer who in the 1950s popularized "The Wayward Wind"
1926   **Charles Bluhdorn.** American corporation executive
1927   **Rachel Roberts.** Welsh motion-picture actress
1934   **Sophia Loren.** Italian motion-picture actress who won the Academy Award for her performance in *Two Women* (1961)
1951   **Guy Lafleur.** Professional hockey player
1953   **Randy Grossman.** Professional football player

September 20 – Events

451   The Romans defeated Attila the Hun at Chalons-sur-Marne in France.
1378   The cardinals elected Clement VII pope shortly after they had elected Urban VI. This rivalry caused the "Great Schism of the West" in the Catholic Church that lasted 40 years.
1519   Ferdinand Magellan set sail from Sanlucar, Spain, with five ships and 240 men on his voyage that would become the first trip around the world.
1863   The Battle of Chickamauga ended in victory for the Confederate troops under General Bragg in the Civil War.
1870   Two German armies began a 135-day siege of Paris in the Franco-Prussian War.
1873   The New York Stock Exchange closed its doors as the Panic of 1873 reached its peak.
1881   Chester A. Arthur was sworn in as president, succeeding President James A. Garfield, who had died the previous day.
1906   Upton Sinclair published *The Jungle,* his famous novel that rocked the meat-packing industry and led to the nation's first pure food law.
1920   The comic strip *Winnie Winkle,* by Martin Branner, first appeared.
1973   Billie Jean King, the reigning women's tennis champion, defeated Bobby Riggs, the men's champion 30 years earlier, in a tennis match before 30,492 people in the Houston Astrodome.
1978   Russian cosmonauts Kovalyonok and Ivanchenko broke the space-flight endurance record after 96 days of a flight that would last 139 days.

September 21 – Birthdays

454   **Flavius Actius.** Roman general and statesman
1411   **Richard, Duke of York.** English statesman and father of Kings Richard III and Edward IV

1452   **Girolamo Savonarola.** Florentine preacher and reformer, who was hanged and his body burned in 1498 for his fiery criticism of Pope Alexander VI
1737   **Francis Hopkinson.** Signer of the Declaration of Independence who was a writer, musician, and artist, as well as a lawyer and a political leader
1756   **John Loudon McAdam.** British engineer who originated the macadam type of road surface, and was the first to realize that pavement is useful only as a smooth surface and for keeping the soil dry
1788   **Margaret Mackall Smith Taylor.** Wife of President Zachary Taylor
1855   **Sara Delano Roosevelt.** Mother of President Franklin D. Roosevelt
1863   **John Bunny.** The first comic star of the American screen
1866   **H.G. Wells.** English novelist and historian, noted for works such as *The Time Machine* (1895) and *The War of the Worlds* (1898)
1867   **Henry L. Stimson.** U.S. cabinet member for three presidents: William Howard Taft, Herbert Hoover, and Franklin D. Roosevelt
1876   **Julio Gonzales.** Spanish sculptor
1885   **Harold Tucker Webster.** American cartoonist and creator of Caspar Milquetoast, the titular hero of his comic strip, *The Timid Soul*
1893   **Frank Willard.** American cartoonist and creator of *Moon Mullins*
1903   **Preston Tucker.** American automobile manufacturer noted for the rear-engine Tucker car in the 1940s
1909   **Kwame Nkrumah.** First president of Ghana, 1960-1966
1910   **Eldon Auker.** Professional baseball player
1912   **Chuck Jones.** American cartoon animator, writer, and creator of Bugs Bunny and Porky Pig
1920   **Jay Ward.** American cartoonist and creator with Bill Scott of Bullwinkle Moose (1959)
1924   **Gail Russell.** American motion-picture actress
1930   **Dawn Addams.** English stage, screen, and television actress
1931   **Larry Hagman.** American motion-picture and television actor and son of actress Mary Martin
1935   **Henry Gibson.** American actor and comedian
1942   **Sam McDowell.** Professional baseball player
1944   **Fannie Flagg.** American comedienne and author
1944   **Hamilton Jordan.** White House assistant to President Jimmy Carter
1944   **Charles Harraway Jr.** Professional football player
1947   **Don Felder.** American musician and songwriter with The Eagles
1947   **Stephen King.** American novelist noted for his horror stories, such as *The Stand, Carrie, The Shining*, and *Children of the Corn*
1947   **Reginald Rucker.** Professional football player
1949   **Artis Gilmore.** Professional basketball player
1950   **Bill Murray.** American actor and comedian

1962 **Rob Morrow.** American stage, screen and television actor
1963 **Cecil Fielder.** Professional baseball player who hit 51 home runs in 1990
1968 **Ricki Lake.** American stage, screen, and television actress and syndicated talk show hostess

September 21 – Events

19 BC Virgil, the great Roman poet, died in Rome at age 50.
1327 King Edward II of England was cruelly murdered by two English knights, after being deposed and imprisoned by his wife Isabelle and her lover Mortimer.
1776 Nathan Hale, the famous American patriot of the Revolutionary War, was captured by the British.
1779 The Battle of Baton Rouge ended British hopes of controlling the Mississippi basin in the American Revolutionary War.
1780 Benedict Arnold, the American Revolutionary War traitor, met with British officer John Andre to arrange the surrender to the British of the American fort at West Point.
1792 The French National Convention voted to abolish France's monarchy.
1832 Sir Walter Scott, the great Scottish novelist, died at his Abbotsford, his famous estate, at age 61.
1893 Frank Duryea drove the first successful gasoline-powered car in America, on the streets of Springfield, Mass. It was a one-cylinder model designed by him and his brother Charles.
1897 The famous editorial "Yes, Virginia, there is a Santa Claus" first appeared, in the New York *Sun*.
1937 J.R.R. Tolkien first published *The Hobbit,* the famous forerunner of the epic volumes *The Lord of the Rings.*
1938 The Czechs, yielding to pressure from Britain and France, agreed to cede the Sudetan German area of their country to Hitler. The Czech cabinet then promptly resigned.
1949 The Chinese Communist victors in the Chinese Civil War proclaimed the formation of the People's Republic of China.
1949 West Germany came into existence with the formation of a national cabinet.
1955 Rocky Marciano retained his heavyweight boxing title, knocking out Archie Moore for his 49th professional victory.

September 22 – Birthdays

1515 **Anne of Cleves.** Fourth wife of King Henry VIII of England, and one of the rare ones who was not executed
1694 **Lord Chesterfield.** English statesman and writer (Philip Dormer Stanhope), noted for his 400 witty and sensible letters to his son, published in 1774, soon after Chesterfield's death

1725 **Joseph Siffred Duplessis.** French painter noted for works such as *Benjamin Franklin* (1778)
1765 **Paolo Ruffini.** Italian mathematician and physician noted for his contributions to group theory
1791 **Michael Faraday.** One of the greatest English chemists and physicists, who in 1831 discovered the principle of the electric motor and generator
1878 **Yoshida Shigeru.** Prime minister of Japan after World War II.
1882 **Wilhelm Keitel.** Chief of the German supreme command in World War II, who was tried in Nuremberg and executed
1885 **Erich Von Stroheim.** Austrian-American motion-picture actor and director of both the silent and talking era, noted for his direction of the authentic classic *Greed* (1923)
1891 **Edward Joseph Flynn.** American political leader of the New Deal Era
1894 **Dave Dreyer.** American composer noted for songs such as "Me and My Shadow" and "You Can't Be True, Dear"
1895 **Paul Muni.** Austrian stage and motion-picture actor, who won the Academy Award in 1936 for *The Story of Louis Pasteur*
1902 **Howard Jarvis.** American social activist and principal author of California Proposition 13 to cut taxes
1902 **John Houseman.** Romanian-born director, writer, and actor, who produced Orson Welles's *Citizen Kane* (1941), one of the greatest movies of all time
1903 **Fred Glickman.** American composer and violinist, noted for songs such as "Mule Train"
1904 **Joe Valachi.** American organized crime informant
1909 **David Riesman.** American sociologist and co-author of *The Lonely Crowd*
1912 **Alfred Gwynne Vanderbilt.** American horse breeder and president of the New York Racing Association
1914 **Martha Scott.** American stage, screen, and television actress
1917 **Richard C. Hottelot.** American broadcast journalist
1920 **Bob Lemon.** Hall of Fame baseball player and manager
1927 **Tom Lasorda.** Hall of Fame professional baseball player and manager
1932 **Ingemar Johansson.** Heavyweight boxing champion, 1959-1960
1946 **Larry Dierker.** Professional baseball player and manager
1948 **Mark Phillips.** Husband of England's Princess Anne
1949 **Harold Carmichael.** Professional football player
1951 **Arthur O. Sulzberger Jr.** Publisher of the *New York Times*
1952 **Ken Schroy.** Professional football player
1954 **Shari Belafonte-Harper.** American television and motion-picture and daughter of singer Harry Belafonte

1954   **Paul Kronk.** Australian tennis player
1956   **Debby Boone.** American singer and daughter of singer Pat Boone
1959   **Wally Backman.** Professional baseball player
1960   **Joan Jett.** American singer-musician (*The Runaways*)
1961   **Catherine Oxenberg.** American television and motion-picture actress
1961   **Vince Coleman.** Professional baseball player
1962   **Scott Baio.** American motion-picture and television actor

September 22 – Events

1503   Pius III was elected Roman Catholic pope.
1692   The last persons were hanged in the American colonies for witchcraft, in Salem, Massachusetts.
1776   The famous American patriot Nathan Hale was hanged as a spy by the British. His last words were, "I only regret that I have but one life to lose for my country."
1780   Charles Lynch gave the language the word *lynch* when he announced that he and his countrymen would properly punish the Tories who were plundering their Virginia land.
1792   The French National Convention met and declared France a republic.
1862   President Lincoln issued his preliminary Emancipation Proclamation, stating that if the South did not quit the Civil War by January 1, 1863, he would free the slaves.
1911   Cy Young, baseball's winningest pitcher, won his 511th and last game at age 44, as Young's team, the Boston Braves, beat the Pittsburgh Pirates, 1-0.
1927   Gene Tunney defeated Jack Dempsey in their second match, which was noted for the controversial "long count" in the seventh round.
1940   Japan invaded French Indochina.
1950   Omar Bradley was promoted to five-star general, joining Dwight Eisenhower, Douglas MacArthur, George Marshall and Hap Arnold as America's only five-star generals.
1960   The Sudan Republic became the Republic of Mali.
1964   *Fiddler on the Roof*, the long-running musical, opened on Broadway for the first of 3,242 performances.
1969   Willy Mays of the San Francisco Giants hit his 600th home run, becoming the first player since Babe Ruth to hit this many.
1975   President Gerald Ford escaped a bullet fired at him in San Francisco by would-be assassin Sara Jane Moore.
1981   The U.S. Senate confirmed the nomination of Sandra Day O'Connor to become the first woman justice on the U.S. Supreme Court.

September 23 – Birthdays

63 BC   **Augustus (Octavian).** Roman emperor at the time of Christ, and the founder in 27 B.C. of the Roman Empire as it was known after the end of the Roman Republic of Julius Caesar's time
1745   **John Sevier.** Governor of "The lost state of Franklin" and the first governor of Tennessee
1800   **William Holmes McGuffey.** American educator and clergyman, noted for the McGuffey readers, published from 1836 to 1857
1838   **Victoria Claflin Woodhull.** First woman presidential candidate (1872)
1859   **Thomas Mott Osborne.** American prison reformer and writer, who organized the Mutual Welfare League to help prisoners rebuild their lives
1862   **James W. Blake.** American composer, noted for "Sidewalks of New York"
1884   **Eugene Talmadge.** Governor of Georgia who served three terms and was elected to a fourth but died before being inaugurated
1889   **Walter Lippmann.** American political commentator, columnist, writer, and editor, who won the 1962 Pulitzer Prize
1890   **Friedrich Paulus.** German World War II field marshal who surrendered to the Russians at Stalingrad
1898   **Walter Pidgeon.** American stage and motion-picture actor and veteran of over 200 silents and 70 talkies
1899   **Tom Clark.** U.S. Supreme Court justice, 1949-1967
1900   **Louise Nevelson.** Russian-born American sculptor, best known for her large wooden constructions, or *assemblages*
1902   **Ayatollah Ruhollah Khomeini.** Iranian religious leader and head of the revolutionary government that toppled the Shah
1910   **Elliott Roosevelt.** Son of President Franklin D. Roosevelt
1913   **Stanley Kramer.** American motion-picture producer and director, noted for films such as *High Noon* (1952) and *Judgment at Nuremberg* (1961)
1916   **Aldo Moro.** Prime minister of Italy, 1963-1968
1920   **Mickey Rooney.** American stage, screen, and television actor, with a career of over 65 years
1926   **John Coltrane.** American saxophonist
1932   **Ray Charles.** American pianist, singer, and composer
1938   **Romy Schneider.** Austrian stage and motion-picture actress
1939   **Roy Buchanan.** American guitarist
1943   **Julio Iglesias.** Spanish popular singer and one of the best-selling musical artists in the history of recording, with over 100 million record sales
1949   **Bruce Springsteen.** American singer, guitarist, and songwriter, noted for songs such as "Blinded By the Light"
1952   **Dennis Lamp.** Professional baseball player

1959   **Jason Alexander.** American stage, screen and television actor

September 23 – Events

480 BC   The Battle of Salamis, Greece, the greatest of ancient naval battles, was won by Greece over Persia. Over 1,000 Persian ships were sunk by fewer than 400 Greek vessels.

1492   The crew of Columbus sighted a dove, leading them to think land was near on the first voyage to America.

1588   The Duke of Medina Sidonia's flagship *San Martin* made port at Santander, Spain, with 43 other ships, survivors of the 130-ship Spanish Armada. Some 20 others arrived later.

1642   Harvard College held its first commencement exercises.

1779   John Paul Jones's *Bonhomme Richard* captured the British ship *Serapis*. During the battle when asked to surrender, Jones replied, "I have not yet begun to fight."

1780   British spy John Andre was captured by American militiamen, who found papers on him revealing Benedict Arnold's plot to surrender West Point to the British.

1806   The Lewis and Clark Expedition came to an end as the explorers completed their homeward trip to St. Louis.

1845   The Knickerbocker Baseball Club was organized in New York.

1846   The planet Neptune was discovered with a telescope by Johann Galle from the Urania Observatory in Berlin.

1912   The first Mack Sennett *Keystone Kops Comedy* film was released.

1926   Gene Tunney won the heavyweight championship title from Jack Dempsey in ten rounds in Philadelphia.

1938   At a Godesburg meeting Adolf Hitler demanded of an astonished Neville Chamberlain that the Czechs cede much more of their country to Germany than had been agreed to earlier.

1939   Sigmund Freud, the great psychoanalyst, died of cancer in London at age 83.

1952   Rocky Marciano won the heavyweight championship title from Jersey Joe Walcott with a 13th-round knockout in Philadelphia.

1952   Vice presidential candidate Richard Nixon made his "Checkers speech," in which he referred to his dog Checkers in a television appeal to keep himself on the Eisenhower ticket.

September 24 – Birthdays

15   **Aulus Vitellius.** Emperor of Rome who served less than one year in A.D. 69

1501   **Girolamo Cardano.** Italian physician, mathematician, and astrologer, who though he stole his fellow mathematician Tartaglia's solution to the cubic equation and published it as his own, he was still a mathematical genius who helped lead the way to a solution of the quartic equation

1583   **Albrecht Wenzel von Wallenstein.** Bohemian soldier, one of the most important figures of the Thirty Years' War, and the most famous military commander of his age

1717   **Horace Walpole.** English letter writer, art lover, and author of *The Castle of Otranto* (1764), the first of the so-called Gothic novels

1739   **Grigori Aleksandrovich Potemkin.** Russian statesman and field marshal, and favorite of Catherine the Great

1755   **John Marshall.** The "great chief justice" of the U.S. Supreme Court, and the fourth man to hold the position, 1801-1835

1837   **Mark Hanna.** American industrialist and political kingmaker, who was the power behind President William McKinley's elections

1843   **Adam Willis Wagnalls.** American publisher who with Isaac Funk founded Funk and Wagnalls publishing house (1890)

1871   **Little Dod.** British tennis player and five times Wimbledon singles champion

1884   **Ismet Inonu.** President of Turkey who succeeded Kemal Ataturk in 1938

1889   **Charles C. Mars.** American confectioner who in 1923 founded Mars, Inc., the famous maker of candy bars such as Milky Way and Snickers

1890   **Allen J. Ellender.** U.S. senator, 1935-1980

1896   **F. Scott Fitzgerald.** The leading writer and glittering hero of America's "Roaring Twenties," noted for works such as *The Great Gatsby* (1925) and *Tender Is the Night* (1934)

1907   **Ben Oakland.** American composer and pianist, noted for songs such as "I'll Dance At Your Wedding"

1910   **Dixie Walker.** Professional baseball player

1912   **John Kluczko (Johnny Watson).** American composer noted for songs such as "Racing With the Moon" (with bandleader-lyricist Vaughn Monroe, who adopted it as his theme song)

1921   **Jim McKay.** American television sportscaster

1921   **Larry Markes.** American composer and author, noted for songs such as "Along the Navajo Trail" and "Mad About Him, Sad About Him, How Can I Be Glad Without Him Blues"

1924   **Sheila MacRae.** American comedienne

1930   **John W. Young.** American astronaut and copilot of *Gemini 3*

1931   **Anthony Newley.** English singer and actor

1932   **Joanne Greenberg.** American author noted for the autobiographical novel *I Never Promised You a Rose Garden* (1964)

1936   **Jim Henson.** American puppeteer

1942 **Linda McCartney.** Member of the rock band Wings and wife of Beatle musician Paul McCartney

1946 **Mean Joe Greene.** Professional Hall of Fame football player

1951 **Terry Metcalf.** Professional football player

1952 **Joseph P. Kennedy III.** U.S. Congressman and son of Robert F. Kennedy

1953 **Joe Washington.** Professional football player

1955 **Christopher Wells.** English tennis player

1956 **Hubie Brooks.** Professional baseball player

1964 **Rafael Palmeiro.** Professional baseball player and superstar

September 24 – Events

768 Pepin the Short, King of the Franks and father of the great Charlemagne, died at age 54.

1492 Columbus's fleet met variable winds and calm, and the sailors mistakenly believed they sighted land, on the first voyage to America.

1742 Faneuil Hall in Boston was opened to the public.

1789 Congress passed the First Judiciary Act, providing for an attorney general and a Supreme Court.

1846 Monterrey fell to U.S. general Zachary Taylor in the Mexican War.

1862 Otto von Bismarck became prime minister of Prussia.

1869 Black Friday occurred on Wall Street when Jim Fiske and Jay Gould tried to corner the market on gold. They made $11 million in the resulting crash.

1905 Sweden agreed to Norway's independence.

1906 Victor Herbert's operetta *The Red Mill* had its premiere at the Knickerbocker Theater in New York.

1934 Babe Ruth made his farewell as a New York Yankee player at Yankee Stadium. He had been sold to Pittsburgh as a player-coach.

1955 President Dwight D. Eisenhower suffered a heart attack while vacationing in Denver.

1956 Grace Metalious published her sensational sex novel *Peyton Place*.

1957 President Eisenhower dispatched U.S. troops to Little Rock, Arkansas, to enforce school integration at Central High.

1963 The U.S. Senate ratified the treaty with Great Britain and the Soviet Union limiting nuclear testing.

September 25 – Birthdays

1403 **Louis III.** Duke of Anjou

1599 **Francesco Borromini.** Italian architect, who, with Giovanni Lorenzo Bernini, led the baroque movement

1683 **Jean Philippe Rameau.** French composer and theorist, whose *Treatise of Harmony* (1722) is a landmark in the development of modern theories of harmony

1807 **Alfred Lewis Vail.** American inventor who perfected the code used with Samuel F.B. Morse's telegraph

1877 **Plutarco Elias Calles.** Mexican reformer and president, 1924-1928

1887 **May Sutton Bundy.** First American tennis player to win at Wimbledon (1905)

1897 **William Faulkner.** One of the leading American novelists of the 20th century, noted for works such as *The Sound and the Fury* (1929) and *The Reivers* (1962)

1902 **Al Hoffman.** Russian-born composer noted for songs such as "Heartaches," "Goodnight, Wherever You Are," "There's No Tomorrow," "Papa Loves Mambo," "I Apologize," and "Mairzy Doats"

1905 **Red Smith.** American sports writer

1906 **Dmitri Shostakovich.** One of the leading Russian composers of the 20th century

1917 **Johnny Sain.** Professional baseball player and coach

1918 **Phil Rizzuto.** Hall of Fame professional baseball player and sportscaster

1921 **Robert David Muldoon.** Prime minister of New Zealand

1926 **Aldo Ray.** American motion-picture and television actor

1926 **John Ericson.** American stage, screen, and television actor

1927 **Carl Braun.** Professional basketball player who scored a career total of over 10,000 points

1931 **Barbara Walters.** American television newscaster and interviewer

1932 **Adolfo Suarez Gonzalez.** Prime minister of Spain

1932 **Glenn Gould.** Canadian pianist, noted for his interpretations of the works of Bach

1933 **Hubie Brown.** Professional basketball coach

1933 **Erik Darling.** American singer and musician with The Weavers musical group

1936 **Juliet Prowse.** South African actress and dancer

1944 **Michael Douglas.** American actor, producer, and son of actor Kirk Douglas

1947 **Cheryl Tiegs.** American model and television personality

1949 **Jeff Borowiak.** American tennis player

1951 **Bob McAdoo.** Professional basketball player

1952 **Mark Hamill.** American motion-picture and television actor

1952 **Christopher Reeve.** American motion-picture actor

1957 **Glenn Hubbard.** Professional baseball player

1961 **Heather Locklear.** American television actress (*Melrose Place*)

1965 **Scottie Pippen.** Professional basketball player

1968 **Will Smith.** American motion-picture actor

September 25 – Events

1493 Christopher Columbus left Cadiz, Spain, on his second voyage to America with 17 ships and 1,000 men.

1513 Spanish explorer Vasco Nunez de Balboa discovered the Pacific Ocean from a mountaintop in what is now Panama.

1555 The Peace of Augsburg legalized the Lutheran-Roman Catholic split in Germany.

1690 America's first newspaper, *Publick Occurrences,* a four-page "newspaper," was published in Boston by Benjamin Harris.

1775 American Revolutionary War hero Ethan Allen was captured by the British as he led an attack on Montreal.

1789 The U.S. Congress proposed 12 amendments to the Constitution and sent them to the states for ratification. Ten of them were ratified and became the Bill of Rights in 1791.

1804 The 12th Amendment to the Constitution went into effect, providing for separate electoral ballots for the offices of president and vice president.

1890 Mormon President Wilford Woodruff issued a church statement formally renouncing polygamy.

1890 Congress established Yosemite National Park in California.

1919 President Woodrow Wilson collapsed from fatigue and nervous tension in Pueblo, Colorado, while on a speaking tour of the West attempting to sell the League of Nations to the public.

1955 The comic strip *Dondi,* by Gus Edson and Irwin Hasen, first appeared.

1957 Nine black students who had been forced to withdraw from Central High School in Little Rock, Arkansas, were escorted to classes with 300 U.S. Army troops standing guard.

1962 Sonny Liston won the heavyweight boxing title by knocking out Floyd Patterson in the first round in Chicago.

September 26 – Birthdays

1580 **Francisco de Quevedo.** The leading Spanish humanist of the 1600s, and author of *Life of the Swindler* (1626)

1651 **Francis Daniel Pastorius.** German lawyer and scholar, who founded Germantown, Pennsylvania, in 1683

1729 **Moses Mendelssohn.** Jewish philosopher and grandfather of the great composer Felix Mendelssohn

1774 **Johnny Appleseed.** American pioneer (John Chapman) who became a legendary figure because of the ardent way he distributed apple seeds and sprouts in central and northern Ohio in the early 1800s

1783 **Jane Taylor.** English poet known for *Twinkle Twinkle, Little Star*

1791 **Theodore Gericault.** French artist noted for vivid pictures of horses and of events of his day

1849 **Ivan Petrovich Pavlov.** Nobel Prize-winning Russian physiologist, noted for the concept of the conditioned reflex

1862 **Arthur Bowen Davies.** American painter and illustrator and member of the group of realistic painters known as The Eight

1869 **Winsor McCay.** American cartoonist noted for many comic creations, the most famous of which is *Gertie, the Trained Dinosaur*

1870 **Christian X.** King of Denmark during the Nazi occupation in World War II

1875 **Edmund Gwenn.** Veteran American stage and screen actor, who won an Academy Award for his part in *Miracle on 34th Street* (1947)

1888 **T.S. Eliot.** One of the most important poets of the 20th century, and author of such works as *The Waste Land* (1922) and *Murder in the Cathedral* (1935)

1888 **J. Frank Dobie.** American author and educator, and a leading collector of Texas lore and folk tales

1891 **Charles Munch.** Conductor of the Boston Symphony Orchestra, 1949-1962

1895 **George Raft.** American stage, screen, and television actor with a 50-year career

1897 **Paul VI.** Roman Catholic pope, 1963-1978

1898 **George Gershwin.** Popular American composer, noted for such works as *Rhapsody in Blue* (1924) and *Porgy and Bess* (1935), the most popular opera ever written by an American

1901 **Ted Weems.** American bandleader of the Big Band Era and composer of songs such as "The Martins and the Coys"

1915 **Frankie Brimsek.** Hall of Fame hockey player

1919 **Barbara Britton.** American motion-picture actress

1925 **Bobby Shantz.** Professional baseball player

1925 **Marty Robbins.** American country singer

1926 **Julie London.** American singer and actress

1927 **Patrick O'Neal.** American stage, screen, and television actor

1934 **Greg Morris.** American television actor

1946 **Christine Todd Whitman.** Governor of New Jersey

1947 **Lucius Allen.** Professional basketball player

1947 **Lynn Anderson.** American country music artist

1948 **Olivia Newton-John.** Australian popular music singer and actress

1949 **Jane Smiley.** American novelist noted for works such as *A Thousand Acres* for which she won the Pulitzer Prize in 1992

1951 **David Casper.** Professional football player

1957 **Linda Hamilton.** American motion-picture and television actress

1962 **Melissa Sue Anderson.** American television actress

September 26 – Events

1580   Sir Frances Drake, the great English seaman, reached Plymouth, England, returning from his round-the-world voyage, the second such trip in history.

1777   The British occupied Philadelphia in the Revolutionary War.

1789   Thomas Jefferson was appointed first secretary of state, John Jay first chief justice, Samuel Osgood first postmaster-general, and Edmund Randolph first attorney general.

1815   The Holy Alliance was signed in Paris, pledging most of the monarchs of Europe to act in accordance with Christian principles.

1820   The famous pioneer Daniel Boone died in Missouri at the age of 85.

1889   Emile Berliner, the noted German-American inventor, obtained the first U.S. patent on a flat disc Gramophone.

1892   John Philip Sousa, the great American composer and bandmaster, presented his first public concert, playing for the first time his "Liberty Bell March."

1914   The Federal Trade Commission was established by Congress.

1934   The Cunard liner *Queen Mary* was launched.

1937   Bessie Smith, "Empress of the Blues," died in a car crash in Coahama, Mississippi.

1938   Adolf Hitler, in a speech at the Sportpalast in Berlin, promised that if the "Czech problem" were solved, he would have no further territorial claims in Europe.

1950   United Nations troops captured Seoul, Korea, from the North Koreans in the Korean War.

1960   Presidential candidates John F. Kennedy and Richard M. Nixon met in Chicago for the first of their historic television "Great Debates."

1969   The Beatles released "Abbey Road," the last album they recorded.

1971   Hirohito became the first Japanese emperor to set foot on U.S. soil, meeting President Nixon in Alaska.

September 27 – Birthdays

1389   **Cosimo de Medici.** Italian ruler of Florence and grandfather of Lorenzo de Medici (The Magnificent)

1601   **Louis XIII.** King of France, 1610-1643

1627   **Jacques Benigne Bossuet.** French preacher, theologian, and historian, and one of the greatest masters of eloquence in sermons

1655   **Domenico Guglielmini.** A founder of the Italian school of hydraulics

1722   **Samuel Adams.** American revolutionary patriot, one of the organizers of the Boston Tea Party, and the leading spokesman for American independence

1783   **Agustin de Iturbide.** Emperor of Mexico for ten months, 1922-1923

1792   **George Cruikshank.** English artist and caricaturist, noted for his illustrations for the books of Charles Dickens, Oliver Goldsmith, Henry Fielding, and Miguel de Cervantes

1809   **Raphael Semmes.** Rear admiral in the Confederate Navy who commanded the famous ship *Alabama* in the Civil War

1840   **Thomas Nast.** One of the greatest American political cartoonists of all time, noted especially for popularizing the Democratic donkey and originating the Republican elephant symbols

1840   **Alfred Thayer Mahan.** American admiral, one of the world's great authorities on sea power, and the author of the famous book *The Influence of Sea Power upon History, 1660-1783* (1890)

1842   **Henry Alden Sherwin.** American entrepreneur who with Edwin Porter Williams founded the Sherwin-Williams Paint Co. in 1870

1874   **Myrtle Reed.** American author noted for *Lavender and Old Lace* (1902)

1881   **William J. Clothier.** American Hall of Fame tennis player and 1900 Singles Champion of the United States

1885   **Joseph McCarthy.** American lyricist noted for songs such as "You Made Me Love You," "I'm Always Chasing Rainbows," and "Alice Blue Gown"

1898   **Sam Ervin.** U.S. senator and chairman of the Senate committee investigating the Watergate charges in 1973

1898   **Vincent Millie Youmans.** American composer noted for songs such as "No, No, Nanette," "Tea for Two," "I Want to Be Happy," "More Than You Know," "Time on My Hands," and "The Carioca"

1901   **Beasley Smith.** American composer, author, and pianist, noted for songs such as "That Lucky Old Sun," "Beg Your Pardon," "The Old Master Painter," and "Night Train to Memphis"

1907   **Whitlow Wyatt.** Professional baseball player

1914   **Catherine Marshall.** Wife of religious leader Peter Marshall and author of *A Man Called Peter* (1951)

1914   **Jim Lee Howell.** Professional football player

1917   **Louis Auchinloss.** American lawyer and novelist, and author of works such as *The Great World and Timothy Colt* (1956)

1919   **Charles H. Percy.** U.S. senator

1920   **William Conrad.** American motion-picture and television actor and star of the long-running TV series *Cannon*

1922   **Arthur Penn.** American writer and stage and motion-picture director, noted for films such as *The Miracle Worker* (1962)

1923   **Jayne Meadows.** American television actress

1924   **Bud Powell.** American pianist, composer, and modern jazz pioneer

1927   **Gardner Dickinson.** Professional golfer

1930   **Dick Hall.** Professional baseball player

1934   **Wilford Brimley.** American motion-picture and television actor

1934	**Greg Morris.** American television actor (*Mission Impossible*)
1934	**Dick Schaap.** American sportscaster
1938	**Don Farmer.** American broadcast journalist
1939	**Kathy Whitworth.** Professional golfer
1948	**Meat Loaf.** American musician and actor (born Marvin Aday)
1949	**Mike Schmidt.** Professional baseball player and Hall of Famer with 548 career home runs
1959	**Shaun Cassidy.** American singer and actor

September 27 – Events

1066	William the Conqueror, with a Norman army of 5,000 men, set sail from France for England, to claim the English throne.
1825	George Stephenson, in England, operated the first locomotive to haul a passenger train.
1854	The first great Atlantic Ocean liner disaster occurred when the steamship *Arctic* sank with 300 people aboard.
1917	Edgar Degas, the famous French painter, died in Paris at age 83.
1938	The Cunard liner *Queen Elizabeth* was launched at Glasgow.
1939	Warsaw surrendered to the Nazis in World War II.
1940	Germany, Italy, and Japan signed the Pact of Berlin, a ten-year mutual military aid agreement.
1950	Ezzard Charles retained his heavyweight championship title by defeating Joe Louis, the former champion, who was trying to come back from retirement.
1954	NBC's *Tonight Show* made its television debut with Steve Allen as its host.
1954	A U.S. Senate select committee recommended a Senate vote of censure against Senator Joseph R. McCarthy for "contemptuous conduct" and abuse of the committee.
1959	A typhoon hit the main Japanese island of Honshu, killing some 5,000 people.
1964	The Warren Report on the assassination of President Kennedy was released. It concluded that Lee Harvey Oswald had acted alone in the murder.
1998	Mark McGwire of the St. Louis Cardinals hit his record-setting 69th and 70th home runs to end the 1998 season as the Cardinals beat the Montreal Expos, 6-3.

September 28 – Birthdays

1565	**Alessandro Tassoni.** Italian writer, poet, and critic
1573	**Michelangelo Merisi da Caravaggio.** The greatest naturalistic painter of the early 1600s
1612	**Michel Anguier.** French sculptor
1803	**Prosper Merimee.** French author best known for his novelettes, one of which, *Carmen* (1845), was the source for Georges Bizet's famous opera of the same name

1839	**Frances Elizabeth Willard.** American women's rights pioneer and temperance leader
1840	**George Wilbur Peck.** American journalist who wrote the Peck's Bad Boy stories
1841	**Georges Clemenceau.** French premier during World War I
1856	**Kate Douglas Wiggin.** American writer and author of *Rebecca of Sunnybrook Farm* (1903)
1856	**Edward Herbert Thompson.** American archaeologist who explored the great Mayan city of Chichen Itza in the early 1900s
1863	**Carlos I.** King of Portugal, 1889-1908
1871	**Pietro Badoglio.** Italian World War II general, who succeeded Mussolini as head of state in 1943
1880	**Ralph Flanders.** U.S. senator who initiated the successful movement to censure Senator Joseph McCarthy for his senatorial behavior in 1954
1881	**Evelyn Sears.** Hall of Fame tennis player and first U.S. women's squash champion (1928)
1892	**Elmer Rice.** American dramatist and champion of personal freedom, noted for plays such as *The Adding Machine* (1923)
1901	**William S. Paley.** First president and chairman of the board of CBS
1902	**Ed Sullivan.** American television's "King of Variety," 1947-1971, and host of the long-running show *Toast of the Town*
1905	**Max Schmeling.** World heavyweight champion, 1930-1932
1907	**Turk Edwards.** Hall of Fame professional football player
1909	**Al Capp.** American cartoonist and creator of the comic strip *Li'l Abner* (1934)
1913	**Alice Marble.** American Hall of Fame tennis player, and one of the greatest women champions of all time
1915	**Ethel Rosenberg.** U.S. citizen who with her husband Julius was the first to be executed for espionage (1953)
1916	**Peter Finch.** British stage and motion-picture actor
1919	**Tom Harmon.** Professional football superstar and sportscaster
1923	**William Windom.** American stage and television actor
1923	**Marcello Mastroianni.** Italian stage and motion-picture actor
1926	**Jerry Clower.** American comedian
1934	**Walter Blum.** American jockey
1934	**Brigitte Bardot.** French motion-picture actress and "sex kitten" of the 1950s and 1960s
1935	**Bruce Crampton.** Professional golfer
1948	**Melvin Gray.** Professional football player
1950	**John Sayles.** American motion-picture director and writer noted for the novel *Union Dues* (1977)
1954	**Steve Largent.** Professional football player and Hall of Famer
1955	**Gina Ponce.** Mexican tennis player
1968	**Moon Unit Zappa.** American singer and daughter of musician Frank Zappa

1972 **Gwyneth Paltrow.** American stage and screen actress and daughter of actress Blythe Danner and director Bruce Paltrow

September 28 – Events

48 BC Pompey the Great, the noted Roman general, was murdered in Egypt, one day before his 58th birthday.

1066 William the Conqueror and his Norman army arrived in England, landing at Pevensey.

1542 Juan Rodriguez Cabrillo, a Portuguese explorer employed by Spain, discovered California.

1781 American forces under George Washington began the siege of Yorktown, the last battle of the Revolutionary War.

1850 The flogging of sailors in the U.S. Navy was abolished.

1864 The First International, the first workers' organization, was formed in London.

1891 Herman Melville, one of America's greatest novelists, died in New York City at age 72.

1904 Police arrested a woman on Fifth Avenue in New York City for smoking a cigarette.

1920 Eight Chicago White Sox players were indicted for throwing the 1919 World Series to Cincinnati. This "Black Sox" scandal led to the appointment of a baseball commissioner.

1924 Two U.S. Army planes completed the first round-the-world flight in 175 days, but only 15 flying days.

1939 Germany and Russia partitioned Poland in World War II.

1951 Allie Reynolds pitched his second no-hitter of the season, as the New York Yankees beat the Boston Red Sox, 8-0.

1967 Walter Washington became the first mayor of Washington, D.C.

1978 Pope John Paul I died in the 34th day of his reign.

September 29 – Birthdays

106 BC **Pompey The Great.** Statesman and general of the Roman Empire, and chief rival of Julius Caesar

1518 **Tintoretto (Jacopo Robusti).** One of the last great Venetian painters of the Italian Renaissance

1547 **Miguel de Cervantes.** The greatest Spanish writer in history, and author of *Don Quixote* (1605), one of the great works in world literature

1640 **Antoine Coysevox.** The leading French sculptor during the latter part of the reign of Louis XIV

1703 **François Boucher.** French painter noted for works such as *The Interrupted Sleep* (1750)

1725 **Robert Clive.** British soldier and founder of British rule in India

1758 **Lord Horatio Nelson.** Great Britain's greatest admiral and naval hero, whose great victory at Trafalgar over the French and Spanish fleets in 1805 established England's rule of the seas

1759 **William Beckford.** English writer and collector of books and pictures

1803 **Charles François Sturm.** Noted French mathematician

1810 **Elizabeth Cleghorn Gaskell.** English writer, best known for her novel *Cranford* (1853)

1831 **John McAllister Schofield.** Commander of the Union forces in the Civil War that captured Wilmington, North Carolina, and successfully defended Franklin, Tennessee

1838 **Henry Hobson Richardson.** First American architect to achieve international fame, and the dominant U.S. architect of the 1870s and 1880s

1864 **Miguel de Unamuno.** Spanish essayist, poet, novelist, dramatist, and the leading humanist of modern Spain

1866 **Gus Weyhing.** Professional baseball pitcher who won 264 games in his career

1887 **Billy Bevan.** Australian-born motion-picture actor, noted for his roles in some 70 Mack Sennett comedies and for his numerous character roles

1891 **Marquis James.** American author noted for works such as *The Raven: A Biography of Sam Houston* (1930) and *Andrew Jackson: Portrait of a President* (1938)

1897 **Herbert Agar.** American author and journalist

1901 **Enrico Fermi.** Great Italian physicist who designed the first atomic piles and produced the first nuclear chain reaction in 1942

1901 **Richard B. Smith.** American lyricist noted for songs such as "Winter Wonderland"

1902 **Miguel Aleman.** President of Mexico, 1946-1952

1903 **Fred Nehar.** American cartoonist noted for *Life's Like That* (1934)

1907 **Gene Autry.** American singer, songwriter, and one of the most famous cowboy actors in motion-picture history

1908 **Greer Garson.** Irish-American motion-picture actress and superstar of the 1940s

1910 **Virginia Bruce.** Leading lady of Hollywood films of the 1930s and early 1940s

1911 **Henry Ellsworth Vines.** American Hall of Fame tennis player and 1932 Wimbledon singles champion

1912 **Michelangelo Antonioni.** Italian motion-picture director, noted for films such as *Blow-Up* (1966) and *Zabriskie Point* (1970)

1916 **Trevor Howard.** British stage, screen, and television actor with a career of over 40 years

1922 **Lizabeth Scott.** American stage and motion-picture actress

1923 **Bum Phillips.** Professional football coach

1925 **John Tower.** U.S. senator

1927 **Paul McCloskey.** U.S. congressman

1930 **Richard Bonynge.** Australian conductor and musicologist

1931 **Anita Ekberg.** Swedish motion-picture actress

1935 **Jerry Lee Lewis.** American rock-and-roll singer and pianist

1939	**Larry Linville.** American actor who played Frank Burns on the TV version of M*A*S*H
1942	**Madeleine Kahn.** American actress and comedienne
1943	**Lech Walesa.** Polish labor leader (in the Solidarity movement) and president of Poland
1948	**Bryant Gumbel.** American sportscaster and television host on NBC's *Today* show and CBS's *The Early Show*
1953	**Warren Cromartie.** Professional baseball player
1956	**Sebastian Coe.** English runner who broke three world records—for the 800 meter, the 1500 meter, and the one mile distances—within 42 days in 1979
1960	**Wendy White.** American tennis player
1969	**Kelly Robbins.** Professional golfer
1970	**Natasha Gregson Wagner.** American motion-picture and TV actress and daughter of actress Natalie Wood and stepdaughter of actor Robert Wagner

September 29 – Events

440	Saint Leo I, The Great, was elected Roman Catholic pope.
1513	Spanish explorer Vasco Nunez de Balboa waded into the Pacific Ocean he had discovered four days earlier from a mountaintop, and claimed it for Spain.
1530	Andrea del Sarto, the great Italian painter, died in Florence at age 44.
1789	The U.S. War Department established a regular army with the strength of several hundred men.
1829	London's reorganized police force, which later became Scotland Yard, went on duty.
1902	Emile Zola, the noted French novelist, died in Paris at age 62.
1910	Winslow Homer, the great American painter, died in Prout's Neck, Maine, at age 74.
1913	Rudolf Diesel, the inventor of the diesel engine, mysteriously disappeared from a German ship bound for England, and was never seen again.
1918	Bulgaria surrendered to the Allies in World War I.
1918	The Allies scored a decisive breakthrough of the Hindenburg Line in the Argonne Forest in World War I.
1930	Lowell Thomas, the great American traveler and commentator, began his nightly radio news program, which would be carried by NBC or CBS until 1976.
1938	Neville Chamberlain, Edouard Daladier, Adolf Hitler, and Benito Mussolini met at Munich to determine the fate of Czechoslovakia. In the first hour they agreed to dismember it.
1963	The second session of Vatican II opened in Rome.
1978	Pope John Paul I was found dead in his Vatican apartment after only 34 days in office.

September 30 – Birthdays

1594	**Sieur de Saint-Amant.** One of the most original of French early 17th century poets
1802	**Antoine Jerome Alard.** French chemist who in 1826 discovered the element bromine
1861	**William Wrigley Jr.** American businessman who founded the William Wrigley chewing gum company (1891)
1865	**William Jerome.** American author, actor, and singer, noted for lyrics such as "Chinatown, My Chinatown," "Get Out and Get Under the Moon," and "And the Green Grass Grew All Around"
1875	**Fred Fisher.** German-American composer noted for songs such as "Peg O' My Heart" and "Dardanella"
1882	**Hans Geiger.** German physicist who invented the Geiger counter
1882	**George Bancroft.** American stage and motion-picture actor
1896	**Fred Howard Wright.** American composer, author, and singer, noted for songs such as "The Strawberry Roan" and "My Pretty Quadroon"
1905	**Michael Powell.** English motion-picture director and screenwriter with a 50-year career
1905	**Johnny Allen.** Professional baseball pitcher with a won-loss record of 15-1 in 1937
1908	**David Oistrakh.** The leading Russian violinist of the mid-twentieth century
1912	**Kenny Baker.** American singer and actor
1915	**Lester Maddox.** Governor of Georgia, 1967-1971
1921	**Deborah Kerr.** English motion-picture actress and leading star of the 1950s and 1960s
1924	**Truman Capote.** American novelist and playwright, noted for works such as *Breakfast at Tiffany's* (1958) and *In Cold Blood* (1966)
1926	**Robin Roberts.** Hall of Fame baseball player
1928	**Elie Wiesel.** American journalist and author
1932	**Johnny Podres.** Professional baseball player
1932	**Angie Dickinson.** American motion-picture and television actress
1934	**Freddie King.** American blues singer and guitarist
1935	**Johnny Mathis.** American singer
1936	**James Sasser.** U.S. senator and ambassador
1943	**Jody Powell.** White House press secretary under President Carter
1944	**Marilyn McCoo.** Member of the Fifth Dimension singing group
1950	**Victoria Tennant.** English motion-picture actress
1951	**Catherine Ball.** American swimmer who set the 100-meter breast stroke record of 1 minute 14.2 seconds in 1968
1954	**John Drew.** Professional basketball player
1964	**Crystal Bernard.** American motion-picture and television actress
1980	**Martina Hingis.** Swiss tennis player and superstar

September 30 – Events

420 Saint Jerome, one of the great scholars of the early Christian church, died at age 80.

1492 Christopher Columbus completed three weeks with no sight of land on his first voyage to America. This was the longest voyage yet made out of sight of land.

1568 Sweden's King Eric XIV was deposed after years of insanity.

1630 The first execution took place in America as John Billington was hanged in Plymouth, Massachusetts, for fatally shooting John Newcomin.

1791 Wolfgang Amadeus Mozart's great opera *The Magic Flute* had its premiere in Vienna.

1846 Dr. William Thomas Green Morton, a dentist in Charleston, Massachusetts, became the first to extract a tooth with the help of anesthesia.

1868 The Spanish Revolution of 1868 ended in the establishment of a provisional government under Generals Francisco Serrano and Juan Prim.

1927 Babe Ruth hit his record-setting 60th home run of the season in New York's Yankee Stadium.

1935 George Gershwin's great opera *Porgy and Bess* had its world premiere at the Colonial Theater in Boston.

1938 The Munich agreement was signed by Adolf Hitler, Neville Chamberlain, Edouard Daladier, and Benito Mussolini, destroying Czechoslovakia. Chamberlain at the London airport called it "peace for our time."

1939 The first football game was televised, between Fordham University and Waynesburg College.

1953 Earl Warren was named chief justice of the U.S. Supreme Court by President Eisenhower.

1954 The submarine *Nautilus*, the first atomic-powered vessel, was commissioned by the U.S. Navy at Groton, Connecticut.

1955 James Dean, American motion-picture actor, was killed in an automobile crash at age 24.

1982 The long-running television show *Cheers* premiered on NBC.

1984 Mike Witt pitched a perfect game (no batter reached base), as the California Angels beat the Texas Rangers, 1-0. It was only the 14th perfect game in baseball history.

1998 The U.S. government ended fiscal year 1999 with a surplus of $70 billion, the first surplus since the Lyndon Johnson administration.

10
October

October, the tenth month of the year, got its name from *Octobris,* the Latin word for *eighth,* because in the original Roman calendar it was the eighth month. When Romulus added October to his calendar he first gave it 30 days, but almost immediately he changed its length to 31 days. Caesar gave it 30 days in his Julian Calendar in 45 B.C., but in 8 B.C. Augustus restored it to its present length of 31 days. The Roman Senate tried to rename October *Antoninus* after a Roman emperor, *Faustinus* after his wife, and *Tacitus* after the great Roman historian, but all three attempts failed since the people continued to call it October.

Columbus Day is an October holiday commemorating Columbus's discovery of America on October 12, 1492. It is now celebrated on the second Monday of the month. Halloween is October 31, as is Reformation Day, celebrated by Protestants to mark the day in 1517 when Martin Luther nailed his 95 Theses of protest to the door of a church in Wittenberg, Germany. Six United States Presidents, John Adams, Rutherford B. Hayes, Chester A. Arthur, Theodore Roosevelt, Dwight D. Eisenhower, and Jimmy Carter, were born in October.

The October birthstones are the opal and the tourmaline, and the special flowers are the calendula and the cosmos.

October 1 – Birthdays

1207 **Henry III.** King of England, 1216-1264, whose 56-year reign was one of the longest in history, and who built the new Westminster Abbey as his most enduring monument

1507 **Giacomo Da Vignola.** Italian architect who succeeded Michelangelo as the architect in charge of building St. Peter's Basilica

1620 **Claes Berchem.** Dutch painter

1685 **Charles VI.** Holy Roman Emperor, 1711-1740, and father of the great Austrian empress Maria Theresa

1730 **Richard Stockton.** Member of the Continental Congress and New Jersey signer of the Declaration of Independence

1754 **Paul I.** Strange, and perhaps crazy, czar of Russia, 1796-1801, and son of Catherine the Great

1781 **James Lawrence.** U.S. naval commander of the *Chesapeake,* whose dying command, "Don't give up the ship," became a watchword of the U.S. Navy

1832 **Caroline Lavinia Scott Harrison.** First wife of President Benjamin Harrison

1881 **William E. Boeing.** American industrialist and founder of the Boeing Airplane Company in 1916

1885 **Louis Untermeyer.** American poet, critic, and editor who edited some 18 collections of poetry and wrote an autobiography, *From Another World* (1939)

1889 **Alice Joyce.** American motion-picture actress of silents and early talkies who was known as "The Madonna of the Screen"

1890 **Stanley Holloway.** English stage and screen actor in over 100 films

1893 **Faith Baldwin.** American novelist

1893 **Cliff Friend.** American composer, author, and pianist, noted for songs such as "When My Dreamboat Comes Home" and "The Merry-Go-Round Broke Down"

1899 **William Allan Patterson.** American aviation pioneer

1902 **Joseph Rines.** American composer and author, noted for songs such as "Halo, Everybody, Halo" and "Ajax, the Foaming Cleanser," two well-known commercials of his day

1904 **Vladimir Horowitz.** Russian-born American piano virtuoso

1904 **Terry Shand.** American composer, author, and conductor, noted for songs such as "I Double Dare You" and "Dance With a Dolly"

1907 **Hiram Fong.** U.S. senator

1909 **Everett Sloane.** American stage and motion-picture actor

1910 **Bonnie Parker.** Notorious American outlaw and killer who was gunned down by the FBI in 1934 with her partner Ciyde Barrow

1911 **Fletcher Knebel.** American columnist and author

1914 **Daniel J. Boorstin.** American social historian, educator and Librarian of Congress (1975-1987), noted for his three-volume work, *The Americans*

1920 **Walter Matthau.** American stage, screen, and television actor

1921 **James Whitmore.** American stage, screen, and television actor

1922 **Ernest Altschuler.** American composer noted for songs such as "I Left My Heart in San Francisco" (with George Cory)

1924 **Jimmy Carter.** 39th U.S. president

1924 **William Rehnquist.** U.S. Supreme Court chief justice

1927 **Tom Bosley.** American motion-picture and television actor

1928 **Laurence Harvey.** English motion-picture actor

1933 **Richard Harris.** Irish-born motion-picture and television actor

1933 **George Peppard.** American motion-picture and television actor

1935 **Julie Andrews.** English-born singer and stage and motion-picture actress

1936 **Stella Stevens.** American motion-picture actress

1936 **Edward Villella.** American ballet dancer and actor

1938 **Paul Gillette.** American author noted for *Play Misty for Me* (1971)

1939 **George Archer.** Professional golfer

1945 **Rod Carew.** Professional baseball Hall of Famer and six-times batting champion

1950 **Randy Quaid.** American motion-picture and television actor and brother of actor Dennis Quaid

1950 **Conrad Dobler.** Professional football player

1955 **Jeff Reardon.** Professional baseball player

1963 **Mark McGwire.** Professional baseball player and superstar who hit 70 home runs in 1998

October 1 – Events

331 BC Alexander the Great defeated Persian emperor Darius III in the Battle of Arbela in Mesopotamia, in one of the fifteen decisive battles of history.

1422 King Charles VI of France died in Paris at age 53.

1553 Mary I ("Bloody Mary") of England was crowned in Westminster Abbey.

1800 Spain ceded Louisiana to France in a secret treaty.

1880 John Philip Sousa, the great bandleader and composer, became leader of the U.S. Marine Band, which under his guidance became one of the finest in the world.

1903 The first baseball World Series began in Boston between the Boston Red Sox and the Pittsburgh Pirates. Pittsburgh won, 7-3, but Boston won the series, five games to three.

1908 The famous Model T Ford, or "Tin Lizzie," was first put on sale by Henry Ford at a price of $850.

1931 New York's Waldorf-Astoria Hotel opened to the public.

1932 Babe Ruth allegedly called his home run off Chicago pitcher Charlie Root by pointing to the stands before lining a homer there in the third game of the 1932 World Series.

1933 The comic strip *Smilin' Jack,* by Zack Mosley, first appeared.

1938 Adolf Hitler occupied the Sudetenland of Czechoslovakia in accordance with the infamous Munich Pact that he had concluded the previous day.

1943 The comic strip *Kerry Drake,* by Alfred Andriola, first appeared.

1946 Nineteen top Nazis were found guilty in Nuremberg of war crimes. Rudolf Hess and six others were sentenced to prison, and 12, including Hermann Goering, were sentenced to death.

1949 Mao Tse-tung took over as Chairman of the People's Government Council in Peking, China.

1961 Roger Maris of the New York Yankees hit his record 61st home run of the season off Boston's Tracy Stallard at Yankee Stadium, breaking Babe Ruth's record of 60 set in 1927.

1962 Johnny Carson started his 29-year tenure as host of NBC's *Tonight Show.*

1963 The cult horror movie *Night of the Living Dead* had its world premiere in Pittsburgh.

1971 Walt Disney World opened in Orlando, Florida.

1984 Peter Ueberroth became Commissioner of Baseball, succeeding Bowie Kuhn.

October 2 – Birthdays

1452 **Richard III.** The last Yorkist king of England, 1483-1485, whose reign brought on the revolt that ended the Wars of the Roses

1800 **Nat Turner.** American slave who led Nat Turner's Rebellion in 1831, the largest slave revolt in American history

1831 **Edward L. Godkin.** Irish-born American editor who in 1865 founded *The Nation,* a liberal weekly newspaper that soon established itself as one of the most influential periodicals in America

1832 **Sir Edward Burnett Tyler.** Father of anthropology in the English-speaking world

1847 **Paul von Hindenburg.** World War I military leader and president of Germany, 1925-1934

1851 **Ferdinand Foch.** French field marshal and supreme Allied commander in World War I, acclaimed by many to be the greatest Allied general of the war

1865 **Dan Casey.** Professional baseball player who was said to be the inspiration for Ernest Thayer's famous poem "Casey at the Bat"

1869 **Mohandas K. Gandhi.** Indian nationalist and religious leader, honored by Indians as the *Mahatma* (Great Soul) and the father of their nation

1871 **Cordell Hull.** U.S. secretary of state under President Franklin D. Roosevelt

1877 **Carl T. Hayden.** American statesman who served Arizona for 56 years in both houses of Congress

1879 **Wallace Stevens.** American poet whose *Collected Poems* won the 1955 Pulitzer Prize

1890 **Groucho Marx.** American actor, member of the Marx Brothers comedy team, and one of America's greatest comedians

1895 **Bud Abbott.** Straight man of the famous Abbott and Costello comedy team of the 1940s and 1950s

1904 **Graham Greene.** English novelist, noted for works such as *This Gun for Hire* (1936) and *The Third Man* (1950)

1904 **Lal Bahadur Shastri.** Prime minister of India, 1964-1966

1909 **Alex Raymond.** American cartoonist and creator in 1934 of *Flash Gordon*

1926 **Frances Farenthold.** American educator and political activist

1928 **Spanky McFarland.** American child movie star noted for the *Our Gang* comedies (later reissued on TV as *The Little Rascals*)

1932 **Maury Wills.** Professional baseball player who stole 104 bases in 1962, a record at the time

1937 **Johnnie Cochran.** American lawyer who successfully defended O.J. Simpson in his murder trial in 1995

1940 **Rex Reed.** American film critic and actor

1945 **Don McLean.** American singer and songwriter

1948 **Donna Karan.** American fashion designer

1951 **Sting.** English musician, singer and songwriter

1967 **Thomas Muster.** Austrian tennis player and winner of the French Open in 1995

October 2 – Events

1187 The Moslems, led by their great warrior Saladin, captured Jerusalem, which brought about the Third Crusade.

1780 Major John Andre, the British officer who collaborated in Benedict Arnold's treachery, was hanged as a spy at Tappan, New York.

1835 The Texas Revolution began with a battle between U.S. settlers and Mexican cavalry near the Guadalupe River.

1889 The first Pan-American Conference, which included all the independent countries of the Western Hemisphere, was held in Washington, D.C.

1905 The keel was laid in secrecy in Portsmouth, England, for the construction of H.M.S. *Dreadnaught,* which was to make existing battleships obsolete.

1938 Bob Feller, the Cleveland Indians' great pitcher, struck out a record 18 men in a game against the Detroit Tigers.

1939 Organized Polish resistance ceased as the Germans and Russians completed the partition of Poland in World War II.

1950 The comic strip *Peanuts,* by Charles Schulz, made its first appearance.

1967 Thurgood Marshall was sworn in as the first black member of the U.S. Supreme Court.

October 3 – Birthdays

1554 **Sir Fulke Greville.** English writer, courtier, and statesman

1800 **George Bancroft.** U.S. historian and "Father of American History," who as secretary of the Navy in 1845 helped establish the U.S. Naval Academy at Annapolis

1803 **John Gorrie.** American physician and inventor who patented the first machine for mechanical refrigeration (1851) and is considered by some to be the inventor of air conditioning

1818 **Alexander Macmillan.** Co-founder of Macmillan and Company publishers

1854 **William Crawford Gorgas.** The world's leading sanitation expert of his time, who made possible the building of the Panama Canal by destroying mosquitoes that carried yellow fever and malaria

1859 **Eleonora Duse.** Italian dramatic actress, noted as "the greatest actress of her time"

1867 **Pierre Bonnard.** French painter noted for his rich textures and vivid colors, an example of which is *The Green Blouse* (1919)

1872 **Fred "Cap" Clarke.** Hall of Fame professional baseball player and manager with 2,675 career hits

1886 **Alain-Fournier.** French novelist (Henri Alban Fournier)

1890 **Henry Hull.** American stage and screen actor who created the role of Jeeter Lester in the original Broadway production of *Tobacco Road*

1900 **Thomas Wolfe.** American novelist, noted for *Look Homeward, Angel* (1929) and *You Can't Go Home Again* (1940), published after his death

1908 **Johnny Burke.** Famous American lyricist, noted for songs such as "Moonlight Becomes You," "Personality," "Swinging on a Star," and "Pennies From Heaven"

1911 **Sir Michael Hordern.** British character actor with a 50-year career in motion pictures and television who was voted TV Actor of the Year in 1957

1916 **James Herriot.** Scottish veterinarian and author, noted for *All Creatures Great and Small* (1972)

1916 **David A. Mann.** American composer and author, noted for songs such as "Somebody Bad Stole de Wedding Bell," "Dearie (You're Much Older Than I)," and "There, I've Said It Again"

1924 **Harvey Kurtzman.** American cartoonist and creator of *Little Annie Fanny* in *Playboy* magazine

1925 **Gore Vidal.** American novelist, playwright, and pungent observer, noted for works such as *The Best Man* (1960), *Myra Breckenridge* (1968), and *Lincoln* (1984)

1933 **Neale Fraser.** Australian tennis player and Wimbledon singles champion in 1960

1938 **Eddie Cochran.** Early American rock-and-roll musician

1941 **Chubby Checker.** American pop singer and recorder of "The Twist," which sold millions and led to the dance of the same name

1943 **Jeff Bingaman.** U.S. senator
1947 **Lindsey Buckingham.** American musician with Fleetwood Mac
1951 **Dave Winfield.** Professional baseball player and superstar
1953 **Pat Day.** American jockey with over 6,000 wins
1954 **Dennis Eckersley.** Professional baseball player
1959 **Fred Couples.** Professional golfer

October 3 – Events

1226 Saint Francis of Assisi, the great Roman Catholic churchman and founder of the Franciscan order, died at his beloved Portiuncula chapel at age 44.
1656 Miles Standish, the great Pilgrim leader, died at age 72.
1863 President Lincoln proclaimed the last Thursday in November Thanksgiving Day.
1906 The great British battleship H.M.S. *Dreadnaught* was completed in Portsmouth, England.
1913 President Woodrow Wilson signed the income tax bill into law, to be retroactive to March 1, 1913.
1919 President Wilson suffered a paralytic stroke that left him an invalid for the rest of his life.
1922 Rebecca L. Felton of Georgia became the first U.S. woman senator, having been appointed to serve the remainder of Thomas E. Watson's term.
1935 Italian troops invaded Ethiopia in one of the preludes to World War II.
1941 With German troops advancing toward Moscow, Adolf Hitler declared that Russia was defeated and "will never rise again."
1955 The television show *Captain Kangaroo,* with actor Bob Keeshan in the title role, made its debut. It was to run for nearly 30 years to December, 1984.
1962 U.S. astronaut Wally Schirra, Jr., made six space orbits in *Sigma 7.*
1974 Frank Robinson was named manager of the Cleveland Indians, as the first African American to manage a major league baseball team.
1990 One million Germans passed before the Reichstag building in Berlin, celebrating the reuniting of Germany.

October 4 – Birthdays

1289 **Louis X.** King of France, 1314-1316
1379 **Henry III.** King of Castile before its merger with Aragon to form Spain
1472 **Lucas Cranach (the Elder).** One of the leading German painters of the Renaissance
1550 **Charles IX.** King of Sweden, 1604-1611, who restored Lutheranism as Sweden's state religion
1720 **Giovanni Battista Piranesi.** Italian etcher, architect, and archaeologist, who had a wide influence on etchers for 100 years
1810 **Eliza McCardle Johnson.** Wife of President Andrew Johnson

1814 **Jean François Millet.** French painter famous for his rural life paintings, such as *The Gleaners* and *The Man with the Hoe*
1822 **Rutherford B. Hayes.** 19th U.S. president
1858 **Michael Idvorsky Pupin.** Hungarian-born American physicist who had 34 patents, and whose autobiography, *From Immigrant to Inventor* (1923), won the 1924 Pulitzer Prize
1861 **Frederic Remington.** American painter and sculptor, best known for his action-filled paintings of the western plains
1862 **Edward Stratemeyer.** American author who wrote the *Rover Boys* adventure novels and formed the Stratemeyer Literary Syndicate of writers using various pen names to flesh out his ideas and produce many series of stories such as *Tom Swift, The Bobbsey Twins,* and *Nancy Drew*
1880 **Damon Runyon.** American writer and author of *Guys and Dolls* (1932)
1895 **Buster Keaton.** One of the great deadpan heros of the silent screen who made the transition to the talkies and had a career of nearly 50 years
1910 **Frank Crosetti.** Professional baseball player and coach
1914 **Brendan Gill.** American critic and author noted for his many contributions to *The New Yorker*
1917 **Jan Murray.** American comedian
1923 **Charlton Heston.** American stage, screen, and television actor with a career of over 40 years
1928 **Alvin Toffler.** American futurologist and author of *Future Shock*
1928 **Torben Ulrich.** Danish tennis player
1941 **Anne Rice.** American author noted for works such as *The Vampire Chronicles*
1941 **Jackie Collins.** American author (*Hollywood Wives,* 1983) and sister of actress Joan Collins
1941 **Robert Wilson.** American playwright and producer
1943 **Owen Davidson.** Australian tennis player
1944 **Tony LaRussa.** Professional baseball player and manager
1946 **Susan Sarandon.** American motion-picture actress

October 4 – Events

1535 The first complete English translation of the Bible was published by Miles Coverdale, a bishop of Exeter, England.
1582 The Gregorian Calendar, introduced by Pope Gregory XIII, was announced to go into effect in most Catholic countries, with the following day, October 5, to become October 15, 1582.
1669 Rembrandt, the great Dutch painter, died in Amsterdam at age 63.
1769 Bangor, Maine, was settled.
1777 The British defeated the Americans under George Washington in the Battle of Germantown, near Philadelphia, in the Revolutionary War.

1853 Turkey declared war on Russia, starting a conflict which became the Crimean War when England and France joined the Turks the following March.

1905 Calvin Coolidge married Grace Anna Goodhue.

1931 The comic strip *Dick Tracy,* by Chester Gould, first appeared.

1940 Adolf Hitler and Benito Mussolini met at the Brenner Pass in the Tyrol where Hitler bragged that "The war is won!"

1943 The plan for the "extermination of the Jews" is under way, announced SS fuehrer Heinrich Himmler in a speech to his associates.

1957 Russia launched *Sputnik I,* the first man-made satellite.

1970 American rock singer Janis Joplin died at age 27.

October 5 – Birthdays

1703 **Jonathan Edwards.** Famous minister of Puritan New England, who was the leading intellectual figure in colonial America

1712 **Francesco Guardi.** Italian painter

1713 **Denis Diderot.** French satirist, encyclopedist, brilliant conversationalist, and one of the major philosophers of the Age of Reason

1752 **Nathan Bowen.** American cabinetmaker

1824 **Henry Chadwick.** American journalist who wrote baseball's first book of rules as well as a history of the game in the 1860s, and was hailed by many as "The Father of the Game"

1830 **Chester A. Arthur.** 21st U.S. president

1840 **John Addington Symonds.** English poet, biographer, and historian

1848 **Edward Livingston Trudeau.** Famous pioneer in the antituberculosis movement in the U.S.

1864 **Louis Lumiere.** French pioneer in photographic manufacturing, who with his brother Auguste invented the *cinematographe,* a combination motion-picture camera, printer, and projector

1882 **Robert Hutchings Goddard.** American scientist and "father of modern rocketry," who launched the first liquid-fueled rocket in 1926

1895 **Walter Bedell Smith.** American World War II general

1902 **Ray Kroc.** American businessman who made McDonald's Hamburgers into an international chain

1902 **Larry Fine.** American comedian and actor and one of the original Three Stooges

1904 **John Hoyt.** American character actor in motion-pictures and television

1904 **T. Murray Mencher.** American composer noted for songs such as "Merrily We Roll Along"

1908 **Robert Trout.** American television newscaster

1908 **Joshua Logan.** American motion-picture director and playwright, noted for the direction of films such as *Picnic* (1956) and *Camelot* (1967)

1914 **Eugene Fodor.** American writer of travel guide books

1917 **Lew Worsham.** Professional golfer

1919 **Donald Pleasance.** English motion-picture actor

1922 **Bill Keane.** American cartoonist and creator of *Family Circus* (1960)

1923 **Glynis Johns.** South African motion-picture actress

1923 **Philip Berrigan.** American priest and social activist

1924 **Bill Dana.** American comedian, actor, and author

1929 **Richard F. Gordon Jr.** American astronaut on *Gemini 11* (1966) and *Apollo 12* (1969), which landed on the moon

1930 **Skip Homeier.** American stage, screen, and television actor

1933 **Diane Cilento.** Australian stage, screen, and television actress

1936 **Vaclav Havel.** Czech playwright, political activist and first president of the Czech Republic

1936 **Odie Smith.** Professional basketball player

1937 **Barry Switzer.** College and professional football coach

1948 **Aurelio Lopez.** Professional baseball player

1949 **Norman Holmes.** American tennis player

1951 **Karen Allen.** American motion-picture actress

1963 **Laura Davies.** Professional golfer and U.S. Women's Open Champion in 1987

October 5 – Events

1795 Napoleon was appointed second in command of the Army of the Interior, paving the way for his assuming power in France.

1813 Tecumseh, the great Shawnee chief, was killed while aiding the British in the Battle of the Thames in Upper Canada in the War of 1812.

1823 Leo XII was crowned Roman Catholic pope.

1892 The Dalton brothers, a notorious Western gang of outlaws, tried their last holdup, in Coffeyville, Kansas. All the gang members except one were killed in the ensuing fight.

1918 The Allied armies broke the Hindenburg Line in World War I.

1921 The first World Series baseball game was broadcast on the radio, with sports writer Grantland Rice giving the play by play between the New York Yankees and the New York Giants.

1931 Clyde Pangborn and Hugh Herndon completed the first non-stop flight across the Pacific Ocean, arriving in the state of Washington 41 hours after leaving Japan.

1937 President Franklin D. Roosevelt called for a "quarantine" of the aggressor nations, Germany and Italy.

1947 President Harry S. Truman made the first presidential telecast address from the White House.

1953 Earl Warren was sworn in as the 14th Chief Justice of the U.S. Supreme Court.

1962 The Beatles released their first hit single, "Love Me Do."

1969 The *Monty Python Show* made its debut in England.

1974 David Kunst returned to Waseca, Minnesota, completing a four-year walking trip around the world that began June 10, 1970.

October 6 – Birthdays

1289 **Wenceslas III.** King of Hungary, 1301-1304
1510 **John Caius.** English humanist and physician
1773 **Louis-Philippe.** King of France, 1830-1848
1816 **William Batchelder Bradbury.** American musician and songwriter noted for songs such as "Jesus Loves Me" (1859) and "Sweet Hour of Prayer" (1860)
1820 **Jenny Lind.** Swedish operatic soprano known as the "Swedish Nightingale"
1831 **Richard Dedekind.** German mathematician noted among other things for the "Dedekind cut"
1846 **George Westinghouse.** American inventor responsible for the adoption of alternating current for use in the United States
1847 **Adolf von Hildebrand.** German sculptor
1859 **Frank Augustus Seiberling.** American businessman who founded Goodyear Tire and Rubber Co.
1866 **Reginald Aubrey Fessenden.** American physicist who demonstrated the first radio-transmission (1900) and made the first radio broadcast of phonograph music (1906)
1887 **Martin Luis Guzman.** Mexican writer of the Mexican Revolutionary period
1887 **Le Corbusier.** Swiss-born architect (Charles-Edouard Jeanneret), considered by many to be the greatest of the 20th century
1893 **Milton Ager.** American composer and pianist, noted for songs such as Franklin D. Roosevelt's theme song, "Happy Days Are Here Again" (with Jack Yellen), "Ain't She Sweet," and "Auf Wiedersehen"
1896 **Joseph M. Davis.** American composer noted for songs such as "Daddy's Little Boy" and "Basin Street Blues"
1902 **Jack Sharkey.** World heavyweight champion, 1932-1933
1905 **Helen Wills Moody.** One of the greatest women tennis players of all time (also known as Helen Wills), who won the Wimbledon title a record eight times and the U.S. title seven times
1906 **Janet Gaynor.** American motion-picture actress and superstar, who won the first Academy Award ever given for best actress (1927-1928)
1908 **Carole Lombard.** American motion-picture actress, and one of Hollywood's most talented and glamorous stars of the 1930s
1914 **Thor Heyerdahl.** Norwegian adventurer and writer, and author of *Kon-Tiki* (1950) and *Aku-Aku* (1958)
1922 **Helen Roark.** American tennis player
1923 **Lowell Thomas Jr.** American author, television producer, and son of the famous news commentator
1925 **Shana Alexander.** American writer and journalist

1930 **Hafez Assad.** President of Syria
1939 **Melvyn Bragg.** English author noted for the film script for *Jesus Christ Superstar* (1973)
1942 **Britt Eklund.** Swedish-born motion-picture actress
1942 **Jerry Grote.** Professional baseball player

October 6 – Events

891 Formosus was elected Roman Catholic pope.
1536 William Tyndale, the great English Protestant leader and translator of the Bible, was burned at the stake as a heretic.
1683 The first permanent German settlement in America was made at Germantown, Pennsylvania.
1889 Thomas A. Edison first exhibited his kinetoscope, a device for producing moving pictures.
1890 The Mormon Church in Utah outlawed the practice of polygamy.
1892 Alfred Lord Tennyson, the great English poet, died near Haslemore, Surrey, at age 83.
1915 Austro-German forces invaded Serbia in World War I.
1927 The first "talking" film, *The Jazz Singer,* starring Al Jolson, had its world premiere at New York's Warner Theater.
1938 Dr. Eduard Benes, under Nazi pressure, resigned the presidency of Czechoslovakia and left for Great Britain to fight for the freedom of his country.
1973 War erupted in the Middle East as Egyptian and Syrian forces attacked Israel.
1981 Egyptian President Anwar Sadat was murdered by Islamic extremists who opened fire on him in his reviewing stand during a parade on the anniversary of the 1973 war with Israel.

October 7 – Birthdays

1491 **Frederick I.** King of Denmark
1573 **Archbishop William Laud.** The dominant figure in the Church of England during the persecution of the Puritans in the time of King Charles I
1576 **John Marston.** English dramatist and essayist of the Shakespearean age
1675 **Rosalba Carriera.** Italian painter
1734 **Sir Ralph Abercromby.** English army commander
1849 **James Whitcomb Riley.** American poet who wrote his most popular works in the dialect of his home state, Indiana, and became famous as the *Hoosier Poet*
1866 **Martha McChesney Berry.** Founder of the Berry Schools in Georgia for mountain boys and girls
1885 **Niels Bohr.** Nobel Prize-winning Danish physicist, noted for the Bohr theory of the atom
1888 **Henry A. Wallace.** Secretary of agriculture and vice president under President Franklin D. Roosevelt
1897 **Elijah Muhammad.** Spiritual leader of the Black Muslim movement

1900 **Heinrich Himmler.** Head of Adolf Hitler's *Gestapo,* and principal director of the systematic killings in World War II concentration camps

1901 **Ralph Rainger.** American composer and pianist, noted for songs such as "Ebb Tide," "Blue Hawaii," and Bob Hope's theme song, "Thanks for the Memory" (1938)

1901 **Prince Souvanna Phouma.** Laotian leader who helped negotiate Laos' independence from France in 1947-1949

1904 **Chuck Klein.** Hall of Fame baseball player

1905 **Andy Devine.** American motion-picture and television actor

1905 **Meyer Levin.** American writer and novelist noted for works such as *Rosemary's Baby* and *The Stepford Wives*

1907 **Helen MacInnes.** Scottish-born American author

1911 **Vaughn Monroe.** American singer and conductor of the Big Band Era, who wrote his own theme song, "Racing With the Moon" (with composer Johnny Watson)

1914 **Alfred Drake.** American singer, actor, and director

1914 **Sarah Churchill.** English actress and daughter of Sir Winston Churchill

1917 **Reginald Smythe.** English cartoonist and creator of *Andy Capp* (1957)

1917 **June Allyson.** American stage and motion-picture actress with a 40-year career

1926 **Diana Lynn.** American motion-picture and television actress

1927 **Al Martino.** American singer, pianist, and actor

1931 **Desmond Tutu.** South African black clergyman, social activist, and 1984 Nobel Peace Prize winner

1934 **Willie Naulls.** Professional basketball player with over 11,000 career points

1943 **Oliver North.** Lt. Colonel in the U.S Marines and central figure in the 1986 Iran-Contra scandal of the Reagan administration

1951 **John "Cougar" Mellencamp.** American rock musician

1955 **Yo-Yo Ma.** American musician and cello virtuoso

1957 **Jayne Torvill.** English Olympic figure skater

October 7 – Events

1492 A second mistaken shout of "Land Ho!" created great disappointment among Columbus's crew on the first voyage to America.

1571 Spain and its allies defeated the Turks in the famous Battle of Lepanto, the last great battle of oar-driven ships, marking a turning point of Moslem power in Europe.

1765 The Stamp Act Congress met in New York to consider colonial grievances against England.

1777 The Americans repulsed the British in the Second Battle of Freeman's Farm in the Revolutionary War.

1780 The American frontiersmen defeated the British in the Battle of Kings Mountain (South Carolina).

1816 The *Washington,* the world's first double-decked steamboat, arrived in New Orleans.

1849 Edgar Allan Poe, the great American writer and poet, died in Baltimore at age 40.

1889 Barnard College was opened, six months after the death of its founder, Frederick Augustus Porter Barnard.

1916 Georgia Tech beat Cumberland University, 222-0, in the most staggering intercollegiate football defeat in history.

1940 German troops entered Romania "by invitation" to reorganize the Romanian army and take the Ploesti oil fields.

1949 Iva d'Aquino was sentenced to prison for her propaganda broadcasts for Japan as *Tokyo Rose* during World War II.

1960 John F. Kennedy and Richard M. Nixon held their second "Great Debate" in the 1960 presidential election.

1968 The Motion Picture Association of America adopted its film-rating system.

1984 Walter Payton of the Chicago Bears broke Jim Brown's National Football League career rushing record of 12,312 yards set in 1966.

October 8 – Birthdays

1585 **Heinrich Schutz.** German composer noted for works such as the opera *Dafne* (1626) and *Musikalische Exequien,* the first German requiem (1636)

1609 **John Clarke.** American colonist who helped found Portsmouth, Rhode Island, in 1638, and Newport, Rhode Island, in 1639.

1697 **Cornelis Troost.** Dutch painter

1832 **Walter Kittredge.** American composer noted for "Tenting on the Old Camp Ground" (1862)

1838 **John M. Hay.** U.S. secretary of state, 1898-1905, best known for his Open-Door Policy in China

1846 **Elbert Henry Gary.** American industrialist and lawyer, who was the chief organizer of the United States Steel Corporation (1901), and for whom the city of Gary, Indiana, was named

1868 **Max Slevogt.** German painter

1869 **J. Frank Duryea.** Co-inventor with his brother Charles of the first successful gasoline-powered automobile in America

1876 **Hugh Doherty.** Irish tennis superstar, who won the Wimbledon singles title five consecutive years (1902-1906), and who with his brother Reginald dominated the game in their day

1882 **Harry Kirby McClintock.** American composer, author, and singer, noted for songs such as "The Big Rock Candy Mountain" and "Lonesome Trail"

1890 **Eddie Rickenbacker.** America's flying hero and "Ace of Aces," who shot down 22 enemy planes and 4 balloons in World War I

1895 **Juan Peron.** President of Argentina, 1946-1955 and 1973-1974

1910 **Gus Hall.** Leader of the American Communist Party in the 1940s and 1950s

1910 **Wally Moses.** Professional baseball player

1912 **Jorge Amado.** Brazilian novelist

1912 **John Gardner.** Secretary of health, education, and welfare under President Lyndon Johnson, and founder in 1970 of the citizens' group, Common Cause

1916 **Spark Masayuki Matsunaga.** U.S. senator

1936 **Rona Barrett.** Entertainment reporter and Hollywood gossip columnist

1938 **Fred Stolle.** Australian tennis star who won four Wimbledon titles

1941 **Paul Hogan.** Australian movie-picture and television actor

1941 **Jesse Jackson.** American civil rights leader and candidate for the Democratic Party's nomination for president in 1984 and 1988

1943 **R.L. Stine.** American author of teen horror fiction, noted for the *Goosebumps* series

1943 **Chevy Chase.** American comedian and actor

1946 **Paul Splittorff.** Professional baseball player

1949 **Enos Cabell.** Professional baseball player

1949 **Sigourney Weaver.** American stage and motion-picture actress and daughter of Pat Weaver, the president of NBC who launched *The Today Show* and *The Tonight Show*

1952 **Edward Zwick.** American motion-picture and television director and screenwriter, noted for his direction of *Glory* (1989)

1956 **Stephanie Zimbalist.** American television actress and daughter of actor Efrem Zimbalist, Jr.

October 8 – Events

451 The fourth Ecumenical Council of the Roman Catholic Church opened in Rome.

1769 Captain James Cook rediscovered New Zealand. (It had been discovered in 1642 by Abel Tasman, but he and his Dutch settlers tried to keep its discovery secret from the English.)

1869 Franklin Pierce died in Concord, New Hampshire, at age 64.

1871 The Great Fire of Chicago started when, according to legend, a cow kicked over a lantern in a barn owned by Mrs. O'Leary at 137 De Koven Street.

1882 "The public be damned," said industrialist William H. Vanderbilt, when questioned about running his railroad in the public interest.

1895 Englebert Humperdinck's opera, *Hansel and Gretel,* had its American premiere at Daly's Theater in New York.

1904 George M. Cohen's immortal "Give My Regards to Broadway" was first sung publicly in his musical play *Little Johnny Jones.*

1904 The first automobile race for the Vanderbilt Cup was won by George Heath, driving a Panhard.

1918 U.S. soldier Alvin York killed over 20 German soldiers and captured 132 others in World War I. He became famous as Sergeant York, but he was only a corporal at the time.

1923 Germany's post-war inflation made one United States penny worth 6,250,000 paper marks.

1930 Laura Ingalls became the first woman to fly across the U.S., as she completed a nine-stop journey from Roosevelt Field, NY to Glendale, California.

1934 Bruno Richard Hauptmann was indicted for murder in the death of Charles Lindbergh's infant son.

1956 Don Larsen pitched the only perfect game (no runner reached base) in World Series history, as the New York Yankees beat the Brooklyn Dodgers, 2-0.

1967 Che Guevara, the Cuban revolutionary, was captured and killed by Bolivian troops in the Bolivian jungle.

1983 Carlos Buhler, Kim Momb, and Louis Reichardt, followed later by the rest of their American team, scaled the East Face of Mount Everest, a sheer wall regarded before as unscalable.

1998 The U.S. House of Representatives voted, largely along party lines, to approve a full-scale, open-ended impeachment investigation of President Clinton's conduct in the Monica Lewinsky affair.

October 9 – Birthdays

1757 **Charles X.** King of France, 1824-1830

1782 **Lewis Cass.** U.S. Army officer and Democratic presidential candidate in 1848

1835 **Camille Saint-Saens.** French composer with a prodigious output of music, the best known of which is probably his opera *Samson and Delilah* (1877)

1860 **Leonard Wood.** American commander of the "Rough Riders" in the Spanish-American War

1863 **Edward William Bok.** American writer and journalist, who as editor of the *Ladies' Home Journal* was called "a lay preacher to the largest congregation in the United States"

1873 **Charles Rudolph Walgreen.** American druggist who founded the Walgreen drugstore chain in 1909

1884 **Martin Johnson.** American explorer and documentary filmmaker

1888 **Irving Cummings.** American motion-picture actor and director associated with over 100 movies

1889 **Rube Marquard.** Hall of Fame baseball pitcher who won 19 consecutive games for the New York Giants in 1912

1890 **Aimee Semple McPherson.** American evangelist and early radio preacher

1891 **Otto Schnering.** American candy manufacturer who originated the Baby Ruth candy bar named for President Cleveland's daughter

1898 **Joe Sewell.** Hall of Fame baseball player and the most difficult batter in history to strike out

1899	**Bruce Catton.** American historian, journalist, and author of numerous Civil War books such as *A Stillness at Appomattox,* which won the 1954 Pulitzer Prize
1900	**Alistair Sim.** Scottish stage, screen, and television actor with a career that spanned 45 years
1903	**Walter O'Malley.** American baseball executive who moved the Brooklyn Dodgers to Los Angeles
1906	**Leopold Senghor.** Poet, statesman, and president of Senegal
1908	**Jim Folsom.** Flamboyant populist governor of Alabama (1947-1951, 1955-1959), who refused to use racism as a campaign tool at a time when others were building careers on it
1908	**Jacques Tati.** French motion-picture actor, master of pantomime, and director
1911	**Joe Rosenthal.** American photojournalist who took the famous World War II picture of the marines raising the flag on Iwo Jima
1914	**Edward Andrews.** American stage, screen, and television actor
1918	**E. Howard Hunt.** One of the better known participants in the Watergate break-in
1924	**Arnold Risen.** Professional basketball player
1929	**Ernest Morial.** First black mayor of New Orleans
1938	**Russell Myers.** American cartoonist and creator of *Broom Hilda*
1940	**Gordon Humphrey.** U.S. senator
1940	**John Lennon.** Member of the Beatles musical group and superstar on his own
1940	**Joe Pepitone.** Professional baseball player
1941	**Trent Lott.** U.S. senator and Majority Leader succeeding Bob Dole
1941	**Brian Lamb.** Cable television executive and interviewer with C-SPAN
1944	**Fred Patek.** Professional baseball player
1949	**Jackson Browne.** American rock singer
1950	**Brian Downing.** Professional baseball player
1953	**Peanut Louie.** American tennis player
1958	**Mike Singletary.** Professional football player and All-Pro defensive lineman for the Chicago Bears
1964	**Martin Jaite.** Argentine tennis player
1965	**Scott Bakula.** American stage, screen and television actor

October 9 – Events

1000	Leif Ericson, the great Norse explorer, became the first European to land in North America, which he called Vinland. (The date is celebrated as Leif Ericson Day in Norway.)
1469	Fra Filippo Lippi, the great Italian painter, died in Spoleto, Italy, at age 63.
1470	King Henry VI was restored to the English throne by the Earl of Warwick.
1635	Religious dissident Roger Williams was banished from the Massachusetts Bay Colony because of his belief in religious and political liberty. He later founded Rhode Island.

1701	Yale College was founded by ten Connecticut clergymen. (It got its present name in 1718 when Elihu Yale contributed money and books to the school.)
1855	Joshua C. Stoddard of Worcester, Massachusetts, patented the first calliope.
1871	The Great Fire of Chicago burned itself out, after sweeping over 17,000 buildings, and leaving 98,000 people homeless.
1888	The Washington Monument in Washington, D.C., was opened to the public.
1905	The great French actress Sarah Bernhardt, in flinging herself off the castle parapet in *Tosca,* injured her leg so severely that it eventually had to be amputated.
1919	The Cincinnati Reds won the World Series, defeating the heavily-favored Chicago White Sox. Eight members of the White Sox team were later charged with throwing the series in what became known as the "Black Sox" scandal.
1936	The first generator at Hoover Dam (originally Boulder Dam) was switched on.
1958	Pope Pius XII died in Rome at age 82.
1973	Elvis and Priscilla Presley were divorced in Santa Monica, California.

October 10 – Birthdays

1560	**Jacobus Arminius.** Theologian and minister of the Dutch Reformed Church, who tried unsuccessfully to liberalize the severe Dutch Calvinistic views on predestination
1684	**Jean Antoine Watteau.** French romantic painter, whose masterpiece, *Pilgrimage to the Island of Cythera*, currently hangs in the Louvre in Paris.
1731	**Henry Cavendish.** Famous English physicist and chemist who first showed that water was a compound of hydrogen and oxygen, and who discovered many fundamental laws of electricity
1738	**Benjamin West.** American painter famous for his large pictures of historical subjects, which were scorned by his contemporary, the noted Gilbert Stuart, as West's "ten-acre" pictures
1813	**Giuseppe Verdi.** Leading Italian opera composer of the 19th century, whose works are performed more often today than those of any other opera composer
1830	**Isabella II.** Queen of Spain, 1833-1868
1833	**John Mohler Studebaker.** American wagon and vehicle maker who with his brothers Henry and Clement formed the Studebaker company that eventually became one of the great U.S. automakers
1845	**George Saintsbury.** English literary critic and historian
1861	**Fridtjof Nansen.** Norwegian explorer and statesman who in 1888 crossed Greenland from east to west, a feat declared by experts as impossible

1882 **Jack Francis Mahoney.** American lyricist noted for songs such as "When You Wore a Tulip and I Wore a Big Red Rose"

1890 **Richard Howard.** American composer and author noted for songs such as "Somebody Else Is Taking My Place"

1892 **Earle Ensign Dickson.** American inventor noted for the Band-Aid (1924)

1900 **Helen Hayes.** American actress and "First Lady of the American Theater"

1901 **Alberto Giacometti.** Swiss sculptor and leader of the surrealism movement, noted for his long, thin human figures

1903 **Vernon Duke.** American composer noted for works such as "April in Paris"

1906 **Paul Creston.** American composer, author, and conductor

1908 **Johnny Green.** American bandleader and composer of hit songs such as "Body and Soul," "I Cover the Waterfront," and "Coquette"

1909 **Johnny Marks.** American composer and author, noted for songs such as "Rudolph the Red-Nosed Reindeer," "A Holly Jolly Christmas," "Silver and Gold," and "Everything I've Always Wanted"

1911 **Leo Mannes (Zeke Manners).** American composer and singer, noted for songs such as "Pennsylvania Polka"

1913 **Claude Simon.** French novelist

1918 **Thelonious Monk.** American pianist and composer of jazz songs such as "Round Midnight" and "Blue Monk"

1920 **Frank Sinkwich.** Heisman Trophy winner (1942) and professional football superstar

1924 **James Clavell.** Australian-American author, playwright and screenwriter known for *Shogun* (1975)

1926 **Richard Jaeckel.** American motion-picture actor

1930 **Adlai E. Stevenson III.** U.S. senator in the 1970s and son of Adlai Stevenson, the Democratic candidate for president in 1952 and 1956

1930 **Harold Pinter.** English playwright and screenwriter, noted for works such as *The Dumb Waiter* (1957) and *Homecoming* (1965)

1937 **Bruce Devlin.** Professional golfer

1946 **Gene Tenace.** Professional baseball player

1946 **Ben Vereen.** American actor, dancer, and singer

1958 **Tanya Tucker.** American singer noted for the hit song *Delta Dawn* (1973)

1969 **Brett Favre.** Professional football quarterback and only NFL member to win three Most Valuable Player awards

October 10 – Events

1492 On the first voyage to America, Christopher Columbus's crew, after a near mutiny, agreed to sail on for three more days and then turn back if land were not found. It was—two days later.

1845 The United States Naval Academy opened at Annapolis, Maryland.

1858 The first Butterfield Overland Mail coach reached San Francisco from St. Louis.

1886 A tailless dress coat for men was introduced for the first time at the Tuxedo Park Club in New York. It shocked the guests but soon became commonplace as the "tuxedo."

1911 Chinese revolutionaries under Dr. Sun Yat-sen rebelled against the Manchu dynasty, which they overthrew by the end of the year.

1920 Bill Wambsganss made an unassisted triple play for Cleveland in a World Series game against Brooklyn when he caught a line drive, touched second to double the runner going to third and tagged the runner coming to second from first.

1931 Kahlil Gibran, the great Lebanese-American poet and author of *The Prophet*, died at age 48.

1935 George Gershwin's opera *Porgy and Bess* opened on Broadway.

1938 Germany completed the occupation of the Sudetenland in Czechoslovakia in accordance with the Munich agreement.

1943 Generalissimo Chiang Kai-shek was sworn in as president of China.

1963 The limited nuclear test ban treaty went into effect between the United States and Russia.

1973 Vice President Spiro Agnew resigned, pleading "no contest" to a tax evasion charge. He was only the second American vice president to resign.

October 11 – Birthdays

1738 **Arthur Phillip.** British admiral who settled Sydney, Australia, with convicts in 1788

1759 **Mason Locke (Parson) Weems.** American clergyman who in about 1800 wrote the first popular biography of Washington, *The Life and Memorable Actions of George Washington*

1821 **Sir George Williams.** A young English clerk who founded the YMCA

1835 **Theodore Thomas.** Noted American conductor

1844 **Henry John Heinz.** Founder of the H.J. Heinz company

1849 **William Knox D'Arcy.** Founder of the Iranian oil industry

1872 **Harlan Fiske Stone.** One of the great Supreme Court justices, who served as associate justice, 1925-1941, and as chief justice, 1941-1946

1882 **Robert Nathaniel Dett.** Canadian-born composer noted for "Mammy" (1912)

1884 **Eleanor Roosevelt.** U.N. diplomat, humanitarian, and wife of President Franklin D. Roosevelt

1885 **François Mauriac.** French novelist and 1952 Nobel Prize winner

1887 **Willie Hoppe.** The greatest billiard player of all time and the winner of 51 world titles between 1906 and 1952

1897 **Nathan F. Twining.** U.S. World War II Air Force general, and chairman of the Joint Chiefs of Staff, 1953-1960

1902	**Charles Revson.** Co-founder of Revlon corporation
1902	**Leon Belasco.** Russian-born motion-picture character comedian in some 60 pictures
1908	**Red Rolfe.** Professional baseball player and manager
1910	**Joseph Alsop.** American newspaper columnist
1918	**Jerome Robbins.** One of the most popular choreographers of the 20th century, with credits such as *The King and I, Westside Story,* and *Fiddler on the Roof*
1925	**Elmore John Leonard Jr.** American author noted for *Get Shorty* (1990)
1932	**Dottie West.** American singer
1939	**Maria Bueno.** Brazilian tennis superstar and winner of three Wimbledon singles titles
1950	**Patty Murray.** U.S. senator

October 11 – Events

732	Charles Martel (Charles the Hammer), the great Frankish leader, defeated the Moors in the famous Battle of Tours, ending the Moorish advance into Europe.
1531	Huldreich Zwingli, Swiss Protestant leader, was killed in the Battle of Kappel, between the Catholic cantons and the Protestants.
1737	One of the greatest earthquakes in world history occurred in Calcutta, India, killing some 300,000 people.
1779	Polish general Casimir Pulaski died from wounds suffered two days earlier while fighting for American independence in the siege of Savannah, Georgia.
1809	The great explorer Meriwether Lewis died in the wilds of Tennessee at age 35 on his way to Washington to report to President Madison. His death was ruled a suicide but the suspicion that he was murdered persists to this day.
1811	The first steam-propelled ferry service began, as inventor John Stevens put his ferryboat, the *Juliana,* into operation between New York City and Hoboken, New Jersey.
1890	The Daughters of the American Revolution was founded in Washington, D.C.
1936	*Professor Quiz,* the first national quiz program on radio, started its long run on CBS.
1941	General Hideki Tojo, the leader of the extremist Japanese military group, became premier of Japan.
1962	The first session of Vatican II was opened in Rome by Pope John XXIII.
1968	*Apollo 7,* the first manned Apollo flight, was launched with astronauts Schirra, Eisele, and Cunningham aboard.
1973	Two Pascagoula, Mississippi, dockworkers, Charles Hickson and Calvin Parker, claimed to have been kidnapped by weird creatures and examined for three days in a UFO.
1975	NBC's comedy series *Saturday Night Live* made its debut with a cast known as "Not Ready for Prime Time Players."
1979	American physicist Allan McLeod Cormack and British engineer Godfrey Newbold Hounsfield won the Nobel Prize for medicine for their development of the CAT scan.

October 12 – Birthdays

1537	**Edward VI.** Son of King Henry VIII by his third wife, Jane Seymour, and king of England, 1547-1553
1775	**Lyman Beecher.** American Presbyterian minister and father of the noted writer Harriet Beecher Stowe and the famous preacher Henry Ward Beecher
1803	**Alexander Turney Stewart.** American merchant who founded the A.T. Stewart Department Store, the world's first true department store
1840	**Helena Modjeska.** Noted Polish actress
1844	**George Washington Cable.** American author and reformer, noted for his books about old French New Orleans
1848	**William Leggett.** American football pioneer who with William Gummere established the rules and organized the first game (1869)
1860	**Elmer Ambrose Sperry.** American inventor and manufacturer, noted for his development of the gyroscope
1866	**Ramsay MacDonald.** Two times prime minister of Great Britain—in 1924 as the first Labour party prime minister, and in 1929-1935
1872	**Ralph Vaughan Williams.** The dominant English composer of the first half of the 20th century
1891	**Perle Mesta.** Prominent Washington, D.C., hostess and U.S. ambassador
1891	**Nelly Sachs.** German-born Nobel Prize-winning poet and dramatist, noted for works such as *Eli: A Miracle Play of the Sufferings of Israel* (1950)
1896	**Eugenio Montale.** Perhaps the greatest Italian poet of the 20th century, noted for works such as *The Storm and Other Poems*
1905	**Rick Ferrell.** Hall of Fame baseball player
1906	**Joe Cronin.** Hall of Fame baseball player and president of the American League
1912	**Sol Marcus.** American composer, author, and conductor, noted for songs such as "I Don't Want To Set the World on Fire" and "When the Lights Go On Again All Over the World"
1923	**Jean Nidetch.** American businesswoman who in 1963 founded Weight Watchers International
1932	**Dick Gregory.** American comedian and civil rights leader
1932	**Jake Garn.** U.S. senator
1935	**Sam Moore.** Soul singer of the Sam and Dave duo
1935	**Luciano Pavarotti.** Noted Italian opera singer and one of the greatest tenors of the late 20th century

1936	**Tony Kubek.** Professional baseball player and sports announcer
1942	**Melvin Franklin.** American singer with The Temptations
1944	**Jack Marin.** Professional basketball player
1950	**Susan Anton.** American motion-picture actress
1951	**Sally Little.** Professional golfer
1957	**Jerry Butler.** Professional football player

October 12 – Events

1492	At 2 A.M. lookout Rodrigo de Triana shouted "Tierra!" as Columbus's fleet discovered America. The land sighted was San Salvador (now Watling Island or perhaps Samana Cay).
1492	Piero della Francesca, the great Italian painter, died in Borgo San Sepolcro at an approximate age of 72.
1518	Martin Luther was interrogated on his Protestant views by Cardinal Cajetan at Augsburg.
1768	The first printed notice of the song "Yankee Doodle" appeared in the New York *Journal.*
1870	Robert E. Lee, the great Confederate general, died in Lexington, Virginia, at age 63.
1895	Charles Blair MacDonald won the first amateur golf tournament played in the United States.
1899	President S.J. Paulus "Oom Paul" Kruger of the Transvaal issued an ultimatum to the Boers of the Orange Free State, which precipitated the Boer War that began two days later.
1920	Construction began on the Holland Tunnel linking New York City and Jersey City.
1950	Senator Estes Kefauver's Subcommittee to Investigate Interstate Crime opened its hearings.
1960	Soviet premier Nikita Khrushchev pounded his desk with a shoe during a dispute at a United Nations General Assembly session.
1973	President Nixon named Congressman Gerald Ford to become vice president, succeeding Spiro Agnew, who had resigned.

October 13 – Birthdays

1474	**Mariotto Albertinelli.** Italian painter
1750	**Molly Pitcher.** American Revolutionary War heroine who took the place of her fallen husband in the Battle of Monmouth
1769	**Horace H. Hayden.** Founder of the first dental college
1821	**Rudolf Virchow.** German pathologist, anthropologist, and statesman, considered to be the father of pathology
1852	**Lily Langtry.** British actress known as the Jersey Lily, and a stage favorite in England and the United States in the late 19th century
1863	**Tod B. Galloway.** American composer and singer, noted for songs such as "The Whiffenpoof Song" and "Little Boy Blue"
1876	**Rube Waddell.** Hall of Fame baseball pitcher with a sensational career earned run average of 2.16

1877	**Theodore Bilbo.** U.S. senator from Mississippi, 1935-1947
1885	**Harry Hershfield.** One of the "grand old men" of the American comic strip, and creator of *Abie the Agent*
1889	**Ira Schuster.** American composer, author, and pianist, noted for songs such as "A Shanty in Old Shanty Town" and "Did You Ever Get That Feeling in the Moonlight?"
1891	**Irene Rich.** American stage and radio actress, and leading lady of the Hollywood silent screen
1900	**Gerald Marks.** American composer noted for songs such as "Is It True What They Say About Dixie?"
1909	**Herblock (Herbert Lawrence Block).** One of the most famous 20th-century American political cartoonists
1910	**Ernest Kellogg Gann.** American author of 23 books including works such as *The High and the Mighty* and *Twilight for the Gods*
1910	**Art Tatum.** Nearly blind American pianist and great jazz virtuoso
1915	**Cornell Wilde.** American motion-picture actor
1917	**Laraine Day.** American motion-picture actress
1921	**Yves Montand.** Italian-French stage and motion-picture actor
1924	**Nipsey Russell.** American comedian and actor
1925	**Margaret Thatcher.** Great Britain's first woman prime minister
1931	**Eddie Mathews.** Hall of Fame baseball player with a career total of 512 home runs
1935	**Chi Chi Rodriguez.** Professional golfer
1936	**Donald F. McHenry.** U.S. ambassador to the United Nations under President Carter
1941	**Paul Simon.** American singer and guitarist of the Simon and Garfunkel duo, and one of America's most successful songwriters
1942	**Jerry Jones.** American businessman and owner of the Dallas Cowboy football team
1942	**Pamela Tiffin.** American motion-picture actress
1950	**Barbara Hawcroft.** Australian tennis player
1952	**Elaine Garzarelli.** American financial advisor and stock analyst
1959	**Marie Osmond.** American singer and actor
1969	**Nancy Kerrigan.** American skater and Olympic medalist

October 13 – Events

54	Emperor Claudius died from poison given him by his physician Xenophon and his empress Agrippina, and Nero became emperor of Rome.
1399	Henry IV, the first English king of the House of Lancaster, was crowned.
1775	The American Navy was established by the Second Continental Congress.
1792	George Washington laid the cornerstone of the White House, known in the beginning as the President's House.

1843   The Jewish organization B'nai B'rith was founded in New York City.

1860   The first aerial photograph in the United States was taken from a balloon over Boston.

1903   Boston defeated Pittsburgh to win the first World Series in history, five games to three.

1924   Alfred Lunt and Lynn Fontanne began their famous joint stage careers in New York in the opening of *The Guardsman.*

1943   Italy declared war on her former World War II Axis partner, Nazi Germany.

1959   *Explorer 7* was launched from Cape Canaveral.

1960   John F. Kennedy and Richard M. Nixon held their third "Great Debate" in the 1960 presidential election.

1962   Edward Albee's great play *Who's Afraid of Virginia Woolf?* opened on Broadway.

1973   Gerald Ford was sworn in as vice president, succeeding Spiro Agnew, who had resigned.

1982   The International Olympic Committee announced that it would restore Jim Thorpe's two 1912 Olympic gold medals stripped from him for playing minor league baseball in 1911.

October 14 – Birthdays

1006   **Geoffrey Martel.** Count of Anjou

1606   **Joan Maetsuyker.** Governor general of the Dutch East Indies, 1653-1678

1633   **James II.** King of England, 1685-1688

1644   **William Penn.** Quaker leader and founder of Pennsylvania

1734   **Francis Lightfoot Lee.** American Revolutionary War patriot and signer of the Declaration of Independence

1863   **Annie Laurie (Winifred Sweet).** Noted American newspaperwoman with the San Francisco *Examiner*

1872   **Sol Hess.** American comic strip cartoonist and creator in 1923 of *The Nebbs*

1882   **Eamon De Valera.** Leader in Ireland's fight for independence, and head of the government as prime minister, president of Ireland, and of the Irish Free State for most of the years, 1937-1959

1888   **Katherine Mansfield.** English short story writer, noted for collections such as *The Garden Party* (1927)

1890   **Dwight D. Eisenhower.** 34th U.S. president and commander of the Allied European forces in World War II

1892   **Sumner Welles.** Undersecretary of state and trusted aide to President Franklin D. Roosevelt

1893   **Lois Lenski.** American author and illustrator of children's books, who received the Newberry Medal in 1946 for *Strawberry Girl*

1894   **E.E. Cummings.** American poet and writer, noted for disregarding the rules of punctuation (he wrote his name e e cummings), and noted for works such as *The Enormous Room* and *Poems 1923-1954*

1896   **Oscar Charleston.** Professional baseball player and Hall of Famer based on his career in the Negro leagues

1896   **Lillian Gish.** The greatest actress of the silent screen and one of the true giants of Hollywood, with a career of over 80 years

1900   **W. Edwards Deming.** American management consultant whose advice enabled Japan to become an economic giant after World War II

1901   **Harry A. Stuhldreher.** One of the famed Four Horsemen of the Notre Dame football team

1906   **Hannah Arendt.** German-born writer, newspaper correspondent, and historian

1910   **John Wooden.** Highly successful American basketball coach

1911   **Le Duc Tho.** North Vietnamese official who negotiated the Vietnam armistice with the United States

1914   **Harry Brecheen.** Professional baseball pitcher who won three games for the St. Louis Cardinals against the Boston Red Sox in the 1946 World Series

1917   **Thomas Geoffrey Bibby.** English archaeologist who developed carbon dating

1928   **Roger Moore.** English motion-picture and television actor

1930   **Stella Castellucci.** American composer, author, and harpist

1930   **Joseph-Desire Mobutu.** President of Zaire

1931   **Istvan Gulvas.** Hungarian tennis player

1938   **Farah Diba Pahlevi.** Shahbanou of Iran and wife of Iranian Shah Mohammed Reza Pahlevi

1938   **John Dean.** Central Watergate figure in the implication of President Nixon

1939   **Ralph Lauren.** American fashion designer and nine-time winner of the Coty, the fashion industry's most prestigious honor

1941   **J.C. Snead.** Professional golfer

1943   **Lance Rentzel.** Professional football player

1946   **Al Oliver.** Professional baseball player

1947   **Bob Kuechenberg.** Professional football player

1947   **Charles Joiner.** Professional football player

1948   **Ed Figueroa.** Professional baseball player

1950   **Sheila Young.** American speed skater, cyclist, and 1976 Olympic gold medal winner

1956   **Beth Daniel.** Professional golfer

October 14 – Events

996   Hugh Capet, the French king who founded the Capetian line, died in Paris at age 56.

1066   William the Conqueror defeated Harold Godwinson (Harold II), heir to the English throne, in the famous Battle of Hastings, which resulted in the Norman conquest of England.

1586   Mary, Queen of Scots, went on trial in England for plotting to kill Queen Elizabeth I. She was later found guilty and beheaded.

1793	French queen Marie Antoinette was brought to trial on a charge of treason by the French revolutionists. She was executed two days later.
1806	Napoleon routed the armies of Prussia in the Battles of Jena and Auerstad.
1899	The Boer War began as the Orange Free State and the South African Republic declared war on Britain.
1912	Theodore Roosevelt was shot by a would-be assassin in Milwaukee, while campaigning for president. He made his speech anyway and was then rushed to a hospital to recuperate.
1930	Ethel Merman made her Broadway debut in the premiere of George Gershwin's musical comedy *Girl Crazy*.
1944	Erwin Rommel, the famous German World War II field marshal, committed suicide after being implicated in the plot to kill Hitler.
1947	American pilot Charles Yeager became the first man to break the sound barrier, reaching a speed of 670 miles per hour—Mach 1.015—in a Bell X-1 rocket airplane.
1960	John F. Kennedy first suggested the idea of the Peace Corps, in a campaign speech at the University of Michigan.
1971	Iran held an elaborate celebration to mark the 2,500th anniversary of the founding of the Persian Empire by Cyrus the Great.

October 15 – Birthdays

70 BC	**Virgil.** The greatest poet of the Roman Empire
1608	**Evangelista Torricelli.** Italian mathematician and physicist, noted for his invention in 1643 of the barometer
1775	**John Vanderlyn.** American artist
1784	**Thomas Hastings.** American composer noted for "Rock of Ages"
1785	**Jose Miguel Carrera.** The first president of Chile
1814	**Mikhail Yuryevich Lermontov.** Russian poet and novelist and outstanding leader of the late Romantic period
1830	**Helen Hunt Jackson.** American poet, novelist, and author of *Ramona* (1884)
1844	**Friedrich Nietzsche.** German classical scholar and philosopher, author of *Thus Spake Zarathustra* (1883-1885), and the originator of the "God is Dead" religious philosophy
1847	**Ralph Blackelock.** American landscape painter noted for works such as *Sunset* and *Moonrise*
1858	**John L. Sullivan.** Famous American bare-knuckle fighter and world heavyweight boxing champion, 1882-1892, known as the "Great John L."
1871	**Frederick Knight Logan.** American composer and conductor, noted for songs such as "Missouri Waltz," "Rose of My Heart," and "Moonlight Waltz"
1878	**Paul Reynaud.** French prime minister in June 1940 when France fell in World War II

1879	**Jane Darwell.** American actress who played Ma Joad in *The Grapes of Wrath* (1940), and appeared in over 200 films in a 50-year career
1881	**P.G. Wodehouse.** Noted British-American humorist, novelist, and short-story writer
1882	**Ballard MacDonald.** American composer and author, noted for songs such as "Back Home In Indiana," "Beautiful Ohio," and "Trail of the Lonesome Pine"
1897	**Ben L. Trace.** American composer, author, and singer, noted for songs such as "You Call Everybody Darling" and "Sweet Dreams, Sweetheart"
1899	**William Claire Menninger.** American psychiatrist and co-founder of the Menninger Clinic
1900	**Boris Aronson.** Russian-born painter, sculptor, and designer
1900	**Fritz Feld.** German stage, screen, and television actor with a career of over 60 years
1900	**Mervyn LeRoy.** American motion-picture producer and director, noted for films such as *Little Caesar* (1931) and *The Wizard of Oz* (1939)
1903	**Otto Ludwig Bettmann.** American historian and founder of the Bettmann Archives (1941)
1905	**C.P. Snow.** British novelist and scientist
1908	**John Kenneth Galbraith.** Noted American economist and author of *The Affluent Society* (1958)
1909	**Mel Harder.** Professional baseball player
1917	**Alan Wendell Livingston.** American composer and author, noted for songs such as "I Taut I Taw a Puddy Tat" and "That's All Folks"
1917	**Arthur Schlesinger Jr.** Noted American historian, and Pulitzer Prize winner in 1966 for the biography *A Thousand Days: John F. Kennedy in the White House*
1920	**Claude Monteux.** American flutist and conductor
1921	**Mario Puzo.** American writer, and author of *The Godfather*
1924	**Lee Iacocca.** American automobile executive with Ford and later Chrysler
1926	**Evan Hunter.** American novelist noted for works such as *The Blackboard Jungle*
1926	**Jean Peters.** American motion-picture and television actress
1937	**Linda Lavin.** American actress noted for her starring role in the long-running television show *Alice*
1942	**Penny Marshall.** American actress and comedienne
1945	**Jim Palmer.** Professional Hall of Fame baseball player
1946	**Richard Carpenter.** American singer of The Carpenters duo
1951	**Roscoe Tanner.** American tennis player noted for his powerful serve
1953	**Beverly D'Angelo.** American motion-picture actress noted for her role of Patsy Cline in *Coal Miner's Daughter* (1980)
1953	**Tito Jackson.** American singer and guitarist with The Jackson 5 musical group

1955	**Victor Pecci.** Paraguayan tennis player
1959	**Sarah Ferguson.** Duchess of York and former wife of England's Prince Andrew

October 15 – Events

1582	The Gregorian Calendar of Pope Gregory XIII went into effect in most Catholic countries, with this day, which would have been October 5, becoming October 15, 1582.
1590	Urban VII was elected Roman Catholic pope.
1783	The brothers Jacques and Joseph Montgolfier sent up the first balloon carrying a man (J.F. Pilatre de Rozier), in Paris.
1846	Ether was used for the first time in a public demonstration, by Dr. William Thomas Green Morton in extracting a tooth in Boston, Massachusetts.
1858	The last Lincoln-Douglas debate was held in Alton, Illinois, before an audience of 6,000 people.
1894	Alfred Dreyfus, a French army officer, was arrested on the false charge of spying for Germany, in the famous Dreyfus case of political injustice.
1901	Geraldine Farrar, the brilliant American soprano, made her debut at the Berlin Opera House as Marguerite in *Faust*.
1905	The comic strip *Little Nemo in Slumberland*, by Winsor McKay, first appeared.
1914	The Clayton Anti-Trust Act became law.
1917	Mata Hari, the most famous spy of World War I, was executed in Paris by a firing squad of Zouaves.
1928	The German dirigible *Graf Zeppelin* arrived in the United States on its first commercial flight.
1945	Pierre Laval, the French World War II traitor, swallowed poison in a suicide attempt, but was revived and shot by a firing squad.
1946	Hermann Goering, the Nazi World War II Reichsmarshal, committed suicide by taking poison a day before his scheduled execution.
1948	Gerald Ford married Elizabeth "Betty" Bloomer.
1951	The long-running television series *I Love Lucy*, starring Lucille Ball and Desi Arnaz, premiered on CBS.
1964	Cole Porter, the noted American popular music composer, died at age 72.
1964	Nikita Khrushchev was ousted as premier and first secretary of the Russian Communist party.

October 16 – Birthdays

1430	**James II.** King of Scotland, 1437-1460
1483	**Gaparo Contarini.** Venetian Humanist scholar and theologian
1620	**Pierre Puget.** The most original of the French baroque sculptors
1708	**Albrecht von Haller.** Swiss biologist and father of experimental physiology
1758	**Noah Webster.** American educator famous for compiling *Webster's Dictionary*, the finest English dictionary of its time

1797	**James Thomas Brudenell Cardigan.** English general who led the charge of the Light Brigade in 1854 in the Crimean War
1806	**William Pitt Fessenden.** U.S. senator who helped found the Republican party in the 1850s
1815	**Francis Richard Lubbock.** One of the early governors of Texas
1854	**Oscar Wilde.** Irish wit, poet, and dramatist, noted for works such as *The Importance of Being Earnest* (1895)
1874	**Reginald Doherty.** Irish tennis player and four times Wimbledon singles champion, 1897-1900
1877	**Lee Laurie.** American sculptor known for the bronze Atlas in Rockefeller Center in New York City
1881	**William Harridge.** President of baseball's American League in the 1940s
1886	**David Ben-Gurion.** Israel's first prime minister after it became independent in 1948
1888	**Eugene O'Neill.** America's greatest playwright
1890	**Paul Strand.** American photographer and documentary filmmaker
1898	**William O. Douglas.** U.S. Supreme Court justice, 1939-1975
1900	**Goose Goslin.** Hall of Fame baseball player
1905	**Rex Bell.** American motion-picture actor
1906	**Cleanth Brooks.** American author and critic, noted for *Modern Rhetoric* (1949), with Robert Penn Warren
1906	**George Martin Lott.** American Hall of Fame tennis player
1908	**Robert Ardney.** American dramatist and scientist
1908	**Enver Hoxha.** Albanian dictator, 1944-1985
1912	**Clifford Hansen.** U.S. senator
1916	**Charles Everett Koop.** American physician and U.S. Surgeon General under Presidents Reagan and Bush
1916	**Kathleen Winsor.** American novelist noted for *Forever Amber* (1945)
1921	**Linda Darnell.** American motion-picture actress
1925	**Angela Lansbury.** English-born American stage, screen, and television actress, and star of the long-running TV series *Murder, She Wrote*
1927	**Gunter Grass.** German novelist and poet, noted for *The Tin Drum* (1959)
1929	**Nicholas von Hoffman.** American journalist, writer, and television personality
1931	**Charles Colson.** Aide to President Nixon who was convicted in the Watergate scandal
1940	**Barry Corbin.** American television and motion-picture actor
1940	**Dave De Busschere.** Professional Hall of Fame basketball player and superstar
1941	**Tim McCarver.** Professional baseball player and announcer
1941	**Mel Counts.** Professional basketball player
1945	**Suzanne Somers.** American television and motion-picture actress
1948	**Richard Caster.** Professional football player

1949   **John Mengelt.** Professional basketball player
1955   **Lynn Cain.** Professional football player
1958   **Tim Robbins.** American stage and motion-picture actor
1959   **Kevin McReynolds.** Professional baseball player
1969   **Juan Gonzalez.** Professional baseball player and superstar

October 16 – Events

1553   Lucas Cranach, the Elder, the great German painter, died in Weimar 12 days after his 81st birthday.
1793   French queen Marie Antoinette was executed on the guillotine by the revolutionists.
1813   The Battle of the Nations began at Leipzig between Napoleon and an Allied force of five countries.
1815   Napoleon was exiled to St. Helena, where he remained for the rest of his life.
1845   Edgar Allan Poe read his new poem, *The Raven,* to a Boston audience, but he did it in such a "singularly didactic" way that his listeners walked out on him.
1846   Boston dentist William T.G. Morton publicly demonstrated the use of ether as an anesthetic, as Dr. John Warren operated on a patient's jaw at Massachusetts General Hospital.
1859   John Brown, the noted abolitionist, made his famous raid on the U.S. arsenal at Harpers Ferry, Virginia.
1916   Margaret Sanger opened the world's first birth control clinic, in New York City.
1925   The Locarno (Switzerland) Conference ended, with the delegates having signed seven treaties outlawing willful aggression in Europe and providing a neutral zone in the Rhineland.
1933   The comic strip *Dan Dunn,* by Norman Marsh, appeared for the first time.
1934   The Chinese Communists began their "Long March" to the province of Shensi, where they planned to continue their struggle against Chiang Kai-shek.
1944   *The Robe,* the best-selling book by Lloyd Douglas, was first published.
1946   Ten top Nazis, including former foreign minister, Joachim von Ribbentrop, were hanged in Nuremburg for war crimes.
1962   President John F. Kennedy revealed to insiders in the United States government the existence of a Soviet missile buildup in Cuba.
1964   China joined the world's nuclear club, detonating its first atomic bomb.
1978   John Paul II was elected Roman Catholic pope.

October 17 – Birthdays

1582   **Johann Gerhard.** Leading theologian of his era
1696   **Augustus III.** King of Poland
1725   **John Wilkes.** English journalist and politician

1780   **Richard Mentor Johnson.** U.S. vice president, 1837-1841, who claimed to have killed the famous Indian chief Tecumseh
1813   **Georg Buchner.** German writer, often considered a forerunner of the naturalism movement of the late 1800s
1846   **Joseph L. Hudson.** English businessman who founded the J.L. Hudson company
1859   **Childe Hassam.** American painter noted for works such as *Union Square, New York* (1890)
1859   **Buck Ewing.** Hall of Fame baseball player
1885   **Isak Dineson.** Danish author who wrote most of her works in English, and who is known for novels such as *Out of Africa* (1937)
1886   **E.W. Goodpasture.** American pathologist who developed a vaccine for mumps (1931)
1893   **Spring Byington.** American stage, screen, and television actress, who appeared in some 100 movies in a 40-year career
1895   **Doris Humphrey.** Pioneer of the American modern dance
1900   **Yvor Winters.** American poet and critic
1903   **Irene Ryan.** American motion-picture and television actress noted for her role as Granny in the long-running series *The Beverly Hillbillies*
1903   **Nathanael West.** American novelist noted for works such as *The Day of the Locust* (1939)
1905   **Claude Binyon.** American motion-picture director and screenwriter who wrote the famous 1929 *Variety* headline about the stock market crash, "Wall Street Lays an Egg"
1905   **Jean Arthur.** American stage, screen, and television actor and comedienne
1906   **Paul Derringer.** Professional baseball player
1912   **Jack Milton Owens.** American composer, author, and singer, noted for songs such as "The Hut Sut Song"
1912   **John Paul I.** Roman Catholic pope who served only 34 days before his death in 1978
1914   **Jerry Siegel.** American comic strip writer, and co-creator with Joe Shuster of *Superman*
1915   **Arthur Miller.** A leading American playwright, and author of *Death of a Salesman* (1949)
1916   **Virgil Franklin Partch.** American cartoonist noted for the strip *Big George*
1917   **Marsha Hunt.** American motion-picture and television actress
1918   **Rita Hayworth.** Sensuous queen of Hollywood films of the 1940s
1920   **Montgomery Clift.** American stage and motion-picture actor and superstar of the 1950s and early 1960s
1927   **Tom Poston.** American actor and comedian
1927   **Johnny Klippstein.** Professional baseball player
1928   **Julie Adams.** American motion-picture and television actress
1928   **Jim Gilliam.** Professional baseball player
1930   **Jimmy Breslin.** American newspaper columnist and writer

| 1933 | **William A. Anders.** American astronaut who participated in *Apollo 8*, the first manned flight to orbit the moon |

1933   **William A. Anders.** American astronaut who participated in *Apollo 8*, the first manned flight to orbit the moon

1939   **Evel Knievel.** American dare-devil performer

1942   **Jim Seals.** American singer and songwriter with Seals and Crofts

1947   **Ronald Johnson.** Professional football player

1948   **George Wendt.** American actor noted for his role as Norm in the longrunning TV show *Cheers*

1948   **Margot Kidder.** Canadian motion-picture actress

1962   **Mike Judge.** American cartoonist and creator of *The Beavis and Butt-head* TV show (1993)

October 17 – Events

1529   Cardinal Wolsey was dismissed from office by King Henry VIII of England because of his disapproval of Henry's affair with Anne Boleyn.

1777   The Americans gained a decisive victory at Saratoga in the Revolutionary War, with British general John Burgoyne surrendering his entire army of some 6,000 men.

1849   Frederic Chopin, the great Polish composer, died of tuberculosis in Paris at age 39.

1855   Henry Bessemer patented his Bessemer process for making steel.

1914   Babe Ruth married Helen Woodford in Ellicot City, Maryland.

1919   The Radio Corporation of America (RCA) was incorporated.

1931   Al Capone, the best-known racketeer in the United States, was convicted of income tax evasion and sentenced to 11 years in prison.

1933   The great German scientist Albert Einstein entered the U.S. as a refugee from Hitler's Germany.

1945   Juan Peron staged a coup in Buenos Aires, and seized power as absolute dictator of Argentina.

1974   The Oakland A's won their third straight World Series, beating the Los Angeles Dodgers four games to one.

1978   The New York Yankees won an unprecedented four straight games, after losing the first two, to defeat the Los Angeles Dodgers in the World Series.

1989   An earthquake measuring 7.1 on the Richter scale hit the San Francisco-Oakland area, killing 67 people, injuring over 3700, and causing $5.6 billion in damage.

October 18 – Birthdays

1405   **Pius II.** Roman Catholic pope, 1458-1464

1595   **Edward Winslow.** A founder of the Plymouth colony in Massachusetts, whose marriage to Susanna White was the first wedding performed in the new colony

1631   **Michael Wigglesworth.** Puritan pastor, doctor, and poet of colonial New England, best known for his poem "The Day of Doom: or, A Poetical Description of the Great and Last Judgment" (1662)

1632   **Luca Giordano.** Neapolitan painter

1697   **Canaletto.** Italian painter (born Giovanni Antonio Canal)

1777   **Heinrich von Kleist.** German writer and playwright, noted for works such as *The Broken Jug* (1808)

1785   **Thomas Love Peacock.** English novelist and poet noted for works such as *Headlong Hall* (1816) and *Crotchet Castle* (1831)

1799   **Christian Friedrich Schonbein.** German chemist who discovered and named ozone

1831   **Frederick III.** King of Prussia, second emperor of modern Germany (for three months in 1888), and father of Wilhelm II, the German World War I kaiser

1839   **Thomas B. Reed.** Speaker of the U.S. House of Representatives, 1889-1891 and 1895-1899, whose autocratic control of the House resulted in his nickname, "Czar Reed"

1848   **Candy Cummings.** Hall of Fame baseball pitcher who is said to have invented the curve ball around 1867

1859   **Henri Louis Bergson.** Nobel Prize-winning French philosopher, noted for works such as *Time and Free Will* (1889)

1878   **James Truslow Adams.** Pulitzer Prize-winning American historian, noted for works such as *The Epic of America* (1931)

1884   **Burt Shotton.** Professional baseball player and manager

1896   **Frederick Hollander.** German composer noted for "Falling in Love Again" (1930)

1896   **Nat Holman.** American basketball coach known as "Mr. Basketball"

1902   **Miriam Hopkins.** American stage and motion-picture actress with a 45-year career

1905   **Felix Houphouet-Boigny.** First president of the Ivory Coast

1906   **Sidney Kingsley.** American dramatist who won a Pulitzer Prize for *Men in White* (1933)

1914   **Waldo Salt.** Hollywood screenwriter who won an Academy Award for *Midnight Cowboy* (1969) and shared another for *Coming Home* (1978)

1918   **Robert William Troup Jr.** American composer, author, and pianist, noted for songs such as "Route 66," "Daddy," and "The Girl Can't Help It"

1919   **Pierre Elliott Trudeau.** Three times prime minister of Canada from 1968 to 1984

1921   **Jesse A. Helms.** U.S. senator

1923   **Melina Mercouri.** Greek motion-picture actress

1926   **John Morris.** American composer who wrote the music for Mel Brooks' films and for such musicals as *Bye Bye Birdie*

1926   **Chuck Berry.** American rock and roll singer and songwriter

1927   **George C. Scott.** American stage, screen, and television actor, who won the Academy Award for *Patton* (1970)

1928   **Keith Jackson.** American television sportscaster

1929 **Violetta Barrios de Chamorro.** President of Nicargua who defeated the Sandinistas in the election of 1990

1929 **Hilliard Elkins.** Broadway play producer

1930 **Frank Carlucci.** Secretary of Defense under President Reagan

1939 **Lee Harvey Oswald.** Presumed assassin of President John F. Kennedy

1939 **Mike Ditka.** Professional football player, coach and Hall of Famer

1942 **Willie Horton.** Professional baseball player

1947 **Laura Nyro.** American popular song composer

1948 **Ntozake Shange.** American poet and playwright

1949 **George Hendrick.** Professional baseball player

1951 **Pam Dawber.** American television actress

1956 **Martina Navratilova.** Czechoslovakian-American tennis player and superstar

1958 **Thomas Hearns.** American heavyweight boxer

1961 **Wynton Marsalis.** American jazz trumpeter

1961 **Erin Moran.** American actress

1968 **Michael Stich.** German tennis player

October 18 – Events

514 The great Mayan city of Chichen Itza was first occupied by the Itzas.

768 Charlemagne and his brother Carloman were crowned co-rulers of the Franks, after the death of their father, Pepin the Short.

1667 Brooklyn was chartered under the name *Brueckelen* by the governor of New Netherlands, Mathias Nicolls.

1685 The Edict of Nantes, which gave Protestants equal rights with Catholics in France, was revoked by Louis XIV, resulting in thousands of Huguenots leaving France.

1767 Charles Mason and Jeremiah Dixon completed their surveying of the Mason and Dixon Line between the Maryland and Pennsylvania colonies.

1813 Napoleon was defeated as the Battle of the Nations at Leipzig ended. Napoleon escaped but his rule of Europe was ended.

1859 U.S. troops under Colonel Robert E. Lee stormed the firehouse at Harpers Ferry, Virginia (now West Virginia), and arrested John Brown, who had raided the arsenal earlier.

1867 Alaska was formally transferred to the United States, as the American flag replaced the Russian flag at Sitka.

1873 Columbia, Princeton, Rutgers, and Yale officials drew up the first rules for intercollegiate football.

1898 The United States formally took over Puerto Rico from Spain.

1912 The Treaty of Lausanne was signed, giving Italy control of Libya.

1924 Grantland Rice coined the name "The Four Horsemen" for Notre Dame football players, Stuhldreher, Miller, Crowley, and Layden, after their impressive win over Army.

1926 Bing Crosby, the great American popular singer, recorded his first record, "I've Got the Girl."

1931 Thomas A. Edison, the world's greatest inventor, died at age 84.

1944 Russian troops entered Czechoslovakia in World War II.

1950 Connie Mack, the Grand Old Man of Baseball, announced his retirement as manager of the Philadelphia Athletics after 67 years in the game.

1969 The U.S. government banned the use of the artificial sweeteners cyclamates because of evidence they caused cancer in rats. This claim was recanted in 1989.

October 19 – Birthdays

1433 **Marsilio Ficino.** Italian philosopher and translator of Plato

1605 **Sir Thomas Browne.** English physician and writer

1741 **Choderlos de Laclos.** French writer

1784 **Leigh Hunt.** English poet, journalist, and editor, noted for the poem "Abou Ben Adhem"

1810 **Cassius Marcellus Clay.** American politician and prominent abolitionist

1859 **Alfred Dreyfus.** French army officer unjustly imprisoned in the famous Dreyfus Affair

1861 **William J. Burns.** Prominent American detective and founder of the William J. Burns International Detective Agency

1862 **Auguste Lumiere.** French pioneer in photochemistry, who with his brother Louis Jean invented the *cinematographe,* a combination motion-picture camera, printer, and projector

1871 **Walter Bradford Cannon.** First neurologist to use X-rays in physiological studies

1876 **Mordecai "Three Finger" Brown.** Hall of Fame baseball pitcher with an amazing 2.03 career earned run average

1882 **Umberto Boccioni.** The greatest Italian sculptor of the early 1900s, noted for works such as *Unique Forms of Continuity in Space*

1885 **Charles Edward Merrill.** American businessman and founder in 1914 of Merrill Lynch, Pierce, Fenner and Beane (now Smith)

1889 **Fannie Hurst.** American novelist and short story writer, popular in the 1920s and 1930s

1895 **Lewis Mumford.** American social critic and historian, and author of *The City in History*, which won the National Book Award for 1961

1901 **Arleigh A. Burke.** American admiral and chief of naval operations, 1955-1961

1909 **Robert Beatty.** Canadian motion-picture and television actor

1911 **George Cates.** American composer noted for the music for "Auf Wiedersehen"

1918 **Russell Kirk.** American writer and lecturer

1918 **Robert Strauss.** Democratic Party leader and national chairman in 1980

1922   **Jack Anderson.** American newspaper columnist and television commentator

1926   **Edward Lewis Wallant.** American novelist noted for works such as *The Pawnbroker* (1961)

1931   **John LeCarre.** English novelist noted for *The Spy Who Came in from the Cold* (1963) and *The Looking Glass War* (1965)

1931   **Sandy Alomar.** Professional baseball player and father of baseball players Sandy Alomar Jr. and Roberto Alomar

1932   **Robert Reed.** American television and motion-picture actor

1938   **Renata Adler.** Italian-American novelist noted for works such as *A Year in the Dark* and *Pitch Dark*

1945   **John Lithgow.** American stage, screen and television actor

1949   **Lynn Dickey.** Professional football player

1955   **Martin Robinson.** English tennis player

1962   **Evander Holyfield.** American boxer and twice heavyweight champion (1990-1992 and 1993)

1967   **Amy Carter.** Daughter of President Jimmy Carter

October 19 – Events

202 BC   The Romans under Scipio Africanus defeated Hannibal's army of Carthaginians and Numidians in the Battle of Sama in the Second Punic War.

439   Gaiseric, King of the Vandals, seized the Roman city of Carthage, and made it his capital.

1453   The English surrendered Bordeaux to France in the Hundred Years' War.

1469   Ferdinand II, King of Aragon, and Isabella I, Queen of Castile, were married in Valladolid, Spain.

1630   The first general court in New England was held, in Boston.

1745   Jonathan Swift, the great British writer, died in Dublin at age 77.

1765   The Stamp Act Congress, called by the colonies in New York, declared that the British stamp taxes could not be enforced without the people's consent.

1774   Outraged citizens of Annapolis, Maryland, destroyed the British brig *Peggy Stewart* and its cargo of tea in reprisal for the tea tax.

1781   British General Cornwallis surrendered to General Washington at Yorktown, Virginia, ending the last major battle of the Revolutionary War.

1807   Sir Humphry Davy, the great English chemist, announced his discovery of the element sodium.

1812   Napoleon evacuated Moscow with only 110,000 men left in his 600,000-man Grande Armee.

1879   Thomas A. Edison invented the electric light.

1944   Marlon Brando made his New York stage debut in the Broadway hit *I Remember Mama*.

1950   United Nations forces captured the North Korean capital of Pyongyang in the Korean War.

1967   U.S. spacecraft *Mariner 5* passed within 2,500 miles of Venus.

1987   Stocks crashed on the New York Stock Exchange as the Dow Jones Industrial Average dropped 508 points, or 22.6%, with a volume of 604 million shares, all record numbers.

October 20 – Birthdays

1620   **Aelbert Cuyp.** Dutch painter noted for works such as *Landscape with Cattle*

1632   **Sir Christopher Wren.** The greatest English architect of his time

1677   **Stanislaw I.** King of Poland

1784   **Viscount, Henry Templeton Palmerston.** English statesman who served as foreign secretary and as prime minister during the Crimean War

1854   **Arthur Rimbaud.** French poet and adventurer

1859   **John Dewey.** American philosopher and educator

1874   **Charles Ives.** American composer who won the 1947 Pulitzer Prize for his *Symphony No. 3*, composed in 1911 but not performed until 1946

1882   **Bela Lugosi.** Hungarian-American motion-picture actor, noted for his portrayal of Count Dracula

1891   **Jomo Kenyatta.** First prime minister (1963) and first president, 1964-1978, of Kenya

1895   **Morrie Ryskind.** American columnist and playwright noted for works such as *Let 'Em Eat Cake* (1933, with George S. Kaufman)

1897   **Adolph Deutsch.** American composer who wrote the score of *Oklahoma!*

1900   **Wayne Morse.** U.S. senator in the 1950s and 1960s

1901   **Frank E. Churchill.** American composer noted for songs such as "Who's Afraid of the Big Bad Wolf?" and "Whistle While You Work"

1905   **Frederick Dannay.** American writer, who, with Manfred B. Lee, published under the pen name Ellery Queen

1906   **Crockett Johnson.** American cartoonist and creator of the comic strip *Dondi* (1941)

1908   **Stuart Hamblen.** American composer and singer, noted for songs such as "It Is No Secret," "This Ole House," and "Open Up Your Heart and Let the Sun Shine In"

1908   **Arlene Francis.** American stage, screen, and television actress

1913   **Grandpa Jones.** American television personality and banjo player on the longrunning TV show *Hee Haw*

1918   **Roy L. Ash.** American industrialist and co-founder of Litton Corporation

1925   **Art Buchwald.** American newspaper columnist and humorist

1928   **Joyce Brothers.** American psychologist and television personality

1930   **David Hall.** U.S. senator

1931   **Mickey Mantle.** The greatest switch hitter in baseball history, with a career total of 536 home runs

1932   **Roosevelt Brown.** Hall of Fame professional football player

1932 **William Christopher.** American television actor noted for his role of Father Mulcahy in *M*A*S*H*

1935 **Jerry Orbach.** American stage, screen and television actor, noted for the long-running TV show *Law and Order*

1950 **Isaac Curtis.** Professional football player

1952 **Melanie Mayron.** American television and motion-picture actress

1953 **Keith Hernandez.** Professional baseball player

1954 **Lee Roy Selman.** Hall of Fame professional football player

October 20 – Events

1740 Maria Theresa ascended the Austrian throne, causing the War of the Austrian Succession.

1803 The U.S. senate ratified the Louisiana Purchase.

1853 Benjamin Harrison married Caroline Lavinia Scott.

1873 P.T. Barnum, the great American showman, opened his *Hippodrome* in New York City.

1879 Thomas A. Edison's electric light bulb, which he had just invented the previous day, still burned all day. It lasted until he raised its voltage on the following day.

1903 A joint commission ruled in favor of the United States in settling the boundary dispute between Alaska and Canada.

1935 The "Long March" of 20,000 Chinese under Mao Tse-Tung ended, completing a 6,000-mile flight from Kiangsi to the province of Shensi. They were fleeing from the Chinese Nationalists for an entire year.

1944 The U.S. Sixth Army landed on Leyte in the Philippines, as General Douglas MacArthur issued the proclamation, "I have returned."

1964 Herbert Hoover died in New York at age 90, the highest age attained by any American president except John Adams.

1968 Former first lady Jacqueline Kennedy married Aristotle Onassis, the Greek shipping magnate.

1973 President Nixon fired special Watergate prosecutor Archibald Cox, setting off a nation-wide storm of protest.

October 21 – Birthdays

1581 **Il Domenichino.** Italian painter (born Domenico Zampieri)

1760 **Hokusai Katsushika.** One of the best-known Japanese color-print artists

1772 **Samuel Taylor Coleridge.** English poet of the romantic movement, and author of "The Rime of the Ancient Mariner," one of the greatest poems in English literature

1785 **Henry Miller Shreve.** Pioneer American steamboat captain and founder of Shreveport, Louisiana

1790 **Alphonse de Lamartine.** French poet, statesman, and man of letters

1808 **Samuel Francis Smith.** American clergyman, editor, and poet, who wrote the words to the patriotic song "America" (1831)

1833 **Alfred Bernhard Nobel.** Norwegian chemist who invented dynamite and founded the Nobel Prizes

1876 **Jay Norwood "Ding" Darling.** American political cartoonist

1892 **Albert Boni.** American publisher who started the Modern Library series (1917)

1909 **Bill Lee.** Professional baseball player

1912 **Sir Georg Solti.** English conductor with a career of nearly 50 years

1917 **Dizzy Gillespie.** American trumpeter and composer

1928 **Whitey Ford.** Hall of Fame pitcher who broke Babe Ruth's record by pitching 33 consecutive scoreless World Series innings in 1960-1962

1928 **Vern Mikkelsen.** Professional basketball player with over 10,000 career points

1929 **Ursula K. LeGuin.** American fantasy novelist noted for her *Earthsea* trilogy: *A Wizard of Earthsea, The Tombs of Atuan,* and *The Farthest Shore*

1939 **Boro Jovanovic.** Yugoslavian tennis player

1943 **Brian Piccolo.** Professional football player

1948 **Bill Russell.** Professional baseball player

1949 **Benjamin Netanyahu.** Prime minister of Israel who succeeded Yitzhak Rabin when he was assassinated

1956 **Carrie Fisher.** American actress and daughter of singer Eddie Fisher and actress Debbie Reynolds

October 21 – Events

1520 Ferdinand Magellan, on the first around-the-world voyage, entered the strait now called the Strait of Magellan.

1797 The United States frigate *Constitution* (Old Ironsides) was launched at the Boston Navy Yard.

1805 British admiral Horatio Nelson defeated the French and Spanish in the Battle of Trafalgar, one of the greatest naval battles in history. He was killed, however, in the action.

1907 Franz Lehar's operetta, *The Merry Widow,* had its New York premiere at the Amsterdam Theater.

1917 Soldiers of the First Division of the U.S. Army training in Luneville, France, became the first Americans to see action on the front lines of World War I.

1944 The U.S. First Army captured Aachen, the first German city to fall into Allied hands in World War II.

1959 The Solomon R. Guggenheim Museum in New York City was dedicated.

1960 John F. Kennedy and Richard M. Nixon held their fourth and last "Great Debate" in the 1960 presidential election.

1973 Oil-producing Arab states placed an embargo on oil for the United States.

1976   The Cincinnati Reds defeated the New York Yankees, becoming the first National League team since 1922 to win two consecutive World Series.

1998   The New York Yankees defeated the San Diego Padres, 3-0, sweeping the 1998 World Series and setting a season's record of 125 victories including the post-season games.

October 22 – Birthdays

1689   **John V.** King of Portugal

1738   **James Manning.** Baptist clergyman who founded Brown University in 1764

1811   **Franz Liszt.** One of the greatest Hungarian composers and the most celebrated pianist of the 1800s

1818   **Charles M.R. Leconte de Lisle.** French poet

1843   **Stephen Moulton Babcock.** American agricultural chemist who devised in 1890 a test for measuring butterfat in milk

1844   **Sarah Bernhardt.** One of the greatest actresses in the history of the stage

1854   **James A. Bland.** American songwriter noted for "Carry Me Back to Old Virginny" (1878), which was adopted as the official state song of Virginia in 1940

1880   **Joe Carr.** American football executive and one of the founders of the National Football League (1919)

1885   **Giovanni Martinelli.** Italian opera singer and actor, who was a leading tenor with the New York Metropolitan Opera Company in more than 50 operas

1887   **John Reed.** American poet, adventurer, and journalist, who wrote the eyewitness account *Ten Days that Shook the World* (1919), of the Bolsheviks' seizure of power in Russia

1891   **Sir James Chadwick.** English physicist who won the 1935 Nobel Prize for his discovery of the neutron (in 1932)

1899   **William Morris Jr.** American talent agent and founder of the William Morris Agency

1900   **Edward R. Stettinius Jr.** Secretary of state under Presidents Franklin Roosevelt and Truman, who was a leader in organizing the United Nations

1903   **Curly Howard.** American comedian and actor, and one of the original Three Stooges

1904   **Constance Bennett.** American motion-picture actress and daughter of matinee idol Richard Bennett

1905   **Joseph Kosma.** Hungarian composer noted for works such as "Autumn Leaves"

1907   **Jimmie Foxx.** First baseball player after Babe Ruth to hit 500 career home runs

1912   **Harry Callahan.** American photographer

1917   **Joan Fontaine.** One of Hollywood's leading actresses of the 1930s and 1940s, and sister of actress Olivia de Havilland

1918   **Harry Walker.** Professional baseball player

1919   **Doris Lessing.** English novelist noted for works such as *Canopus in Argos,* a sequence of fantastic novels set in space

1920   **Timothy Leary.** American scientist, radical, and "visionary prophet"

1922   **John Chafee.** U.S. senator

1925   **Robert Rauschenberg.** American artist and a founder of the pop art school

1925   **Slater Martin.** Professional basketball player and Hall of Famer

1925   **Dory Previn.** American songwriter

1935   **Judy Devlin Hashman.** One of the greatest players in the history of women's badminton and winner of 56 national championships

1937   **Bobby Seale.** American black militant

1938   **Christopher Lloyd.** American stage, screen and television actor

1938   **Derek Jacobi.** English stage, screen and television actor

1939   **Tony Roberts.** American stage, screen, and television actor

1941   **Wilbur Wood.** Professional baseball player

1942   **Annette Funicello.** American actress and "Mouseketeer"

1943   **Catherine Deneuve.** French motion-picture actress

1944   **Mike Wynn.** Professional golfer

1952   **Patti Davis.** American author and daughter of President Reagan

1954   **Jamie Quirk.** Professional baseball player

1955   **Gary Green.** Professional football player

1961   **Barbara Potter.** American tennis player

1966   **Valeria Golino.** Italian motion-picture actress

October 22 – Events

741   French king Charles Martel, the grandfather of the great emperor Charlemagne, died at age 53.

1303   Benedict XI was elected Roman Catholic pope.

1746   Princeton University received its charter from George II of England.

1797   Andre Jacques Garnerin became the first man to drop from a balloon in a parachute, over the Parc Monceau in Paris.

1836   Sam Houston was inaugurated as the first president of the Republic of Texas.

1883   The Metropolitan Opera House in New York celebrated its grand opening with a performance of Gounod's opera *Faust.*

1906   Paul Cezanne, the great French painter, died at age 67 in Aix-en-Provence.

1934   The comic strip *Terry and the Pirates,* by Milton Caniff, first appeared.

1934   Pretty Boy Floyd, the notorious outlaw, was gunned down by the FBI in a field in Ohio.

1954   West Germany was accepted as a member of NATO.

1962   President Kennedy announced the Soviet missile buildup in Cuba and ordered an American blockade of the island.

1973 Pablo Casals, the great Spanish cellist and conductor, died in Puerto Rico at age 96.

October 23 – Birthdays

1698 Jacques Ange Gabriel. French architect
1715 Peter II. Czar of Russia, 1727-1730
1734 Nicolas E.R. De la Bretonne. French writer and printer
1750 Thomas Pinckney. American soldier, diplomat, and vice presidential candidate in 1796
1817 Pierre Larousse. Noted French encyclopedist
1835 Adlai E. Stevenson. U.S. vice president, 1893-1897, and grandfather of 1952 and 1956 presidential candidate, Adlai E. Stevenson
1838 Francis Hopkinson Smith. American novelist, painter, and engineer, who built the foundation for the Statue of Liberty
1844 Wilhelm Leibl. German painter
1844 Robert Seymour Bridges. English poet and scholar, who became poet laureate of England in 1913
1861 Marquis Converse. American businessman who founded Converse Rubber Shoe Co. (1908)
1869 John William Heisman. American football player and coach for whom the Heisman Trophy is named
1879 Ernie Erdman. American composer noted for songs such as "Toot, Toot, Tootsie, Goodbye" and "Nobody's Sweetheart"
1883 Hugo Wast. Argentina's most popular novelist
1893 Gummo Marx. American comedian and one of the Marx Brothers
1901 Moe Jaffe. American composer and author, noted for songs such as "Bell Bottom Trousers" and "The Gypsy in My Soul"
1906 Gertrude Ederle. First woman to swim the English Channel (1926)
1913 Bao Dai. Last emperor of Vietnam, 1925-1945
1918 James Daly. American actor and father of actors Tyne and Timothy Daly
1918 Paul Rudolph. American architect
1920 Frank Rizzo. Mayor of Philadelphia in the 1970s
1920 Vern Stephens. Professional baseball player
1920 Bob Montana. American comic strip artist, and creator of *Archie*
1923 Ned Rorem. American Pulitzer Prize-winning composer and teacher
1925 Johnny Carson. American comedian and longtime host of NBC's *Tonight Show*
1931 Diana Dors. English motion-picture actress
1931 Jim Bunning. Professional baseball pitcher who pitched a perfect game (no batter reached base) in 1964
1936 Philip Kaufman. American motion-picture director noted for works such as the 1978 remake of *The Invasion of the Body Snatchers*
1938 John Heinz. Heir to the H.J. Heinz fortune and U.S. senator

1940 Pele (Edson Arantes do Nascimento). Brazilian soccer player and possibly the most famous and highest paid athlete of his time
1942 Michael Crichton. American screenwriter, director and novelist noted for works such as *The Andromeda Strain* and *Jurassic Park*
1943 Milan Holecek. Czechoslovakian tennis player
1956 Dwight Yoakam. American country singer
1959 "Weird Al" Yankovic. American parodist and rhythm and blues singer
1962 Doug Flutie. Heisman Trophy winner in 1984 and professional football superstar

October 23 – Events

4004 BC The earth was created at 9 A.M., in the opinion of Bishop James Ussher, a 17th-century Irish clergyman.
42 BC Marcus Brutus, leader of the plot to murder Julius Caesar, committed suicide.
1386 The University of Heidelberg, the oldest in Germany, was founded.
1915 Twenty-five thousand women marched in New York City demanding the right to vote.
1917 The U.S. Army fired its first shots against the Germans in World War I, near Luneville, France.
1929 Stocks on the New York Stock Exchange lost an average 18.24 points, but stocks, experts said, had reached a "permanently high plateau." The market crashed six days later.
1940 Adolf Hitler conferred in France with Generalissimo Franco, seeking Franco's aid in World War II. Franco squirmed and hedged, but never committed himself.
1942 English general Bernard Montgomery began the Battle of El Alamein against German Field Marshal Erwin Rommel's Afrika Corps.
1944 The World War II Battle for Leyte Gulf began, the biggest naval battle in history. It ended three days later in a crushing defeat of the Japanese by the Americans.
1945 Vidkun Quisling, the Norwegian World War II traitor, was shot by the Norwegians.
1950 Al Jolson, Russian-born American singer, died at age 64.
1955 The South Vietnamese, in their first election, chose Ngo Dinh Diem as premier.
1956 The Hungarian Revolution against Russian rule began.
1970 Gary Gabelich, American racing car driver, drove an automobile a record 631 miles per hour at Bonneville Salt Flats, Utah.
1983 Two hundred and forty-one U.S. marines and sailors were killed in Lebanon by a suicide truck-bomber who crashed into the American compound at Beirut International Airport.

October 24 – Birthdays

51	**Domitian.** Roman emperor, AD 81-96
1632	**Anton Van Leeuwenhoek.** Dutch scientist and microscopist, and first man to observe bacteria
1788	**Sarah Josepha Hale.** American magazine editor and author of "Mary Had a Little Lamb"
1820	**Eugene Fromentin.** French painter
1855	**James Schoolcraft Sherman.** Vice president under President Taft, and first vice president to be renominated (1912) in the history of the Republican party (but he died during the election campaign)
1882	**Dame Sybil Thorndike.** One of the great ladies of the British stage
1890	**Mainbocher.** American fashion designer
1891	**Rafael Trujillo.** Dictator of the Dominican Republic, 1930-1961
1893	**Merian C. Cooper.** American motion-picture director noted for films such as *King Kong* (1933)
1899	**Ferhat Abbas.** Leader of the Algerian National Liberation Front until Algeria was granted its independence from France in 1962
1900	**Ossie Bluege.** Professional baseball player and manager
1902	**Preston Foster.** American stage and screen actor with a career of over 100 films
1904	**Moss Hart.** American playwright and screenwriter, noted for works such as *Act One* (1959)
1911	**Clarence M. Kelley.** Director of the FBI under Presidents Nixon and Ford
1914	**Jackie Coogan.** American motion-picture actor and noted child star
1915	**Tito Gobbi.** Italian baritone
1916	**Bob Kane.** American comic strip artist and creator of *Batman*
1925	**Bobby Brown.** American physician, professional baseball player, and President of the American League
1926	**Y.A. Tittle.** Professional Hall of Fame football player and superstar
1936	**David Nelson.** American motion-picture and television actor
1937	**Juan Marichal.** Hall of Fame baseball player
1938	**Jack H. Watson Jr.** Presidential aide under President Carter
1939	**F. Murray Abraham.** American motion-picture, stage, and television actor who won the Academy Award for best actor in *Amadeus* (1984)
1947	**Kevin Kline.** American motion-picture actor
1948	**Bill Wyman.** British bassist with The Rolling Stones musical group
1950	**Rawley Eastwick.** Professional baseball player
1950	**Tom Myers.** Professional football player
1953	**Omar Moreno.** Professional baseball player

October 24 – Events

1537	Jane Seymour, third wife of King Henry VIII of England, died in childbirth, saving Henry the need for killing her.
1648	The Peace of Westphalia ended the Thirty Years' War between the Catholics and Protestants of various European countries, and effectively destroyed the Holy Roman Empire.
1861	The first transcontinental telegrams were sent, one from California to Washington, D.C., and one from New York to California.
1901	Anna Edson Taylor, a 43-year-old widow, became the first person to go over Niagara Falls in a barrel and live to tell about it.
1904	The first sections of the New York subway were opened to the public.
1922	Benito Mussolini issued his call for the "March on Rome," resulting in his becoming dictator of Italy a few days later.
1929	Prices on the New York Stock Exchange dropped sharply in "a little distress selling." The real collapse came five days later.
1931	The George Washington Bridge, between New York City and New Jersey, was opened to the public.
1939	The first nylon stockings went on sale in the United States, in Wilmington, Delaware.
1940	The 40-hour work week went into effect under the Fair Labor Standards Act of 1938.
1945	The United Nations was formally established with the ratification of its charter by the 29th nation.
1952	General Dwight D. Eisenhower, candidate for president, said that if elected, he would go to Korea to try to end the war there.
1962	Six Soviet ships bound for Cuba "stopped dead in the water" at the edge of the quarantine line enforced by the U.S. Navy in the Cuban Missile Crisis.
1964	Zambia, formerly Northern Rhodesia, became independent.

October 25 – Birthdays

1767	**Benjamin Constant.** Franco-Swiss novelist and political writer
1800	**Thomas Babington Macaulay.** The most widely read English historian of the 1800s
1802	**Richard Parkes Bonington.** English landscape painter
1811	**Evariste Galois.** French mathematician noted for the development of group theory
1825	**Johann Strauss Jr.** Austrian composer and "Waltz King," whose most famous work is probably *On the Beautiful Blue Danube*
1837	**Anna M. Richardson Harkness.** American philanthropist who established the Commonwealth Fund

1838   **Georges Bizet.** French composer whose last and finest work was *Carmen* (1875), perhaps the most popular opera of all time

1864   **John Francis Dodge.** Pioneer American automobile manufacturer, who with his brother Horace founded the Dodge Company and produced the Dodge automobile, one of the first with an all-steel body

1873   **John North Willys.** American industrialist who founded the Willys-Overland motor car company in 1907

1881   **Pablo Picasso.** The most famous painter of the 20th century

1885   **Samuel M. Lewis.** American lyricist noted for songs such as "Rockabye Your Baby With a Dixie Melody," "Five Foot Two, Eyes of Blue," "I'm Sitting on Top of the World," and "In a Little Spanish Town"

1888   **Richard E. Byrd.** U.S. naval officer and polar explorer, who was the first to fly over the North Pole (1926), and who made three expeditions to the South Pole

1889   **Smoky Joe Wood.** Professional fastball pitcher and superstar who won 16 consecutive games in 1912 with the Boston Red Sox

1892   **Leo G. Carroll.** English stage, screen and television actor

1895   **Levi Eshkol.** Prime minister of Israel, 1963-1969, who was in office at the time of the Six-Day War of 1967

1902   **Henry Steele Commager.** American historian and educator, noted for his popular books on American history

1903   **Clay A. Boland.** American composer noted for songs such as "Stop Beatin' 'Round the Mulberry Bush" and "The Gypsy in My Soul"

1904   **Arshile Gorky.** American artist and a leading member of the abstract expressionist movement

1912   **Minnie Pearl.** American comedienne

1917   **Lee MacPhail.** Professional baseball executive and son of noted baseball owner Larry MacPhail

1921   **Michael.** King of Romania, 1927-1930 and 1940-1947

1923   **Bobby Thomson.** Professional baseball player who hit the dramatic home run that gave the New York Giants the pennant in the 1951 playoffs with the Brooklyn Dodgers

1928   **Marion Ross.** American motion-picture and television actress

1935   **Russell Schweickart.** U.S. astronaut who participated in the *Apollo 9* mission

1940   **Bobby Knight.** Noted basketball coach, primarily at Indiana University

1941   **Anne Tyler.** American author noted for works such as *Breathing Lessons* (1989)

1942   **Helen Reddy.** Australian pop singer

1944   **James Carville.** American political consultant, author and strategist for President Clinton in the 1992 election

1945   **Dan Gable.** Professional wrestler

1948   **Dan Issel.** Professional basketball player and Hall of Famer

1948   **Dave Cowens.** Professional Hall of Fame basketball player and superstar

1958   **David Woodley.** Professional football player

1963   **Tracy Nelson.** American movie and TV actress and granddaughter of actors Ozzie and Harriet Nelson

October 25 – Events

1400   Geoffrey Chaucer, the greatest English poet of the Middle Ages, died at approximately 57 years of age.

1415   King Henry V of England, with 13,000 troops, defeated the French army of 50,000 in the Battle of Agincourt (France) in the Hundred Years' War.

1529   Henry VIII of England appointed Sir Thomas More Lord Chancellor, succeeding Cardinal Wolsey, who had been dismissed for not approving Henry's affair with Anne Boleyn.

1555   Charles V, Holy Roman emperor and king of Spain, abdicated rule of The Netherlands.

1760   George III became king of England. He was to serve 60 years and preside over the loss of the American Colonies.

1764   John Adams married Abigail Smith.

1854   The Allies defeated the Russians in the Battle of Balaklava in the Crimean War. It was one of the most famous battles in history because of the charge of the Light Brigade.

1859   Chester A. Arthur married Ellen Lewis Herndon.

1924   The U.S. Navy's *Shenandoah* made the first transcontinental airship voyage.

1936   Germany and Italy formed the Rome-Berlin Axis.

1938   The Chinese Nationalist government fled to Chungking as the Japanese captured Hankow.

1950   Communist China entered the Korean War on the side of the North Koreans.

1971   The United Nations voted to seat the People's Republic of China and to unseat Nationalist China.

October 26 – Birthdays

1466   **Desiderius Erasmus.** The foremost Christian humanist of the Renaissance, noted for *Praise of Folly,* one of the great works of literature

1556   **Ahmad Baba.** Jurist, writer, university chancellor, and cultural leader of the great black Songhay Empire in the late 16th century

1685   **Domenico Scarlatti.** Italian composer, noted for some 550 clavier sonatas, and son of Italian composer Alessandro Scarlatti

1757   **Charles Pinckney.** American diplomat, governor, senator, congressman, and one of the American founding fathers

1759   **Georges Danton.** One of the greatest leaders of the French Revolution

1800	**Helmuth Karl von Moltke.** Prussian military genius who ranked next to Bismarck as a builder of the German Empire
1842	**Vereshchagin.** Russian painter
1849	**Ferdinand Georg Frobenius.** German mathematician noted for the "method of Frobenius" of solving differential equations
1854	**Charles W. Post.** American businessman who founded the Postum Cereal Co. in 1897
1861	**Richard Dudley Sears.** American tennis player and the first U.S. Singles Champion
1863	**Ellsworth Milton Statler.** American hotel proprietor who in 1901 founded the Statler Hotel chain
1866	**Kid Gleason.** Professional baseball player and manager
1902	**Beryl Markham.** English-African aviator noted for her autobiography *West with the Night* (1942) and as the first person to fly solo across the Atlantic from east to west (1936)
1910	**John Cardinal Krol.** Archbishop of Philadelphia
1911	**Mahalia Jackson.** American singer
1912	**Don Siegel.** American motion-picture director noted for *Invasion of the Body Snatchers* (1956)
1913	**Charlie Barnet.** American bandleader of the Big Band Era of the 1930s and 1940s
1916	**François Mitterand.** President of France
1918	**Snuffy Stirnweiss.** Professional baseball player
1919	**Edward Brooke.** First black U.S. senator since Reconstruction, 1967-1979
1919	**Mohammed Reza Pahlavi.** Shah of Iran, 1941-1979
1942	**Bob Hoskins.** British stage and motion-picture actor
1945	**Pat Conroy.** American novelist noted for works such as *The Great Santini* (1976)
1946	**Pat Sajak.** American newscaster, disc jockey, and host of the TV shows *Wheel of Fortune* and *The Pat Sajak Show*
1947	**Hillary Rodham Clinton.** American lawyer and wife of President Bill Clinton
1947	**Jaclyn Smith.** American television actress
1948	**Toby Harrah.** Professional baseball player
1949	**Mike Hargrove.** Professional baseball player and manager
1949	**Steve Rogers.** Professional baseball player
1950	**Chuck Foreman.** Professional football player
1953	**Louis Breeden.** Professional football player

October 26 – Events

899	King Alfred the Great of England died in Wessex, England, at the approximate age of 50.
1676	Bacon's Rebellion in Virginia ended with the death of its leader, Nathaniel Bacon.
1774	The first Continental Congress adjourned in Philadelphia after nearly two months of meetings.
1825	The Erie Canal, the first important man-made waterway in the United States, was opened to traffic, connecting Lake Erie and the Hudson River.
1881	The Earps and Doc Holliday took on the Clantons and McLowrys in the Gunfight at the O.K. Corral in Tombstone, Arizona. Ike Clanton fled and his other cohorts were killed.
1905	Norway became independent of Sweden with a formal treaty dissolving their union.
1944	The Battle for Leyte Gulf ended with the U.S. Pacific Fleet crushing the Japanese fleet. The U.S. lost six ships and the Japanese lost 26 in the battle.
1951	The Conservative Party defeated the Labor Party in England to bring Winston Churchill back as prime minister.
1951	Rocky Marciano knocked out former champion Joe Louis in the eighth round at Madison Square Garden to retain his heavyweight championship.
1958	Pan American World Airways flew its first Boeing 707 jetliner from New York to Paris.
1962	The *Marucla*, sailing under the Russian flag, was stopped by the U.S.S. *Joseph P. Kennedy, Jr.*, and boarded, enforcing the Cuban Missile Crisis quarantine.
1970	The comic strip *Doonesbury*, by Garry Trudeau, first appeared.

October 27 – Birthdays

1401	**Catherine.** Wife of King Henry V of England
1728	**Captain James Cook.** British navigator and famous explorer of the Pacific Ocean
1736	**James Macpherson.** Scottish poet whose alleged translations from a third century Gaelic poet were much admired but were later exposed as fraudulent by Samuel Johnson
1760	**August Gneisenau.** Prussian field marshal and reformer
1782	**Niccolo Paganini.** One of the greatest violinists of all time
1811	**Isaac Merrit Singer.** American manufacturer who, more than any other man, made the sewing machine a universal household appliance
1858	**Theodore Roosevelt.** 26th U.S. president
1870	**Roscoe Pound.** American educator and authority on law, and the best known figure in American legal education in the early 20th century
1872	**Emily Post.** Well-known American authority on social behavior, whose faulty mathematics caused waiters' tips to be raised from 10% to 15%, because, she said, of inflation during World War II
1877	**Walt Kuhn.** American painter
1895	**Robert Paine Scripps.** American journalist, publisher, and son of Edward Wyllis Scripps, the founder of the Scripps newspaper chain
1910	**Jack Carson.** Canadian-born actor and comedian
1911	**Leif Erickson.** American stage, screen, and television actor
1912	**C.L. Sulzberger.** American writer, novelist, and newspaper columnist

1914	**Dylan Thomas.** Welsh poet and writer, noted for works such as *Eighteen Poems* (1934) and *Portrait of the Artist as a Young Dog* (1940)
1918	**Teresa Wright.** American stage and motion-picture actress
1920	**Nanette Fabray.** American stage, screen, and television actress
1922	**Ralph Kiner.** Hall of Fame baseball player whose ratio of 7.1 home runs per 100 times at bat is second only to Babe Ruth's
1923	**Ruby Dee.** American stage, screen and television actress and wife of actor Ossie Davis
1923	**Roy Lichtenstein.** American cartoonist
1925	**Warren M. Christopher.** Secretary of state under President Clinton
1926	**H.R. Haldeman.** Aide to President Nixon, imprisoned for his part in the Watergate scandal
1928	**Terry Horvitz Kovel.** American columnist and antique authority
1928	**Kyle Rote.** Professional football player and sportscaster
1930	**Bill George.** Hall of Fame football player
1932	**Sylvia Plath.** American poet and author whose novel *The Bell Jar* (1962) is an autobiographical account of manic depression which led to her suicide at age 31
1939	**John Cleese.** British actor and comedian noted for the long-running television series *Monty Python's Flying Circus*
1946	**Carrie Snodgress.** American stage, screen, and television actress
1946	**Peter Martins.** Danish ballet dancer
1951	**Jayne Kennedy-Overton.** Actress and television personality
1952	**Pete Vukovich.** Professional baseball player
1954	**Michael D. McCurry.** White House press secretary under President Clinton
1956	**Patty Sheehan.** Hall of Fame professional golfer and first woman to win the U.S. Women's Open and the British Women's Open in the same year (1992)
1958	**Simon Le Bon.** Lead vocalist of the Duran Duran musical group
1964	**Mary Terstegge Meagher.** Hall of Fame Olympic swimmer who won three gold medals and 22 U.S. championships

October 27 – Events

97	Roman emperor Nerva adopted Trajan as his successor.
1553	Michael Servetus, the great Spanish physician and theologian, was burned at the stake after being denounced as a heretic by John Calvin.
1787	The *Federalist* papers, a series of letters under the signature *Publius,* but written by Hamilton, Madison, and Jay, began to appear in the New York *Independent Journal.*

1871	William Marcy "Boss" Tweed, corrupt political dictator of Tammany Hall, was arrested on charges of fraud.
1880	Theodore Roosevelt married his first wife, Alice Hathaway Lee.
1904	The first practical subway started operations, running from the Brooklyn Bridge to 145th Street in New York City.
1917	Jascha Heifetz, the great violinist, made his American debut in Carnegie Hall at age 16.
1920	The League of Nations moved its headquarters from London to Geneva.
1936	Wallis Warfield Simpson, later to be the wife of England's ex-king, Edward VIII, divorced her first husband.
1938	Dupont announced the invention of nylon hosiery.
1961	The United States super aircraft carrier *Constellation* was commissioned.
1997	The Dow Jones lost 554 points, the worst single-day drop in history. Percentage-wise it was only 7.2%, much less than the 22.6% drop of October 19, 1987.

October 28 – Birthdays

1017	**Henry III.** King of Germany, 1039-1056, and Holy Roman emperor, 1046-1056
1435	**Andrea Della Robbia.** Italian sculptor of the early Renaissance noted for the process of glazing terra cottas, passed down to him by his famous uncle, the sculptor Luca Della Robbia
1793	**Eliphalet Remington.** American inventor, noted for the flintlock rifle
1808	**Horace Smith.** American inventor who with Daniel Baird Wesson produced a lever-action pistol and founded (in 1854) the Smith and Wesson Revolver Company
1847	**J. Walter Thompson.** American advertising pioneer who in 1868 founded the J. Walter Thompson agency
1875	**Gilbert H. Grosvenor.** Editor of *The National Geographic Magazine* for more than 50 years
1896	**Howard Hanson.** American composer and educator, and winner of the Pulitzer music prize in 1944
1902	**Elsa Lanchester.** English character actress with a 50-year career in Britain and Hollywood
1903	**Evelyn Waugh.** The most brilliant satirical novelist of his day
1907	**Edith Head.** Hollywood's best-known costume designer
1908	**James Edward Rogan.** American composer, author, and violinist, noted for songs such as "You Started Something" and "Moonlight Mood"
1910	**Francis Bacon.** One of the best-known British painters in the mid-1900s, noted for works such as *Study After Valesquez: Portrait of Pope Innocent X* (1953)
1914	**Jonas Salk.** American physician who developed the Salk polio vaccine

1916 **Willard "Bill" Harris.** American jazz musician

1917 **Joe Page.** Professional baseball player

1924 **Edward George Kean.** American composer, author, and pianist, noted for songs such as "It's Howdy Doody Time"

1925 **Leonard Starr.** American comic strip artist, and creator of *On Stage*

1926 **Bowie Kuhn.** Commissioner of Baseball, 1969-1984

1928 **Tony Franciosca.** American stage, screen, and television actor

1929 **Dody Goodman.** American television actress (*Mary Hartman, Mary Hartman*)

1929 **Joan Plowright.** English stage and screen actress and wife of actor Laurence Olivier until his death

1933 **Suzy Parker.** American model and actress

1937 **Len Wilkens.** Professional basketball player

1939 **Jane Alexander.** American stage and motion-picture actress

1944 **Dennis Franz.** American actor noted for TV roles in *Hill Street Blues* and *NYPD Blue*

1949 **Bruce Jenner.** American Olympic decathlon champion, 1976

1955 **Bill Gates.** Co-founder and chief executive officer of Microsoft Corporation

1957 **Annie Potts.** American stage, screen and television actress

1964 **Paul Wylie.** American Olympic silver medal figure skater

1966 **Juan Guzman.** Professional baseball player

1967 **Julia Roberts.** American motion-picture actress and superstar

October 28 – Events

312 Roman emperor Constantine I, the Great, defeated Maxentius, his major rival in the west, at the Battle of the Milvian Bridge and became undisputed master of Rome.

1491 The last Moorish Emir of Granada consented to surrender the city to Ferdinand and Isabella of Spain within 60 days, removing the Moors from Spain.

1492 Columbus landed in Cuba, at what is now Bahia Bariay, after a few days on San Salvador on his first voyage to America.

1636 Harvard College was founded at Newtowne, Massachusetts, which was renamed Cambridge in 1638.

1646 John Eliot, the famous American missionary to the Indians of Massachusetts, preached his first sermon in America.

1726 Jonathan Swift published *Gulliver's Travels,* one of the greatest satires of world literature.

1886 The Statue of Liberty was dedicated in New York Harbor by President Grover Cleveland.

1918 The Czechoslovak National Committee in Prague proclaimed the establishment of the Republic of Czechoslovakia.

1919 Congress enacted the Volstead Act enforcing Prohibition over President Wilson's veto.

1922 Benito Mussolini's black-shirted Italian Fascists began their march on Rome, resulting in their taking power the following day.

1940 Italy invaded Greece in World War II.

1958 John XXIII was elected Roman Catholic pope.

1962 Russian premier Nikita Khrushchev agreed to remove the Soviet missiles from Cuba, ending the Cuban Missile Crisis.

1983 The United States invaded the island of Grenada for the stated purpose of rescuing the American students there from the Marxist government.

1997 Capping two of the most tumultuous days in Wall Street history, the stock market bounced back from the previous day's disaster with the Dow Jones soaring a record 337 points. A record one billion shares changed hands on the New York Stock Exchange.

October 29 – Birthdays

1740 **James Boswell.** English author, who in 1791 wrote *The Life of Samuel Johnson,* probably the most brilliant biography in the English language

1815 **Daniel Decatur Emmett.** American minstrel performer, and composer of songs such as "Turkey in the Straw," "Old Dan Tucker," and "Dixie" (1859), the war song of the South in the Civil War

1859 **Charles Ebbets.** Baseball executive and long-time owner of the Brooklyn Dodgers baseball team

1879 **Franz von Papen.** German politician who helped Adolf Hitler come to power in 1933

1882 **Jean Giraudoux.** The most prominent French playwright between the two world wars, especially noted for *The Madwoman of Chaillot*

1891 **Fanny Brice.** American singer, dancer, and comedienne, who starred in the *Ziegfeld Follies* and for many years as radio's *Baby Snooks*

1897 **Joseph Goebbels.** Adolf Hitler's minister of propaganda

1898 **Charles Garland.** American Hall of Fame tennis player

1899 **Akim Tamiroff.** Russian-born stage and motion-picture actor

1921 **Bill Mauldin.** Noted American political cartoonist and author

1925 **Dominick Dunne.** American journalist and novelist noted for *The Two Mrs. Grenvilles* (1985)

1925 **Geraldine Brooks.** American motion-picture actress

1927 **Frank Sedgman.** Australian tennis player with six Wimbledon titles

1946 **Peter Green.** English singer and musician with Fleetwood Mac

1947 **Melba Moore.** American singer and actress

1947 **Richard Dreyfuss.** American stage and motion-picture actor

1948	**Kate Jackson.** American television and motion-picture actress
1952	**Byron Bertram.** South African tennis player
1959	**Jesse Barfield.** Professional baseball player
1971	**Wynona Ryder.** American motion-picture actress

October 29 – Events

1618	Sir Walter Raleigh, English writer and adventurer, was beheaded on a trumped-up charge of conspiracy in the Old Palace Yard, Westminster, in London.
1682	William Penn arrived at what is now Chester, Pennsylvania, for the purpose of founding the colony of Pennsylvania.
1863	The International Red Cross flag was adopted.
1884	The Reverend Samuel Burchard, trying to help Republican candidate James G. Blaine, doomed Blaine with his speech blaming the Democrats for "Rum, Romanism, and Rebellion."
1901	Leon Czolgosz was electrocuted for the assassination of President William McKinley.
1916	The comic strip *Rosie's Beau,* by George McManus, first appeared.
1922	Benito Mussolini, with his Fascists, was invited to form an Italian government by King Victor Emanuel III.
1923	Turkey became a republic as its first president, Kemal Ataturk (Mustafa Kemal), took office.
1929	Pandemonium reigned on the New York Stock Exchange, as stock prices collapsed, marking the start of the Great Depression of the 1930s.
1940	The first peacetime military draft in United States history began, as Secretary of State Henry L. Stimson drew the first number—158.
1945	Ballpoint pens first went on sale, at New York's Gimbel Brothers.
1956	Israel invaded Egypt to start the second Arab-Israeli War.
1966	The National Organization for Women was founded.

October 30 – Birthdays

1735	**John Adams.** First vice president and second president of the United States
1751	**Richard Brinsley Sheridan.** Irish dramatist, politician, author of *The School for Scandal* (1777), one of the great comedies of English drama, and creator of Mrs. Malaprop in *The Rivals* (1775)
1762	**Andre Marie de Chenier.** French poet and satirist of the French Revolutionists, who condemned him to death without a trial
1829	**Roscoe Conkling.** U.S. senator and Republican party leader of the "Gilded Age" of the late 1800s
1839	**Alfred Sisley.** French impressionist painter best known for his landscape paintings
1840	**William Graham Sumner.** American sociologist and prolific publicist for Social Darwinism

1867	**Ed Delahanty.** Hall of Fame baseball player who hit over .400 three times in his career
1871	**Paul Valery.** French poet noted for "La Jeune Parque" (1917) and "Le Cimetiere marin" (1920)
1873	**Francisco Madero.** Mexican patriot who issued the call for the Revolution of 1910
1877	**Irma S. Rombauer.** American author of the popular cookbook *The Joy of Cooking* (1931)
1882	**Gunther von Kluge.** German World War II general
1882	**William F. "Bull" Halsey Jr.** American naval officer and, according to General MacArthur, "the greatest fighting admiral" of World War II
1883	**Bob Jones.** American religious leader for whom Bob Jones College is named
1885	**Ezra Pound.** American poet and critic, and one of the most influential and controversial literary figures of his time
1893	**Charles Atlas.** Ex-"97-pound weakling" who became famous for his male physique
1894	**Peter Warlock.** English composer, critic, and editor
1895	**Dickinson Woodruff Richards Jr.** American Nobel Prize-winning physician, who developed a way to diagnose heart diseases by means of a catheter
1896	**Ruth Gordon.** American stage and motion-picture actress with a career of some 70 years
1898	**Bill Terry.** Hall of Fame baseball player who hit .401 in 1930
1914	**Marion Ladewig.** Perhaps the greatest woman bowler in history, who was Woman Bowler of the Year nine times
1914	**Ruth Hussey.** American stage and motion-picture actress
1915	**Fred Friendly.** American television producer and broadcaster
1917	**Bobby Bragan.** Professional baseball player, manager, and executive
1923	**Herschel Bernardi.** American stage and motion-picture actor
1927	**Joe Adcock.** Professional baseball player who hit four home runs and a double in one game in 1954
1932	**Louis Malle.** French motion-picture director with a career of nearly 40 years
1936	**Robert A. Caro.** American author known for *The Path to Power* (a biography of Lyndon Johnson in 1982)
1936	**Jim Perry.** Professional baseball player
1939	**Grace Slick.** American singer with The Jefferson Airplane/Starship musical group
1943	**Henry Winkler.** American motion-picture and television actor
1948	**J.D. Hill.** Professional football player
1950	**Phil Chenier.** Professional basketball player
1951	**Harry Hamlin.** American stage, screen and television actor
1954	**Jo Anne Russell.** American tennis player

1958	**Kevin Pollak.** American motion-picture and television actor and comedian
1962	**Danny Tartabull.** Professional baseball player

October 30 – Events

1340	The Battle of Rio Salado ended forever the Moorish threat to Spain.
1485	Henry Tudor was crowned Henry VIII, King of England.
1768	Wesley Chapel in New York City, the first Methodist church in America, was dedicated.
1847	Henry Wadsworth Longfellow's poem "Evangeline" was first published.
1912	Vice President James Sherman died in office during the presidential campaign of 1912, becoming the only vice president to die while running for reelection.
1914	Turkey joined the Central Powers, Germany and Austria-Hungary, in World War I.
1918	Turkey signed an armistice ending her part in World War I.
1922	Benito Mussolini became dictator of Italy.
1938	Orson Welles caused a national panic when he produced a radio dramatization of H.G. Wells' *The War of the Worlds*.
1953	U.S. General George C. Marshall received the 1953 Nobel Peace Prize and Dr. Albert Schweitzer received the 1952 Nobel Peace Prize (delayed until 1953).
1961	Russia exploded a 58-megaton hydrogen bomb in the Novaya Zemlya area of the U.S.S.R.
1974	Muhammad Ali regained the heavyweight boxing title by defeating champion George Foreman.

October 31 – Birthdays

1424	**Wladyslaw III.** King of Poland, 1434-1444
1599	**Baron Denzil Holles.** English statesman and churchman
1620	**John Evelyn.** English writer, famous for his diary, which he kept from 1641 until his death in 1706
1632	**Jan Vermeer.** One of the great masters of Dutch art in the 17th century, noted for paintings such as *The Milk Maid* and *View of Delft*
1638	**Meindert Hobbema.** Dutch landscape painter, noted for the *Avenue of Middelharnis*
1795	**John Keats.** One of the greatest English poets of all time, noted for works such as "Endymion" (1818) and "Ode on a Grecian Urn" (1819)
1815	**Karl Weierstrass.** German mathematician and a founder of the theory of functions
1827	**Richard Morris Hunt.** American architect noted for introducing the style of the French Gothic chateau to the United States and for designing the pedestal for the Statue of Liberty
1828	**Sir Joseph Wilson Swan.** English physicist and inventor of the dry photographic plate

1860	**Juliette Gordon Low.** Founder of the Girl Scouts of America (1912)
1863	**William Gibbs McAdoo.** Secretary of the treasury during whose term the Federal Reserve System was created (1913-1918)
1883	**Sara Allgood.** Irish stage and motion-picture actress with a 45-year career
1887	**Chiang Kai-shek.** Ruler of China, 1928-1949
1888	**Sir Hubert Wilkins.** Australian explorer, aviator, scientist, and photographer
1900	**Cal Hubbard.** Professional baseball umpire
1900	**Ethel Waters.** American blues singer and actress
1902	**Wilbur Shaw.** American automobile racing driver who won the Indianapolis 500 three times and finished second three times
1912	**Dale Evans.** American actress and wife of cowboy actor Roy Rogers
1915	**James Wechsler.** Editor of the *New York Post* newspaper
1916	**Ken Keltner.** Professional baseball player who helped stop Joe DiMaggio's famous batting streak at 56 with two sparkling fielding plays
1918	**Griffin Bell.** Attorney general under President Carter
1920	**Dick Francis.** Welsh author noted for works such as *Forfeit* (1969)
1922	**Norodom Sihanouk.** King of Cambodia
1922	**Barbara Bel Geddes.** American motion-picture and television actress
1928	**Roy Romer.** Governor of Colorado
1929	**Lee Grant.** American stage, screen, and television actress
1930	**Michael Collins.** U.S. astronaut and Command Module pilot of *Apollo 11*, the first manned lunar landing mission in 1969
1931	**Dan Rather.** American broadcast journalist and television anchor man
1936	**Michael Landon.** American actor, producer, and director, noted for his roles in the TV shows *Bonanza* and *Little House on the Prairie*
1942	**David Ogden Stiers.** American television and motion-picture actor, noted for his role in the long-running TV show *M*A*S*H*
1942	**Dave McNally.** Professional baseball player
1944	**Sally Kirkland.** American stage and motion-picture actress
1948	**Mickey Rivers.** Professional baseball player
1950	**John Candy.** American comedian and motion-picture actor
1950	**Jane Pauley.** Hostess of television's *Today Show* and *Dateline NBC*
1960	**Reza Pahlavi.** Crown prince of Iran and son of Shah Mohammed Reza Pahlavi
1967	**Vanilla Ice.** American rap performer

October 31 – Events

1517 Martin Luther nailed his famous 95 Theses to the door of the Castle Church in Wittenburg, marking the beginning of the Protestant Reformation.

1754 King's College, which later became Columbia University, was founded, the fifth college founded in the United States in colonial times.

1815 Sir Humphry Davy, the great English chemist, invented the miner's safety lamp.

1852 Michael Reagan and Catherine Mulcahy, great grandparents of President Ronald Reagan, were married in St. George's Catholic Church in London.

1864 Nevada was admitted to the Union as the 36th state.

1903 John Barrymore, the great American actor, made his first stage appearance, in *Magda* at the Cleveland Theater in Chicago.

1932 President Herbert Hoover, running for re-election, warned a New York audience that if Franklin D. Roosevelt was elected, "The grass will grow in the streets of a hundred cities."

1941 A German submarine torpedoed the destroyer *Reuben James,* making it the first American ship lost by enemy action in World War II.

1948 The Chinese Communists captured Mukden, Manchuria, in the Chinese Civil War.

1956 Great Britain and France joined the Israeli attack on Egypt, begun two days earlier.

1984 Indian Prime Minister Indira Gandhi was killed at age 66 in New Delhi by her Sikh bodyguards.

11

November

November, the 11th month, gets its name from the Latin *Novembris,* meaning *ninth,* because in the ancient Roman calendar it was the ninth month. In the calendar of Romulus, November had 30 days, which Numa Pompilius reduced to 29 in his calendar. Caesar gave the month 31 days in the Julian Calendar, and Augustus reduced it to 30, its present number when he made his adjustments to the Roman calendar. The Roman Senate offered to name the month for the emperor Tiberius, the successor to Augustus, but he refused, asking, "What will you do if you have thirteen Caesars?"

Special days of November include election day in the United States, the first Tuesday after the first Monday of the month, and Thanksgiving Day, a legal holiday celebrated on the fourth Thursday. All Saints' Day is observed by the Roman Catholic Church on November 1, and Veterans Day, formerly Armistice Day, commemorating the end of World War I, is celebrated on November 11. Five American Presidents, James K. Polk, Zachary Taylor, Franklin Pierce, James A. Garfield and Warren G. Harding, were born in November.

The birthstone for November is the topaz, and the special flower is the chrysanthemum.

November 1 – Birthdays

1500 Benvenuto Cellini. Florentine goldsmith and sculptor, and author of *The Autobiography of Benvenuto Cellini,* one of the great works of world literature

1596 Pietro da Cortona. Italian architect and painter

1636 Nicolas Boileau-Despreaux. French poet and critic, and favorite of King Louis XIV

1757 Antonio Canova. One of the most famous and influential European sculptors of the Napoleonic era, noted for works such as *Perseus* and *Cupid and Psyche*

1757 George Rapp. German religious leader of the Harmonists who founded the village of Harmonie in Indiana, which later became New Harmony

1778 Gustavus IV. King of Sweden, 1792-1809

1798 Sir Benjamin Lee Guinness. Irish brewer

1815 Crawford Williamson Long. First surgeon to use ether as an anesthetic (1842)

1861 Joseph Sill Clark. American Hall of Fame tennis player

1871 Stephen Crane. American novelist and poet, noted for *The Red Badge of Courage* (1895)

1880 Sholem Asch. Polish novelist and playwright

1880 Grantland Rice. One of the greatest sportswriters of all time

1890 James Barton. American stage and motion-picture actor

1903 Max Adrian. Irish stage and screen actor

1907 Larry French. Professional baseball player

1911 Sidney B. Wood. American Hall of Fame tennis player

1920 James J. Kilpatrick. American journalist and author

1924 Victoria De los Angeles. Spanish operatic soprano

1929 Betsy Palmer. American stage, screen, and television actress

1936 Gary Player. Professional golfer

1939 Barbara Bosson. American television actress noted for her role in the long-running series *Hill Street Blues*

1941 Robert Foxworth. American motion-picture and television actor

1942 Larry Flynt. American magazine publisher (*Hustler* magazine)

1947 Ted Hendricks. Hall of Fame football player known as "Mad Stork"

1949 Jeannie Berlin. American actress and screenwriter and daughter of actress Elaine May

1949 Jeff Kinney. Professional football player

1953 Tim Fox. Professional football player

1956 Lyle Lovett. American country singer and songwriter

1960 Fernando Valenzuela. Professional baseball player

1961 **Anne Donovan.** One of the best (and tallest, at six feet eight inches) players in the history of U.S. women's basketball, and winner of two Olympic gold medals

1963 **Demi Moore.** American motion-picture actress

November 1 – Events

1503 Julius II was elected Roman Catholic pope.

1512 Michelangelo's paintings on the ceiling of the Sistine Chapel in St. Peter's Cathedral were first exhibited to the public.

1604 William Shakespeare's great play *Othello* was first presented, at Whitehall Palace in London.

1700 King Charles II of Spain died, leaving his crown in his will to French prince Philip of Anjou, which subsequently led to the War of the Spanish Succession.

1755 The Lisbon earthquake, the worst in Europe in 200 years, destroyed two-thirds of the city and killed more than 60,000 people.

1861 President Lincoln appointed General George B. McClellan to head the United States Army during the Civil War.

1913 Notre Dame defeated Army, 35 to 13, in a football game that featured a new play called the "forward pass." Notre Dame's star end, Knute Rockne, was the receiver a number of times.

1918 The empire of Austria-Hungary was destroyed as the Hapsburg monarchy was ended by a revolution in Hungary.

1923 The German mark fell to 130 billion to the American dollar, as Germany's unbelievable inflation continued.

1929 Former Secretary of the Interior Albert B. Fall was sentenced to one year in prison for his part in the scandals of the Harding Administration.

1950 Two Puerto Rican nationalists attempted to force their way into Blair House to assassinate President Harry S. Truman.

1952 American scientists detonated the first megaton-class hydrogen bomb.

1963 President Ngo Dinh Diem of South Vietnam was assassinated by a military junta which seized the government.

1963 The first United States Christmas stamps went on sale.

November 2 – Birthdays

1470 **Edward V.** King of England, 1482-1483

1699 **Jean Baptiste Simeon Chardin.** One of the greatest French painters of the 18th century

1734 **Daniel Boone.** The most famous American pioneer of colonial times

1755 **Marie Antoinette.** Queen consort of King Louis XVI of France, who was beheaded by the French revolutionaries

1795 **James K. Polk.** 11th U.S. president

1808 **Jules Amedee Barbay D'Aurevilly.** French writer and critic

1815 **George Boole.** Irish logician and mathematician, whose "Boolean algebra" of logic is basic to the design of digital computers

1865 **Warren G. Harding.** 29th U.S. president

1894 **William "Little Bill" Johnston.** American Hall of Fame tennis player and National Champion in 1915 and 1919

1897 **Richard B. Russell.** U.S. senator, 1933-1971

1901 **Paul Ford.** American character actor of stage, screen, and television

1903 **Travis Jackson.** Hall of Fame professional baseball player

1913 **Burt Lancaster.** American motion-picture actor who won an academy award in 1960 for the title role in *Elmer Gantry*

1914 **Johnny Vander Meer.** Professional baseball pitcher who pitched two consecutive no-hit games in 1938

1917 **Ann Rutherford.** American stage and motion-picture actress and leading lady of the 1930s and 1940s

1934 **Ken Rosewall.** Australian tennis superstar and U.S. singles champion in 1956 and 1970

1938 **Patrick Buchanan.** American columnist and television commentator, speech-writer for Presidents Richard Nixon and Ronald Reagan, and candidate for U.S. president

1940 **James K. Bakken.** Professional football player

1941 **Dave Stockton.** Professional golfer

1942 **Stephanie Powers.** American motion-picture and television actress

1942 **Shere Hite.** American cultural researcher, historian, and author of the *Hite Reports* on sex and love

1946 **Tom Paciorek.** Professional baseball player

1958 **Willie McGee.** Professional baseball player

1961 **k.d. lang.** Canadian singer who won a Grammy for "Constant Craving" (1993)

November 2 – Events

1769 Gaspar de Portola, Spanish governor of Baja California, discovered San Francisco Bay.

1783 General George Washington made his Farewell Address to the Continental Army near Princeton, New Jersey.

1889 North Dakota was admitted to the Union as the 39th state, and South Dakota was admitted to the Union as the 40th state.

1917 British Foreign Secretary Arthur Balfour proposed his Balfour Declaration pledging British support for Palestine as a national home for the Jews.

1920 The first regular radio broadcasts began, over station KDKA in Pittsburgh. A major news item was the reporting of the 1920 election returns showing Harding handily defeating Cox.

1930 Haile Selassie was crowned Emperor of Ethiopia at Addis Ababa.

1943   The comic strip *Buz Sawyer*, by Roy Crane, first appeared.

1947   Howard Hughes' *Spruce Goose*, a 200-ton, eight-engine airplane, made its first and only flight, with Hughes at the controls, in Long Beach, California.

1948   Harry S. Truman defeated Thomas E. Dewey in the biggest upset in the history of presidential elections.

1950   George Bernard Shaw, the great British playwright, died at Ayot St. Lawrence, England, at age 94.

1954   Strom Thurmond became the only write-in candidate ever elected to the U.S. Senate.

1976   Jimmy Carter was elected president, defeating incumbent president Gerald Ford.

November 3 – Birthdays

1560   **Annibale Carracci.** Italian painter

1718   **Earl of Sandwich (John Montagu).** English naval officer who ordered a servant to bring him two slices of bread with a piece of roast beef between them, and thus gave his name to the sandwich

1749   **Daniel Rutherford.** Scottish physician who discovered the element nitrogen (in 1772)

1793   **Stephen F. Austin.** Colonizer of Texas for whom the city of Austin was named

1794   **William Cullen Bryant.** The father of American poetry, whose best-known poem is "Thanatopsis" (1817)

1801   **Vincenzo Bellini.** One of the foremost Italian opera composers of his day

1816   **Jubal Early.** Confederate general in the Civil War

1834   **Charles Louis Fleischmann.** Hungarian-American distiller who in 1868 developed Fleischmann's Yeast

1845   **Edward Douglass White.** Ninth chief justice of the U.S. Supreme Court, 1910-1921

1879   **Vilhjalmur Stefansson.** Canadian arctic explorer and writer

1883   **Ford Sterling.** American stage and motion-picture actor who helped Mack Sennett create the Keystone comedies of the silent era

1883   **Alfred Hart Miles.** American lyricist noted for songs such as "Anchors Aweigh"

1893   **Robert Lindley Murray.** American Hall of Fame tennis player and 1918 National Champion

1896   **William Raskin.** American lyricist noted for songs such as "Wedding Bells Are Breaking Up That Old Gang of Mine"

1901   **Leopold III.** King of the Belgians, 1934-1951

1901   **André Malraux.** French novelist noted for works such as *The Royal Way* (1930) and *Man's Hope* (1937)

1908   **Bronko Nagurski.** Hall of Fame professional football player

1909   **James Reston.** American newspaper columnist

1918   **Russell B. Long.** U.S. senator and son of Louisiana governor and senator Huey P. Long

1918   **Bob Feller.** Hall of Fame baseball pitcher who had a record 348 strike-outs in 1946

1921   **Charles Bronson.** American motion-picture actor and Golden Globe Award winner as the world's most popular actor in 1971

1930   **Philip M. Crane.** U.S. congressman

1931   **Monica Vitti.** Italian stage and motion-picture actress

1933   **Michael Dukakis.** Governor of Massachusetts and Democratic candidate for president in 1988

1936   **Roy Emerson.** Australian tennis player and Wimbledon singles champion in 1964 and 1965

1939   **Terrence McNally.** American playwright

1942   **Martin Cruz Smith.** American author noted for *Gorky Park* (1981)

1945   **Ken Holtzman.** Professional baseball player

1949   **Larry Holmes.** World heavyweight champion

1951   **Dwight Evans.** Professional baseball player

1952   **Roseanne.** American television actress and comedienne

1953   **Dennis Miller.** American comedian and television personality

1953   **Larry Herndon.** Professional baseball player

1954   **Atom Ant (Stuart Goddard).** British singer and bassist

1955   **Phil Simms.** Professional football player

1956   **Bob Welch.** Professional baseball player

November 3 – Events

1003   Ethelred the Unready led the English in a massacre of the Danes.

1083   Queen Matilda, wife of William the Conqueror, died.

1493   Christopher Columbus landed in the West Indies, at an island he called Mariagalante, after his flagship, on his second voyage to America.

1640   The Long Parliament met in London. It lasted without a break for 13 years.

1783   The Continental Army was disbanded by Congress.

1814   The Congress of Vienna opened to reshape Europe after the Napoleonic era.

1839   The Opium War began between China and Great Britain.

1848   The Prussian Revolution of 1848 ended with the king's forming a new ministry.

1903   Panama gained its independence from Colombia.

1918   Austria signed an armistice ending its part in World War I.

1936   President Franklin D. Roosevelt was reelected, defeating Alf Landon with a record landslide electoral vote of 523 to 8.

1942   The 1,523 mile-long Alaska Highway was completed, linking Dawson Creen, British Columbia, and Fairbanks, Alaska.

1954   Henri Matisse, the great French artist, died in Nice at age 84.

1957   The Russians launched their second satellite, *Sputnik II,* carrying a dog named Laika, the first animal to be sent into space.

1964 In the first presidential election in which Washington, D.C., citizens were allowed to vote, Lyndon Johnson defeated Barry Goldwater in a landslide.

November 4 – Birthdays

1575 **Guido Reni.** Italian Baroque painter and engraver
1590 **Gerrit Van Honthorst.** Dutch painter who influenced Rembrandt and Hals
1840 **Auguste Rodin.** One of the world's greatest sculptors, and creator of the famous figure *The Thinker*
1841 **Benjamin Franklin Goodrich.** American industrialist who founded the B.F. Goodrich Co. (1880)
1873 **Bobby Wallace.** Hall of Fame baseball player with a 25-year major league career
1874 **Charles Despiau.** French sculptor
1876 **James Earle Fraser.** American sculptor who designed the buffalo nickel
1878 **Jean Schwartz.** Hungarian-born composer and pianist, noted for songs such as "Chinatown, My Chinatown" and "Rockabye Your Baby With a Dixie Melody"
1879 **Will Rogers.** American humorist, columnist, motion-picture actor, and folk hero
1889 **Charles Hackett.** Noted American tenor
1896 **Harry MacGregor Woods.** American composer noted for songs such as "When the Red Red Robin Comes Bob-Bob-Bobbin' Along," "I'm Looking Over a Four Leaf Clover," and "When the Moon Comes Over the Mountain"
1906 **Bob Considine.** American newspaper correspondent and author
1907 **Bennie Benjamin.** Canadian-born composer noted for songs such as "I Don't Want to Set the World on Fire," "Surrender," "Rumors Are Flying," and "Wheel of Fortune"
1907 **Paul Douglas.** American motion-picture actor
1911 **Dixie Lee.** American actress and first wife of singer Bing Crosby
1916 **Walter Cronkite.** Noted American television news broadcaster and commentator
1917 **Gig Young.** American stage and motion-picture actor
1918 **Art Carney.** American motion-picture and television actor
1919 **Martin Balsam.** American motion-picture and television actor
1930 **Kate Reid.** Canadian actress noted for her role as Linda Loman in *Death of a Salesman*
1930 **Dick Groat.** Professional baseball player
1933 **Tito Francona.** Professional baseball player
1943 **Loretta Swit.** American actress noted for her role as Hot Lips in the long-running television show *M*A*S*H*
1943 **Clark Graebner.** American tennis player
1946 **John Cooper.** Australian tennis player
1950 **Markie Post.** American stage, screen and television actress

1955 **Laurie Tenney.** American tennis player
1969 **Matthew McConaughey.** American motion-picture actor

November 4 – Events

1677 William and Mary, the future co-rulers of England, were married.
1825 The Erie Canal was formally opened at New York City when the *Seneca Chief* arrived there. It had started from Buffalo on October 26.
1842 Abraham Lincoln married Mary Todd in Springfield, Illinois.
1847 Felix Mendelssohn, the great German composer, died in Leipzig at age 38.
1862 Richard Gatling patented his "Gatling gun," the first practical quick-firing machine gun developed in the U.S.
1880 James and John Ritty of Dayton, Ohio, patented the first cash register.
1884 Grover Cleveland, by a slim majority of 23,005 votes, was elected president over James G. Blaine.
1922 English archaeologist Howard Carter and his crew discovered the steps leading to the tomb of Tutankhamen, which Carter eventually entered on November 26.
1924 Calvin Coolidge defeated John W. Davis in the presidential election in a landslide.
1952 General Dwight D. Eisenhower was elected president over Adlai E. Stevenson.
1956 The Russian Army crushed the Hungarian Revolt.
1979 Iranian militants, with their government's approval, seized the U.S. embassy in Tehran, taking all the diplomats and personnel hostage.
1980 Ronald Reagan was elected president, unseating President Carter.
1986 A Lebanese newspaper, *Al Shiraa*, started the Iran-Contra scandal by reporting that Robert McFarlane, a representative of the Reagan administration, was negotiating arms for hostages with Iran.
1995 Israeli prime minister Yitzhak Rabin was assassinated by a right-wing Israeli minutes after attending a peace rally.

November 5 – Birthdays

1494 **Hans Sachs.** German poet and composer
1619 **Philips de Koninck.** Dutch painter
1732 **John Glover.** American revolutionary whose "amphibious" regiment took 2400 men of Washington's army across the Delaware in a blinding snowstorm on Christmas night, 1776, to capture Trenton
1779 **Washington Allston.** The first American artist to paint in the romantic tradition of the 1800s, noted for works such as *Belshazzar's Feast* and *The Deluge*

1850 **Ella Wheeler Wilcox.** American poet who in her 1883 poem "Solitude" penned the lines, "Laugh, and the world laughs with you; Weep, and you weep alone"

1855 **Eugene V. Debs.** American labor leader and five time Socialist Party presidential candidate

1857 **Ida M. Tarbell.** American author and noted muckraker of the early 1900s

1876 **Raymond Duchamp-Villon.** French sculptor

1879 **Will Hays.** American political figure and czar of the motion-picture industry

1885 **Will Durant.** American historian, philosopher, and author of *The Story of Philosophy* (1926), and co-author with his wife, Ariel, of *The Story of Civilization*

1891 **Earle "Greasy" Neale.** Noted professional football player and coach

1894 **Beardsley Ruml.** American congressman who proposed the withholding system of income tax payments, which was adopted by Congress in 1943

1895 **Walter Gieseking.** German pianist

1905 **Annunzio Mantovani.** Italian-born conductor

1905 **Joel McCrea.** American motion-picture and television actor with a career of some 50 years

1912 **Roy Rogers.** One of Hollywood's most popular singing cowboy stars

1913 **John McGiver.** American motion-picture and television actor

1913 **Vivien Leigh.** English actress who achieved fame and worldwide popularity in her Academy Award-winning role of Scarlett O'Hara in the motion picture *Gone With the Wind* (1939)

1919 **Myron Floren.** American musician noted for his work with *The Lawrence Welk Show*

1934 **Jeb Stuart Magruder.** Convicted Watergate participant

1941 **Art Garfunkel.** American singer of the Simon and Garfunkel duo

1941 **Elke Sommer.** German motion-picture and television actress

1943 **Sam Shepard.** American playwright

1947 **Peter Noone.** Singer Herman with Herman's Hermits

1951 **Wendy Slaughter.** English tennis player

1952 **Bill Walton.** Professional basketball player and Hall of Famer

1957 **Kellen Winslow.** Professional football player

1959 **Lloyd Moseby.** Professional baseball player

1963 **Tatum O'Neal.** American motion-picture actress and daughter of actor Ryan O'Neal

November 5 – Events

1605 Guy Fawkes was seized as he was about to blow up the English Houses of Parliament in the Gunpowder Plot.

1733 John Peter Zenger began publishing his newspaper, the New York *Weekly Journal.*

1757 Frederick the Great of Prussia, the outstanding commander of his age, decisively defeated the French in the Battle of Rossbach, the greatest battle of the Seven Years' War.

1862 President Lincoln relieved General George B. McClellan of the command of the Army of the Potomac and replaced him with General Ambrose E. Burnside.

1872 American suffragist Susan B. Anthony was arrested and later fined $100 (which she never paid) for trying to vote in the presidential election between U.S. Grant and Horace Greeley.

1895 George B. Selden, the noted American inventor, received the first U.S. patent for a gasoline-powered automobile.

1912 Woodrow Wilson was elected president of the United States over President William Howard Taft and ex-President Theodore Roosevelt.

1914 England and France declared war on Turkey in World War I.

1940 President Franklin D. Roosevelt was elected over Wendell Willkie to an unprecedented third term.

1942 General Bernard L. Montgomery announced that his British Eighth Army had won a complete victory over the Germans in Egypt in World War II.

1974 Ella T. Grasso was elected governor of Connecticut, the first woman to win a gubernatorial office without succeeding her husband.

1996 President Clinton won a second term, defeating former senator Bob Dole, and becoming the first Democrat to be re-elected president since Franklin D. Roosevelt in 1944.

November 6 – Birthdays

1479 **Joanna (the Mad).** Queen of Castile

1671 **Colley Cibber.** English actor, author and poet laureate (1730-1757), who was ridiculed in Alexander Pope's *The Dunciad*

1771 **Aloys Senefelder.** Inventor in 1798 of lithography

1814 **Adolphe Sax.** Belgian musical instrument maker and inventor in 1840 of the saxophone

1825 **Charles Garnier.** French architect

1841 **Nelson W. Aldrich.** U.S. senator and financier

1851 **Charles Henry Dow.** A founder of Dow Jones and Company

1854 **John Philip Sousa.** Famous American bandmaster and "March King," who composed over 100 military marches, such as "Semper Fidelis," "The Washington Post," and "Stars and Stripes Forever"

1861 **James A. Naismith.** Canadian-American teacher who in 1891 invented the game of basketball

1877 **William A. Dillon.** American composer noted for songs such as "I Want a Girl Just Like the Girl That Married Dear Old Dad"

1880 **Robert Edler Von Musil.** Austrian novelist

1882 **Thomas H. Ince.** American motion-picture director, screenwriter and actor who was a pioneer in the history of American movies

1886 **Gus Kahn.** German-born lyricist noted for such songs as "Pretty Baby," "Charley My Boy," "Toot, Toot, Tootsie, Goodbye," "On the Alamo," and "The Waltz You Saved for Me"

1887 **Walter Johnson.** Hardest throwing pitcher in baseball history and winner of 414 career games, second only to Cy Young

1892 **Ole Olsen.** American comedian who with Chic Johnson formed the Olsen and Johnson comedy team

1893 **Edsel Ford.** Only child of industrialist Henry Ford

1908 **Tony Canzoneri.** American Hall of Fame boxer and champion in three weight divisions

1916 **Joseph Bushkin.** American composer noted for such songs as "There'll Be a Hot Time in the Old Town Tonight"

1921 **James Jones.** American novelist and author of *From Here to Eternity*

1923 **Robert Griffin.** U.S. senator

1931 **Mike Nichols.** American motion-picture director, noted for films such as *The Graduate* (1967)

1935 **Johnny Pott.** Professional golfer

1939 **Pat Dye.** College football coach

1941 **Ray Perkins.** Professional football player and college and professional football coach

1946 **Sally Field.** American motion-picture and television actress who won best actress Academy Awards for *Norma Rae* (1979) and *Places in the Heart* (1984)

1953 **John Candelaria.** Professional baseball player

1955 **Maria Shriver.** American television personality and daughter of Sargent Shriver, first director of the Peace Corps

1968 **Kelly Rutherford.** American motion-picture and television actress (*Melrose Place*)

November 6 – Events

1492 Sonni Ali, the founder of the great black African empire of Songhay, drowned in the River Koni.

1860 Abraham Lincoln was elected president over Stephen A. Douglas, John C. Breckinridge, and John Bell.

1861 Jefferson Davis was elected to a six-year term as president of the Confederacy.

1869 Rutgers defeated the College of New Jersey (now Princeton University), 6 to 4, in New Brunswick, New Jersey, in the first college football game.

1882 Lily Langtry, the great English actress known as "The Jersey Lily," made her American debut in New York in the play *An Unequal Match*.

1888 Benjamin Harrison defeated incumbent Grover Cleveland in the presidential election in spite of Cleveland's popular vote majority.

1893 Peter Ilich Tchaikovsky, the great Russian composer, died of cholera in St. Petersburg at age 53.

1900 The presidential ticket of William McKinley and Theodore Roosevelt defeated that of William Jennings Bryan and Adlai E. Stevenson.

1913 Mahatma Gandhi was arrested as he led a march of Indian miners in South Africa.

1917 The October Revolution (October 24 in the old Russian calendar) began in Petrograd, Russia, as the Bolsheviks under Lenin began taking over key points of the city.

1928 Herbert Hoover was elected president, defeating Al Smith.

1938 The comic strip *Red Ryder,* by Fred Harmon, made its first appearance.

1968 The Vietnam peace talks began in Paris.

1984 Ronald Reagan was reelected president over Walter Mondale in a landslide in which he received all the electoral votes except those of Minnesota and the District of Columbia.

November 7 – Birthdays

1598 **Francisco de Zurbaran.** Spanish painter noted for works such as *Still-life with Lemons, Oranges and a Rose* (1633)

1832 **Andrew D. White.** First president of Cornell University and author of the monumental work *A History of the Warfare of Science With Theology in Christendom* (1895)

1867 **Marie Curie.** Polish-born French physicist and co-discoverer, with her husband, Pierre Curie, of the elements radium and polonium

1878 **Lise Meitner.** Austrian physicist who with physicists Otto Hahn and Fritz Strassmann succeeded in splitting the uranium atom in 1938

1879 **Leon Trotsky.** One of the principal leaders of the Bolshevik revolution and the second most powerful man in Russia while Lenin was alive

1890 **Phil Spitalny.** Russian-born composer, conductor, and clarinetist, noted for his "All-Girl Orchestra" of the 1930s and 1940s

1893 **Leatrice Joy.** American actress and leading lady of the 1920s who popularized bobbed hair and was married to matinee idol John Gilbert

1903 **Dean Jagger.** American stage, screen, and television actor with a career of over 50 years

1906 **Eugene Carson Blake.** American church official

1909 **Norman Krasna.** American playwright, screenwriter, producer, and director

1913 **Albert Camus.** French novelist, journalist, and playwright, noted for *The Stranger* (1942) and *The Plague* (1947)

1918 **Billy Graham.** Noted American evangelist and author

1922 **Al Hirt.** American musician

1926 **Dame Joan Sutherland.** British opera singer

1930 **Rudy Boschwitz.** U.S. senator

1937 **Mary Travers.** American singer with the Peter, Paul, and Mary musical group

1938   **Jim Kaat.** Professional baseball player whose career spanned from the 1960s to the 1980s
1943   **Joni Mitchell.** Canadian guitarist and singer
1944   **Joe Niekro.** Professional baseball player and brother of baseball player Phil Niekro
1947   **Sue Mappin.** English tennis player
1951   **Wallace Francis.** Professional football player
1956   **Elvis Peacock.** Professional football player
1964   **Dana Plato.** American actress

November 7 – Events

1504   Christopher Columbus arrived in Sanlucar, Spain, ending his fourth and last voyage to America.
1811   General William Henry Harrison defeated Chief Tecumseh's Shawnee Indians in the Battle of Tippecanoe on the Wabash River.
1848   General Zachary Taylor defeated Lewis Cass in the presidential election.
1874   The Republican Party was first depicted as an elephant, in a cartoon by Thomas Nast in *Harper's Weekly.*
1876   The "stolen presidential election" took place between Samuel J. Tilden and Rutherford B. Hayes. A deal was finally worked out to give Hayes the victory the following March.
1885   The last spike was driven in the Canadian Pacific Railway, linking Canada's east and west coasts.
1910   Victor Herbert's operetta *Naughty Marietta* opened in New York. One of its biggest hits was "Ah, Sweet Mystery of Life."
1916   Jeannette Rankin became the first woman elected to the U.S. House of Representatives.
1916   President Woodrow Wilson was reelected, narrowly defeating Charles Evans Hughes.
1917   The October Revolution ended in Russia (October 25 by the old calendar), as Lenin and his Bolsheviks seized Petrograd.
1940   "Galloping Gertie," the third largest suspension bridge in the world, at Tacoma, Washington, collapsed in a windstorm a few months after its completion.
1944   President Franklin D. Roosevelt won an unprecedented fourth term, defeating Republican Thomas E. Dewey.
1962   Eleanor Roosevelt, the wife of President Franklin D. Roosevelt, died at age 78.
1962   Richard Nixon held his "last press conference," as he called it, telling reporters, "You won't have Nixon to kick around any more."
1989   L. Douglas Wilder won the governor's race in Virginia, becoming the first elected black governor in U.S. history.
1989   David Dinkins was elected New York City's first black mayor.

November 8 – Birthdays

35   **Marcus Nerva.** Emperor of Rome, A.D. 96-98

1086   **Henry V.** King of Germany and Holy Roman Emperor, 1106-1125, and the last of the Salian dynasty
1622   **Charles X.** King of Sweden, 1654-1660, whose reign marked the height of Swedish power in Europe
1656   **Edmund Halley.** English astronomer for whom Halley's Comet was named
1836   **Milton Bradley.** American manufacturer, publisher and father of the Milton Bradley Co.
1847   **Bram Stoker.** British author who wrote *Dracula* (1897), one of the most famous horror stories of all time
1867   **Sadakichi Hartmann.** American art critic
1883   **Charles Demuth.** American painter known for works such as *My Egypt* (1927) and *I Saw a Figure 5 in Gold* (1928)
1884   **Hermann Rorschach.** Swiss psychiatrist who in 1921 developed the Rorschach ink-blot test to evaluate mental illness
1885   **Tomobumi Yamashita.** Japanese general who led the Japanese forces in the Philippines in 1944 and who was executed after World War II for war crimes
1896   **Bucky Harris.** Professional baseball player, manager and Hall of Famer
1897   **Dorothy Day.** Influential American lay Catholic
1900   **Margaret Mitchell.** American author, noted for *Gone With the Wind,* one of the most popular novels of all time, and which was made into one of the greatest motion pictures of all time
1906   **H.C. Hansen.** Danish prime minister
1907   **Tony Cuccinello.** Professional baseball player
1910   **Harnett Kane.** American novelist noted for works such as *New Orleans Woman* (1946)
1913   **Robert Strauss.** American actor and comedian who played Animal in *Stalag 17* (1953)
1914   **Norman Lloyd.** American stage, screen and television actor (*St. Elsewhere*)
1916   **June Havoc.** American stage, screen, and television actress
1921   **Gene Saks.** American stage, screen and television actor and motion-picture director noted for films such as *I Love My Wife*
1922   **Jack Fleck.** Professional golfer
1922   **Christiaan Barnard.** South African surgeon who performed the first heart transplant (1967)
1923   **Jack Kilby.** American electrical engineer who developed the integrated circuit
1924   **Johnny Bower.** Professional Hall of Fame hockey player
1927   **Patti Page.** Popular American singer of the 1950s and 1960s
1929   **Bobby Bowden.** Noted college football coach
1931   **Morley Safer.** American broadcast journalist
1935   **Alain Delon.** French motion-picture actor
1949   **Bonnie Raitt.** American singer and musician
1951   **Mary Hart.** American television hostess (*Entertainment Tonight* and *PM Magazine*)
1952   **John Denny.** Professional baseball player

1953 **Alfre Woodard.** American stage, screen, and television actress

1954 **Rickie Lee Jones.** American singer-artist who won a Grammy for best new artist in 1980

1958 **Terry de Miall Harron.** English musician with the Adam and the Ants musical group

1967 **Courtney Thorne-Smith.** American motion-picture and television actress (*Ally McBeal* and *Melrose Place*)

November 8 – Events

1519 Hernando Cortes, the Spanish conqueror of Mexico, reached Tenochtitlan, the Aztec capital and site of present-day Mexico City.

1674 John Milton, the great English poet, died in London at age 65.

1793 The Louvre in Paris, originally built in stages as a palace, was first opened to the public as a museum.

1837 Mt. Holyoke Seminary for women in South Hadley, Mass., was opened with 80 students.

1864 President Lincoln was reelected, defeating General George B. McClellan.

1880 Sarah Bernhardt, the great French actress, made her American debut in New York in *Adrienne Lecouvreur.*

1887 Doc Holliday, the famous alcoholic Wild West gunslinger, died of tuberculosis in a Colorado sanitarium.

1889 Montana was admitted to the Union as the 41st state.

1892 Grover Cleveland defeated incumbent President Benjamin Harrison, becoming the only president to win two nonconsecutive terms.

1895 Wilhelm Konrad Roentgen, the great German physicist, discovered X rays.

1904 President Theodore Roosevelt won a second term, defeating Democrat Alton B. Parker.

1917 The Second All-Russian Congress of Soviets opened and agreed to ask Germany for peace in World War I.

1923 Adolf Hitler and his Nazis staged the *Beer Hall Putsch* in Munich, a movement to seize the Bavarian government. The attempt failed and Hitler was subsequently jailed.

1932 Franklin D. Roosevelt was elected for his first term, defeating incumbent President Herbert Hoover.

1942 Operation Torch began, as Allied troops under General Dwight D. Eisenhower, landed at Casablanca, Oran, and Algiers in North Africa in World War II.

1960 John F. Kennedy defeated Richard M. Nixon in the presidential election, becoming at 43 the youngest president ever elected.

1970 Tom Dempsey of the New Orleans Saints kicked a record 63-yard field goal.

1994 The Republicans won both Houses of Congress for the first time since 1954.

November 9 – Birthdays

1389 **Isabella of France.** Wife of King Richard II of England

1801 **Gail Borden.** American inventor who developed the first successful milk-condensing process and who founded the Borden Company

1818 **Ivan Turgenev.** One of the three greatest Russian novelists, noted for works such as *Fathers and Sons* (1862) and *Smoke* (1867)

1841 **Edward VII.** Oldest son of Queen Victoria and Prince Albert, and King of England, 1901-1910

1853 **Stanford White.** Prominent American architect who designed the Madison Square Garden in New York (1890)

1869 **Marie Dressler.** Canadian-born stage and motion-picture actress and number one box office attraction in the 1930s

1881 **Herbert T. Kalmus.** American inventor and motion-picture pioneer, noted for his invention of technicolor

1886 **Ed Wynn.** American stage, screen, and television actor and comedian, whose career spanned 40 years

1887 **Gertrude Astor.** American actress and leading lady of Hollywood silents and early talkies

1888 **Jean Monnet.** French economist and architect of the European Common Market

1895 **Mae Marsh.** A leading lady of the silent screen who played "The Little Sister" in *The Birth of a Nation* (1915), and who made the transition to the talkies in a 50-year career

1902 **Anthony Asquith.** English motion-picture director and son of Britain's prime minister, H.H. Asquith

1913 **Hedy Lamarr.** Austrian-born motion-picture actress and leading lady of the 1940s

1915 **Sargent Shriver.** First U.S. Peace Corps director and vice presidential candidate with George McGovern in 1972

1918 **Spiro T. Agnew.** U.S. vice president under President Nixon, and only the second vice president in history (after John C. Calhoun) to resign his office

1918 **Florence Chadwick.** American swimmer and first woman to swim the English Channel in both directions, in 1950 and 1951

1921 **Silvio Conte.** U.S. congressman

1923 **Alice Coachman.** American Hall of Fame high jumper and sprinter, and first black woman to win an Olympic medal (1948)

1923 **Dorothy Dandridge.** American actress, singer, and dancer

1931 **Whitey Herzog.** Professional baseball player and manager

1932 **Frank Selvy.** Professional basketball player

1934 **Carl Sagan.** American astronomer, writer, and television personality

1935 **Bob Gibson.** Hall of Fame baseball pitcher with 3,117 career strikeouts

1936 **Bob Graham.** U.S. senator

1941 **Bruce Gossett.** Professional football player

1942	**Tom Weiskopf.** Professional golfer
1958	**Ted Higuera.** Professional baseball player
1962	**Dion James.** Professional baseball player

November 9 – Events

1389	Boniface IX was crowned Roman Catholic pope.
1799	Napoleon Bonaparte, in the "Coup d'Etat of Eighteenth Brumaire," seized power in France.
1918	Kaiser Wilhelm, the German emperor, abdicated and fled to The Netherlands, as the German government was negotiating the surrender terms with the Allies in World War I.
1923	Adolf Hitler's *Beer Hall Putsch* was crushed and his followers were arrested in Munich. Hitler himself was arrested two days later.
1924	Nellie Tayloe Ross was elected governor of Wyoming, becoming the first woman governor in the United States.
1935	The Congress for Industrial Organization (CIO) was formed by John L. Lewis and other American labor leaders.
1938	Mary Martin, the great American actress, made her debut in the musical comedy *Leave It to Me,* at the Imperial Theater in New York.
1938	Adolf Hitler and Joseph Goebbels set in motion *Crystal Night*—named for the smashed windows—in which Jewish shops and synagogues were burned and ransacked all over Germany by Nazi thugs.
1944	The first operation to save a "blue baby" was performed at Johns Hopkins Children's Hospital.
1953	Dylan Thomas, the noted Welsh poet, died in New York at age 39 while on an American tour.
1953	The Supreme Court upheld a 1922 ruling that the federal antitrust laws do not apply to major-league baseball.
1964	The comic strip *The Wizard of Id,* by Johnny Hart and Brant Parker, first appeared.
1965	The great Northeastern United States power failure occurred, blacking out New York, Boston, Philadelphia, Baltimore, and two provinces of Canada.
1970	General Charles De Gaulle died of a heart attack at age 79.

November 10 – Birthdays

1483	**Martin Luther.** Founder of the Protestant Reformation, and called by some the most influential German who ever lived
1630	**Adriaen Van de Velde.** Dutch painter
1668	**François Couperin.** French composer and musician greatly admired by Johann Sebastian Bach, his great contemporary
1683	**George II.** King of England, 1727-1760, and the last British ruler to lead troops on the battlefield
1697	**William Hogarth.** English painter and engraver, noted for such paintings as *The Rake's Progress* and *The Shrimp Girl*

1730	**Oliver Goldsmith.** Irish-born poet and playwright, noted for works such as the poem "The Deserted Village" (1770) and the famous comedy *She Stoops to Conquer* (1773)
1759	**Friedrich von Schiller.** The greatest German playwright of all time and, with Goethe, one of the two greatest figures of German literature
1852	**Henry Van Dyke.** American clergyman, short-story writer, poet, and essayist
1871	**Winston Churchill.** American novelist, noted for works such as *Richard Carvel* (1899) and *The Crisis* (1901)
1874	**Donald Baxter Macmillan.** American polar explorer who surveyed and charted Greenland and the Canadian Arctic
1879	**Vachel Lindsay.** American poet noted for works such as "Abraham Lincoln Walks at Midnight" (1914)
1880	**Sir Jacob Epstein.** American-born English sculptor whose subjects are noted for their strong and energetic appearance
1889	**Claude Rains.** English stage and motion-picture actor with a career of over 50 years
1893	**John P. Marquand.** American novelist who won the 1938 Pulitzer Prize for *The Late George Apley*
1895	**John Knudsen Northrup.** American aircraft designer and co-founder of Lockheed Aircraft Corporation
1896	**Jimmy Dykes.** Professional baseball player and manager
1906	**Dutch Clark.** Professional football player, coach and Hall of Famer
1909	**Birdie Tebbetts.** Professional baseball player
1913	**Karl Shapiro.** American poet who won the 1945 Pulitzer Prize for *V-Letter and Other Poems*
1919	**George Fenneman.** American radio and television announcer, who was Groucho Marx's straight man on the TV show *You Bet Your Life*
1919	**Moise Tshombe.** President of Katanga and premier of Zaire, 1964-1965
1925	**Richard Burton.** Welsh stage, screen, and television actor and superstar
1934	**Norm Cash.** Professional baseball player
1935	**Roy Scheider.** American stage and motion-picture actor
1939	**Russell Means.** American Indian leader of the 1960s and 1970s
1946	**David Stockman.** U.S. budget director under President Reagan
1947	**David A. Loggins.** American composer and singer, noted for songs such as "The Fool in Me," "Pieces of April," and "One Way Ticket to Paradise"
1949	**Donna Fargo.** American singer
1953	**Larry Parrish.** Professional baseball player
1954	**Bob Stanley.** Professional baseball player
1955	**Jack Clark.** Professional baseball player
1959	**Mackenzie Phillips.** American television actress noted for the long-running series *One Day At a Time*

1963	**Andres Thomas.** Professional baseball player
1968	**Sammy Sosa.** Professional baseball player who hit 66 home runs in 1998 but still finished second to Mark McGwire's 70

November 10 – Events

1630 This was the famous "Day of Dupes" in France, a day when the enemies of Cardinal Richlieu thought he had fallen into disfavor, but when King Louis XIII restored him to power.

1775 The United States Marine Corps was authorized by the Continental Congress.

1798 Alois Senefelder, German inventor, developed the lithographic printing process.

1834 Franklin Pierce married Jane Means Appleton.

1871 Henry M. Stanley, English explorer, discovered the missing missionary David Livingstone in Africa, and greeted him with: "Dr. Livingstone, I presume?"

1888 Fritz Kreisler, the great composer and violinist, made his American debut at age 13 in Steinway Hall in New York.

1918 Kaiser Wilhelm II of Germany arrived in Belgium, asking for asylum, as World War I was ending.

1919 The American Legion held its first national convention, in Minneapolis.

1947 The comic strip *Ferd'nand,* by Henning Dahl Mikkelsen, first appeared in American newspapers.

1961 Stalingrad, Russia, was renamed Volgograd.

1969 The children's show *Sesame Street* made its debut on Public Television.

1977 Louise Brown, the world's first test tube baby, was conceived.

1989 The Berlin Wall was opened by East Germany as the Communist regimes in Eastern Europe continued to topple.

November 11 – Birthdays

1050 **Henry IV.** King of Germany, 1056-1106, who tried to depose Pope Gregory VII, and had to stand barefoot in the snow for three days before Gregory would pardon him (Henry got his revenge later)

1493 **Bernardo Tasso.** Italian courtier, poet, and father of Torquato Tasso, one of the great masters of Italian poetry

1579 **Frans Snyders.** Flemish painter

1679 **Firmin Abauzit.** French theologian

1729 **Louis Antoine de Bougainville.** French navigator who discovered the island of Bougainville in 1768

1781 **Cyrus Alger.** American inventor who produced the first gun ever rifled in America

1821 **Fyodor Dostoevsky.** One of the two or three greatest Russian novelists, whose *Crime and Punishment* (1866) and *The Brothers Karamazov* (1880) are among the world's greatest novels

1836 **Thomas Bailey Aldrich.** American writer

1863 **Paul Signac.** French painter

1868 **Edouard Vuillard.** French painter and decorator

1869 **Victor Emmanuel III.** King of Italy, 1900-1946, during Mussolini's Fascist regime

1872 **Maude Adams.** American stage actress, and one of the greatest of the 1890-1918 era

1882 **Gustaf VI.** King of Sweden who succeeded his father, Gustaf V, in 1950

1885 **George S. Patton Jr.** One of the greatest and most colorful American generals of World War II

1891 **Rabbit Maranville.** Hall of Fame baseball player who played 23 years and 2,670 games

1892 **Al Schacht.** Professional baseball player and "Clown Prince of Baseball"

1894 **Beverly Bayne.** Popular leading lady of Hollywood silent films, who with Francis X. Bushman formed the first important love team of American movies

1898 **Rene Clair.** French producer, director, and writer

1899 **Pie Traynor.** Perhaps the greatest third baseman in baseball history

1899 **Pat O'Brien.** American stage and motion-picture actor, who appeared in 85 films in a career of over 60 years

1900 **Hugh Scott.** U.S. senator and Minority Leader in the 1970s

1903 **Sam Spiegel.** European-born motion-picture director

1904 **Alger Hiss.** U.S. state department official convicted of perjury in a famous case in 1949-1950

1909 **Robert Ryan.** American stage and motion-picture actor

1914 **Howard Fast.** American writer and novelist

1915 **George Case.** Professional baseball player

1915 **William Proxmire.** U.S. senator

1916 **Shelby Foote.** American historian and author noted for works such as *Shiloh* (1952)

1922 **Kurt Vonnegut Jr.** American novelist noted for works such as *Cat's Cradle* (1963) and *Slaughterhouse-Five* (1969)

1925 **Jonathan Winters.** American comedian and actor

1934 **Charles Manson.** American convicted mass murderer and cult leader

1935 **Bibi Andersson.** Swedish motion-picture actress

1937 **Rudy La Russo.** Professional basketball player with 10,000 career points

1940 **Barbara Boxer.** U.S. senator

1941 **Helga Masthoff.** West German tennis player

1945 **Daniel Ortega.** President of Nicaragua in the 1980s

1951 **Fuzzy Zoeller.** Professional golfer

1956 **Ian Craig Marsh.** English musician with the Heaven 17 musical group

1964 **Calista Flockhart.** American television actress (title role in *Ally McBeal*)

1974 **Leonardo DiCaprio.** American motion-picture and television actor

November 11 – Events

1417 Martin V was elected Roman Catholic pope.

1534 The famous Act of Supremacy was passed at King Henry VIII's insistence, making the Church of England a separate institution with the king as its supreme head.

1647 King Charles I of England escaped from Parliament and fled to the Isle of Wight.

1675 Gottfried Wilhelm Leibniz, the great co-inventor with Isaac Newton of the calculus, first set down on paper an equation establishing the symbol for the integral sign.

1831 Nat Turner was hanged for his leadership of the largest slave revolt in American history.

1855 Soren Kierkegaard, the noted Danish theologian, died in Copenhagen at age 42.

1858 James A. Garfield married Lucretia Rudolph.

1889 Washington was admitted to the Union as the 42nd state.

1918 World War I ended at 11 A.M., following the signing of the armistice in a railway car in the Forest of Compiegne, in France.

1921 The Unknown Soldier of the United States was buried in Arlington National Cemetery.

1923 Adolf Hitler was arrested for his part in the *Beer Hall Putsch* in Munich, and was taken to prison.

1933 The first of the great dust storms of the 1930s, which laid waste thousands of acres of land, swept over North Dakota.

1939 Kate Smith sang Irving Berlin's "God Bless America" on her radio show, the first time it had been heard by the public.

1942 German troops occupied the previously unoccupied portion of France in World War II.

1954 Veterans Day was first celebrated in the United States. (It is now observed on the fourth Monday in October.)

1975 Angola gained its independence from Portugal.

1985 The Colombian volcano Nevado del Ruiz erupted, burying the town of Armero and leaving some 15,000 dead, in the worst volcanic disaster in the Western hemisphere in the 1900s.

November 12 – Birthdays

1493 **Baccio Bandinelli.** Florentine sculptor and painter

1615 **Richard Baxter.** One of the greatest English theologians

1770 **Joseph Hopkinson.** American jurist and composer of "Hail Columbia" (1798)

1790 **Letitia Christian Tyler.** First wife of President John Tyler

1815 **Elizabeth Cady Stanton.** Pioneer in the American women's rights movement and first president of the National Woman Suffrage Association

1833 **Alexander Borodin.** Russian composer noted for the opera *Prince Igor,* and whose *Second Symphony* ranks among the best by any Russian composer

1842 **Lord John William Strutt Rayleigh.** One of England's greatest physical scientists

1866 **Sun Yat-sen.** Father of modern China and first president of the Republic of China, in 1912

1870 **Glen MacDonough.** American lyricist noted for songs such as "Forgive and Forget" and "Toyland"

1874 **Bert Williams.** West Indies-born composer and pianist noted for songs such as "Nobody" (1905)

1889 **DeWitt Wallace.** Founder of the *Reader's Digest* (1921)

1891 **Carl Mays.** Professional baseball player

1891 **Richard A. Whiting.** American composer noted for songs such as "Some Sunday Morning," "Sleepytime Gal," "Ain't We Got Fun?" "Beyond the Blue Horizon," "Guilty," and "Too Marvelous for Words"

1903 **Jack Oakie.** American stage and motion-picture actor

1908 **Harry A. Blackmun.** U.S. Supreme Court justice

1917 **Joseph Coors.** American brewery executive

1918 **Jo Stafford.** American singer

1922 **Sunset Carson.** American motion-picture actor

1922 **Kim Hunter.** American motion-picture and television actress

1929 **Grace Kelly.** American motion-picture superstar and Princess of Monaco

1944 **Ken Houston.** Hall of Fame professional football player

1945 **Neil Young.** Canadian singer and guitarist with the Crosby, Stills, Nash, and Young musical group

1950 **Bruce Bochte.** Professional baseball player

1952 **Steve Bartkowski.** Professional football superstar

1954 **Paul McNamee.** Australian tennis player

1957 **Gerry Ellis.** Professional football player

1958 **Dan Petry.** Professional baseball player

1961 **Nadia Comaneci.** Romanian gymnast and darling of the 1976 Olympic Games

November 12 – Events

1035 King Canute of England and Denmark died at Shaftesbury at an approximate age of 39.

1439 Plymouth, England, became the first English town incorporated by Parliament.

1875 The first Harvard-Yale football game was played under the rules that permitted running with the ball and tackling.

1918 After its defeat in World War I, Austria proclaimed itself a separate state independent of Hungary.

1920 In the aftermath of the "Black Sox" scandal, Judge Kenesaw Mountain Landis was appointed the first commissioner of professional baseball.

1927 Joseph Stalin expelled Leon Trotsky from the Central Committee of the Communist party, paving the way for Stalin to become sole ruler of Russia.

1938 In the aftermath of *Crystal Night,* on which Nazi thugs destroyed Jewish shops all over Germany, Adolf Hitler ordered the Jews themselves to pay $400,000,000 for the damages.

1942 British troops captured Tobruk in World War II.

1944 The German battleship *Tirpitz* was destroyed by British bombers in World War II.

1948 The war crimes tribunal sentenced former World War II Japanese premier Hideki Tojo to death.

1954 The Ellis Island immigration station in New York Harbor was closed after processing more than 20 million immigrants beginning in 1892.

1965 The Cowboy Hall of Fame in Oklahoma City inducted its first five members: Theodore Roosevelt, Will Rogers, Charles Russell, Jake McClure, and Charles Goodnight.

1973 Egypt and Israel signed a cease-fire agreement, ending the Middle East War.

November 13 – Birthdays

354 **Saint Augustine.** One of the earliest Christian theologians, and author of *The City of God* and *Confessions,* two of the best-known religious writings of all time

1312 **Edward III.** King of England, 1327-1377, and father of Edward, the Black Prince, one of the greatest warriors in English history

1504 **Philip of Hesse (The Magnanimous).** Father of political Protestantism

1753 **Ippolito Pindemonte.** Italian writer, poet, and translator of Homer's *Odyssey*

1809 **John Adolphus Bernard Dahlgren.** American naval officer who invented the Dahlgren gun that became famous during the Civil War

1814 **Joseph Hooker.** U.S. Civil War general known as "Fighting Joe"

1831 **James Clerk Maxwell.** Great English physicist noted, among other things, for "Maxwell's Laws," which form the basis for modern electromagnetic theory

1833 **Edwin Booth.** Renowned American stage actor of the 19th century, and brother of John Wilkes Booth, the assassin of Abraham Lincoln

1848 **Albert Honore Charles Grimaldi.** Prince of Monaco, marine researcher and founder of the famous Oceanographic Museum

1850 **Robert Louis Stevenson.** One of the world's most popular writers, and author of *Kidnapped* (1886), *Treasure Island* (1883), and *The Strange Case of Dr. Jekyll and Mr. Hyde* (1886)

1853 **John Drew.** Famous American stage actor who played over 100 leading roles in his 50-year career

1856 **Louis Brandeis.** U.S. Supreme Court justice, 1916-1939, and one of the first men to advocate conservation

1872 **Louis Gorham Hupp.** American manufacturer and co-creator of the Hupmobile car (1908)

1875 **James Guilford Swinnerton.** One of the "grand old men" of the American comic strip, and creator of *Little Bears and Tykes*

1890 **Conrad Richter.** American Pulitzer Prize-winning novelist noted for works such as *The Town, The Waters of Kronos,* and *The Trees*

1900 **Alexander King.** American writer, and author of *May This House Be Safe from Tigers*

1904 **Vera Caspary.** American novelist noted for *Laura* (1942)

1906 **Hermione Baddeley.** English stage, television, and motion-picture actress

1910 **William Bradford Huie.** American journalist and author known for *The Execution of Private Slovik* (1954)

1913 **Irving "Deacon" Crane.** American pocket billiards superstar with a career of some 50 years

1915 **Nathaniel Benchley.** American humorist and son of humorist Robert Benchley

1916 **Jack Elam.** American motion-picture actor

1922 **Oskar Werner.** Austrian-born motion-picture actor

1923 **Linda Christian.** Mexican-born motion-picture actress

1930 **Fred Harris.** U.S. senator in the 1960s and 1970s

1932 **Richard Mulligen.** American stage, screen, and television actor who won an Emmy in 1980 for *Soap* and in 1989 for *Empty Nest*

1938 **Jean Seberg.** American motion-picture actress

1941 **Mel Stottlemyre.** Professional baseball player and coach

1947 **Joe Mantegna.** American stage and motion-picture actor

1949 **Roger Steen.** American guitarist with The Tubes

1949 **Whoopi Goldberg.** American stage, screen, and television actress and comedienne

1954 **Scott McNealy.** American business executive and a founder of Sun Microsystems

1955 **Jenny Dimond.** Australian tennis player

1956 **Bill Scanlon.** American tennis player

1959 **Tracy Scoggins.** American stage, screen and television actress

1963 **Vinny Testaverde.** Heisman Trophy winner and professional football superstar

November 13 – Events

1093 Malcolm III MacDuncan, King of Scots, was killed while laying siege to Alnwick in an invasion of England. He was succeeded by his brother Donald Bane.

1460 Prince Henry the Navigator, the great Portuguese promoter of exploration of the 1400s, died at age 66.

1775 American patriots occupied Montreal in the Revolutionary War.

1789 Benjamin Franklin, in a letter to a friend, said, "In this world nothing can be said to be certain except death and taxes."

1868 Gioacchino Antonio Rossini, the great Italian composer, died at Passy, France, at age 76.

1914 The elastic brassiere was patented by American heiress Mary Phelps Jacob.

1921 The motion picture *The Sheik,* starring Rudolph Valentino, was first released. Women fainted in the aisles during the performance.

1927	The Holland Tunnel, linking New York City to Jersey City, was opened to traffic.
1933	The first recorded "sit-down" strike in the United States was staged by workers in the Hormel Packing Company in Austin, Minnesota.
1940	Walt Disney's classic cartoon *Fantasia* was first released.
1941	The British aircraft carrier *Ark Royal* sank in the Mediterranean one day after it had been torpedoed by a German submarine in World War II.
1956	The U.S. Supreme Court struck down Alabama's laws calling for racial segregation on public buses.
1971	U.S. space probe *Mariner 9* went into orbit around Mars and began transmitting pictures of that planet's surface.

November 14 – Birthdays

1650	**William III.** King of England, who with his wife ruled as William and Mary, 1689-1702
1668	**Johann Lucas von Hildebrandt.** Austrian architect
1719	**Leopold Mozart.** Austrian musician who wrote the first important book about violin playing and who was the father of the great composer Wolfgang Amadeus Mozart
1765	**Robert Fulton.** American inventor and builder in 1807 of the *Clermont*, the first commercially successful steamboat
1803	**Jacob Abbott.** American teacher and author of the *Rollo* series of books
1807	**Auguste Laurent.** French chemist
1828	**James B. McPherson.** U.S. Civil War general
1840	**Claude Monet.** Noted French painter and one of the leaders of the Impressionist movement
1863	**Leo Hendrik Baekeland.** American chemist noted for making the first bakelite
1877	**Norman Brookes.** Australian tennis superstar and Hall of Famer
1889	**Jawaharlal Nehru.** First prime minister of India and father of India's first woman prime minister Indira Gandhi
1890	**Raymond Egan.** Canadian songwriter, known for works such as "Sleepy Time Gal" (1925)
1891	**Frederick Grant Banting.** Canadian physician famous for discovering insulin
1896	**Mamie Doud Eisenhower.** Wife of President Dwight D. Eisenhower
1897	**John Steuart Curry.** American painter of the regionalism movement of the 1930s
1900	**Aaron Copland.** American composer noted for works such as *Billy the Kid* (1938) and *Appalachian Spring* (1944)
1904	**Dick Powell.** American motion-picture actor and director
1904	**Marya Mannes.** American novelist and journalist
1906	**Louise Brooks.** American motion-picture actress
1907	**William Steig.** American cartoonist and author

1908	**Joseph R. McCarthy.** U.S. senator who made sensational but unproved charges of Communist subversion in the government in the 1950s
1908	**Harrison Salisbury.** American newspaper columnist
1912	**Barbara Hutton.** Often-married heiress to the Woolworth fortune
1913	**Rosemary DeCamp.** American motion-picture and television actress
1919	**Veronica Lake.** Glamour star of Hollywood films of the 1940s, whose trademark was her long blond hair falling over one of her eyes
1921	**Brian Keith.** American motion-picture and television actor
1923	**Johnny Desmond.** American singer and actor
1924	**Jeri Kelli Sullivan.** American composer, author, and singer, noted for songs such as "Rum and Coca Cola"
1929	**McLean Stevenson.** American television actor, noted for his role in the long-running series, *M*A*S*H*
1929	**Jim Piersall.** Professional baseball player
1930	**Edward H. White.** First U.S. astronaut to walk in space, in 1965
1933	**Fred W. Haise Jr.** American astronaut on the *Apollo 13* mission
1935	**Hussein I.** King of Jordan who succeeded his father Talal in 1952
1945	**Mike Livingston.** Professional football player
1947	**P.J. O'Rourke.** American humorist and author noted for *Parliament of Whores* (1991)
1948	**Prince Charles.** Son of Queen Elizabeth II and heir to the English throne
1955	**Jack Sikma.** Professional basketball player
1962	**Laura San Giacomo.** American stage, screen and TV actress

November 14 – Events

1305	Clement V was crowned. He was the first Roman Catholic pope to reside at Avignon.
1784	Samuel Seabury was consecrated as the first American Episcopalian bishop.
1832	The world's first streetcar, the *John Mason,* made its appearance in New York. It was drawn by two horses on tracks on Fourth Avenue.
1851	Herman Melville's *Moby Dick* was published by Harper and Brothers in New York. It was a failure during Melville's lifetime but is now one of the world's greatest books.
1881	The trial of Charles Guiteau, President James A. Garfield's assassin, opened in Washington, D.C.
1889	Nelly Bly set out from Hoboken, New Jersey, to outdo the hero of *Around the World in Eighty Days*. She succeeded, completing the trip around the world 72 days later.
1896	England repealed the law banning motor vehicles on the highways.

1922	The British Broadcasting Corporation began domestic radio service.
1940	German planes dropped 225 tons of bombs on Coventry, England, in World War II, smashing the heart out of the old city through which Lady Godiva had ridden 900 years earlier.
1942	Captain Eddie Rickenbacker, American World War I ace, was rescued in the Pacific after floating 24 days on a raft, after his plane was forced down on a World War II mission.
1969	*Apollo 12* was launched with the second crew of astronauts, Richard Gordon, Alan Bean, and Charles Conrad, to make a lunar landing.
1972	The Dow Jones Industrial Average closed at 1,003, the first time in its 76-year history that it had closed above 1,000.
1973	Princess Anne of England married Captain Mark Phillips.
1986	The SEC imposed a record $100 million penalty against inside-trader Ivan Boskey and barred him from working again in the securities industry.

November 15 – Birthdays

1397	**Nicholas V.** Roman Catholic pope, 1447-1455, who founded the Vatican Library
1666	**Robert Le Lorrain.** French sculptor
1708	**William Pitt (the Elder).** British statesman known as the "Great Commoner," who transformed Britain into an imperial power
1738	**Sir William Herschel.** British astronomer who in 1781 discovered the planet Uranus, the first planet discovered since prehistoric times
1797	**Thurlow Weed.** American journalist and political leader who was largely responsible for the election of Presidents William Henry Harrison and Zachary Taylor
1862	**Gerhart Hauptmann.** Nobel Prize-winning German dramatist, noted for works such as *The Weavers* (1892) and *Till Eulenspiegel* (1928)
1879	**Lewis Stone.** American stage matinee idol and motion-picture actor in some 200 films
1882	**Felix Frankfurter.** Influential adviser to Presidents Woodrow Wilson and Franklin D. Roosevelt, and U.S. Supreme Court justice, 1939-1962
1887	**Georgia O'Keeffe.** American painter noted for her stark, simple paintings
1887	**Marianne Moore.** One of America's finest woman poets, ranking second perhaps to Emily Dickinson
1891	**Erwin Rommel.** One of the most brilliant German generals of World War II and famed leader of the Afrika Corps
1891	**W. Averell Harriman.** U.S. diplomat, statesman, governor of New York, 1955-1958, and son of industrialist Edward Henry Harriman
1897	**Aneurin Bevan.** English politician and orator noted for his caustic wit and for introducing the British socialized medicine system, in 1948

1906	**Curtis LeMay.** U.S. Air Force general, commander of the Strategic Air Command, 1948-1957, and vice-presidential candidate with third-party candidate George C. Wallace in 1968
1907	**Claus Von Stauffenberg.** German army officer who was one of the leading conspirators in the failed assassination attempt against Hitler in July, 1944
1919	**Inez Eleanor James.** American composer, author, and pianist, noted for such songs as "Vaya Con Dios" and "Come to Baby Do"
1920	**Wayne Thiebaud.** American painter
1925	**Howard Baker.** U.S. senator and Majority Leader, 1981-1985
1928	**Gus Bell.** Professional baseball player
1928	**James Brady.** American writer and television commentator
1929	**Edward Asner.** American stage, screen, and television actor
1932	**Petula Clark.** English singer, songwriter, and actress
1940	**Sam Waterston.** American stage, screen, and television actor
1942	**Daniel Barenboim.** Israeli pianist and conductor
1946	**Janet Lennon.** One of the singing Lennon Sisters
1947	**Bill Richardson.** U.S. congressman and Ambassador to the United Nations under President Clinton
1947	**Bob Dandridge.** Professional basketball player
1950	**Otis Armstrong.** Professional football player

November 15 – Events

1315	The Swiss defeated the Austrians at Mortgarten, consolidating the Everlasting League of the Three Forest Cantons, the nucleus of modern Switzerland.
1777	The Articles of Confederation were adopted by the Continental Congress in York, Pennsylvania.
1806	American explorer Zebulon Pike first sighted Pike's Peak.
1837	Isaac Pitman published his shorthand manual *Stenographic Sound-hand*. Pitman's shorthand eventually became the most popular shorthand of all.
1864	Union general William Tecumseh Sherman burned Atlanta before completing his famous "March to the Sea" in the Civil War.
1881	The Federation of Organized Trades and Labor Unions was organized by Samuel Gompers and others. It was the forerunner of the American Federation of Labor.
1907	*Mr. A. Mutt*, by Bud Fisher, the first successful daily comic strip and the forerunner of *Mutt and Jeff*, made its first appearance, in the San Francisco *Chronicle*.
1917	The Bolsheviks took Moscow in the October Revolution. (It was October by the calendar in use at the time in Russia.)
1920	The first meeting of the League of Nations Assembly was held in Geneva.

1926	NBC made its debut with a four-hour radio broadcast from the Waldorf-Astoria Hotel in New York. It had a network of 24 stations.
1935	Manuel Quezon was inaugurated as the first president of the Philippines.
1959	Herbert Clutter, his wife, and his two children were killed in their home in Holcomb, Kansas, by two robbers, creating the basis for Truman Capote's novel *In Cold Blood*.
1965	Craig Breedlove drove the jet-powered car *Spirit of America* 600.601 miles per hour at Bonneville Salt Flats, Utah, becoming the first to break the 600 mph barrier.
1969	A peaceful demonstration against the Vietnam War was staged in Washington, D.C., by 225,000 protesters.

November 16 – Birthdays

42 BC	**Tiberius.** Emperor emperor, A.D. 14-37, during the adult life of Christ
1766	**Rodolphe Kreutzer.** French composer and virtuoso violinist, to whom Beethoven dedicated his *Sonata in A Major* or *Kreutzer Sonata*
1793	**Francis Danby.** English painter
1811	**John Bright.** English orator, reformer, and statesman, who opposed slavery and England's recognition of the Confederacy in the American Civil War
1839	**Louis Honore Frechette.** Canadian poet of the School of Quebec
1873	**W.C. Handy.** American composer, bandleader, and father of the blues, who wrote "St. Louis Blues" (1914) and "The Memphis Blues" (1912)
1886	**Arthur Krock.** American newspaper columnist
1889	**George S. Kaufman.** American director and playwright, who co-authored the plays *You Can't Take It With You* (1936) and *The Solid Gold Cadillac* (1952)
1894	**Mabel Normand.** American actress and comedienne and superstar of the silent era
1895	**Paul Hindemith.** One of the most important composers of the first half of the 20th century
1896	**Fibber McGee.** American radio personality of the 1930s and 1940s
1896	**Sir Oswald Mosley.** British politician and member of Parliament
1905	**Eddie Condon.** American bandleader and jazz guitarist
1906	**Dan Dowling.** American political cartoonist
1908	**Burgess Meredith.** American stage, screen, and television actor with a career of over 40 years
1916	**Daws Butler.** American entertainer and voice of cartoon characters such as Yogi Bear and Huckleberry Hound
1919	**Anatoly Dobrynin.** Russian diplomat and Ambassador to the United States
1921	**Ben Weisman.** American composer and author, noted for songs such as "Let Me Go Lover" and "Love in the Afternoon"

1926	**Joan Gardner Janis.** American composer, author, and actress
1928	**Clu Gulager.** American motion-picture and television actor
1935	**Elizabeth Drew.** American journalist and author
1941	**Ann McLaughlin.** U.S. Secretary of Labor under President Reagan
1944	**Joanna Pettet.** English-born stage and screen actress
1945	**Martine Van Hamel.** Dutch ballerina
1946	**Jo Jo White.** Professional basketball superstar
1953	**Mary Anne Butke.** Professional golfer
1963	**Zina Garrison.** American tennis player
1964	**Dwight Gooden.** Professional baseball player
1966	**Lisa Bonet.** American television and motion-picture actress
1977	**Oksana Baiul.** Ukrainian skater and 1994 gold medalist

November 16 – Events

1272	King Henry III of England died at age 65, eight years after he had been deposed by reformers.
1532	Spanish conquistador Francisco Pizarro reached Cajamarca, capital of the Inca Empire, where he brought down the empire in a 30-minute fight and captured Emperor Atahualpa.
1864	Union general William Tecumseh Sherman started his "March to the Sea" from Atlanta in the Civil War.
1882	The Milwaukee *Journal* newspaper was founded.
1901	Three automobile racers in Brooklyn achieved a speed of more than a mile a minute, for the first time in history. The fastest, Henry Fournier, drove a mile in 51.8 seconds.
1907	Oklahoma was admitted to the Union as the 46th state.
1933	The United States recognized the Communist government of Russia.
1961	Speaker of the House Sam Rayburn died in Bonham, Texas, at age 79. He had served 49 years in Congress and a record 17 years as Speaker.
1969	A moon rock first went on display, at the Museum of Natural History in New York.

November 17 – Birthdays

1503	**Il Bronzino.** Italian Renaissance painter
1587	**Joost Van den Vondel.** Dutch poet and dramatist
1717	**Jean Le Rond D'Alembert.** French mathematician and scientist, noted for d'Alembert's Principle of motion
1755	**Louis XVIII.** King of France, 1815-1824, known as "the Restoration King" because he ruled after the French Revolution and the execution of his brother, Louis XVI
1788	**Seth Boyden.** American inventor who in 1819 developed patent leather

1790 **August Ferdinand Mobius.** German mathematician, noted for the Mobius strip and as one of the founders of topology

1793 **Sir Charles Eastlake.** English painter

1878 **Grace Abbott.** American pioneer in social work, noted for her part in child labor legislation and in the development of the Social Security Act

1887 **Bernard Law Montgomery.** British World War II field marshal and hero of the Battle of El Alamein

1901 **Lee Strasberg.** Austrian-born motion-picture actor and director

1904 **Isamu Noguchi.** American sculptor noted for works such as *The Seed, View Through Kouros*, and *Strange Bird*

1905 **Mischa Auer.** Russian-born stage and motion-picture actor

1906 **Soichiro Honda.** Japanese industrialist who founded the Honda Motor Co.

1907 **Joe Day.** Hall of Fame golfer

1912 **Bebe Rebozo.** Close friend and associate of President Richard Nixon

1919 **Hershy Kay.** American composer noted for the score of the Broadway play *Evita* (1978)

1923 **Mike Garcia.** Professional baseball player

1925 **Rock Hudson.** American motion-picture and television actor and leading man of the 1950s and 1960s

1930 **Bob Mathias.** American track athlete who won the decathlon at the 1948 and 1952 Olympic games

1937 **Peter Cook.** English actor and irreverent comedian-writer of *Beyond the Fringe* fame

1938 **Gordon Lightfoot.** Canadian singer and composer

1942 **Martin Scorsese.** American motion-picture director, noted for films such as *Alice Doesn't Live Here Anymore* (1975)

1943 **Lauren Hutton.** American motion-picture actress and cover girl

1944 **Danny DeVito.** American motion-picture and television actor

1944 **Tom Seaver.** Professional Hall of Fame baseball pitcher, with over 3,000 career strikeouts

1945 **Elvin Hayes.** Professional basketball superstar and Hall of Famer

1953 **Dino Martin.** American actor and son of singer Dean Martin

November 17 – Events

1558 The glorious Elizabethan Age began as Queen Elizabeth I ascended the throne of England.

1603 Sir Walter Raleigh was imprisoned in the Tower of London where he stayed 12 years. The charge was conspiring to overthrow King James I.

1734 John Peter Zenger was arrested in New York and charged with libel in the famous case that gained the first victory for freedom of the press in the American colonies.

1800 The U.S. Congress convened in Washington, D.C., for the first time.

1805 The Lewis and Clark Expedition reached the Pacific Ocean at the mouth of the Columbia River in the Oregon Territory.

1869 The Suez Canal was opened to traffic.

1891 Ignace Paderewski, the great Polish pianist, made his American debut at New York's new Carnegie Hall.

1917 Auguste Rodin, the great French sculptor, died at Meudon at age 77.

1934 Lyndon B. Johnson married Claudia Alta "Lady Bird" Taylor.

1948 The House of Commons voted to nationalize the British steel industry.

1958 The comic strip *Short Ribs,* by Frank O'Neal, made its first appearance.

1973 President Richard Nixon told an Associated Press meeting that "people have got to know whether or not their president is a crook. Well, I'm not a crook."

November 18 – Birthdays

1584 **Gaspar de Crayer.** Flemish painter

1785 **Sir David Wilkie.** Scottish painter

1786 **Carl Maria von Weber.** The first important composer of German romantic opera, noted for works such as *The Free-shooter* (1821)

1787 **Louis Jacques Mande Daguerre.** French inventor and painter, who perfected the daguerreotype process of making permanent pictures

1810 **Asa Gray.** American botanist, who was the leading authority of his time on the plant life of the United States

1836 **William S. Gilbert.** Collaborator with Sir Arthur Sullivan in the Gilbert and Sullivan operas

1860 **Ignace Jan Paderewski.** Polish pianist, composer, and statesman

1870 **Dorothy Dix.** Newspaper advice columnist (born Elizabeth Meriwether Gilmer) of the 1930s and 1940s

1871 **Amadeo Vives.** Spanish composer of some 100 light operas

1874 **Clarence Day.** American author, noted for *Life with Father* (1935), one of the most popular plays of the 1940s

1882 **Jack Coombs.** Professional baseball player and manager

1882 **D.B. Wyndham Lewis.** British essayist, humorist, and biographer, noted for works such as "On Straw and Other Conceits" (1927) and *Emperor of the West, Charles V* (1932)

1899 **Eugene Ormandy.** Conductor of the Philadelphia Orchestra, 1938-1980

1901 **George Gallup.** Founder of the Gallup Poll

1908 **Imogene Coca.** American actress and comedienne

1909 **Johnny Mercer.** American composer and lyricist, noted for songs such as "Moon River," "In the Cool, Cool, Cool of the Evening," "I'm an Old Cowhand," "On the Atcheson, Topeka, and Santa Fe," and "Autumn Leaves"

1910 **Francis X. Shields.** American Hall of Fame tennis player

1918 **Cameron Mitchell.** American stage, screen, and television actor

1923 **Ted Stevens.** U.S. senator

1923 **Alan B. Shepard Jr.** America's first man in space (May 5, 1961)

1925 **Gene Mauch.** Professional baseball player and manager

1926 **Roy Sievers.** Professional baseball player

1926 **Dorothy Collins.** American popular singer

1939 **Margaret Atwood.** Canadian author noted for works such as *The Handmaid's Tale* (1981)

1939 **Brenda Vaccaro.** American stage, screen, and television actress

1942 **Linda Evans.** American television actress

1948 **Jack Tatum.** Professional football player known as "The Assassin"

1953 **Kevin Nealon.** American actor and comedian noted for his work on TV's *Saturday Night Live*

1962 **Jamie Moyer.** Professional baseball player

1963 **Dante Bichette.** Professional baseball player

1968 **Gary Sheffield.** Professional baseball player

November 18 – Events

1302 Pope Boniface VIII issued the famous bull *Unam Sanctam,* asserting papal authority in Christian society and declaring everyone to be saved must "be subject to the Roman pontiff."

1820 U.S. sea captain Nathaniel Brown Palmer discovered the continent of Antarctica while searching for new seal-fishing grounds.

1852 The Duke of Wellington's funeral was held in London two months after his death. (The funeral was delayed to await the opening of Parliament.)

1865 Mark Twain's story "The Celebrated Jumping Frog of Calaveras County" first appeared, in the New York *Saturday Press.*

1883 Standard time with four time zones was adopted in the United States.

1886 Chester A. Arthur died in New York City at age 56.

1903 The United States and Panama signed a treaty providing for the Panama Canal.

1905 Haakon VII was elected king of Norway.

1922 Marcel Proust, the great French novelist, died in Paris at age 51 just after completing his monumental work, *Remembrance of Things Past.*

1928 Mickey Mouse, perhaps the most beloved cartoon character of all time, was introduced by Walt Disney in *Steamboat Willie* , the first animated cartoon with a sound track.

1966 U.S. Roman Catholic bishops abolished the rule against eating meat on Fridays.

1978 Over 900 members of the People's Temple, a California-based cult, died in Guyana in a mass suicide-murder.

November 19 – Birthdays

1503 **Pier Luigi Farnese.** First duke of Parma

1600 **Charles I.** King of England, 1625-1649, who was beheaded for treason in 1649

1616 **Eustache Le Sueur.** French painter

1752 **George Rogers Clark.** American frontier military leader who won the Northwest Territory from the British during the Revolutionary War

1770 **Bertel Thorvaldsen.** Denmark's greatest sculptor, whose best-known work is the *Lion of Lucerne,* carved in solid rock in Lucerne, Switzerland

1799 **Rene Auguste Caille.** First European to survive a journey to Timbuktu

1805 **Ferdinand Marie De Lesseps.** French promoter of the Suez Canal

1831 **James A. Garfield.** 20th U.S. president

1862 **Billy Sunday.** Professional baseball player who became one of the most famous evangelists of his time

1891 **Clifton Webb.** American stage and motion-picture actor

1897 **Bud Green.** Austrian-born lyricist noted for songs such as "Sentimental Journey," "Alabamy Bound," "That's My Weakness Now," and "Flat Foot Floogie"

1899 **Allen Tate.** American poet, teacher, and novelist

1905 **Tommy Dorsey.** One of the best-known bandleaders of the Big Band Era of the 1930s and 1940s

1907 **Jack Warner Schaefer.** American novelist noted for *Shane* (1949)

1908 **Alan Baxter.** American motion-picture actor

1917 **Indira Gandhi.** Prime minister of India for all but three of the years in the period 1966-1984, and daughter of the great Indian nationalist leader Jawaharlal Nehru

1919 **Alan Young.** English-born motion-picture and television actor noted for the long-running series *Mr. Ed*

1921 **Roy Campanella.** Hall of Fame baseball player and one of the three or four greatest catchers in the history of the game

1926 **Jeane J. Kirkpatrick.** UN ambassador under President Reagan

1933 **Larry King.** American broadcaster, newspaper columnist, and host of *The Larry King Show*

1935 **Jerry Gaylon Foster.** American composer and singer noted for songs such as "Somebody Loves Me"

1936 **Dick Cavett.** American television entertainer

1938 **Ted Turner.** American television executive, sportsman, and founder of Cable News Network (CNN)

1939 **Tom Harkin.** U.S. senator

1941 **Tommy Thompson.** Governor of Wisconsin

1942 **Calvin Klein.** American fashion designer and founder of Calvin Klein Ltd., whose most famous design was his Calvin Klein jeans

1947 **Michael Phipps.** Professional football player

1947 **Bob Boone.** Professional baseball player

1947 **Scott Hunter.** Professional football player

1949 **Ahmad Rashad.** Professional football player and sportscaster

1951 **Wilbur Jackson.** Professional football player

1953 **Richard Todd.** Professional football player

1954 **Kathleen Quinlan.** American stage, screen and television actress

1961 **Meg Ryan.** American actress and leading lady of Hollywood films of the 1980s and 1990s

1962 **Jodie Foster.** American television and motion-picture actress who won the best actress Academy Award for *The Accused* (1988) and a second one for *The Silence of the Lambs* (1991)

November 19 – Events

1493 Columbus discovered Puerto Rico on his second voyage to America, and named it San Juan Bautista.

1828 Franz Schubert, the great Austrian composer, died in Vienna at age 31.

1850 Alfred Lord Tennyson became poet laureate of England, succeeding William Wordsworth.

1863 Abraham Lincoln delivered his famous Gettysburg Address, and "Four score and seven years ago" became part of the American heritage.

1874 The Woman's Christian Temperance Union was organized in Cleveland, Ohio.

1919 The Treaty of Versailles, ending World War I, was rejected by the United States Senate.

1942 The Russians counterattacked at Stalingrad, launching their winter offensive against the Germans along the Don River, in World War II.

1959 Ford Motor Company announced it would no longer produce the Edsel.

1969 The *Apollo 12* module, *Intrepid,* landed on the Ocean of Storms of the moon with astronauts Charles Conrad, Jr., and Alan Bean, in the second moon landing in history.

1977 Egyptian President Anwar Sadat arrived in Israel on his historic mission to seek peace with the Israelis.

November 20 – Birthdays

1602 **Otto von Guericke.** Mayor of Magdeburg, Prussia, who in the 1640s invented the first air pump

1620 **Peregrine White.** The first English child born in New England, on the *Mayflower* in Cape Cod Bay

1726 **Oliver Wolcott.** Connecticut signer of the Declaration of Independence, army commander in the Revolutionary War, and governor of Connecticut, 1796-1797

1752 **Thomas Chatterton.** English poet known for works such as *The Balade of Charitie*

1761 **Pius VIII.** Roman Catholic pope, 1829-1830

1841 **Sir Wilfred Laurier.** First French-Canadian to become prime minister of Canada, 1896-1911

1858 **Selma Lagerlof.** Nobel Prize-winning Swedish novelist, best known for *Gosta Berling's Saga* (1891)

1866 **Kenesaw Mountain Landis.** First commissioner of professional baseball, 1920-1944

1869 **Clark Griffith.** Professional baseball player and long-time owner of the Washington Senators baseball team

1874 **James M. Curley.** American political leader, four-time mayor of Boston and governor of Massachusetts

1884 **Norman Thomas.** U.S. social reformer and six times Socialist Party candidate for president

1885 **Albert Kesselring.** German World War II field marshal who led the German army in the final weeks before the collapse

1890 **Robert Armstrong.** American stage, screen, and television actor with a career of over 40 years

1891 **Jimmy Murphy.** American cartoonist and creator of *Toots and Casper* (1919)

1891 **Reginald Denny.** English stage and motion-picture actor who appeared in over 200 films

1900 **Chester Gould.** American cartoonist and creator of *Dick Tracy* (1931)

1908 **Alistair Cooke.** English-born American reporter and television narrator

1909 **Alan Bible.** U.S. senator, 1954-1975

1916 **Judy Canova.** American actress, singer, and comedienne

1917 **Robert C. Byrd.** U.S. senator and Majority Senator in the 1970s and 1980s

1917 **Bobby Locke.** Professional golfer

1919 **Evelyn Keyes.** American motion-picture actress

1920 **Gene Tierney.** American stage, screen, and television actress

1921 **Phyllis Thaxter.** American stage and motion-picture actress

1925 **Robert F. Kennedy.** U.S. senator, attorney general, and brother of President John F. Kennedy

1926 **Kaye Ballard.** American actress and comedienne

1927 **Estelle Parsons.** American motion-picture and television actress

1929 **Don January.** Professional golfer

1932 **Richard Dawson.** English-born comedian and long-time host of the television game show *Family Feud*

1938 **Dick Smothers.** One of the two Smothers Brothers, American comedians

1942 **Joseph Biden.** U.S. senator

1943 **Veronica Hamel.** American stage and screen actress

1944 **Louie Dampier.** Professional basketball player

1945 **Jay Johnstone.** Professional baseball player

1945 **Rick Monday.** Professional baseball player

1946   **Judy Woodruff.** American broadcast journalist
1946   **Duane Allman.** Guitarist with the Allman Brothers musical group
1956   **Bo Derek.** American motion-picture actress
1959   **Sean Young.** American motion-picture actress

November 20 – Events

1541   John Calvin reorganized the church in Geneva with the Presbyterian constitution.
1542   The first of the "New Laws" of Spain was passed to protect native laborers in America from unscrupulous settlers.
1866   The Grand Army of the Republic held its first national encampment at Indianapolis.
1910   The Mexican Revolution of 1910 began, led by Francisco I. Madero.
1910   Leo Tolstoy, the great Russian novelist, died in the cottage of the station master of the railway station in Astapovo, Russia, at age 82. He was waiting for the train when he became ill.
1914   The United States Department of State first required photographs to be attached to passports.
1940   Hungary joined the Axis powers in World War II.
1943   U.S. marines landed on Tarawa, beginning one of the most savage battles of World War II.
1945   Twenty-four Nazi leaders went on trial before an international war crimes tribunal in Nuremberg, Germany.
1947   Elizabeth, the future queen of Great Britain, married Philip Mountbatten, formerly Prince Philip of Greece, in Westminster Abbey.
1947   The long-running television show *Meet the Press* first went on the air. It was moderated by Lawrence Spivak until November 1975.
1950   United Nations forces in Korea reached the Manchurian border.
1953   Texas millionaire Hugh Roy Cullen gave over $2 million to the University of Houston because of its 37-7 victory over Baylor.
1967   The United States population reached 200 million.
1969   The Nixon administration announced a halt to residential use of the pesticide DDT as part of a total phaseout.
1975   Spain's Generalissimo Francisco Franco died two weeks before his 83rd birthday, after ruling as a dictator since 1936.

November 21 – Birthdays

1495   **John Bale.** English bishop and author of *Kynge Johan,* the first English history play
1659   **Henry Purcell.** English composer noted for *Dido and Aeneas* (1680), the first English opera, and which contains "Dido's Lament," one of the most beautiful songs of sorrow in opera

1694   **Voltaire (François Marie Arouet).** French philosopher and writer, who was one of the greatest 18th-century thinkers, and who wrote *Candide* (1759), one of the great works of world literature
1729   **Josiah Bartlett.** A leading American patriot during the Revolutionary War and one of the New Hampshire signers of the Declaration of Independence
1787   **Sir Samuel Cunard.** Founder of the Cunard steamship line
1834   **Frederick Weyerhaeuser.** American lumberman and founder of the Weyerhaeuser timber company in 1870
1834   **Hetty Green.** American financier and "Witch of Wall Street," who at the time of her death was the richest woman in the world
1889   **Leon Flatow.** American composer noted for "Popeye the Sailor Man"
1898   **Rene Magritte.** Belgian surrealist painter noted for works such as *Golconda* (1953)
1904   **Coleman "Bean" Hawkins.** American musician, who was the first important tenor saxophonist in jazz
1905   **Freddie Lindstrom.** Professional baseball player
1907   **Jim Bishop.** American newspaper columnist and author
1912   **Eleanor Powell.** American motion-picture actress and dancer
1916   **Sid Luckman.** Professional football superstar and Hall of Famer
1920   **Ralph Meeker.** American stage, screen, and television actor
1920   **Stan Musial.** Hall of Fame baseball player and winner of seven batting championships
1921   **Vivian Blaine.** American actress and singer
1937   **Marlo Thomas.** American television and motion-picture actress and daughter of actor and singer Danny Thomas
1940   **Natalia Makarova.** Russian ballerina
1941   **Juliet Mills.** English stage, screen and motion-picture actress, daughter of actor John Mills and sister of actress Hayley Mills
1944   **Earl Monroe.** Professional Hall of Fame basketball superstar known as "The Pearl"
1945   **Goldie Hawn.** American motion-picture and television actress
1953   **Tina Brown.** English editor of *Vanity Fair* and *New Yorker*
1956   **Cherry Jones.** American stage, screen, and television actress, and Tony award winner for *The Heiress*
1961   **Mariel Hemingway.** American motion-picture and television actress and grand-daughter of writer Ernest Hemingway
1966   **Troy Aikman.** Professional football player and superstar
1969   **Ken Griffey Jr.** Professional baseball player and superstar
1974   **Karrie Webb.** Australian golfer and LPGA leading money winner in 1996

November 21 – Events

235 St. Anterus became Roman Catholic pope.

1620 The *Mayflower* arrived at what is now Province-town Harbor in Massachusetts, and the Mayflower Compact was signed by the Pilgrims on board the ship (November 11, Old Style).

1789 North Carolina ratified the Constitution, becoming the 12th state to do so.

1844 Charles Goodyear patented his rubber vulcanization process.

1864 President Lincoln wrote his famous letter of condolence to Mrs. Lydia Bixby, whose five sons had been killed in battle.

1874 Johann Strauss's operetta *Die Fledermaus* began its first American run, at the Thalia Theater in New York.

1877 Thomas A. Edison announced his invention of the phonograph, which he named a "talking machine."

1922 Rebecca L. Felton of Georgia was sworn in as the first U.S. woman senator. Her term, the unexpired term of the late Senator Thomas E. Watson, ended the next day.

1925 The great Red Grange played his last varsity football game with the University of Illinois before turning professional with the Chicago Bears.

1934 *Anything Goes*, one of Cole Porter's greatest musicals, opened at the Alvin Theater on Broadway.

1942 The Alaska highway across Canada was formally opened.

1964 The Verazano-Narrows Bridge between Staten Island and Brooklyn was opened to traffic.

1973 White House attorney Fred Buzhardt revealed the existence of an 18½ minute gap in one of the key Watergate tapes.

November 22 – Birthdays

1515 **Mary of Guise.** Wife of King James V of Scotland

1643 **Robert Cavalier, Sieur de La Salle.** The greatest French explorer of North America, who claimed the entire Mississippi Valley for France

1744 **Abigail Smith Adams.** Wife of President John Adams and first hostess of the White House

1808 **Thomas Cook.** Innovator of conducted tours and founder of Thomas Cook and Son travel agency

1819 **George Eliot (Mary Ann Evans).** One of the greatest English novelists of the 19th century, and author of *Middlemarch: A Study of Provincial Life* (1871-1872) and *Silas Marner* (1861)

1842 **Jose Maria de Heredia.** French poet

1857 **George Robert Gissing.** English novelist, noted for *New Grub Street* (1891)

1868 **John Nance Garner.** U.S. vice president under President Franklin D. Roosevelt, 1933-1941

1869 **Andre Gide.** Nobel Prize-winning French author, noted for works such as *Strait Is the Gate* (1909)

1877 **Endre Ady.** Greatest Hungarian lyric poet of the 20th century

1890 **Charles de Gaulle.** The outstanding French patriot, general, and statesman of the 20th century

1891 **Edward L. Bernays.** American public relations pioneer, author, and nephew of the noted psychologist Sigmund Freud

1893 **Johnny Dundee.** Hall of Fame American boxer and Featherweight champion (1923-1925)

1899 **Walter Berndt.** American cartoonist noted for the comic strip *Smitty* (1922-1973)

1899 **Wiley Post.** Pioneer American aviator who was the first man to fly around the world alone, and who piloted the plane in which he and humorist Will Rogers were killed in Alaska in 1935

1899 **Hoagy Carmichael.** One of America's leading composers, noted for such classics as "Stardust," "Lazy Bones," "Old Rockin' Chair," "Up a Lazy River," and "Georgia On My Mind"

1901 **Roy Crane.** American cartoonist and creator of *Captain Easy, Wash Tubbs*, and *Buz Sawyer*

1902 **Al J. Neiburg.** American composer and author, noted for songs such as "I'm Confessin' That I Love You" and "It's the Talk of the Town"

1907 **Dick Bartell.** Professional baseball player

1912 **Doris Duke.** Often-married heiress to the Duke tobacco fortune

1913 **Charles F. Berlitz.** Language expert and author

1913 **Benjamin Britten.** British composer famous for his vocal music, especially his operas, such as *Peter Grimes, Billy Budd,* and *The Turn of the Screw*

1918 **Ray Walston.** American stage, screen and television actor and comedian

1918 **Claiborne Pell.** U.S. senator

1921 **Rodney Dangerfield.** American comedian with the byword "I get no respect"

1924 **Geraldine Page.** American stage, screen, and television actress

1926 **Lew Burdette.** Professional baseball player

1935 **Michael Callan.** American motion-picture and television actor, dancer, and singer

1938 **Henry Lee.** Chinese-born forensic scientist

1938 **Charles Johnson.** Professional football player

1940 **Terry Gilliam.** American director, screenwriter and actor noted for his work with the long-running TV series *Monty Python's Flying Circus*

1941 **Tom Conti.** British stage, screen and television actor

1943 **Billie Jean King.** American tennis superstar and six times women's singles champion at Wimbledon

1950 **Greg Luzinski.** Professional baseball player

1958 **Jamie Lee Curtis.** American motion-picture actress and daughter of actor Tony Curtis and actress Janet Leigh

1967 **Boris Becker.** German tennis player who by winning the 1985 Wimbledon championship became at 17 the youngest player to win a tennis Grand Slam tournament

November 22 – Events

1497 Vasco da Gama, the great Portuguese navigator, rounded the Cape of Good Hope on his historic trip to India.

1718 Blackbeard (Edward Teach), the famous British pirate, was caught by the British Navy off the North Carolina coast, and killed by 25 bullet wounds in his body.

1852 French citizens voted to establish the Second French Empire under Emperor Napoleon III.

1880 Lillian Russell, the great American actress, made her vaudeville debut at Tony Pastor's Theatre in New York City.

1900 Sir Arthur Sullivan, the noted English operetta composer, died in London at age 58.

1906 The International Radio Telegraphic Convention, meeting in Berlin, adopted the SOS distress signal. SOS does not stand for anything; it was convenient to send by wireless.

1909 Helen Hayes, the great American stage actress, made her New York debut at age nine in the play *In Old Dutch,* at the Herald Square Theater.

1935 The first transpacific airmail flight began, as the *China Clipper* left San Francisco for Manila with 100,000 letters.

1942 The comic strip-within-a-strip "Fearless Fosdick," by Al Capp, first appeared in *Li'l Abner.*

1943 President Roosevelt, Prime Minister Churchill, and Generalissimo Chiang Kai-shek opened the Cairo Conference in Egypt.

1963 President John F. Kennedy was shot at 12:30 p.m. in Dallas, Texas, while riding in a caravan in an open-top automobile. He died at 1 p.m. C.S.T.

1975 Juan Carlos I was installed King of Spain, two days after the death of dictator Francisco Franco.

1980 Mae West, one of the most famous American actresses, died at age 88.

November 23 – Birthdays

912 **Otto I (The Great).** King of Germany, A.D. 936-983, who was the first king to become Holy Roman Emperor (A.D. 961)

1608 **Francisco Manuel de Melo.** Portuguese soldier, diplomat, and poet

1616 **John Wallis.** English mathematician who contributed to the origins of calculus

1749 **Edward Rutledge.** Member of the Continental Congress, governor of South Carolina (1798-1800), and signer of the Declaration of Independence

1804 **Franklin Pierce.** 14th U.S. president

1834 **James Thomson.** English Victorian poet noted for *The City of Dreadful Night* (1874)

1859 **Billy the Kid (William H. Bonney).** Notorious outlaw of the American West

1862 **Sir Gilbert Parker.** Canadian novelist

1876 **Manuel de Falla.** Spanish composer, noted for works such as the ballet *The Three Cornered Hat* (1919), one of the finest works of contemporary Spanish music

1878 **Holcombe Ward.** American tennis player and U.S. Singles Champion in 1904

1878 **Ernest J. King.** American fleet admiral, who, as commander-in-chief of the U.S. Navy in World War II, directed the greatest naval fleet in history

1883 **Jose Clemente Orozco.** One of Mexico's greatest and best-known painters

1887 **Boris Karloff.** English-born American actor with a 50-year career of some 140 films, the most notable of which was *Frankenstein,* in 1931

1888 **Harpo Marx.** American comedian and the member of the Marx Brothers comedy group who always pretended to be mute

1896 **Ruth Etting.** American singer, actress, and pioneer radio and recording star of the 1920s and 1930s

1902 **Victor Jory.** American stage and motion-picture actor who typically played evil-eyed heavy roles in a career of over 40 years

1910 **Hal Schumacher.** Professional baseball player

1915 **Ellen Drew.** American motion-picture actress and leading lady of the 1940s and 1950s

1923 **Art Wall Jr.** Professional golfer with a record 41 career holes-in-one

1927 **Otis Chandler.** Publisher of the Los Angeles *Times*

1928 **Jerry Bock.** American composer and member of Songwriters Hall of Fame, who teamed with lyricist Sheldon Harnick to write songs such as "Sunrise, Sunset" from *Fiddler on the Roof*

1930 **William E. Brock.** U.S. senator and Secretary of Labor under President Reagan

1934 **Lew Hoad.** Australian tennis superstar and Wimbledon singles champion, 1956-1957

1940 **Luis Tiant.** Professional baseball player

1947 **Toshiro Sakai.** Japanese tennis player

1950 **Charles E. Schumer.** U.S. congressman and senator

1955 **Mary Landrieu.** U.S. senator and daughter of ex-Mayor Moon Landrieu of New Orleans

November 23 – Events

1644 John Milton, the great English poet, published his greatest prose work, "Areopagitica," a defense of freedom of the press.

1774 Massachusetts began organizing the Minutemen, so called because they were prepared to fight "at a minute's notice."

1863 The Battle of Chattanooga began and resulted two days later in Union control of Tennessee in the Civil War.

1876 Harvard, Yale, Princeton, and Columbia formed the American Intercollegiate Football Association, the first college football conference.

1889 The first jukebox made its debut, in San Francisco at the Palais Royale Saloon. It was devised by Louis Glass and had four listening tubes with a coin slot for each tube.

1903 Enrico Caruso, the great Italian tenor, made his American debut in *Rigoletto* at the Metropolitan Opera House in New York.

1936 The first edition of *Life* magazine was published by Henry R. Luce.

1940 The Greeks drove the last of the Italian invaders from their country in World War II.

1940 Romania joined the Axis powers in World War II.

1942 Congress established SPARS, the U.S. Coast Guard Women's Reserve. The name SPAR came from the first letters of the motto and its translation, Semper Paratus (Always Ready).

1943 U.S. marines captured Tarawa after one of the bloodiest battles of World War II.

1960 U.S. weather satellite *Tiros II* was launched.

1971 The People's Republic of China was seated in the U.N. Security Council.

1980 President Jimmy Carter warned the Iranians of "extremely grave" consequences if any of the American hostages in the American embassy in Teheran were harmed.

November 24 – Birthdays

1391 **Charles of Valois-Orleans.** Duke of Orleans and one of the greatest poets of France

1632 **Baruch Spinoza.** One of the greatest Dutch philosophers of the 17th century (also known as Benedict Spinoza)

1655 **Charles XI.** King of Sweden, 1660-1697

1713 **Father Junipero Serra.** Franciscan missionary who in 1769 founded the first mission in California (then called Upper California)

1713 **Laurence Sterne.** English clergyman who became famous for the novel *The Life and Opinions of Tristram Shandy, Gentleman* (1760-1767)

1784 **Zachary Taylor.** American hero of the Mexican War and 12th U.S. president

1815 **Grace Darling.** English heroine who saved nine survivors of a shipwreck off the English coast on September 7, 1838

1848 **Lilli Lehmann.** German operatic soprano and leading member of the Berlin Royal Opera and the Metropolitan Opera Company of New York

1849 **Frances Eliza Hodgson Burnett.** English-born American author noted for the novels *Little Lord Fauntleroy* (1886) and *The Secret Garden*

1853 **Bat Masterson.** Noted lawman of the American West

1864 **Henri de Toulouse-Lautrec.** French painter noted for his lively pictures of Paris night life and for his lithographs and posters

1868 **Scott Joplin.** American composer and performer of ragtime music, credited with the first ragtime opera, *A Guest of Honor* (1903)

1875 **Ed Rose.** American lyricist noted for songs such as "Baby Shoes" and "Oh Johnny, Oh Johnny, Oh"

1877 **Alben W. Barkley.** U.S. vice president under President Truman

1887 **Erich von Manstein.** German World War II field marshal

1888 **Dale Carnegie.** American lecturer, author and pioneer in the field of public speaking, noted for the best-selling book *How to Win Friends and Influence People* (1936)

1890 **George E. Stratemeyer.** American World War II general

1896 **Corinne Griffith.** American motion-picture actress and "the world's most beautiful woman" in the silent screen era

1897 **"Lucky" Luciano.** Notorious American racketeer

1905 **Harry Barris.** American composer noted for songs such as "Mississippi Mud" and "Wrap Your Troubles in Dreams"

1908 **Harry Kemelman.** American author noted for works such as *Friday the Rabbi Slept Late* (1965)

1911 **Joe "Ducky" Medwick.** Hall of Fame baseball player with a .324 lifetime batting average

1912 **Garson Kanin.** American director, screenwriter and playwright noted for works such as *The True Glory* (1945)

1914 **Geraldine Fitzgerald.** Irish-born stage and motion-picture actress with a career of some 50 years

1917 **Howard Duff.** American motion-picture and television actor

1920 **Elmo Zumwalt Jr.** American naval officer, and youngest four-star admiral in U.S. history

1921 **John V. Lindsay.** Mayor of New York City, 1966-1974

1923 **Scott Meredith.** American literary agent

1925 **William F. Buckley Jr.** American columnist, author, and television show host

1930 **Bob Friend.** Professional baseball player

1938 **Oscar Robertson.** One of professional basketball's greatest players and Hall of Famer, known as the "Big O"

1942 **Marlin Fitzwater.** White House press secretary for Presidents Reagan and Bush

1943 **Dave Bing.** Professional basketball player

1946 **Ted Bundy.** American serial killer who confessed to over 20 murders of women

1948 **Rudy Tomjanovich.** Professional basketball player

1948 **Steve Yeager.** Professional baseball player

November 24 – Events

1564 Pope Pius IV published the *Index of Prohibited Books*.

1642 Abel Janszoon Tasman, the famous Dutch navigator, discovered the island of Tasmania.

1655 Use of the *Book of Common Prayer* was prohibited in England by Oliver Cromwell.

1832	South Carolina passed the Ordinance of Nullification, declaring the federal tariff statute null and void. (The ordinance was rescinded in March 1833.)
1859	Charles Darwin, the famous evolutionist, published his book *The Origin of Species.*
1859	Adelina Patti, the great operatic soprano, made her world debut in *Lucia di Lammermoor* at the Academy of Music in New York City.
1871	The National Rifle Association was incorporated and Major General Ambrose E. Burnside was named as its first president.
1874	Barbed wire was patented by its inventor, Joseph F. Glidden, of De Kalb, Illinois.
1918	The comic strip *Gasoline Alley,* by Frank King, first appeared.
1944	U.S. Air Force B-29 superfortress bombers raided Tokyo, from Saipan for the first time.
1947	The Hollywood 10, screen writers and officials, were cited for contempt of Congress for refusing to say if they were Communists. They were later blacklisted and imprisoned.
1963	Jack Ruby shot and killed Lee Harvey Oswald, the presumed assassin of President Kennedy, on live TV in Dallas.
1969	*Apollo 12* splashed down in the Pacific, returning from the second manned trip to the moon.
1971	A skyjacker calling himself D.B. Cooper leaped from a Boeing 727 with $200,000 and a parachute, in the most successful skyjacking of all time. Cooper was never found.

November 25 – Birthdays

1562	**Lope de Vega.** The most important playwright of Spain's Golden Age, who wrote more plays (at least 400 with estimates up to 2200) than any other author in history
1609	**Henrietta Marie.** French wife of King Charles I of England
1835	**Andrew Carnegie.** American steel industrialist and philanthropist, noted for founding the Carnegie Corporation of New York and Carnegie Technical Schools (now Carnegie-Mellon University)
1844	**Karl Benz.** German automobile pioneer who designed and built the world's first practical automobile powered by an internal combustion engine and who founded Benz and Company
1846	**Carry Nation.** American temperance advocate famous for her hatchet attacks on barrooms
1870	**Maurice Denis.** French painter
1874	**Joe Gans.** World lightweight boxing champion, 1902-1908, known as the "Old Master"
1881	**John XXIII.** Roman Catholic pope, 1958-1963, who called the Second Vatican Council (1962)
1890	**Isaac Rosenberg.** English poet
1893	**Joseph Wood Krutch.** American writer, drama critic, and teacher

1895	**Anastas Ivanovich Mikoyan.** First vice premier of Russia, and Russian president, 1964-1965
1895	**Ludvick Svoboda.** Czech national hero of the two World Wars, and president of Czechoslovakia, 1968-1975, after the crushing by Russia of the 1968 Czech revolt
1896	**Virgil Thomson.** American composer and critic, who won the 1949 Pulitzer Prize for the music for the movie *Louisiana Story*
1899	**W.R. Burnett.** American novelist and screenwriter, noted for scripts such as *Little Caesar, High Sierra,* and *The Asphalt Jungle*
1900	**Helen Gahagan Douglas.** Broadway leading lady and opera singer of the 1920s and 1930s, and U.S. congresswoman, 1945-1949
1900	**Arthur Schwartz.** American popular music composer and motion-picture producer who, with Howard Dietz, wrote songs such as "Dancing in the Dark" and "That's Entertainment"
1904	**Jessica Royce Landis.** American stage and screen actress
1914	**Joe DiMaggio.** One of the greatest outfielders in baseball history, with a record 56 game hitting streak in 1941
1919	**Steve Brodie.** American motion-picture actor
1920	**Ricardo Montalban.** Mexican-born motion-picture and television actor
1927	**Jeffrey Hunter.** American motion-picture actor
1933	**Kathryn Grant.** American motion-picture actress and wife of singer Bing Crosby
1940	**Joe Gibbs.** Professional football coach with three Super Bowl victories
1945	**John McVie.** English musician with the Fleetwood Mac musical group
1947	**John Larroquette.** American motion-picture and television actor (*Night Court*)
1951	**Bucky Dent.** Professional baseball player
1960	**Amy Grant.** American Christian rock singer
1960	**John F. Kennedy Jr.** Son of President Kennedy
1963	**Bernie Kosar.** Professional football player
1971	**Christina Applegate.** American motion-picture actress

November 25 – Events

1277	Nicholas III was elected Roman Catholic pope.
1780	The British frigate *Hussar* sank in New York Harbor with 900,000 gold guineas aboard. (There is no record that it was ever recovered.)
1783	The last British red coats in the United States left New York City, after the Revolutionary War.
1795	William Henry Harrison married Anna Symmes.
1851	The first YMCA branches were organized in North America, at Montreal and Boston.
1863	The Battle of Lookout Mountain began in Tennessee. It ended two days later in victory for the Union.

1899 The Baghdad Railway Commission was signed, giving a German company the right to build a railway from Constantinople to Baghdad to Basra.

1903 Bob Fitzsimmons became the first to win three different boxing championships, defeating George Gardner for the light heavyweight title.

1907 Mary Garden, the great American singing actress, made her American debut in *Thais* at the Manhattan Opera House in New York.

1920 Station WTAW, College Station, Texas, broadcast the first play-by-play radio account of a football game, between the University of Texas and Texas A & M.

1921 Hirohito became regent five years before becoming emperor of Japan.

1955 Bill Haley's "Rock Around the Clock" topped the United Kingdom's singles chart, the first rock and roll record to do so.

1963 President John F. Kennedy was buried at Arlington National Cemetery.

1986 The Iran-Contra affair erupted as President Reagan revealed that profits from secret arms sales to Iran had been diverted illegally to Nicaraguan rebels (the contras).

November 26 – Birthdays

1607 **John Harvard.** American minister and philanthropist for whom Harvard University was named

1731 **William Cowper.** English poet, noted for works such as "The Olney Hymns" (1779) and "The Task" (1785)

1807 **William Sydney Mount.** First native-born American painter to make a career of genre painting, noted for works such as *Bargaining for a Horse* (1835)

1858 **Israel Abrahams.** British Jewish scholar

1861 **Albert B. Fall.** Secretary of the Interior under President Warren G. Harding, who was sent to prison for accepting bribes in the notorious Teapot Dome Scandal

1866 **Hugh Duffy.** Professional baseball player who hit .438 in 1894, the highest ever under the current rules

1876 **Willie Haviland Carrier.** American inventor who developed the first practical air-conditioning process (1911)

1879 **Charles W. Goddard.** Author of *Perils of Pauline*

1888 **Ford Beebe.** American motion-picture director with a 40-year career

1891 **Anne Nichols.** American playwright noted for *Abie's Irish Rose* (1922)

1894 **Norbert Wiener.** American mathematician and logician, and founder of cybernetics

1895 **Bill W. (William Griffith Wilson).** Co-founder with Dr. Bob of Alcoholics Anonymous (1935)

1900 **Bruno Richard Hauptmann.** Convicted kidnapper and murderer of Charles A. Lindbergh's infant son in 1932

1905 **Emlyn Williams.** Welsh actor, playwright, screenwriter, and director

1906 **Bob Johnson.** Professional baseball player

1907 **Frances Dee.** American motion-picture actress and wife of actor Joel McCrea

1909 **Vernon "Lefty" Gomez.** Hall of Fame baseball pitcher who had a career won-lost percentage of .649

1911 **Samuel Herman Reshevsky.** American chess master and one of the greatest players of the 20th century

1912 **Eric Severeid.** Influential American newscaster and commentator

1912 **Eugene Ionesco.** Romanian-born French dramatist, noted for works such as *The Bald Soprano* (1948) and *The Pedestrian in the Air* (1962)

1916 **Bob Elliott.** Professional baseball player

1919 **Frank Fletcher.** American cartoonist who continued the comic strip *Bringing Up Father* (Sunday page) when its creator, George McManus, died in 1954

1922 **Charles Schulz.** American cartoonist and creator of *Peanuts,* one of the most successful of all American comic strips

1924 **George Segal.** American sculptor noted for his realistic, life-size plaster figures

1925 **Eugene Istomin.** American virtuoso pianist

1933 **Robert Goulet.** American singer and actor

1938 **Rich Little.** Canadian-born impressionist and actor

1938 **Tina Turner.** American singer

1942 **Jan Stenerud.** Professional football player and Hall of Famer

1947 **Larry Gura.** Professional baseball player

1947 **Roger Wehrli.** Professional football player

1947 **Richie Hebner.** Professional baseball player

1952 **Wendy Turnbull.** Australian tennis player

1954 **Roz Chast.** American cartoonist and illustrator

1962 **Chuck Finley.** Professional baseball player

November 26 – Events

885 Danish Vikings attacked Paris and were paid by the Frankish emperor Charles the Fat not to destroy the city as they had in A.D. 845 and 856.

1789 The first national Thanksgiving Day was proclaimed by President George Washington to observe the adoption of the U.S. Constitution.

1825 The first collegiate social fraternity, Kappa Alpha, was organized at Union College in Schenectady, New York.

1864 Edwin Booth, the great American actor, opened his run of Shakespeare's *Hamlet* at the Winter Garden Theater in New York.

1894 Nicholas II, the last czar of Russia, married Alexandra of Hesse.

1922 Howard Carter first saw inside the tomb of Tutankhamen at Luxor in Egypt's Valley of the Kings, making one of the greatest archaeological discoveries in history.

1928	The comic strip *Jane Arden,* by Monte Barrett and Frank Ellis, first appeared.
1941	Secretary of State Cordell Hull submitted American proposals to the Japanese "peace" envoys in Washington, D.C., less than two weeks before the Japanese attacked Pearl Harbor.
1950	Communist China entered the Korean War, opening a great offensive against United Nations troops, forcing a general retreat.
1973	Rosemary Woods, President Richard Nixon's personal secretary, told a federal court she had mistakenly caused the 18½ minute gap in one of the key Watergate tapes.

November 27 – Birthdays

1701	**Anders Celsius.** Swedish astronomer who in 1742 devised the Celsius, or centigrade, temperature scale
1746	**Robert Livingston.** American statesman who helped draw up the Declaration of Independence, administered the oath of office to George Washington, and negotiated the Louisiana Purchase
1865	**Jose Asuncion Silva.** Colombian poet
1874	**Eugene Walter.** American dramatist noted for *Trail of the Lonesome Pine* (1911)
1874	**Bill Wambsganss.** Professional baseball player who made the only unassisted triple play in World Series history (1920)
1874	**Chaim Weizmann.** First president of Israel, 1949-1952
1874	**Charles A. Beard.** Noted American historian and author
1884	**Jose de Creeft.** American sculptor
1901	**Ted Husing.** American sports announcer
1903	**Mona Washbourne.** English stage, screen, and television actress
1909	**James Agee.** American novelist and scriptwriter, noted for the Pulitzer Prize-winning novel *A Death in the Family* (1957), and for movie scripts such as *The African Queen*
1912	**David Merrick.** American Broadway producer of such hits as *Hello Dolly!*
1917	**Buffalo Bob Smith.** American entertainer and creator and star of TV's *Howdy Doody* (1947-1960)
1921	**Alexander Dubcek.** Czech leader whose liberal reforms alarmed the Russians and led to the Russian occupation of Czechoslovakia in 1968
1925	**Marshall Thompson.** American motion-picture and television actor
1937	**Gail Sheehy.** American journalist and author, noted for the best-selling book *Passages*
1939	**Dave Giusti.** Professional baseball player
1940	**Bruce Lee.** American motion-picture and television actor
1941	**Eddie Rabbitt.** American country singer and songwriter noted for sngs such as "Kentucky Rain"
1942	**Jimi Hendrix.** American guitarist and singer
1949	**Jim Price.** Professional basketball player
1950	**Donald Strock.** Professional football player
1952	**Ike Harris.** Professional football player
1956	**Curtis Dickey.** Professional football player
1957	**Caroline Kennedy (Schlossberg).** Daughter of President John F. Kennedy
1958	**Mike Scioscia.** Professional baseball player
1971	**Ivan Rodriguez.** Professional baseball player and the American League's Most Valuable in 1999

November 27 – Events

8 BC	Horace (Quintus Horatius Flaccus), the great Roman lyric poet, died at Venusia, in Apulia, at age 56.
1095	Pope Urban II addressed the Council of Clermont, calling for the first Crusade to deliver the Holy Land from the Moslems.
1582	William Shakespeare and Anne Hathaway were issued a marriage license. He was 18 and she was 26.
1875	The Hoosac Tunnel, the first long railroad tunnel in America, was completed through the Berkshire Hills in western Massachusetts.
1889	Curtis P. Brady received the first permit to drive a car through New York's Central Park, contingent on his not "frightening horses" in the park.
1901	The Army War College, the highest educational institution of the U.S. Army, was founded in Washington, D.C. It was moved to Carlisle Barracks, Pennsylvania, in 1951.
1910	Pennsylvania Station, the largest railway terminal in the world at the time, opened in New York City.
1942	The French fleet at Toulon was scuttled by its crews to keep the Germans from taking it in World War II.
1945	General George C. Marshall was dispatched to China by President Harry S. Truman to try to reconcile the Nationalists and the Communists.
1953	Eugene O'Neill, America's great playwright, died in Boston at age 65.
1970	Diego Velasquez's *Portrait of Juan de Pareja* sold at auction at Christie's in London for $5,544,000, a record price for a painting at the time.
1973	The U.S. Senate voted 92-3 to confirm Gerald R. Ford to succeed Spiro Agnew as vice president.

November 28 – Birthdays

1628	**John Bunyan.** English preacher and writer noted for *The Pilgrim's Progress* (1678)
1632	**Jean Baptiste Lully.** Italian-born French composer, who wrote the first significant French operas, and influenced the work of Johann Sebastian Bach and George Frederick Handel
1757	**William Blake.** Brilliant, unconventional English poet and painter, noted for such famous lines as "Tyger! Tyger! burning bright"
1793	**Carl Jonas Love Almqvist.** One of the most prolific of all Swedish writers

1820   **Friedrich Engels.** German social scientist, journalist, and professional revolutionary, noted for his close collaboration with communist Karl Marx

1829   **Anton Gregor Rubenstein.** Russian composer and the greatest pianist of the 19th century

1832   **Sir Leslie Stephen.** English essayist, biographer, critic, and editor

1866   **David Warfield.** Noted American stage actor

1880   **Alexander Alexandrovich Blok.** Russian poet and dramatist

1881   **Stefan Zweig.** Austrian poet and novelist, noted for novels such as *Amok* (1922) and biographies such as *Marie Antoinette* (1932)

1887   **Ernst Rohm.** Organizer of Adolf Hitler's SA (storm troops)

1894   **Brooks Atkinson.** American journalist, author, and critic

1895   **Jose Iturbi.** Spanish-born American conductor and piano virtuoso

1904   **Nancy Mitford.** English writer known for her witty novels and essays (such as *Love in a Cold Climate* and *Pursuit of Love*)

1904   **James O. Eastland.** U.S. senator from the 1940s through the 1970s

1912   **Morris Louis.** American painter

1925   **Gloria Grahame.** American stage, screen, and television actress with a 40-year career

1929   **Berry Gordy.** American songwriter and founder of Motown Records

1931   **Hope Lange.** American motion-picture and television actress

1936   **Gary Hart.** U.S. senator and candidate in 1984 and 1988 for the nomination of the Democratic Party for president

1942   **Paul Warfield.** Professional football superstar and Hall of Famer

1946   **Susan Spencer.** American television news correspondent

1948   **Romana Guerrant.** American tennis player

1950   **Ed Harris.** American stage, screen and television actor

1953   **Sixto Lezcano.** Professional baseball player

1958   **Dave Righetti.** Professional baseball player

1959   **Judd Nelson.** American motion-picture actor

1965   **Matt Williams.** Professional baseball player

November 28 – Events

1520   Ferdinand Magellan entered the Pacific Ocean after a month in the Strait of Magellan on his voyage around the world. He gave the new ocean the name Pacific because it was so calm.

1582   William Shakespeare married Anne Hathaway at Stratford-on-Avon.

1678   Catherine of Braganza, wife of England's King Charles II, was accused of treason for having no children.

1680   Gian Lorenzo Bernini, Italian sculptor who designed the great plaza of St. Peter's Church in Rome, died at age 82.

1780   Maria Theresa, Empress of Austria and Hungary, died at age 63.

1859   Washington Irving, one of America's greatest early writers, died in Sunnyside, New York, at age 76.

1863   The U.S. celebrated the first Thanksgiving Day set aside by President Lincoln's proclamation of October 3, 1863.

1895   J. Frank Duryea won the first gasoline-automobile race in America, between Chicago's Jackson Park and Evanston, Ind., averaging seven mph in a car he and his brother Charles built.

1919   American-born Lady Astor was elected the first woman member of the British Parliament.

1925   The Grand Ole Opry, Nashville's famed home of country music, made its radio debut on station WSM.

1929   Richard E. Byrd began his famous flight across the South Pole. On the next day he and his pilot would become the first men to fly over the pole.

1942   The Cocoanut Grove night club in Boston burned, with nearly 500 people losing their lives. Among them was the famous cowboy actor Buck Jones.

1943   The Tehran Conference of World War II began with President Roosevelt, Prime Minister Churchill, and Premier Stalin in attendance.

November 29 – Birthdays

1781   **Andres Bello.** South American poet and scholar

1797   **Gaetano Donizetti.** Italian operatic composer, noted for works such as *Lucia di Lammermoor* (1835) and *Don Pasquale* (1843)

1803   **Christian Doppler.** German physicist who discovered the Doppler effect, which is the apparent change in the frequency of sound or light waves caused by motion

1811   **Wendell Phillips.** American orator, reformer, and famous crusader for abolition in the pre-Civil War period

1816   **Morrison Remick Waite.** Seventh chief justice of the U.S. Supreme Court, 1874-1888

1832   **Louisa May Alcott.** American writer noted for *Little Women,* one of the best-loved stories in American literature

1849   **Sir Ambrose Fleming.** British scientist noted for inventing the diode vacuum tube (1904)

1858   **Robert Abbott Hadfield.** English metallurgist who in 1882 invented manganese steel, an early form of stainless steel

1875   **Stanley Murphy.** Irish-born lyricist noted for songs such as "Put On Your Old Gray Bonnet" and "Be My Little Baby Bumble Bee"

1895   **Busby Berkeley.** American choreographer and director with a 50-year movie career

1895   **William V.S. Tubman.** President of Liberia, 1943-1971

1895 Yakima Canutt. American actor and stuntman, whose exploits became legendary

1897 John Alexander. American stage and motion-picture actor

1898 C.S. Lewis. British author of over 30 science fiction, religion, and fantasy literature books

1911 Walter Kent. American composer and author, noted for songs such as "I'll Be Home for Christmas," "The White Cliffs of Dover," and "Come Rain Come Shine"

1917 Merle Travis. American guitarist

1918 Madeleine L'Engle. American author noted for *A Wrinkle in Time*

1922 Minnie Minoso. Professional baseball player who came back after many years of retirement when he was in his 50s, making him the oldest player in major league history

1923 Frank Reynolds. American broadcast journalist

1927 Vin Scully. Hall-of-Fame sportscaster

1928 Paul Simon. U.S. senator and candidate for the Democratic nomination for president in 1988

1933 John Mayall. British blues musician

1933 David Reuben. American author, noted for *Everything You Always Wanted to Know About Sex*

1933 James Rosenquist. American painter

1934 Willie Morris. American writer and novelist

1940 Chuck Mangione. American composer and rock and jazz musician

1947 Joe Inman. Professional golfer

1950 Mike Easler. Professional baseball player

1960 Cathy Moriarty. American motion-picture actress

1960 Howard Johnson. Professional baseball player

1969 Mariano Rivera. Professional baseball pitcher and super closer

November 29 – Events

1226 Louis IX (Saint Louis) assumed the throne of France.

1314 King Philip IV of France died at age 46 after a reign of 29 years.

1515 After a disastrous war for the Swiss, a pact of "perpetual peace" was signed between France and Switzerland.

1516 Giovanni Bellini, the noted Italian painter, died in Venice at age 66.

1643 Claudio Monteverdi, the great Italian composer, died in Venice at age 76.

1887 Josef Hoffmann, the noted Polish pianist, made his American debut at the Metropolitan Opera House in New York.

1890 The first Army-Navy football game was played at West Point, with Navy winning, 24-0.

1924 Giacomo Puccini, the great Italian opera composer, died in Brussels of throat cancer at age 65.

1929 Commander Richard E. Byrd completed the first flight over the South Pole.

1932 Cole Porter's song "Night and Day" was first publicly sung at the Ethel Barrymore Theater in New York.

1945 Yugoslavia became a republic as Marshal Tito abolished the monarchy.

1947 The United Nations voted to end British control of Palestine and divide the country into an Israeli state and an Arab state.

1952 President-elect Dwight D. Eisenhower went to Korea to observe the war effort there, keeping a campaign promise he had made.

1963 President Lyndon B. Johnson appointed a commission headed by Supreme Court Chief Justice Earl Warren to investigate the assassination of President John F. Kennedy.

November 30 – Birthdays

1466 Andrea Doria. Genoese statesman and foremost naval leader of his time

1508 Andrea Palladio. Italian Renaissance architect whose work inspired Thomas Jefferson in the design of Monticello

1554 Sir Philip Sidney. Author, courtier, and soldier during the reign of Queen Elizabeth I of England, whose greatest work is *Astrophel and Stella* (in the early 1580s)

1636 Adriaen van de Velde. Dutch painter

1667 Jonathan Swift. English author, churchman, and the greatest satirist in the English language, whose book *Gulliver's Travels* (1726) is a masterpiece of world literature

1809 Mark Lemon. English publisher and founder of *Punch* magazine

1810 Oliver Fisher Winchester. Developer of the Winchester rifle

1817 Theodor Mommsen. Nobel Prize-winning German historian, noted for his monumental work *History of Rome* (1854-1856)

1819 Cyrus W. Field. American financier who promoted the first telegraph cable across the Atlantic Ocean, between Ireland and Newfoundland (1857-1866)

1825 Adolphe William Bouguereau. French painter noted for works such as *The Proposal* (1872)

1835 Mark Twain. The greatest humorist in American literature (born Samuel Langhorne Clemens), and creator of *Tom Sawyer* and *Huckleberry Finn*

1874 Lucy Maud Montgomery. Canadian novelist famous for *Anne of Green Gables* (1908)

1874 Sir Winston Churchill. British World War II prime minister and one of the greatest statesmen in world history

1889 Edgar Douglas Adrian. British electrophysiologist noted for nerve cell discoveries

1898 Firpo Marberry. Professional baseball player

1907 Jacques Barzun. American teacher, historian, and author, noted for works such as *Teacher in America* (1945)

1920   **Virginia Mayo.** Glamorous beauty of Hollywood films of the 1940s and 1950s

1923   **Efrim Zembalist Jr.** American motion-picture and television actor

1924   **Shirley Chisholm.** The first black woman to serve in the U.S. Congress (1969)

1924   **Allan Sherman.** American comedian

1926   **Richard Crenna.** American motion-picture and television actor

1929   **Dick Clark.** American television host, producer, and actor

1930   **G. Gordon Liddy.** American government official, writer, and Watergate figure

1932   **Robert Vaughn.** American motion-picture and television actor

1936   **Abbie Hoffman.** American revolutionary and leader of the Yippies in the 1960s

1937   **Richard Threlkeld.** American broadcast journalist

1945   **Roger Glover.** Welsh singer with the Deep Purple musical group

1947   **Mandy Patinkin.** American stage and motion-picture actor and singer

1947   **David Mamet.** American playwright

1949   **Jim Chones.** Professional basketball player

1950   **Paul Westphal.** Professional basketball player

1952   **Steve McCullum.** Professional football player

1955   **Billy Idol.** British rock singer

1955   **Clarence Harmon.** Professional football player

1962   **Bo Jackson.** Professional baseball and football player

November 30 – Events

70   Saint Andrew, one of the Twelve Disciples of Christ, was martyred on an X-shaped cross during the reign of Vespasian. The day is celebrated as St. Andrew's feast day.

1016   England's King Edmund Ironside was murdered at age 26, resulting in King Canute's ascending the throne of England and Denmark.

1290   John de Baliol was crowned King of Scotland, following the death of seven-year-old Queen Margaret, who had succeeded her grandfather, King Alexander III.

1628   John Bunyan, the great English author of *The Pilgrim's Progress,* was baptized. He was probably born three days earlier.

1700   Charles XII, Sweden's great king, defeated the Russians at Narva in a half hour and took 6,000 prisoners.

1782   The Americans and British signed a preliminary peace treaty in Paris, ending the Revolutionary War.

1900   Oscar Wilde, the noted British writer, died in France at age 46, penniless and in debt, but with his wit intact. "I am dying beyond my means," he said, on his deathbed.

1905   Japan took Port Arthur in northern China after winning the Russo-Japanese War.

1922   Sarah Bernhardt, the great French actress, made her last appearance, playing in *Daniel* in Turin, Italy.

1939   Russian troops invaded Finland in violation of a nonaggression pact between the two countries.

1940   Lucille Ball and Desi Arnaz, the popular film entertainers, eloped to Greenwich, Connecticut.

1949   The Chinese Communists captured the Chinese Nationalists' World War II capital of Chungking in the Chinese Civil War.

1956   Floyd Patterson knocked out Archie Moore in the fifth round in Chicago to win the heavyweight boxing title.

1967   South Yemen gained its independence from Britain.

12

December

December is the 12th month of the year, but its name comes from the Latin *Decembris,* meaning *tenth.* The name was appropriate when December was added to the Roman calendar by Romulus, since at the time it was the tenth and last month. Romulus gave the month 30 days, which was changed to 29 when Numa Pompilius issued his calendar. In the Julian Calendar, December had 30 days, and when Augustus adjusted the calendar he gave it its present 31 days. The emperor Commodus tried to change the name of the month to *Amazonius* in honor of his mistress, who he said had once been painted as an Amazon. This attempt, as well as a number of others, failed to catch on, and December, though misnamed, is still with us.

Christmas is doubtless the most famous holiday of December, and the important Jewish holidays of Hanukkah often also occur in the month. Other special days are December 6, when many Europeans celebrate the Feast of Saint Nicholas and exchange gifts, Forefathers' Day on December 21, commemorating the landing of the Pilgrims at Plymouth Rock on that date in 1620, and, of course, New Year's Eve on December 31. Also, three American Presidents, Martin Van Buren, Andrew Johnson and Woodrow Wilson, were born in December.

The birthstones of December are the turquoise and the zircon, and the special flower is the poinsettia.

December 1 – Birthdays

1716	**Etienne Maurice Falconet.** French sculptor
1761	**Marie Gresholtz Tussaud.** Swiss modeler in wax, who in 1802 founded Madame Tussaud's Exhibition, the famous wax museum in London
1765	**William Hill Brown.** American author noted for *The Power Of Sympathy* (1789)
1792	**Nikolai Lobachevsky.** Russian mathematician who invented non-Euclidean geometry (simultaneously with, but independently of, Polish mathematician Janos Bolyai)
1844	**Princess Alexandra.** Daughter of King Christian IX of Denmark and wife of King Edward VII of England

1876	**George Creel.** American author and newspaperman
1877	**Rex Beach.** Prominent American author of Western novels
1879	**Lane Bryant.** American businessman and founder in 1904 of the Lane Bryant clothing stores
1882	**Ed Reulbach.** Professional baseball pitcher with a career earned run average of 2.28
1886	**Rex Stout.** American detective-story writer, noted for the Nero Wolfe mysteries
1896	**Ray Henderson.** American composer, author, and pianist, noted for songs such as "Alabamy Bound," "Button Up Your Overcoat," "Sonny Boy," "Bye Bye Blackbird," and "Life Is Just a Bowl of Cherries"
1899	**Robert Welch.** Founder of the John Birch Society
1910	**Dame Alicia Markova.** The first great English ballerina
1911	**Walter Alston.** Manager of the Brooklyn and Los Angeles Dodgers baseball team for 22 years
1912	**Cookie Lavagetto.** Professional baseball player
1913	**Mary Martin.** One of the major talents of the American musical stage, motion-picture actress, and mother of actor Larry Hagman
1917	**Marty Marion.** Professional baseball player
1923	**Stansfield Turner.** Director of the CIA under President Carter
1923	**Dick Shawn.** American comedian and comic actor noted for such roles as Adolf Hitler in Mel Brooks's spoof *The Producers*
1933	**Violette Verdy.** French ballerina
1935	**Lou Rawls.** American soul singer and motion-picture actor
1935	**Woody Allen.** American motion-picture actor, director, screenwriter, play-wright, and jazz clarinetist
1939	**Dianne Lennon.** One of the singing Lennon Sisters
1939	**Lee Trevino.** Professional golfer
1940	**Richard Pryor.** American actor and comedian
1944	**John Densmore.** American drummer with the Doors musical group
1945	**Bette Midler.** American singer and actress

1946	**Gilbert O'Sullivan.** Irish pop singer and song-writer
1948	**Ian Fletcher.** Australian tennis player
1948	**George Foster.** Professional baseball player
1952	**Treat Williams.** American stage, screen and television actor
1960	**Carol Alt.** American model, noted cover girl, and actress

December 1 – Events

1455   Lorenzo Ghiberti, noted Italian sculptor and goldsmith, died in Florence at age 77.

1648   The English army seized King Charles I and turned him over to Parliament for trial. He was executed the following year.

1822   Pedro I, son of King John VI of Portugal, became emperor of Brazil.

1824   The electoral college vote resulted in no presidential candidate receiving a majority in the 1824 election. The U.S. House of Representatives later chose John Quincy Adams.

1878   The first telephone was installed in the White House.

1909   The first Christmas Club saving plan was introduced by a bank, the Carlisle Trust Company, in Carlisle, Pennsylvania.

1913   The first drive-in automobile service station was opened, in Pittsburgh.

1919   Lady Nancy Astor, American wife of Waldorf Astor, became the first woman to serve in the British Parliament, succeeding her husband in the House of Commons.

1924   The first performance of George Gershwin's *Lady Be Good* was given at the Liberty Theater in New York, starring Fred and Adele Astaire.

1939   La Guardia Airport in New York was opened to the public.

1943   The Tehran Conference ended with a communique expressing Allied determination to destroy the German armies in World War II.

1955   Rosa Parks, a black woman, sat on a front bus seat usually reserved for whites in Montgomery, Ala., which started the civil rights movement led by Dr. Martin Luther King, Jr.

1990   The English Channel Tunnel ("Chunnel") breakthrough was made as workers from the English side and the French side joined each other in the drilling.

December 2 – Birthdays

1694	**William Shirley.** Colonial governor of Massachusetts, 1741-1756
1825	**Pedro II.** Second and last emperor of Brazil, 1841-1889
1859	**Georges Seurat.** Noted French artist who developed *pointillism,* a system of painting using uniform-sized dots side by side instead of brushstrokes

1863	**Charles Ringling.** One of the Ringling brothers who built a small troupe of performers into the world's largest circus
1884	**Ruth Draper.** American monologist and mono-dramatist
1885	**George Minot.** American physician, who was one of the world's great authorities on blood diseases
1891	**Otto Dix.** German painter
1891	**Larry Gilbert.** Professional baseball player and manager
1895	**Warren William.** American stage and motion-picture actor with a 25-year career
1896	**Georgi Konstantinovich Zhukov.** Russian World War II marshal who organized the defense of Moscow and the victory at Stalingrad, and led the Russian forces that captured Berlin
1897	**Walter Hoving.** Chairman of the board of Tiffany's in New York
1899	**John Rhodes Cobb.** American racing driver who drove a piston-powered automobile 394.196 miles per hour in 1947 for the world's record
1902	**Arnold Bernhard.** American publisher and founder of Value Line, Inc., the world's largest investment advisory service
1909	**Joseph P. Lash.** American author noted for the biography *Eleanor and Franklin*
1915	**Adolph Green.** American librettist, screenwriter, actor and lyricist
1923	**Maria Callas.** American-born soprano and one of the best-known opera singers of the 1960s and 1970s
1924	**Alexander Haig Jr.** American general, aide to President Nixon, and secretary of state under President Reagan
1925	**Julie Harris.** American stage, screen, and television actress
1931	**Edwin Meese.** Attorney general under President Reagan
1939	**Harry Reid.** U.S. senator
1940	**Willie Brown.** Hall of Fame professional football player
1946	**Gianni Versace.** Italian fashion designer
1952	**Michael McDonald.** American singer and songwriter with Doobie Brothers
1954	**Stone Phillips.** NBC news broadcaster noted for his work on TV's *60 Minutes*
1962	**Tracy Austin.** American tennis player
1973	**Monica Seles.** Yugoslavian-American tennis player and youngest woman to win the French and the Australian Opens

December 2 – Events

1547   Hernando Cortes, Spanish conqueror of Mexico, died near Seville at age 62.

1804   Napoleon crowned himself Emperor of the French, when he snatched the crown from Pope Pius VII, who was in the act of crowning him, and placed it on his head himself.

1805	Napoleon crushed the Allied armies in the Battle of Austerlitz, in one of his most brilliant victories.
1816	The Philadelphia Savings Fund Society, the first savings bank in the United States, opened for business.
1823	President James Monroe, in a message to Congress, proclaimed the historic Monroe Doctrine.
1851	Louis Napoleon Bonaparte (Napoleon III) seized power in France in a *coup d'etat*.
1859	John Brown was hanged in Charles Town, Virginia (now West Virginia), on charges of treason for his famous raid on Harpers Ferry.
1886	Theodore Roosevelt married his second wife, Edith Kermit Carow.
1927	Henry Ford unveiled his Model A Ford, successor to the famed Model T.
1941	Advance units of General von Bock's German army penetrated to the suburbs of Moscow in World War II, the nearest the Germans came to taking the city.
1942	The world's first controlled, self-sustaining nuclear reaction was achieved at the University of Chicago by the Manhattan Engineering team led by Enrico Fermi.
1952	General Dwight D. Eisenhower, U.S. president-elect, arrived in Korea, keeping his campaign pledge to go there.
1954	The U.S. Senate voted to censure Senator Joseph R. McCarthy for "contemptuous" conduct and abuse of Senate members.
1970	The last anti-evolution teaching law in the U.S., that of Mississippi, was voided by the courts.
1982	The world's first permanent artificial heart was implanted, at the University of Utah Medical Center in the chest of retired dentist Barney Clark.

December 3 – Birthdays

1368	**Charles VI.** King of France, 1380-1422
1596	**Nicolo Amati.** Famous Italian violinmaker, who also trained other great violinmakers, including Antonio Stradivari and Andrea Guarneri
1753	**Samuel Crompton.** English weaver, who invented the spinning mule, so called by him because it was a cross between the spinning jenny and the water frame
1755	**Gilbert Stuart.** America's first great portrait painter, who became famous for his unfinished portrait of George Washington, probably the best-known portrait in America
1766	**Robert Bloomfield.** English poet noted for works such as "The Farmer's Boy" (1800)
1805	**Constantin Guys.** French watercolorist and draftsman
1812	**Hendrik Conscience.** Flemish romantic novelist
1826	**George B. McClellan.** U.S. Civil War general and presidential candidate against President Lincoln in 1864

1833	**Carlos Juan Finlay.** Chief sanitary officer of Cuba, 1902-1908, who was the first man to present evidence that yellow fever was transmitted by mosquitoes
1838	**Cleveland Abbe.** American meteorologist prominent in the founding of the U.S. Weather Bureau
1857	**Joseph Conrad.** Polish-born English author, famous for his novels about the sea, such as *Lord Jim* (1900) and *The Nigger of the 'Narcissus'* (1897)
1883	**Anton von Webern.** Austrian composer
1895	**Anna Freud.** Austrian psychoanalyst and daughter of the great psychoanalyst Sigmund Freud
1903	**John von Neumann.** Hungarian-born American mathematician and prominent contributor to the development of computers
1909	**Dana Suesse.** American composer, author, and musician, noted for songs such as "Whistling in the Dark," "The Night Is Young and You're So Beautiful," and "You Ought to Be in Pictures"
1921	**John Doar.** Special counsel to the House Judiciary Committee during the Nixon impeachment hearings
1923	**Tom Fears.** Hall of Fame football player
1927	**Phyllis Curtin.** American operatic soprano
1930	**Jean-Luc Godard.** One of the great French motion-picture directors of the 20th century
1930	**Andy Williams.** American singer and television entertainer
1937	**Bobby Allison.** Professional hockey superstar
1947	**Jim Plunkett.** Professional football player and superstar
1948	**Ozzy Osbourne.** British rock singer
1951	**Rick Mears.** American racing car driver who won the Indianapolis 500 four times
1955	**Brigitte Cuypers.** South African tennis player
1957	**Kathy Jordan.** American tennis player
1961	**Daryl Hannah.** American motion-picture actress
1965	**Katarina Witt.** German Olympic gold medalist figure skater
1968	**Brendan Fraser.** American motion-picture actor

December 3 – Events

1639	Jonas Bronck purchased from the Indians the land that later became known as the Bronx, New York, because the Broncks lived there.
1818	Illinois was admitted to the Union as the 21st state.
1833	Oberlin College at Oberlin, Ohio, the first coeducational college in the United States, was opened.
1894	Robert Louis Stevenson, the great English novelist, died on the island of Samoa at age 44 of a stroke.
1910	Mary Baker Eddy, founder of the Church of Christ, Scientist, died at age 89.
1948	Whitaker Chambers claimed to have microfilm copies of secret government documents hidden in a pumpkin and given to him by Alger Hiss.
1967	South African surgeon Dr. Christiaan Bernard performed the first human heart transplant in history in Cape Town, South Africa, on 55-year-old Louis Washkansky.

1971 India launched a full-scale land, sea, and air attack on Pakistan, without a declaration of war.

1976 The 600-year-old monarchy in Laos was abolished as the Communists took control of the government.

1979 Iranian voters ratified a new constitution establishing the Islamic government and making Ayatollah Khomeini leader for life.

1984 More than 4,000 people were fatally strickened after a cloud of poisonous gas escaped from a pesticide plant operated by a Union Carbide subsidiary in Bhopal, India.

December 4 – Birthdays

1383 **Felix V.** The last Roman Catholic antipope (one improperly elected, who sets himself up as pope in opposition to the regularly elected pope), 1439-1449

1584 **John Cotton.** American Puritan minister who wrote the catechism *Milk for Babes* (1646)

1795 **Thomas Carlyle.** Scottish essayist and historian and one of the greatest social philosophers of Victorian England, who wrote the monumental work *The French Revolution* (1837)

1835 **Samuel Butler.** English author best known for the satirical novel *Erewhon* (1872) and for his other major work *The Way of All Flesh* (1903, published after his death)

1860 **George Albert Hormel.** Founder in 1892 of the George A. Hormel meat-packing company

1861 **Lillian Russell.** American singer and actress, and "one of the most beautiful women of the American stage" during "The Gay Nineties"

1861 **James Thornton.** English-born composer, author, and entertainer, noted for songs such as "When You Were Sweet Sixteen"

1866 **Wassily Kandinsky.** Noted Russian artist, generally considered to be the first abstract painter

1868 **Jesse Burkett.** Hall of Fame baseball player who hit .423 in 1895, .410 in 1896, and .402 in 1899

1875 **Rainer Maria Rilke.** Czechoslovakian-born German poet regarded as one of the giants of modern literature

1880 **Gar Wood.** Developer of the PT boats of the U.S. Navy in World War II

1881 **Charles Wakefield Cadman.** American composer noted for *From the Land of Sky-Blue Water* (1908)

1885 **Grover Arnold Magnin.** American chain store executive and son of the founder of I. Magnin and Company

1889 **Buck Jones.** One of Hollywood's most popular cowboy stars of all time, who was a leading man in the 1920s and 1930s

1890 **Bob Shawkey.** Professional baseball player and manager

1892 **Francisco Franco.** Dictator of Spain, 1936-1975

1893 **Sir Herbert Read.** English poet and critic

1896 **Lawrence Stock.** American composer and author, noted for songs such as "Blueberry Hill," "You're Nobody 'Til Somebody Loves You," and "You Won't Be Satisfied Until You Break My Heart"

1897 **Robert Redfield.** American cultural anthropologist

1921 **Deanna Durbin.** Canadian-born actress and singer and internationally popular screen star of the late 1930s and early 1940s

1926 **Lee Dorsey.** American soul singer

1930 **Harvey Kuenn.** Professional baseball player

1931 **Jaye P. Morgan.** American singer and television personality

1932 **Horst Buchholz.** German-born motion-picture actor

1932 **Thomas Morgan Edwards.** American composer noted for the scores of such TV shows as *Gunsmoke, Twilight Zone,* and *Have Gun, Will Travel*

1937 **Max Baer Jr.** American actor, producer (noted for his role as Jethro in the long-running TV show *The Beverly Hillbillies*) and son of boxer Max Baer

1941 **Marty Riessen.** American tennis player

1944 **Dennis Wilson.** American drummer with the Beach Boys musical group

1948 **Randel Vataha.** Professional football player

1949 **Jeff Bridges.** American motion-picture actor and son of actor Lloyd Bridges

1957 **Lee Smith.** Professional baseball player

1964 **Marisa Tomei.** American motion-picture actress who won the Academy Award for best supporting actress in 1992 for *My Cousin Vinny*

December 4 – Events

771 Carloman, Charlemagne's brother and co-ruler of the Franks, died, leaving their empire to Charlemagne.

1154 Adrian IV became Roman Catholic pope, the only Englishman ever chosen.

1674 Father Jacques Marquette, the great French explorer and missionary, built the first house in what is now Chicago.

1679 Thomas Hobbes, the great English philosopher, died at Hardwick, Derbyshire, at age 91.

1783 George Washington bade farewell to his officers of the Continental Army at Fraunces Tavern in New York City: "With a heart full of love and gratitude, I now take leave of you."

1839 The Whig Party held its first national convention, nominating as its candidates in the 1840 election, General William Henry Harrison and John Tyler, "Tippecanoe and Tyler, too."

1851 The "December 4 Massacre" occurred in Paris, as the government suppressed an uprising against Emperor Napoleon III.

1912 The comic strip *Polly and Her Pals,* by Cliff Sterrett, first appeared.

1918 President Woodrow Wilson sailed for France to attend the Versailles peace conference, becoming the first president to visit a foreign country while in office.

1943 The Second Cairo Conference in World War II was held with President Roosevelt, Prime Minister Churchill, and President Inonu of Turkey attending.

1960 Alan Jay Lerner's *Camelot* opened on Broadway and became a favorite of President-elect Kennedy, whose term in office later became known as the "brief shining moment" of Camelot.

1963 The second session of Vatican II ended. One of its documents allowed the use of the local language in place of Latin in parts of the Mass.

December 5 – Birthdays

1443 **Julius II.** Roman Catholic pope, 1503-1513, who began the construction of St. Peter's Basilica in 1506

1751 **Pierre Philippe Thomire.** French sculptor

1782 **Martin Van Buren.** Eighth U.S. president, and the first who was a United States citizen at birth

1811 **David Van Nostrand.** American publisher who founded the D. Van Nostrand publishing house

1830 **Christina Rossetti.** English poet and sister of the famous poet Dante Gabriel Rossetti

1839 **George Armstrong Custer.** American army general who was killed and his unit wiped out by Indians in the Battle of the Little Bighorn ("Custer's last stand") on June 25, 1876

1859 **Sir John Jellicoe.** British Grand Fleet commander at the Battle of Jutland in 1916, the only major engagement of World War I between the British and German fleets

1879 **Clyde Vernon Cessna.** American aircraft manufacturer who founded Cessna Aircraft Co.

1890 **Fritz Lang.** Noted Austrian-born motion-picture director with a career of over 40 years

1897 **Nunnally Johnson.** American motion-picture director and producer, and one of the screen's most prolific and highly respected writers, noted for scripts such as *The Grapes of Wrath* (1940)

1901 **Werner Karl Heisenberg.** German physicist, noted for the uncertainty principle of atomic theory

1901 **Walt Disney.** American producer of animated cartoons, movies, and television shows, and creator of *Mickey Mouse* and *Donald Duck,* two of the best-loved cartoon characters in American history

1902 **Strom Thurmond.** U.S. senator and third-party presidential candidate in 1948

1903 **Arnold Gingrich.** American publisher and founder of *Esquire* magazine

1904 **Betty Smith.** American author noted for *A Tree Grows in Brooklyn* (1943)

1905 **Gus Mancuso.** Professional baseball player

1906 **Otto Preminger.** Famous Austrian-born motion-picture director, noted for the controversial *The Moon Is Blue* (1953), and for such works as *Anatomy of a Murder* (1959)

1922 **Don Robertson.** American songwriter noted for "Please Help Me I'm Falling"

1934 **Joan Didion.** American novelist, journalist, and screenwriter

1935 **Calvin Trillin.** American author noted for works such as *If You Can't Say Something Nice* (1987)

1936 **Chad Mitchell.** American singer of the Chad Mitchell Trio

1946 **Jose Carreras.** Spanish operatic tenor

1949 **Lanny Wadkins.** Professional golfer

1954 **Gary Roenicke.** Professional baseball player

1955 **Art Still.** Professional football player

1957 **Art Monk.** Professional football player

1963 **Carrie Hamilton.** American stage, screen, and television actress, and daughter of comedienne Carol Burnett

December 5 – Events

1484 Pope Innocent VIII issued the bull *Summis desiderantes,* initiating harsh measures against "witches" and "magicians."

1776 Phi Beta Kappa, the first scholastic fraternity in America, was founded at the College of William and Mary in Williamsburg, Virginia.

1791 Wolfgang Amadeus Mozart, the great Austrian composer, died in poverty at age 35. He was buried in an unmarked grave, the location of which is now unknown.

1812 Napoleon left the remnants of his Grande Armee in Smorgonie, Russia, to hasten back to Paris to put down the rumored revolts against him in France.

1831 Former president John Quincy Adams took his seat in the House of Representatives, the only ex-president to serve in that capacity.

1848 The California gold discovery, which led to the Gold Rush of 1849, was announced by President Polk in a message to Congress.

1870 Alexander Dumas the Elder, the noted French novelist, died at Marly-le-Roi at age 68.

1929 The American League for Physical Culture, the first United States nudist group, was organized.

1933 Amendment 21 to the U.S. Constitution was proclaimed, repealing Prohibition.

1934 Sixty-two persons were executed in Russia for "plotting" against the Stalin regime.

1936 England's King Edward VIII announced his decision to abdicate to marry Wallis Warfield Simpson.

1955 The AF of L and CIO, the two major American labor unions, merged to form the AFL-CIO. George Meany became its first president.

1994 Congressman Newt Gingrich was elected the first Republican Speaker of the House in 40 years.

December 6 – Birthdays

1421   **Henry VI.** The last king of England from the House of Lancaster, 1422-1461 and 1470-1471

1478   **Baldassare Castiglione.** Italian Renaissance writer, best known for *The Book of the Courtier* (about 1518), which became a guide for social refinement in Spain, France, and England, as well as Italy

1732   **Warren Hastings.** First British governor-general of India, 1774-1785

1778   **Joseph Louis Gay-Lussac.** Noted French chemist and physicist, who discovered the law (now called Charles' Law) that deals with the effect of temperature on gases

1792   **William II.** King of the Netherlands, 1840-1849

1822   **John Eberhard Faber.** A founder of the Eberhard Faber Pencil Company

1833   **John Singleton Mosby.** Famous Confederate ranger during the Civil War

1841   **Frederic Bazille.** French painter

1859   **E.H. Sothern.** One of the great dramatic actors of the American theater

1867   **Karl Bitter.** American sculptor

1870   **William S. Hart.** American stage and motion-picture actor, who was the first, and perhaps the most famous, cowboy actor of Hollywood Westerns

1876   **Frederick S. Duesenberg.** Pioneer American automobile manufacturer, who with his brother Augie designed the first Duesenberg cars

1883   **Thomas Elmer Braniff.** American airline executive and founder of Braniff International Airways

1886   **Joyce Kilmer.** American author and poet, most famous for the short poem "Trees" (1913)

1892   **Lynn Fontanne.** English-born actress who with her husband, Alfred Lunt, formed one of the greatest acting teams in the history of the American theater

1893   **Lou Little.** Professional football player

1896   **George Trafton.** Hall of Fame professional football player

1896   **Ira Gershwin.** Noted American lyricist, who collaborated in much of his work with his famous brother, composer George Gershwin

1898   **Alfred Eisenstaedt.** Noted American photographer

1898   **Gunnar Myrdal.** Swedish sociologist and economist, who gained fame for the book *An American Dilemma: The Negro Problem and Modern Democracy* (1944)

1899   **Jocko Conlan.** Hall of Fame baseball umpire

1900   **George Eugene Uhlenbeck.** Indonesian physicist who helped develop the concept of electron spin

1903   **Hardie Albright.** American stage and motion-picture actor, and Hollywood leading man of the 1930s and 1940s

1903   **Tony Lazzeri.** Professional baseball player and member of the great New York Yankee teams of the Babe Ruth and Lou Gehrig era

1905   **James J. Braddock.** World heavyweight champion, 1935-1937

1906   **Agnes Moorehead.** American motion-picture and television actress

1908   **Baby Face Nelson.** American criminal of the 1930s

1909   **Stan Hack.** Professional baseball player and manager

1913   **Eleanor Holm.** American swimmer who held 12 national titles and won the 100-meter backstroke race in the 1932 Olympics

1920   **Dave Brubeck.** American pianist and composer

1921   **Otto Graham.** Hall of Fame football player who played in ten consecutive title games with the Cleveland Browns

1924   **Wally Cox.** American comedian and actor

1927   **Patsy Mink.** U.S. congresswoman

1943   **Ingrid Bentzer.** Swedish tennis player

1945   **Larry Bowa.** Professional baseball player and manager

1948   **Don Nickles.** U.S. senator

1953   **Tom Hulce.** American stage and screen actor noted for the title role in *Amadeus*

1962   **Janine Turner.** American stage and television actress

December 6 – Events

1362   Urban V was crowned Roman Catholic pope.

1492   Christopher Columbus discovered Hispaniola on his first voyage to America.

1506   Niccolo Machiavelli, the great Italian writer and statesman, created a Florentine militia, the first Italian national army.

1648   Colonel Thomas Pride's soldiers arrested and excluded 95 members of Parliament opposed to trying Charles I for treason. The remaining members formed the "Rump Parliament."

1847   Abraham Lincoln took his seat as a representative in the 30th U.S. Congress.

1864   Salmon P. Chase was appointed chief justice of the U.S. Supreme Court by President Lincoln.

1877   Thomas A. Edison shouted "Mary had a little lamb" into the horn of his newly-invented phonograph, which, to the amazement of his shop foreman, repeated Edison's words.

1882   Anthony Trollope, the popular English novelist, died of a stroke brought on, it was said, by over-hearty laughter.

1884   Construction of the Washington Monument was completed after four years of work by Army engineers.

1889   Jefferson Davis, the former president of the Confederacy, died in New Orleans at age 81.

1917   Finland declared its independence from Russia, after the Russian Bolshevik Revolution.

1941   President Roosevelt sent a personal note to Emperor Hirohito of Japan seeking to dispel the "dark clouds" threatening war. (Japan attacked Pearl Harbor the next day.)

1973   Congressman Gerald Ford was sworn in as vice president of the United States, succeeding Spiro Agnew who had resigned in disgrace.

December 7 – Birthdays

1542   **Mary, Queen of Scots.** The last Roman Catholic ruler of Scotland, who in 1587 was beheaded on orders of Queen Elizabeth I of England

1598   **Gian Lorenzo Bernini.** Italian sculptor and architect, designer of the great plaza of St. Peter's Church, and probably the most famous artist of the 17th century

1784   **Allan Cunningham.** Scottish poet

1823   **Leopold Kronecker.** Polish mathematician, noted for his work in the theory of algebraic numbers and for the Kronecker delta, named in his honor

1863   **Pietro Mascagni.** Italian opera composer, noted for the verismo style that he made famous in *Cavalleria Rusticana* (1888), his greatest work

1863   **Richard Warren Sears.** American merchant and co-founder with Alvin C. Roebuck of Sears, Roebuck, and Company

1873   **Willa Cather.** American novelist, noted for works such as *O Pioneers!* (1913), *My Antonia* (1918), and *Death Comes for the Archbishop* (1927)

1879   **Rudolph Friml.** Austrian-born composer of operettas such as *The Firefly, Rose Marie,* and *The Vagabond King,* and for songs such as "Donkey Serenade" (1937)

1888   **Joyce Cary.** One of the leading British novelists of the 1900s, noted for works such as *Herself Surprised* (1941) and *The Horse's Mouth* (1944)

1888   **Heywood Campbell Broun.** One of America's most widely read newspaper columnists of the 1920s and 1930s

1892   **Fay Bainter.** American stage and motion-picture actress and Academy Award winner in 1938 for best supporting actress in *Jezebel*

1894   **Stuart Davis.** American painter and illustrator noted for works such as *Garage Lights* (1931) and *Seme* (1953)

1905   **Clarence Nash.** American entertainer and the voice of Donald Duck in animated cartoons

1908   **John Hope Doeg.** American Hall of Fame tennis player

1910   **Richard Franko Goldman.** American composer and bandleader noted for "A Sentimental Journey" (1941)

1910   **Rod Cameron.** Canadian-born motion-picture and television actor with a 40-year career

1911   **Denny Galehouse.** Professional baseball player

1912   **Louis Prima.** American musician

1915   **Eli Wallach.** American stage and motion-picture actor

1923   **Ted Knight.** American television actor

1924   **Mario Soares.** Leader of Portugal's Socialist Party after the death of dictator Antonio Salazar in 1968

1925   **Max Zaslofsky.** Professional basketball player

1928   **Noam Chomsky.** American linguistics expert and political theorist

1930   **Dan Sikes.** Professional golfer

1931   **Bobby Osborne.** American bluegrass singer

1932   **Ellen Burstyn.** American stage, screen, and television actress

1934   **Judi Dench.** British stage, screen and television actress in both leading lady and supporting player roles

1937   **Thad Cochran.** U.S. senator

1942   **Harry Chapin.** American singer and songwriter noted for works such as "Taxi" (1972)

1942   **Alex Johnson.** Professional baseball player and American League batting champion in 1970

1947   **Johnny Bench.** Hall of Fame baseball player, noted as one of the greatest catchers in the game's history

1956   **Larry Bird.** Professional basketball superstar

1967   **Tino Martinez.** Professional baseball player

December 7 – Events

43   Cicero, the great Roman orator and statesman, was assassinated by agents of Mark Antony.

1787   Delaware became the "First State" of the Union, when it ratified the U.S. Constitution.

1793   Madame du Barry, mistress of King Louis XV of France, was guillotined at age 47 by the French republicans.

1842   The New York Philharmonic gave its first concert, performing Beethoven's *Fifth Symphony,* the *Overture* from Weber's *Oberon,* and part of the score of Beethoven's *Fidelio.*

1917   The U.S. 42nd, or "Rainbow," Division arrived in France in World War I.

1941   Shortly before 8 A.M., Hawaiian time, Japanese naval and air forces suddenly attacked Pearl Harbor, plunging the United States into World War II.

1965   The Roman Catholic Church and the Eastern Orthodox Churches removed the sentences of excommunication they had imposed on each other in 1054.

1970   Rube Goldberg, the great American cartoonist, died at age 87.

1988   A major earthquake, 6.9 on the Richter scale, devastated Armenia in the Soviet Union, killing some 25,000 people.

December 8 – Birthdays

65 BC   **Horace (Quintus Horatius Flaccus).** One of the most familiar and admired of the Roman poets

1626   **Christina.** Queen of Sweden, 1632-1654, whose court included Rene Descartes, the famous French mathematician and philosopher

1708   **Francis I.** Holy Roman Emperor, 1745-1765, and husband of Maria Theresa, the great queen of Austria

1765 Eli Whitney. American inventor, noted for his invention of the cotton gin (1793) and for making guns by using machinery, which marked the beginning of mass production

1815 Adolf von Menzel. German painter and printmaker

1816 August Belmont. American financier, founder of the banking house of August Belmont and Company, and grandfather of the original owner of the famous race horse Man O' War

1832 Bjornstjerne Bjornson. Norwegian novelist and dramatist and the great national poet of Norway

1861 William Crapo Durant. American automobile manufacturer and founder of General Motors (1908)

1861 Aristide Maillol. French sculptor noted for the serene balanced style of his figures, which were almost exclusively female, such as *The Mediterranean* (1901)

1862 Georges Feydeau. French writer

1865 Jean Sibelius. Finnish composer and musician, noted for *Finlandia* and his seven symphonies

1868 Norman Douglas. British writer best known for his witty, satirical novel *South Wind* (1917)

1881 Albert Gleizes. French painter

1885 Kenneth Lewis Roberts. American novelist and essayist, noted for works such as *Northwest Passage* (1937) and *Lydia Bailey* (1947)

1886 Diego Rivera. Mexican painter and outstanding leader in the birth of mural art in Mexico

1890 Bohuslav Martinu. Czechoslovakian composer

1894 E(lsie). C. Segar. American cartoonist and creator of *Popeye* (1929), one of the most successful comic strip characters in history

1894 James Thurber. American writer, cartoonist, and perhaps America's finest humorist since Mark Twain

1902 Oswald Jacoby. One of the greatest American bridge players of the 20th century

1904 Wilmer Lawson Allison. American Hall of Fame tennis player

1906 Richard Llewellyn. Welsh novelist noted for *How Green Was My Valley* (1940)

1911 Lee J. Cobb. Outstanding American character actor of the stage, screen, and television

1913 Delmore Schwartz. American poet

1925 Sammy Davis Jr. American actor, singer, and dancer

1930 Maximilian Schell. Austrian-born stage, screen, and television actor and director

1933 Flip Wilson. American comedian and actor

1933 John Green. Professional basketball player

1936 David Carradine. American motion-picture and television actor, and son of actor John Carradine

1937 James MacArthur. American motion-picture and television actor, and adopted son of playwright Charles MacArthur and actress Helen Hayes

1939 James Galway. Noted Irish flutist

1942 Bob Love. Professional basketball player

1943 Jim Morrison. American singer with The Doors musical group

1945 Julie Heldman. American tennis player

1946 John Rubinstein. American actor and son of pianist Arthur Rubinstein

1947 Greg Allman. American singer with the Allman Brothers musical group

1953 Kim Basinger. American motion-picture and television actress

1959 Mark Dickson. American tennis player

1964 Teri Hatcher. American actress who played Lois in TV's *Lois and Clark: The New Adventures of Superman*

1967 Sinead O'Connor. Irish singer

December 8 – Events

877 Louis II, the Stammerer, was crowned King of France.

1854 Pope Pius IX defined the doctrine of the Immaculate Conception.

1863 President Lincoln announced his plans for Reconstruction of the South, one feature of which was to pardon Southerners who would take an oath of loyalty to the United States.

1864 Pope Pius IX issued the *Syllabus of Errors,* which, among other things, denied the equality of Catholicism and Protestantism.

1886 The American Federation of Labor (AF of L) was created by the reorganization of the Federation of Organized Trades and Labor Unions.

1940 The House of Commons suffered heavy damage as 400 German planes raided London in World War II.

1941 President Roosevelt declared December 7, 1941, "a date that will live in infamy," and asked Congress to declare war on Japan. The declaration of war was signed at 4:10 P.M.

1949 Generalissimo Chiang Kai-shek fled with his Nationalist government to Formosa, surrendering mainland China to the Chinese Communists.

1953 President Eisenhower proposed his "atoms for peace" plan, providing for nations to pool their atomic information and materials for peaceful purposes.

1965 The fourth and final session of the ecumenical council Vatican II ended.

1978 Golda Meir, former prime minister of Israel, died at age 80.

1980 John Lennon, famous member of the Beatles musical group, was assassinated in New York City at the age of 40.

1987 President Ronald Reagan and Soviet leader Mikhail Gorbachev signed a landmark treaty banning intermediate-range nuclear missiles, in a meeting in Washington, D.C.

December 9 – Birthdays

1594 **Gustavus II.** King of Sweden, 1611-1632 (known also as Gustavus Adolphus), who laid the foundations of the modern Swedish state

1608 **John Milton.** One of the greatest poets of the English language, whose *Paradise Lost* (1667) is one of the world's greatest epics

1717 **Johann Winckelmann.** German archaeologist and art historian

1842 **Peter Kropotkin.** Russian prince and noted anarchist of the late 1800s

1848 **Joel Chandler Harris.** American writer and creator of the famous character *Uncle Remus*

1871 **Joe Kelley.** Hall of Fame professional baseball player

1897 **Hermione Gingold.** English stage, screen, and television actress, with a career of over 70 years

1898 **Emmett Kelly.** Noted American circus clown, famous for his sad-faced tramp

1902 **Margaret Hamilton.** American actress in over 75 movies and as many stage plays, best remembered as the Wicked Witch of the West in *The Wizard of Oz* (1939)

1903 **Matty Malneck.** American composer and violinist, noted for songs such as "Hey, Good Lookin'"

1905 **Dalton Trumbo.** American screenwriter and author noted for the novel *Johnny Got His Gun* (1939) and for the script *Roman Holiday* (originally credited to another writer because Trumbo was on Hollywood's infamous Black List)

1906 **Freddy Martin.** American bandleader of the Big Band Era

1909 **Douglas Fairbanks Jr.** American motion-picture and television actor, and son of the silent screen's most beloved hero

1911 **Broderick Crawford.** American stage, screen, and television actor with a career of some 45 years

1912 **Thomas P. "Tip" O'Neill.** Speaker of the U.S. House of Representatives

1915 **Elisabeth Schwarzkopf.** Polish-born lyric soprano, who was highly successful in the 1940s and 1950s as a concert and opera singer

1916 **Kirk Douglas.** American stage and motion-picture actor with a career of some 50 years

1922 **Redd Foxx.** American motion-picture and television actor

1925 **Dina Merrill.** American stage, screen, and television actress and daughter of Marjorie Merriweather Post, heiress of the Post cereal fortune

1926 **Luis Miguel Dominguin.** Professional bullfighter

1928 **Dick Van Patten.** American stage, screen, and television actor

1929 **John Cassavetes.** American motion-picture and television actor, director, and screenwriter

1930 **Buck Henry.** American actor, author, and television comedy script writer

1931 **Cliff Hagan.** Hall of Fame professional basketball player with over 13,000 career points

1932 **Bill Hartak.** American jockey with five Kentucky Derby winners

1938 **Deacon Jones.** Hall of Fame professional football player

1941 **Beau Bridges.** American motion-picture actor and son of actor Lloyd Bridges

1942 **Dick Butkus.** Professional football superstar and actor

1944 **Del Unser.** Professional baseball player

1947 **Tom Daschle.** U.S. senator and Minority Leader

1947 **Steve Owens.** Professional football player

1949 **Tom Kite.** Professional golfer

1950 **Joan Armatrading.** West Indian-born singer and guitarist

1953 **John Malkovich.** American stage and screen actor

1954 **Renata Tomanova.** Czechoslovakian tennis player

1955 **Otis Birdsong.** Professional basketball player

1957 **Donny Osmond.** American singer and actor

December 9 – Events

1531 The Virgin of Guadalupe allegedly appeared to an Indian boy, Juan Diego, on Tepeyac Hill near Mexico City, and caused a picture of herself to appear on his cloak.

1641 Sir Anthony Van Dyck, the great Flemish painter, died in London at age 42.

1793 Noah Webster published *The American Minerva,* New York's first daily newspaper.

1824 The armies of Simon Bolivar and Antonio Jose de Sucre defeated the Spaniards at Ayacucho, ending the Latin-American wars of independence.

1854 Alfred Lord Tennyson published his famous poem "The Charge of the Light Brigade."

1884 Levant M. Richardson of Chicago patented the ball-bearing roller skate.

1905 Church and state were separated by law in France, breaking the church-state connection established in 1801 by Napoleon and Pope Pius VII.

1917 British troops under General Viscount Allenby captured Jerusalem from the Turks in World War I.

1934 Ethiopian and Italian soldiers clashed at Wai Wai, providing the pretext for Italy's later invasion of Ethiopia.

1958 The John Birch Society was founded by Robert Welch, a retired business executive.

1965 Branch Rickey, the great baseball executive, died eleven days before his 84th birthday.

1984 Eric Dickerson of the Los Angeles Rams gained his 2,007[th] yard, breaking O.J. Simpson's single-season NFL record, as the Rams beat the Houston Oilers, 27-16.

1992 British Prime Minister John Majors announced that Prince Charles and Princess Diana were separating. They later obtained a divorce.

December 10 – Birthdays

1538 **Battista Guarini.** Italian Renaissance court poet

1610 **Adriaen van Ostade.** Dutch painter and print-maker of the Baroque period

1787 **Thomas Hopkins Gallaudet.** Pioneer American teacher of deaf-mutes, and founder of the Hartford School for the Deaf (1817)

1804 **Karl Gustav Jacob Jacobi.** Noted German mathematician who was famous for the development of elliptic functions

1805 **William Lloyd Garrison.** American journalist and reformer who became famous in the 1830s for his denunciations of slavery

1822 **Cesar Franck.** French composer best known for his *Symphony in D minor* (1888)

1830 **Emily Dickinson.** One of the greatest American poets, noted for lines such as "I'm nobody! Who are You?" (published in 1891)

1851 **Melvil Dewey.** American librarian who in 1876 developed the library classification method known today as the Dewey Decimal System

1870 **Pierre Louys.** French novelist and poet

1870 **Adolph Loos.** Austrian architect

1879 **Ernest Howard Shepard.** English artist and illustrator of A.A. Milne's *Pooh* books

1883 **Andrei Vishinsky.** Russian prosecutor in the Communist Party purge trials of the 1930s and chief delegate to the U.N. in the early 1950s

1886 **Victor McLaglen.** English character star in some 150 silent and sound movies

1891 **Harold Alexander.** British World War II field marshal who commanded the evacuation of Dunkerque and was supreme Allied commander in the Mediterranean area

1893 **Lew Brown.** American songwriter noted for songs such as "Button Up Your Overcoat" and "Beer Barrel Polka"

1902 **Vito Marcantonio.** American Congressman noted in the 1940s and 1950s for his left-wing views

1903 **Una Merkel.** American motion-picture actress in over 50 films

1911 **Chet Huntley.** American television newscaster who teamed with newscaster David Brinkley in the Huntley-Brinkley Report of the 1950s and 1960s

1912 **Philip Hart.** U.S. senator in the 1960s and 1970s

1913 **Morton Gould.** American composer, conductor, and arranger, known for his clever use of American folk and popular music

1914 **Dorothy Lamour.** American motion-picture actress and one of Hollywood's most popular stars of the 1930s and 1940s

1923 **Harold Gould.** Noted American character actor of film and television

1950 **Lloyd Neal.** Professional basketball player

1952 **Susan Dey.** American model and actress

1960 **Kenneth Branagh.** Irish stage and film actor and director

December 10 – Events

1520 Martin Luther burned the *Bull Exsurge* issued against him by Pope Leo X, demanding that he recant.

1607 Captain John Smith left Jamestown on the trip in which Pocahontas allegedly saved his life by intervening with her father, the Indian chief Powhatan.

1817 Mississippi was admitted to the Union as the 20th state.

1832 President Andrew Jackson proclaimed his nonrecognition of South Carolina's Ordinance of Nullification and ordered warships and troops concentrated near Charleston.

1848 Louis Napoleon, the nephew of Napoleon I, was elected president of France with 5.5 million votes out of 7.5 million cast.

1869 The Territory of Wyoming authorized women to vote and hold office, the first U.S. state or territory to do so.

1896 Alfred Nobel, the noted Swedish chemist, died at age 63. The Nobel Prizes, established by him, are awarded on this date in his honor.

1898 The Treaty of Paris ended the Spanish-American War, making Cuba independent and ceding Guam, Puerto Rico, and the Philippine Islands to the United States.

1901 The first Nobel Prizes were awarded.

1906 President Theodore Roosevelt was awarded the Nobel Prize for peace for his mediation in the Russo-Japanese War.

1910 Giacomo Puccini, the great Italian composer, attended the world premiere of his opera, *The Girl of the Golden West,* at the Metropolitan Opera House in New York.

1913 Leonardo da Vinci's masterpiece, the *Mona Lisa,* was recovered two years after it was stolen from the Louvre Museum in Paris.

1915 Henry Ford produced his one millionth Model T automobile.

1917 Father Edward Joseph Flanagan founded Boys Town near Omaha, Nebraska.

1920 The Nobel Peace Prize for 1919 was awarded to President Wilson for his part in the World War I peace treaty and for establishing the League of Nations.

1931 Jane Addams, the noted American reformer, became the first American woman to win the Nobel Peace Prize, sharing the honor with Nicholas M. Butler.

1941 Japanese forces captured Guam and invaded the Philippine Islands, landing in northern Luzon in World War II.

1941 The British battleships *Prince of Wales* and *Repulse* were sunk by the Japanese in World War II.

1950 Ralph Bunche, American statesman, became the first black American to win the Nobel Peace Prize.

1958 The first domestic passenger jet flight took place in the United States, inaugurated by National Airlines from New York to Miami.

December 11 – Birthdays

1475 **Leo X.** Roman Catholic pope who was in office when Martin Luther started the Protestant Reformation, and who was the second son of Lorenzo the Magnificent of the Medici family

1803 **Louis Hector Berlioz.** French conductor and composer noted for such works as the *Fantastic Symphony* (1830) and *The Damnation of Faust* (1846)

1810 **Alfred de Musset.** French poet, dramatist, and novelist, noted chiefly for his plays *Comedies et Proverbes* (1840)

1822 **George David Cummins.** Founder of the Reformed Episcopal Church

1843 **Robert Koch.** German physician, noted for establishing bacteriology as a separate science

1854 **Old Hoss Radbourn.** Hall of Fame professional baseball player

1882 **Fiorella La Guardia.** Famous mayor of New York City from 1934 to 1945

1882 **Max Born.** German physicist who shared the 1954 Nobel prize for physics for his contributions to quantum theory

1890 **Mark Tobey.** American painter

1892 **John Augustus Larson.** American inventor who made one of the first lie detectors, or polygraphs (1921)

1905 **Gilbert Roland.** Mexican-born motion-picture actor with a career of over 50 years

1908 **Elliott Carter Jr.** American composer

1910 **Carlo Ponti.** Italian motion-picture producer, noted for films such as *Two Women* (1960) (starring his wife, actress Sophia Loren) and *Dr. Zhivago* (1965)

1914 **Bill Nicholson.** Professional baseball player

1918 **Alexander Solzhenitsyn.** Nobel Prize-winning Russian novelist (*The Gulag Archipelago*) exiled from his country because of charges of slander by the Soviet government

1923 **Betsy Blair.** American stage and motion-picture actress

1924 **Doc Blanchard.** Noted football player, particularly with the great Army teams of the World War II years

1930 **Jean-Louis Trintnignant.** French motion-picture actor

1931 **Rita Moreno.** Puerto Rican-born actress, singer, and dancer

1938 **Frederick Cox.** Professional football player

1941 **Max Baucus.** U.S. senator

1943 **John F. Kerry.** U.S. senator

1943 **Donna Mills.** American motion-picture and television actress

1946 **Linda Day George.** American actress

1949 **Teri Garr.** American motion-picture and television actress

1950 **Christine Onassis Andreadis.** Heiress and daughter of Greek shipping magnate Aristotle Onassis

1951 **Robert Cochran.** American skiing champion

1953 **Bess Armstrong.** American motion-picture and television actress

1954 **Jermaine Jackson.** American singer and bassist with The Jackson 5 musical group

1958 **Nikki Sixx.** American rock musician with Motley Crue

1964 **David Schools.** Rock musician with the group Widespread Panic

December 11 – Events

1695 Captain William Kidd, the famous Scottish pirate, was commissioned a privateer (captain of an armed ship) by King William III of England to capture certain notorious pirates.

1718 Charles XII, the great king of Sweden, was killed in the siege of Fredrikstad, Norway, at the age of 36.

1719 The first recorded sighting of the Aurora Borealis occurred in New England.

1816 Indiana was admitted to the Union as the 19th state.

1844 An anesthetic (nitrous oxide, or laughing gas) was first used in dentistry, when American dentist Dr. Horace Wells used it on himself before having his tooth extracted.

1872 Pinckney Benton Stewart Pinchback became the first black governor in U.S. history, as he took office as acting governor of Louisiana.

1904 President Theodore Roosevelt stated that he would "not accept another nomination" for the presidency, an action he was later to regret.

1911 Great Britain under Prime Minister Herbert Asquith passed the first National Health Insurance act.

1936 King Edward VIII abdicated in order to marry Mrs. Wallis Simpson, and his brother George VI became King of England.

1941 Germany and Italy declared war on the United States, followed by a U.S. declaration of war on them.

1946 John D. Rockefeller, Jr., announced his donation of a six-block parcel of land along the East River in New York City as a site for the United Nations headquarters.

December 12 – Birthdays

1745 **John Jay.** First U.S. Supreme Court chief justice

1775 **William Henry.** English chemist for whom Henry's law of gases was named

1786 **William L. Marcy.** U.S. senator noted for the political slogan "To the victor belong the spoils"

1791 **Marie Louise.** Austrian princess and second wife of Napoleon Bonaparte

1805 **Henry Wells.** Co-founder with William G. Fargo in 1852 of Wells, Fargo & Company

1821 **Gustave Flaubert.** French writer whose first and greatest work, *Madame Bovary* (1857), is considered by many to be the world's "perfect novel"

1863 **Edvard Munch.** Norwegian artist noted for his paintings and lithographs depicting man as helpless, isolated, and tormented by emotions, a prime example of which is *The Scream* (1893)

1864 **Arthur Brisbane.** One of the first syndicated newspaper columnists in the United States, noted for his columns *Today* and *This Week,* which appeared in the 1920s and 1930s

1866 **George Swinnerton Parker.** American businessman who with his brothers formed Parker Brothers Co., noted for board games such as Monopoly and Clue

1875 **Karl Rudolf Gerd von Rundstedt.** One of Hitler's ablest World War II field marshals, who directed The Battle of the Bulge in 1944

1879 **Laura Hope Crews.** American stage and motion-picture actress, noted for her role as Aunt Pittypat in *Gone With the Wind*

1881 **Harry Morris Warner.** One of the Warner Brothers who founded the motion-picture company of the same name

1881 **Arthur Garfield Hays.** American lawyer and civil liberties leader, who assisted Clarence Darrow in the famous Scopes Trial of 1925

1883 **Cliff Sterrett.** American comic strip cartoonist and creator of *Polly and Her Pals*

1893 **Edward G. Robinson.** American stage and motion-picture actor with a brilliant 50-year career

1894 **Philip Drinker.** American educator and engineer who invented the iron lung (1929)

1906 **Zack Mosley.** American comic strip cartoonist and creator of *Smilin' Jack*

1912 **Henry Armstrong.** The only boxer to hold three world championships at the same time—the welterweight, the lightweight, and the featherweight titles (1937)

1915 **Frank Sinatra.** American singer, actor, and superstar performer for over 50 years

1918 **Eugene Leonard Burdick.** American author who, with William J. Lederer, wrote *The Ugly American* (1958)

1923 **Bob Barker.** American television game show host

1924 **Edward I. Koch.** Mayor of New York City

1927 **Robert Norton Noyce.** American scientist who developed an etching method to print transistors on silicon waters and who with Gordon Moore, founded Intel Corp. (1968)

1928 **Helen Frankenthaler.** American abstract expressionist painter

1929 **John Osborne.** English playwright and screenwriter, noted for his play *Look Back in Anger,* which was made into a movie in 1959

1932 **Bob Pettit.** Professional Hall of Fame basketball superstar and the first to score 20,000 career points

1936 **Lucia Bassi.** Italian tennis player

1938 **Connie Francis.** American singer and actress

1940 **Tom Hayden.** American social activist

1941 **Dionne Warwick.** American soul singer

1943 **Grover Washington Jr.** American jazz musician, composer and arranger

1945 **Ralph Garr.** Professional baseball player

1946 **Emerson Fittipaldi.** Brazilian race car driver and two time winner of the Indianapolis 500

1948 **Randy Smith.** Professional basketball player

1950 **Gorman Thomas.** Professional baseball player

1952 **Kathy Rigby.** American gymnast, television and stage actress, and first U.S. woman gymnast to win a medal in world competition (1970)

1952 **David Jaynes.** Professional football player

1953 **Rafael Septien.** Professional football player

1970 **Jennifer Connelly.** American model and motion-picture and TV actress

December 12 – Events

1398 Tamerlane, the feared Mongol conqueror, sacked Delhi, India, and massacred most of its 100,000 inhabitants.

1787 Pennsylvania ratified the Constitution, becoming the second state of the Union.

1850 *The Wide, Wide World*, by Susan Warner, was published. It is considered by many publishers to be the first U.S. "best seller."

1870 Joseph H. Rainey of South Carolina became the first black U.S. Congressman.

1871 Wild Bill Hickok was fired as marshall of Abilene, Kansas, for mistakenly killing a law officer.

1889 Robert Browning, the great English poet, died in Venice at age 77.

1897 The comic strip *The Katzenjammer Kids,* by Rudolph Dirks, first appeared.

1901 The message *S* was received from Cornwall, England, by Guglielmo Marconi in St. John's, Newfoundland, the first long-distance wireless message.

1925 The world's first motel, the "Motel Inn," opened in San Luis Obispo, California.

1937 Japanese planes sank the U.S. gunboat *Panay* in the Yangtze River in China. Their government apologized and paid a two million dollar indemnity.

1947 John L. Lewis withdrew his United Mine Workers from the AF of L.

1953 U.S. Major Chuck Yeager flew a Bell X-1A jet plane at a record two-and-a-half times the speed of sound.

1963 Kenya became independent of Great Britain.

1968 Tallulah Bankhead, the noted American actress, died at age 65.

December 13 – Birthdays

1520 **Sixtus V.** Roman Catholic pope, 1585-1590, who established the Vatican Press, and urged King Philip of Spain to launch the Spanish Armada against England.

1553 **Henry IV.** The first Bourbon king of France, 1589-1610, noted for the famous Edict of Nantes

1560 **Maximilien de Bethune Sully.** French minister of King Henry IV, and the first important person to hold the position of minister to a French king

1797 **Heinrich Heine.** One of the most popular writers in German literature, noted especially for his poem "The Lorelei," published in his *Book of Songs* (1827)

1816 **Werner von Siemens.** German engineer who developed an electroplating process and invented a dynamo, and for whom (with his brother Wilhelm) the *siemens*, the electrical unit of conductance is named

1818 **Mary Todd Lincoln.** Wife of President Abraham Lincoln

1835 **Phillips Brooks.** American clergyman best known as the composer of the famous Christmas carol "O Little Town of Bethlehem," first sung in 1868

1887 **Alvin "Sergeant" York.** American World War I hero who killed more than 20 Germans and forced 132 others to surrender on October 8, 1918

1890 **Marc Connelly.** American playwright, journalist, and stage director, best known for *The Green Pastures* (1930), perhaps America's most popular religious drama

1897 **Drew Pearson.** American muckraking newspaper columnist of the 1940s and 1950s

1903 **Carlos Montoya.** Noted Spanish guitarist

1910 **Van Heflin.** American stage and motion-picture actor in over 50 films

1912 **Curt Jurgens.** German stage and motion-picture actor in over 100 films

1913 **Archie Moore.** World light-heavyweight champion, 1952-1962

1914 **Alan Bullock.** English author best known for *Hitler: A Study in Tyranny* (1952), one of the earliest and best biographies of the Nazi dictator

1914 **Larry Parks.** American motion-picture actor

1915 **Balthazar Johannes Vorster.** Prime minister of the Republic of South Africa, 1966-1978

1915 **Ross Macdonald.** American writer noted for works such as *The Dark Tunnel* (1944) and *Meet Me at the Morgue* (1953)

1918 **William Vukovitch Sr.** American automobile racer

1920 **George P. Shultz.** American cabinet member in the Nixon, Ford, and Reagan administrations

1920 **Don Taylor.** American motion-picture actor and director

1923 **Larry Doby.** Professional baseball player and first black player in the American League

1925 **Dick Van Dyke.** American actor and comedian

1926 **Carl Erskine.** Professional baseball player

1927 **Christopher Plummer.** Canadian-born stage, screen, and television actor

1930 **Robert Joseph Prosky.** American stage, screen and television actor

1934 **Richard Darryl Zanuck.** American motion-picture producer and executive, and son of the noted producer Darryl F. Zanuck

1935 **Lindy McDaniel.** Professional baseball player

1941 **John Davidson.** American singer and actor

1943 **Ferguson Jenkins.** Professional baseball superstar

1947 **Lemar Parrish.** Professional football player

December 13 – Events

1250 Holy Roman Emperor Frederick II, the brilliant ruler of the Middle Ages, died in Fierentino 13 days short of his 56th birthday.

1294 Pope Celestine V abdicated under the persuasion of Cardinal Benedetto Gaetano, who succeeded him as Pope Boniface VIII.

1466 Donatello, the great Italian sculptor, died in Florence at an approximate age of 80.

1545 The first session of the Council of Trent met in Trent, a city in the Austrian Tyrol, to restate the doctrines of the Roman Catholic Church.

1577 Sir Francis Drake left Plymouth, England, beginning the second round-the-world voyage in history.

1642 Abel Tasman, the great Dutch navigator, discovered New Zealand.

1648 The "Rump" Parliament (96 members were arrested by the army and excluded) voted to try King Charles I of England for treason.

1784 Samuel Johnson, the great English man of letters, died in London at age 75.

1809 Dr. Ephraim McDowell performed America's first abdominal operation, removing a 22-pound ovarian tumor from Mrs. Jane Todd Crawford in Danville, Kentucky.

1862 The Confederates under General Robert E. Lee dealt the Union forces under General Ambrose Burnside a crushing defeat in the Battle of Fredericksburg in the Civil War.

1928 George Gershwin's *An American in Paris* was performed for the first time, by the New York Philharmonic Symphony Orchestra.

1937 Japanese soldiers captured Nanking, the former Chinese capital, in the Sino-Japanese War.

1975 Australians elected Malcolm Fraser's Liberal-National Country Party to office in a landslide victory over the Labor Party.

December 14 – Birthdays

1503 **Nostradamus (Michel de Notredame).** French astrologer and physician, famous for his prophecies and for his book *Centuries* (1555), a series of prophecies in verse

1546 **Tycho Brahe.** Noted Danish astronomer and associate of the great astronomer Johannes Kepler

1610 **David Teniers the Younger.** Flemish painter noted for works such as *Country Fair* (1641), *Tavern Scene* (1645), and *The Picture Gallery of Archduke Leopold Wilhelm* (1653)

1727	**François Hubert Drouais.** French painter
1775	**Philander Chase.** American Episcopal priest who founded Kenyon College (1824)
1824	**Pierre Cecille Purvis de Chavannes.** French artist and the most popular mural painter of the 1800s
1895	**George VI.** King of England, 1936-1952, who ruled during World War II, having succeeded his brother Edward VIII, who abdicated
1895	**Paul Eluard.** French poet
1896	**Jimmy Doolittle.** Noted American flier who led the first bombing raid on Tokyo in World War II (1942)
1897	**Margaret Chase Smith.** First woman to be elected to both houses of the United States Congress
1901	**Henri Cochet.** French tennis player and one of the Four Musketeers who dominated French tennis in the 1920s and early 1930s (the other Musketeers were Rene Lacoste, Jacques Brugnon and Jean Borotra)
1901	**Paul I.** King of Greece, 1947-1964
1911	**Hans Pabst von Ohain.** German engineer and inventor of the first practical jet engine
1911	**Spike Jones.** American composer, drummer, and leader of the band, Spike Jones and His City Slickers
1914	**Morey Amsterdam.** American comedian, actor, and writer
1915	**Benjamin Wilfred Loewy.** American composer, author, and leading tenor in musical comedy, plays, and on the radio
1917	**Dan Dailey.** American actor and dancer
1918	**James Aubrey.** American television executive
1919	**Shirley Jackson.** American novelist and short-story writer, noted for works such as *The Lottery* (1949)
1922	**Don Hewitt.** American television executive and creator in 1968 of CBS's *60 Minutes*
1922	**Charley Trippi.** Professional football player and Hall of Famer
1932	**Charlie Rich.** American country singer
1935	**Lee Remick.** American stage, screen, and television actress and attractive leading lady
1935	**Abbe Lane.** Latin American singer
1946	**Patty Duke.** American stage, screen, and television actress, billed also as Patty Duke Astin
1946	**Stan Smith.** American tennis player and 1972 Wimbledon singles champion
1949	**Bill Buckner.** Professional baseball player
1953	**Vijay Amritraj.** Indian tennis player
1954	**Ib Andersen.** Danish ballet dancer
1956	**Tony Nathan.** Professional football player
1965	**Craig Biggio.** Professional baseball player

December 14 – Events

867	Adrian II was elected Roman Catholic pope.
872	John VIII was elected Roman Catholic pope.

1799	George Washington died at Mount Vernon at age 67. After he indicated to his secretary his burial instructions, he said "'Tis well," felt for his own pulse, and then died.
1812	Marshal Michel Ney, Napoleon's second in command, crossed the Nieman River after the Russian campaign with a tattered army of 30,000 men out of the original 600,000-man Grande Armee.
1819	Alabama was admitted to the Union as the 21st state.
1861	Prince Albert, husband of England's Queen Victoria, died of typhoid fever at age 42.
1910	The Carnegie Endowment for International Peace was established with a gift from Andrew Carnegie of $10 million, to "hasten the abolition of international war."
1911	Raold Amundsen, the great Norwegian explorer, discovered the South Pole.
1918	Women first voted in a British election. Complete woman suffrage was not granted in Great Britain, however, until 1928.
1962	U.S. space probe *Mariner 2* approached Venus, transmitting to Earth information about the planet's atmosphere and surface temperature.
1967	King Constantine II of Greece went into exile after unsuccessfully trying to overthrow the military junta that had ruled Greece since the preceding April.
1986	The experimental aircraft *Voyager,* piloted by Dick Rutan and Jeana Yeager, took off from Edwards Air Force Base on the first non-stop, non-fueled flight around the world.

December 15 – Birthdays

37	**Nero.** Roman emperor who allegedly fiddled while Rome burned
1734	**George Romney.** English portrait painter noted for works such as *Death of Wolfe* (1763) and *Lady Hamilton as a Bacchante* (1783)
1832	**Alexandre Gustave Eiffel.** French engineer who designed the 984-foot Eiffel Tower in Paris (1889)
1852	**Antoine Henri Becquerel.** French physicist who shared the 1903 Nobel Prize for physics with Pierre and Marie Curie for the discovery of natural radioactivity
1859	**Ludovic Lazarus Zamenhof.** Polish oculist who invented the universal language Esperanto
1861	**Charles Edgar Duryea.** American automobile pioneer who with his brother Frank built the first successful gasoline-powered automobile in America (1893)
1861	**Pehr Evind Svinhufvud.** First chief of state of an independent Finland
1888	**Maxwell Anderson.** American playwright and screenwriter, noted for works such as *Elizabeth the Queen* (1930), *Key Largo* (1939), and *The Bad Seed* (1955)

1892 **David Wendell Guion.** American composer noted for songs such as "Home on the Range" and "Wild Geese"

1892 **John Paul Getty.** American industrialist, founder of Getty Oil Company, and one of the richest men of his time

1904 **Kermit Bloomgarden.** American motion-picture producer

1907 **Oscar Niemeyer.** Brazilian architect noted for the design of the principal buildings of Brasilia, the new capital of Brazil

1911 **Nicholas Dallis.** American cartoonist and co-creator of *Rex Morgan, M.D.*

1918 **Jeff Chandler.** American motion-picture actor

1930 **Edna O'Brien.** Irish writer

1933 **Tim Conway.** American actor and comedian

1940 **Nick Buoniconti.** Professional football player

1944 **Stan Bahnson.** Professional baseball player

1946 **Art Howe.** Professional baseball player and manager

1948 **Charles Scott.** Professional basketball player

1950 **Don Johnson.** American motion-picture and television actor, noted for his role in the long-running series *Miami Vice*

1950 **Jonathan Keyworth.** Professional football player

1965 **Helen Slater.** American stage and motion-picture actress

1967 **Mo Vaughn.** Professional baseball player

December 15 – Events

687 Sergius I (Saint Sergius) was elected Roman Catholic pope.

1675 Jan Vermeer (Vermeer van Delft), the great Dutch painter, died at age 43.

1685 Izaak Walton, the noted English writer and fisherman, died in Winchester at age 90. He fished until he was 83.

1791 The U.S. Bill of Rights became law, having been ratified by the states.

1792 The Insurance Company of North America issued the first life insurance policy in America.

1864 The Battle of Nashville began in the Civil War. It ended the next day in a decisive Northern victory.

1890 Sioux Indian Chief Sitting Bull was shot and killed at the Standing Rock Reservation in South Dakota by federal troops.

1939 The great motion picture *Gone With the Wind* had its world premiere in Loew's Theater in Atlanta.

1944 A plane carrying bandleader and U.S. Army major Glenn Miller disappeared during a World War II flight over the English Channel.

1945 Prince Fumimaro Konoye of Japan committed suicide to avoid facing trial as a war criminal.

1948 Alger Hiss, the former State Department official, was indicted on two perjury counts by a Federal Grand Jury.

1961 Former Nazi Adolf Eichmann was sentenced to death in Jerusalem for World War II crimes committed against the Jews.

1971 The United States government announced the first devaluation of the dollar since the 1930s.

1978 President Carter announced that the United States would recognize China on January 1, 1979.

December 16 – Birthdays

1485 **Catherine of Aragon.** The first of the six wives of King Henry VIII of England, and the daughter of Ferdinand and Isabella of Spain

1716 **Thomas Gray.** English poet noted for "Elegy Written in a Country Churchyard" (1751), perhaps the best-known poem in the English language

1742 **Gebhard Leberecht von Blucher.** Prussian marshal whose arrival with reinforcements helped the British defeat Napoleon at Waterloo

1770 **Ludwig van Beethoven.** Perhaps the greatest composer in musical history, and certainly one of the two or three greatest

1775 **Jane Austen.** The world's first great woman novelist, noted for works such as *Pride and Prejudice* (1813), *Emma* (1816), and *Northanger Abbey* (1818)

1790 **Leopold I.** First King of the Belgians, 1831-1865

1863 **George Santayana.** Spanish-born American philosopher, poet, and critic, who also wrote the popular novel *The Last Puritan* (1936)

1882 **Sir Jack Hobbs.** English cricketer

1899 **Sir Noel Coward.** English playwright and actor, noted for such works as the song "Mad Dogs and Englishmen" and the play *Blithe Spirit* (1941)

1900 **V(ictor) S(awden) Pritchett.** English novelist noted for works such as *Mr. Beluncle* (1951)

1901 **Margaret Mead.** American anthropologist and writer, noted for her studies of the cultures of the Pacific Islands, the United States, and Russia

1916 **William Lester Strickland.** Noted American mathematician, U.S. government scientist, and businessman

1917 **Arthur C. Clarke.** English writer of science fiction and nonfiction, noted for works such as *Childhood's End* (1953)

1918 **Murray Kempton.** American editor and writer

1928 **Philip K. Dick.** American novelist noted for works such as *The Man in the High Castle*

1936 **Morris S. Dees Jr.** American lawyer and civil rights activist who won a huge court settlement against the Ku Klux Klan

1939 **Liv Ullmann.** Outstanding dramatic actress of Swedish and international motion-pictures, who gained fame in the 1960s and 1970s as the star of a number of Ingmar Bergman productions

1941 **Lesley Stahl.** American broadcast journalist

1951 **Jean Fuget Jr.** Professional football player

1951 **Mike Flanagan.** Professional baseball player

1952	**Susan Estrich.** American lawyer, educator and the first woman to direct a major political campaign (for Dukakis for president in 1988)
1961	**Jon Tenney.** American stage, screen and television actor
1962	**William "Refrigerator" Perry.** Professional football player

December 16 – Events

882	Marinus I was elected Roman Catholic pope, replacing the murdered John VIII.
1653	Oliver Cromwell became Lord Protector of England.
1689	Parliament passed the English Bill of Rights.
1773	The "Boston Tea Party" took place in Boston Harbor, as 40 to 50 colonists disguised as Indians broke open 340 chests of tea in three British ships and dumped the tea into the harbor.
1809	Napoleon divorced Josephine in order to marry a younger woman to give him an heir for his empire.
1838	The Boers in South Africa crushed the Zulu king Dingaan.
1864	The Civil War Battle of Nashville ended with Union general Thomas smashing Confederate general Hood's army and ending Southern resistance in the West.
1893	Czech composer Antonin Dvorak attended the world premiere of his *New World Symphony* at Carnegie Hall in New York.
1905	*Variety*, a weekly show business periodical, was published for the first time.
1916	Grigori Rasputin, the Russian "mad Monk," was poisoned by a group of noblemen bent on ridding Russia of his corrupting influence. He lived until December 30 when he was shot.
1944	The Germans attacked the Americans in the Ardennes (Belgium), beginning the Battle of the Bulge in World War II.
1965	W. Somerset Maugham, the noted English author, died at Villa Mauresque in Switzerland at age 91.

December 17 – Birthdays

1632	**Anthony Wood.** British antiquarian
1732	**John Townsend.** American cabinetmaker
1734	**William Floyd.** Leader in the struggle for American independence, and a New York signer of the Declaration of Independence
1734	**Maria I.** Queen of Portugal, 1777-1816
1749	**Domenico Cimarosa.** Italian composer, noted for such works as *The Secret Marriage* (1792)
1778	**Sir Humphry Davy.** English chemist noted for the invention of the Davy lamp, a miner's safety lamp, and for first isolating the elements sodium, potassium, barium, calcium, magnesium, and strontium
1797	**Joseph Henry.** American physicist and pioneer in electromagnetism, for whom the unit *henry* of electrical inductance is named

1807	**John Greenleaf Whittier.** One of the best-known American poets, noted for such works as "Barefoot Boy" (1856) and "Snow-Bound" (1866)
1830	**Jules de Goncourt.** French novelist, art critic, and diarist, who with his brother Edmond wrote *Germinie Lacerteux* (1864), one of the earliest examples of naturalism in fiction
1853	**Sir Herbert Beerbohm Tree.** One of the great figures of the English theater, and half brother of writer Max Beerbohm
1873	**Ford Madox Ford.** English author of complex and symbolic novels, the best known of which form the series *Parade's End* of the 1920s
1874	**William Lyon Mackenzie King.** Three times prime minister of Canada, 1921-1926, 1926-1930, and 1935-1948, and grandson of noted Canadian politician William Lyon Mackenzie
1894	**David Butler.** American motion-picture and stage director with a 40-year career
1894	**Arthur Fiedler.** Conductor of the Boston Pops Orchestra, 1930-1980
1903	**Erskine Caldwell.** American novelist noted for such works as *Tobacco Road* (1932) and *God's Little Acre* (1933)
1904	**Paul Cadmus.** American painter and etcher
1906	**William McChesney Martin Jr.** American broker and chairman of the Federal Reserve System during the Eisenhower and Kennedy administrations
1908	**Willard Frank Libby.** Nobel Prize-winning American chemist who discovered carbon 14 (1947) and the process of carbon dating
1910	**Jimmy Caras.** Hall of Fame pocket billiards player
1926	**Patrice Wymore.** American stage and motion-picture actress
1926	**Allan V. Cox.** American geophysicist known for his study of the earth's magnetic poles
1929	**William Safire.** American journalist and author
1930	**Bob Guccione.** Publisher of *Penthouse* magazine
1940	**Eddie Kendricks.** American singer with The Temptations
1942	**Paul Butterfield.** American blues harmonica player
1957	**Bob Ojeda.** Professional baseball player

December 17 – Events

63	Lazarus died again (according to Biblical theory).
1187	Clement III was elected Roman Catholic pope.
1830	Simon Bolivar, the great South American liberator, died at age 47.
1892	Peter Ilich Tchaikovsky's famous ballet *The Nutcracker* was first presented, at the Maryinsky Theater in St. Petersburg.
1903	The Wright brothers, Wilbur and Orville, made the world's first airplane flight, at Kitty Hawk, N.C. Orville went first and Wilbur flew the longest of their four flights.
1919	Pierre Auguste Renoir, the great French painter, died in Provence at age 78.

1925	General Billy Mitchell was court-martialed for advocating a strong air force in defiance of his superiors. He later was given the Congressional Medal of Honor (1946).
1933	The Chicago Bears beat the New York Giants, 23-21, in the first world championship football game.
1936	Edgar Bergen, one of the most famous ventriloquists of all time, made his debut in New York with his dummy Charlie McCarthy.
1939	The German pocket battleship *Graf Spee* was scuttled in Montevideo Harbor on orders of Adolf Hitler to keep the British from taking her in World War II.
1971	Bangladesh became independent of Pakistan.

December 18 – Birthdays

1633	**Willem van de Velde (the Younger).** Dutch painter
1707	**Charles Wesley.** The famous hymn writer of Methodism, who wrote some 6,000 hymns, and was the brother of Methodist Church founder John Wesley
1709	**Elizabeth.** Empress of Russia, 1741-1762, and daughter of Peter the Great
1835	**Lyman Abbott.** American Congregational preacher and editor, who popularized the reconciliation of evolution with the Biblical account of creation
1856	**Sir Joseph John Thomson.** English physicist who in 1897 discovered the electron
1859	**Francis Thompson.** British poet noted for "The Hound of Heaven" (1893)
1861	**Edward MacDowell.** American composer and pianist noted for such short piano pieces as "To a Wild Rose" and "To a Water Lily"
1863	**Francis Ferdinand.** Austrian archduke whose assassination in Serbia in 1914 led to World War I
1870	**Hector Hugh Munro.** British writer who wrote under the pen name Saki, noted for works such as *Beasts and Super-Beasts* and *The Square Egg*
1879	**Paul Klee.** Swiss-German artist and one of the greatest and most original masters of modern painting
1886	**Chu Teh.** Founder of the Chinese Communist army
1886	**Ty Cobb.** One of the two or three greatest baseball players in history (with Babe Ruth and Willie Mays, perhaps), with a record .367 lifetime batting average
1890	**Edwin Howard Armstrong.** American electrical engineer noted for his invention of FM radio broadcasting (frequency modulation) in 1933, and for the superheterodyne circuit which became widely used in radio receivers
1897	**Fletch Henderson.** American bandleader
1904	**George Stevens.** American motion-picture director who won Academy Awards for *A Place in the Sun* (1951) and *Giant* (1956), and who directed the famous Western *Shane* (1953)

1907	**Christopher Fry.** English dramatist who wrote in verse works such as *The Lady's Not for Burning* (1949)
1908	**Dame Cecilia Johnson.** English stage and motion-picture actress noted as the romantic heroine of *Brief Encounter* (1945)
1910	**Abe Burrows.** Broadway play producer and dramatist
1911	**Jules Dassin.** American motion-picture director, noted for works such as *The Naked City* (1948) and *Never on Sunday* (1960)
1913	**Alfred Bester.** American author and science fiction novelist best known for *Tiger! Tiger!*
1913	**Willy Brandt.** Mayor of West Berlin after World War II and chancellor of West Germany in the 1970s
1916	**Betty Grable.** American actress and "pin-up girl" of World War II GIs
1916	**Douglas Fraser.** President of the United Automobile Workers in the 1970s and early 1980s
1917	**Ossie Davis.** American actor, director, and playwright who wrote and starred in the play *Purlie Victorious* (1961) and the film version *Gone Are the Days!* (1963)
1927	**Ramsey Clark.** Son of U.S. Supreme Court Justice Tom Clark, and U.S. Attorney General under President Lyndon Johnson
1930	**Bill Skowron.** Professional baseball player
1931	**Gene Shue.** Professional basketball superstar with over 10,000 career points
1932	**Roger Smith.** American motion-picture and television actor
1943	**Keith Richards.** British guitarist with The Rolling Stones musical group
1946	**Greg Landry.** Professional football player
1947	**Steven Spielberg.** American motion-picture director noted for films such as *Jaws, E.T.,* and *Raiders of the Lost Ark*
1950	**Leonard Maltin.** American film historian and author, noted for works such as the popular editions of *TV Movies and Video Guide*
1952	**Stan Fritts.** Professional football player
1953	**Johnny Gray.** Professional football player
1955	**Ray Liotta.** American motion-picture and television actor
1956	**Jerry Robinson.** Professional football player
1963	**Lori McNeil.** American tennis player
1964	**Brad Pitt.** American motion-picture actor
1966	**Kiefer Sutherland.** English motion-picture actor and son of actor Donald Sutherland
1971	**Arantxa Sanchez Vicario.** Spanish tennis player

December 18 – Events

| 1534 | The Act of Supremacy, making the Church of England a separate institution and establishing the king as its supreme head, was formally accepted by King Henry VIII. |

1737 Antonio Stradivari, the greatest violinmaker of all time, died at an approximate age of 93 in Cremora, Italy.

1787 New Jersey became the third state when it ratified the U.S. Constitution.

1812 Napoleon reached Paris after 13 days of traveling incognito from Russia after his disastrous invasion of that country.

1813 The British captured Fort Niagara in the War of 1812.

1865 The 13th Amendment to the Constitution was proclaimed, ending slavery in the United States.

1915 President Woodrow Wilson married his second wife, Edith Bolling Galt.

1931 Legs Diamond (John Thomas), the American gangland boss, was shot and killed by his enemies, contradicting his earlier remark that "the bullet hasn't been made that can kill me!"

1935 Dr. Eduard Benes was elected president of Czechoslovakia.

1956 Japan joined the United Nations.

1969 Great Britain abolished capital punishment.

December 19 – Birthdays

1683 **Philip V.** King of Spain, 1700-1724, whose elevation to the Spanish throne caused the War of the Spanish Succession

1814 **Edwin M. Stanton.** Secretary of war under President Lincoln

1849 **Henry Clay Frick.** American industrialist and philanthropist

1852 **Albert A. Michelson.** American physicist who established the speed of light as a constant, and who in 1907 became the first American to win the Nobel prize in physics

1861 **Constance Garnett.** English translator noted for her translation into English of Russian classics, particularly those of Tolstoy and Dostoevsky

1861 **Italo Svevo.** Italian novelist and pioneer of the psychological novel in Italy

1865 **Minnie Maddern Fiske.** One of America's leading stage actresses for more than 60 years

1868 **Eleanor H. Porter.** American author known for the children's *Pollyanna* books

1879 **Beals Coleman Wright.** American Hall of Fame tennis player and U.S. singles champion in 1905

1884 **Ernie Burnett.** American composer noted for "My Melancholy Baby"

1888 **Fritz Reiner.** One of the greatest symphony orchestra and operatic conductors of his time

1888 **Walter Donovan.** American composer and pianist noted for songs such as "One Dozen Roses" and "Aba Daba Honeymoon"

1894 **Ford Frick.** National League president, 1934-1951, and Commissioner of Baseball, 1951-1965

1902 **Sir Ralph Richardson.** Eminent British character actor of stage and screen with a career of over 60 years

1906 **Leonid Brezhnev.** Russian head of state who succeeded Khrushchev in 1964 and served until the early 1980s

1907 **H. Allen Smith.** American humorist

1910 **Jean Genet.** French novelist and playwright known for his violent, complex plays

1912 **Michel Andre.** French actor and playwright and son of actor Marcel Andre

1915 **Carlton Franklin Stutz.** American composer noted for songs such as "Little Things Mean a Lot" and "Jamestown Suite"

1920 **David Susskind.** American television producer and talk show host

1923 **Gordon Jackson.** Scottish motion-picture and television actor

1924 **Edmond Purdom.** English stage and motion-picture actor

1926 **Bobby Layne.** Professional football superstar and Hall of Famer

1927 **Al Kilgore.** American cartoonist and creator of the comic strip *Bullwinkle*

1933 **Cicely Tyson.** American stage, screen, and television actress

1934 **Al Kaline.** Hall of Fame baseball player

1941 **Maurice White.** Musician and singer with the Earth, Wind, and Fire group

1943 **William C. DeVries.** American surgeon who implanted the first artificial heart in a human being, on Barney Clark on December 2, 1982

1946 **Robert Urich.** American television actor

1947 **Janie Fricke.** American country singer

1957 **Kevin McHale.** Professional basketball player

1958 **Limahl.** British singer with the Kajagoogoo musical group

1962 **Clay Parker.** Professional baseball player

1963 **Jennifer Beals.** American motion-picture actress

December 19 – Events

1732 Benjamin Franklin began publishing *Poor Richard's Almanac.*

1776 Thomas Paine published the first installment of *The American Crisis* in the *Pennsylvania Journal.* The essay opened with the words: "These are the times that try men's souls."

1777 George Washington's army retired to Valley Forge for the "Winter of Despair" of 1977-1978 in the Revolutionary War.

1843 The great novelist Charles Dickens published *A Christmas Carol*, one of the most famous stories ever written.

1848 Emily Brontë, the great English novelist, died of tuberculosis at age 30.

1851 J.M.W. Turner, the noted English painter, died in Chelsea at age 76.

1871 Birmingham, Alabama, was incorporated.

1919 The comic strip *Thimble Theater,* by E.C. Segar, first appeared. The fabled Popeye figure, however, was not added to its cast until January 17, 1929.

1924	William Green succeeded Samuel Gompers as president of the American Federation of Labor.
1941	Adolf Hitler dismissed his chief of staff, General Heinrich von Brauchitsch, and assumed personal command of the German Army himself.
1946	Ho Chi Minh, Indochinese Nationalist leader, began his guerrilla war against the French.
1950	General Dwight D. Eisenhower was appointed commander of the NATO forces.
1959	Walter Williams, the last surviving veteran of the Civil War, died at age 117. He had fought in the Confederate Army.
1972	*Apollo 17* splashed down in the Pacific, completing the 9th trip to the moon.
1974	Nelson A. Rockefeller was sworn in as the 41st vice president of the United States.
1998	The House of Representatives impeached President Clinton on near-party-line votes on two charges, perjury before a grand jury and obstruction of justice. Two other charges by the House Judiciary Committee were dropped.

December 20 – Birthdays

1629	**Pieter De Hooch.** Dutch artist noted for works such as *The Mother* and *Interior with Figures*
1738	**Clodion.** French sculptor
1838	**Edwin Abbott.** English clergyman, writer, and author of *Flatland*
1867	**Pudge Heffelfinger.** Professional football player
1868	**Harvey Firestone.** Pioneer rubber manufacturer and founder of the Firestone Tire and Rubber Company
1871	**Henry Kimball Hadley.** American conductor and composer
1875	**Charley Grapewin.** American stage and motion-picture actor who played Jeeter Lester in *Tobacco Road,* and appeared in 100 movies and countless plays during a 60-year career.
1876	**Walter Sydney Adams.** American astronomer
1881	**Branch Rickey.** Professional baseball executive who devised the farm system, and broke the color line by bringing to the game the first black player, Jackie Robinson, in 1947
1886	**Hazel Hotchkiss Wightman.** American tennis player for whom the Wightman Cup was named, four times U.S. champion, and one of the greatest women players in history
1888	**Fred Merkle.** Professional baseball player unfairly called "bonehead" for failing to advance from first to second, subsequently losing the game after the winning run had scored on a hit to the center field wall
1888	**Abe Olman.** American composer and pianist, noted for songs such as "Oh Johnny Oh," "Down Among the Sweltering Palms," "Down by the O-Hi-O," and "Come Back to Waikiki"
1894	**Sir Robert Gordon Menzies.** Australian prime minister, 1939-1941 and 1949-1966

1895	**Suzanne K. Langer.** American philosopher and educator, and author of *Philosophy in a New Key*
1898	**Irene Dunne.** American stage, screen, and television actress, and one of Hollywood's top-ranking stars until her retirement in the 1950s
1899	**John J. Sparkman.** U.S. senator and candidate for vice president on Adlai Stevenson's ticket in 1952
1900	**Ted Fiorito.** American bandleader and songwriter, known for "Toot, Toot, Tootsie, Goodbye"
1900	**Gabby Hartnett.** Hall of Fame baseball player and manager
1901	**Robert Jemison Van de Graaff.** American physicist and inventor of the electrostatic generator, or Van de Graaff generator
1902	**Sidney Hook.** American philosopher and writer
1902	**Max Lerner.** Russian-born American writer and lecturer
1905	**Albert Dekker.** American stage and motion-picture actor and director, with a 40-year career
1907	**Horace Coy Poe.** American lyricist noted for songs such as "The Object of My Affection" and "What's the Reason I'm Not Pleasin' You"
1907	**Paul Francis Webster.** American lyricist noted for songs such as "Doctor, Lawyer, Indian Chief," "Secret Love," "Somewhere My Love," "Love Is a Many-Splendored Thing," and "The Shadow of Your Smile"
1910	**Charlie "The Bomber" Conacher.** Hall of Fame professional hockey player
1914	**Harry F. Byrd Jr.** U.S. senator and son of the long-time senator from Virginia
1918	**Audrey Totter.** American radio, motion-picture, and television actress
1922	**George Roy Hill.** American motion-picture director who won the Academy Award for *The Sting* (1973)
1927	**Dean Burch.** American political figure and FCC chairman under President Nixon
1941	**Dave Stallworth.** Professional basketball player
1942	**Robert Hayes.** Professional football player
1946	**Uri Geller.** Israeli psychic noted for reading minds and moving watch hands without touching them
1947	**Peter Criss.** American singer and musician with KISS
1949	**Cecil Cooper.** Professional baseball player
1949	**Oscar Gamble.** Professional baseball player
1952	**Jenny Agutter.** English ballet dancer and actress

December 20 – Events

44 BC	Cicero, the great Roman orator and statesman, delivered his third *Philippic* (one of 14 speeches against Mark Antony) in the Roman Senate.
1334	Benedict XII was elected Roman Catholic pope. He was the third of the Avignon popes.
1606	Captain John Smith and 120 colonists left London bound for America. They were to reach the Chesapeake Bay in April and found the Jamestown colony in May of 1607.

1690	Englishman Job Charnock of the East India Company founded Calcutta, India.
1790	The first successful U.S. cotton mill began operations, in Pawtucket, Rhode Island.
1803	Louisiana was officially transferred from French to United States control, following the Louisiana Purchase.
1860	South Carolina voted to secede from the Union, the first state to do so.
1880	Broadway became the "Great White Way," as it was illuminated by electricity for the first time.
1917	Communist dictator V.I. Lenin ordered the creation of the *Cheka,* a Russian secret police force designed to establish rule by terror.
1928	The Ethel Barrymore Theater, the first named for a living person, opened in New York City.
1941	Admiral Ernest J. King was appointed commander-in-chief of the United States Fleet in World War II.
1968	The noted American author, John Steinbeck, died at age 66.

December 21 – Birthdays

1401	**Masaccio (Tommaso Guidi).** The greatest painter in Florence during the early Renaissance, whose art was studied by both Michelangelo and Raphael
1639	**Jean Racine.** One of the greatest French playwrights of all time
1804	**Benjamin Disraeli.** One of Great Britain's greatest prime ministers, 1868 (ten months) and 1874-1880, who improved the common citizen's lot at home and extended the empire to its zenith abroad
1815	**Thomas Couture.** French painter
1872	**Albert Payson Terhune.** American author noted for his stories about dogs, especially collies
1879	**Joseph Stalin.** Dictator of the U.S.S.R., 1929-1953
1891	**John W. McCormack.** Speaker of the U.S. House of Representatives, 1962-1971
1892	**Walter Hagen.** One of the superstars of professional golf, who won the U.S. Open in 1914 and the British Open four times in the 1920s
1896	**Konstantin Rokossovsky.** Russian World War II commanding general who successfully defended Moscow against the Germans
1905	**Harry Revel.** English-born composer and pianist, noted for songs such as "Did You Ever See a Dream Walking?" "With My Eyes Wide Open I'm Dreaming," and "Just the Way You Are"
1909	**George Ball.** American statesman and diplomat of the Kennedy and Johnson Administrations
1911	**Josh Gibson.** Hall of Fame baseball player who was one of the greatest hitters in the so-called Negro leagues
1917	**Heinrich Boll.** German novelist, essayist and short-story writer, noted for works such as the novel *Billiards at Half-Past Nine* (1959)

1918	**Kurt Waldheim.** Fourth secretary-general of the United Nations and President of Austria, who was accused of engaging in Nazi atrocities during World War II
1922	**Paul Winchell.** American ventriloquist
1926	**Joe Paterno.** Noted college football coach
1935	**Phil Donahue.** American television talk show host
1937	**Jane Fonda.** American motion-picture actress, daughter of actor Henry Fonda, and Academy Award winner as best actress for *Klute* (1971) and *Coming Home* (1978)
1940	**Frank Zappa.** American avant-garde rock guitarist and composer, chosen as Pop Musician of the Year in 1970, 1971, and 1972
1944	**Michael Tilson Thomas.** American conductor, pianist and composer
1946	**Carl Wilson.** American guitarist with the Beach Boys musical group
1948	**Dave Kingman.** Professional baseball player who hit over 400 career home runs
1948	**Elliott Maddox.** Professional baseball player
1949	**Patti Hogan.** American tennis player
1952	**Joaquin Andujar.** Professional baseball player
1954	**Chris Evert.** American tennis superstar and one of the game's all time greatest women players, particularly on clay
1959	**Florence Griffith Joyner.** American track star and gold and silver Olympic medalist
1960	**Andy Van Slyke.** Professional baseball player
1960	**Roger McDowell.** Professional baseball player

December 21 – Events

1124	Honorius II was elected Roman Catholic pope.
1620	After a month of exploring the Massachusetts coast, the Pilgrims in the *Mayflower* landed at Plymouth. The passengers disembarked 5 days later after further exploration.
1864	General William Tecumseh Sherman's Union troops occupied Savannah, Georgia, completing his famous "March to the sea" in the Civil War.
1879	News of Thomas A. Edison's invention of the electric light was announced, astounding the world.
1881	Benjamin Disraeli, the famous English prime minister, died in London on his 77th birthday.
1898	The element radium was discovered by French scientists Marie and Pierre Curie.
1913	The first crossword puzzle was published, in the New York *World.* It was compiled by journalist Arthur Wynne and had 32 clues.
1914	The first feature-length silent film comedy, *Tillie's Punctured Romance,* was released, starring Charlie Chaplin and Marie Dressler, and directed by Mack Sennett.
1937	Walt Disney's animated motion picture *Snow White and the Seven Dwarfs* was shown for the first time.
1944	Horse racing was banned in the United States for the duration of World War II.

1945	General George S. Patton, the great American World War II general, died at age 60 of injuries suffered in an automobile accident.
1953	Ex-Premier Mohammed Mossadegh of Iran was convicted of trying to lead a revolt against the Shah.
1958	General Charles de Gaulle was elected first president of the French Fifth Republic.
1968	*Apollo 8* was launched with astronauts Frank Borman, William A. Anders, and James Arthur Lovell Jr. aboard to orbit the moon.
1988	A bomb exploded aboard a Pan Am Boeing 747 over Lockerbie, Scotland, killing 270 persons.
1991	The Soviet Union faded into history as 11 of the 12 Soviet republics proclaimed the birth of a commonwealth at Alma-Ata, Kazakhstan. Only Georgia failed to join. (The Baltic states had already been granted independence.)

December 22 – Birthdays

1696	**James Edward Oglethorpe.** English army officer who was the founder (1733) and first governor of Georgia
1723	**Karl Friedrich Abel.** German symphonist
1727	**William Ellery.** One of the Rhode Island signers of the Declaration of Independence and a member of the Continental Congress
1768	**John Crome.** English painter noted for works such as *Boulevard des Italiens* (1815)
1802	**Sara Coleridge.** English author of children's verse, and daughter of the poet Samuel Taylor Coleridge
1831	**Charles Stuart Calverley.** English poet and parodist
1856	**Frank B. Kellogg.** U.S. secretary of state who won the 1929 Nobel Peace prize for his work in framing the Kellogg-Briand Peace Treaty of 1928
1858	**Giacomo Puccini.** One of the five greatest opera composers of all time, noted for works such as *La Boheme* (1896), *Tosca* (1900), and *Madame Butterfly* (1904)
1862	**Connie Mack.** Hall of Fame baseball player, manager, and owner, known as the "grand old man" of baseball
1869	**Edwin Arlington Robinson.** Pulitzer Prize-winning American poet, noted for works such as "The Man Who Died Twice" (1925) and "Tristram" (1928)
1885	**Edgar Varese.** Franco-American composer
1885	**Deems Taylor.** American composer and music critic
1888	**J. Arthur Rank.** British motion-picture magnate who for a quarter of a century owned more than half of the British studios and more than 1000 theaters
1901	**Andre Kostelanetz.** American conductor of popular and classical music
1907	**Dame Peggy Ashcroft.** British stage and screen actress and noted Shakespearean interpreter

1908	**Max Bill.** Swiss artist
1908	**Giacomo Manzu.** Italian sculptor
1912	**Lady Bird Johnson.** Wife of President Lyndon B. Johnson
1916	**Charley Boswell.** American golfer, blinded from World War II wounds, with numerous U.S. Blind Golfers Association wins
1917	**Gene Rayburn.** American actor and television show host
1922	**Jim Wright.** U.S. congressman and Speaker of the House, who because of ethics charges in 1989 became the only speaker in history to resign in mid-term
1924	**Ruth Roman.** American stage and motion-picture actress and short story writer
1936	**Hector Alizondo.** Noted American character actor of stage, screen and television
1938	**Matty Alou.** Professional baseball player
1944	**Steve Carlton.** Hall of Fame baseball pitcher and superstar with a career total of over 3,500 strikeouts and 300 career wins
1945	**Diane Sawyer.** American television reporter
1948	**Steve Garvey.** Professional baseball player
1949	**Robin Gibb.** English singer and songwriter with The Bee Gees
1949	**Squeaky Fromme.** Charles Manson follower and attempted assassin of President Ford in 1975
1949	**Guy Ray.** Professional football player
1951	**Jan Stephenson.** Professional golfer
1954	**Ken Landreaux.** Professional baseball player
1955	**Lonnie Smith.** Professional baseball player
1962	**Ralph Fiennes.** British stage and motion-picture actor
1968	**Lauralee Bell.** American television actress (*The Young and the Restless*)

December 22 – Events

69	Roman Emperor Vitellius was killed in a street battle in Rome by soldiers of Vespasian, who succeeded Vitellius as emperor.
1775	The Continental Navy was established by the Continental Congress with Ezek Hopkins, a former New England sea captain, as the first commander-in-chief.
1807	Congress passed the Embargo Act, designed to cut off trade with Europe and bring the warring nations of Britain and France to reason.
1864	Union General William T. Sherman sent President Lincoln the message, "I beg to present you as a Christmas gift the city of Savannah."
1880	George Eliot (Mary Ann Evans), the noted English novelist, died at age 61.
1894	The United States Golf Association was organized.
1894	Alfred Dreyfus was found guilty of spying against France in the famous Dreyfus case. He was released in 1906 and pronounced innocent after an imprisonment on Devil's Island.

1944	"Nuts," said American General Anthony McAuliffe to German demands that he surrender at Bastogne in the Battle of the Bulge in World War II.
1962	"Telstar," by the Tornadoes, became the first record by a British musical group to top the U.S. charts.
1968	North Korea released 82 members of the U.S. intelligence ship Pueblo, eleven months after their seizure.
1989	Romania's hard-line president, Nicolae Ceausescu, was toppled from power in a popular uprising.

December 23 – Birthdays

1174	**Louis I.** Duke of Bavaria
1682	**James Gibbs.** British architect
1732	**Sir Richard Arkwright.** British inventor and manufacturer, noted for a water-powered spinning machine
1777	**Alexander I.** Czar of Russia, 1801-1825, who formed the coalition that defeated Napoleon
1790	**Jean François Champollion.** French Egyptologist who in 1822 deciphered the Rosetta stone
1804	**Charles Augustin Saint-Beuve.** French critic, poet, and novelist
1805	**Joseph Smith.** Founder and first president of the Mormon Church, officially called the Church of Jesus Christ of Latter-Day Saints (in 1830)
1812	**Samuel Smiles.** Scottish writer best known for *Self Help* (1859), which enshrined the Victorian values associated with the "gospel of work"
1819	**George Barnard.** American photographer
1856	**James Buchanan Duke.** American businessman and philanthropist, who organized the American Tobacco Company (1890) and established the Duke Endowment (1924)
1857	**Edward Reynolds Pease.** Co-founder of the Fabian Society (1884), a group of British socialists
1860	**Harriet Monroe.** American poet, editor, and founder of *Poetry: A Magazine of Verse* (1912)
1870	**John Marin.** American painter, famous for his water-color landscapes, such as *Off Stonington* (1921)
1885	**Vincent Sardi.** Noted Italian-American restauranteur
1900	**Otto Soglow.** American cartoonist and creator of the comic strip *The Little King* (1934)
1907	**James Roosevelt.** Oldest son of President Franklin D. Roosevelt
1907	**Barney Ross.** World lightweight boxing champion, 1933-1935, and welterweight champion, 1934 and 1935-1938
1907	**Don McNeill.** American radio show host on the Don McNeill Breakfast Club
1908	**Yousuf Karsh.** Armenian-born Canadian photographer who made the famous picture of Winston Churchill used on commemorative stamps by six countries

1911	**James Gregory.** American stage, screen and television actor, noted for his role in the long-running series *Barney Miller*
1918	**Helmut Schmidt.** Chancellor of West Germany in the 1970s
1918	**Jose Greco.** One of the most famous Spanish dancers of his time
1922	**Calder Willingham.** American writer noted for works such as *End As a Man* (1947)
1929	**Dick Weber.** Prominent American bowler
1933	**Akihito.** Emperor of Japan who succeeded Hirohito
1935	**Paul Hornung.** Professional football superstar and Hall of Famer
1943	**Jerry Koosman.** Professional baseball player
1943	**Elizabeth Hartman.** American stage and motion-picture actress
1946	**Helen Gourlay.** Australian tennis player
1948	**Jack Raphael Ham.** Hall of Fame professional football player
1948	**Susan Lucci.** American actress noted for her role in *All My Children* as Erica Kane, "the queen of soap-opera bitches"
1952	**William Kristol.** American publisher and political commentator
1971	**Corey Haim.** American television actor

December 23 – Events

619	Boniface V became Roman Catholic pope.
1783	George Washington resigned his commission as commander-in-chief of the army and retired to Mount Vernon.
1823	The most popular Christmas poem in America, "A Visit from St. Nicholas," also known as "'Twas the Night Before Christmas," was published by its author, Clement Clarke Moore.
1834	George Hansom patented the Hansom cab, a horse-drawn one-seated vehicle that served as a big-city taxi in the 1800s.
1863	William Makepeace Thackeray, the great English novelist, died in London at age 52.
1888	Vincent Van Gogh, the great Dutch painter, cut off one of his own ears during an epileptic seizure. He also threatened to kill the painter Paul Gauguin who was visiting him.
1913	The United States Federal Reserve System was established, as President Wilson signed the Glass-Owen Currency Act.
1928	The National Broadcasting Company (NBC) established a permanent coast-to-coast radio network.
1938	A new kind of music, *boogie-woogie,* was introduced in Carnegie Hall by two pianists, Meade Lewis and Albert Ammons.
1941	Wake Island surrendered to the Japanese in World War II.
1947	The transistor was invented by Walter H. Brattain, John Bardeen and William Shockley of Bell Labs.
1948	Ex-Premier Hideki Tojo of Japan was hanged in Tokyo as a war criminal.

1953 Lavrenty P. Beria, head of the dreaded Soviet secret police, was executed in a purge of top Russian officials.

1986 The *Voyager*, piloted by Dick Rutan and Jeana Yeager, completed its non-stop, round-the-world flight, landing at Edwards Air Base in California.

December 24 – Birthdays

3 BC **Servius Sulpicius Galba.** Emperor of Rome, A.D. 68-69

1167 **John (Lackland).** King of England, 1199-1216, who was forced to approve the Magna Carta in 1215

1491 **Saint Ignatius Loyola.** Spanish nobleman who in 1534 founded the Society of Jesus, better known as the Jesuits

1745 **Benjamin Rush.** American physician, patriot, reformer, and Continental Army surgeon-general

1754 **George Crabbe.** English poet noted for works such as *The Library* (1781) and *The Village* (1783)

1791 **Augustine Eugene Scribe.** French dramatist noted for the tragedy *Adrienne Lecouvreur* (1849) and for some 400 other dramatic pieces

1809 **Kit Carson.** Famous American frontiersman, hunter, guide, and soldier

1818 **James P. Joule.** English physicist who shared in the discovery of the law of conservation of energy, and for whom the unit of work, or energy, the *joule,* is named

1822 **Charles Hermite.** Noted French mathematician for whom the Hermite Polynomials are named

1822 **Matthew Arnold.** One of the greatest poets of Victorian England, noted for works such as "Dover Beach"

1845 **George I.** King of Greece, 1863-1913, who succeeded Otto, the first king of Greece, and who was the ancestor of every later Greek king

1880 **Johnny Gruelle.** Creator of *Raggedy Ann*

1881 **Juan Ramon Jimenez.** Nobel Prize-winning Spanish poet (1956), whose masterpiece is "Platero and I" (1917)

1893 **Harry Warren.** American composer noted for songs such as "The Lullaby of Broadway," "Jeepers Creepers," "Chattanooga Choo Choo," and "I've Got a Gal in Kalamazoo"

1903 **Ad Reinhardt.** American painter

1903 **Joseph Cornell.** American sculptor

1905 **Howard Hughes.** American financier, aviator, and one of the richest men of his time

1907 **Adam Rapacki.** Polish socialist and economist

1907 **I.F. Stone.** American publisher

1909 **Mike Mazurki.** Austrian-American motion-picture actor

1910 **William Hayward Pickering.** American physicist and head of the team that developed *Explorer I*, the first U.S. satellite

1930 **Robert Joffrey.** American choreographer

1931 **Mary Higgins Clark.** American novelist noted for works such as *The Cradle Will Fall* (1980), *I'll Be Seeing You* (1993), and *You Belong to Me* (1998)

1957 **Ian Burden.** British musician with the Human League group

December 24 – Events

640 John IV was elected Roman Catholic pope.

1492 Columbus lost his flagship, the *Santa Maria,* which was wrecked on a reef near the present Cap-Haitien in Haiti, on his first voyage to America.

1524 Vasco da Gama, the Portuguese explorer who first sailed to India around the Cape of Good Hope, died in Cochin, India, at age 55.

1814 The United States and Great Britain signed the Treaty of Ghent, ending the War of 1812.

1818 Joseph Mohr wrote the words to the famous Christmas carol "Silent Night," and Franz Gruber composed the music and presented it at the midnight mass.

1822 Dr. Clement Clarke Moore first read his newly-written poem, "A Visit from St. Nicholas," to his children. He published it a year later.

1865 The Ku Klux Klan was founded at Pulaski, Tennessee, as a social group for war veterans.

1871 Giuseppe Verdi's great opera *Aida* had its world premiere in Cairo, Egypt.

1920 Enrico Caruso, the great Italian operatic tenor, made his last appearance at the Metropolitan Opera House in New York in *La Juive.*

1920 The comic strip *Sappo,* by E.C. Segar, first appeared.

1942 French Admiral Jean Darlan, administrator of North Africa, was assassinated by a young anti-Vichy French patriot in World War II.

1943 General Dwight D. Eisenhower was appointed supreme commander of Operation Overlord (the invasion of Normandy) by President Roosevelt and Prime Minister Churchill.

1951 Libya was declared independent by the United Nations.

1968 U.S. spacecraft *Apollo 8* flew around the moon, broadcasting a Christmas message to earth.

December 25 – Birthdays

4 BC **Jesus Christ.** Founder of the Christian religion (December 25 is traditional, and the year is scholars' best guess, since Christ was born in the age of Herod the Great, who died in 4 B.C.)

1564 **Abraham Bloemaert.** Dutch painter

1717 **Pius VI.** Roman Catholic pope, 1775-1799

1721 **William Collins.** English poet

1801 **Wesley Harper.** One of the four Harper brothers who founded the famous publishing house of Harper and Brothers

1821 **Clara Barton.** American humanitarian "Angel of the Battlefield," and founder in 1881 of the American Red Cross

1847 **James D. Kelly.** Composer of the U.S. Navy's anthem, "Anchor's Aweigh"

1855 **Pud Galvin.** Hall of Fame baseball pitcher who was the first to win 300 career games and who won 46 games in the 1883 season

1863 **Charles Pathe.** French industrialist and film pioneer, and cofounder with his brothers of the Pathe film company

1876 **Giuseppe De Luca.** Italian baritone

1878 **Louis Chevrolet.** American Hall of Fame auto racer, who helped organize the Chevrolet Motor Co. and designed its first automobile

1881 **Sir John Greer Dill.** British World War II chief of staff

1883 **Maurice Utrillo.** French artist known for his paintings of Paris street scenes

1885 **Paul Manship.** American sculptor best known for *Prometheus* in Rockefeller Center in New York City

1886 **Kid Ory.** American trombonist, composer, and jazz musician

1887 **Conrad Hilton.** American businessman who in 1946 organized the Hilton Hotel Systems

1888 **David Lawrence.** American journalist and publisher

1892 **Dame Rebecca West.** English journalist, novelist, and critic, noted for works such as *Henry James* (1916) and *The Birds Fall Down* (1966)

1893 **Robert Leroy Ripley.** American cartoonist who in 1918 created Ripley's *Believe It or Not*

1895 **Arthur H. Gibbs.** American composer and pianist, noted for songs such as "Runnin' Wild"

1899 **Raphael Soyer.** American artist noted for works such as *Portrait of Hugo Kastor* (1957)

1899 **John Bowers.** American actor and handsome leading man of Hollywood silents

1899 **Humphrey Bogart.** American motion-picture actor who has become a Hollywood legend

1902 **Barton MacLane.** American motion-picture and television actor who appeared in over 200 films

1906 **Ernst August Friedrich Ruska.** German engineer who invented the electron microscope

1906 **Clark Clifford.** Special counsel and speechwriter to President Truman and secretary of defense under President Lyndon Johnson

1907 **Cab Calloway.** American singer and actor

1908 **Ben Chapman.** Professional baseball player and manager

1908 **Quentin Crisp.** British author with the motto "I never, never work. Work does age you."

1911 **Burne Hogarth.** American artist who succeeded Harold Foster in drawing the comic strip *Tarzan*

1912 **Tony Martin.** American singer and actor

1918 **Anwar Sadat.** President of Egypt in the 1970s and early 1980s, who signed the historic Camp David peace agreement between Egypt and Israel

1924 **Moktar Ould Daddah.** First president of Mauretania

1924 **Rod Serling.** American writer and creator of television's *Twilight Zone*

1925 **Ned Garver.** Professional baseball player

1927 **Nellie Fox.** Professional baseball player

1935 **Little Richard (Penniman).** American soul and rock singer

1937 **Kelly Isley.** American singer with the Isley Brothers

1942 **Françoise Durr.** French tennis player

1943 **Howard Twilley Jr.** Professional football player

1945 **Gary Sandy.** American television actor

1945 **Ken Stabler.** Professional football superstar

1946 **Jimmy Buffett.** American singer, and songwriter known for works such as "Margaritaville" (1977)

1946 **Norman Bulaich.** Professional football player

1946 **Larry Csonka.** Professional football superstar and Hall of Famer

1948 **Barbara Mandrell.** American country singer and television entertainer

1949 **Sissy Spacek.** American motion-picture actress

1950 **Manny Trillo.** Professional baseball player

1954 **Annie Lennox.** British singer with the Eurythmics musical group

1955 **William Andrews.** Professional football player

1956 **Billy Martin.** American tennis player

1958 **Rickey Henderson.** Professional baseball superstar

December 25 – Events

336 The first recorded celebration of Christmas on December 25 took place in Rome.

800 Charlemagne was crowned the first Holy Roman Emperor by Pope Leo III in Rome.

1066 William the Conqueror was crowned King of England.

1170 Thomas à Becket, the archbishop of Canterbury, excommunicated all those who assisted at the coronation of English King Henry II. Becket was murdered four days later.

1356 Holy Roman Emperor Charles IV issued the famous *Golden Bull*, which regulated imperial elections.

1776 George Washington and his men made their famous crossing of the Delaware River to Trenton, New Jersey, where the next morning they wiped out the entire Hessian garrison.

1818 The famous Christmas carol "Silent Night," written the previous day by Josef Mohr and Franz Gruber, was first publicly sung, by Gruber in the midnight mass in Oberndorff, Germany.

1868 President Andrew Johnson proclaimed an unconditional pardon and amnesty to all who "participated in the late rebellion."

1922 Russian Communist leader V.I. Lenin dictated the *Lenin Testament*, asking his comrades to remove Joseph Stalin as party general secretary, but he was too ill to carry it out.

1926	Hirohito became Emperor of Japan.
1936	Chiang Kai-shek was released 12 days after being kidnapped by mutinous war lords in China.
1941	British troops at Hong Kong surrendered to the Japanese in World War II.
1943	The British Navy sank the German battleship *Scharnhorst* off the coast of Norway in World War II.
1946	W.C. Fields, the great American motion-picture actor and comedian, died at age 67.
1977	Charlie Chaplin, the famous American comedian, died at age 88.
1991	The Soviet Union died officially as Michail Gorbachev resigned. The Russian flag was raised over the Kremlin as the Soviet flag was lowered.

December 26 – Birthdays

1194	**Frederick II.** Holy Roman Emperor, 1215-1250, known as "The Amazement of the World," and one of the most brilliant rulers of the Middle Ages
1792	**Charles Babbage.** English mathematician who developed the idea of a digital computer in the 1830s, and whose principles are used in modern computers
1823	**John Elliott Cairnes.** English economist
1829	**Patrick Sarsfield Gilmore.** Irish-American bandmaster and songwriter noted for "We Are Coming, Father Abraham, 300,000 More" (1862) and "When Johnny Comes Marching Home" (1863)
1837	**George Dewey.** American admiral who won fame as the "hero of Manila" in the Spanish-American War
1838	**Clemens Alexander Winkler.** German chemist who discovered the element germanium in 1886
1891	**Henry Miller.** American novelist noted for works such as *Tropic of Cancer* (1934) and *Tropic of Capricorn* (1939)
1893	**Mao Tse-tung.** Leader of the Chinese Communist revolution and first ruler of the People's Republic of China (also known as Mao Zedong)
1906	**Elisha Cook.** American stage and motion-picture actor
1914	**Richard Widmark.** American stage, screen, and television actor with a career of over 40 years
1917	**Rose Mary Wood.** Personal secretary to President Nixon
1921	**Steve Allen.** American comedian, writer, actor, and first star of NBC's *Tonight Show*
1926	**Doris Lilly.** American writer
1927	**Stu Miller.** Professional baseball pitcher who was once blown off the mound by the wind in an All Star game in San Francisco's Candlestick Park
1927	**Alan King.** American comedian and actor
1940	**Phil Spector.** American songwriter and record producer
1948	**Carlton Fisk.** Professional baseball player and superstar
1948	**Chris Chambliss.** Professional baseball player

1948	**Dave Rader.** Professional baseball player
1954	**Jerry Eckwood.** Professional football player
1954	**Ozzie Smith.** Professional baseball player and superstar
1956	**Susan Butcher.** American athlete who was the fastest woman ever to complete the Iditarod Trail Sled Dog Race (11 days, 1:53.23, in 1990)

December 26 – Events

795	Leo III was elected Roman Catholic pope.
1559	Pius IV was elected Roman Catholic pope.
1620	After spending five days in Cape Cod Bay, the *Mayflower* anchored at Plymouth harbor and the Pilgrims disembarked to found the Plymouth colony.
1776	After crossing the Delaware River, Washington and his men surprised the 1,000 Hessians at Trenton, New Jersey, taking all of them prisoner.
1799	Light-Horse Harry Lee eulogized George Washington as being "first in war, first in peace, and first in the hearts of his countrymen."
1825	The Decembrist Revolt in St. Petersburg, Russia's first modern revolution, was put down by government cannons.
1845	Marthasville, Georgia, changed its name to Atlanta.
1865	James Nason of Franklin, Massachusetts, was awarded a patent for his invention of the coffee percolator.
1908	Jack Johnson became the first black heavyweight boxing champion, defeating Tommy Burns in the 14th round in Sydney, Australia.
1944	The U.S. Third Army of General George S. Patton relieved the 101st Airborne Division, which had been surrounded by the Germans at Bastogne, Belgium, in the Battle of the Bulge.
1972	Harry S. Truman died in Independence, Missouri, at age 88.
1996	Six-year-old beauty queen JonBenet Ramsey was found murdered in her family's home in Boulder, Colorado.

December 27 – Birthdays

1571	**Johannes Kepler.** German astronomer who discovered three fundamental laws of planetary motion, one of which is that the earth and the other planets travel in orbits around the sun
1773	**Sir George Cayley.** English scientist considered to be the father of modern aeronautics
1793	**Alexander Laing.** Scottish explorer who explored the Niger Basin in 1822
1806	**Ramon Cabrera.** Spanish general who supported the Carlist, or Roman Catholic Church party position favoring Don Carlos to inherit the Spanish throne
1822	**Louis Pasteur.** One of the world's greatest scientists and originator of the process of pasteurization

1879 **Sydney Greenstreet.** English stage and motion-picture actor, noted for his urbane brand of villainy which made him one of the classic film heavies of all time

1883 **Cyrus Eaton.** American industrialist known as the "last of the tycoons"

1895 **Robert H. Ellsworth.** American composer noted for songs such as "Carmelita" and "Somebody Else Is Taking My Place"

1897 **Ivan Stepanovich Konev.** Russian World War II field marshal whose troops were the first Russians to meet American forces in Germany, on the Elbe River

1901 **Marlene Dietrich.** German-born stage and motion-picture actress and one of the screen's true immortals

1905 **Sam Coslow.** American songwriter noted for works such as "Cocktails for Two" (1934)

1906 **Oscar Levant.** American pianist, composer, actor, and self-declared genius, who made over 100 recordings and wrote three autobiographical books

1910 **Charles Olson.** American avant-garde poet

1911 **Anna Russell.** English-born composer, author, singer, and comedienne, noted for works such as "Anna Russell Sings?"

1915 **William H. Masters.** American physician noted for human sexuality studies

1924 **James A. McClure.** U.S. senator

1927 **Anne Armstrong.** American ambassador to England under President Nixon

1933 **Dave Marr.** Professional golfer

1935 **Bernard Lanvin.** French fashion designer

1943 **Cokie Roberts.** American television news journalist and co-hostess, and daughter of former Congresspersons Hale and Lindy Boggs

1943 **Roy White.** Professional baseball player

1944 **Tracy Nelson.** American country singer

1948 **Gerard Depardieu.** French motion-picture actor

1951 **Arthur Kent.** American television broadcast journalist

1952 **Craig Reynolds.** Professional baseball player

December 27 – Events

537 The third Cathedral of Santa Sophia at Constantinople was dedicated. The first two were destroyed, but this one is still in use, a masterpiece of Byzantine architecture.

1831 Charles Darwin set out on the H.M.S. *Beagle* on his exploratory trip to the Galapagos, where he formulated his theory of evolution.

1900 Carry Nation, the famous temperance advocate, conducted her first big saloon raid, in Wichita, Kansas.

1903 "Sweet Adeline," by Henry Armstrong and Richard Gerard, was sung for the first time, in New York City.

1904 *Peter Pan*, the famous play of J.M. Barrie, was first performed, at the Duke of York's Theatre in London.

1927 Jerome Kern's *Showboat* was performed for the first time, at the Zeigfield Theater in New York.

1932 New York's Radio City Music Hall was opened to the public.

1937 Maurice Ravel, the great French composer, died in Paris at age 62, following a brain operation.

1948 Joseph Cardinal Mindszenty, Primate of Hungary, was arrested for espionage by the Communists.

1968 *Apollo 8* splashed down in the Pacific Ocean after orbiting the moon on Christmas Day.

1979 Russian troops invaded Afghanistan, executed its president, Hafizullah Amin, and replaced him by former Deputy Premier Babrak Karmal.

1981 Hoagy Carmichael, the noted American songwriter, died in Rancho Mirage, California, at age 82.

December 28 – Birthdays

1856 **Woodrow Wilson.** 28th U.S. president

1860 **Harry Bache Smith.** American lyricist noted for songs such as "The Sheik of Araby," "Yours Is My Heart Alone," and "Gypsy Love Song"

1865 **Felix Vallotton.** Swiss painter

1888 **Martin Branner.** American cartoonist and creator of the strips *Louie* (1919) and *Winnie Winkle* (1920)

1894 **Alfred Sherwood Romer.** American evolutionist and paleontologist

1896 **Roger Sessions.** One of America's foremost composers, noted for works such as *The Trial of Lucullus* (1947)

1899 **Abner Silver.** American composer and author, noted for songs such as "How Green Was My Valley," "My Home Town Is a One Horse Town," and "On the Beach at Bali-Bali"

1900 **Ted Lyons.** Hall of Fame baseball player

1905 **Cliff Arquette.** American entertainer known as "Charlie Weaver"

1905 **Earl "Fatha" Hines.** American jazz musician

1906 **Tommy Bridges.** Professional baseball player and superstar of the 1930s and 1940s

1908 **Lew Ayres.** American motion-picture actor and leading man of the 1930s, with a 50-year career

1911 **Sam Levenson.** American humorist and author

1913 **Lou Jacobi.** Canadian stage, screen and television actor

1914 **Lee Bowman.** American stage, screen, and television actor

1920 **Steve Van Buren.** Professional football superstar

1925 **Hildegarde Knef.** German stage and motion-picture actress, acclaimed by some as "the thinking man's Marlene Dietrich" (Made some early movies as Hildegard Neff)

1927 **Simon Raven.** English novelist, playwright, and journalist

1929	**Owen Bieber.** President of the United Auto Workers union, elected in 1983
1932	**Manuel Puig.** Argentine author noted for *Kiss of the Spider Woman* (1979)
1933	**Charles Portis.** American author noted for *True Grit* (1968)
1934	**Dame Maggie Smith.** English stage and screen actress and supremely gifted comedienne
1946	**Bill "Spaceman" Lee.** Professional baseball player
1946	**Hubert Green.** Professional golfer
1946	**Edgar Winter.** American rock musician
1947	**Aurelio Rodriguez.** Professional baseball player
1949	**John Milner.** Professional baseball player
1950	**Alex Chilton.** American singer with The Box Tops
1952	**Ray Knight.** Professional baseball player
1954	**Denzel Washington.** American stage, screen and television actor and Academy Award winner for supporting actor in *Glory* (1989)
1981	**Elizabeth Jordan Carr.** First U.S. test-tube baby

December 28 – Events

418	Boniface I became Roman Catholic pope.
1688	The "Glorious Revolution" ended with the arrival in London of William and Mary to assume the throne of England.
1732	*Poor Richard's Almanack* was first advertised for sale by its author, Benjamin Franklin.
1832	Vice-President John C. Calhoun resigned from his office, the first vice president to do so.
1846	Iowa was admitted to the Union as the 29th state.
1869	Chewing gum was patented by William F. Semple, a dentist from Mount Vernon, Ohio.
1895	The Lumiere brothers, Auguste and Louis, demonstrated their *cinematographe* in the Grand Cafe in Paris in the first commerical presentation of a movie.
1897	Edmond Rostand's play *Cyrano de Bergerac* opened in Paris.
1945	Theodore Dreiser, the great American novelist, died at age 74.
1958	Johnny Unitas led the Baltimore Colts to a 23-17 win over the New York Giants in the first sudden death in professional football history, to win the NFL championship.

December 29 – Birthdays

1695	**Jean Baptiste Pater.** French painter noted for works such as *The Fair at Bezons* (1733)
1721	**Madame Jeanne A.P. De Pompadour.** Influential mistress of King Louis XIV of France
1729	**Benjamin Burt.** American silversmith
1766	**Charles Macintosh.** British chemist and inventor of waterproof fabrics, for whom the mackintosh jacket was named
1800	**Charles Goodyear.** American inventor who discovered the process of vulcanizing rubber
1808	**Andrew Johnson.** 17th U.S. president

1809	**William Ewart Gladstone.** One of the most famous British political leaders of the 19th century, during which he served as prime minister four times
1816	**Carl Friedrich Wilhelm Ludwig.** German physiologist
1859	**Venustiano Carranza.** First president of the new Mexican Republic in 1915
1874	**Mark Charles Honeywell.** American inventor, manufacturer, and founder of Honeywell Heating, one of the forerunners of the present Honeywell company
1876	**Pablo Casals.** Spanish cellist and one of the outstanding string players of the 20th century
1877	**Bert Leighton.** American composer, author, and singer, noted for songs such as "Frankie and Johnny" and "Ain't Dat a Shame"
1879	**Billy Mitchell.** American army general and pioneer advocate of a separate U.S. Air Force, who was first court-martialed and later pardoned for his outspoken views
1881	**Jess Willard.** World heavyweight boxing champion, 1915-1919
1898	**Jules Bledsoe.** American actor, composer, and singer
1907	**Robert C. Weaver.** First black U.S. cabinet member, under President Kennedy
1915	**Robert Ruark.** American novelist
1917	**Tom Bradley.** First black mayor of Los Angeles
1920	**Viveca Lindfors.** Swedish stage and motion-picture actress with a 40-year career
1937	**Mary Tyler Moore.** American motion-picture and television actress
1938	**Jon Voight.** American stage, screen, and television actor and Academy Award winner for *Coming Home* (1978)
1939	**H. Wayne Huizenga.** American businessman who developed Blockbuster Video into the largest business of its kind
1947	**Dick Dell.** American tennis player
1947	**Ted Danson.** American motion-picture and television actor, noted for his role in the long-running TV show *Cheers*
1950	**Joe Gilliam.** Professional football player
1959	**Paula Poundstone.** American actress and comedienne

December 29 – Events

1170	Thomas à Becket, Archbishop of Canterbury, was murdered while at vespers in Canterbury Cathedral by four knights of King Henry II.
1775	The famous English actress Sarah Siddons made her debut in David Garrick's Drury Lane Theatre in London.
1825	Jacques Louis David, the great French painter, died in Brussels at age 77.
1845	Texas was annexed to the United States as the 29th state.

1848   The first gas lights were installed in the White House.

1851   The first Young Men's Christian Association (YMCA) in the United States opened its doors in Boston.

1890   The Wounded Knee massacre took place in South Dakota, as more than 200 Sioux men, women, and children were killed by U.S. troops.

1934   Japan renounced the Washington Naval Treaty of 1922 and the London Naval Treaty of 1930.

1940   President Franklin D. Roosevelt, in a "Fireside Chat," said that in aiding Britain the United States must "be the great arsenal of democracy."

December 30 – Birthdays

41   **Titus.** Roman emperor, A.D. 79-81, during whose reign the Collosseum was completed

1514   **Andreas Vesalius.** Italian anatomist and the first person to describe the human body completely

1847   **John Peter Altgeld.** Illinois reformist governor, 1893-1897

1851   **Asa Griggs Candler.** American industrialist who bought the Coca Cola company in 1891 for $2,300 and made it into the greatest soft drink company in the world

1865   **Rudyard Kipling.** English novelist and poet, noted for works such as the poem "Recessional" (1897) and the novel *Kim* (1905)

1867   **Simon Guggenheim.** American philanthropist who established the John Simon Guggenheim Memorial Foundation in 1925

1872   **William A. Larned.** American tennis player and seven times U.S. Singles Champion

1873   **Alfred E. "Al" Smith.** Four times governor of New York and U.S. presidential candidate in 1928

1884   **Hideki Tojo.** Japanese World War II premier who was later executed for war crimes

1895   **Lin Yutang.** Chinese scholar and writer

1904   **Dmitri Kabalevsky.** Russian composer

1906   **Sir Carol Reed.** English motion-picture director, noted for films such as *The Third Man* (1949) and *Oliver!* (1968)

1910   **Dennis Morgan.** American motion-picture actor in over 50 films

1911   **Jeanette Nolan.** Noted American character actress of stage, screen, radio, and television, and wife of actor John McIntire

1912   **Margaret Wade.** Noted American basketball player and first woman inducted into the Basketball Hall of Fame (1984)

1914   **Louis Oliveira.** Brazilian-born composer and author, noted for lyrics such as "Tico Tico"

1914   **Bert Parks.** American actor and television host

1916   **Marie Wilson.** American motion-picture and television actress

1919   **Jo Van Fleet.** American stage and motion-picture actress

1928   **Jack Lord.** American motion-picture and television actor and star of the long-running series *Hawaii 5-O*

1928   **Bo Diddley.** American blues guitarist

1934   **Russ Tamblyn.** American actor and dancer

1935   **Sandy Koufax.** Hall of Fame baseball player and first pitcher to pitch four no-hit games

1937   **John Hartford.** American singer, musician and composer, noted for "Gentle on My Mind" (1967)

1937   **Paul Stookey.** American singer and guitarist with the Peter, Paul, and Mary musical group

1942   **Michael Nesmith.** American singer with The Monkees musical group

1946   **Patty Smith.** American singer who with Bruce Springsteen wrote "Because the Night" (1978)

1947   **Steve Mix.** Professional basketball player

1949   **John Smith.** Professional football player

1956   **Patricia Kalember.** American stage, screen, and television actress

1957   **Matt Lauer.** Host of NBC's *Today* show, who succeeded Bryant Gumbel

1959   **Tracey Ullman.** English-born actress, singer, and comedienne

1961   **Ben Johnson.** Canadian runner labeled "the fastest man on earth," who was disqualified in the 1988 Olympics 100 meter dash for using steroids

1975   **Tiger Woods.** Professional golfer superstar and youngest to win the Masters tournament (1997)

December 30 – Events

1703   A Japanese earthquake and fire destroyed Edo (Tokyo) and killed 200,000 people.

1852   Rutherford B. Hayes married Lucy Ware Webb, later known as "Lemonade Lucy" because she served lemonade in the White House rather than the hard liquor of the U.S. Grant era.

1853   The Gadsden Purchase treaty was signed with Mexico, permitting the U.S. to annex a strip of land south of the Gila River.

1896   Jose Rizal, the Filipino hero, was shot by a Spanish firing squad.

1911   Dr. Sun Yat-sen was elected the first president of the Republic of China.

1916   Grigori Rasputin, the Russian "Mad Monk," was shot to death by Prince Felix Yusupov, two weeks after poisoning him had failed to work.

1922   The Union of Soviet Socialist Republics was formed by the Communists, following Lenin's proclamation, beginning with four constituent republics. It lasted until its breakup in 1991.

1922   V.I. Lenin proclaimed the establishment of the Union of Soviet Socialist Republics.

1948   Cole Porter's musical comedy *Kiss Me Kate*, based on Shakespeare's play *The Taming of the Shrew*, opened on Broadway, and became Porter's longest-running musical.

1963   The John F. Kennedy half dollar was authorized by Congress.

December 31 – Birthdays

1320   **John Wycliffe.** A leading English philosopher in religion and politics during the Middle Ages, whose followers with his help translated the Bible into English about 1382

1491   **Jacques Cartier.** French explorer whose daring explorations were the basis for French claims to Canada

1738   **Charles Cornwallis.** British general defeated by George Washington at Yorktown, Virginia, in the last battle of the Revolutionary War

1815   **George G. Meade.** U.S. Civil War general who commanded the victorious Union Army at the Battle of Gettysburg in 1863

1842   **Giovanni Boldini.** Italian painter

1857   **King Kelly.** Hall of Fame baseball player

1860   **John Taliaferro Thompson.** U.S. brigadier general who invented the Thompson submachine gun, or Tommy gun

1869   **Henri Matisse.** French painter and one of the most influential artists of the 20th century

1870   **Tom Connolly.** Noted major league umpire

1880   **George C. Marshall.** American World War II chief of staff and secretary of state for whom the Marshall Plan was named

1885   **Edgar Leslie.** American composer and author, noted for songs such as "For Me and My Gal," "Among My Souvenirs," "A Little Bit Independent," and "It Looks Like Rain in Cherry Blossom Lane"

1894   **Pola Negri.** German-born motion-picture actress and one of the reigning queens of Hollywood in the 1920s and 1930s

1904   **Nathan Milstein.** One of the greatest violinists of his time

1905   **Jule Styne.** English-born composer, noted for songs such as "It's Magic," "Three Coins in the Fountain," "Diamonds Are a Girl's Best Friend," "I'll Walk Alone," and "Five Minutes More"

1908   **Simon Wiesenthal.** Noted Nazi hunter

1919   **Tommy Byrne.** Professional baseball player

1933   **Chryssa (Vardea).** Greek-born artist

1937   **Sir Anthony Hopkins.** British stage, screen and television actor and Academy Award winner (1992) for his role in *The Silence of the Lambs*

1941   **Sarah Miles.** English motion-picture actress

1942   **Andy Summers.** English guitarist with The Police musical group

1943   **John Denver.** American singer, songwriter, guitarist, and actor

1943   **Ben Kingsley.** British motion-picture actor who won the Academy Award for Best Actor in *Gandhi* (1982)

1946   **Cliff Richey.** American tennis player

1946   **Diane Von Furstenberg.** Noted fashion designer

1948   **Donna Summer.** American rock singer

1950   **Golden Richards.** Professional football superstar

1959   **Val Kilmer.** American stage and screen actor

1961   **Rick Aguilera.** Professional baseball player

1963   **Scott Ian.** Rock musician with the group Anthrax

December 31 – Events

1375   Giovanni Boccaccio, the great Italian writer and humanist, died in Certaldo, Italy, at age 62.

1384   John Wycliffe, the noted English philosopher, died following a paralytic stroke at age 64.

1418   Rouen surrendered to King Henry V of England in the Hundred Years' War, after a two-month siege in which the English starved out the defending French.

1805   Napoleon abandoned the French Revolutionary Calendar.

1859   The comic weekly *Vanity Fair* began publication in New York.

1879   Thomas A. Edison gave his first public demonstration of his incandescent lamp to a New Year's Eve crowd in Menlo Park, New Jersey.

1923   The chimes of Big Ben, the great bell in the clock tower of the Houses of Parliament in London, were first broadcast on the radio.

1926   Harry Houdini, the great magician, died of a ruptured appendix at age 52.

1929   Big bandleader Guy Lombardo, with his Royal Canadians, began the tradition of broadcasting dance music on New Year's Eve in New York City.

1941   Admiral Chester W. Nimitz became commander of the U.S. Pacific Fleet in World War II.

1943   Frank Sinatra began a singing engagement at New York's Paramount Theater, which established him as the idol of the nation's "bobbysoxers."

1946   President Harry S. Truman officially proclaimed the end of World War II.

1972   Roberto Clemente, the great baseball player, was killed in an airplane crash at age 38, while aiding Nicaraguan earthquake survivors.

1974   Private U.S. citizens were allowed to buy and own gold for the first time in 40 years.

Index

Page numbers in italics refer to birthdays.

About the Author

David E. Johnson was born in Chatham, Louisiana, on August 16, 1927, and received a B.S. degree in Electrical Engineering and a B.A. degree in Mathematics, both from Louisiana Tech University in 1949. He also received an M.S. degree and a Ph.D. degree in Applied Mathematics in 1952 and 1958, respectively, from Auburn University, and spent the 1961-1962 academic year at Stanford University, as a post-graduate National Science Faculty Fellow. He taught mathematics for six years at Louisiana Tech University and electrical engineering for 21 years at Louisiana State University. After retiring from L.S.U. in 1983, he taught mathematics at Birmingham-Southern College, from which he retired (again) in 1994. He served in the U.S. Navy in 1945-1946 and in the U.S. Army in 1952-1954.

Professor Johnson has published over 40 technical articles and authored or co-authored 43 books, including *A Funny Thing Happened on the Way to the White House* (Beaufort Books, 1983) and *Electric Circuit Analysis*, Third Edition (Prentice-Hall, 1997).